THE HANDY HISTORY ANSWER BOOK

From the Stone Age
to the Digital Age

FOURTH EDITION

Stephen A. Werner, Ph.D.

VISIBLE
INK
PRESS

Detroit

THE HANDY HISTORY ANSWER BOOK

Visible Ink Press®
43311 Joy Rd., #414
Canton, MI 48187–2075

Visible Ink Press is a registered trademark of Visible Ink Press LLC.

Most Visible Ink Press books are available at special quantity discounts when purchased in bulk by corporations, organizations, or groups. Customized printings, special imprints, messages, and excerpts can be produced to meet your needs. For more information, contact Special Markets Director, Visible Ink Press, www.visibleink.com, or 734–667–3211.

Managing Editor: Kevin S. Hile
Art Director: Mary Claire Krzewinski
Typesetting: Marco Divita
Proofreaders: Larry Baker, Rebecca Brown–Gregory, and Shoshana Hurwitz
Indexer: Larry Baker

Front cover images: Machu Picchu (Martin St-Amant), Confucius (*Encyclopedia Britannica*), Elizabeth I (Woburn Abbey collection), U.S. Capitol (Martin Falbisoner).

Back cover images: Champs Elysees during French Liberation (Library of Congress), Joan of Arc (Musée Dobrée), John F. Kennedy family (Cecil W. Stoughton).

ISBN: 978–1–57859–680–5

Cataloging-in-Publication data is on file at the Library of Congress.

Printed in the United States of America.

10 9 8 7 6 5 4 3 2 1

About the Author

Stephen A. Werner, Ph.D., has over thirty years of experience teaching as a college adjunct in the St. Louis area. He has taught courses on human civilization, mythology, religion, and popular culture: including courses on Frank Sinatra, Elvis Presley, and Route 66. Dr. Werner does not think in terms of separate academic disciplines; rather, he sees them as all connected. History is more than kings, wars, and generals; it includes art, literature, religious beliefs, and the culture of ordinary people.

Dr. Werner is the author of *The Handy Christianity Answer Book*, which was also published by Visible Ink Press, and *How to Study Religion: A Guide for the Curious* (Cognella Academic Publishers). His other books include *Life Hurts: An Exploration of the Pain and Suffering of Life* and the satirical work *Elvis and Apocalypse*, both published by Press, Press, Pull—St. Louis.

As a teacher and writer, Werner lives by the concept that real learning is an exciting adventure. If it is not exciting, then one needs to hunt around for more interesting topics or better ways to learn. Most children want to learn. If an adult has lost that eagerness, then it needs to be found and can be found.

Also from Visible Ink Press

The Handy Accounting Answer Book
by Amber K. Gray
ISBN: 978-1-57859-675-1

The Handy African American History Answer Book
by Jessie Carnie Smith, Ph.D.
ISBN: 978-1-57859-452-8

The Handy American Government Answer Book: How Washington, Politics, and Elections Work
by Gina Misiroglu
ISBN: 978-1-57859-639-3

The Handy American History Answer Book
by David L. Hudson, Jr.
ISBN: 978-1-57859-471-9

The Handy Anatomy Answer Book, 2nd edition
by Patricia Barnes-Svarney and Thomas E. Svarney
ISBN: 978-1-57859-542-6

The Handy Answer Book for Kids (and Parents), 2nd edition
by Gina Misiroglu
ISBN: 978-1-57859-219-7

The Handy Art History Answer Book
by Madelynn Dickerson
ISBN: 978-1-57859-417-7

The Handy Astronomy Answer Book, 3rd edition
by Charles Liu, Ph.D.
ISBN: 978-1-57859-419-1

The Handy Bible Answer Book
by Jennifer R. Prince
ISBN: 978-1-57859-478-8

The Handy Biology Answer Book, 2nd edition
by Patricia Barnes Svarney and Thomas E. Svarney
ISBN: 978-1-57859-490-0

The Handy Boston Answer Book
by Samuel Willard Crompton
ISBN: 978-1-57859-593-8

The Handy California Answer Book
by Kevin Hile
ISBN: 978-1-57859-591-4

The Handy Chemistry Answer Book
by Ian C. Stewart and Justin P. Lamont
ISBN: 978-1-57859-374-3

The Handy Christianity Answer Book
by Stephen A. Werner, Ph.D.
ISBN: 978-1-57859-686-7

The Handy Civil War Answer Book
by Samuel Willard Crompton
ISBN: 978-1-57859-476-4

The Handy Communication Answer Book
by Lauren Sergy
ISBN: 978-1-57859-587-7

The Handy Diabetes Answer Book
by Patricia Barnes-Svarney and Thomas E. Svarney
ISBN: 978-1-57859-597-6

The Handy Dinosaur Answer Book, 2nd edition
by Patricia Barnes-Svarney and Thomas E. Svarney
ISBN: 978-1-57859-218-0

The Handy English Grammar Answer Book
by Christine A. Hult, Ph.D.
ISBN: 978-1-57859-520-4

The Handy Forensic Science Answer Book: Reading Clues at the Crime Scene, Crime Lab, and in Court
by Patricia Barnes-Svarney and Thomas E. Svarney
ISBN: 978-1-57859-621-8

The Handy Geography Answer Book, 3rd edition
by Paul A. Tucci
ISBN: 978-1-57859-576-1

The Handy Geology Answer Book
by Patricia Barnes-Svarney and Thomas E. Svarney
ISBN: 978-1-57859-156-5

The Handy History Answer Book, 4th edition
by Stephen A. Werner, Ph.D.
ISBN: 978-1-57859-680-5

The Handy Hockey Answer Book
by Stan Fischler
ISBN: 978-1-57859-513-6

The Handy Investing Answer Book
by Paul A. Tucci
ISBN: 978-1-57859-486-3

The Handy Islam Answer Book
by John Renard, Ph.D.
ISBN: 978-1-57859-510-5

Photo Sources

52 Pickup (Wikicommons): p. 163.
AgnosticPreachersKid (Wikicommons): p. 395.
Architect of the Capitol: p. 95.
Art Institute of Chicago: p. 426.
Associated Press: p. 371.
Associated Press/Murray Becker: p. 525.
Auschwitze Album: p. 187.
B & O Museum: p. 343.
Bain News Service: p. 154.
Andrew Balet: p. 584.
Biblioteca Nacional de España: p. 158.
BigSteve (Wikicommons): p. 233.
Binarysequence (Wikicommons): p. 597.
Boston Public Library: p. 332.
Bridgeman Art Library: p. 74.
Brooklyn Museum: p. 151.
Viktor Bulla: p. 228.
Don Camillo: p. 268.
CDC Public Health Image Archive: p. 553.
Cflm001 (Wikicommons): p. 212.
H. D. Chadwick: p. 511.
Adam Cuerden: p. 137.
Dbachmann (Wikicommons): p. 20.
Sophie Delar: p. 577.
European Solidarity Centre: p. 388.
Executive Office of the President of the United States/Annie Liebovitz: p. 220.
Federal Bureau of Investigation: p. 326.
Finnish Museum of Photography: p. 500.
Fletcher6 (Wikicommons): p. 595.
Flickr: p. 347.
Gandhiserve.org: p. 260.
Francesco Gasparetti: p. 49.
German Federal Archives: p. 170.
Giorces (Wikicommons): p. 475.
Mikael Häggström: p. 555.
Hermitage Museum: p. 422.
Hoodinski (Wikicommons): p. 105.
IAEA Imagebank: p. 535.
Joel Levine: p. 399.

Library of Congress: pp. 77, 87, 132, 138, 140, 149, 160, 166, 236, 322, 328, 357, 368, 380, 397, 403, 448, 455, 483, 590.
Los Angeles County Museum of Art: p. 285.
Louvre Museum: p. 424.
Amritpal Singh Mann: p. 305.
MapMaster (Wikicommons): p. 30.
MerlinUK (Wikicommons): p. 18.
C. Messier: p. 265.
Hamid Mir: p. 217.
Musée Dobrée: p. 68.
Museum of Modern Art, New York: p. 429.
Myworkforwiki (Wikicommons): p. 16.
NASA: pp. 501, 513.
NASA/WMAP Science Team: p. 579.
Nationaal Archief: p. 470.
National Gallery of Art: p. 317.
National Gallery of Victoria: p. 418.
National Library of Wales: p. 47 (right).
National Maritime Museum: p. 572.
National Portrait Gallery, London: pp. 66, 79, 313, 574.
National Portrait Gallery, United States: pp. 117 (right), 280, 378.
Naval Museum of Madrid: p. 93.
Daniel Nicoletta: p. 408.
Jamling Tenzing Norgay: p. 496.
The Official CTBTO Photostream: p. 243.
Mario Roberto Durán Ortiz: p. 498
Peter Potrowl: p. 468.
Royal Collection, England: p. 63.
Royal Library, Turin: p. 414.
RR Auctions: p. 450.
Seasonsinthesun (Wikicommons): p. 250.
Shutterstock: pp. 2, 5, 7, 8, 10, 11, 23, 24, 25, 28, 32, 33, 45, 52, 53, 55, 57, 61, 80, 85, 89, 91, 106, 107, 120, 126, 175, 177, 178, 190, 221, 231, 235, 244, 248, 252, 266, 287, 292, 298, 316, 338, 352, 360, 376, 384, 401, 416, 434, 435, 438, 453, 457, 459, 461, 472, 477, 481,

485, 504, 516, 521, 523, 528, 532, 537, 561, 563, 564, 566, 568, 570.
Smithsonian Institution: p. 323.
South African History Online: p. 390.
Statens Museum for Kunst: p. 428.
Matthew Trump: p. 122.
Tuskegee University Archives/Museum: p. 575.
Uffizi Gallery: p. 47 (left).
U.S. Air Force: p. 203.
U.S. Army Africa Historical Image Archive: p. 206.
U.S. Army Center of Military History: p. 180.
U.S. Department of Defense: pp. 184, 207.
U.S. Department of State: p. 240.
U.S. Environmental Protection Agency: p. 530.
U.S. Farm Security Administration/Arthur Rothstein: p. 518.
U.S. Geological Survey: p. 508.
U.S. government: pp. 191, 198, 200.
U.S. Marine Corps: p. 215.
U.S. National Archives and Records Administration: pp. 108, 113, 183, 194, 195, 373, 488, 550.
U.S. Signal Corps: p. 173.
Rosemary Wardley: p. 344.
Wellcome Images: p. 544.
Whitmer Gallery of Western Art: p. 147.
Wide World Photos: p. 499.
Roger Wollstadt: p. 239.
World Economic Forum: p. 391.
Wu Daozi: p. 254.
Yale University Art Gallery: p. 350.
The Yorck Project: p. 269.
Public domain: pp. 35, 37, 41, 42, 64, 69, 70, 71, 73, 98, 100, 110, 115, 117 (left), 119, 127, 130, 134, 144, 227, 258, 272, 273, 276, 278, 290, 294, 296, 302, 319, 334, 341, 254, 363, 383, 394, 398, 405, 420, 432, 444, 445, 446, 451, 464, 465, 473, 479, 482, 492, 495, 539, 542, 546, 549, 552, 557, 581, 585, 587, 588, 593.

Contents

Introduction

Welcome to this journey through history! I have written *The Handy History Answer Book* in a clear and straightforward style that does not assume the reader has extensive prior knowledge of history. The first chapter, "History Basics," explores the importance of knowing history and gives you, the reader, many suggestions on how to learn history in a way that keeps it interesting. The first half of the book then follows history in the normal chronological way, starting with the prehistoric past, then moving on to the ancient past and working up to the modern world and current events.

Because so much has happened in human history across the globe, I have made some choices on what to cover. Thus, *The Handy History Answer Book* will focus mostly, though not exclusively, on the events in the ancient Mediterranean world, then Europe, and then the United States.

The three opening chapters are "The Ancient Mediterranean to Middle Ages Europe," "The Middle Ages and the Renaissance in Europe," and "Empires, Kingdoms, Dynasties, and Nations." You will learn about Vandals and Vikings and crusades and cathedrals. The journey then shifts to North America with the chapters "The First Americans," "European Colonies and the Early United States," and "The American Civil War." Readers will learn about early Native peoples, such as the mound builders; the conquests of the Europeans; the birth of the United States; and the war that nearly destroyed it.

The next chapters investigate the American story from the mid-1800s, through the 1900s, and up to the present. Events in the United States, American participation in global history, and important recent events across the world are described in four chapters: "America from the Civil War to World War I," "The World Wars," "America after World War II," and "The Twenty-first Century." Two chapters follow, covering other world history: "Russia and the Soviet Union" and "Asian History and Culture."

The second half of *The Handy History Answer Books* looks at history by exploring thirteen different topics. How humans make sense of their lives is found in the chapters

"Philosophy" and "Religion." Two chapters delve into the history of key elements in society: "The Law" and "Economics and Business." You will learn about the greatest "Trial of the Century" (There was more than one!), the Triangle Trade, and the Ponzi scheme of Bernie Madoff that ripped off countless people. Next comes a discussion of how mostly ordinary people struggled to change the social conditions around them: "Human Rights Issues" and "Political and Social Movements." You learn about historical struggles against slavery, for workers rights, and for equal rights.

Two chapters follow that delve into human creative and artistic expression: "Western Art, Photography, and Architecture," and "Music, Dance, and Theater." "Expressions of Human Culture" and "Exploration" look at the need of many people to express themselves, and the human desire to push boundaries and discover new worlds and new things. The chapter "Disasters" stands on its own as it covers both natural and man-made disasters. The final two chapters examine human intellectual accomplishments to understand the world around them and to better control natural things—often, for the benefit of humans: "Medicine and Disease" and "Science and Invention."

I hope at the end of this journey your curiosity will be stoked to keep exploring the fascinating realm of human history. Also, you will have learned about the many human missteps and wrongs done through ignorance and blindness, as well as through greed and ambition. Perhaps you can be among those who know history well enough to help guide us into the future as we humans face daunting problems such as how to assure that all people prosper in a worldwide economy and how to respond to global climate change.

Go forth and explore history!

—Stephen Werner (May 2020)

HISTORY BASICS

WHY STUDY HISTORY?

Why study history?

History is fascinating! As you explore this book, hopefully you will agree. The goal of this book is to increase your interest in history.

Our present world has been shaped by history. Understanding today's events requires understanding the history behind them. For example, political events in the Middle East often make the news. However, the problems behind current conflicts often have been developing over decades or centuries. Most conflicts today are based on unresolved issues from the past.

The United States of America today is shaped by its history: the conflict between settlers and Native Americans, the Revolutionary War, the extensive use of enslaved people from Africa, the arrival of millions of European immigrants, the building of railroads, the Civil War, industrialization, the fight for worker rights, World War I and World War II, the fight for civil rights, the Vietnam War, 9/11, and everything that happened in between these events. Often, the only way to understand the present is to understand the history that got us to the present.

Also, history is all around us if you look for it. Are there monuments, historic houses, or historic sites near you? Do an Internet search for historic sites in your town, city, state, or region. Are there historic buildings or historic neighborhoods near you? Are there any old buildings around you? What about monuments of historic events or statues of famous people near you? Are there statues near you that you have driven by many times but never taken the time to figure out what the person did to wind up being remembered with a statue? Are there old cemeteries near you that you can explore? Often, historic cemeteries have guides to the important people buried there. What museums can you find that cover local history?

Do you explore history when you travel? For many people, the most interesting part of travel is exploring the history of other places. For example, Civil War battlefields can be found in many parts of the country. (The states with the most such sites are Virginia, Tennessee, and Missouri.)

When you travel, do an online search for interesting historical sites. Or get a printed road atlas of the United States. Each state has its own map, and all kinds of interesting places to see and explore are marked in red.

What does the word "history" mean?

For most people, the word "history" refers to things that happened to humans in the past. Thus, to study history is to study past events involving humans. Natural history refers to animals and plants. Geological history describes how the earth was shaped and goes back long before humans. Cosmic history tries to understand the universe.

What gets confusing is that technically the word "history" means the "writings describing past events." This can only happen when humans began writing, which probably began about 7,000 years ago. Thus, anything before writing is called "prehistory," meaning before history.

For example, 10,000 years ago in North America, people were hunting mastodons— giant ancestors of the elephant. But these people had no written language, so we call this period "prehistory." Many people find this confusing since human hunting of mastodons took place a long time ago. Isn't that history? You can use the word either way; just know that there are two different understandings of the word.

But isn't history boring?

Those who love history find it fascinating to understand what happened in the past and how things are interconnected. Unfortunately, many people have found history boring. Sadly, some history teachers in grade school, high school, and college have made history boring and tedious. The problem is that history can be very complicated. Sometimes, teachers give too much detail that comes off as boring, without enough focus on the big issues that make it so interesting.

The trick is getting the right level of detail for your individual level of interest. So, for example, in a museum you do not have to read all the written information given with the artifacts if it is too detailed. Find what interests you and build on that. In reading, try to find articles and books with the right level of detail to keep you interested.

Learning history doesn't have to be boring. It's only really dull if the person teaching it doesn't understand how to make the past come alive. The story of humanity's past is actually a fascinating tale!

Does the saying "There is nothing new under the sun!" apply to studying history?

The Book of Ecclesiastes in the Bible states:

> What has been is what will be,
> and what has been done is what will be done;
> there is nothing new under the sun (1:9 NRSV)

Many current events seem so unique. Yet, in the past many similar things have happened. Admittedly, some events are unprecedented in history, such as Charles Lindbergh flying solo across the Atlantic Ocean in 1927 or Neil Armstrong walking on the moon in 1969. However, many other events seem to be replays of past events and often leave one wondering: "Why weren't the lessons from the past learned?" Looking at the past to see how similar events have played out can often give one a clue how to proceed in the future.

For example, there are many examples in the past when military action was taken based on faulty or distorted information. This should lead those deciding to take military action to be more cautious and always be aware that they could be mistaken. Such caution was not observed in the American decision to invade Iraq in 2003. The invasion was justified by the claim that Iraq had chemical and biological weapons—weapons of mass destruction (WMD)—which turned out not to be true.

As Spanish philosopher George Santayana (1863–1952) stated: "Those who cannot remember the past are condemned to repeat it."

What role have aliens played in human history?

No role! There is zero historical evidence that aliens from outer space have visited the earth. Also, there is no scientific evidence that aliens exist despite much effort trying to find other life in space. Advanced telescopes continue to search the universe. Only in the last thirty years have planets been found beyond our solar system. It is typically assumed that if life exists in outer space, it would exist on a planet. Although over 4,000 planets have been found, no evidence of alien life has been found.

Also, since the 1930s, radio telescopes (this field is known as radio astronomy) have been listening to outer space. All kinds of radiation have been detected within the range of radio wavelengths, which helps us understand the universe; however, nothing has been heard that would indicate intelligent beings out in space.

Unfortunately, cable TV shows such as *Ancient Aliens* explore claims that aliens have visited the earth. However, reputable historians and scientists have not supported such claims.

Some have made the claim that aliens built the pyramids of Egypt, since ancient humans could not have moved such large stones. There are stones in the pyramids of Giza in Egypt that weigh over thirty tons. A Hummer you might see on the street typically weighs over three tons. To many modern people, it seems impossible that ancient people with no machinery could move a thirty-ton block. But it turns out they could. It

3

took hundreds of people to drag the stone. But it could be done. They did not need aliens to help them.

Also, some cultures, such as the ancient Mayans, practiced head shaping. The head of an infant was wrapped in such a way that over the years of growing up, the skull would grow in a distorted way and become elongated. The result is that occasionally skulls can be found that are very oddly shaped. These are not aliens; these people were the elites of their societies.

What makes studying history a challenge?

Two things make the study of history challenging. First, there is so much history to learn about; and second, history is often complicated.

Here is an example of this complexity. Abraham Lincoln is known for the Emancipation Proclamation, which freed slaves. However, Lincoln's views on slavery shifted and changed many times. It is not correct to say Lincoln opposed slavery throughout his political career; it is far more complicated than that! Also, the Emancipation Proclamation only freed slaves in areas not under Lincoln's control.

As for the quantity of history, yes, there is lots of history to study. Many people find the exploration of history to be a lifetime adventure. With so much history, everyone should be able to find interesting people and events to learn about.

What have been some problems in studying and teaching American history in the past?

There are four main problems:

1. The First Problem

In the past there was often a tendency to focus on American history with its roots in Europe and ancient cultures around the Mediterranean. The strength of this approach is that it explored in detail some of most important influences on American culture. The problem is that important cultures with very long histories, such as in India and China, did not get enough attention. Traditional cultures in Africa and the South Pacific also did not get enough attention.

Today, many people live in more culturally diverse places in America. Many of us regularly encounter people from other countries and other cultures. Some of these people

What was the book *Chariots of the Gods?*

The idea that aliens visited the earth was promoted by the popular 1968 book *Chariots of the Gods? Unsolved Mysteries of the Past* by Erich von Däniken, which has sold over seventy million copies. However, historians and scientists have rejected all his claims. Furthermore, Däniken has been accused of plagiarism.

were born in other countries; for others, their parents or grandparents were born in other countries. Some places, such as New York City, are incredibly diverse.

Unfortunately, many people find this diversity threatening or frightening despite the fact that America was built by immigrants, most of whom spoke languages other than English when they arrived. However, much of this fear is based on ignorance about these other cultures. Learning the history of the rest of the world is important to overcome this ignorance. In particular, it is important to know more about China since it has so much economic influence around the world.

2. The Second Problem

In exploring American history, often the history and role of Native Americans has been minimized despite the fact that twenty-six state names and countless towns and counties are named using Native American words. Native Americans are an important part of the American story, and more attention should be given to their history, culture, legacy, and presence today.

Also, Native American history is filled with figures such as Sacagawea, Osceola, Tecumseh, Crazy Horse, Sitting Bull, and Geronimo. The dramatic stories of these people and events such as the Trail of Tears and Wounded Knee Massacre are worth knowing.

Lastly, Native Americans represent an important part of American society today, especially in states such as Arizona, New Mexico, Alaska, and South Dakota.

3. The Third Problem

The role of African Americans in building America has often been overlooked. For example, the culture and economy of the South before the Civil War was totally based on the production and sale of cotton. African American slaves grew and picked the cotton. Slaves built the plantations and did most of the domestic work in the plantation mansions.

Wall Street is named for a wall built across the lower tip of Manhattan. Slaves built that wall. The stock exchange created there often traded stocks of companies that shipped slaves, molasses, and rum. Molasses and rum were made from sugar, grown in the Caribbean by slave labor.

In the decades after the Civil War, African Americans made important contributions in science, literature, sports, music, entertainment, and the fight for civil rights.

The role of Native Americans in our history is, unfortunately, often overlooked in U.S. classrooms.

5

4. The Fourth Problem

The role of women has been ignored or downplayed when discussing the past. In recent decades, many writers, scholars, teachers, and historians have worked to shed light on the role and contributions of women.

INTERESTING WAYS TO STUDY HISTORY

Is Wikipedia a reliable source on history?

Yes, Wikipedia has generally reliable articles about history. The biggest problem is that often the Wikipedia articles are too detailed. For example, at the time of this writing, the Wikipedia article on the important religious leader Martin Luther is over 12,000 words long. This makes it hard to use for a person who wants a quick and basic introduction of the life and work of Martin Luther.

The article does include a short summary at the beginning, which is helpful, but that summary uses the word "sacerdotalism," which will throw off a lot of readers. (If you click on "sacerdotalism," you will get an explanation of over eight hundred words.)

Is the Internet helpful for studying history?

Some historical topics have decent websites that explain what happened. However, many websites are not well written. Hunt around. However, it is sad that for many important topics, there should be several great websites from which to choose, yet unfortunately many are of poor quality.

Another problem is that many sites that are supposed to be educational are loaded with advertising. This is particularly regrettable since the promise of the Internet was that it could be of great use as an educational tool. For many websites, the advertising has outstripped the educational use.

What else can I do to learn more history?

Read books on history! Go to your local library and browse the history section. If you cannot find what you are looking for, ask a staff member. Or ask a staff member for suggestions.

A surprising place to get short and clear introductory books on history topics is in the "juvenile" section of a library. Many of the history and science books are excellent if you want a good, short introduction to a topic. Also, they have lots of books with drawings and photos that make learning easier. If you feel embarrassed checking out these books, just say, "They're for my nephew." The DK educational books are excellent—short and to the point, with great pictures, drawings, and graphics.

The best way to discover history is to read books on history! You don't even have to buy them; just go to your local library.

Browse the history section of a bookstore to see all the interesting topics out there. Tragically, because of Amazon, most bookstores have closed. However, some still exist, so go find one and visit it to see all the amazing books available.

I do not have time to read books. How else can I learn about history?

If you have little time to sit down and read, try audiobooks, which work on many different electronic devices. Audiobooks are great for when you are driving, jogging, or walking the dog. Your local library can lend you CDs to play or audiobooks to download for free. There are a number of online services that provide audiobooks.

Admittedly, some books on history can be a bit long—requiring twenty or more hours. (For example, Ron Chernow's 2005 book *Alexander Hamilton* runs thirty-six hours. Many readers have found it a great read. Others have chosen a quicker route to learn about this monumental figure in American history—by seeing the musical *Hamilton*.) However, if you get a good book that is interesting, you might be surprised how quickly on your daily drive to and from work you can complete it.

Also, if you start an audiobook but discover it is not keeping your interest, you do not have to finish it! Find something else! The trick in learning history is to find interesting topics to explore. And there are plenty of them.

Any other suggestions for learning history?

Talk to older people. Ask them about their lives and experiences.

Pay attention to what is happening in the news. Look for current events that are shaped by past history.

Is YouTube a good source for history lessons?

Lots of history documentaries wind up on YouTube. As with music on YouTube, in many cases these videos are put up without getting permission from the creators of the video or paying royalties. In other cases, the creators might be grateful that their work is getting viewed. Explore YouTube by clicking on the "history" category. Like everything on the Internet, you have to use some judgment. There is some junk and misleading material. But there are also many high-quality, informative historical documentaries out there.

So the next time you have time to spare and an electronic device in front of you, instead of playing games or doing mindless things, pull up a history documentary and learn something!

What is *American Experience*?

American Experience is an excellent series of documentaries produced by PBS (Public Broadcasting Service). They can be seen on your public television station or on the *American Experience* web page. These documentaries are easy ways to learn about history.

American Experience has had over thirty seasons. Look at the Wikipedia article "List of *American Experience* episodes" to see all the fascinating topics that you can explore.

Who is Ken Burns?

Ken Burns is a filmmaker who has created award-winning documentaries on American history. Some of his more important films are:

- *The Civil War* (1990, nine episodes)
- *Baseball* (1994, 2010, ten episodes)
- *Jazz* (2001, ten episodes)
- *The War* (World War II, 2007, seven episodes)
- *The Vietnam War* (2017, ten episodes)
- *Country Music* (2019, eight episodes)

Are there some good movies about history?

Many movies are based on historical events. Some portray history accurately, and some do not. In this book, a number of movies will be suggested that are excellent ways to learn about important events and figures. Here are a few examples:

- *All Quiet on the Western Front* (1931)
- *Gandhi* (1982)

Filmmaker Ken Burns is renowned for his history movies and miniseries.

- *Apollo 13* (1995)
- *Lincoln* (2011)

What are some movies that do not give an accurate view of history?

Although not at all accurate, these movies *are* entertaining!

- *The Three Stooges Meet Hercules* (1962)
- *Start the Revolution without Me* (1970)
- *Mel Brooks History of the World: Part 1* (1981)
- *Abraham Lincoln: Vampire Hunter* (2012)

I am confused about the centuries. Why are the 1600s known as the seventeenth century? Why are we in the twenty-first century when the years start with "20"?

Below is a list of the years of each century C.E. There are two ways of assigning the years to a century: starting with a "0" year or starting with a "1" year. The "1" system is the more technically correct; however, most people think in terms of the "0" year system.

Notice that the first century includes the years from 1 to 99. (There was no "0" year in the first century.) That means the second century is from 100 to 199, not the years starting with 200. The years starting with 200 become the third century. It can be totally confusing, but study the list, and it will make sense. (If there were no years 1–99, there would be no problem as the century numbers would line up with year numbers.)

Years	Century	Years	Century
1–99 (1–100)	1st	1000–1099 (1001–1100)	11th
100–199 (101–200)	2nd	1100–1199 (1101–1200)	12th
200–299 (201–300)	3rd	1200–1299 (1201–1300)	13th
300–399 (301–400)	4th	1300–1399 (1301–1400)	14th
400–499 (401–500)	5th	1400–1499 (1401–1500)	15th
500–599 (501–600)	6th	1500–1599 (1501–1600)	16th
600–699 (601–700)	7th	1600–1699 (1601–1700)	17th
700–799 (701–800)	8th	1700–1799 (1701–1800)	18th
800–899 (801–900)	9th	1800–1899 (1801–1900)	19th
900–999 (901–1000)	10th	1900–1999 (1901–2000)	20th
		2000–2099 (2001–2100)	21st

To better understand the problem, imagine a three-story building with five rooms on each floor. One could number the rooms on the first floor as 1–5. The second floor would be rooms 101–105, and the third-floor rooms 201–205. But this would be very confusing to someone looking for room 203, which would be on the third floor, not the second floor. To avoid this problem, buildings with several floors simply avoid using the numbers 1 to 99. However, in studying history, we cannot dump years 1 to 99 because so many important things happened in the first century.

HUMAN ORIGINS

Since history is about humans, what is the origin of humans?

There are two very different versions of the story of human origins. One version comes from a literal reading of the first chapters of the Book of Genesis in the Bible. The other version comes from science.

What does the Bible say about the origins of humans?

The book of Genesis, which is found in both the Christian Bible and the Jewish Bible, tells two stories of the origins of humans. In the first story, God creates the earth, sun, moon, stars, plant life, and animal life in six days. Humans are created on the sixth day:

> Then God said: Let us make human beings in our image, after our likeness. Let them have dominion over the fish of the sea, the birds of the air, the tame animals, all the wild animals, and all the creatures that crawl on the earth. God created mankind in his image; in the image of God he created them; male and female he created them. (1:26–27)

The second story:

> Then the LORD God formed the man out of the dust of the ground and blew into his nostrils the breath of life, and the man became a living being.
>
> …
>
> The man gave names to all the tame animals, all the birds of the air, and all the wild animals; but none proved to be a helper suited to the man. So the LORD God cast a deep sleep on the man, and while he was asleep, he took out one of his ribs and closed up its place with flesh. The LORD God then built the rib that he had taken from the man into a woman. When he brought her to the man, the man said:

> This one, at last, is bone of my bones
> and flesh of my flesh;
> This one shall be called "woman,"
> for out of man this one has been
> taken. (2:7, 20–23 NABRE)

Although the early Bible stories contain no dates, many Christians have worked their way back through the Bible and place the creation story at about 4000 B.C.E. This would mean that the whole universe and humans are about 6,000 years old. And in this reading of the Bible, there is no evolution, nor would there be time for evolution in such a short period.

Creationists believe in the biblical version of humanity's origins, including the story of Adam and Eve and the Garden of Eden.

Science says the earth is 4.6 billion years old. Who is right: science or the Bible? The key is how to read the Bible.

What are the different approaches to reading the Bible?

There are two approaches to reading the Bible: the literalist approach and the nonliteralist approach.

What is the literalist view on reading the Bible?

Literalists believe that the Bible should be taken literally because it is the Word of God. Typically, literalists also believe that the Bible is "God's words." This is the idea that God told the biblical writers what to write down, word for word. Therefore, if God told them what to write, there cannot be any mistakes in the Bible. Thus, if the Bible says the earth is 6,000 years old, it is 6,000 years old! (A literalist might argue that God would know how old the earth is because he was there at creation; Stephen Hawking was not!) Typically, literalists do not believe in evolution since it is not mentioned in the Bible.

In the Bible, there is the story of Jonah, who was thrown overboard from a ship. Jonah was swallowed by a big fish and lived in the belly of the fish for three days before being spat out. Literalists believe this actually happened. This approach to reading the Bible is the literalist view.

Sometimes, literalists are called "fundamentalists."

What do you call the nonliteralist view of the Bible?

The nonliteralist view for reading the Bible can be called the contextualist view. The word "contextualist" is a new term to make this simpler. The older term for this approach to reading the Bible is the "historical-critical method." A person who reads the Bible in its context is called a "contextualist."

The contextualist view holds that humans wrote the Bible. To understand any human writing, speech, or communication, one has to understand the "context" or setting. If someone says to me, "You are such a stupid idiot!" I have to know the context to know how to interpret the remark. Is someone who does not like me calling me a stupid idiot!", Is it a friend just teasing me? Is someone who really loves me just mad at me? If I am a boss, do I need to fire the employee who called me a stupid idiot? Am I an actor in a play? How you would understand "You are such a stupid idiot!" totally depends on the context.

Fundamentalist Christians interpret the Bible literally, which can lead to beliefs such as the world is 6,000 years old.

The view of contextualists is that if humans wrote the Bible, there could be historical mistakes. If four different humans wrote the story of Jesus, there will be differences in how they tell the story. Ancient people did not have science to explain the world around them, so they often told myths. Typically, contextualists think that the stories in the first part of the Book of Genesis are religious myths and not a scientific or historical description of how the universe came into being.

Contextualists believe the story of Jonah was meant to teach a lesson. It turns out the Book of Jonah is a very profound teaching story about religious hatred. Contextualists do not believe that Jonah actually lived in the belly of a fish for three days since that would be physically impossible. Contextualists believe you have to try to think like ancient people, who had no science and very little written history, and no archeology to know about what happened before them. There are two kinds of contextualists.

What are the two kinds of contextualists?

1. Those contextualists who believe the Bible was written solely by humans. In this view, the Bible is an interesting ancient religious text but nothing more than that.

2. Those contextualists who believe the Bible was written by humans but inspired by God. The Bible is God's message written by humans in their own words using ancient styles of literature. The Bible is "God's Word"—meaning God's message but not "God's words."

So, how many views are there on how to read the Bible?

There are three basic views on how to read the Bible:

- Literalist view
- Contextualist view—solely a human product
- Contextualist view—a human product inspired by God

  Which view makes more sense to you?

What does science say about humanity's origins?

According to science, the species of *Homo sapiens* (the human species) evolved over many millions of years from less developed animals. Understanding this evolution of humans is challenging for two reasons: 1) human evolution was a complicated and at times convoluted process, and 2) scientists—especially paleontologists and geneticists—continue to discover new pieces of the complex history of the evolutionary history of humans. What follows is a simplified description of current scientific thought on the evolution of humans.

The first piece of the puzzle is the widely recognized similarities between humans and apes. Humans share over 98 percent of their DNA with chimpanzees, gorillas, and bonobos. Among all mammals, one group is the primates, which includes humans, apes, monkeys, lemurs, and tarsiers. Evidence of early apes goes back ten million years. About

> ## Who is Lucy?
>
> In November 1974, American Donald C. Johanson (1943–) made one of paleoan-thropology's most widely publicized finds when he discovered a partial skeleton in Ethiopia in Africa. More than three million years old, the female skeleton of an *australopithecine* was the most complete hominid fossil ever found, although the skull was not recovered. The creature stood three and a half feet tall and, although apelike, had definitely walked upright. Johanson officially announced his find in 1979 as "Lucy," named for the Beatles song "Lucy in the Sky with Diamonds," which was popular in the camp at the time the fossil was found.

nine million years ago, the gorillas split off, and about six million years ago, the chimpanzees split off, leaving the line called hominids.

About 3.5 million years ago, several species of hominids called *Australopithecines* appeared. Possibly, they evolved as they moved from tropical rainforest out onto the savannah and began walking upright. They lived from about 2.5 million to 1.4 million years ago.

From the *Australopithecines* came early humans such as *Homo habilis* (*homo* means "human" or "man"). *Homo habilis* evolved about 2.8 million years ago. This appears to be the first species to use stone tools.

Homo erectus came next, appearing about 1.8 million years ago. This species led to our species, *Homo sapiens* (which means "thinking man"). However, a separate species, *Homo neanderthalensis*, called Neanderthal Man, also evolved. Of these four "homo" species, only humans, *Homo sapiens*, survived.

Homo sapiens appeared about 200,000 years ago in Africa. About 90,000 years ago, they moved into Asia and Europe. However, some of the *Homo sapiens* in Europe intermingled and had children with the still existing *Neanderthals*. Today, many people in Europe have Neanderthal DNA.

Did humans evolve from monkeys?

No. Although humans and monkeys share a common evolutionary line that split many millions of years ago, humans did not evolve from monkeys.

Will more be learned about human evolution?

Yes. Scientists continue to work to figure out the story of human evolution. Many branches of science are working on the problem, such as archeology, paleontology, and genetic biology. Also, more bones of human ancestors are being found.

THE ANCIENT MEDITERRANEAN TO MIDDLE AGES EUROPE

STONE, BRONZE, AND IRON AGES

What are the different time periods for ancient humans?

To try to organize our understanding of time, scholars have created several ages based on the tools used by various peoples of the distant past: the Stone Age, the Bronze Age, and the Iron Age. Each different age represents an advance in technology. This system was created by Danish archeologist Christian Jürgensen Thomsen (1788–1865). Here are the year ranges for the three periods:

- Stone Age: 3.4 million to 3300 B.C.E.
- Bronze Age: 3300 to 1200 B.C.E.
- Iron Age: 1200 B.C.E. to 800 C.E.

Keep in mind that these dates are not precise and that technology varied from place to place. For centuries, one area of the globe might have been using bronze tools and weapons, while in other places, iron tools and weapons were used.

The Stone Age is the prehistoric period and is split into the "Old Stone Age," "Middle Stone Age," and "New Stone Age." These are often called the Paleolithic, Mesolithic, and Neolithic ages. ("Paleo" is from the Greek word for old or ancient, and "lithic" is from the Greek word for stone. "Meso" means middle, and "neo" means new.)

The period of history—according to the strict definition—begins during the Bronze Age, when many cultures began using writing. In describing the time of the Bronze Age onward, historians organize history by different ancient cultures, such as Egyptian, Mesopotamian, Greek, Indian, and Chinese.

What happened in the Stone Age?

In the Old Stone Age, humans were evolving from their apelike ancestors into modern-looking hunter-gatherers. They began making and using stone tools. Somewhere in this long period, humans learned to control and use fire. By the Middle Stone Age, humans began living in permanent settlements and developing agriculture.

In the New Stone Age, humans learned to produce food rather than collect it. People were no longer dependent on hunting, fishing, and gathering wild fruit and nuts for subsistence. They learned to cultivate crops, domesticate animals, make pottery, weave textiles from fiber and hair, and produce more sophisticated tools and weapons by hammering, grinding, and polishing granite, jasper, and other hard stones. More substantial houses and communities, even fortified villages, came into being, laying the foundation for the great civilizations that would follow.

What is the Bronze Age?

Near the end of the New Stone Age, craftsmen in the Middle East learned to make tools and weapons from the metal copper. The world's earliest known manmade copper objects—beads, pins, and awls—were fabricated in the area that today is Turkey and Iran around 8000 B.C.E. Use of copper eventually led to the discovery of adding tin to melted copper to produce bronze. Bronze is much harder than copper, and it can be sharpened; thus, it is an excellent material for making tools and weapons.

Use of bronze began in the region that is today Turkey, Iraq, and Iran. In the ensuing centuries, the use of bronze spread west to Egypt, north into Europe, and east in Asia, including India, China, Korea, and Japan. In addition to tools and weapons, bronze was used in cooking utensils and for creating art.

When did the Iron Age begin?

Copper melts at a lower temperature than iron ore, so humans had to learn to create hotter fires to smelt iron ore. Then they learned the process of casing or steeling iron, by repeatedly reheating wrought iron in a charcoal fire and then hammering it, so it became harder than bronze but also kept its hardness after long use. The next technological improvement to create harder iron was the process of quenching it, which involved repeatedly plunging the hot iron into cold water.

Because bronze was scarce, it was also costly. Consequently, it was not until iron came into use that humans extended their

Early human history is divided into the Stone, Bronze, and Iron Ages, indicating the type of materials being used for tools and weapons.

control over nature. For this reason, iron has been called the "democratic metal." Widespread use of iron tools meant a general increase in living standards. For example, iron axes brought about the clearing of forests for cultivation. Iron tools could be used for sheep shearing and cloth cutting, and iron was used to create the lathe, the most fundamental machine tool. In a lathe, a piece of wood is spun as an iron blade cuts it, producing things such as spindles and spokes for wooden wheels.

ANCIENT EGYPTIAN CULTURE

What is the history of ancient Egypt?

In 3100 B.C.E., the two kingdoms of Upper Egypt and Lower Egypt were united. (Upper Egypt was upstream on the Nile, and Lower Egypt was downstream. Since the Nile flows to the North, Upper Egypt is below Lower Egypt on maps.) There is debate among Egyptian scholars whether the king who united Egypt and became the first king was named Menes or Narmer. The Egyptian kings, known as pharaohs, were believed to be both human and divine. The living pharaoh was seen as the embodiment of the sun god Ra.

Menes (or Narmer) created the first dynasty. Some thirty Egyptian dynasties would follow. A dynasty is a ruling family who holds the throne for several generations. Egyptian history can be broken into three main periods called the Old Kingdom, Middle Kingdom, and New Kingdom. Here is an overview. All dates are B.C.E.

Dates	Events
7000–3100	Independent villages along the Nile
3100–2686	First dynasties
3100	Unification of Egypt and hieroglyphics first used
2686–2181	Old Kingdom at Memphis
2667–2648	Imhotep builds first pyramid for Zoser
2650–2514	Great pyramids and Sphinx built at Giza
2181–2055	First Intermediate Period
	Small independent states
2055–1650	Middle Kingdom at Thebes
1650–1550	Second Intermediate Period
	Hyksos invasion from East and then the Hyksos expelled
1550–1069	New Kingdom
1352–1336	Reign of Akhenaton at Tell el-Armarna
1334–1325	Reign of Tutankhamen
1279–1213	Reign of Ramesses II
	Huge building projects: Luxor, Karnak, Abu Simbel
1069–715	Third Intermediate Period
715–332	Late or Decline Period.

Dates	Events
	Assyrians invade and then the Persians invade
332	Alexander the Great ends Egyptian Kingdom
332–30	Ptolemaic Period under the Greeks
51–30	Cleopatra
30	Romans conquer Egypt

What are the great pyramids of Egypt?

The great pyramids and the Sphinx were built at Giza, outside of the modern city of Cairo, Egypt. The three pyramids were the tombs for pharaohs Khufu, Menkaure, and Khafre and were built in the Old Kingdom. The most famous pharaohs who came later were Tutankhamen—King Tut—and Ramesses. However, in the time of King Tut and Ramesses, the great pyramids were already over 1,200 years old. The pyramids were already ancient history to them!

King Tut is one of the most famous Egyptian pharaohs. Was he an important Egyptian ruler?

No; in fact, King Tut's reign was relatively unimportant in the vast history of ancient Egypt. A ruler of the Eighteenth Dynasty, Tutankhamen (c. 1342–1325 B.C.E.) was in power from age nine until his death at the age of eighteen—a nine-year period that would be of little significance were it not for the 1922 discovery of his tomb in the Valley of the Kings near ancient Thebes (present-day Luxor). Of the twenty-seven pharaohs buried near Thebes, only the tomb of the minor king, Tutankhamen, was spared from looting through the ages. Having not been opened since ancient times, the tomb still contained its treasures.

In the antechamber, English archeologist Howard Carter (1874–1939) found more than 600 artifacts, including funerary bouquets, sandals, robes, cups and jars, a painted casket, life-sized, wooden statues of Tutankhamen, animal-sided couches, remnants of chariots, and a golden throne. In the burial chambers, a team of archeologists discovered four golden shrines and the golden coffin containing the royal mummy of Tutankhamen—complete with a golden mask covering his head and shoulders. (Do an on-

A stone statue of Ramesses II guards the front of Luxor Palace in Thebes, Egypt. The ruins were discovered half buried in the 1880s.

18

line image search for "King Tut treasure" to see what was in the tomb, including the golden mask of King Tut. The blue stripes on the mask are made from the stone lapis lazuli.)

Who was the greatest ruler of ancient Egypt?

Ramesses II (1303 B.C.E.–1213 B.C.E.)—also known as Ramesses the Great—may be the greatest of all ancient Egyptian pharaohs, or rulers. Many referred to him as the "Great One" or the "Great Ancestor." He took command of the empire as a teenager and ruled for more than sixty years. Many famous temples and monuments were completed during his reign, a testament to his power and influence. He lived until he was ninety years old. Numerous other pharaohs took the name Ramesses, but none could match his accomplishments or power.

The mummy of Ramesses II can be seen in Cairo's Egyptian Museum. The head and hands have been unwrapped, so one can see the actual over–3,000-year-old face of Ramesses II. (Do online image searches for "Ramesses II mummy" and "Ramesses II buildings.")

ANCIENT GREEK CULTURE

What are the time periods for the ancient Greek world?

The time frame for the ancient Greek world runs from roughly 3000 to 146 B.C.E. and can be broken down as follows:

Dates	Events
3000–1200 B.C.E.	The Minoan and Mycenaean Periods
1200–800 B.C.E.	The Dark Ages
800–500 B.C.E.	The Archaic Period
500–323 B.C.E.	The Classical Period
323–146 B.C.E.	The Hellenistic Period
146 B.C.E.	The Roman Conquest of Greece

Who were the Minoans?

Ancient Greek civilization began with the Minoans, Europe's first advanced civilization. The Minoans were a prosperous and peaceful people who flourished on the Mediterranean island of Crete from about 3000 to 1450 B.C.E. (Find the island of Crete on the map.) They are believed to be the first people to produce an agricultural surplus, which could be exported. The Minoans built structures from stone, plaster, and timbers; painted walls with brilliant frescoes; made pottery; wove and dyed cloth; constructed stone roads and bridges; and built highly advanced drainage systems and aqueducts. In the city of Knossos, the royal family had a system for showers and even had toilets that could be flushed.

Why are they called the Minoans?

We do not know what these ancient people on Crete called themselves, and their writings cannot be deciphered. However, Greek mythology tells the story of King Minos, who lived on Crete. From this story came the label of "Minoans."

How did the Minoan culture collapse?

Historians debate the cause of the collapse of the Minoan culture. The island of Crete suffered from earthquakes, the effects of volcanoes in the region, and a tsunami wave. Ecological damage, such as deforestation, may have also played a role. However, the final catastrophe was an invasion by the Mycenaeans from the Greek mainland.

Who were the Mycenaeans?

The Mycenaeans flourished from about 1650 to 1200 B.C.E., carrying forth the culture and skills they had learned from the Minoans. The Mycenaeans were skilled horsemen, charioteers, and accomplished sailors who ruled the Aegean Sea. Mycenaean culture revolved around its fortified palaces, called acropolises, which were built on hills. Mycenaean cities included Mycenae, Argos, Corinth, Sparta, and the then small cities of Athens and Thebes.

What was the Trojan War?

In about 1200 B.C.E., the Mycenaeans attacked the city of Troy, which was considered the key to access to the profitable trade by ship with peoples around the Black Sea. Thus began the Trojan War.

The map below shows the location of Troy, protecting the Hellespont, the narrow strait of water now called the Dardanelles, which connects to the Sea of Marmara and then the Bosporus strait, which allows ships to sail from the Aegean Sea to the Black Sea.

How do we know about the Trojan War?

Archeology has confirmed the destruction of the city of Troy by the Myceneans around 1200 B.C.E. Beyond that, all the stories of the Trojan War come from ancient Greek writings, such as the *Iliad*. However, the *Iliad* is considered mythology since it contains many stories about Greek gods and goddesses.

In the stories, Agamemnon led an army that besieged Troy for ten years. The stories include Greek heroes, such as Odysseus and Achilles, and the Trojan hero Hector.

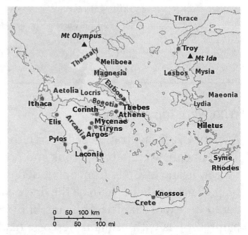

A modern map of the area where the Trojan War occurred, including what is now modern Greece, indicates where ancient Troy once stood in what is now northwestern Turkey.

What is the tale about the Trojan horse?

The story of the Trojan horse comes from Greek, and later Roman, mythology. It is told in the *Aeneid* by Latin writer Virgil. It is also mentioned in the earlier writing the *Odyssey* by Homer. However, both writings are considered mythology. In the story, the Greeks build a wooden horse big enough to hold a squad of soldiers. The Greeks trick the Trojans into taking the horse into the city and into thinking the war is over. That night, the soldiers come out of the horse, open the gates of the city so the Greeks can come in, and destroy the city and kill or enslave the population.

There is no way to know whether or not there actually was a Trojan horse used to destroy Troy. Some suggest the Greeks might have used a battering ram or siege machine shaped like a horse, or perhaps it was a ship with hidden soldiers given as a gift to the Trojans.

Who were the Dorians?

Soon after the Trojan War, the Mycenaeans were overrun by the Dorians, who had the advantage of iron swords. Coming from the northwestern part of the Greek mainland, the Dorians moved southward, where they sacked and burned the great Mycenaean cities and conquered the wealthy sea traders, throwing Greece into the period known as the Dark Ages, which lasted from 1200 to about 800 B.C.E.

The Dorians rejected the life of the great Mycenaean cities in favor of their nomadic shepherding and hunting life. A tribal people, they possessed a harsh sense of justice, and the period was marked by feuds between clans. Men typically carried weapons—now made of iron. The Dorians ended the Bronze Age and ushered in the Iron Age.

Why is this period called the "Dark Ages"?

During the Dark Ages, there is little evidence of Greek civilization; the script used by the Mycenaeans disappeared, and art, which had prospered during the Mycenaean Age, declined. Under Dorian rule, numerous Mycenaean cities were abandoned, and many regions and islands seem to have been depopulated. There is no evidence of trade with other countries. Poverty had overtaken the Greeks.

As the Dorians took possession of the Greek mainland, a few Mycenaean communities survived in remote areas, such as the city of Athens, which became a haven for those who hoped for a return to the former civilization. Other Mycenaeans crossed the Aegean Sea and settled on the coast of Asia Minor (what today is Turkey). All these refugees spoke Ionian Greek.

What was the Greek Archaic Period (800–500 B.C.E.)?

In the Archaic Period, the Ionian Greeks attempted to hold on to the refined civilization of the Bronze Age. They commemorated the greatness of the past in song and verse, in-

21

cluding Greek poet Homer's *Iliad* and *Odyssey*. (The "Expressions of Human Culture" chapter will have more to say on Homer and these important writings.) These epics were combined with eighth-century poet Hesiod's *Theogony,* an account of the creation of the universe and the generations of the gods, to give rise to a new Greek religion based on the god Zeus and eleven other gods, who were believed to reside on Mount Olympus in northeastern Greece. Hesiod lived around 700 B.C.E., and Homer lived around 800 B.C.E.

What was the Classical Period of ancient Greece?

This was the period of 500–323 B.C.E., in which ancient Greece achieved its greatest accomplishments. The classical Greeks, who called themselves the Hellenes and their land Hellas, influenced western civilization more than any other people. Their contributions to every field of endeavor remain with us today, more than 2,000 years later.

Greek thought shaped science, medicine, philosophy, art, literature, architecture and engineering, mathematics, music, drama, language, and politics. The classical Greeks believed in individual freedom, reasoning, and truth and that everything should be done in moderation. They also held that people should find time for both work and play and should balance the life of the mind with the exercise of the body.

The Greeks took the early alphabet of the Phoenicians—an ancient sea people— and adapted it to the Greek language. The Greeks then started writing down the works of Homer and Hesiod and poets, historians, playwrights, and philosophers.

Among the great Greek philosophers were Socrates, Plato, and Aristotle. (See the "Philosophy" chapter.) Greek literature included the passionate love poems of Sappho. The Greeks also wrote plays: the tragedies of Aeschylus, Sophocles, and Euripides, which continue to be studied by students today, along with the comedies of Aristophanes and Menander. The classical Greeks loved to speak, and oratory is considered by some to be their highest form of prose. Orators known to the modern world were Antiphon, Lysias, Isocrates, and Demosthenes.

Herodotus (c. 484–c. 425 B.C.E.), called the "Father of History," left the modern world with an account of the Persian Wars (499–449 B.C.E.), a conflict between the Greek city-states and the Persian Empire. The Greeks also gave humankind the "Father of Medicine" in physician Hippocrates, who taught that doctors should use reason to determine the cause of illness and should study the patient's appearance, behavior, and lifestyle to diagnose and treat illnesses and injuries. (His "Hippocratic Oath" will be discussed in the "Medicine and Disease" chapter.) Greek scientists included Thales and Pythagoras; scientist-philosophers included Leucippus and Democritus. And, of course, the Greeks gave modern culture the Olympic Games.

Who was Pericles?

Pericles (495–429 B.C.E.) was a leading Greek statesman who led Athens during the height of its powers. Called "the first citizen of Athens," Pericles led his country at the

The Parthenon in Athens was a temple for the goddess Athena. Constructed from 447 to 432 B.C.E., it is an important example of Doric architecture and is one of the most popular tourist attractions in Greece to this day.

beginning of the Peloponnesian War with the city of Sparta. He fostered democracy and encouraged the growth of various forms of art and architecture.

Pericles also built the Parthenon, the famous temple of Athena on the Acropolis in Athens. According to Greek mythology, Athena was a virgin. The Greek word for virgin is *parthénos*, so the temple is called the Parthenon.

What disasters befell Athens at the peak of its glory?

Two disasters hit Athens: a plague and the Peloponnesian War. In 430 B.C.E. Athens was hit by a terrible plague that would eventually kill a third of the city's citizens, including its ruler, Pericles. The deaths from the plague would weaken Athens as it fought the Peloponnesian War with the city-state of Sparta.

The war, which lasted from 431 to 404 B.C.E., is named for the lower part of Greece, which is called Peloponnesus. (Sparta is in Peloponnesus.) The war signaled the end of the golden age of Greece. The war, which took place in three phases, ended with the destruction of the Athenian naval fleet in a fierce sea battle. Athens was left in ruins.

What happened to Athens after the Peloponnesian War?

While the Greek city-states were in decline due to war, Greece's neighbor to the north, Macedonia, was growing more powerful. In 353 B.C.E. Macedonian king Philip II (382–336 B.C.E.) launched an attack on Greece. The war that resulted did not end until 338 B.C.E., when Greece was finally conquered.

When Philip was killed, his twenty-year-old son, Alexander, came to power. Alexander then began a ten-year campaign to conquer the Persian Empire. By the time he was thirty years old, Alexander had conquered much of the known world, expanding his empire from Egypt to India.

Why was Macedonian king Alexander known as "the Great"?

Alexander the Great (356–323 B.C.E.) has passed through history as a legendary figure, a reputation attributable to the fact that he conquered virtually all the known world in his day. In effect, he was king of the world.

As the son of King Philip II, Alexander had an upbringing and education befitting a young Greek prince. He was tutored by Greek philosopher Aristotle (384–322 B.C.E.) and was trained in athletics and war. His studies of Greek literature and art would later combine with his skill as a warrior to produce a formidable conqueror, who spread Hellenism (Greek culture) throughout the known world.

At age sixteen, Alexander began running the government of Macedonia while his father waged military campaigns to expand his kingdom. At seventeen, Alexander joined his father on the battlefield, where he commanded a section of the army that defeated Thebes. When Philip was assassinated in 336 B.C.E., Alexander acted quickly to assert his claim to the throne. He continued to carry out his father's campaigns, securing Greece and the Balkan Peninsula. He followed this with an all-out offensive on the Persian Empire, long the enemy of Greece. Supremely courageous and confident in his own abilities as well as in his troops (which numbered in the tens of thousands), by the fall of 331 B.C.E., Alexander had defeated the Persian army and along the way claimed Egypt.

The centuries-old Persian Empire crumbled, and the young Macedonian king proclaimed himself "Lord of Asia." Still, he pressed on, claiming Afghanistan and then India. He was poised to take the Arabian Peninsula, but in 323 B.C.E., he died of fever at age thirty-three.

Although Alexander is remembered as "the Great," many of the people he conquered would not give him that honor. Others referred to him as "the accursed." His vast king-

This replica of a Greek trireme shows that it was quite an impressive vessel for its day.

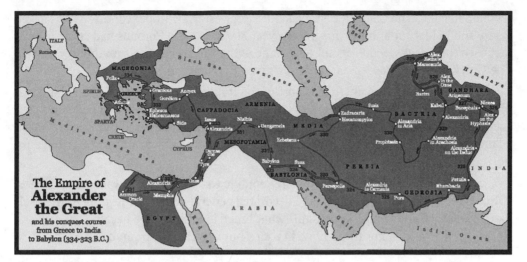

The Empire of
Alexander the Great
and his conquest course
from Greece to India
to Babylon (334-323 B.C.)

This map shows the farthest extent of Alexander the Great's empire.

dom, which he had ruled leniently but nevertheless authoritatively, was divided among his former generals.

What is the Hellenistic period of ancient Greek history?

The Hellenistic period, from 323 to 146 B.C.E., lasted from the death of Alexander to the conquest of Greece by the Romans. The Roman period followed. The term "Hellenistic" refers to Greek political control and Greek culture. The word comes from the name of the upper part of Greece, Hellas. (The term has nothing to do with the figure of Greek mythology Helen of Troy.)

ANCIENT ROMAN CULTURE

What is the early history of Rome?

In 753 B.C.E., the city of Rome was established. (Legend has it that the city was founded by Romulus.) Situated on wooded hills above the Tiber River, about fifteen miles from the sea, Rome enjoyed the advantages of access to trade routes while having natural protection from aggressors since the location was very defensible. Agriculture prospered in the area, as did manufacturing and mining.

In 509 B.C.E., noblemen established the Roman Republic. The government was headed by two elected officials, called consuls. Since they shared power, a certain measure of balance was ensured in that either one could veto the actions of the other. And the posts were brief: each elected official served for only one year. These heads of state were guided by the Roman Senate, which was made up of senior statesmen. There were also assemblies in which the people had a voice.

In 390 B.C.E., the Gauls (a Celtic people from western Europe) captured and sacked Rome and held it for a short time. By the year 300 B.C.E., the Romans had come in contact with the Greeks, adopting not only some of their ideas but their mythology as well. The Greek gods and goddesses were soon given Roman names.

By 275 B.C.E., Rome controlled most of the Italian peninsula. Their homeland stable, the Romans set their sights on overseas expansion, and between 264 and 146 B.C.E., they fought the Punic Wars in order to gain territory. They conquered the Mediterranean islands of Sicily, Sardinia, and Corsica; part of Gaul; much of Spain; and Carthage (in northern Africa).

In the last century B.C.E., the Roman Republic was torn by civil wars. In the chaos, Julius Caesar came to power. He was a decorated general known for leading Roman soldiers to victory and conquest in Gaul (what today is France). He became the ruler of Rome, serving as dictator from 49 to 44 B.C.E., but was then murdered.

Why was Julius Caesar murdered?

The Roman general and statesman Julius Caesar (100–44 B.C.E.) was stabbed to death in the Senate house by a group of men, including some of his former friends, who viewed him as an ambitious tyrant and a threat to the Roman Republic. The event illustrates the controversy about Julius Caesar.

While some clearly viewed him as a demagogue who forced his way into power, others considered the patrician-born Caesar a man of noble character who defended the rights of the people in an oligarchic state—where the government was controlled by a few people who had only their own interests in mind. This divided opinion has followed Caesar throughout history.

The date of the assassination, March 15, became famous based on a line from William Shakespeare's play *Julius Caesar* (written in 1599), where a prophet warns Julius Caesar to "beware the ides of March." "Ides" was the middle of the month.

After Caesar's death in 44 B.C.E., a triumvirate was formed to rule Rome, with Lepidus, Octavian, and Mark Antony sharing power. Mark Antony is remembered for his relationship with the Egyptian queen Cleopatra. In the end, Octavian, the grandnephew of Caesar, became the Roman emperor in 27 B.C.E. He took the name of Augustus, which translates into "revered one."

Who were the most important rulers of the Roman Empire?

The 500 years of the Roman Empire (27 B.C.E. to 476 C.E.) gave history some of its most noteworthy—and most diabolical—leaders. The major emperors are names that are familiar to almost every student of Western civilization:

Emperor	Years Reigned
Augustus	27 B.C.E.–14 C.E.
Tiberius	14–37 C.E.

Emperor	Years Reigned
Caligula	37–41 C.E.
Claudius	41–54 C.E.
Nero	54–68 C.E.
Trajan	98–117 C.E.
Marcus Aurelius	161–180 C.E.
Diocletian	284–305 C.E.
Constantine I	306–337 C.E.

Under Augustus's rule began the 200 years of the Pax Romana (the "Roman Peace"), a period of relative peace with little warfare; consequently, Rome was able to turn its attention to the arts, literature, education, and trade.

As second emperor of Rome, Tiberius came under the influence of Roman politicians. Tiberius was the adopted son of Emperor Augustus, and he had been carefully schooled and groomed to take on the leadership role. Ultimately, he became a tyrannical ruler; the final years of his reign were marked by viciousness and cruelty.

Upon Tiberius's death, his nephew Caligula ascended to the throne. For a short time, Caligula ruled with moderation; however, not long after he came to power, he fell ill and thereafter exhibited the erratic behavior for which he is well known. Most scholars agree that Caligula must have been crazy. He was murdered in 41 C.E., and Claudius (also a nephew to Tiberius) was then proclaimed emperor. (Some speculate that Caligula might have suffered from lead poisoning, which can cause brain damage. Wine was often kept in jugs made of lead, and water pipes were also made of lead.)

Claudius renewed the expansion of Rome, waging battle with Germany, Syria, and Mauretania (present-day Algeria and Morocco), and conquering half of Britain. Though his administration was reportedly well run, he had his enemies; among them was his niece, Agrippina the Younger, who is believed to have murdered him in 54 C.E. after making sure her son, Nero, would be the next ruler.

In Nero, the early Roman Empire had perhaps its most despotic ruler. Though his early years in power were marked by the efficient conduct of public affairs, in 59 C.E., he had his mother assassinated (she reportedly had tried to rule through her son), and Nero's legacy from that point forward is one of ruthless behavior. He was involved in murder plots, ordered the deaths of many Romans, instituted the persecution of Christians, and led an extravagant lifestyle that emptied the public coffers. He was declared a public enemy by the Roman Senate and in the year 68 C.E. took his own life.

Trajan is best known for his military campaigns, which expanded Rome's territory. He was also a builder—constructing bridges, roads, and many buildings.

Why is Emperor Marcus Aurelius important?

When Marcus Aurelius ascended to emperor, he had already been in public office for more than twenty years. A man of great experience, he was reportedly both learned and of gentle character. His generals put down revolting tribes, and in addition to winning victories along the Danube River, his troops also fought barbarians in the north. He is also known for writing an important book of Stoic philosophy, the *Meditations*.

By the third century C.E., Roman armies had conquered so many peoples that the empire stretched across Europe and included the entire Mediterranean coast of Africa as well as parts of the Middle East. During this time of power and expansion, trade thrived over a vast network of roads and sea routes, which extended to China, India, and Africa. The Roman government issued and controlled coins made of gold, silver, copper, and bronze.

What were the Punic Wars?

The Punic Wars were three major campaigns that Rome waged to expand its empire. Messina, a city on the island of Sicily, was the site of the First Punic War, which began in 264 B.C.E. when warring factions in the city called for assistance from both Carthage and Rome. The Carthaginians arrived first from North Africa and secured the city. But the Romans, who had girded their navy for the battle, arrived and drove the Carthaginians out (in 241 B.C.E.), conquering Sicily. Messina became a free city allied with Rome.

The Second Punic War (218–201 B.C.E.) was largely fought over control of Spain. When the great Carthaginian general Hannibal captured the Roman-allied city of Sa-

One of the largest empires to have ever existed, the Roman Empire encircled the Mediterranean Sea, reaching from Africa to the British Isles and from Spain to the Middle East at its height.

gunto, Spain, in 218 B.C.E., he crossed the Alps and invaded Italy, where he was met by and then defeated the Roman armies. The deciding battle in the Second Punic War was fought in the North African town of Zama (southwest of Carthage) in 202 B.C.E. It was there that the Romans under General Scipio Africanus (236–183 B.C.E.) crushed the Carthaginians under Hannibal. Rome exacted payments from Carthage, and Carthage was also forced to surrender its claims in Spain. In 201 B.C.E. the two powers signed a peace treaty, which held for five decades.

Why is Hannibal considered so important?

Hannibal (247 B.C.E.–183 B.C.E.) is considered a skilled military leader and strategist far ahead of his times, who sometimes led his Carthaginian troops to victories over much larger Roman forces. For example, in 216 B.C.E., he and his troops engaged and trapped a much larger Roman force of more than 85,000 troops in Cannae during the Second Punic War. Hannibal and his troops killed more than 50,000 Roman soldiers—probably the most devastating defeat Roman soldiers ever suffered.

Eventually, Hannibal was forced to retreat, as the Romans had too many resources. Rome won the Second Punic War in 201 B.C.E., and Hannibal fled to present-day Turkey. He eventually committed suicide rather than surrender to the Romans.

What happened in the Third Punic War?

The Third Punic War erupted in 149 B.C.E., when the Carthaginians rebelled against Roman rule. By 146 B.C.E., Carthage, which had been richer and more powerful than Rome when the Punic Wars began, was completely destroyed.

Who were some of the famous later emperors?

Diocletian had served as an army commander before becoming emperor. To effectively rule the expansive territory, he divided it into four regions, each with its own ruler, though he himself remained the acknowledged chief. Two years before he abdicated the throne in 305 C.E., he began the persecution of Christians—a surprising move since he had long been friendly toward them. Unlike his predecessors who died in office, Diocletian had a retirement, which he reportedly spent gardening. He enjoyed raising cabbages far more than ruling as emperor.

Constantine the Great is notable for reuniting the regions that Diocletian had created, bringing them all under his rule by 324. He was also the first Roman emperor to convert to Christianity.

Theodosius I (347–395), also called "the Great," is known to many since he was the last to rule the united Roman Empire (from 379 to 395). In 395, upon the death of Emperor Theodosius, the Roman Empire was divided into two: East and West. In 476, after suffering a series of attacks from nomadic Germanic tribes, Rome fell.

How was Rome "sacked"?

After the split of the Roman Empire in 395, the Western Roman Empire continued to weaken, and Rome became the subject of a series of brutal attacks by Germanic tribes. In 410 the Visigoths moved into Italy and looted Rome; in 455 the Vandals thoroughly ravaged the city; finally, in 476 the city fell when the Germanic chieftain Odoacer (433–493) forced Romulus Augustulus (c. 460–?), the last ruler of the empire, from the throne. By this time, however, Germanic chiefs had already taken Roman lands and di-

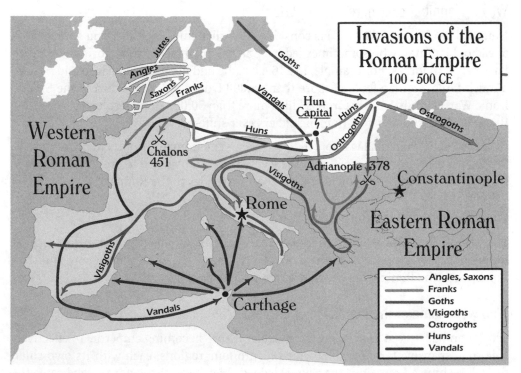

The Roman Empire was under constant risk of invasion from barbarian tribes in the north, including the Visigoths, Franks, Vandals, and others. Eventually, these invaders would reach the city of Rome, sacking it on several occasions as the empire gradually weakened and then fell.

vided them into several smaller kingdoms. The year 476 marks the official collapse of the Western Roman Empire.

What is the legacy of ancient Rome?

Since the Romans borrowed and adapted the ideas of the Greeks, with whom they had come into contact in about 300 B.C.E. and later conquered in 146 B.C.E., the culture of ancient Rome is sometimes called Greco-Roman. Over the course of centuries, Romans spread their ideas throughout their vast empire.

They also developed a legal code, which outlined basic principles while remaining flexible enough that lawyers and judges could interpret the laws, taking into consideration local customs and practices. The *Code of Justinian*, the *Corpus Juris Civilis* of 529 C.E., later became the model for legal systems in Europe and Latin America.

Roman armies built a network of roads, aqueducts, and tunnels, putting in place an infrastructure that outlasted the empire. Many Roman aqueducts and bridges still stand.

Latin, the Roman language, remained the language of educated Europeans for more than 1,400 years, while the Latin-based (or Romance) languages of Italian, French, Spanish, Portuguese, and Romanian took over everyday communication. The economic system put in place during the height of the Roman Empire, with a centrally controlled money supply, also had a lasting effect.

Though the empire had crumbled by 476 C.E., its cultural, social, and economic establishments continued to have validity well into the Middle Ages.

Why is it called the Byzantine Empire?

An ancient Greek colony called Byzantium was settled on the Bosporus. The Bosporus is a narrow strait or natural channel that connects the Black Sea in the east to the Mediterranean Sea in the west. (Sailing west, one would cross the Sea of Marmara, the Dardanelles, and the Aegean Sea to get to the Mediterranean Sea.) The location of the colony is in what today is Turkey. Because of its location along the shipping trade routes, the colony would become a great city, later called Constantinople. Today, it is called Istanbul. The original name of the colony would become the name of the Byzantine Empire.

What is the Byzantine Empire's role in history?

The Byzantine Empire (330 or 395 to 1453) is considered a link between ancient and modern civilizations. Though the empire was constantly fighting off invaders, plagued by religious controversies, and marred by political strife, as the heir of the Roman world, it allowed for the customs of Greco-Roman civilization to mix with those of the East and with Christianity.

Why was Constantine I called "the Great"?

Roman emperor Constantine the Great (c. 272–337) is credited with no less than beginning a new era in history. His father, Constantius, was ruler of the Roman Empire when he died in 306. Though Constantine was named emperor by Roman soldiers, a power struggle ensued. During a battle near Rome in 312 at the Milvian Bridge, Constantine, who had always been sympathetic toward Christians, reportedly saw a vision in the sky. Inspired by the vision, he and his troops won the battle against those trying to stop him from becoming emperor. Constantine emerged from the conflict both converted and victorious.

For the next twelve years, Constantine ruled the Western Roman Empire, while Licinius (also tolerant to Christians) ruled the Eastern Roman Empire. But a struggle between the two emperors ended in death for Licinius and, beginning in 325, Constantine ruled as sole emperor.

During Constantine's reign, Christians gained freedom of worship, and the Christian Church became legal. In 325 he convened the Council of Nicaea. At the council, the Nicene Creed was created, which stated the essential beliefs of Christians. Many Christians today still follow the beliefs of the Creed.

Constantine also moved the capital of the Roman Empire to Byzantium. He named the city after himself: Constantinople, meaning "Constantine's city." (Today, the city is Istanbul in Turkey.) By moving the capital, he laid the foundation for the Byzantine Empire.

This bronze statue of Constantine the Great was created by artist Philip Jackson and unveiled in 1998 in York, England. It commemorates his ascension to the throne in 306 C.E.

When did the Byzantine Empire begin?

The Byzantine Empire was a continuation of the Roman Empire—its citizens even called themselves Romans. Some historians date the beginning of the empire to 330 C.E., when Constantine moved the capital from Rome to Byzantium and renamed the city Constantinople. (Other historians date the beginning to 395 C.E., when the empire was divided into East and West, followed by the fall of Rome in 476.)

Constantine was succeeded by nearly one hundred rulers over the course of more than 1,000 years of Byzantine rule. At its height, during the sixth-century reign of Justinian I from 483 to 565, the empire included parts of southern and eastern Europe, northern Africa, and the Middle East. The Byzantine Empire ended when the Ottoman Turks conquered Constantinople in 1453.

What is the Hagia Sophia?

The Hagia Sophia was built as a magnificent Orthodox Christian church with a massive dome. The words *hagia sophia* mean "holy wisdom." Built by Emperor Justinian I, it was completed in the year 537 C.E. For a thousand years, it was the largest church in the world. It stands today in the city of Istanbul in modern Turkey, although at the time it was built, the city was called Constantinople. In the year 1453, the Muslim Ottoman Turks conquered the region, and the Hagia Sophia was converted into a mosque. Four

An Eastern Orthodox cathedral for nearly a thousand years, the Hagia Sophia was the largest building in the world when it was completed in the sixth century. Today, it is a stunning museum in Istanbul, Turkey.

towers, called "minarets," were added. Five times a day, men called "muezzins" would go to the top of the towers to call Muslims to prayer. In 1935, the Hagia Sophia became a museum and is visited by many tourists each year.

THE TRIBAL PEOPLES OF EUROPE

Who were the Celts?

The Celts were an Indo-European people who by 500 B.C.E. had spread across what is now France, Italy, Portugal, Spain, and the British Isles and by 200 B.C.E. had expanded as far as present-day Bulgaria and Greece. When the Romans conquered much of Europe (about 300 B.C.E.), many Celts were absorbed into the Roman Empire. However, those Celts living in Ireland, Scotland, Wales, southwest England, and Brittany (in northwestern France) were able to maintain their cultures, and it is in these regions that people of Celtic origin still live today.

Their society was divided among three classes: commoners, the educated, and aristocrats. They formed loose federations of tribes, raised crops and livestock, used the Greek alphabet to write their own language, and were among the first peoples in northern Europe to make iron. They never formed one united nation, however, so that when Roman armies swept across Europe, the Celtic tribes were overrun.

How were the Gauls related to the Celts?

The ancient Gauls were a Celtic people who occupied the ancient country of Gaul (an area that today consists of France, Belgium, Luxembourg, part of Germany, and part of the Netherlands). The Gauls were led by priests, called Druids.

Over several centuries, the Gauls fought the Romans, and then, under Julius Caesar, the Romans conquered all of Gaul with the defeat of the chief of the Gauls, Vercingetorix, in 52 B.C.E. Gaul became part of the Roman Empire. Very likely, a million or more Gauls were killed or died of disease and famine under the conquest of Julius Caesar. Perhaps a million were enslaved.

Julius Caesar described the military campaign in his *Commentarii de bello Gallico* (*Commentaries on the Gallic War*).

Who were the Huns?

The Huns were a nomadic central Asian people, who in the middle of the fourth century C.E. moved westward and conquered the local peoples. Unified by the ruler Attila the Hun in 434, the Huns gained control of a large part of central and eastern Europe. The Italian countryside was ravaged in the process, and many people sought refuge on the numerous islands in the Lagoon of Venice; the settlement later became the city of Venice. With the death of Attila in 453, the subjects of the Huns revolted and defeated them.

Who was Attila the Hun?

While Attila (c. 406–453) may have possessed some of the worthwhile qualities of a military leader, the king of the Huns was no doubt a ruthless and fierce figure. He is believed to have ascended through the ranks of the Hun army, coming to power as the leader of the nomadic group in 434. By this time, the Huns (who originated in central Asia) had occupied the Volga River valley in the area of present-day western Russia.

At first, like his predecessors, he was wholly occupied with fighting other barbarian tribes for control of lands. But under Attila's leadership, the Huns began to extend their power into central Europe. He waged battles with the Eastern Roman armies, and, after murdering his older brother and coruler Bleda in 445, went on to trample the countries of the Balkan Peninsula and northern Greece—causing terrible destruction along the way. As Attila continued westward with his bloody campaigns, which each Hun fought using his own weapons and his own savage technique, he nearly destroyed the foundations of Christianity.

The leader of the Huns from 434 to 453, Attila the Hun was the most feared invader throughout Europe.

But the combined armies of the Romans and the Visigoths defeated Attila and the Huns at Châlons (in northeastern France) in June 451, which is known as one of the most decisive battles of all time. From there, Attila and his men moved into Italy, devastating the countryside before Pope Leo I (c. 400–461) succeeded in persuading the brutal leader to spare Rome. (For this and other reasons, Leo was later canonized, becoming Saint Leo.) Attila died suddenly—and of natural causes—in 453, just as he was again preparing to cross the Alps and invade Italy anew.

Who were the barbarians?

The term refers to any of the Germanic tribes that, beginning about 400, repeatedly attacked Rome, eventually conquering it and dividing the territories of the Western Roman Empire into many kingdoms. The Germanic tribes included the Goths, the Vandals, the Franks, the Lombards, the Angles, and the Saxons.

Who were the Goths?

The Goths divided into two groups: a western group known as the Visigoths and an eastern group known as the Ostrogoths. Theodoric (c. 454–526) became the ruler of the Ostrogoths in 493, and it was under his leadership that the group invaded northern Italy.

In 378 the Visigoths rebelled against the Roman authorities. On horseback, they fought the battle of Adrianople (in present-day Turkey), destroying a Roman army and killing Rome's eastern emperor, Valens (c. 328–378). The Visigoths' introduction of the cavalry (troops trained to fight on horseback) as part of warfare determined European military, social, and political development for the next thousand years.

The Visigoths moved into Italy, and under the leadership of their ruler, Alaric (c. 370–410), sacked Rome in 410, an event that signaled the beginning of the end of the Roman Empire. The Visigoths moved into Gaul and then the Iberian Peninsula (present-day Spain and Portugal). The city of Toledo was established as their capital. Roderick (or Rodrigo), the last Visigoth king, was defeated and killed in 711 during a battle with the Muslims (Moors), who invaded from northern Africa and then conquered most of the Iberian Peninsula.

Who were the Vandals?

Around the year 100 C.E., the Vandals had settled in what today is Poland. In time, they were threatened by the Huns, so the Vandals moved west, overrunning Gaul (present-day France), Spain, and northern Africa, where they eventually settled. In 455, led by the powerful King Genseric, the Vandals ravaged Rome. Their pillage was so thorough that the word "vandal" would be used to describe anyone who willfully destroys property.

Who were the Franks?

The Franks were yet another Germanic people. Their most important early king was Clovis I (c. 466–511). Under this cruel and cunning king, the Franks soon controlled much of Europe, including the land that is today France, Belgium, and Germany. (In case you have not guessed it, France is named after the Franks.) Under the influence of his wife, Clotilde, Clovis converted to Catholic Christianity. Soon, most of his people would also convert.

Who were the Lombards?

The Lombards, too, were a Germanic tribe who moved from the area that today is Germany, then moved south into what today is Austria, and then moved into much of Italy. In 754, Pope Stephen II (714–757) appealed to the powerful Franks for help. Under the rule of Pepin III (called Pepin the Short; c. 714–768), the Franks defeated the Lombards. The northern region of Italy, Lombardy, is named for them.

What is the origin of the word "barbarian"?

The word comes from the ancient Greeks; possibly, it referred to the language of people the Greeks did not understand: their language sounded like "bar … bar.…"

Who were the Angles and Saxons?

The Angles were a Germanic tribe that settled in England, where they joined the Saxons (also a Germanic-speaking people). Together, they became known as Anglo-Saxons. The name "England" comes from the older name *Englaland*, meaning "Land of the Angles."

Who were the Vikings?

The Vikings, also called Norsemen, were fierce, seafaring warriors who originated in Scandinavia (today the countries Norway, Sweden, and Denmark). Beginning in the late 700s, they raided England, France,

The Vikings often attacked cities and towns not to take them over and expand an empire but simply to loot them. This illustration depicts the 845 siege of Paris in which the Vikings defeated Charles the Bald, took a ransom of gold and silver, and then left.

Germany, Ireland, Scotland, Italy, Russia, and Spain. They also reached Greenland, Iceland, and even North America long before the Europeans. (Ruins of a Norse settlement were found on the northeastern coast of Newfoundland, Canada.) The Viking raiders were greatly feared.

What was the importance of Viking ships?

The Viking ship was designed to sail on open oceans on rough seas, yet the boats had a shallow draft, which meant they did not go that deep into the water and could sail in shallow waters. Thus, not only could Vikings raid and plunder coastal settlements and cities, they could also go up rivers and raid cities far from the coast. All major cities were built on rivers. For example, the Vikings in 845, led by the chieftain Ragnar, sailed 120 ships over 200 miles up the Seine River to attack and plunder Paris.

The Vikings converted to Christianity around the year 1000, about the same time that the kingdoms of Norway, Denmark, and Sweden were established. Under the Danish leader Canute, Vikings conquered England in 1016 and ruled it as part of Denmark until 1042.

Who were the Normans?

The Normans were Vikings who in the mid-800s invaded northern France, ousting the Franks. The region came to be known as Normandy. In 1066, the Norman duke William (the Conqueror; 1027–1087) sailed across the English Channel, and in the Battle of Hastings, defeated the army of King Harold Godwinson and claimed the English throne.

THE RISE OF ISLAM

What are the origins of the religion of Islam?

In the year 570, Muhammad was born in the city of Mecca in what today is Saudi Arabia. According to Muslim tradition, at the age of forty, he began receiving revelations from the archangel Gabriel. In the next years, a new religion, Islam, would be built on these revelations. Eventually, the revelations would be written down as the holy book of Islam, the Qur'an. Muhammad would be honored as the final prophet of Allah's message. Allah is the Arabic word for God.

Muhammad died in 632. In the next centuries, his followers would spread Islam over the Mideast, North Africa, and what today is Spain. There would be numerous conflicts as the Islamic world and the Christian world clashed. (Islam will be covered in more detail in the "Religion" chapter.)

THE MIDDLE AGES AND THE RENAISSANCE IN EUROPE

SETTING THE STAGE FOR THE MIDDLE AGES

What happened after the collapse of the Roman Empire?

The Roman Empire collapsed for many reasons. One of the key reasons was the arrival of the tribal peoples, also called the Barbarians, who began carving up pieces of the Roman Empire. Over the centuries, these peoples, such as the Goths, the Vandals, the Franks, and the Anglo-Saxons, settled in Europe. In time, these peoples were all Christianized and then created kingdoms. These Christianized kingdoms became medieval Europe. Several important missionaries brought Christianity to these tribal peoples.

Why is Benedict important?

Benedict, often called St. Benedict, was born in 480 and died in either 543 or 547. He set up several monasteries in Italy. Most importantly, he wrote a guidebook on being a monk called the *Rule of St. Benedict*. His rule book became so influential that he is often called the founder of Western monasticism. One group of monks, called the Order of St. Benedict, are still around today.

However, Benedict did not invent Christian monasticism. Early Christian men and women living the monastic life existed in the second century. Famous monks, such as St. Antony and the Desert Fathers in Egypt, lived in the third and fourth centuries. By the time of Benedict, there were many Christian monasteries and a long history of Christian monasticism.

The *Rule of St. Benedict* is important because it became so influential. In writing his rule, Benedict tried to find a middle way of moderation. He wanted to avoid practices that were overzealous or fanatical, such as demands for extreme fasting. The problem with such practices is that they are very hard to maintain over the long term. On the other hand, Benedict wanted to avoid a monastic life that was too easy and that would encourage laziness and invite distractions from a life of prayer.

The motto of St. Benedict was *ora et labora,* which means "pray and work." Monks were required to spend most of their time in prayer either in community or by themselves. Yet, monks were also required to work to support themselves. Initially, Benedict imagined monks supporting themselves through manual labor and farm work. He wanted to get away from monasteries that were supported solely by donations.

He expected his monks to live a simple life without possessions for fear that possessions would distract them from the spiritual life and also because more possessions would require more money to buy them.

Who are some important Christian missionaries of this period?

St. Augustine of Canterbury (d. 604) brought Christianity to England. He is a different person from Augustine of Hippo (354–430). St. Boniface (c. 675–754) brought Christianity to the Germanic tribes. One legend tells how he chopped down the sacred tree of Thor (called Donar in German) in a village. When he was not struck dead by lightning, the villagers believed his god was more powerful than Thor, so they converted.

St. Cyril (826–869) and St. Methodius (815–885) were two brothers who are known as the "apostles to the Slavs" for their missionary work with the Slavic people in Eastern Europe. They created a special alphabet for translating the Bible. Called the Cyrillic alphabet, it is named after Cyril. Today, the script is used for languages such as Russian.

Who was Saint Patrick?

Saint Patrick is known as the "Apostle of Ireland" for helping to bring Christianity to Ireland. He lived in the late 400s. He grew up in Great Britain but was captured by Irish pirates at about the age of sixteen. He worked as a slave for the next six years until he escaped to his family in Britain. He became a priest and returned to Ireland as a mis-

Why is the shamrock the symbol of St. Patrick?

There is a legend that Patrick used the shamrock to teach people about the Trinity. Just as the shamrock has three leaves, the Trinity has three persons in one God. However, since the legend first appears in writing in the 1700s, there is serious doubt whether Saint Patrick actually used the shamrock as a teaching device.

The feast of Saint Patrick is March 17. Many people use shamrocks as decorations to remember Saint Patrick, especially in areas that have populations with an Irish heritage. Ironically, many bars decorate with shamrocks as people celebrate St. Patrick's Day by drinking, with little interest in the religious beliefs supposedly behind the symbol.

sionary. He eventually became a bishop. He is remembered for bringing Christianity to Ireland.

Who was Gregory the Great?

Gregory lived from c. 540 to 604 and became the bishop of Rome in 590. He did much to shape the influence and authority of the bishop of Rome over Western Christianity, which included his efforts to send out missionaries in Europe. He is called Pope Gregory I, although the word "pope" was not in use in his time for the bishop of Rome. His numerous writings have survived, including his sermons and letters. The Gregorian chant, a style of music used by monks for chanting the Psalms from the Bible, is named after him.

Later, in the Middle Ages, the pope in Rome would become a key figure in religion and politics in Europe for many centuries.

Who was Charles Martel?

In 719, Charles Martel (c. 688–741), known as Charles the Hammer, united the lands of the Franks under his rule. He is most famous for his victory at the Battle of Tours in 732 in which he defeated a Muslim army led by Abd al-Rahman al-Ghafiqi coming from the area that today is Spain.

Although some see this battle as key in stopping Islam from overtaking more of Europe, there is much uncertainty about the exact location of the battle, the size of the armies, and the significance of the battle.

A statue of Charles Martel can be found at Versailles. His victory at the Battle of Tours helped halt Muslim expansion into Europe.

THE MIDDLE AGES

When is the beginning of the Middle Ages?

There are different views on when to mark the beginning of the Middle Ages. A common beginning point is the fifth century with the decline of the Roman Empire. Although in the past, the term "Dark Ages" was often used for the period between the Roman Empire and medieval Christian Europe, the term is avoided today. The Middle Ages is also called the Medieval Period.

The year 800 marks an important year in the early Middle Ages. In that year, the king of the Franks, Charlemagne, was crowned the holy Roman emperor by Pope Leo III. The pope wanted to recreate an empire on the model of the old Roman emperor, only this time, it would be a Christian empire. Charlemagne did create a large kingdom that would include what are known today as France, Germany, and part of Italy. However, the Holy Roman Empire never lived up to its name. It was very small compared to the original Roman Empire. It was not that Roman, and although Charlemagne and the succeeding rulers were Christians, their conduct was often anything but holy.

However, the title and role of the holy Roman emperor would last in Europe through 1806. Over the centuries, the holy Roman emperors, who would be French, Spanish, and German, would have great influence over what happened in Europe.

Who was Charlemagne?

Charlemagne (742–814), or Charles the Great, became king of the Franks after his father, Pepin the Short (c. 714–768, son of Charles Martel), and his brother died. Charles then began expanding his kingdom. He sometimes employed brutal tactics in bringing people and regions under control, such as mass executions to subdue Saxon rebellions.

In Latin he was called *Carolus Magnus*, which means Charles the Great. (Carol, Carl, and Charles are related names. The empire of Charles is called the Carolingian Empire,

The 1861 painting by Friedrich Kaulbach titled *Imperial Coronation of Charlemagne* reverentially depicts the Frankish king being crowned emperor of the Romans in 800 by Pope Leo III.

and the time frame is the Carolingian Period.) As a patron of the arts, literature, and science, Charlemagne revived Western Europe after the decline of the Roman Empire.

How did people in the Middle Ages see the world?

To better understand this period, one must note that most people, but not all, thought the world was flat. They also thought that the sun, moon, and stars were small objects a few miles up in the air. Most people had no idea that Earth was a planet in a vast, vast universe. So, most people believed Heaven was "up there, beyond the stars" and that Hell was down below Earth. By the Middle Ages, the concepts of Heaven and Hell were well developed.

During the Middle Ages, scholars argued that the meaning of life on Earth lay primarily in its relation to an afterlife. Therefore, they believed that art for its own sake had no value, and they even frowned on the recognition of individual talent. For this reason, many of the great artworks of the Middle Ages were created anonymously.

What are the characteristics of medieval times?

Although the Middle Ages were shadowed by poverty, ignorance, economic chaos, bad government, and the plague, it was also a period of cultural and artistic achievement. For example, the university originated in medieval Europe (the first university was established in 1158 in Bologna, Italy). The period was marked by the belief, based on the Christian faith, that the universe was an ordered world, ruled by an infinite and all-knowing God. This belief persisted even through the turmoil of wars and social upheavals, and it is evident in the soaring Gothic architecture (such as the Cathedral of Chartres, France), the poetry of Dante Alighieri (1265–1321), the philosophy of St. Thomas Aquinas (1225–1274), the Gregorian chant, and the music of such composers as Guillaume de Machaut (c. 1300–1377).

What was the structure of feudal society?

With the breakup of the Roman Empire, a system called feudalism developed. What follows is a simplified description of the feudal social structure. It was often more complicated than this and often varied from place to place.

Kings—At the top was the king. In theory, all the land in the kingdom was his. He would then give or lease large sections of the land to men called lords or barons.

Lords—The land of each lord was called a manor. In exchange for land, the lord had to serve in the royal court and provide knights for the king. Lords gave some of their land to knights. Lords were wealthy landowners during the Middle Ages, and their manors were self-sufficient estates. The lord would lease land to peasants who would farm it; in return, the peasants would pay the lord in taxes, in services, or in kind (with crops or goods). In addition to farmland, a manor would typically have meadows, woodlands, and a small village. The lord presided over the entire manor and all the people living there. As the administrator of the land, he collected taxes and presided over legal matters. But the manors were not military entities; in other words, the lord did not promise protection to the peasants living on his land. As such, the manors were purely socioeconomic (as opposed to fiefs, which were social, economic, and political units).

Knights—Knights were warriors who were typically given land by a lord in exchange for promises to protect the lord, his family, and the lord's manor.

Serfs—At the bottom were the serfs, also called villeins. They had to provide the lord with labor and food. They had few rights. They were bound to the manor and could not leave without the lord's permission. They even had to have the lord's permission to marry. Serfs lived lives of hard work and poverty.

Slaves—In a number of places, slaves also existed.

What were fiefs?

A fief was an estate that a lord owned, governed, and protected. A fief consisted of several manors (each of which might have had its own lord) and their villages, along with all buildings on the land as well as the peasants (serfs) who worked the land, served at court, or took up arms on behalf of the lord. The lord of the fief, called a feudal lord, would secure the allegiance of the manorial lords (sometimes called seigniors), who would in turn secure the allegiance of the peasants.

In short, land was exchanged for loyalty; this was feudalism, the political and economic system of the Middle Ages. The word "feud" is of Germanic origin and means "fee"; in repayment for the land they lived on and the protection they received from the lord, serfs were expected to pay the lord fees—in the form of money (taxes), services, or goods.

What were vassals?

In the Middle Ages, a vassal was anyone who was under the protection of another and therefore owed and avowed not only allegiance but a payment of some sort to their protector. Peasants (serfs and village commoners) were always vassals to a lord—whether it was the lord of the manor or the lord of the fief. But the lord of the manor was himself a vassal—to the lord of the fief. As kingdoms were created, with many fiefs within their jurisdiction, the feudal lords became the vassals of the kings.

MONASTICISM

What is monasticism?

Monasticism is the life of monks living in monasteries devoting their lives to prayer.

Did Christians invent monasticism?

Christians did not invent monasticism. Buddhist monks had been living the monastic life for 500 years before Jesus. The monastic tradition in Hinduism is even older.

There do not seem to be many monks around today. Why was it important?

Although monks and monasteries are few and far between today, for most of Christian history, monasteries were extremely important. In the Middle Ages, there were thousands of monasteries all across Europe from small ones of a dozen or so men to enormous monasteries with hundreds of men. Monasteries served both religious and societal functions in their time. For example, in many families, the eldest son would alone inherit the family farm because if the land were divided among all the sons, the pieces each had would be too small to farm. After the eldest son got the family land, what would happen to the younger sons? One answer was to send them to monasteries.

Monks and monasteries were once common throughout Europe, but where once there were thousands of them, today, there are just a couple hundred Trappist and Benedictine monasteries.

What is the monastic life?

To understand the monastic life, one must start by recognizing that this tradition came from a view of God as harsh and demanding. The culture that supported the monastic life saw the Christian life as very difficult. If one wanted to follow Christ completely, then one had to withdraw from ordinary life and devote oneself to prayer.

Also, keep in mind that effective birth control is a modern reality, so becoming celibate and giving up sex freed one from all the demands of having and raising children. This freed one up to follow God completely. It is sometimes difficult for modern people to appreciate the reasons for celibacy.

Monks were not married. *Mono* in Greek means "one," and from this comes the word "monk." Monks were alone in terms of not being married, although they usually lived in communities with other monks. A monk lives in a "monastery." A monk lives a "monastic" life. The head of a monastery is called the "abbot." This comes from the word for father, "abba." Sometimes, a monastery is called an "abbey."

Women who wanted to follow the monastic life lived in monasteries for women called "convents." They were called "nuns." The head of a convent was called "Mother Superior." She might also be called an "abbess." For both men in monasteries and women in convents, they lived a life closed off from the outside world in what is called a "cloister."

In London many centuries ago, there was an abbey. The road in front of it was called Abbey Road. The recording studio for the Beatles was on Abbey Road, so the Beatles named one of their famous albums *Abbey Road*.

How did one become a monk?

To become a monk, a man took three vows. (A vow is a promise.) The three vows were celibacy (no marriage and no sex), poverty (to not own anything), and obedience (to the abbot). In a monastery, most men were not priests and called each other "brother." A few became priests, and they would be called "father."

Nuns took the same vows, although the first vow was called "chastity." The nuns called each other "sister," although the leader of the convent was often called "mother."

What did the monks do?

The most important duty of the monks and sisters in convents was to pray. The sequence of prayers was called the Divine Office. Eight times during the day and night, monks and nuns went to the chapel to pray with their community. Two passages from Psalm 119 were cited for determining the number of times to pray during a twenty-four-hour period: "At midnight I rise to praise you because of your righteous judgments" (v. 62) and "Seven times a day I praise you because your judgments are righteous" (v. 164, NABRE).

The traditional times of prayer were as follows:

- Midnight, called Matins, Vigils, Nocturns, or the Night Office. (The French word *matin* means "morning.")

- Lauds or Dawn Prayer at Dawn, or 3 A.M. ("Lauds" is based on the Latin word for praise.)

- Prime or Early Morning Prayer at the First Hour, typically at 6 A.M.

- Terce or Mid-Morning Prayer at the Third Hour, typically at 9 A.M.

- Sext or Midday Prayer at the Sixth Hour, typically at 12 noon.

- None or Mid-Afternoon Prayer at the Ninth Hour, typically at 3 P.M. (The words "prime," "terce," "sex," and "none" are based on the Latin words for first, third, sixth, and ninth hours of the day.)

- Vespers or Evening Prayer, typically at 6 P.M.

- Compline or Night Prayer, typically at 9 P.M.

The core prayers of the Divine Office were the Psalms. At each prayer time, one or more of the Psalms was chanted. Often, they were chanted in choir style, with one side of the chapel or church saying one line of the psalm with the next line chanted by the other side of the chapel. It went back and forth from one side to the other until the psalm was completed.

The Canticle of Zachariah, also called the Benedictus, from the Gospel of Luke was usually chanted during morning prayers; the Canticle of Mary, called the Magnificat, also from the Gospel of Luke, was chanted at Vespers. Typically, the Psalms would be chanted as music. The most common style of monastic music was called a Gregorian chant.

MEDIEVAL LITERATURE AND ARCHITECTURE

What is the famous book about the afterlife written by Dante in the Middle Ages?

The Italian writer Dante Alighieri (1265–1321) wrote *The Divine Comedy,* describing the medieval view of the afterlife. The word "comedy" does not mean it is a humorous story but rather that it has a happy ending. *The Divine Comedy* is a poem made up of 100 parts called "cantos," which are divided into three sections: Inferno—Hell, Purgatorio—Purgatory, and Paradiso—Paradise or Heaven.

In the poem, Dante is led through Hell and Purgatory by the Roman writer Virgil. Beatrice, Dante's image of the ideal woman, leads him through Paradise.

What is *The Canterbury Tales*?

The Canterbury Tales was written by Geoffrey Chaucer between the years 1387 and 1400. The book is a collection of stories told by pilgrims on their way to the shrine of Thomas

Two of Europe's most famous authors are Dante Alighieri (left), who composed *The Divine Comedy*, and Geoffrey Chaucer, author of *The Canterbury Tales.*

Becket in Canterbury, England. *The Canterbury Tales* gives a window into the late medieval feudal world. A number of the characters are religious figures, such as the Parson, the Monk, the Friar, the Pardoner, the Summoner, nuns, priests, and the Prioress (a woman in charge of a convent). The characters are all introduced in the Prologue.

Chaucer did not write about ideal models of these various religious roles. Rather, he describes monks and friars who are ignoring the precepts of their religious orders. Chaucer does this because they make for more interesting characters. A monk or friar who followed the rules and spent all his time praying would actually be quite boring.

Some of the more popular tales are "The Miller's Tale," "The Reeve's Tale," "The Wife of Bath's Tale," and "The Pardoner's Tale." Although Chaucer wrote *The Canterbury Tales* in English, he used a much older form of English that modern readers find difficult to read. Chaucer also wrote in verse style. So, rather than read the original, most readers today prefer a prose version in modern English. (Verse is short lines, such as in a poem. Prose is in the form of paragraphs.)

What are the Gothic cathedrals?

About a hundred Gothic cathedrals were built in Europe in the Middle Ages. The Gothic style includes pointed arches, extensive use of stained glass, and flying buttresses to support the wall. The Gothic movement began with the Church of St. Denis outside of Paris. The leader of this church, Abbot Suger (1081–1151), had been influenced by the writings of an early Christian monk named Pseudo-Dionysius, who saw light as God's essence. Suger wanted to open the church walls to include lots of window space for colorful, stained glass windows. The trick was to design buttresses in the walls to hold up the roof and ceiling of the cathedral. The buttresses held the weight, which meant the walls could be opened up for glass.

Do an image search for "St. Denis Paris," and then a search for "flying buttresses." Two of the most famous Gothic cathedrals are Notre Dame in Paris and Chartres Cathedral in the town of Chartres, France. Take a look at them online. Notre Dame suffered a devastating fire in 2019, though it is being restored.

THE CRUSADES

What were the Crusades?

The Crusades were a series of military campaigns in the Middle Ages undertaken by European Christians to conquer the Holy Land—Jerusalem and the surrounding territory. At that time, various Muslim rulers held the area. The First Crusade began in 1095. The last Crusade ended in 1272.

The First Crusade conquered Jerusalem but with great bloodshed. The Muslims then retook Jerusalem, and subsequent Crusades failed to reconquer it. By 1291, all the territory that had been conquered during the Crusades was in Muslim hands.

What happened in the First Crusade?

The First Crusade lasted from 1095 to 1099. In response to the letter of Emperor Alexius, Pope Urban II, in an open-air sermon in Clermont, France, called for a crusade on November 27, 1095. He wanted an army to rescue the Holy Land. He gave exaggerated accounts of Muslim atrocities against Christians. He offered pardon of sins for those on the crusade and freedom from their debts. Part of the motivation for Pope Urban was his hope that a crusade would unite the Christian kingdoms in Europe and stop the fighting between them.

In the wake of the Crusaders' conquest of so much territory, including Jerusalem, the Muslims started organizing to fight back. The Muslims' first step in 1144 was to reconquer the city of Edessa (today in modern Turkey), which the Crusaders conquered on their way to Jerusalem.

A statue of Saladin at the Egyptian Military Museum in Cairo shows the sultan who created an empire that spanned Egypt, Syria, Upper Mesopotamia, Yemen, western Saudi Arabia, and northern Africa.

What happened in the Second Crusade?

The Second Crusade lasted from 1147 to 1149. In response to the fall of Edessa, Pope Eugene III called for the Second Crusade. The pope commissioned the fiery Bernard of Clairvaux to preach the crusade and build up support. Kings Conrad III and Louis VII led the Crusader army. There was dissension and distrust among the various Christian armies. They decided to attack the city of Damascus even though the city was an ally of Jerusalem, which the Crusaders held. Although they laid siege to Damascus, the Crusaders eventually gave up and went home. The whole crusade was a debacle.

What happened after the Second Crusade?

The Muslim ruler Saladin came to power. In 1187 he conquered Jerusalem. He then destroyed much of the Crusader states.

What happened in the Third Crusade?

The Third Crusade lasted from 1187 to 1192. It was led by German emperor Frederick I (Frederick Barbarossa), King Philip II of France, and King Richard I of England, the Lionheart. Frederick drowned en route. Richard and Philip conquered the city of Acre, which is today in northern Israel. Richard made a deal with Saladin: Richard could rebuild the Crusader states, but Jerusalem remained under Saladin's control. The story of Robin Hood in England takes place while Richard is on this crusade.

What happened in the Fourth Crusade?

The Fourth Crusade lasted from 1202 to 1204. It was led by Count Baldwin. To get the city of Venice to pay for the ships he needed, he agreed to attack the Christian city of Zara, a trade rival of Venice. The Crusaders then attacked the Christian city of Constantinople. They looted and sacked the city in 1204.

What is the legacy of the Fourth Crusade?

The sacking of Constantinople greatly weakened it so that it would eventually be taken over by the Muslim Ottoman Turks in 1453. Ironically, defending Christian Constantinople and its surrounding territory had been the original catalyst for starting the Crusades.

The sacking of Constantinople led to great resentment on the part of Eastern Orthodox Christians toward Roman Catholic Christians. In some places the resentment still lingers. For many people today, the Fourth Crusade is one of several important illustrations of the fundamental immorality and unchristian nature of the Crusades.

What was the Fifth Crusade?

This crusade, which lasted from 1217 to 1221, was called by Pope Innocent III and led by King John of Jerusalem. His army sailed to Egypt to move toward Jerusalem from the west. The Crusaders conquered the Egyptian city of Damietta. At this point, the sultan, fearing the Crusaders, offered them the city of Jerusalem. However, the pope's representative, Cardinal Pelagius, overruled John and insisted that they attack Jerusalem.

The Crusader armies had to wait for more troops to arrive. In the meantime, the army was destroyed by floods on the Nile and the Egyptian army. The crusade was a failure.

What was the Children's Crusade of 1212?

The story of the Children's Crusade is a mix of legend and fact, with no one sure what exactly happened. The legend is that a large band of children, perhaps 30,000, set out to free the Holy Land. They were assuming that the Muslim armies would surrender Jerusalem to a band of peaceful children. When the children arrived at the Mediterranean Sea, they were offered passage on ships. However, they were sold into slavery instead.

The historical evidence points to two groups of peasants of all ages. Both set out, but both groups fell apart before leaving Europe.

What was the Sixth Crusade?

This crusade, which lasted from 1228 to 1229, was led by German emperor Frederick II. Frederick did not want to go on a crusade but was forced by Pope Innocent III. Once he got to the Holy Land, Frederick made a deal with the Muslims, called the Treaty of Jerusalem, and got control of Jerusalem. However, neither the Christians nor the Muslims liked the deal. Frederick eventually left and returned to Europe to protect his kingdom back home. In 1244, the Muslims retook Jerusalem.

What was the Seventh Crusade?

This crusade, which lasted from 1248 to 1254, was led by King Louis IX, who would later become St. Louis. (The well-known city in Missouri is named after him.) Louis IX conquered the Egyptian city of Damietta. However, he was then captured. He paid a large ransom for his freedom and then returned with his forces to France.

What was the Eighth Crusade?

This crusade, which occurred in 1270, was also led by King Louis IX. The plan was to take North Africa and then conquer Jerusalem. It failed, and King Louis died of the plague in North Africa.

What was the Ninth Crusade?

This crusade, which lasted from 1271 to 1272, was led by Prince Edward of England and achieved nothing. Some historians list it as a second phase of the Eighth Crusade. In the next years, Muslim armies conquered all Crusader strongholds in what had been the Crusader states. The last to fall was the city of Acre in 1291.

What is the legacy of the Crusades today?

When people today make the claim that most wars have been fought over religion, the Crusades become their primary example. The truth is that most wars are fought over political and economic issues.

However, the Crusades illustrate a problem that has occurred many times over the centuries when religion is used to promote very unreligious policies. A recent example is the 1995 genocide by Christian Serbians of Muslims from Bosnia and Herzegovina.

The Crusades also played an important role in creating friction between some Muslims and some Christians, which is still around today. However, the big source of resentment by some Muslims of the Mideast toward Western countries has to do with the economic, political, and military domination of many countries of the Mideast by both the British and then the Americans in the twentieth century. For example, in the Mideast, Britain and America have been involved in the overthrow of governments in Iran, Iraq, Syria, and Egypt. Most Americans do not know this history, but people in the regions do.

ENGLAND

What is the Magna Carta?

The Magna Carta, one of the most famous documents in British history, was signed by King John (1167–1216) in June 1215. He had been forced to sign it. Drawn up by English barons who were angered by the king's encroachment on their rights, the charter has been credited with no less than ensuring personal liberty and putting forth the rights of the individual, which include the guarantee of a trial by jury: "No freeman shall be arrested and imprisoned, or dispossessed, or outlawed, or banished, or in any way molested; nor will be set forth against him, nor send against him, unless by the lawful judgment of his peers, and by the law of the land."

An 1875 illustration by John Leech shows King John II refusing to sign the Magna Carta when it was first presented to him.

The document, to which John was forced to put his seal, asserted the rights of the barons, churchmen, and townspeople and provided for the king's assurance that he would not encroach on their privileges. In short, the Magna Carta stipulated that the king, too, was subject to the laws of the land.

The Magna Carta had a provision for a Great Council, to be comprised of nobles and clergy, who would approve the actions of the king and ensure the tenets set forth in the charter were upheld. It is credited with laying the foundation for a parliamentary government in England.

After signing it, John immediately appealed to Pope Innocent III (1160 or 1161–1216), who issued an annulment of the charter. Nevertheless, John died before he could further fight it, and the Magna Carta (which means "Great Charter") was later upheld as the basis of English feudal justice. It is still considered by many to be the cornerstone of constitutional government.

RELIGIOUS STRUGGLES IN THE MIDDLE AGES

What was the Investiture Struggle?

Also called the Investiture Controversy, it is the name for the power struggle between kings and popes over who got to select bishops and abbots—the heads of monasteries. The pope wanted to choose all the bishops and abbots in Europe, whereas kings wanted to choose the bishops and abbots in their lands so they could pick clergy who would support their political and economic policies. At that time, bishops and abbots were often influential because they controlled large tracts of land and had economic and political influence.

The struggle for supremacy peaked in 1075, when Pope Gregory VII (c. 1020–1085), who wanted to protect the Church from the influence of Europe's powerful leaders, issued a decree against lay investitures, meaning that no one except the pope could name bishops or heads of monasteries. (A king was not a member of the clergy and was thus a layperson. Investiture is the process of choosing and installing an abbot or bishop.) German king Henry IV (1050–1106), who was fighting for political power, took exception to Gregory's decree and challenged it, asserting that the kings should have the right to name the bishops. The pope excommunicated Henry. Though he later sought—and was granted—forgiveness by Gregory, the struggle did not end there. Henry soon regained political support, deposed Gregory (in 1084), and set up an antipope (Clement III), who in turn crowned Henry IV, Holy Roman Emperor

What was the Great Schism?

For some centuries, tension had been growing between Western Christianity under the leadership of the pope in Rome and Eastern Orthodox Christianity. A key issue was that the Eastern Christians did not believe that the pope was the head of the universal church.

Also, there was a controversy over a word added to the Latin version of the Nicene Creed. There was also much misunderstanding between the two sides.

In 1054, things came to a head when Pope Leo IX excommunicated Patriarch Michael Cerularius (the head bishop) of Constantinople. Cerularius responded by excommunicating the pope. This break between the Western and Eastern Christian churches is called the Great Schism or the East-West Schism. (The word "schism" refers to a break or division, especially within churches.) These two branches of Christianity have remained divided up to the present. However, starting in the mid-twentieth century, many efforts have been made to promote respect and understanding between them.

The Western part became the Roman Catholic Church. The Eastern part became the Christian Orthodox churches, which

The Eastern Orthodox Church came about because of the Great Great Schism, when the pope in Rome split with leader of the church in Constantinople.

today are usually identified by nationality, such as the Greek Orthodox Church, Russian Orthodox Church, and the Orthodox Church in America.

What was the Filioque Controversy?

The Latin Church added the word "filioque" to the Nicene Creed. The word means "and the Son" and was used in the sentence: "We believe in the Holy Spirit, the Lord, the giver of life, who proceeds from the Father and the Son." The Eastern Orthodox Church insisted that the Creed only described the Holy Spirit as proceeding from the Father. This disagreement is known as the Filioque Controversy.

What was the place of Jews in the Middle Ages?

Jews played an important role in medieval Europe. Jews increased in numbers, although they were a minority of the overall population. The dominant Christian culture tolerated Judaism because of the Jewish background of Jesus. However, there were many laws and restrictions against Jews. For instance, Jews were often forbidden from owning property or belonging to the guilds, the equivalent of labor unions.

In some places, Jews were required to wear clothes that identified them as Jews. Sometimes, they were required to wear yellow stars. In some cities, Jews were required to live in specific areas called ghettos. Also, under penalty of death, Jews were forbidden to convert Christians to Judaism.

In many places, there was significant anti-Semitism, which occasionally flared up into violence. During the Crusades, peasant armies massacred Jews in several cities.

Is there a connection between Jews and banking that developed in this period?

In several passages in the Bible, the lending of money at usury is forbidden. Usury is to charge interest, so technically, Christians were forbidden from charging interest on loans. However, Jews understood this rule to mean that Jews could not lend money to other Jews at interest. However, they could lend to non-Jews, so by this quirk in interpreting this rule of the Bible, some Jews found themselves as moneylenders in the medieval world. The problem was that in the growing economies of the Middle Ages, no one was willing to lend money unless there was some interest to cover the risk for lending the money.

Keep in mind that in the Middle Ages, no consumer-protection laws existed. Many people today are not great at figuring percentages; most people in the Middle Ages could not do math. Not surprisingly, there was often mistrust and anger toward Jewish moneylenders, in some cases legitimate and in other cases not legitimate.

Today, modern Christians get around the biblical prohibition on lending money at usury by saying that usury means exorbitant interest rates. Although this is a helpful way around the issue, it ignores the original Bible intent that all charging of interest was forbidden.

THE RENAISSANCE

Why is the Renaissance considered a time of rebirth?

The term "renaissance" is from the French word for "rebirth," and the period from 1350 to 1600 C.E. in Europe was marked by the resurrection of ancient Greek and Roman ideals; the flourishing of art, literature, and philosophy; and the beginning of modern science. (Ancient Greek and Roman cultures are called "classical.") However, the "Renaissance" label was given to this period many centuries later.

Italians believed themselves to be the true heirs to Roman achievement. For this reason, it was natural that the Renaissance began in Italy, where the ruins of ancient civilization provided a constant reminder of their classical past and where other artistic movements, such as Gothic, had never taken firm hold.

How did the Renaissance begin?

In northern Italy, a series of city-states developed, including Florence, Rome, Venice, and Milan, that gained prosperity through trade and banking, and as a result, a wealthy class of businessmen emerged. These community leaders admired and encouraged creativity, patronizing artists who might glorify their commercial achievement with great buildings, paintings, and sculptures. The most influential patrons of the arts were the Medicis,

Florence, Italy, is considered the birthplace of the Renaissance, a time of cultural revitalization. after the long, difficult Dark Ages.

55

a wealthy banking family in Florence. Members of the Medici family supported many important artists, including Botticelli and Michelangelo. Guided by the Medici patronage, Florence became the most magnificent city of the period.

One way that patrons encouraged art was to sponsor competitions in order to spur artists on to more significant achievement. In many cases, the losers of these contests went on to greater fame than the winners. After his defeat in the competition to create the bronze doors of the Baptistery of Florence Cathedral, architect Filippo Brunelleschi (1377–1446) made several trips to take measurements of the ruined buildings of ancient Rome. When he returned to Florence, he created the immense *il duomo* (dome) of the Santa Maria del Fiore Cathedral, a classically influenced structure that became the first great monument of the Renaissance.

How is the attitude of the Renaissance characterized?

The artists and thinkers of the Renaissance, like the ancient Greeks and Romans, valued earthly life, glorified man's nature, and celebrated individual achievement. These new attitudes combined to form a new spirit of optimism, the belief that man was capable of accomplishing great things.

This outlook was the result of the activities of the wealthy mercantile class in northern Italy, who, aside from supporting the arts and letters, also began collecting the classical texts that had been forgotten during the Middle Ages. Ancient manuscripts were taken to libraries, where scholars from around Europe could study them. The rediscovery of classical texts prompted a new way of looking at the world.

As mentioned before, during the Middle Ages, scholars had argued that the meaning of life on Earth lay primarily in its relation to an afterlife. Therefore, they believed that art for its own sake had no value, and they even frowned on the recognition of individual talent. In contrast, Renaissance artists and thinkers studied classical works for the purpose of imitating them. As an expression of their new optimism, Renaissance scholars embraced the study of classical subjects that addressed human concerns. These "humanities," as they came to be called, included language and literature, art, history, rhetoric, and philosophy.

Above all, humanists, those who espoused the values of this type of education, believed in humankind's potential to become well versed in many areas. During this era, people in all disciplines began using critical skills as a means of understanding everything from nature to politics. Today, a person who is knowledgeable in many fields is called a "Renaissance man" or "Renaissance woman."

Which artists and thinkers are considered the greatest minds of the Renaissance?

The great writers of the Renaissance include the Italian poet Petrarch (1304–1374), who became the first great writer of the Renaissance and was one of the first proponents of the concept that a "rebirth" was in progress; Florentine historian Niccolò Machiavelli (1469–1527), who wrote the highly influential work *The Prince* (1513); English drama-

What is the importance of St. Peter's Basilica in Rome?

St. Peter's Basilica in Rome is the largest church in the world. Famous Renaissance architects Donato Bramante, Michelangelo, Carlo Maderno, and Gian Lorenzo Bernini designed the church itself as well as St. Peter's Square in front of it. For many Catholics, it is one of the holiest places on Earth. Tradition holds that it was built on the burial site of St. Peter the Apostle.

tist and poet William Shakespeare (1564–1616), whose works many view as the culmination of Renaissance writing; Spain's Miguel de Cervantes (1547–1616), who penned *Don Quixote* (1605), the epic masterpiece that gave birth to the modern novel; and Frenchman François Rabelais (c. 1483–1553), who is best known for writing the five-volume novel *Gargantua and Pantagruel*.

The great artists of the Renaissance include the Italian painters/sculptors Sandro Botticelli (1445–1510), whose works include *The Birth of Venus*; Leonardo da Vinci (1452–1519), whose *Mona Lisa* and *The Last Supper* are among the most widely studied works of art; Michelangelo Buonarroti (1475–1564), whose sculpture *David* became the symbol of the new Florence; and Raphael Sanzio (1483–1520), whose *School of Athens* is considered by art historians to be the complete statement of the High Renaissance.

What do the words "cathedral" and "basilica" mean?

The word "cathedral" comes from the word "cathedra," which means "throne" or "seat." Every cathedral has a chair in the front for the bishop of the diocese. So, a cathedral is the bishop's church. The word "basilica" is used for a specific style for a large church. Although St. Peter's in Rome is the church of the pope, it is not a cathedral even though the pope is the bishop of Rome. The pope's cathedral is a different church in Rome—St. John Lateran.

What is the importance of Renaissance art?

When many people hear the word "Renaissance," they immediately think of the great painters like da Vinci and Raphael and great sculptors like Michelangelo. (These artists and their work will be explored in the chapter "Western Art, Photography, and Architecture.")

EMPIRES, KINGDOMS, DYNASTIES, AND NATIONS

THE OTTOMAN EMPIRE

What was the Ottoman Empire?

The Ottoman Empire was a vast Turkish state founded in the thirteenth century by the Osmani Turks, who were led by descendants of Osman I (c. 1258–c. 1323). By the middle of the next century, the Ottoman Empire consisted roughly of modern-day Turkey (the terms "Turkey" and "Ottoman Empire" are used interchangeably). The empire was expanded further by conquests during the 1400s, including the conquest of the Byzantine Empire and the city of Constantinople in 1453. Eventually, Constantinople would be called Istanbul, from the Greek words meaning "to the city."

At its height, the Ottoman Empire extended over an area that included the Balkan Peninsula (present-day Slovenia, Croatia, Bosnia and Herzegovina, Montenegro, Kosovo, Serbia, Macedonia, Romania, Bulgaria, Albania, Greece, and Turkey), Syria, Egypt, Iraq, the northern coast of Africa, Palestine, and parts of Arabia, Russia, and Hungary. The Turks established a Muslim empire that would remain a formidable force and influence in the region and in Europe for the next three centuries.

During the 1500s and 1600s, the Ottoman Empire was the most powerful in the world. It reached its most glorious heights during the reign of Suleiman the Magnificent (1494–1566), who ruled from 1520 to 1566. It was he who added parts of Hungary to the Ottoman territory. He also tried to take Vienna but failed. He did succeed in strengthening the Ottoman navy, which dominated the Mediterranean Sea. Suleiman was not only an expansionist but also a patron of the arts and a builder. He ordered the construction of mosques (to spread the Islamic religion throughout the empire), bridges, and public works.

What was the later history of the Ottoman Empire?

By the time World War I began in 1914, the Ottoman Empire had been in decline for some 300 years and only consisted of Asia Minor, parts of the Middle East, and part of the Balkan Peninsula. As one of the losing Central Powers of World War I, the Ottoman Empire was dissolved in 1922 by the peace treaties that ended the war, and much of its territory was divided up by France and Britain.

THE HABSBURGS

Who were the Habsburgs?

The Habsburgs (also spelled Hapsburg) were arguably Europe's most powerful royal family. They supplied Europe with a nearly uninterrupted stream of rulers for more than 600 years. The first member of the family to bear the name was Count Werner I (1025–1096). It was Werner's descendant, Rudolf I (1218–1291), who was elected king of Germany and the Holy Roman Empire in 1273. When Rudolf conquered Austria three years later, he established that country as the family's new home.

Austria, Bohemia, Germany, Hungary, and Spain were among the European states ruled by the house of Habsburg. With only one exception, the Habsburg family also ruled the Holy Roman Empire from 1440 until 1806.

Why were Spain's King Ferdinand and Queen Isabella so powerful?

The 1469 marriage of Ferdinand (1452–1516) and Isabella (1451–1504) brought the previously separate Spanish kingdoms of Aragon and Castile under joint control. Together, the monarchs went on to rule Spain and expand their realm of influence. Both were deeply religious yet politically ambitious.

It was Ferdinand and Isabella who in 1478 established the infamous Spanish Inquisition, a court that imprisoned or killed Catholics suspected of not correctly following religious teachings. While the Inquisition was initially aimed at finding and punishing Muslims and Jews who had converted to Catholicism but who were thought to be insincere, soon all Spaniards came to fear its power.

In 1482, the monarchs undertook a war with the (Muslim) Moors and in 1492 conquered the last Moorish stronghold at Granada in the southern part of Spain. The Moors were forced to flee to Africa. Ferdinand and Isabella wanted to create a completely Catholic kingdom. Not only were Muslim Moors driven out but so were Jews in that fateful year of 1492. Forced out, the Spanish Jews, called Sephardim, went to North Africa, the Middle East, and eventually to North America.

Ferdinand and Isabella also financed the voyage of Christopher Columbus, who would arrive in the New World in 1492. The monarchs believed that the new lands would

King Ferdinand and Queen Isabella are depicted receiving Christopher Columbus, who was requesting they fund his expedition to Asia, which, of course, landed Columbus in the New World instead.

not only add to their authority but would also provide new territory for the spread of Catholicism. The Spaniards soon emerged as a formidable sea power in the Atlantic.

When Ferdinand died in 1516, his grandson Charles (1500–1558) became the king of Spain as Charles I. However, in 1519 he also became the holy Roman emperor as Charles V. He was a Habsburg, and under his reign the Habsburg influence reached its high-water mark. Charles ruled over Spain, much of Europe, and the Spanish territories in the New World. Under his rule, the Spanish conquered Mexico (by Hernán Cortés, 1485–1547) and Peru (by Francisco Pizarro, c. 1475–1541). The Catholic Charles resisted the influence of the Protestant Reformation; dealt with his lifelong rival Francis I (1494–1547), king of France; and opposed the Ottoman Turks, who were at the height of their power during his reign.

What happened to the Habsburg rule?

In 1867 the Habsburg Empire was reorganized as the Austro-Hungarian monarchy. That monarchy was dissolved in 1918, after World War I, with the Treaty of Versailles establishing new boundaries for the successor states.

ENGLAND

What happened with England's royal "houses"?

This is the list of the ten royal houses of England:

Royal House	Years Reigned
Normandy	1066–1135
Blois	1135–1154
Plantagenet	1154–1399
Lancaster	1399–1471
York	1471–1485
Tudor	1485–1603
Stuart	1603–1649, restored 1660–1714
Hanover	1714–1901
Saxe-Coburg	1901–1910
Windsor	1910–

Two contending branches of the House of Plantagenet—the houses of Lancaster and York—vied for the crown in the infamous War of the Roses (1455–1485). The struggle finally ended when Henry VII (1457–1509, a Lancaster) ascended the throne and married into the House of York, reuniting the two sides of the family under the newly minted House of Tudor.

The Tudors were a famous lot, remembered for the reigns of Henry VIII (1509–1547) and his daughters, Mary I (1553–1558) and Elizabeth I (1558–1603).

Who was Henry VIII of England?

Henry VIII (1491–1547), the king of England, was a devout Catholic and a supporter of the pope. Henry even wrote an essay condemning Martin Luther and his teaching, for which the pope called Henry the "Defender of the Faith." However, Henry did not have a son. Henry desperately wanted a son to take the throne when he died. He feared a civil war if there were no clear successor to the throne.

Henry's wife was Catherine of Aragon (1485–1536) from Spain. Catherine bore a daughter, Mary, but no son. Henry decided he would need another wife who could provide him a son. (At the time, they did not understand the process of conception—that it is the sperm of the male that determines the gender of a child.)

Henry asked the pope for an annulment to end his marriage so he could leave Catherine and marry Anne Boleyn. Normally, the pope would have agreed to such an annulment; however, the pope was under pressure from the Spanish to not annul the marriage. The Spanish wanted to keep the Spanish Catherine on the throne of England. The pope refused Henry's request.

Henry's response was to break away from the Catholic Church and create the Church of England, also known as the Anglican Church. He became head of this church. Henry soon found other benefits of breaking away from the pope. At the time, all European countries paid taxes to the pope in Rome. Henry could now keep that tax money in England. Also, any legal cases involving clerics or church property could be appealed to courts in Rome, which were favorable to the Catholic Church. Now, all such cases had to stay in England and be resolved in English courts.

Although Martin Luther rejected the idea of monks in monasteries as not biblical, Henry saw a practical advantage to getting rid of monasteries in England. Many of the monasteries were very large properties. Henry suppressed the monasteries, closed them down, and gave the land to lords who supported him. The lords then created large estates. On some of these estates today, the old ruins of the medieval monasteries can still be seen. Some estates retained the names of the monasteries that were closed. Note the name of the popular PBS TV series *Downton Abbey*. An abbey is a monastery.

However, beyond these changes, the Church of England retained many of the elements of the Roman Catholic Church in terms of belief and liturgical practices. Many Christians in England were happy with things this way, while many others wanted more changes.

Who were the six wives of Henry VIII?

Henry VIII divorced Catherine and married Anne Boleyn. However, Anne did not produce a son. She was accused of being unfaithful to Henry and was beheaded. Four more wives followed. The six wives were:

- Catherine of Aragon—She gave birth to Mary. Henry had their marriage annulled.

- Anne Boleyn—She gave birth to Elizabeth. Anne was beheaded.

- Jane Seymour—She gave birth to Edward. She died twelve days later.

- Anne of Cleves—Henry had their marriage annulled.

- Catherine Howard—She was beheaded.

- Catherine Parr—She became a widow when Henry died.

Their fates can be remembered as "divorced, beheaded, died, divorced, beheaded, lived."

Shown in this 1531 portrait, King Henry VIII was an athletic, handsome man when he was younger. He is remembered for creating the Church of England, expanding the power of the king, and his tendency to execute wives.

63

Did Henry's son become king? What about his daughters?

Yes, his son Edward became King Edward VI (1537–1553). He became king in 1547 at age nine. He died at age fifteen.

Henry's daughter Mary (1516–1558) took the throne in 1553 when Edward died. She tried to undo the religious changes of Henry VIII and take England back to the Catholic Church. During her reign, she burned over 280 religious dissenters at the stake. Her opponents called her "Bloody Mary."

In 1558 Elizabeth became queen. She took up the effort of Henry to create a Protestant England. She also executed many religious dissenters.

Why did Queen Elizabeth I have an entire age named after her?

Ascending the throne in 1558, Queen Elizabeth (1533–1603) remained in power for forty-five years, during which England dominated the seas to become a European power. Colonization began, with Sir Walter Raleigh (1554–1618) and others establishing British settlements in North America. Culture flourished, with the likes of William Shakespeare (1564–1616), Christopher Marlowe (1564–1593), and Sir Edmund Spenser (1552–1599) producing literary masterpieces. Industry and commerce boomed. This was the Elizabethan Age, one of England's most prosperous times.

One of the most well-known events of Elizabeth's reign was England's defeat of the Spanish Armada in July–August 1588. This event has an interesting twist. In the summer of 1588, the "invincible" Spanish fleet, which was en route to invade England, had been dispatched by none other than Spain's Philip II (1527–1598), Mary Tudor's former husband. Though the English were severely outnumbered (having only thirty-four ships to Spain's 132), they were aided by weather and defeated the Spanish Armada. This victory at sea opened the world to English trade and colonization.

Who became the ruler of England after the death of Elizabeth?

Queen Elizabeth was the last of the Tudor rulers, who are credited with strengthening the monarchy in England. They were succeeded by the House of Stuart in 1603, when James I (1566–1625), who ruled from 1603 to 1625, ascended the throne. It is this James who gave the world the King James Version of the Bible. He is also

The daughter of Henry VIII and Anne Boleyn, Elizabeth I was one of England's greatest monarchs. She died without an heir, however, ending the rule of the House of Tudor.

notable for having been the son of Mary, Queen of Scots (1542–1587), whom Elizabeth I had reluctantly put to death.

Who was Mary, Queen of Scots?

Mary Stuart was born in 1542 to James V of Scotland, who ruled from 1513 to 1542, and his wife, Mary of Guise. When Mary was just six days old, her father died, making the infant a queen. Her mother ruled the country as a regent until 1561, when Mary officially took on her duties. She was, by all reports, a beautiful and charming young woman whose courage and mettle would be tested by time. When she ascended the throne, she inherited her mother's struggle with the Protestants, who were led by John Knox (1513–1572), a former Catholic priest who was involved in the Reformation.

As a Roman Catholic, Mary was subject to harsh verbal attacks issued by Knox, who denounced the pope's authority and the practices of the Church. But this was not the worst of her troubles. In 1565 Mary wed her English cousin, Lord Darnley (1545–1567), in an attempt to secure her claim to the English throne as successor to Elizabeth I, also her cousin.

But Mary's ambitions would be her undoing. She quickly grew to dislike her husband, who became aligned with her Protestant opponents and successfully carried out a plot to murder—in her presence—Mary's adviser, David Rizzio (c. 1533–1566). Surprisingly, Mary and Darnley reconciled shortly thereafter (a politically savvy move on her part), and she conceived a child, James, who was born in 1566. Darnley had enemies of his own, and one year later he was murdered. Mary promptly married the Earl of Bothwell (1534–1578), with whom she had fallen in love well before becoming a widow. Bothwell was accused of Darnley's murder, and though he was acquitted, his marriage to the queen shocked Scotland. The people took up arms, forcing Mary to abdicate the throne in 1567. She was twenty-five years old.

Who were all Stuarts who ruled England?

Elizabeth I died in 1603. The next kings and queens were from the House of Stuart, interrupted by the period of the Commonwealth of England.

How did Mary, Queen of Scots, die?

Fleeing to England, Mary, Queen of Scots, was given refuge by Elizabeth I. Though she was technically a prisoner, Mary nevertheless was able to conspire with Elizabeth's enemies—including English Catholics and the Spanish—in attempts to kill her. When one such plot was discovered in 1586, Mary was charged for her involvement in it and was put on trial. Found guilty, she was put to death in 1587, though Elizabeth hesitated to take such action.

The Stuarts

Ruler	Years Reigned
James I	1603–1625
Charles I	1625–1649
The Commonwealth of England	1649–1660
Oliver Cromwell	1653–1658 (Lord Protector)
Richard Cromwell	1658–1659 (Lord Protector)
Charles II	1660-1685
James II	1685–1688
Mary II	1689–1694
William II (William of Orange, husband of Mary II)	1689–1702
Anne	1702–1714

Why was Oliver Cromwell important to British history?

English soldier and statesman Oliver Cromwell (1599–1658) was a key player in a chain of events that shaped modern British government. The events began when Charles I (1600–1649), from the House of Stuart, ascended the throne in 1625 and shortly thereafter married a French Catholic princess, immediately raising the ire of his Protestant subjects. This was not the end of England's problems with King Charles. After repeated struggles with the primarily Puritan Parliament, Charles dismissed the legislative body in 1629 and went on to rule without it for eleven years. During this period, religious and civil liberties were seriously diminished, and political and religious strife prevailed.

One of the most famous figures in English history, Oliver Cromwell led the fight to depose Charles I and briefly ruled as Lord Protector of the Commonwealth of England.

Fearing the king's growing power, Parliament moved to raise an army, and soon civil war broke out (1642–1648). Like the French Revolution (1789–1799), fought 150 years later, the struggle in England was largely one between a king who claimed to rule by divine right and a government body (in this case Parliament) that claimed the right to govern the nation on behalf of the people.

From this chaos emerged the leader Oliver Cromwell. After two years of indecisive battles in the English civil war, Cromwell led his parliamentary army troops to victories at Marston Moor (1644) and Naseby (1645), which resulted in Charles's surrender. But when Charles escaped his captors in 1647, the fighting was briefly renewed.

The war ended in 1648, and the king was tried the following year. Cromwell was among those leading the charge to have Charles executed. The king's opponents had their way and, having abolished the monarchy, soon established the Commonwealth of England, installing Cromwell as "Lord Protector."

Though Cromwell endeavored to bring religious tolerance to England and was somewhat successful in setting up a quasidemocratic government (he declined to take the title of king in 1657), his leadership was constantly challenged by those who wished to restore the Stuart monarchy. When Cromwell died in 1658, he was succeeded by his son, Richard (1626–1712), whose talents were not up to the challenges put to the Lord Protector. The movement to restore the monarchy—particularly the Stuart line—gained impetus, and Richard Cromwell was soon dismissed and went to live outside of England for the next twenty years.

Charles II (1630–1685), the son of Charles I, ascended the throne in 1660, beginning the eight-year period known as the Restoration. Both Charles and his brother, James II (1633–1701), who succeeded him in 1685, worked to reassert the absolutism of the Stuart monarchy. But both kings butted heads with Parliament, particularly when it came to financial matters.

Finally, in 1688, James II was deposed in the so-called Glorious Revolution. William III (1650–1702), grandson of Charles I, and his wife, Queen Mary II (1662–1694), daughter of James II, were placed on the throne the following year. Though the House of Stuart remained in power, there was an important hitch: Parliament compelled William and Mary to accept the Bill of Rights (of 1689), which asserted that the Crown no longer had absolute power in England and that it must rule responsibly through the nation's representatives sitting in Parliament. Thus, the English civil war (also called the Protestant Revolution) and the influence of Oliver Cromwell and other parliamentarians laid the foundation for England's constitutional monarchy.

What was the Bill of Rights of 1689?

The English Bill of Rights was presented to King William and Queen Mary as a condition of their ascension to the throne. The document not only described certain civil and political rights and liberties as "true, ancient, and indubitable," but it also ironed out how the throne would be succeeded. This point was of critical importance to the future

How old is the British Parliament?

The legislative assembly of Great Britain has roots dating back to the Middle Ages, when a great council, known as the Curia Regis, advised the king. This body was made up of nobility and clergy. The body evolved over time and progressively gained more power to govern. Eventually, the House of Commons became the governing body of Great Britain.

of England—the article stipulated that no Roman Catholic would rule the country. Since the Bill of Rights served to assert the role of Parliament in the government of England, it is considered one of the seminal documents of British constitutional law. It also is considered a key precursor to the U.S. Bill of Rights.

What would happen to the royal houses of England in later centuries?

A Stuart descendant, George I (1660–1727), established the House of Hanover, which originated in Germany. Queen Victoria (1819–1901), who presided over the Victorian Age, was of the House of Hanover. She was succeeded by her son, Edward VII (1841–1910), who established the House of Saxe-Coburg. Technically, this is the royal house still at the helm today, though the name of the house was changed to Windsor during World War I. Since England was fighting the Germans, they removed the German family name.

FRANCE

Who was Joan of Arc?

Joan of Arc (Jeanne d'Arc in French; c. 1412–1431) was a young peasant girl who claimed she received visions from the archangel Michael and several saints telling her to support French king Charles VII (1403–1461) and to help free France from English domination. Although she was poor and illiterate, she asked for armor and a horse to lead the forces. She was sent to the French city of Orléans, then under siege by the English. She rallied the French, and the siege was lifted. Several more French victories followed, which led to Charles VII being crowned as king in the French city of Reims. This set the stage for the ultimate French victory.

During the Hundred Years' War, Joan of Arc was a heroine to France, inspiring her nation to eventually oust the English from their country.

However, Joan was captured by Burgundians, who handed her over to the English. She was tried by Pierre Cauchon (1371–1442), the pro-English bishop of Beauvais, and accused of both heresy and cross-dressing. She had worn men's clothing as a disguise so as not to be captured, and then in prison, she wanted to wear pants because she felt it gave her some protection from being raped by the guards. Found guilty in a trial that was rigged against her, she was burned at the stake on May 30, 1431. She was about nineteen years old.

Who was the Sun King?

The Sun King was a name given to French king Louis XIV, or Louis the Great, who reigned for more than seventy years. Louis the Great (1638–1715) engaged France in several wars, most notably the Franco-Dutch War, the War of Devolution, the War of the Spanish Succession, and the War of the League of Augsburg. He was supported by the Divine Right of Kings and trained in the art of politics by Cardinal Jules Mazarin (1602–1661). Upon Mazarin's death, Louis assumed total power and continued to make France, arguably, the most dominant power in the world at that time.

In 1456 Pope Callixtus III (1378–1458) authorized a church court to examine the trial. Joan was found innocent of all the false charges that had been made against her and was declared a martyr. She would become a Catholic saint in 1920. In the middle of the twentieth century, "Joan" would become a popular name for Catholic girls.

Several movies have been made about her, including *The Passion of Joan of Arc* (1928), a silent film; *Joan of Arc* (1948), starring Ingrid Bergman; and *The Messenger: The Story of Joan of Arc* (1999).

Who was Cardinal Richelieu?

Armand Jean du Plessis, duke of Richelieu—and best known as Cardinal Richelieu (1585–1642)—was a leading political leader and religious figure in France. A bishop in the Catholic Church, he also achieved great success in politics, serving as King Louis XIII's chief adviser. He consolidated power domestically in France by bringing nobles into line. He also was a master at foreign policy, not only centralizing power in France but also undermining the Habsburg dynasty (France's chief rival for dominance in Europe). Richelieu's vision and execution were essential to French successes in the seventeenth century, including the later dominance of France as the world power under King Louis XIV (1638–1715), also known as Louis the Great.

FRENCH REVOLUTION

How long did the French Revolution last?

The Revolution lasted some ten years, and it grew increasingly violent as it progressed. It began in mid-1789 when the government found itself nearly bankrupt, and due to festering discontent among the commoners and the prosperous middle class, the crisis quickly grew into a movement calling for reform.

What was the Oath of the Tennis Court?

It was the oath taken in June 1789 by a group of representatives of France's third estate who, having been rejected by King Louis XVI (1754–1793) and the first and second estates, vowed to form a French national assembly and write their own constitution. The pledge set off a string of events that began the French Revolution.

French society had long been divided into three classes, called "estates": members of the clergy were the first estate, nobles comprised the second, and everyone else made up the third. When philosophers such as Jean-Jacques Rousseau (1712–1778) came along and challenged the king's supreme authority by promoting the idea that the right to rule came not from God but from the people, it fueled the discontent felt by the long-suffering peasants and the prosperous middle class, who paid most of the taxes to run the government but who had no voice in it. In short, these people were the disenfranchised third estate.

A government financial crisis brought on by the expense of war forced King Louis XVI to reluctantly call a meeting of the representatives of all three estates, called the Estates General, which had last convened in 1614. During the May 5, 1789, meeting at Versailles, the third estate attempted to seize power from the nobility, the clergy, and the king by insisting that the three estates be combined to form a national assembly in which each member had one vote; since the third estate had as many representatives as the other two combined, the people would at last have a voice. When the attempt failed,

Members of France's Third Estate are shown here taking the Oath of the Tennis Court in 1789, rejecting the king and helping to set off the French Revolution.

the representatives of the third estate gathered on a Versailles tennis court, where they vowed to change the government. Louis XVI began assembling troops to break up the meeting. Meantime, an armed resistance movement had begun to organize. The situation came to a head on July 14, 1789, with the storming of the Bastille in Paris. (The Bastille was an old fortress being used as a prison.)

What was the Rights of Man declaration?

In 1789 the French assembly wrote the Declaration of the Rights of Man and of the Citizen, meant to flesh out the revolutionary cry of "liberty, equality, and fraternity." Influenced by the U.S. Declaration of Independence (1776) as well as the ideas of the Enlightenment, the document guaranteed religious freedom, the freedom of speech and the press, and personal security. It proclaimed that man has natural and inalienable rights, which include "liberty, property, personal security, and resistance to oppression...." The declaration further stipulated that "no one may be accused, imprisoned, or held under arrest except in such cases and in such a way as is prescribed by law" and that "every man is presumed innocent until he is proved guilty...." The declaration was subsequently written into the preamble of the French Constitution (1791).

What was the Reign of Terror?

The revolution started with high ideals, but the chaotic situation led to the Reign of Terror from 1793 to July 1794. During this short period, revolutionary leader Maximilien de Robespierre (1758–1794) led a tribunal that arrested, tried, and put to death more than 17,000 people—most of them by guillotine.

In the reforms that followed the 1789 Oath of the Tennis Court and the capture of the Bastille, France was transformed into a constitutional state, and French subjects became French citizens. An elected legislature (the Constituent Assembly) was given control of the government. Robespierre was elected first deputy from Paris and was the leader of the radical popular party. In this new era, those who had been associated with the old regime or those who opposed the French Revolution became the subjects of persecution.

Did Marie Antoinette really say, "Let them eat cake"?

No, the widely quoted phrase was incorrectly attributed to her. Nevertheless, the legend is not far from fact. Unhappy in her marriage to Louis XVI, king of France, she pursued her own pleasurable interests with abandon. Despite the economic problems that plagued France at the time, she lived an extravagant lifestyle, which included grand balls, a "small" palace at Versailles, theater, gambling, and other frivolities. She was completely disinterested in the affairs of the nation.

In January 1793, King Louis XVI (1754–1793) and his wife, Marie Antoinette (1755–1793), were executed, beginning the Reign of Terror that saw thousands more (mostly those of the aristocracy and clergy) suffer a similar fate at the hands of the revolutionaries. To escape certain death, many fled the country; this included top-ranking military officials, which made room for the rapid advancement of young military officers, such as Napoleon Bonaparte (1769–1821).

The Reign of Terror ended on July 28, 1794, when Robespierre himself was put to death. As he had gained power and influence, the revolutionary leader also had become increasingly paranoid, even putting two of his friends to death in 1794.

What was the Brumaire coup d'état?

The French revolutionary government stayed in power until it was overthrown on November 9, 1799, by a coup d'état. This coup put Napoleon Bonaparte (1769–1821) in power as one of three consuls intended to head the government and marked the end of the French Revolution.

Why was it called the Brumaire coup?

The French had created a new calendar called the French Republican Calendar that was used from 1793 to 1805. Traditional month names were replaced with names based on nature:

- Vendémiaire (vintage)
- Brumaire (mist)
- Frimaire (frost)
- Nivôse (snowy)
- Pluviôse (rainy)
- Ventôse (windy)
- Germinal (seed)
- Floréal (flower)
- Prairial (meadow)
- Messidor (harvest)
- Thermidor (heat)
- Fructidor (fruit)

Part of what was October and November became Brumaire.

What are the details on Napoleon's coup?

While Napoleon was in Egypt and Syria, waging military campaigns on behalf of the French government, there was growing discontent back home with the Directory, the group of five men governing France. Napoleon received word that France might soon be under attack by the Second Coalition (the second in a series of six alliances that

What is a *coup d'état*?

The term is French for a "hit to the head." The term is used to describe the quick overthrow of a government. Typically, a coup is done illegally.

formed in Europe in order to stave off French domination). Leaving his troops, Napoleon hurried home, where he was welcomed as a hero. Aided by his brother, Lucien Bonaparte (1775–1840), and French revolutionary leader Emmanuel-Joseph Sieyès (1748–1836), Napoleon carried out a coup d'état, overthrowing the Directory. A consulate was formed, with the young Napoleon becoming first consul; the other consuls had little influence, acting primarily as advisers to the ambitious Napoleon.

After the chaos and violence of the previous decade, the French people looked to Napoleon as a strong leader who could bring order to the country. They did not know that the thirty-year-old possessed a seemingly insatiable hunger for power, which would soon transform the government into a dictatorship. After a brief peace, Napoleon declared himself emperor of France on December 2, 1804, by which time he had already begun a series of wars to gain more power in Europe.

When did the Napoleonic Wars begin?

The Napoleonic Wars began shortly after Napoleon Bonaparte took power and lasted until 1815, when he was finally defeated at the Battle of Waterloo. Ever the general, Napoleon had used his power to keep France at war throughout his reign.

After a brief peace, Napoleon in May 1800 marched across the Alps to defeat the Austrians, ending a war that had begun eight years earlier. Britain, fearing a growing European power on the continent, had declared war on France in 1793; by 1802, having grown tired of battle, the country agreed to peace with Napoleon in the Treaty of Amiens. But the calm in Europe was not to last.

By 1803 the diminutive but power-hungry Napoleon (nicknamed the Little Corporal) had begun to plot an invasion of Britain. Declaring himself emperor of France in 1804, he initiated a series of campaigns across Europe, and by 1806 most of the continent was under his control. He remained, of course, unable to beat the British, whose superior navy gave them supremacy at sea.

What effect did the Napoleonic Wars have on the United States?

Needing cash to pay for his wars, Napoleon sold the massive territory of Louisiana to Thomas Jefferson in 1803. The deal was called the Louisiana Purchase.

What happened at Trafalgar?

Cape Trafalgar, on the southwest coast of Spain, was in 1805 the scene of a decisive victory for Great Britain over Napoleon

Napoleon Bonaparte ruled France from 1804 to 1814 and built an empire that encompassed much of Europe until it collapsed after a series of wars.

Bonaparte's navy. France and Britain had been at war with each other since 1793. Napoleon remained determined to conquer Britain, just as he had most of continental Europe. But when his fleets met those of decorated English admiral Horatio Nelson (1758–1805), the defeat and destruction of Napoleon's navy ended the emperor's hopes of invading England.

The confrontation at Trafalgar was the culmination of a two-year game of cat and mouse between Nelson's fleets and the French under the direction of Admiral Pierre-Charles Villeneuve (1763–1806), whose sole objective was to invade Britain. To prevent this from happening, in 1803 Nelson began a two-year blockade of Villeneuve and the French Navy at Toulon, France (on the Mediterranean coast). When the French fleets escaped Toulon, attempting to lure the British out to sea, Nelson chased them all the way across the Atlantic—to the West Indies and back—before the showdown off Spain's coast, where the French were joined by Spanish fleets. Meantime, the British Navy continued to protect the coast of England, leaving no opportunity for invasion by the French.

On October 21, 1805, seeing the enemy sailing out of Trafalgar, Nelson formed his fleet of twenty-eight ships into two columns, intending to divide and conquer the combined French and Spanish force of thirty-three ships. About noon that day, as they prepared for the confrontation, Admiral Nelson sent out one of the most famous commands of naval history: "England expects that every man will do his duty."

While the British prevailed, destroying Napoleon's fleet in less than four hours' time, Nelson was fatally wounded by a sharpshooter, and the English navy hero died just as victory was his. The brave Nelson had seen fate coming: the night before Trafalgar, he had revised his will, and just before the battle had begun, he told Captain Henry Blackwood (1770–1832), "God bless you, Blackwood, I shall never speak to you again." Nevertheless, Nelson died knowing that he had won, uttering the still famous words, "Thank God, I have done my duty."

How was Admiral Nelson honored for his victory?

The popular and busy Trafalgar Square in London honors the victory of Admiral Horatio Nelson. In the center of the square is a column topped by a statue of Nelson.

Why did the Russians burn Moscow because of Napoleon?

The September 14, 1812, torching of their own city was directed by Tsar Alexander I

Possibly the greatest naval hero in English history is Admiral Horatio Nelson, who was a brilliant strategist who led the British fleet to numerous victories during the Napoleonic Wars.

(1777–1825), who wished to prevent Napoleon Bonaparte (1769–1821) and his invading armies from reaping the benefits of anything Russian. Through a series of wars, Napoleon had dominated most of Europe by 1805. In 1805 and 1807, Russia suffered major losses in battles with Napoleon's armies. In the face of these defeats, Alexander had made peace with Emperor Napoleon in the first Treaty of Tilsit (1807) in order to buy time so that Russia could better prepare for future conflicts.

By 1812, Russia, its economy dependent on exports, resumed trade with Great Britain, Napoleon's archenemy. This prompted the return of Napoleon's troops to Russia. The French emperor marched into Russia with a force of as many as 685,000 men, but the Russians still delivered Napoleon a crushing defeat. The Russian army relied on guerrilla warfare tactics against the French and followed a scorched-earth policy as the French moved into Russia.

The Russians destroyed everything in front of the path of the French Army, especially crops and food supplies. In the days of Napoleon, armies were not supplied with food from their home country; rather, they took food from the lands they invaded. As Napoleon once said, "An army marches on its stomach," referring to the importance of food supplies, which the Russians now intended to deny the French. Finally, when the French Army reached Moscow, they found a burned and abandoned city with no supplies to get through the winter. Napoleon was forced to retreat in frigid weather, where his army dealt with famine, disease, and constant attacks by Russian forces. His forces suffered great losses: only 27,000 survived.

What well-known piece of classical music remembers the French defeat by the Russians?

Almost seventy years after the event, the famous Russian composer Pyotr Ilyich Tchaikovsky (1840–1893) wrote his "1812 Overture" to commemorate the Russian victory. The piece is fifteen minutes long and includes cannon fire and ringing chimes. It also contains music themes representing the victorious Russians and the defeated French.

Today, in the United States, the piece is often performed on Independence Day and sometimes performed with firework displays.

The various alliances (called coalitions) formed by European countries against Napoleon eventually broke him. After he had been defeated in Russia in 1812, the European powers that had long been held in submission by Napoleon formed a sixth and final coalition against him: Great Britain, Russia, Sweden, Prussia, and Austria met Napoleon's army at the momentous Battle of the Nations at Leipzig, Poland, from October 16 to 19, 1813. Napoleon was defeated there in what is sometimes called the War of Liberation, and he retreated to France.

The following March, the allies making up the Sixth Coalition took Paris, and Napoleon's generals were defeated. He abdicated the throne on April 6. However, that was not the end of the Napoleonic era.

What were Napoleon's Hundred Days?

The term refers to Napoleon Bonaparte's last one hundred days as ruler of France. Having been defeated by his enemies and abdicating the throne, Napoleon was exiled to the island of Elba in the Mediterranean Sea. There, he heard of the confusion and discontent that came after he had descended the throne.

He then left Elba and, with more than 1,000 men, arrived on the French coast at Cannes and marched inland to Paris. Hearing of his arrival, the new Bourbon king, Louis XVIII (1755–1824), fled. On March 20, Napoleon began a new reign, but it was only to last until the European allies defeated him again at the Battle of Waterloo, June 12 through 18, the last battle of the Napoleonic Wars.

After that battle, Napoleon was permanently exiled to the British island of St. Helena (far off the coast of Africa), where he remained until his death in 1821. In 1861 his body was entombed at Les Invalides in Paris, where his tomb can be seen today.

Why is Napoleon still controversial?

Even history has not been able to sort out the widely disparate opinions of the diminutive French ruler. And both his detractors and the apologists continue to publish their arguments and supporting research. The most obvious point on which most scholars agree centers on the fact that, first and foremost, Napoleon Bonaparte was a military man. Here opinion divides. Not long after Napoleon assumed power, he proceeded to keep France—and the rest of Europe—at war for more than ten years.

From the French perspective, Napoleon was a great man, a brilliant strategist who could not only muster his troops but could keep them motivated to fight one campaign after another. The targets of these campaigns—England, Russia, Austria, Germany, Spain, and Portugal among them—view Napoleon in quite a different light. Researchers from these countries have seen and rendered Napoleon's dark side, calling him a megalomaniac and a psychopath and even seeing him as a forerunner of Adolf Hitler.

To further complicate the matter of how history views Napoleon, before he declared himself emperor for life and launched his military conquests throughout the continent and beyond, Napoleon enjoyed a brief period in which many Europeans—not just the French—believed him to be a hero. After all, he assumed leadership of France after the

What popular song, named for the place of Napoleon's defeat, launched the career of one of the greatest European pop groups?

The song is "Waterloo" by ABBA. The song won the 1974 Eurovision Song Contest for the group, which helped ABBA's rise in the charts. It was a Number 1 hit in several countries and sold six million copies. It would be used in the hit musical *Mamma Mia*.

hideous period of Robespierre's Terror and the ineffectual government of the Directory, and then he proceeded to make peace with the Americans, the Russians, and the British. Many believed Napoleon was just the man to bring order to the chaos France had known since the storming of the Bastille, and he extended an olive branch to France's long-time enemies. It looked like he would restore order at home and abroad. Of course, this honeymoon did not last. By 1805 the leader many had looked to in hopes he would end the turmoil only became the cause of more turmoil. His compulsive war-making soon swept over the continent, ultimately uniting various countries in an effort to rid Europe of the scourge that was Napoleon and his Grand Army.

OTHER IMPORTANT DEVELOPMENTS

What was the Crimean War?

The Crimean War was fought from 1853 to 1856 between Russian forces and the allied armies of Britain, France, the Ottoman Empire (present-day Turkey), and Sardinia (part of present-day Italy). The Crimean Peninsula, which juts out into the Black Sea and is part of Ukraine, was the setting for many of the battles. The source of the conflict was Russia's continued expansion into the Black Sea region to gain strategic and commercial advantages. The British and the French wanted to limit Russia's influence.

This photo by Roger Fenton of a battlefield in the Crimea shows the land strewn with canonballs. It is one of the most famous pictures from the war.

But Russia was unable to muster the strength it needed to combat the powerful alliance formed by the European countries and the Ottoman Empire. The war was ended with the signing of the Treaty of Paris (1856), which required Russia to surrender lands it had taken from the Ottoman Empire and abolished Russian navy and military presence in the Black Sea region. It was the first conflict that was covered by newspaper reporters at the front.

What is the origin of the modern nation of Greece?

In 1453, the Ottoman Turks conquered Constantinople (present-day Istanbul, Turkey), and they soon moved westward to bring the Greek peninsula under their control. Hundreds of years later, in 1770, the Greeks tried to overthrow the Turks and were aided in this effort by Russian Tsarina Catherine the Great, whose aim it was to replace Muslim rule with Orthodox Christian rule throughout the Near East. But the effort was unsuccessful, and it was fifty years before the Greeks would rise again to assert their independence.

On March 25, 1821, the Greeks, led by the archbishop of Patras, proclaimed a war of independence against the Turks. Soon, Egypt had thrown its military support behind the Turks, but even the combined force could neither defeat the Greeks nor squelch the revolution.

In 1827, Britain, France, and Russia, all sympathetic to the Greek cause, came to their aid. In October of that year, a combined fleet of the three European powers defeated the Turk and Egyptian fleet in the Battle of Navarino, off the Peloponnese Peninsula. But the deciding moment came when Russia declared war on the Ottoman Empire in 1828, and the Ottoman Turks turned their attention to fighting the Russians. The following year, the Egyptians withdrew from Greece. In March 1830, the London Protocol was signed by Britain, France, and Russia, recognizing an independent Greece. Weary from the fighting, the Ottoman Turks accepted the terms of the proclamation later that year.

THE HOUSE OF WINDSOR

How did the House of Windsor originate?

The origins of Windsor, the family name of the royal house of Great Britain, can be traced to the 1840 marriage of Queen Victoria (who ruled from 1837 to 1901) to her first cousin Albert, the son of the Duke of Saxe-Coburg-Gotha (in present-day Germany). As a foreigner, Prince Albert had to overcome the distrust of the British public, which he did by proving himself to be a devoted husband to Queen Victoria and by demonstrating his genuine concern in Britain's national affairs. Although the husband of Victoria, Albert was not crowned as king.

Victoria and Albert had nine children. Their oldest son, Albert Edward (1841–1910), became King Edward VII upon Victoria's death in 1901. But Edward's reign lasted only until 1910, when he died, and his son, George V (1865–1936), ascended the throne.

George was king during World War I, and, in 1917, with Britain and Germany bitter enemies, he denounced his ties and claims to Germany, superseding his grandfather's (Prince Albert's) family name of Wettin and establishing the House of Windsor.

Thus, George V was the first ruling member of the House of Windsor. His son became king as Edward VIII (1894–1972), but he abdicated the throne in 1936, after reigning for less than a year, so that he could marry American socialite Wallis Simpson (1896–1986). Edward's brother, George VI (1895–1952), became king upon Edward's abdication. He would work tirelessly during World War II to keep up the morale of the British people. (The 2010 movie *The King's Speech* describes the struggles of George VI to overcome his problem with stuttering so he could make an important live radio broadcast in 1939 on Britain's declaration of war on Germany.)

When George VI died in 1952, his daughter became Queen Elizabeth II (b. 1926).

Which British monarch has ruled the longest?

Up until 2016, it was Queen Victoria (1819–1901), who remained on the throne of England for a whopping sixty-four years. (Queen Elizabeth II broke Victoria's record in 2016.)

Victoria became queen in June 1837 upon the death of her uncle, King William IV (1765–1837). Since she was but a teenager at the time, during the early years of her reign, she relied on the guidance of the prime minister, the tactful Lord Melbourne (William Lamb; 1779–1848), whom she counted as a friend. After marrying Prince Albert (1819–1861) in 1840, she also sought out advice from him and his adviser. But by 1850 she had grown confident in her abilities, and she managed the country's affairs with authority. Later in her reign, Prime Ministers Benjamin Disraeli (1804–1881) and William Gladstone (1809–1898) gradually secured increased authority for that office—without alienating the queen. It is for this reason that she is often seen as the first modern monarch, of which she remains a lasting symbol. Queen Victoria celebrated her diamond jubilee in 1897 amid an outpouring of public support. She remained on the throne four more years until her death in 1901.

During her sixty-four-year reign, Victoria presided over the rise of industrialization in Great Britain as well as British imperialism abroad. Architecture, art, and literature flourished, in part due to the in-

This 1875 painting of the British monarch by Heinrich von Angeli was one of Queen Victoria's favorites.

fluence and interests of Prince Albert. It was the prince who, in 1851, sponsored the forward-looking Great Exhibition at London's Crystal Palace. It was the first international exposition—a world fair. The grand Crystal Palace remained a symbol of the Victorian Age until it was destroyed by fire in 1936.

The PBS series *Victoria* is a great look at the life of Victoria.

Who was Lady Di?

Diana Spencer (1961–1997) has been known as "Lady Di," the "People's Princess," and "Princess Diana." Diana came to the world's attention when she became engaged to Prince Charles (1948–), Prince of Wales. Their short courtship led to a royal wedding in July 1981. The beautiful, classy, and fashionable Diana had what seemed to be a fairy-tale marriage to a

Queen Elizabeth II, as of 2020, has served as England's monarch for sixty-eight years, four years longer than Queen Victoria, the previous record-setter.

prince. The elaborate wedding was broadcast on television. In time, the couple had two sons, William and Harry. As Princess of Wales, Diana worked to create awareness of the AIDS crisis and the dangers of land mines left in war zones.

However, her marriage was deeply troubled by their incompatibility and her husband's infidelity. She also struggled with depression and bulimia. Their marriage struggles became tabloid headlines. They divorced in 1996.

Tragically, in August 1997, she died in a car crash in a road tunnel in Paris. Her partner, Dodi Fayed, also died. Initially, the crash was blamed on paparazzi photographers chasing the car. An investigation determined that the driver of her car, Henri Paul, who also died in the accident, was intoxicated and under the effects of prescription drugs, which caused him to crash while speeding.

Her televised funeral was watched worldwide, with her friend, Elton John, singing a tribute to her.

THE EUROPEAN UNION

What is the European Union?

After the devastation of Europe in World War I and World War II, many leaders sought an alternative to the system of nationalist states with all their political, economic, and military rivalries. Discussions began on uniting European countries in a new way. An

80

early phase was the creation of the European Coal and Steel Community in 1951, which made up six countries.

The European Union (EU) came into its present form with the Maastricht Treaty of 1992. In 2002 the EU began issuing its own banknotes, called the Euro, which are used in nineteen of the member countries. The 2009 Lisbon Treaty was the next step in the development of the EU. Currently, there are twenty-seven members of the EU; Great Britain left the EU on January 31, 2020.

The benefit of the European Union is that it created an internal market so that people, goods, services, and capital could move freely among the EU countries. In the past, separate countries had borders that made it difficult for people to move and for goods and services to cross borders. The EU is able to create common policies for all member nations on such things as trade, farming, fishing, labor policies, and environmental policies.

What is Brexit?

Brexit is from the words "British" and "exit." In a June 2016 referendum, 52 percent of United Kingdom citizens voted to leave the European Union. For several years there has been much political turmoil over Brexit, as those on both sides hold very strong views. It has deeply divided the United Kingdom.

One aspect of the problem is that it is not easy to leave the European Union. For several decades, the British economy has been closely aligned with the economies of other EU countries. There is no easy way to entangle things.

Proponents of Brexit believe that freeing the United Kingdom will free its economy to lead to great prosperity. Opponents predict that the result will be just the opposite, and people will be worse off.

In a December 2019 election, the Conservative Party won an eighty-seat majority in Parliament. The Conservatives, led by Prime Minister Boris Johnson (1964–), strongly supported Brexit. On January 31, 2020, the United Kingdom left the European Union, although many of the details of the separation and future relationship between the United Kingdom and the European Union have yet to be worked out.

THE FIRST AMERICANS

When did people first migrate to North America?

The first people came to what we call North America from Asia, perhaps as early as 30,000 years ago. They crossed a land bridge between what is now Russia and Alaska. (Look at a map if you need a geography refresher.) At that time, there was more ice on Earth, and, thus, the oceans were lower. Several waves of Asians crossed over until about 10,000 years ago. Over many centuries, these immigrants and their descendants spread out over all of North America and Central America, and by about 8000 B.C.E., they had reached the southern tip of South America, a place called Tierra del Fuego.

Do an online image search for "prehistoric animals North America" to see some of the animals these early people encountered. Sadly, many of the animals were hunted to extinction by these early peoples with their stone weapons.

Initially, these peoples were wandering hunters and gatherers. Eventually, many different Native American cultures, languages, and societies developed in the Americas. Some became settled farmers raising maize (corn). Maize was a grass that was domesticated about 9,000 years ago in present-day Mexico.

In time, a number of great civilizations developed with organized life in cities, such as in North America: the Adena culture, starting about 1000 B.C.E., and the Mississippian culture, starting about 800 C.E. In Central America, the Mayan culture began about 2000 B.C.E. and the Aztec culture about 1300 C.E. In South America, the Incan Empire arose in 1438.

Are there places where one can see evidence of these ancient peoples?

Thousands of archeological sites exist, and hundreds are open to the public. Here is a small sample of sites for cultures that built mounds:

- At Poverty Point in northeastern Louisiana, many of the original earthworks remain that were built between 1800 and 1200 B.C.E.

- Serpent Mound in southern Ohio is a 1,348-foot-long mound shaped like a snake. Burial mounds in the area date from the Adena culture (800 B.C.E.–100 C.E.).

- Hopewell Culture National Historic Park is a site of mounds in southern Ohio built between 200 B.C.E. and 500 C.E. There are numerous earthworks in the area.

- At Newark Earthworks in central Ohio, large circles and an octagon-shaped mound built between 100 and 500 C.E. can be seen. The original Native American site covered 3,000 acres.

- Moundville Archaeological Park in central Alabama is a Mississippian culture site occupied from 1000 to 1450 C.E.

- Cahokia Mounds (a 10-minute drive from St. Louis, Missouri, into Illinois) was the site of the largest city in North America until Philadelphia passed it in size in the 1870s. Perhaps as many as 40,000 people lived at Cahokia. Many of the mounds, including the spectacular Monks Mound, can be seen today. The city reached its peak in about 1100 C.E. but was abandoned by 1300 C.E.

EMPIRES OF MESOAMERICA AND SOUTH AMERICA

Why are the cultures of Mesoamerica and South America sometimes called "Pre-Columbian"?

Pre-Columbian simply means "before Columbus," so the term refers to the time before 1492. The arrival of Columbus, followed by the Spanish conquerors (called conquistadors) and then settlers, brought great, and often tragic, change to Native peoples in the Americas.

What are the empires of Mesoamerica and South America?

A number of great civilizations developed that built large cities, organized complex societies, and left behind monumental buildings, such as temples and pyramids. The most important cultures in Mesoamerica were Teotihuacan, the Mayas, and the Aztecs. In South America,

What is Mesoamerica?

The region of Mexico and Central America is called Mesoamerica, meaning "middle America." Today, it consists of the countries of Mexico, Guatemala, Belize, El Salvador, Honduras, Nicaragua, Costa Rica, and Panama. (Look at a map online.)

the major culture was the Incans. However, this history is extremely complicated, and there are dozens of minor cultures, such as the Olmecs, the Zapotecs, the Toltecs, and the Miztecs. Making it even more complicated is that archeologists find it difficult to sort out the different cultures since all of these various groups shared much in common.

Imagine future archeologists trying to sort out the differences between Chinese culture and American culture in the present age. Many products that Americans buy are made in China. Many Americans enjoy Chinese food. In China, one can find many American fast-food restaurants. There is even the Shanghai Disney Resort and the Hong Kong Disneyland Resort. Many Chinese enjoy American music and dress like Americans. So, how does one separate out the two different cultures even though the people of these two cultures use different languages and have two very different histories?

For what are the Olmecs known?

The Olmecs are best known for the large, carved heads they created. Eighteen of these heads still exist, and they range in height from 4 feet to 11 feet.

What about *The Simpsons*?

In episode 22 of season 2 of *The Simpsons*, Bart donates his blood to save the life of Mr. Burns. In belated gratitude, Mr. Burns gives Bart an Olmec head. The head shows up in almost twenty later episodes.

THE MAYA EMPIRE

Who were the Maya?

The Maya were an agricultural people who settled in southern Mexico and Central America. Their territory covered Mexico's Yucatan Peninsula, Belize, much of Guatemala,

The ruins of Tikal in modern-day Guatemala are an example of how the Mayans were clearly an advanced civilization.

and parts of Honduras and El Salvador. They developed a civilization that was highly advanced. The Maya produced remarkable architecture (including flat-topped pyramids, temples, and towers that are still visited by tourists today), art (including sculpture, painting, and murals), and their own writing system—probably the first in the Western Hemisphere.

They used this system to record time, astronomical events, their history, and religion (they believed in more than 160 gods). They also developed an advanced mathematics as well as a 365-day calendar believed by some to be even more accurate than the Gregorian calendar in use today. (They also had a 260-day religious calendar.)

When did the Maya Empire exist?

As noted above, the first peoples arrived in North America as long as perhaps 30,000 years ago. In the Archaic Period (28,000 to 2500 B.C.E.), these people settled and began creating different cultures in North, Central, and South America. The Mayan culture then emerged. Its history can be divided into three periods:

Period	Years
Preclassic Mayan (Formative Period)	2500 B.C.E. to 250 C.E.
Classic Mayan	250 C.E. to 900 C.E.
Postclassical Mayan	900 C.E. to 1540s C.E.

Maya culture spread throughout Mesoamerica. City-centers were developed at Copan (Honduras); Palenque, Uxmal, and Chichen Itza (Mexico); and Piedras Negras, Uaxactun, and Tikal (Guatemala). Scholars believe that Tikal was home to some 50,000 people and was not only a center for government, education, economics, and science but was also a spiritual mecca for the Maya. At its peak, the Maya population numbered some fourteen million.

In the postclassical period, Mayan culture began to decline. There are many possible reasons for the decline, such as famine and disease, rebellion by the people against harsh leaders, fighting between Mayan groups, or ecological damage. Some suggest that deforestation and drought were the real reasons. A long period of drought led to smaller crop yields, so more land was cleared to plant more land to compensate for lower yields.

However, there was another possible cause of deforestation. The Mayans built magnificent temples and pyramids that were bright white. The white exteriors required covering the structures with lime plaster. Powdered lime for the plaster was created by

What do the Mayans have to do with Luke Skywalker?

A camera shot of the Mayan pyramids at Tikal was used in the movie *Star Wars: A New Hope* as the site of a rebel base on the moon of Yavin 4.

burning limestone rocks. It took perhaps five tons of trees to create one ton of lime. Thus, the environmental impact of so many buildings covered in white lime plaster must have been great. (There is a brief scene in Mel Gibson's 2006 movie *Apocalypto* that shows Mayan peasants making lime.)

THE AZTEC EMPIRE

Who were the Aztecs?

The Aztecs founded their central city of Tenochtitlan (the site of Mexico City) in about 1325. A poor, nomadic people before their arrival in Mexico's central region, the Aztecs believed the Lake Texcoco marsh was a prophetic place to settle. A prophecy told them to look for an eagle eating a snake, sitting on a cactus. When they saw such a scene, they knew where to settle. (That image would wind up on the Mexican flag.) Before they built it into a great city, they first had to fill in the swampy area, which they did by creating artificial islands.

In addition to constructing the impressive trade and cultural center of Tenochtitlan, the Aztecs were farmers, astronomers, mathematicians, and historians who recorded the events of their civilization. In the 1500s, when the Spanish first saw the remarkable city of Tenochtitlan—with its system of causeways, canals, bridges, and aqueducts—they called it the Venice of the New World. In fact, it was better than most cities in Europe, yet they set about destroying it.

In 1521 the Spanish attacked the great city of Tenochtitlan (seventeenth-century painting by unknown artist).

The Aztec religion was pantheistic, meaning they worshipped many gods. Given that, it is not surprising that when the Spanish conquistadors arrived, at first, the Aztecs believed they were gods (or, at least, the heavenly hosts of their long-awaited god Quetzalcoatl) and even welcomed them with gifts.

Did the Aztecs do human sacrifice?

The Aztecs practiced extensive human sacrifice. They believed that the cosmos was unstable and that the sun might not rise if human sacrifice were not offered to the gods. At some events, hundreds of victims captured in wars and raids were sacrificed. The victims were dragged to the tops of pyramids, where a priest would cut them open with a flint knife and rip out their hearts, which were offered up as "precious cactus fruits" to the gods.

Who was Montezuma? Who was Moctezuma?

Many people have learned of the Aztec king Montezuma, who was conquered by the Spanish. It turns out the correct way to spell and pronounce the name is "Moctezuma." And there were two Aztec kings with the name.

Moctezuma I (1398–1469) was a leading Aztec ruler who expanded the empire and consolidated power in a skillful manner. During his nearly thirty-year reign, the empire achieved several conquests of neighboring lands and generally prospered.

Moctezuma II (1466–1520) was a later Aztec emperor who also accomplished great things during his reign. In fact, many historical sources say that the Aztec Empire was at its zenith in terms of size during his reign. However, Moctezuma and the Aztec Empire fell victim to the Spanish conquistador Hernán Cortés, who conquered the empire and plundered its vast riches for the Spanish Crown.

THE INCA EMPIRE

Who were the Incas?

The Incas developed one of the most extensive empires in all the Americas. During the hundred years before the arrival of the Europeans, the Incas expanded their territory along the western coast of South America to include parts of present-day Peru, Ecuador, Colombia, Bolivia, Chile, and Argentina. Though it was a vast region, it was nevertheless a closely knit state ruled by a powerful emperor, called the Inca. The government was subdivided down to the local level, but because the emperor required total obedience from his subjects, local rulers were kept in check. (Do online image searches for "map of Incan Empire" and "Machu Picchu.")

The Incans developed an infrastructure that included a network of roads, bridges, ferries, and irrigation systems. They, too, built impressive edifices, demonstrating their abilities as engineers. They built the magnificent city of Machu Picchu high in the moun-

The citadel in the Andes Mountains known as Machu Picchu is a famous site of the Incan Empire.

tains. The Incas were also skilled craftspeople, working with gold, silver, and textiles. Like the Aztecs, the Incas worshipped many gods, such as the creator god Viracocha.

Spanish explorer Francisco Pizarro (c. 1475–1541) conquered the Inca Empire in the 1530s. The Spanish looted the empire of its gold and silver.

DISCOVERY OF THE NEW WORLD

Who were the first Europeans to reach North America?

The Norwegian-born Viking, or Norseman, Leif Eriksson (c. 970–c. 1020) was the first European to set foot on North American soil. He was the son of navigator Erik the Red, who founded a Norse settlement in Greenland. About that same time, another Norseman, Bjarni Herjólfsson, who was driven off course on his way from Iceland to Greenland, became the first European to sight North America, but he did not go ashore.

About 1001, Leif set out from Greenland with a crew of thirty-five men and landed on the southern end of Baffin Island, due north of the province of Quebec. The expedition likely made it to what today is Newfoundland and Labrador. In time, a Viking settlement would be built there at L'Anse aux Meadows.

The first authenticated European landing in North America was in 1500, when Portuguese navigator Gaspar Côrte-Real (c. 1450–c. 1501) explored the coast of Labrador and Newfoundland. A year later, he made a second trip to North America but never returned home.

What were the different groups of Native Americans?

When Europeans arrived, some 500 different Native American nations or tribes existed in North America. It was an incredibly diverse world! Here is a list of the better-known tribes, grouped by regions.

Arctic—Present-day northern Alaska, Canada, and Greenland. Aleut, Inuit, and Yupik; these people are also called Eskimos.

Subarctic—Present-day Canada. Cree, Naskapi, and Ojibwa (Chippewa).

Northeast Woodlands—Present-day states of the northeast and the Great Lakes region into Canada. Delaware, Fox, Huron, Illinois, Iroquois, Mahican, Massachuset, Miami, Mohigan, Nipissing, Ottawa, and Shawnee.

Southeast—Present-day Florida, Georgia, Alabama, and Tennessee. Cherokee, Chickasaw, Choctaw, Creek, and Seminole. These people were later called the Five Civilized Tribes.

Great Plains—The prairies between the Mississippi River and the Rocky Mountains. Blackfoot, Cheyenne, Comanche, Crow, Dakota, Lakota, Missouri, Omaha, and Pawnee.

Northwest Coast—The Pacific Coast of Oregon, Washington, and Canada. Chinook, Haida, Kwakiutl, Tillamook, and Tlingit.

Plateau—Present-day Montana, Idaho, and eastern parts of Washington and Oregon. Klamath, Nez Perce, Salish, Walla Walla, and Yakama.

Great Basin—Present-day Idaho, Nevada, and Utah. Bannock, Shoshone, Ute, and Washo.

California—Chumash, Hupa, Karuk, Miwok, and Mohave.

Southwest—Present-day Arizona, Colorado, New Mexico, Texas, and Utah. Pueblo peoples—such as the Hopi and Zuni—Navajo, and Apache. Previous people: Anasazi—the cliff dwellers.

What was Columbus trying to do when he set out on his famous journey?

To understand Columbus, one must look at a map of the world or, better yet, a globe. If you do not have a globe, open Google Maps and zoom out until you see the round Earth. Then locate Europe and India. Europeans greatly valued spices from India. Although spices made food taste better, they also covered up the bad taste of the spoiled food that people often ate. For centuries, spices traveled along the land trade routes between India and Europe. However, at the time of Columbus, the Turks had cut off the trade routes. Columbus came up with his bold idea that he could sail west from Europe across the Atlantic and eventually reach India. Now, rotate the earth map to see what Columbus had in mind. Columbus did not know that the two continents later to be called North and

South America existed. He also miscalculated the size of Earth.

Many scholars of his time knew that Earth was round. It is an obvious conclusion if you watch a ship sail away into the distance. Although the ship gets smaller, it also disappears from the bottom up, indicating a curvature to Earth. Critics of Columbus pointed out that it would be impossible to take enough food and water to sail from Europe to India; Earth was too big. They were right. (It is a commonly held myth that Columbus alone believed the world was round, while his skeptics believed it was flat.) However, Columbus believed Earth was much smaller than it was, so he imagined he could cross to India. Instead, he landed in the New World. Thinking they had found India, the Spanish would soon call the Native peoples "Indians," and they named the islands in the Caribbean Sea that Columbus discovered the West Indies.

Once revered in the United States as the famous explorer who "discovered America" in 1492, Christopher Columbus is now known to be just one of many explorers who reached the New World.

What were the different journeys of Columbus?

Christopher Columbus (born Cristoforo Colombo; 1451–1506) was born in Italy but moved to Portugal, where he married and had a son. Since Portugal was the leading seafaring nation of Europe at that time, he first proposed his idea to the king of Portugal, who turned him down. In 1484, he took his plan to the Spanish monarchs, King Ferdinand (1452–1516) and Queen Isabella (1451–1504), but they too refused to back him. Columbus persisted, and in 1492, the Spanish king and queen agreed to sponsor the explorer's plan because they wanted to restore trade with the Far East and because, as devout Christians, they shared a desire to advance the Christian religion. In short, the monarchs saw that there were both material and religious advantages for backing Columbus's expedition.

Columbus set sail from southwest Spain on August 3, 1492, and he sighted land on October 12 of that year. Going ashore, he named it San Salvador (today, it is one of the Bahamas). With his fleet of three vessels, the *Niña*, the *Pinta*, and the *Santa Maria*, Columbus then continued west and south, sailing along the north coast of Cuba and Haiti (which he named Hispaniola). When the Santa Maria ran aground, Columbus left a colony of about forty men on the Haitian coast, where they built a fort, which, being Christmastime, they named La Navidad (*Navidad* means "Christmas" in Spanish).

91

In January 1493, Columbus set sail for Spain, arriving back in March with a few Native Americans as well as some belts, aprons, bracelets, and gold on board. News of his successful voyage spread rapidly, and Columbus journeyed to Barcelona, Spain, where Ferdinand and Isabella triumphantly received him.

On his second voyage, which he undertook in September 1493, he sailed with a fleet of seventeen ships and some 1,500 men. In November, he reached Dominica, Puerto Rico, and the Virgin Islands. Upon returning to Haiti (Hispaniola), Columbus found that Native peoples had destroyed the colony at La Navidad. In December 1493, he made a new settlement at Isabella (present-day Dominican Republic, the eastern end of Hispaniola), which became the first European town in the New World. Before returning to Spain in 1496, Columbus also landed at Jamaica.

On his third voyage in May 1498, Columbus reached Trinidad, just off the coast of South America. On his fourth and last trip, he found the island of Martinique before arriving on the North American mainland at Honduras (in Central America). It was also on this voyage, in May 1502, that he sailed down to the Isthmus of Panama—finally believing himself to be near China. However, Columbus suffered many difficulties, and in November 1504, he returned to Spain for good. He died two years later in poverty and neglect.

What controversies surround Christopher Columbus?

The first controversy is that for centuries Columbus was called "the discoverer of the New World," when in reality the Native peoples living in the Americas before the arrival of Columbus were the true discoverers of these lands.

The second controversy is that Columbus was called back from the New World twice (on his second and third voyages) to be investigated for his dealings with Native Americans, including numerous charges of cruelty.

The final and most important controversy is that after Columbus came the conquistadors. In the next centuries, much land in Central and South America would be taken from the Native peoples. The Aztec and Incan empires would be destroyed. Many millions of Native peoples would be killed or enslaved as the Spanish looted the land of gold and silver in one of the greatest thefts of all time. However, the biggest killers of Native peoples were the diseases the Spanish brought, such as smallpox and measles.

Where can the name of Columbus be seen today?

Some twenty towns and cities in the United States are named after him. A Catholic men's group is called the Knights of Columbus. His name is the basis for the name "Columbia." Columbia is seen as the personification of the United States. Columbia shows up as the name of cities and towns, the District of Columbia, Columbia University in New York, Columbia Pictures, and Columbia Records.

Because of the controversies, in some places in the United States, monuments and statues of Christopher Columbus are coming under public scrutiny.

Who were the conquistadors?

The Spaniards who arrived in North and South America in the late 1400s and early 1500s were just that—conquerors of the American Indians and their lands. The Spanish encountered the Aztec of Mexico, the Maya of southern Mexico and Central America, and the Inca of western South America. By the mid-1500s, these Native peoples had been conquered and their populations decimated by the Spanish conquistadors. The conquest happened in two ways: first, the Spaniards rode on horseback and carried guns, while their native opponents were on foot and carried crude weapons, such as spears and knives; and second, the European adventurers brought illnesses (such as smallpox and measles) to which the native populations of the Americas had no immunities, causing the Native peoples to become sick and die.

By 1535, conquistadors such as Francisco Pizarro (c. 1475–1541), Hernán Cortés (1485–1547), and Vasco Núñez de Balboa (1475–1519) had claimed the southwestern United States, Mexico, Central America, and much of the West Indies (islands of the Caribbean) for Spain.

What was the claim to fame of Núñez de Balboa?

Vasco Núñez de Balboa was a Spanish explorer best known for laying claim as the first European to lead an expedition in the New World with the purpose of seeing the Pacific Ocean. He set sail for the New World, eventually landing in modern-day Colombia. He established the first colonial settlement constructed by the conquistadors in mainland America at Santa María la Antigua del Darién. Núñez de Balboa became governor of the area. He also crossed the Isthmus of Panama in 1513 and became the first European to see the Pacific Ocean from the New World. In years past, he was often credited as the "discoverer" of the Pacific Ocean.

What plants did the Europeans discover in the New World?

The lands of the Western Hemisphere yielded many plants unknown in Europe.

Vasco Núñez de Balboa was the first European to lead an expedition across Central America to the Pacific Ocean in 1513.

93

On Christopher Columbus's first voyage in 1492, he became the first European to discover maize (corn), sweet potatoes, capsicums (peppers), plantains, and pineapples. Subsequent expeditions found potatoes, wild rice, squash, tomatoes, cacao (chocolate beans), peanuts, cashews, and tobacco. These plants, many of which had been developed and cultivated by the American Indians, were carried back to Europe, and their cultivation spread to suitable climates throughout the world.

The crops also made their way to Asia. It is hard to imagine certain styles of Chinese cooking without peppers, just as it is hard to imagine Italian pasta without tomato sauce.

However, the Europeans brought animals to the New World: horses, cattle, sheep, goats, pigs, and chickens. They later brought plants from Europe and the East back to the Americas, including rice, sugar, indigo, wheat, and citrus fruits—all of which became important crops.

How was Cortés able to claim Mexico for the Spaniards?

On behalf of the Spanish, Hernán Cortés (1485–1547) claimed Mexico after conquering its native peoples. In 1519, Cortés landed on the eastern coast of Mexico and founded the city of Veracruz. From there, he marched inland, making an alliance with the Tlaxcalan Indians (who had fought wars against the powerful Aztecs in central Mexico). On November 8 of that year, Cortés marched into Tenochtitlan (later Mexico City) and took hostage the Aztec leader Mocteczuma II.

Cortés then continued to Mexico's west coast. When he returned to Tenochtitlan, he found the Aztecs in revolt against the Spaniards. Fierce fighting ensued, and by the end of June, Moctezuma II was dead. This period of warfare is still remembered today by Mexicans as *la noche triste* (the sorrowful night). It was not until the following year, in August 1521, that Cortés, after a four-month battle, claimed Mexico City, and the land came under control of the Spanish.

Who was Ponce de León?

Juan Ponce de León (1474–1521) was a Spanish conquistador who explored Puerto Rico for the Spanish crown and would later become governor of Puerto Rico. (*Puerto Rico* is

How did America get its name?

"America" is derived from the name of Italian navigator Amerigo Vespucci (1454–1512), who took part in several early voyages to the New World (in 1497, 1499, 1501, and 1503). German mapmaker Martin Waldseemüller (c. 1470–c. 1520) labeled the land "America" because he knew that Vespucci was the first to realize that the Spanish had actually arrived in a New World—not in the Far East as other explorers (including Columbus) had thought. Historians today are unsure of Vespucci's role as an explorer.

Spanish for "rich port.") Ponce de León traveled north to explore the mainland, which he named La Florida, which translates as "Flowery Land." He searched in Florida for the mythical Fountain of Youth, which was believed to have water that would stop aging.

Who was Hernando de Soto?

Hernando de Soto (c. 1500–1542) was part of a brutal Spanish expedition that crushed the Inca Empire (in what is now Peru). He returned to Spain a hero. King Charles I (1500–1558) then appointed him governor of Cuba and authorized him to conquer and colonize the region that is now the southeastern United States.

Arriving in Florida in 1539, de Soto and an army of about 600 men headed north in search of gold and silver. They traveled through present-day Georgia, through North and South Carolina, through the Great Smoky Mountains, and into Tennessee, Georgia, and Alabama. After defeating the Choctaw leader Tuscaloosa in 1540 in south-central Alabama, the Spaniards headed north and west into Mississippi. They crossed the Mississippi River on May 21, 1540, and de Soto died later that same day. His army continued without him, reaching Mexico in 1541.

Who was the explorer Vázquez de Coronado?

Francisco Vázquez de Coronado (c. 1510–1554) set out in 1540 from Mexico with 300 Spanish troops as well as some Native peoples in search of gold and treasure. They made

Artist William Henry Powell depicts Hernando de Soto seeing the Mississippi for the first time in this romanticized 1853 painting. In reality, de Soto and his expedition were known for their cruel treatment of the Incas and other native peoples.

it into the region where Arizona and New Mexico lie today. There, they captured the Zuni people but found no gold. Coronado's men became the first Europeans to see the Grand Canyon and to travel up the Rio Grande Valley. In 1546, Coronado was accused of cruelty in his treatment of Native peoples.

What was the impact on Native Americans of the arrival of the Spanish?

When the Spanish arrived in the New World, the continents of North and South America were filled with many Native peoples. There were over 500 different Native American nations with over 300 different languages.

However, the arrival of the Spanish had a devastating impact on the Native peoples. The Spanish operated under a medieval mindset that the people on the land belonged to whomever owned the land. Thus, since the Spanish claimed they owned the conquered land, the people living on it had no rights. The Spanish killed and enslaved many Native Americans.

However, the bigger killers were the diseases the Spanish brought, such as smallpox, measles, and cholera, to which the Native peoples had no resistance. It is estimated that the population of indigenous Americans declined by 90 percent in the centuries after the arrival of the Spanish.

Destruction of the lives of Native peoples would continue under the British and the French.

COLONIAL AMERICA

What were the Spanish holdings in the New World?

New Spain comprised much of the Spanish possessions in the New World during the colonial period. At its height, New Spain included what are today the states of California, Nevada, Utah, Arizona, New Mexico, Texas, and Florida. It also included all of Mexico and Central America and many islands in the Caribbean, such as Cuba and Puerto Rico. In addition to the land of New Spain, the Spanish also controlled the northern and southern parts of South America.

In 1821, a Mexican rebellion ended Spanish rule there, and the colonial empire of New Spain was dissolved. By 1898 Spain had relinquished all its possessions in North America.

What were the French holdings in the New World?

The French possessions in North America, called New France, consisted of the colonies of Canada, Acadia, and Louisiana. The first land claims were made in 1534 by French explorer Jacques Cartier (1491–1557) as he sailed the St. Lawrence River in eastern Canada. In 1604, Pierre Dugua de Mons (c. 1558–1628) established a settlement at Acadia (in present-day Nova Scotia, Canada). French claims later extended the region to include what are today the province of New Brunswick and the eastern part of the state of Maine. After founding Quebec in 1608, explorer Samuel de Champlain (c. 1567–1635) penetrated the interior (present-day Ontario) as far as Lake Huron, extending French land claims westward.

In 1672 French-Canadian explorer Louis Jolliet (1645–1700) and French Catholic missionary Père Jacques Marquette (1637–1675) became the first Europeans to discover the upper part of the Mississippi River. (Marquette University in Milwaukee is named for the explorer.) Ten years later, French explorer René-Robert Cavelier, Sieur de La Salle (1643–1687) followed the Mississippi to the Gulf of Mexico, claiming the river valley for France and naming it Louisiana in honor of French king Louis XIV. While the French expanded their North American claims, most French settlers lived in Canada. France lost Canada to Great Britain in the Seven Years' War (1756–1763).

Louisiana changed hands numerous times before it was finally sold to the United States under President Thomas Jefferson in 1803 as the Louisiana Purchase. Louisiana was far larger than the land that is the current state of Louisiana. Louisiana initially included land from the Gulf of Mexico, into what is today Canada, and from the Mississippi to the Rockies. French culture and influence in these areas remain prevalent today.

What was the Lost Colony?

The Lost Colony was the second English colony established in America. It was set up in 1587 on Roanoke Island, off the coast of North Carolina; however, by 1590 it had disappeared without a trace.

The first colony, which was also on Roanoke Island, was set up in 1585 by 100 men sent there by Sir Walter Raleigh (1554–1618). They eventually abandoned the site and returned to England.

Who are the Cajuns?

The French settled much of the eastern part of Canada in land they called New France. The colony of Acadia grew up in what are today known as the provinces of New Brunswick and Nova Scotia. Its capital at Port Royal was founded in 1605. In time, the British fought to take control of Canada, and many Acadians resisted the British. During the French and Indian War, in what became known as the Great Expulsion (1755–1764), the British expelled some 11,500 Acadians. Many were deported to other British colonies, while others were sent to Britain and France from where they migrated to Louisiana, which was under Spanish control at the time. In Louisiana, they created a distinct culture with a distinctive dialect, Cajun food, and Cajun music that can all be found in the area today. The word "Acadian" has become "Cajun."

In the spring of 1587, the next group arrived. Their leader, John White, went back to England for supplies. When he finally returned in 1590, he found that the colony was abandoned.

The only clue that White found was the word "Croatoan," which had been engraved on a tree. The Croatoan, or Hatteras, were friendly Indians who lived on an island south of Roanoke Island. White set out to see if the colonists had joined the Hatteras Indians, but weather prevented the search, and his expedition returned to England instead.

Two theories explain what might have become of the lost colonists. In one theory, the colonists left Roanoke to go to Chesapeake Bay but then perished at the hands of the Indians. Other evidence suggests that the colonists became integrated into several Indian tribes living in North Carolina.

Who were the Pilgrims?

The Pilgrims were early settlers who sought religious freedom and self-government in the New World. Since theirs was a religious journey, they described themselves as pilgrims. In fact, they were Separatists—Protestants who separated from the Anglican Church (the Church of England) to set up their own church. In 1609, they fled their home in England and settled in Holland. Fearing their children would lose contact with

Throughout much of U.S. history, the first Thanksgiving has been treated with idealism. In fact, relations between the Pilgrims and local Mashpee Wampanoag Tribe were rather tense, although the Indians did share food with the settlers.

their own culture and accept Dutch culture, the group decided to voyage to America to establish their own community. In 1620, they arrived on the rocky western shore of Cape Cod Bay, Massachusetts.

Their transatlantic crossing took sixty-six days aboard the *Mayflower*. There were 102 settlers on the ship, only some thirty-five of whom were Pilgrims; the rest were merchants. On November 21, the Pilgrims drafted the Mayflower Compact, an agreement by which the forty-one signatories (the men aboard the *Mayflower*) formed a body politic authorized to enact and enforce laws for the community. They voted religious leader John Carver (1576–1621) as governor. Though their colonial charter from the London Company specified they were to settle in Virginia, they decided to establish their colony at Cape Cod, well outside the company's jurisdiction. By December 25, the Pilgrims had chosen the site for their settlement and began building at New Plymouth.

The first year was difficult, and the Pilgrims faced many hardships: thirty-five more colonists arrived aboard the *Fortune*, putting a strain on already limited resources; sicknesses such as pneumonia, tuberculosis, and scurvy claimed many lives, including that of Governor Carver; and the merchants in the group challenged the purity of the settlement. Having secured a new patent from the Council of New England in June 1621, the lands of New Plymouth Colony were held in common by both the Pilgrims and the merchants. However, this communal system of agriculture proved unsuccessful, and in 1624 William Bradford (1590–1657), who had succeeded Carver as governor, granted each family its own parcel of land. The Wampanoag Indians, who had previously occupied the land settled by the Pilgrims, proved friendly and were helpful advisers in agricultural matters. In 1626, the Pilgrims bought out the merchants' shares and claimed the colony for themselves.

The Pilgrims successfully governed themselves according to the Scriptures, and Plymouth Colony remained independent until 1691, when it became part of Massachusetts Bay Colony—which had been founded by the Puritans.

How were the Puritans different from the Pilgrims?

The Puritans created the Massachusetts Bay Colony. The Puritans wanted to purify the Anglican Church, while the Pilgrims were Separatists who had left the Anglican Church. Puritan leader John Winthrop (1588–1649) would become the governor. In 1630, they settled in what is today Boston and Salem, Massachusetts, establishing a Puritan Commonwealth. By 1643, more than 20,000 Puritans arrived in Massachusetts in what is called the Great Migration. Puritans also settled in Rhode Island, Connecticut, and Virginia during the colonial period.

The Puritan movement had developed in England during the 1500s, and they were influenced by the teachings of reformer John Calvin (1509–1564). When King James I (1566–1625) ascended the throne of England in 1603, he was the first ruler of the house (royal family) of Stuart. The Stuart monarchs, particularly James's successor, King Charles I (1600–1649), tried to enforce absolute adherence to the High Church of Anglicanism and viewed the Puritan agitators as a threat to the authority of the crown. As a result, many Puritans fled England.

What were the Dutch colonial holdings?

New Netherlands was the only Dutch colony on the North American mainland. It consisted of lands surrounding the Hudson River and the lower Delaware River (now the states of New York, New Jersey, and Delaware). Explorers from the Netherlands first settled the area in about 1610. In 1624, the Dutch West India Company officially founded the colony of New Netherlands. The Dutch colonial official Peter Minuit (1580–1638) purchased the island of Manhattan from the American Indians for an estimated $24 in trinkets. The colonial capital of New Amsterdam was established there.

The Dutch held the colony until 1664, when it was conquered by the English under the direction of the duke of York, the brother of King James II. Under British control, the area was divided into the colonies of New Jersey and New York, and New Amsterdam became New York.

What are the origins of slavery in America?

The roots of slavery in North America date back to about 1400, when Europeans arrived in Africa. At first, the result of African contact with Europeans was positive, opening trade routes and expanding markets. Europeans profited from Africa's rich mineral and agricultural resources and, for a while, abided by local laws governing their trade. Africans benefited from new technologies and products brought by the Europeans. But the relationship between the two cultures soon turned disastrous as the Europeans saw the economic potential of enslaving human beings. Often, people displaced by warfare within Africa would be caught and enslaved.

By the mid-1600s, triangular patterns of trade emerged. The most common route began on Africa's west coast, where ships picked up enslaved people. The second stop was the Caribbean islands—predominately the British and French West Indies—where the enslaved were sold to plantation owners who needed slave labor to grow crops, such as sugar. The traders on the ships used the profits from selling slaves to purchase sugar, molasses, to-

The first slave auction in North America was held in New Amsterdam in 1655 as depicted in this 1895 painting by Howard Pyle.

> ### What nineteenth-century ship became a symbol of slavery and the abolitionist movement?
>
> On the Spanish ship *La Amistad* (Spanish for "friendship") in 1839, enslaved Africans revolted against their captors. The ship had been headed from Havana to another city in Cuba. The enslaved—led by Joseph Cinqué—headed north and were captured by a U.S. ship near Long Island.
>
> Litigation ensued over the status of the Africans. The case eventually reached the U.S. Supreme Court, which ruled in *United States v. Amistad* that the Africans were illegally transported. The result was that the Africans were freed and headed back to their homeland. The story was made into the 1997 film *Amistad*.

bacco, and coffee. These raw materials were then transported north to the third stop, New England, where a rum industry was thriving. (Rum is made from fermenting sugar or molasses and then distilling it. Rum became the biggest export from New England.) There, ships were loaded with the spirits before traders made the last leg of their journey back across the Atlantic to Africa's west coast, where the process began again.

Other trade routes operated as follows: 1) manufactured goods were transported from Europe to the African coast; enslaved people to the West Indies; and sugar, tobacco, and coffee back to Europe, where the route began again; and 2) lumber, cotton, and meat were transported from the colonies to southern Europe; wine and fruits to England; and manufactured goods to the colonies, where the route began again. There were as many possible routes as there were ports and demand for goods.

The tragic result of the triangular trade was the transport of an estimated ten million black Africans. Sold into slavery, these human beings were often chained below deck and allowed only brief, if any, periods of exercise during the transatlantic crossing, which came to be called the Middle Passage. Conditions for the enslaved people were brutal and improved only slightly when traders realized that should they perish during the long journey across the ocean, it would adversely affect their profits upon arrival in the West Indies.

After economies in the islands of the Caribbean crashed at the end of the 1600s, many enslaved people were sold to plantation owners on the North American mainland, initiating another tragic trade route. The slave trade was abolished in the 1800s, putting an end to the forced migration of Africans to the Western Hemisphere.

When did the first Africans arrive in the British colonies of North America?

In 1619, a Dutch ship carrying twenty Africans landed at Jamestown, Virginia. This event is often seen as the beginning of slavery in the British colonies, which would later become the United States.

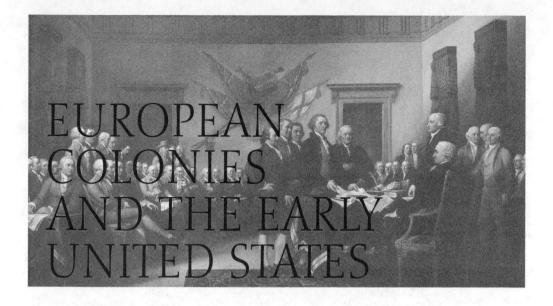

EUROPEAN COLONIES AND THE EARLY UNITED STATES

COLONIALISM

Where were the European colonies in North America?

By the 1600s, the French had taken the land north of the British colonies. The French controlled Canada, the land around the Great Lakes, and Louisiana. The British claimed the land on the Atlantic coast of what today is Maine down to Georgia. The Spanish controlled Florida, Mexico, and the Caribbean.

How did the British come to control much of North America during colonial times?

British and French explorers laid claim to many parts of what is now the United States. During the late 1600s and into the mid-1700s, the two European powers fought a series of four wars in their struggle for control of territory in North America. Three of the wars broke out in Europe before they spread to America, where British and French colonists fought King William's War (1689–1697), Queen Anne's War (1702–1713), and King George's War (1744–1748). King William's War saw no gains for either side. After Queen Anne's War, however, both sides signed the Treaty of Utrecht, in which France ceded Newfoundland, Acadia, and the Hudson Bay territory to Britain.

The struggle between England and France was not settled until a fourth war, the French and Indian War (1754–1763), from which Britain emerged the victor.

What was the religion of British colonies?

The British would establish colonies along the Eastern Seaboard from Georgia in the South to Massachusetts in the North, which included the land that would eventually become Maine. Since most of the immigrants from Britain were Protestants, most of the colonies were Protestant. For example, the Anglican Church was the official religion in

Virginia. Maryland, an exception, was established as a Catholic colony. However, Protestants eventually took control and took away the religious freedom of Catholics. The colony of Pennsylvania was set up by a Quaker, William Penn.

What were the original thirteen British colonies?

Here are the thirteen colonies listed chronologically from when they were established:

Original Thirteen Colonies

Colony	Year Established
Virginia	1607
New York	1626
Massachusetts Bay (included Maine)	1630
Maryland	1633
Rhode Island	1636
Connecticut	1636
New Hampshire	1638
Delaware	1638
North Carolina	1653
South Carolina	1663
New Jersey	1664
Pennsylvania	1682
Georgia	1732

What was the French and Indian War?

The French and Indian War (1754–1763) was the last major conflict in North America before the Revolutionary War. For decades, Britain and France had steadily expanded their territories into the Ohio River valley. Since the fur trade prospered in this region, both countries wished to control it. As the French encroached on their territory, the British governor sent an ultimatum to them, delivered by none other than George Washington (1732–1799). But the French did not intend to back down. In 1754, Washington (now a lieutenant colonel) and 150 troops established a British outpost at present-day Pittsburgh, not far from the French Fort Duquesne. That spring and summer, fighting broke out.

Washington met the French, and though he and his troops mustered a strong resistance, there were early losses for the British. But a reinvigorated British force, under the leadership of Britain's secretary of state, William Pitt (1759–1806), took French forts along the Allegheny River in western Pennsylvania and met French troops in battle at Quebec. In 1755, Washington was made colonel and led the Virginia troops in defending the frontier from French and Indian attacks. Though the British finally succeeded in occupying Fort Duquesne in 1758, fighting continued until 1763, when the Treaty of Paris ended the war.

The British won the spoils, gaining control of all French lands in Canada as well as French territories east of the Mississippi River, except for New Orleans. (The city was

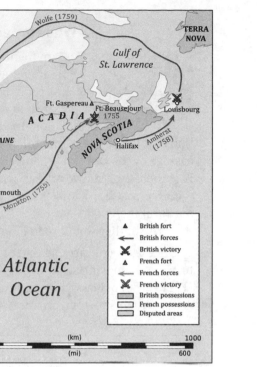

The French and Indian War was a conflict between Britain and France (and their Indian allies) for control over the abundant fur-trading regions around the Ohio River valley.

ceded to Spain, along with its holdings west of the Mississippi; Spain had become an ally to France late in the war, in 1762.) In exchange for Havana, Cuba, Spain turned over Florida to the British. France, which had once controlled a vast region of America, retained only two small islands off the coast of Newfoundland, Canada, and the two Caribbean islands of Martinique and Guadeloupe.

However, the cost of fighting the war left Great Britain and France in debt. The British decided to tax the American colonies, in part because the war had protected the colonies. Resentment of the taxes would lead to the American Revolution. The French debt would weaken the French monarchy and help lead to the French Revolution.

AMERICAN REVOLUTION

What were the Intolerable Acts?

The so-called Intolerable Acts, also known as the Coercive Acts, were five laws passed by the British Parliament early in 1774. Intended to assert British authority in the Massachusetts colony, the measures were seen as punishment for the Boston Tea Party (December 1773). In brief, the laws enacted the following: 1) closure of the port of Boston;

Who started the Boston Tea Party?

Many believe that on December 13, 1773, it was patriot Samuel Adams (1722–1803) who gave the signal to the men, who may have numbered more than one hundred and were dressed as Indians, to board the ships in Boston Harbor and dump the tea overboard. Adams was a leader in the agitation that led up to the event. The show of resistance was in response to the recent passage by the British Parliament of the Tea Act, which allowed the British-owned East India Company to "dump" tea on the American colonies at a low price and also required that the colonists pay a duty for said tea. Colonists feared the act would put local merchants out of business and that if they conceded to pay the duty to the British, they would soon be required to pay other taxes as well.

Once the ships carrying the tea had arrived in Boston Harbor, the colonists tried to have them sent back to England. But when Governor Thomas Hutchinson (1711–1780) of Massachusetts refused to order the return of the ships, patriots organized their show of resistance, which came to be known as the Boston Tea Party.

2) an English trial for any British officer or soldier who was charged with murder in the colonies; 3) a change to the charter of Massachusetts such that the council had to be appointed by the British and that town meetings could not be held without the (British-appointed) governor's permission; 4) the requirement that the colonists house and feed British soldiers; and 5) the extension of the province of Quebec southward to the Ohio River.

While the British intention was to bring the Massachusetts colony under control, the result was instead to unite all the colonies in opposition to British rule. In this regard, the acts are seen as a precursor to the American Revolution (1775–1783).

Why were there two Continental Congresses?

The First Continental Congress convened on September 5, 1774, in Philadelphia, Pennsylvania. The meeting was largely a reaction to the so-called Intolerable Acts (or the Coercive Acts), which British Parliament had passed to control Massachusetts after the rebellion of the Boston Tea Party (December 1773). Sentiment grew among the colonists that they would need to band together to challenge British authority. Twelve of the thirteen colonies dispatched fifty-six delegates to meet in Philadelphia. Delegates included Samuel Adams (1722–1803), George Washington (1732–1799), Patrick Henry (1736–1799), John Adams (1735–1826), and John Jay (1745–1829).

The First Continental Congress petitioned the king, declaring that the British Parliament had no authority over the American colonies, that each colony could regulate its own affairs, and that the colonies would not trade with Great Britain until Parliament rescinded its trade and taxation policies. The petition stopped short of proclaiming independence from Great Britain, but the delegates agreed to meet again if necessary.

However, King George III (1738–1820) was determined that the British Empire be preserved at all costs. He believed that if the empire lost the American colonies, there may be a domino effect, with other British possessions encouraged to also demand independence. He feared these losses would render Great Britain a minor state rather than the power it was. With Britain unwilling to lose control in America, in April 1775 fighting broke out between the British soldiers—the redcoats—and patriots at Lexington and Concord, Massachusetts.

As a result, the colonies again sent representatives to Philadelphia, convening the Second Continental Congress on May 10. Delegates—including George Washington, John Hancock (1737–1793), Thomas Jefferson (1743–1826), and Benjamin Franklin (1706–1790)—organized and prepared for the fight, creating the Continental Army and naming Washington as its commander in chief. With armed conflict already underway, Congress nevertheless moved slowly toward proclaiming independence from Britain: On July 10, two days after issuing a declaration to take up arms, Congress made another appeal to King George III, hoping to settle the matter without further conflict. The attempt failed, and the following summer, the Second Continental Congress approved the Declaration of Independence, breaking off all ties with the mother country.

A statue commemorating Paul Revere's famous ride stands near the Old North Church in Boston. Revere was made famous by Longfellow's poem, but fellow riders William Dawes and Dr. Samuel Prescott should be remembered as well.

Why is Paul Revere's ride so well known?

The April 1775 event was famous in its own right but was memorialized by American writer Henry Wadsworth Longfellow (1807–1882) in his poem "Paul Revere's Ride":

> Listen, my children, and you shall hear
> Of the midnight ride of Paul Revere,
> On the eighteenth of April, in Seventy-five;
> Hardly a man is now alive
> Who remembers that famous day and year....

Revere rode that night—on a borrowed horse. He left Boston at about 10:00 P.M. and arrived in Lexington at midnight to warn Samuel Adams and John Hancock, who were wanted for treason, that British soldiers were coming. The next day, the battles of Lexington and Concord were fought, starting the Revolutionary War in America.

As an American patriot, Revere (1735–1818) was known for his service as a special messenger, so much so that by 1773, he had already been mentioned in London newspapers. Revere also participated in the Boston Tea Party in 1773.

What other patriot rode that night to warn about the British invasion?

William Dawes (1745–1799) also rode from Boston to Lexington to warn Samuel Adams and John Hancock of the pending British invasion and threat. Dawes and Revere both arrived in Lexington. They later rode together to Concord with Dr. Samuel Prescott. The three riders dispersed when they ran into a group of British soldiers. While Paul Revere is a household name, Dawes has been largely ignored.

Did the American colonies have any allies in their fight against the British?

Yes. France, a longtime rival of Great Britain, was a key ally to the Americans, supplying them with some 90 percent of their gunpowder. France also controlled numerous

---

Who was Benedict Arnold?

Benedict Arnold (1741–1801) was an American military leader who later defected to Great Britain in 1780. His name has become an eponym, as Benedict Arnold refers to a traitor.

Arnold had successes for the American Continental Army, winning battles at Saratoga. However, he was denied certain promotions and felt that he would be better off switching sides. He negotiated with the British about surrendering West Point. The plan leaked, and American forces led by George Washington nearly captured Arnold. He escaped and actively campaigned as a British officer. He later moved to London.

> ## Why was Bunker Hill important in the American Revolution?
>
> The June 1775 battle on the hills outside Boston proved to be the bloodiest battle of the war. After the fighting in April at Lexington and Concord, more British troops arrived in Boston in late May. The Americans fortified Breed's Hill, near Bunker Hill, and on June 17, the British were ordered to attack the Americans there. The patriots, who needed to conserve ammunition, were given the famous direction not to fire until they saw the whites of their enemies' eyes. The patriots succeeded in driving the British back on their first two charges. But on the third charge, the patriots fled. The Battle of Bunker Hill resulted in more than 1,000 injured or dead British soldiers and 400 American soldiers killed or wounded.

ports and helped American ships with safety and supplies. Thousands of French troops assisted in the war effort as well.

Who was Rochambeau?

Jean-Baptiste Donatien de Vimeur, the Comte de Rochambeau (1725–1807), was a French military leader and noble who assisted the American colonists in the American Revolutionary War against the British. He had previously fought in the Seven Years' War, distinguishing himself at the Battle of Minorca.

In 1780, Rochambeau was given command of a special French force of more than 7,000 French troops who were sent with the task of helping General George Washington in his fight against the British. He helped Washington win the Battle of Yorktown with a decisive victory over British military leader Charles Cornwallis (1738–1805).

Were all the battles of the American Revolution waged in the Northeast?

No; there was also fighting in the southern colonies. But the struggle between the American colonists and the British was further complicated in the South by the presence of slaves. Landowners feared that any fighting in the vicinity would inspire slaves to revolt against them. Knowing this, the British believed they could regain control of the southern colonies more readily than those in the north.

In November 1775, the British governor of Virginia offered to free any slaves who would fight for the British. As many as 2,000 black slaves accepted the offer and took up arms. But there were also patriots in the South: It was Virginian Patrick Henry (1736–1799) who uttered the famous words, "Give me liberty, or give me death."

In late February 1776, patriot forces confronted and defeated pro-British colonists near Wilmington, North Carolina. The British troops who were sailing from Boston, Massachusetts, to North Carolina to join the loyal colonists arrived too late to help. They instead sailed on to Charleston, South Carolina, which was also the scene of fighting that summer.

What does the Declaration of Independence say?

The U.S. Declaration of Independence, adopted July 4, 1776, has long been regarded as history's most eloquent statement of the rights of the people. In it, not only did the thirteen American colonies declare their freedom from Britain, they also addressed the reasons for the proclamation (naming the "causes which impel them to the separation") and cited the British government's violations of individual rights, saying "the history of the present King 'George III' of Great Britain is a history of repeated injuries and usurpations," which aimed to establish "an absolute Tyranny over these States."

The opening paragraphs go on to state the American ideal of government, an ideal that is based on the theory of natural rights. The Declaration of Independence puts forth the fundamental principles that a government exists for the benefit of the people and that "all men are created equal." As the chairman of the Second Continental Congress committee that prepared the Declaration of Independence, it was Thomas Jefferson (1743–1826) who wrote the first draft for the Second Continental Congress.

The most oft-cited passage is the following:

We hold these truths to be self-evident, that all men are created equal, that they are endowed by their Creator with certain unalienable Rights, that among these are Life, Liberty and the pursuit of Happiness. That to secure these rights, Governments are instituted among Men, deriving their just powers from the con-

This painting by artist John Trumbull is probably the most famous image of the signing of the U.S. Declaration of Independence. The painting can be found today hanging at the U.S. Capitol rotunda.

sent of the governed, That whenever any Form of Government becomes destructive of these ends, it is the Right of the People to alter or to abolish it, and to institute new Government, laying its foundation on such principles and organizing its powers in such form, as to them shall seem most likely to effect their Safety and Happiness.

Although there was heated discussion on the subject of slavery at the Second Continental Congress, slavery was not addressed in the final version of the Declaration of Independence despite the claim that "all men are created equal."

Who are considered the Founding Fathers of the United States?

The term is used to refer to a number of American statesmen who were influential during the revolutionary period of the late 1700s. Though definitions vary, most include the authors of the Declaration of Independence and the signers of the U.S. Constitution among the nation's Founding Fathers.

Of the fifty-six members of the Continental Congress who signed the Declaration of Independence, the most well known are John Adams (1735–1826) and Samuel Adams (1722–1803) of Massachusetts, Benjamin Franklin (1706–1790) of Pennsylvania, John Hancock (1737–1793) of Massachusetts, and Thomas Jefferson (1743–1826) of Virginia.

The thirty-nine men who signed the U.S. Constitution on September 17, 1787, include notable figures such as George Washington (1732–1799), who would go on to become the first president of the United States; Alexander Hamilton (1755–1804), who, as a former military aid to Washington, went on to become the first U.S. secretary of the treasury; and James Madison (1751–1836), who is called the "Father of the Constitution" for his role as negotiator and recorder of debates between the delegates. At eighty-one years of age, Franklin was the oldest signer of the Constitution and was among the six statesmen who could claim the distinction of signing both it and the Declaration of Independence.

What were the Articles of Confederation?

This American document was the forerunner to the U.S. Constitution (1788). Drafted by the Continental Congress at York, Pennsylvania, on November 15, 1777, the Articles of

---

Why did John Hancock go down in history as the notable signer of the Declaration of Independence?

Most Americans know that when they're putting their "John Hancock" on something, it means they're signing a document. Hancock was one of the fifty-six men who signed their names to the historic document; since he was president of the Second Continental Congress, he signed the declaration first. Hancock also had the largest signature of the men who signed the famous document.

Confederation went into effect on March 1, 1781, when the last state, Maryland, ratified them. The articles had shortcomings that were later corrected by the Constitution. They provided the states with more power than the central government, stipulating that Congress rely on the states both to collect taxes and carry out the acts of Congress.

How was the Constitution created?

It is largely thanks to Alexander Hamilton (1755–1804) that the articles were thrown out. Realizing that they made for a weak national government, Hamilton led the charge to strengthen the central government—even at the expense of the states. Eventually, he won the backing of George Washington (1732–1799), James Madison (1751–1836), John Jay (1745–1829), and others, which led to the convening of the Philadelphia Constitutional Convention, where the ineffectual Articles of Confederation were thrown out and the Constitution was drafted.

Which Founding Father later became the first chief justice of the U.S. Supreme Court?

John Jay served as the country's first chief justice of the U.S. Supreme Court from 1789 to 1795. A widely respected statesman, Jay held numerous positions, including delegate to the Continental Congress, president of the Continental Congress, minister to Spain, secretary of foreign affairs (under President George Washington), special envoy to Great Britain, and chief justice. Washington named Jay chief justice, but Jay eventually left that position to serve as governor of New York—a position he coveted more.

Who was Samuel Huntington?

Samuel Huntington (1731–1796) was a leading early American statesman from Connecticut. He served as chief justice of the Connecticut Supreme Court and as governor of Connecticut—his last public office. But Huntington was also the first president of the Continental Congress when the Articles of Confederation were ratified. Thus, some have made the claim that he was technically the first president of the United States.

THE U.S. CONSTITUTION

What was the Virginia Plan?

It was the famous plan drafted by James Madison and put forth by the Virginia delegates to the Constitutional Convention, which convened on May 25, 1787. After taking a few days to set the ground rules and elect officers, the delegation from Virginia, led by Edmund Jennings Randolph (1753–1813), proposed a plan to write an all-new constitution rather than attempting to revise and correct the weak Articles of Confederation. There was opposition (sometimes called the New Jersey Plan), and the issue was debated for weeks. Eventually, a majority vote approved the Virginia Plan, and the delegates began work drafting a document that would provide a strong national government for the United States.

Who wrote the U.S. Constitution?

In spirit, the U.S. Constitution was created by all of the fifty-five delegates to the meeting that convened on May 25, 1787, in Philadelphia's Independence Hall. Thomas Jefferson called the Constitutional Convention "an assembly of demigods"—and with good cause, as the delegates were the young nation's brightest and best. Even in such stellar company, the document did have to be written. While many had a hand in this process, it was New York lawyer and future American politician and diplomat Gouverneur Morris (1752–1816) who actually took on the task of penning the Constitution, putting into prose the resolutions reached by the convention.

The U.S. Constitution went into effect in 1789. It defines the branches of the federal government, the separation of powers, and the powers of the states versus the central government. A landmark document in world government, it has influenced the constitutions of many other countries since its writing.

Morris had the considerable help of the records that James Madison of Virginia had kept as he managed the debates among the delegates and suggested compromises. In that capacity, and because he designed the system of checks and balances among the legislative (Congress), the executive (the president of the United States), and the judicial (Supreme Court) branches, Madison had considerable influence on the document's language, quite rightfully earning him the designation "Father of the Constitution."

The original document, drafted by Morris, is preserved in the National Archives Building in Washington, D.C. While the Constitution has been amended by Congress, the tenets set forth therein have remained with Americans for more than two centuries, and they have provided proof to the countries of the world that a constitution outlining the principles and purposes of its government is necessary to good government.

When was the U.S. Constitution ratified?

The Constitution was ratified by the required nine states by June 21, 1788. It went into effect the following year, superseding the Articles of Confederation (1781).

What was the goal of the Lewis and Clark expedition?

The expedition, which began in 1804 and took more than two years to complete, had three purposes: to chart a route that would be part of a passage between the Atlantic and

Pacific oceans, to trace the boundaries of the territory obtained in the Louisiana Purchase, and to lay claim to the Oregon Territory.

Thomas Jefferson (1743–1826) was president of the United States at the time, and he believed that a route could be found between St. Louis and the West Coast. As early as 1801, Jefferson had conceived of the idea that the Missouri and Columbia rivers might be followed west, leading to the Pacific. The journey would also be a reconnaissance mission; information would be collected about the vast region, and communications would be set up with its inhabitants. On April 30, 1803, the United States bought the Louisiana Territory from France. The purchase extended from the Mississippi River in the east to the Rocky Mountains in the west and from the Gulf of Mexico in the south to British America (Canada) in the north. Napoleon Bonaparte, who desperately needed cash for his wars, sold the land to the United States at what in retrospect was a bargain price.

Jefferson soon picked his private secretary, Virginia-born Meriwether Lewis (1774–1809), to lead the westward expedition. Lewis then chose as his co-leader William Clark (1770–1838), who had served in the U.S. Army. Beginning in the summer of 1803, Lewis and Clark undertook the necessary preparations for the overland journey. These included studying the classification of plants and animals, learning how to determine geographical position by observing the stars, and recruiting qualified men (mostly hunters and soldiers) for the expedition. (Do an online image search for "map of Lewis and Clark expedition.")

On May 14, 1804, the Lewis and Clark expedition left just north of St. Louis and headed up the Missouri River to its source. They then crossed the Great Divide and followed the Columbia River to its mouth (in present-day Oregon) at the Pacific Ocean, where they arrived in November 1805—one and a half years after they had set out. They arrived back in St. Louis on September 23, 1806, having gathered valuable information on natural features of the country, including its flora, fauna, and the Indian tribes who lived there.

The expedition had been helped by the addition (in what is now North Dakota) of a Shoshone Indian woman named Sacagawea (c. 1786–1812). Lewis and Clark had hired her husband, French-Canadian trader Toussaint Charbonneau (1767–1843), as an interpreter during the winter of 1804–1805.

WAR OF 1812

What caused the War of 1812?

The war between the young United States and powerful Great Britain largely came about because of France. After the French Navy was crushed by the British under Admiral Horatio Nelson (1758–1805) at the Battle of Trafalgar, Napoleon turned to economic warfare in his long struggle with the British. He directed all countries under French control not to trade with Great Britain. Its economy dependent on trade, Britain struck back by imposing a naval blockade on France, which soon interfered with U.S. shipping. The

United States had tried to remain neutral, but the interruption of shipping to and from the continent and the search and seizure of ships posed significant problems to the American export business.

In 1807, Great Britain issued Orders in Council that required even neutral vessels destined for a continental port to stop first in England. Napoleon responded by decreeing that any neutral vessel that had submitted to British search could be seized. A further problem was that the British Navy had expanded its number of ships but did not have enough sailors. So, when the British stopped an American ship, they often took American sailors and forced them to work on British ships. This was called "impressing" sailors, meaning to press or force them to work on ships against their will.

Sometimes viewed by historians as a branch of the Napoleonic Wars, the War of 1812 has the United States, which was an ally of France, fighting the British. Both sides had several Indian tribes providing support in the war, which at one point saw the British invade Washington, D.C., and burn down the White House.

Back in America, the people of New England, the region most dependent on shipping, nevertheless vehemently opposed a war with the British. But the country's economy was depressed as a result of the interruption of exports, and the U.S. Congress declared war on June 18, 1812. In these days before telegraph and radio, the United States did not know that two days before, on June 16, Britain had withdrawn its Orders in Council, lifting its policy of shipping interference, which had been the chief reason for the war declaration.

Who were the War Hawks?

The War Hawks were a group of Republicans in the U.S. Congress who advocated war with Great Britain because they were tired of the failure of diplomacy to resolve maritime problems with the British. They also opposed British aid to American Indians. Under War Hawk leader Henry Clay (1777–1852), Congress soon passed resolutions to strengthen the army and navy. When called upon by President James Madison to declare war on the British in June of 1812, it was the War Hawks who swung the close vote. Thus, the War of 1812 began. Some historians believe the true motive behind the War Hawks was not resolution of the shipping problems but rather the desire to annex parts of southern Canada to the United States.

Who said, "We have met the enemy and they are ours"?

It was Captain Oliver Hazard Perry (1785–1819) who wrote the famous words in a letter to General William Henry Harrison (1773–1841) after defeating the British at the Battle of Lake Erie in September 1813. An improvised U.S. squadron commanded by Captain Perry, twenty-eight years old, achieved the victory during the War of 1812. The message he sent to Harrison (who later became president) was: "We have met the enemy and they are ours: two ships, two brigs, one schooner, and one sloop."

When did the War of 1812 end?

The two countries engaged in fighting for the next two and a half years. At one point, British troops entered Washington, D.C., and burned the White House. In December 1814, the Treaty of Ghent officially ended the war. But once again, poor communication led to fighting: two weeks after the treaty was signed, troops in New Orleans, unaware of this event, fought for control over the Mississippi River in the worst battle of the entire conflict: the Battle of New Orleans, with Andrew Jackson (1767–1845) leading the American forces. Though both the United States and Great Britain claimed victory in the War of 1812, neither side had gained anything.

What is privateering?

Privateering is the hiring of privately owned ships and their crews to fight during battle. The practice, which dates to the 1400s, continued well into the 1800s, eventually being replaced by the development of strong navies. Privateers were, essentially, gunboats for hire. They played a crucial role in the American Revolutionary War (1775–1783) after the Second Continental Congress authorized their use on March 18, 1776, enabling the colonists to capture about 600 British ships. The Americans would again employ privateers in the War of 1812 (1812–1814).

But during times of peace, some privateers turned to pirating, which at least in part prompted European nations to sign the Treaty of Paris of 1856, which ended the Crimean War (1853–1856) and outlawed privateering. Since the United States had relied on privateers in the past and had yet to develop its own navy, the Americans did not sign the treaty. While there was some privateering during the American Civil War (1861–1865), the need for them soon subsided as navies developed—by enlistment and draft. Privateering has not been used in more than one hundred years.

What was the Creek War?

The Creek War—sometimes called the Red Stick War—was a war between different tribes of the Creek Nation conducted during the War of 1812. Sometimes, it is considered part of the War of 1812. The Red Sticks were a group of Creeks (sometimes called

What song remembers the Battle of New Orleans?

The 1959 song by Johnny Horton, "The Battle of New Orleans," was a popular hit in its day. It sold over a million copies as a single (making it a gold record) and earned Horton a Grammy Award for Best Country and Western Performance and composer Jimmy Driftwood for Song of the Year.

Upper Creeks) who opposed assimilation and concessions to the U.S. government. They opposed the Lower Creeks, who were more willing to accede to the U.S. government.

A military commander from Tennessee named Andrew Jackson (1767–1845) earned praise for his bravery and skill in leading U.S. troops and Lower Creek troops in several victories over the Upper Creeks. His most famous victory in the Creek War occurred at the Battle of Horseshoe Bend in central Alabama. Jackson later catapulted from war hero to two terms as U.S. president.

What two other American military leaders achieved success during the time of the War of 1812 and later became U.S. presidents?

William Henry Harrison (1773–1841) and Zachary Taylor (1784–1850) later served as the ninth and twelfth presidents of the United States, respectively. Both gained fame during the War of 1812.

Harrison earned acclaim during the war for his battles with Tecumseh, the legendary Shawnee Indian chief, who opposed U.S. expansion and was willing to fight to defend his peoples. In a series of conflicts—sometimes called Tecumseh's War—Tecumseh (1768–1813) achieved several victories. However, Harrison engaged Tecumseh's warriors at the Battle of Tippecanoe in November 1811 near Battle Ground, Indiana. The battle was inconclusive, but Harrison claimed it was a great victory.

When he later ran for president with his running mate John Tyler (1790–1862), their campaign slogan and song was "Tippecanoe and Tyler too." Harrison only served

Zachary Taylor (left) and William Henry Harrison were two heroes of the War of 1812 who also would become presidents of the United States. Sadly, Harrison died of a fever only 31 days after his inauguration.

thirty-one days in office—the shortest tenure in the history of the presidency—because the sixty-eight-year-old died of pneumonia.

Zachary Taylor also served in the War of 1812, earning acclaim for successfully defending Fort Harrison from attack by Shawnee Indians led by Tecumseh. For his bravery, he received a promotion to major. Taylor, whose nickname was "Old Rough and Ready," also served during the Black Hawk War, the Second Seminole War, and the Mexican–American War. Like Harrison, Taylor served briefly as U.S. president; he took office in March 1849 and died of a stomach ailment in July 1850.

Who were the expansionists?

Not long after the colonies won the American Revolution and founded the United States of America, a nationalistic (super-patriotic) spirit emerged in the hearts of many citizens of the new country. Eager to spread American ideals, many looked westward, northward, and southward to expand the territory of the Union beyond the original thirteen states. These people were called expansionists. Not only did they favor the settlement of the frontier, but some advocated seizure of the southwest (from Spain and later from Mexico), Florida (from Spain), the Louisiana Territory (from France), and the Northwest Territories and even Canada (from Britain). By the 1840s, the doctrine of Manifest Destiny, which stated that the United States had a God-given right and duty to expand its territory and influence throughout North America, took hold.

The fires of expansionism were fanned by population growth during the 1800s. Pioneer settlement of the Great Plains and the Old Northwest (the present-day states of Ohio, Michigan, Indiana, Illinois, Wisconsin, and part of Minnesota) resulted in an increase in farmland and overall crop production; Yankee ingenuity resulted in inventions such as the cotton gin (1793) and the McCormick reaper (1831), which improved the processing and harvesting of raw materials, such as cotton and grain; and a continuous influx of immigrants from Europe supplied labor for the factories that had popped up across New England and the mid-Atlantic states. All these factors combined to create rapid population growth. In the two decades between 1840 and 1860 alone, the population of the United States more than doubled, increasing from just over seventeen million to more than thirty-eight million.

Though the Eastern Seaboard cities grew, a system of new canals, steamboats, roads, and railroads opened the interior to increased settlement. By 1850, almost half the population lived outside the original thirteen states.

However, the movement west meant taking land from the Native American tribes who had lived on these lands going back thousands of years. The conquest of the Native Americans is a sad and tragic part of American history.

Many Americans also wanted to take land from Canada, which at the time was a colony of Great Britain. This was one of the reasons for the War of 1812. Although largely unknown to many Americans today, during the war, the United States made several unsuccessful invasions into Canada.

However, the spirit of expansionism resulted in the United States' relatively speedy acquisition of North American territories that had belonged to Spain, Mexico, France, and the British. By 1853, the United States owned all the territory of the present-day contiguous states, and by the end of the century, it owned all the territory of its present-day states—including Alaska (purchased from Russia in 1867) and Hawaii (annexed in 1898).

What was the Trail of Tears?

The Trail of Tears was the government-enforced western migration of the American Indians in the 1830s. As an increasing number of white settlers moved inland from the coastal areas, they laid claim to Native American homelands; conflicts ensued. The government's solution was to relocate the Indians to make room for the pioneers. As many as 20,000 members of the Cherokee Nation were forced from tribal lands in Georgia, Alabama, and Tennessee and were escorted west by federal troops under the command of General Winfield Scott (1786–1866) along an 800-mile trail that followed the Tennessee, Ohio, Mississippi, and Arkansas rivers to Indian territory in Oklahoma, north of the Red River.

The journey took between 93 and 139 days, and the movement westward was called the Trail of Tears not only because it was a journey the Native peoples did not wish to make, to a place where they did not wish to go, but because an estimated 2,000 to 8,000 people—mostly infants, children, and the elderly—died en route. The deaths were primarily caused by sickness, including measles, whooping cough, pneumonia, and tuberculosis.

Escorted in waves, it was a full year before the Cherokee had been relocated; some 1,000 had refused to leave their tribal lands in the Southeast. This forced migration resulted in the fragmentation and weakening of the tribe.

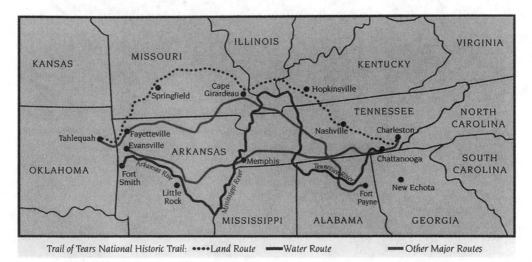

Trail of Tears National Historic Trail: ••••Land Route ▬▬Water Route ▬▬Other Major Routes

This map shows the various land and water routes taken by Native Americans who were forced off their ancestral lands by President Andrew Jackson. Thousands died during the forced relocation.

Were the other forced removals of Native Americans from this area?

Yes, four other tribes who lived in the Southeast were also affected. (Many other tribes outside this area were also removed at various times.)

Forced Removal of Native Tribes

Tribe	Years	Number Forced to Move	Deaths
Choctaw	1831–1836	12,500	2,000–4,000
Seminole	1832–1842	2,833	700
Creek	1834–1837	19,600	3,500
Cherokee	1836–1838	20,000	2,000–8,000
Chickasaw	1837–1847	over 4,000	500–800

What does "Remember the Alamo" mean?

The saying was a rallying cry for Texans in their war for independence from Mexico. The movement for independence had begun in the winter of 1835 to 1936, when the people of Texas decided to cut off relations with Mexico, and soon turned into a war when the Mexican government sent a force of some 4,000 troops, under the command of General Antonio López de Santa Anna (1794–1876), to squelch the rebellion. From the Mexican perspective, these settlers, who had been invited into Mexico, were now trying to break away and steal part of Mexico. As the Mexican Army approached, the force of about 150 men who were determined to defend the city of San Antonio retreated to the Alamo, a Spanish mission built in the previous century.

The Alamo is now a popular historic museum and attraction in San Antonio that is visited by about two and a half million tourists every year!

There, they were joined by another fifty men but were still no match for the Mexicans, who kept the Alamo under siege for thirteen days—from February 23 to March 6, 1836. The Texans, low on ammunition, ceased to return fire. On the morning of March 6, Santa Anna's troops seized the Alamo. The fierce frontiersmen, Davy Crockett (1786–1836) among them, are believed to have fought using the butts of their rifles. All the Texans who fought that day at the Alamo died.

Meantime, General Sam Houston (1793–1863) had assembled his forces, and, with the rallying cry "Remember the Alamo," he set out to face the Mexican Army and secure independence. This he did, at San Jacinto, Texas, on April 21, 1836, in a quick and decisive battle that had caught Santa Anna's troops by surprise. The following day, the Mexican general was captured and made to sign a treaty giving Texas independence.

What caused the Mexican–American War?

The two-year war (1846–1848) was fought over the United States' annexation of Texas. The events that led up to the conflict began in 1837, when President Andrew Jackson recognized Texas as independent. Sam Houston, president of the Republic of Texas, felt that protection against a Mexican invasion may be necessary, so he eyed annexation to the United States. In the meantime, Mexican president Antonio López de Santa Anna warned that such an action on the part of the United States would be "equivalent to a declaration of war against the Mexican Republic." The Mexicans viewed Texas as land that had been stolen from Mexico.

President John Tyler (1790–1862) signed a joint resolution from Congress inviting Texas to join the Union in March 1845, three days before leaving office. Mexico responded by breaking off diplomatic relations with the United States. A border dispute made the situation increasingly tenuous: Texas claimed that its southern border was the Rio Grande River, while Mexico insisted it was the Nueces River, situated farther north. In June, new president James K. Polk (1795–1849) ordered Brigadier General Zachary Taylor (1784–1850) to move his forces into the disputed area. In November, the U.S. government received word that Mexico was prepared to talk. Polk dispatched Congressman John Slidell (1793–1871) to Mexico. However, upon arrival in Mexico City, Slidell was refused the meeting; President José Joaquín Herrera (1792–1854) had bowed to political pressure, opposing discussions with the United States.

Polk then sent General Taylor and his army to advance through the disputed territory to the Rio Grande. Meanwhile, Mexico overthrew President Herrera, putting into office the fervent nationalist General Mariano Paredes y Arrillaga (1797–1849), who reaffirmed Mexico's claim to Texas and pledged to defend Mexican territory.

How and when did the United States declare war?

In May 1846, Polk's Cabinet met and approved the president's recommendation to ask Congress to declare war. The next day, news arrived in Washington that on April 25, 1846, a sizeable Mexican force had crossed the Rio Grande and surrounded a smaller

American reconnaissance party. Eleven Americans were killed, and the rest were wounded or captured. (Critics of the war would argue that sending the U.S. military into that area had been used to provoke Mexico to respond militarily so that the Mexican response could be used as an excuse to declare war on Mexico. In other words, Mexico was set up so they could be blamed for starting the war, which in the end led to the loss of over half of the land of Mexico.)

Polk delivered a message to Congress, concluding, "Mexico has … shed American blood upon the American soil.… War exists … by the act of Mexico herself." By the time the war was officially declared on May 13, 1846, General Taylor had already fought and won key battles against the Mexicans.

What did the United States gain from the Mexican–American War?

The Mexican–American War officially ended when the U.S. Senate ratified the Treaty of Guadalupe Hidalgo in March 1848. By the treaty, Mexico relinquished roughly half its territory to the United States. Mexico also recognized the Rio Grande as its border with Texas.

Mexico received payments in the millions from the United States. Five years later, under the terms of the Gadsden Purchase of 1854, the United States purchased a small portion of land from Mexico for another $10 million, which was widely regarded as further compensation for the land lost in the war.

Many Mexicans see their loss of land as a theft by the United States, which was legitimized by the Treaty of Guadalupe Hidalgo. From the loss of Texas to the Treaty of Guadalupe Hidalgo, in twelve years, Mexico lost 55 percent of its land, which

The United States secured huge land concessions from Mexico after the war, gaining much of what is now considered the American Southwest.

What was the deal with Santa Anna's leg?

In 1838, Santa Anna was in a battle against the French at Veracruz, Mexico, and got hit in the leg by cannon fire. His leg was amputated. However, he insisted that his leg be buried with full military honors in the Cathedral in Mexico City. He then had a prosthetic leg made of cork. In 1844, Santa Anna lost power, and an unhappy Mexican mob dug up his real leg and dragged it through the streets.

When he later regained power, his leg (or a substitute) was reburied with more honors and ceremonies. Sometimes, in parades he would remove his prosthetic leg and wave it to the crowds to show what he had sacrificed for Mexico.

Then, in 1848, during the Mexican–American War, American troops captured his prosthetic leg. That leg is currently on display in the Illinois State Military Museum in Springfield. The American troops later captured a second leg, which was a wooden peg leg. Apparently, they used it as a baseball bat.

included the present states of California, Nevada, Utah, part of Colorado, Arizona, New Mexico, and Texas.

What does "Fifty-four forty or fight" mean?

The slogan refers to a dispute between the United States and Great Britain over Oregon Country, which an 1818 treaty allowed both nations to occupy. This was the territory that began at 42 degrees north latitude (the southern boundary of present-day Oregon) and extended north to 54 degrees, 40 minutes north latitude (in present-day British Columbia). During the 1830s and early 1840s, American expansionists insisted that U.S. rights to the Oregon Country extended north to latitude 54 degrees, 40 minutes, which was then the recognized southern boundary of Russian America (roughly present-day Alaska).

The eleventh president of the United States, James K. Polk (1795–1849), used the slogan in his political campaign of 1844. After he was elected, Polk settled the dispute with Great Britain (in 1846), and the boundary was set at 49 degrees north, the northern boundary of what is today Washington State and the border between the United States and Canada. This agreement—reached without the fight threatened in the slogan—gave the United States the territory that is present-day Washington, Oregon, and Idaho as well as parts of Montana and Wyoming.

THE AMERICAN PARTY SYSTEM

What were the first political parties in the United States?

The first political parties were the Federalists and the Democratic-Republicans. The Federalists favored a strong central government, favored the mercantile and banking interests, and often took a pro-Great Britain position (at least compared to their opponents).

The Democratic-Republicans favored a less powerful central government, retention of power by the states, and the interests of farmers and those of the lower and middle class, and they often took a foreign policy stance more in alignment with France.

Earlier, there were political leaders known as Anti-Federalists, but the Federalists and the Democratic-Republicans were the first political parties after the U.S. Constitution was signed.

Who were the Whigs?

They were members of political parties in Scotland, England, and the United States. The name is derived from *whiggamore* (meaning "cattle driver"), which was a derogatory term used in the seventeenth century to refer to Scottish Presbyterians who opposed King Charles I of England (1600–1649). Charles, who ruled from 1625 to 1649, was deposed in a civil war, then tried in court, convicted of treason, and beheaded. The British Whigs, who were mostly merchants and landed gentry, supported a strong Parliament. They were opposed by the aristocratic Tories, who upheld the power of the king. After 1832, the British Whigs became part of the Liberal Party.

At about the same time, the Whig Party in the United States emerged as one of the two major American political parties. The other was the Democratic Party (that Americans still know today), which supported President Andrew Jackson, nicknamed "Old Hickory," for reelection in 1832. Though Jackson's first term of office was controversial, the Whigs were unable to elect their candidate, Henry Clay (1777–1852), of the so-called Southern "Cotton" Whigs, so Jackson went on to a second term.

In the election of 1840, the Whigs, whose leadership had succeeded in uniting the party, finally put their candidate in the White House: William Henry Harrison. However, he died after only thirty-two days in office, and his successor, John Tyler, alienated the Whig leaders in Congress, who then ousted Tyler from the party. In 1848 the Whigs put Zachary Taylor (nicknamed "Old Rough and Ready") in the White House, but two years later, he, too, died in office. His successor, Millard Fillmore (1800–1874), remained loyal to the Whigs, but there were problems within the party. The last Whig presidential candidate was General Winfield Scott ("Old Fuss and Feathers"; 1786–1866) in 1852, but he was defeated by Franklin Pierce (1804–1869). Shortly thereafter, the Whig Party broke up over the slavery issue; most of the Northern Whigs joined the Republican Party, while most of the Southern "Cotton" Whigs joined the Democratic Party.

How did the Republican Party begin?

The Republican Party, one of the two principal political parties of the United States today, was founded in 1854 by those opposing the extension of slavery into new territories. It also included Nativists, who opposed immigrants and Catholics. The party mustered enough support to elect their candidate in 1860, Abraham Lincoln (1809–1865).

During the 1880s, party members nicknamed themselves the Grand Old Party; the vestige of this nickname is still around today as the GOP. There have been nineteen Republican presidents.

How did the Democratic Party begin?

The other—and older—principal party in the United States today, the Democratic Party, was founded around electing Thomas Jefferson (1743–1826) to office in 1800 (defeating incumbent Federalist president John Adams). The party's platform favored personal liberty and the limitation of federal government. Installing Jefferson in office, the party—then called the Democratic-Republicans—successfully saw its candidates elected to the White House for the next twenty-five years. In 1828, they became known simply as Democrats, dropping the suffix.

If you count from Andrew Jackson to Barack Obama (1961–), there have been fourteen presidents who were Democrats (covering fifteen administrations since Grover Cleveland was elected in two nonconsecutive terms).

THE AMERICAN PRESIDENCY

Why does the president of the United States give a State of the Union Address?

The U.S. Constitution requires the president to annually present a joint session of Congress (attended by representatives and senators) with a status report on the nation. Presidents George Washington and John Adams, the first and second presidents, delivered their messages in person. Thereafter, the State of the Union was sent as a written message, which was read in Congress. But President Woodrow Wilson (1856–1924) delivered his messages in person, including that of January 1918, when he delivered the Fourteen Points—his formulation of a peace program for Europe once World War I had ended. Since Franklin D. Roosevelt (1882–1945) held office (beginning in 1933), all U.S. presidents have made formal addresses to Congress.

What state is known as the "Cradle of Presidents"?

Ohio is known as the "Cradle of Presidents" because it is home to eight presidents: William Henry Harrison, Ulysses S. Grant, Rutherford B. Hayes, James A. Garfield, Benjamin Harrison, William McKinley, William Howard Taft, and Warren G. Harding. Three Ohio presidents in a row—Grant, Hayes, and Garfield—followed each other in succession as the eighteenth, nineteenth, and twentieth presidents, respectively.

What was the Kitchen Cabinet of Andrew Jackson?

It was the name given to President Andrew Jackson's unofficial group of advisers, who reportedly met with him in the White House kitchen. The group included Secretary of State Martin Van Buren (1782–1862), who went on to become vice president and later

Today, most Americans watch the State of the Union Address given by the president on television. The Constitution requires the president to give such an address annually.

president; Francis Preston Blair Sr. (1791–1876), editor of the *Washington Globe*, who was active in American politics and later helped get Abraham Lincoln elected to office in 1860; and Amos Kendall (1789–1869), a journalist who was also a speechwriter for Jackson and went on to become U.S. postmaster general. The Kitchen Cabinet, was influential in formulating policy during Jackson's first term (1829–1833). Many believe he relied on the wisdom of the Kitchen Cabinet members because his real Cabinet which he convened infrequently, had proved ineffective. But Jackson, the seventh president of the United States, drew harsh criticism for relying on his cronies in this way. When he reorganized the Cabinet in 1831, the Kitchen Cabinet disbanded.

Jackson's favoritism to his circle of friends did not end with the Kitchen Cabinet, however. During his presidency, the "spoils system" was in full force. Jackson gave public offices as rewards to many of his loyal supporters. Though the term "spoils system" was popularized during Jackson's terms in office (it was his friend, Senator William Marcy [1786–1857], who coined the phrase when he stated, "to the victor belong the spoils of the enemy"), Jackson was not the first president to grant political powers to his party's members. And the practice continued through the nineteenth century. However, beginning in 1883, laws were passed that gradually put an end to, or at least limited, the spoils system.

AMERICAN IMMIGRATION

What prompted widespread Irish emigration in the mid-1800s?

In 1845, Ireland's potato crop failed. Though crop failures in Europe were widespread at the time, the blight in Ireland was particularly hard-hitting because of the reliance on a single crop, potatoes, as the primary source of sustenance. The Great Famine that resulted lasted until 1848. The effect was a drastic decline in the Irish population—due both to deaths and emigration. Between 700,000 and one million people died in Ireland during the Great Famine. And between 1846 and 1854 alone, 1.75 million left the country in search of a better life elsewhere. Three-quarters of those sailed to the United States. However, the ships were often called "coffin ships" because so many died during the journey.

When were the major waves of immigration to the United States?

The first wave of immigration was during colonial times, when most new arrivals to North America were from England. But other European countries were represented as well, including France, Germany, Ireland, Italy, the Netherlands, Sweden, and Wales. By 1700, roughly a quarter million people lived in the American colonies. By the beginning of the American Revolution (1775–1783), the number had climbed to 700,000.

Some of these new arrivals had been encouraged to immigrate by Virginia's headright system: Englishmen who could pay their own Atlantic crossing were granted fifty acres of land; each of their sons and servants were also granted an additional fifty acres. Other colonies also adopted the headright system, with the land amounts varying in each.

Other immigrants in this first wave were poor and could not afford the price of the transatlantic passage; by signing a contract agreeing to work as an indentured servant for a specific period (typically three to seven years), their future master paid their fare. At the end of this period, the servant became a freeman, and the former master usually granted land, tools, or money. During the American Revolution and for several decades after, the flow of immigrants into the new country slowed.

A second wave of immigration began in 1820. During the next fifty years, nearly

There were many reasons the Irish left their island over the course of the nineteenth century, including political and religious persecution, but in the 1840s it was famine caused by crop failures that led to immigrants traveling abroad, including to the United States.

7.5 million newcomers arrived in the United States. Many were Irish who escaped the effects of the Great Famine back home, settling in cities along the eastern U.S. seaboard. Cities such as Boston, New York, and Philadelphia had large Irish populations. The Irish would play significant roles in areas such as the police force and the Catholic clergy. New Orleans would also receive many Irish immigrants. The ships taking cotton to Liverpool, England, would offer cheap passage to New Orleans.

An equal number (roughly a third) were German, who settled the nation's interior farmlands, particularly the Midwest. The cities of Cincinnati, Milwaukee, and St. Louis would become known as the German Triangle.

What later waves of immigration came in the next decades?

Between 1881 and 1920, a third wave brought more than twenty-three million immigrants to American shores. These new arrivals were largely from eastern and southern Europe, such as Italians and Poles. German immigration reached its peak in 1882. In 1883, the United States saw the peak of immigration from Denmark, Norway, Sweden, Switzerland, the Netherlands, and China. In 1902, U.S. immigration set new records as people from Italy, Austria-Hungary, and Russia made the transatlantic journey.

Between 1920 and 1965, immigration slowed. In the last three and a half decades of the twentieth century and into the twenty-first, a fourth wave of immigration has taken place. In the spring of 1998, the U.S. Census Bureau released a report citing that 9.6 percent of American residents are foreign-born, or roughly one in every ten. Fourteen million immigrants entered the United States between 2000 and 2010.

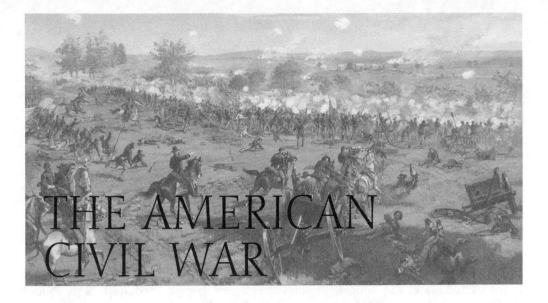

THE AMERICAN CIVIL WAR

THE ANTISLAVERY MOVEMENT

Which U.S. state was the first to abolish slavery?

Vermont, in 1777, adopted a state constitution prohibiting slavery. The first document of its kind in the United States, it read, "No male person, born in this country, or brought from over sea, ought to be holden by law, to serve any person, as a servant, slave or apprentice, after he arrives to the age of twenty-one years, nor female, in like manner, after she arrives to the age of eighteen years, unless they are bound by their own consent, after they arrive to such age, or bound by law, for the payment of debts, damages, fines, costs, or the like." Vermont's constitution also gave suffrage (the right to vote) to all men, regardless of race.

Vermonters were the first to put a black legislator in the state house, when Alexander Twilight (1795–1857) was elected as a representative in 1836. Twilight also earned another first when he graduated from Vermont's Middlebury College to become the first black person in the nation to earn a college degree.

When was the slave trade outlawed?

The slave trade ended in Britain in 1807, when authorities agreed with the growing number of abolitionists (those who argued that slavery was immoral and violated Christian beliefs) and outlawed the trade. In 1833, slavery was abolished throughout the British colonies. In the United States, the slave trade was prohibited in 1808, but possessing slaves was still legal. An illegal trade in slaves continued in the United States until Britain stepped up its enforcement of its antislavery law by conducting naval blockades and surprise raids off the African coast, effectively closing the trade. The slave trade finally came to an end after it was outlawed in 1870 throughout the Americas.

When did the antislavery movement begin?

In the United States, the campaign to prohibit slavery strengthened in the early 1800s. Abolitionists, believing slavery to be morally wrong and in violation of Christian beliefs, called for an end to the system, which had become critical to the agrarian economy of the southern states, where plantations used slaves to produce cotton, tobacco, and other crops for domestic and international markets.

Who were the leaders of abolition?

Leaders of the antislavery movement included journalist William Lloyd Garrison (1805–1879), founder of the influential antislavery journal *The Liberator* and the American Anti-Slavery Society (established 1833); brothers Arthur (1786–1865) and Lewis (1788–1873) Tappan, prominent New York merchants who were also founders of the American Anti-Slavery Society; and Theodore Dwight Weld (1803–1895), leader of student protests, organizer of the American and Foreign Anti-Slavery Society, and author of *The Bible against Slavery* (1837). Another leading abolitionist, escaped freed slave Frederick Douglass (1818–1895), wrote his autobiography, *Narrative of the Life of Frederick Douglass, An American Slave*, which inspired many to join the abolitionist movement.

Underground Railroad conductor Harriet Tubman (c. 1822–1913) worked against slavery by helping to free hundreds of blacks

By any definition of the word, Harriet Tubman was a heroine of the Civil War era. She led over a dozen missions on the Underground Railroad to rescue some seventy slaves, and during the war, she was a spy and scout for the Union.

who escaped slavery in the South and headed for northern states and Canada. Writers such as Harriet Beecher Stowe (1811–1896), author of *Uncle Tom's Cabin* (1851–1852), helped strengthen the abolitionist cause and were instrumental in swaying public sentiment.

What was the Underground Railroad?

It did not involve trains, and it was not underground. Rather, it was a network of routes and safe houses that allowed enslaved people to escape slave states and go to free states and Canada. People escaping usually traveled at night, walking or riding in wagons. People called "conductors" would guide the travelers from one safe house to another. Perhaps 100,000 enslaved people escaped on the Underground Railroad.

What did the founding of the country of Liberia in Africa have to do with the antislavery movement?

Surprisingly, a number of those who opposed slavery believed that once slaves were free, they should be sent back to Africa. With this goal in mind, members of the American Colonization Society (organized 1816–1817) made land purchases on the West African coast. The holdings were named Liberia, a Latin word meaning "freedom." The first black Americans arrived there in 1822. But the society's plan was controversial; other abolitionists and blacks opposed it, as they believed the only answer to the question of slavery was to eradicate it from the United States and extend the full rights of citizenship to the freed slaves in their new American home.

Nevertheless, by 1860, 11,000 people freed from slavery in the United States had been settled there; eventually, a total of 15,000 made the transatlantic voyage to a secured freedom in Liberia. The country was established as an independent republic on July 26, 1847.

What did lawmakers do to resolve the slavery question before the Civil War?

In the mid-1800s, the divide widened between the northern free states and the southern slave states. The government tried but was unable to bring resolution; rather, its efforts seemed geared toward maintaining the delicate North-South political balance in the nation. The fight over slavery played out in the next decades and eventually led to the Civil War. Here are some parts of this complicated history.

After the Mexican War (1846–1848), Congress argued over whether slavery should be extended into Texas and the western territories gained in the peace treaty of Guadalupe Hidalgo, which ended the war. Lawmakers arrived at the Compromise of 1850, which allowed for Texas to be admitted to the Union as a slave state, California to be admitted as a free state (without slavery), voters in New Mexico and Utah to decide the slavery question themselves, the slave trade to be prohibited in Washington, D.C., and for passage of a strict fugitive slave law to be enforced nationally.

Four years later, as it considered how to admit Kansas and Nebraska to the Union, Congress reversed an earlier decision (part of the Missouri Compromise of 1820) that had declared the territories north of the Louisiana Purchase to be free, which set up a dangerous situation in the new states. The slavery status of Kansas and Nebraska would be decided by popular vote in each state. Nebraska was settled mostly by people opposing slavery, called "Free Soilers." In Kansas some antislavery groups were called "Jayhawkers." However, settlers from both the North and the South poured into Kansas, which became the setting for violent conflicts between proslavery and antislavery forces. However, keep in mind that although Free Soilers did not want slavery in their state, they did not want free blacks either.

Both sides tried to swing the vote by sending "squatters" to settle the land. Conflicts resulted, with most of them around the Kansas border with Missouri, where slavery was legal. In one incident, on May 24, 1856, ardent abolitionist John Brown (1800–1859) led a massacre in which five proslavery men were brutally murdered as they slept. The act had been carried out in retribution for earlier killings of freemen in Lawrence, Kansas: Brown claimed his was a mission of God. Brown disagreed with abolitionists who refused to fight against slavery, stating, "These men are all talk. What we need is action—action!"

Newspapers dubbed the series of deadly conflicts, which eventually claimed more than fifty lives, "Bleeding Kansas." The situation proved that neither congressional compromises nor the doctrine of popular sovereignty would solve the nation's deep ideological differences.

Who was John Brown?

In the hands of some activists, the antislavery movement became violent. In 1859, John Brown led a raid on the armory at Harpers Ferry (in present-day West Virginia), which proved a failed attempt to emancipate slaves by force.

At Harpers Ferry, Brown had hoped to lead a movement to liberate slaves. He attacked the armory to get guns to arm freed slaves. Although he and his twenty-one men captured the armory, they were quickly surrounded by local militiamen, farmers, and Marines—led by Robert E. Lee, who eventually killed or captured all the raiders who had not escaped earlier.

While in prison, Brown wrote several letters that were published in newspapers. In the North, he was hailed by some as a sacrificial martyr in the cause for ending slavery. In the South, he was reviled. Many in the South feared that there

Abolitionist John Brown led a raid on the Harper's Ferry armory in 1859 in an attempt to arm slaves for a rebellion. He was captured and hanged for treason.

would be more attempts to free slaves with armed rebellions. Brown was convicted and hanged.

In addition to Lee, army officer James Ewell Brown "Jeb" Stuart was involved in the fight. Witnesses of the execution of Brown included Thomas Jackson, who would later be the famous general "Stonewall" Jackson; John Wilkes Booth, the later assassin of Abraham Lincoln; and American poet Walt Whitman. Brown's raid greatly increased tensions between the North and South.

THE CIVIL WAR

Was the Civil War fought because of slavery?

With nineteen free states and fifteen slave states making up the Union, Abraham Lincoln had called the country "a house divided"—even before he became president. Slavery was central to the conflict, but other issues helped set the stage for it.

By the mid-1800s, important differences had developed between the South and the North. The economy in the South was based on agriculture, while the North was industrialized; the ideals and lifestyles of each region reflected these economic realities. The political party system was in disarray in mid-1850s America. The disorder prompted feelings of distrust for the elected politicians who set national policy. Also, there were different views of relationship between the federal government and the states.

However, slavery was the main reason outweighing all other factors. The economy of the South was built on slavery, and Southerners saw Lincoln as a threat to their economic system.

How did the Civil War begin and end?

Abraham Lincoln (1809–1865) was elected president in November 1860. Very quickly, Southern states started to secede, fearing that Lincoln would jeopardize slavery despite the fact that Lincoln supported the idea of continuing to allow slavery in those states that already had it. South Carolina was the first (in December of that year). In January 1861, five more states followed: Mississippi, Florida, Alabama, Georgia, and Louisiana. When representatives from the six states met the next month in Montgomery, Alabama, they established the Confederate States of America and elected Mississippi senator Jefferson Davis (1808–1889) president. Two days before Lincoln's inauguration, Texas joined the Confederacy. (Virginia, Arkansas, North Carolina, and Tennessee joined in April, shortly after the Civil War had already begun.)

The Civil War began on April 12, 1861, when Southern troops fired on Fort Sumter, a U.S. military post in Charleston, South Carolina. Brutal fighting would continue for four years. On April 9, 1865, General Robert E. Lee (1807–1870) surrendered his ragged Confederate troops to General Ulysses S. Grant (1822–1885) of the Union at Appomattox Court House, Virginia. The war had not only been between the states, it had also been between brothers: the conflict divided the nation. The Civil War took more American lives than any other war in American history.

A photo taken in 1863 shows a bombed-out Fort Sumter occupied by the Confederates.

What are some of the more important battles of the Civil War?

There were over 10,000 military confrontations ranging from small skirmishes to the major battles, fought in twenty-three states. Between 620,000 and 750,000 soldiers died, which is more deaths than the combined total of deaths in all other American wars. In the Civil War, far more soldiers died from sickness—such as diarrhea and dysentery—than died from combat wounds. An estimated 50,000 civilians also died in the Civil War.

Here are ten of the most important battles and military actions of the war:

U.S. Civil War Events of Note

Battle	Date
The Battle of Fort Sumter	April 12, 1861
The Battle of Bull Run/The Battle of First Manassas	July 21, 1861
The Battle of Shiloh/The Battle of Pittsburg Landing	April 6, 1862, to April 7, 1862
The Peninsular Campaign/The Seven Days' Battles	June 25, 1862, to July 1, 1862
The Battle of Antietam	September 17, 1862
The Battle of Chancellorsville	April 30, 1863, to May 6, 1863
The Battle of Gettysburg	July 1, 1863, to July 3, 1863
The Fall of Atlanta/The Battle of Atlanta	July 22, 1864
Sherman's March to the Sea	November 15, 1864, to December 21, 1864
The Surrender at Appomattox	April 9, 1865

What battle is sometimes called the bloodiest battle in the Civil War?

The Battle of Stones River (in Murfreesboro, Tennessee) is sometimes called the bloodiest battle of the Civil War because of the high percentage of losses on each side. Union commander William Rosecrans (1819–1898) and Confederate leader Braxton Bragg (1817–1876) engaged in a series of conflicts that left nearly 13,000 Union casualties and nearly 12,000 Confederate casualties. The conflict left no clear winner, though historians have said that the Union gained morale by driving the Confederates from Murfreesboro into a retreat southward.

Did all Southern lawmakers leave Washington once the South seceded?

All but one left. Even after the South seceded and the first shot of the war was fired at Fort Sumter, South Carolina, Senator Andrew Johnson (1808–1875) of Tennessee opted not to leave the Union. The fact that Johnson did not stick with the state he represented may seem a surprising move, but it reveals one of his most fundamental and fiercely held beliefs: an unswerving trust in the Constitution. Consequently, he viewed secession as not only treasonous but illegal.

His decision to remain with the Union proved politically advantageous to Johnson, a Democrat. In 1862, President Abraham Lincoln appointed him military governor of Tennessee. When Abraham Lincoln sought reelection in 1864, he chose Johnson to be his running mate, replacing incumbent vice president Hannibal Hamlin. Lincoln and Johnson won the election, but Johnson held the vice presidential job for a scant six weeks before Lincoln was assassinated (April 14) and Johnson assumed the presidency.

Who were the most important generals of the war?

Union Generals	Confederate Generals
Ulysses S. Grant (1822–1885)	Robert E. Lee (1807–1870)
William Tecumseh Sherman (1820–1891)	Stonewall Jackson (1824–1863)
George Gordon Meade (1815–1872)	Nathan Bedford Forrest (1821–1877)
Philip Sheridan (1831–1888)	James Ewell Brown "Jeb" Stuart (1833–1864)

Why did President Lincoln issue the Emancipation Proclamation before the end of the Civil War?

As the war raged between the Confederacy and the Union, victory seemed far away. In August of 1862, things seemed grim for the federal troops when they were defeated at the Second Battle of Bull Run in Virginia. But on September 17, with the Battle of Antietam in Maryland, the Union finally forced the Confederates to withdraw across the Potomac into Virginia. That September day was the bloodiest of the war. President Abraham Lincoln decided that this withdrawal was successful enough for him to make his proclamation, and he called a Cabinet meeting to present to his advisers the preliminary Emancipation Proclamation. Lincoln's main purpose in writing the proclamation was to weaken the South by undermining its slave labor force. If emancipated, enslaved people would flee the Southern plantations, thereby crippling the Southern economy.

The official Emancipation Proclamation was issued on January 1, 1863. This final version differed from the preliminary one in that it specified emancipation was to be affected only in those states that were in rebellion (i.e., the South). This key change had been made because the president's proclamation was based on congressional acts giving him authority to confiscate rebel property and forbidding the military from returning slaves of rebels to their owners. Also, in the border states of Missouri, Kentucky, West Virginia, Maryland, and Delaware, slavery was still practiced. Lincoln feared that freeing the enslaved people in those states, especially Missouri and Kentucky, could lead to those states seceding.

Abolitionists in the North criticized the president for limiting the scope of the edict to those states in rebellion, for it left open the question of how enslaved people and their owners in the loyal (Northern) states should be dealt with. Nevertheless, Lincoln had made a stand, which served to change the scope of the Civil War to a war against slavery.

On January 31, 1865, just over two years after the Emancipation Proclamation, Congress passed the Thirteenth Amendment, banning slavery throughout the United States. Lincoln, who had lobbied hard for this amendment, was pleased with its passage. The Confederate states did not free their four million enslaved people until after the Union was victorious and General Lee surrendered on April 9, 1865. (The excellent 2012 film *Lincoln* tells the story of the struggle to pass the Thirteenth Amendment.)

Why was the battle at Gettysburg important?

The 1863 battle, fought when the two sides met accidentally in the southern Pennsylvania town, was a turning point in the Civil War. From July 1 to 3, General George Meade (1815–1872) led his troops (about 90,000 strong) to defeat the advancing Confederate troops (numbering some 75,000) under General Robert E. Lee (1807–1870). The Union win effectively stopped Lee's invasion of the North.

Confederate Lt. Gen. James Longstreet (1821–1904) disagreed with General Lee's tactics, especially Pickett's Charge, an infantry assault of 12,500 Confederate soldiers trying to take Cemetery Ridge. The Confederates got to the Union lines. (Some see this moment as the high mark of the Confederacy.) However, the Confederate attack was repulsed and driven back with great loss of life.

Casualties were high, with Union troops suffering 3,155 killed, 14,531 wounded, and 5,369 captured or missing and Confederate troops suffering 4,708 killed, 12,693 wounded, and 5,830 captured or missing.

As the Confederate troops left the battlefield, General Meade did not follow up and pursue the retreating Confederates. Very likely, he could have captured most of Lee's men and equipment. Despite repeated pleas from Lincoln, Meade let the Confederate Army escape.

What was the Gettysburg Address?

On November 19, 1863, President Abraham Lincoln made the historical address at Gettysburg, as he dedicated part of the battlefield as a national cemetery. His words became legendary:

The 1887 painting by Thure de Thulstrup depicts a scene from the Battle of Gettysburg, a turning point of the war that marked the farthest advance the South made into Union territory.

Four score and seven years ago our fathers brought forth on this continent, a new nation, conceived in Liberty, and dedicated to the proposition that all men are created equal.

Now we are engaged in a great civil war, testing whether that nation, or any nation so conceived and so dedicated, can long endure. We are met on a great battlefield of that war. We have come to dedicate a portion of that field, as a final resting place for those who here gave their lives that that nation might live. It is altogether fitting and proper that we should do this.

But, in a larger sense, we can not dedicate—we can not consecrate—we can not hallow—this ground. The brave men, living and dead, who struggled here, have consecrated it, far above our poor power to add or detract. The world will little note, nor long remember what we say here, but it can never forget what they did here. It is for us the living, rather, to be dedicated here to the unfinished work which they who fought here have thus far so nobly advanced. It is rather for us to be here dedicated to the great task remaining before us—that from these honored dead we take increased devotion to that cause for which they gave the last full measure of devotion—that we here highly resolve that these dead shall not have died in vain—that this nation, under God, shall have a new birth of freedom—and that government of the people, by the people, for the people, shall not perish from the earth.

137

What Union general rode Civil War success to the presidency?

General Ulysses S. Grant (1822–1885) served as the commanding general of the Union Army and rode that popularity to a successful political career, culminating with two terms as the eighteenth U.S. president (1869–1877). Grant had previously served with distinction in the Mexican–American War (1846–1848).

Grant suffered some setbacks during the war but eventually achieved success in taking Confederate strongholds in Vicksburg, Mississippi, and Chattanooga, Tennessee. He earned the respect of President Lincoln, who named him chief of all Union armies in March 1864. Grant later famously took Richmond, Virginia, and fought Confederate forces until Robert E. Lee surrendered in April 1965.

Shown here in 1870, when he was president, Ulysses S. Grant was a hero of the Civil War whose presidency was marked by both scandals and successes.

During his presidency, Grant fought the Ku Klux Klan and worked to protect the rights of African Americans in the South during the period called Reconstruction. His tenure was also plagued by several corruption scandals by those who served below him, although Grant himself was not involved in the corruption.

As he was dying of throat cancer, he wrote *Personal Memoirs of Ulysses S. Grant*, which sold widely and was hailed by critics.

How were the Southern states brought back into the Union?

Even before the Civil War had ended, politicians in Washington, D.C., considered the difficult problem of how to rejoin the seceding states with the North. Some lawmakers felt the Southern states should be treated as if they were territories that were gained through war. Others, including both Abraham Lincoln and Andrew Johnson, reasoned that since secession was illegal, the South belonged—and always had—to the Union, and, therefore, the states ought to be brought back into their "proper relationship" with the federal government. They favored punishing the Southern leaders—but not the states themselves.

President Lincoln developed his 10 percent plan: As soon as 10 percent of a state's population had taken an oath of loyalty to the United States, the state would be allowed to set up a new government. But Congress opposed it, proclaiming the policy too mild, and responded by passing the Wade-Davis Bill (June 1864), making the requirements for statehood more rigid. Instead of Lincoln's 10 percent, Congress required that a majority of voters in each state would need to swear their loyalty in an "ironclad oath" before

What is the most famous movie set during the Civil War?

*G*one with the Wind is the epic 1939 movie set in Atlanta and its environs before, during, and after the Civil War. It was produced by David O. Selznick, directed by Victor Fleming, and starred Vivien Leigh as Scarlett O'Hara, Clark Gable as Rhett Butler, Leslie Howard as Ashley Wilkes, and Olivia de Havilland as Melanie Wilkes. *Gone with the Wind*, which was based on the 1936 novel by Margaret Mitchell, won ten Academy Awards, including Best Picture, Best Director, Best Adapted Screenplay, and Best Actress. Hattie McDaniel won Best Supporting Actress, the first African American to win an Academy Award. The film was immensely popular, and, when adjusted for inflation, it is the highest-grossing film in history.

statehood could be restored. Furthermore, the bill stipulated that the constitution of each state had to abolish slavery and that Confederate military leaders were to be prohibited from holding political office and otherwise disenfranchised. Lincoln opposed the bill and neither signed nor returned it before Congress was dismissed, and so the Wade-Davis measure failed to become law.

When Lincoln was assassinated the following April, the matter remained unsettled. His successor, President Andrew Johnson, soon put forth a plan to readmit the states. He called for each state constitution to abolish slavery and repudiate the Confederate war debt; furthermore, a majority of voters in each state needed to vow allegiance to the Union. Once a state had reorganized itself under this plan, Johnson required the state legislature to approve the Thirteenth Amendment (abolishing slavery in the United States). When Congress reconvened in December 1865 for the first time since Lincoln's assassination, all former Confederate states except Texas had complied with the president's specifications for statehood.

But these new states had also set up Black Codes, severely restricting the rights of blacks. These would later be called Jim Crow laws. Furthermore, there was violence against blacks by white Southerners—including members of the newly formed Ku Klux Klan, a secret white organization that spread terror across the South.

Congress became determined to fight the readmission of the Southern states by Johnson's lenient standards, and it refused to seat any representatives from the South. The move angered President Johnson, and political volleying between the legislature and the executive office began. Ultimately, it was Congress that determined the process by which the Southern states were readmitted.

By the summer of 1868, the legislatures of seven (of eleven) Southern states had approved the Fourteenth Amendment. The remaining four states—Georgia, Mississippi, Texas, and Virginia—complied with the requirements for statehood by 1870, at which time the Union was restored and Congressional representatives from the South were again welcomed in Washington.

In the intervening period (between Congress's rejection of President Johnson's plan for statehood and the ratification of the Fourteenth and Fifteenth amendments), military administrators governed the South, protecting people and property and overseeing the reorganization of government in each state.

RECONSTRUCTION

What was Reconstruction?

Reconstruction was the twelve-year period (1865–1877) of rebuilding that followed the Civil War. The last battle over, the South lay in ruins. Food and other supplies were scarce, people were homeless, city centers had been destroyed, schools were demolished, railways were torn up, and government was nonexistent. Furthermore, the nation had new citizens to enfranchise—and protect—the freed slaves. There was also the question of how to readmit each Southern state to the Union.

In short, the nation's wounds needed to heal. But the long years of the Reconstruction brought only more divisiveness and quarrels. This time, the battlefield was not Gettysburg or Chattanooga but Washington, D.C. President Andrew Johnson, a Southern Democrat and former owner of enslaved people, squared off with Congress, led

The rail yard in Atlanta, Georgia, lies in ruins after the Civil War in this photograph. The economic and social challenges involved in rebuilding the South were daunting, and the Reconstruction efforts often sowed resentment instead of gratitude among Southerners that in many ways lingers today.

by a radical Republican faction. As described above, the two branches of the government fought over who should guide Reconstruction policy. Johnson favored a more tolerant and swifter approach to reuniting the nation, but his measures failed to protect the country's black citizens. Congress proceeded more cautiously, setting up military administrators in the South as an interim form of government until readmission of the states could be affected. In the end, Congress won out by overriding President Johnson's vetoes again and again.

Congress passed the Civil Rights Act of 1866, which took a first step toward enfranchising the black population by guaranteeing the legal rights of the formerly enslaved; the Reconstruction Acts (1867), outlining how each Southern state would be readmitted to the Union; the Freedmen's Bureau Bill, which extended the life of the wartime agency in order to help Southern blacks and whites get back on their feet; and adopted the Thirteenth, Fourteenth, and Fifteenth amendments (the so-called Civil War amendments). Since the South was based on agriculture, the economy slowly recovered, eventually becoming more industrial. Public schools were established in each state. And the state governments became more open than they had been, with more offices up for election rather than appointment. In addition, blacks were guaranteed the vote—and the right to run for office.

But there was great resistance to all these measures. In Southern states, a terrorist campaign broke out. Tens of thousands of African Americans were killed during this period. Many black schools and churches were burned. African Americans who tried to vote were intimidated or sometimes murdered. Those who did vote were often forced to vote for the white Democrats or lose their jobs. In this period, there were a number of armed attacks against African Americans organizing to assert their rights. Such events were often labeled as riots when, in effect, they were massacres.

Many historians believe that the controversy that ensued in the years that followed the Confederate surrender at Appomattox (April 1865) laid the groundwork for segregation and other injustices that brought on the civil rights movement. Many also believe that the problems are still with the country today.

The problem was that many Southerners had trouble accepting that they had lost the war. They also did not agree with the idea of treating African Americans as equals in society. Furthermore, great resentment existed over the destruction wrought by the Union Army in the South—in particular, the actions under Union general William Tecumseh Sherman. Over 150 years later, these attitudes have changed dramatically for many people. However, some people still hold them.

Who were carpetbaggers?

"Carpetbagger" was a derisive term that referred to Northerners who arrived in the South in the early days of Reconstruction. Even though many of these Northern businessmen intended to settle in the South, Southerners viewed them as outsiders and, worse, as opportunists who only intended to make a quick profit before returning north.

"**S**calawag" was a derogatory term used by white Southerners to refer to those white Southerners who supported or were sympathetic to the goals of the Republican lawmakers during Reconstruction. It also referred to Southern Republicans or whites who supported black rights. The Republican Party was the object of much contempt in the American South for many decades.

They were called carpetbaggers because many carried carpetbags as luggage; some Southerners even quipped that these Northerners could carry all their belongings in a carpetbag, implying that they were nothing more than transients. Nevertheless, Northerners who relocated to the South following the Civil War played an important role during Reconstruction. Some came to build schools for African Americans. Others, aided by the black vote, gained public office and impacted state and local policy. But others proved to be corrupt. Because of the latter, the term "carpetbagger" became synonymous with a meddling, opportunistic outsider.

This is confusing. Don't most African Americans vote Democrat these days?

The Southern states were controlled by the Democratic Party before the Civil War and long after it. Many or most white Southern Democrats supported segregation and Jim Crow laws that took away the freedoms of African Americans, did not want African Americans to vote, and did not support civil rights. However, civil rights legislation in the 1950s and 1960s was promoted by Democratic presidents: Harry S. Truman, John F. Kennedy, and Lyndon B. Johnson. By the mid-1960s, many Southern Democrats moved away from the Democratic Party because of its promotion of civil rights and started voting Republican. In the 1960s, as more African Americans could vote, they embraced the Democratic Party, which had pushed for civil rights. Today, in Southern states, most whites who vote, vote Republican; and most African Americans who vote, vote the Democratic ticket.

AMERICA FROM THE CIVIL WAR TO WORLD WAR I

THE SIOUX UPRISING

What was the Sioux Uprising?

Also called the Dakota War of 1862, the uprising took place during the Civil War in August and September 1862 in southwestern Minnesota, when the Sioux there suddenly had been forced to give up half their reservation lands. Crop failures made their situation even worse. While the government debated over whether it would make the payments it owed to Native American nations in gold or in paper currency, the Sioux were also without money. The U.S. agent at the Sioux reservation refused to give out any food to the Native Americans until money arrived from Washington. The Sioux people were hungry and angry, and white observers could see there was trouble coming and warned the government.

The situation soon erupted in August, when four young men having a shooting contest suddenly fired into a party of whites, killing five people. The Sioux refused to surrender the four men to the authorities, and, under the leadership of Chief Little Crow (c. 1820–1863), they raided white settlements in the Minnesota River valley. A small U.S. military force sent out against the Sioux was annihilated. White settlers fled the region in panic.

On September 23, Minnesota sent out 1,400 men, who defeated Little Crow at the Battle of Wood Lake. The raids had already claimed the lives of 490 white civilians. Thirty-three Sioux were killed in the fighting with the military. While most of the Native Americans who had taken up arms fled to the Dakotas, the government began to round up Native men suspected of participating in the campaign against white settlers. More than 300 men were tried and sentenced to death, many on flimsy evidence.

Episcopal bishop Henry Whipple (1822–1901) interceded on their behalf, making a personal plea to President Abraham Lincoln. The bishop was able to get 265 death sentences reduced to prison terms. But thirty-eight Sioux men, accused of murder or rape, were hung in a public ceremony on December 26, 1862. The Sioux reservation lands were broken up, and the remaining Sioux were dispersed.

The events during and after the uprising were brutal for both sides, but many observers viewed the mistreatment of the Sioux as the cause of the conflict. One missionary, after witnessing the harsh way the policy with the Native Americans had been carried out, wrote to Bishop Whipple, saying, "If I were an Indian, I would never lay down the war club while I lived."

PRESIDENT ANDREW JOHNSON

Who was Andrew Johnson?

As described in the previous chapter, Andrew Johnson (1808–1875) served as Abraham Lincoln's vice president for Lincoln's second term. When Lincoln was assassinated, Johnson became president.

Why was President Andrew Johnson impeached?

In late February 1868, nine articles of impeachment were brought against Andrew Johnson over political and ideological differences between the president and Congress.

An illustration from *Harper's Weekly* shows President Johnson being tried by the U.S. Senate. Johnson was the first president to be impeached in U.S. history.

Johnson—self-educated, self-made, and outspoken—inspired people to either love or hate him. A Southern Democrat in the U.S. Senate, he broke bonds of home and party when he swore allegiance to the Union after the outbreak of the Civil War. This he did because of his strong personal belief that the Southern states had violated the U.S. Constitution when they seceded from the Union. Soon, this Tennessean and former Democrat shared the Union Party ticket with Republican Abraham Lincoln as he ran for reelection to the presidency in the fall of 1864.

Inaugurated in March 1965, Vice President Johnson became President Johnson that fateful mid-April day when Lincoln was shot as he sat watching a play at Washington, D.C.'s Ford's Theatre. But Johnson's troubles had begun earlier. As he and Lincoln took the oath of office weeks before, Johnson appeared to be drunk. Some attributed this to the fact that he was recovering from typhoid fever, but one journalist labeled him a "drunken clown," and a group of senators began calling for his resignation. Lincoln met with his vice president for the first—and what would turn out to be the last—time on April 14, just hours before Lincoln's life was claimed by assassin John Wilkes Booth (1838–1865).

How was Andrew Johnson as president?

As president, Johnson's true colors shined through. Again allegiant to his homeland, his policies toward Southern states were lenient; ever class-conscious, he used the power of his office to demonstrate to the Southern aristocrats, whom he openly despised, just how far a poor man from North Carolina had come; as a states' rights advocate, he was ever-watchful of any congressional bills that might impinge upon the freedoms of the individual states, and, as a racist, he proved reticent to grant rights or protection to blacks.

All these traits combined to create sticking points between Johnson and Congress. In February 1866, Congress voted to extend the life of the Freedmen's Bureau, a War Department agency that assisted blacks and whites. But Johnson vetoed the measure, and Congress was unable to overturn his veto. Later that year, Congress passed the Civil Rights Act of 1866, a bill that extended citizenship to freed slaves and guaranteed them "equal protection of the laws." Believing this piece of legislation overstepped the boundaries of central government (he felt this sort of lawmaking was up to each state), he again vetoed it. But this time, Congress mustered the votes it needed to overturn a presidential veto. It was the first of many veto overrides during Johnson's administration. Feeling Johnson was ill-equipped to run the nation, Congress moved its meeting time so that it could keep an eye on the executive branch. Meantime, Congress was guiding Reconstruction policy. The Southern states were being run by their military administrators, reporting to General Ulysses S. Grant.

In 1867, Congress passed a law, the Tenure of Office Act, preventing the president from removing any Cabinet member without Congress's permission. By this time, Congress had already begun to consider whether Johnson ought to be impeached. That fall,

President Johnson pardoned many Confederate generals and officials, further raising the ire of Congress and the nation. Johnson's popularity was waning.

The following February, Johnson attempted to replace Edwin Stanton (1814–1869) as secretary of war. Stanton, who was favored by Congress, refused to leave his office, physically chaining himself to his desk. Congress viewed Johnson's move as a violation of the Tenure of Office Act and proceeded to hold impeachment hearings in the House of Representatives. Within a few days, the House approved a resolution of impeachment. On March 13, the trial began in the Senate. On May 19, the Senate voted on one of the articles of impeachment—it was considered to be the one most likely to receive the two-thirds majority vote required to convict the president. The measure failed—by one vote. Subsequent votes resulted in the same tally.

While many believe Johnson was an inadequate and unpopular president who made numerous mistakes while in office, many others believe he was not guilty of the high crimes and misdemeanors called for in Article 2 (Section 4) of the Constitution. In fact, the law that he was accused of breaking, the Tenure of Office Act, was later overturned as unconstitutional.

THE BATTLE OF THE LITTLE BIGHORN

What was "Custer's Last Stand"?

The term refers to the defeat of General George A. Custer (1839–1876) at the Battle of Little Bighorn on June 25, 1876. (It is known as the Battle of the Greasy Grass by Native Americans. The battle took place at a river known both as the Greasy Grass and the Little Bighorn.) Custer had a national reputation as a Civil War general and Indian fighter in the West, and when he and his troops were outnumbered and badly beaten by the Sioux, led by Sitting Bull (c. 1831–1890)—just as the country was about to celebrate the hundredth anniversary of the Declaration of Independence—the result was a stunning reversal in the national mood.

Little Bighorn was part of a series of campaigns known collectively as the Sioux War. Several events led to the Battle of the Greasy Grass. The Sioux were nontreaty Native Americans, which meant they had refused to accept the white-dictated limits on their territory. They were outraged at the repeated violation of their lands by the onrush of miners to new gold strikes in the Black Hills of South Dakota. Furthermore, there had been eight attacks by the Sioux on the Crow, who were living on reservation land. Finally, Sitting Bull, the chief of the Hunkpapa band of Sioux, refused government demands that he and his people return to reservation lands.

Meanwhile, unbeknownst to the government's military strategists, by the spring of 1876, Sitting Bull had been joined in his cause by other groups of northern Plains tribes, including Cheyenne and Lakota warriors led by Crazy Horse (c. 1840–1877). With the government ready to use force to return Sitting Bull and his band of Sioux to reservations, the stage was set for a dramatic conflict.

There have been many paintings of General Custer's las dramatic battle, including this romanticized on by artist Edgar Samuel Paxson from 1899.

In June 1876, Custer rode into Montana Territory with his Seventh Cavalry to meet the Sioux. Despite orders to simply contain the Native Americans and prevent their escape, he decided to attack. Custer did not know that he and his men were badly outnumbered. Having divided his regiment into three parts, Custer rode with about 225 men against a force of at least 2,000—the largest gathering of Native American warriors in Western history.

Custer's men started firing into the camp. The warriors counterattacked, driving Custer and his men up a hillside, where they were all killed. After the fight, the various tribes disbanded and returned to their designated territories. Sitting Bull and his band retreated into Canada. Returning to the United States five years later, in 1890, Sitting Bull was killed as he was being arrested.

The battle became the subject of countless movies, books, and songs. It is remembered by some Native Americans as a galvanizing force—proof that brave men who fight for what they believe can win.

What happened at Wounded Knee?

In 1890, a band of Miniconjou Lakota and Hunkpapa Lakota led by Spotted Elk left their reservation. The U.S. Calvary caught up with them and led them to Wounded Knee in South Dakota, where they camped. The next day, the soldiers went through the camp to

147

take away any weapons. A gun went off, and the troops who had encircled the camp started shooting. When the shooting stopped, between 250 and 300 Lakota were dead—most of whom were not armed. Twenty-five soldiers were also killed. Almost all the Lakota were massacred.

This tragic moment represented the end of the free life of the Native Americans on the plains and the end of the Indian Wars.

Who was Black Elk?

Black Elk (1863–1950) was a medicine man (or holy man) of the Oglala Lakota people. He lived through the times of the Battle of the Greasy Grass and Wounded Knee Massacre. The story of his life is told in *Black Elk Speaks: Being the Life Story of a Holy Man of the Oglala Sioux, as told through John G. Neihardt*, first published in 1932.

THE SPANISH–AMERICAN WAR

What caused the Spanish–American War?

The 1898 war, which lasted only a matter of months (late April to mid-August), was fought over the liberation of Cuba. During the 1870s, the Cuban people rebelled against Spanish rule. But once that long rebellion had been put down, peace on the Caribbean island did not hold. Worsening economic conditions prompted revolution in 1895. American leaders, the bloody American Civil War (1861–1865) still in their memories, feared that while the Cuban rebels could not win their battle against the Spanish, neither were the Spanish strong enough to fully put down the insurrection. Meanwhile, the American public, fed by a steady stream of newspaper accounts—often exaggerated or completely fictitious reporting about oppressive conditions on the island—increasingly supported U.S. intervention in the Cuban conflict.

In November 1897, President William McKinley (1843–1901) did intervene, but it was through political, rather than military, pressure. As a result, Spain granted Cuba limited self-government within the Spanish empire. However, the move did not satisfy the Cuban rebels, who were determined to achieve independence from Spain; the fighting continued. Rioting broke out in Havana, and in order to protect Americans living there, the United States sent the battleship *Maine* to the port on January 25, 1898. On February 15, an explosion blew up the *Maine*, killing more than 200 people.

Blame for the blast was promptly—and history would later conclude wrongly—assigned to Spain. (Very likely, it blew up because of an explosion of the gunpowder magazines in the ship.) While President McKinley again made several attempts to pressure Spain into granting Cuba full independence, it was to no avail. On April 19, the U.S. Congress passed a joint resolution recognizing an independent Cuba, disclaiming American intention to acquire the island, and authorizing the use of the American Army and

Navy to force Spanish withdrawal. On April 25, the United States formally declared that the country was at war with Spain.

In the months that followed, American forces battled the Spanish and Spanish loyalists in Cuba and the Spanish-controlled Philippines. There was also military activity on Puerto Rico; however, the American forces there met little resistance. Once the Spanish surrendered Santiago, Cuba, after the battle at San Juan Hill in July 1898, it would only be a matter of weeks before a cease-fire was called and an armistice was signed (on August 12), ending the brief war.

What was the charge up San Juan Hill?

On July 1, 1898, during the Spanish–American War, Colonel Theodore Roosevelt (1858–1919) led his American troops, known as the Rough Riders, on an attack of the Spanish blockhouse (a small fort) on San Juan Hill near Santiago, Cuba. Newspaper reports made Roosevelt and the Rough Riders into celebrities, and even after he became a U.S. president, Teddy Roosevelt boasted, "San Juan was the great day of my life."

San Juan Hill was part of a two-pronged assault on Santiago. While the Rough Riders regiment attacked the Spanish defenses at San Juan Hill and Kettle Hill, another American division led by General Henry Lawton (1843–1899) captured the Spanish fort at El Caney. The success of the two initiatives on July 1 combined to give the Americans command over the ridges surrounding Santiago. By July 3, the American forces had destroyed the Spanish fleet under the command of Admiral Pascual Cervera y Topete (1839–1909). On July 17, the Spanish surrendered the city.

Roosevelt can be seen at center after the victory at San Juan Hill in this 1898 photograph. Colonel Roosevel actually took San Juan Heights and Kettle Hill.

What happened to the Philippines after they were ceded by Spain?

The United States gained control of the Philippines in the Treaty of Paris (1898). Some Americans questioned whether the United States should own colonies given the principles that led America to seek independence.

The Philippines was soon embroiled in a conflict similar to the one in Cuba, which had developed into the Spanish–American War: Filipinos, determined to achieve independence, revolted in an uprising that lasted from 1899 to 1901. A civil government was established in the Philippines in 1901, and in November 1935, the Commonwealth of the Philippines was officially established.

Though the victory was critical to the outcome of the war, the assault on Kettle Hill and San Juan Hill had come at a high price: 1,600 American lives were lost in a battle that had seen American troops—black and white—fight the Spanish shoulder to shoulder.

How did the war end?

The Treaty of Paris, signed December 10, 1898, ended the Spanish–American War. The treaty provided for Cuba's full independence from Spain. It also granted control of Guam and Puerto Rico to the United States. The pact further stipulated that the United States would pay Spain $20 million for the Philippine Islands.

ASSASSINATIONS

How many U.S. presidents have been assassinated?

Four American presidents have been assassinated while in office: Abraham Lincoln, James Garfield, William McKinley, and John F. Kennedy. (The Kennedy assasination will be described in more detail in the chapter "America after World War II.")

Abraham Lincoln (1809–1865) was shot on the evening of April 14, 1865, as he sat in the presidential box of Ford's Theatre in Washington, D.C., watching a performance of *Our American Cousin*. The man who fired the shot was actor John Wilkes Booth (1838–1865), who then jumped onto the stage, fell (breaking a leg), and limped away, calling out, "*Sic semper tyrannis*" (a Latin phrase meaning "Thus always to tyrants"). The president lived through the night, attended by family. He died just after 7:00 A.M. on April 15. On April 26, a search party found Booth in a Virginia barn, where he was fatally shot.

Booth shot Lincoln because Booth was an ardent supporter of the Southern cause. Ironically, reconciliation of the North and South might have gone much smoother if Lincoln had not been shot.

James Garfield (1831–1881) was en route to a class reunion at Williams College (Williamstown, Massachusetts) on July 2, 1881, when his assailant fired two shots at him in a Washington, D.C., train station. The shooter was Charles J. Guiteau (1841–1882), who held a grudge against the president. One of Guiteau's bullets had only grazed the president; the other was fixed in his back, and doctors were unable to locate it.

Today, the president's life would have been spared. However, in 1881, he died of infection, likely caused by unsterile fingers and instruments used to repeatedly probe the wound trying to find the bullet. At the time, the ideas of germ theory and sterilization were known, but many doctors, including Willard Bliss, the doctor working on Garfield, rejected such innovations.

Garfield lived eighty days after the shooting, dying at a cottage on the New Jersey shore on September 19. He was succeeded in office by Vice President Chester Arthur (1829–1886). Guiteau's trial lawyer would later claim that Garfield's assassin was insane, but it was an unsuccessful plea for his life. In 1882, Guiteau was convicted and hanged.

On September 6, 1901, President William McKinley (1843–1901) was attending a reception in Buffalo, New York, where the previous day, he had delivered a speech. As he approached a man to shake his hand, the fellow fired two shots at McKinley. One bullet delivered only a minor flesh wound, but the other lodged in his stomach. Surgeons operated, but gangrene and infection set in, claiming the president's life the morning of September 14. He was succeeded in office by Vice President Theodore Roosevelt (1858–1919). The shooter was identified as avowed anarchist Leon F. Czolgosz (1873–1901); he was tried, convicted, and put to death in 1901.

IMMIGRATION

What is the importance of Ellis Island?

Ellis Island, in New York, is the most famous entry point for immigrants. Over twelve million people who emigrated to the United States in the nineteenth and early twentieth centuries entered there. However, many millions of other immigrants to America did not come through Ellis Island.

On January 1, 1892, the Federal Immigration Station opened on the island—in the shadows of the Statue of Liberty. The island had previously been a fort and, later, an arsenal. The Ellis Island facility, which by 1901 consisted of thirty-five

Immigrants arriving at Ellis Island in 1908. Getting into the country was an unpleasant process that included an often humiliating medical examination.

buildings, was the country's chief immigration station. Its heaviest use was in processing the influx of immigrants who arrived between 1892 and 1924. The facility was closed on November 29, 1954, when immigration quotas had drastically reduced the number of incoming people, and the mass-processing center was no longer needed. In 1965, Ellis Island was designated a national historic site, which can be visited today.

What did immigrants experience at Ellis Island?

The Ellis Island immigration depot was a processing center for third-class ship passengers arriving in New York Harbor. (Immigration officials on board their ships processed most first- and second-class passengers.) The new arrivals were ferried from their transatlantic vessels to Ellis Island, where they disembarked and were guided in groups into registration areas in the Great Hall, a room 200 feet long and 100 feet wide. There, they were questioned by government officials, who determined their eligibility to land.

Upon completing the registration process, newcomers were ushered into rooms, where doctors examined them. The processing was extremely businesslike—to the point of being dehumanizing. Processing typically took between three and five hours. An estimated 98 percent of those arriving at Ellis Island were allowed into the country. The remaining 2 percent were turned back for medical reasons (as U.S. health officials tried to keep out infectious diseases) or for reasons of insanity or criminal record. Other facilities at the Ellis Island Immigration Station included showers that could accommodate as many as 8,000 bathers a day, restaurants, railroad-ticket offices, a laundry, and a hospital. At its peak, the Ellis Island station processed some 5,000 immigrants and nonimmigrating aliens (visitors) daily.

THE EARLY TWENTIETH CENTURY

What was the temperance movement?

Temperance was an American movement that began in the mid-1800s to outlaw the manufacture and consumption of alcoholic beverages, which many viewed as a corrupting influence on American family life. By 1855, growing public support to ban liquor resulted in thirty-one states making it illegal to some degree. But many sought a national policy of temperance. During the 1870s, temperance became one of the cornerstones of the growing women's movement. As the nation's women, joined by other activists, mobilized to gain suffrage (the right to vote), they also espoused sweeping cultural changes.

In 1874, a group of women established the Woman's Christian Temperance Union (WCTU); in 1895, the Anti-Saloon League was formed. Such societies, which grew out of a fundamentalist spirit, found an increasing voice and eventually influenced legislators, many of whom were "dry" candidates that the societies had supported, to take federal action. Even President Woodrow Wilson (1856–1924) supported prohibition as one of the domestic policies of his New Freedom program. (Candidates who supported prohibition were called "drys," and those who opposed it were called "wets.")

Those pushing to make liquor illegal argued that it often destroyed individuals and families. Drinking often led to financial problems, as paychecks were wasted on liquor. It was also a frequent factor in domestic abuse of spouses and children. Heavy drinking also made it difficult for some to hold jobs, and drunks often got in trouble with others and with the law. Heavy drinking often led to health problems and even death. Thus, it was believed that banning liquor would greatly reform society.

What was Prohibition?

In January 1919, the Eighteenth Amendment to the U.S. Constitution (1788) was ratified, forbidding people to make, sell, or transport "intoxicating liquors" in the United States and in all territories within its jurisdiction. In October, Congress passed the Volstead Act to enforce it. But government nevertheless found Prohibition difficult to enforce. Bootleggers (who made their own moonshine—illegal spirits, often distilled at night), rumrunners (who imported liquor, principally from neighboring Canada and Mexico), and speakeasies (underground establishments that sold liquor to their clientele) proliferated. Soon, organized crime ran the distribution of liquor in the country to citizens who had not lost their taste for alcoholic beverages. Prohibition was a failure on many levels.

The problem with Prohibition is that it had a limited effect on the demand for alcohol, and when people could not buy legal liquor, they often bought illegal liquor. This made a lot of people lawbreakers. Also, making liquor illegal just made it more expensive, which in turn created an incentive for the manufacture, sale, and smuggling of illegal liquor; this led to worse criminal types getting involved. (Many people have noted that making narcotics illegal has had the same effects.) Al Capone (1899–1947), one of most infamous American gangsters, gained power and wealth by his control over the sale of illegal liquor in Chicago during Prohibition.

The government now found itself with a big problem. As the Federal Bureau of Investigation (FBI) and police worked to control and end mob violence, and as the country suffered through the early years of the Great Depression, lawmakers in Washington reconsidered the amendment.

Which U.S. president held the first press conference?

President Woodrow Wilson was the first president to routinely assemble the press to answer questions for the public. On March 15, 1913, shortly after his inauguration, he called the first presidential press conference. More than one hundred news reporters attended the event. Decades later, President John F. Kennedy (1917–1963) became known for his frequent use of the televised press conference to directly communicate with Americans.

On February 20, 1933, the U.S. Congress proposed that the Eighteenth Amendment be repealed. Approved by the states in December of that year, the Twenty-first Amendment declared the Eighteenth Amendment null, and the manufacture, transportation, and consumption of alcoholic beverages was again legal in the United States, ending the thirteen-year period of Prohibition.

What happened in September 1920 in New York?

In 1920, a bomb explosion on September 16 ripped through the J. P. Morgan Bank Building in New York City, killing thirty-nine people (thirty of them instantly), injuring 300 more, and causing $2 million in property damage. The bomb had been carried by a horse-drawn carriage into the heart of America's financial center just before midday, and it exploded as nearby church bells tolled noon. Among the victims were passersby in the street and people working at their desks, including some high-ranking personnel at J. P. Morgan. Suspicion centered around anarchists, some of whom were questioned by the police and the Federal Bureau of Investigation (FBI). But no culprit was ever found. Until September 11, 2001, that event was the deadliest bombing in New York City history. The explosion was an expression of anticapitalist sentiment.

What was Teapot Dome?

Teapot Dome was a notorious political scandal that was on a level with Watergate (1972). While the early 1920s abuses of power affected President Warren G. Harding (1865–1923), it was not Harding who was implicated in the crimes. Albert Bacon Fall (1861–1944), Harding's secretary of the interior, secretly transferred government oil lands at Elk Hills, California, and Teapot Dome, Wyoming, to private use, and he did so without a formal bidding process. Fall leased the Elk Hills naval oil reserves to American businessman Edward L. Doheny (1856–1935) in exchange for an interest-free "loan" of $100,000. Fall made a similar arrangement with another businessman, Harry F. Sinclair (1876–1956) of Sinclair Oil Corporation—leasing the Teapot Dome reserves in exchange for $300,000 in cash, bonds, and livestock.

The scandal was revealed in 1922, and committees of the U.S. Senate and a special commission spent the next six years sorting it all out. By the time the hearings and investigations were concluded in 1928, Harding had died; Fall had resigned

Because of the Teapot Dome scandal, Secretary of the Interior Albert Fall became the first U.S. Cabinet member to be sent to prison.

from office and taken a job working for Sinclair; all three players—Doheny, Sinclair, and Fall—had faced charges; and the government had successfully sued the oil companies for the return of the lands. The punishments were light considering the serious nature of the charges. Fall was convicted of accepting a bribe, fined $100,000, and sentenced to a year in prison, while Doheny and Sinclair were both indicted but later acquitted of the charges against them, which included conspiracy and bribery.

THE WORLD WARS

WORLD WAR I

What was World War I called before there was a World War II?

The war from 1914 to 1918 was called the "Great War." It was the largest war up to that point in history. Many hoped it would be the last such war. It wasn't. When the Germans invaded Poland in 1939, another war began. The Great War became World War I, and the new war became World War II.

The Great War would also be the largest human undertaking in history—up to that point—yet none of the countries involved wanted a world war that would last four years, and almost none of the political leaders saw it coming, yet they stumbled into it. Here is how that happened.

How did World War I begin?

The Great War was sparked by the June 28, 1914, assassination of Archduke Franz Ferdinand of Austria-Hungary (1863–1914). However, the war in Europe had been precipitated by several developments. National pride had been growing among Europeans; nations increased their armed forces through drafts; and colonialism continued to be a focus of the European powers as they competed for control of lands in far-off places. At the same time, weapons and other implements of war had been improved by industry and science, making them deadlier than ever.

On that June day in the city of Sarajevo (then the capital of Austria-Hungary's province of Bosnia and Herzegovina), when a gunman named Gavrilo Princip (1894–1918) shot down Archduke Franz Ferdinand and his wife, it was not surprising that Austria-Hungary responded with force. Princip was known to have ties to a Serbian terrorist organization, the Black Hand, that was connected to military officers in the Kingdom

157

of Serbia. Although the assassination took place within their territory, Austria-Hungary blamed the nearby country of Serbia. Austria-Hungary feared that the Greater Serbian movement might grow and wreck their empire.

What events followed the assassination of Archduke Franz Ferdinand?

Things happened very quickly after the assassination:

July 23—Austria-Hungary sent an ultimatum to the Kingdom of Serbia with ten specific demands. Most were about suppression of anti-Austrian propaganda in Serbia. However, Serbia had a long connection to Russia. Russia warned that if military action were taken against Serbia, the Russian army would respond.

July 25— Urged by Great Britain and Russia, Serbia accepted all but two demands. Austria-Hungary declared the Serbian reply unsatisfactory. Probably, they wanted a war on Serbia. Russians asked Austria to modify terms and warned that if Austria marched on Serbia, Russia would mobilize.

July 26—A proposal was made by British foreign minister Sir Edward Grey for a conference of Great Britain, France, Germany, and Italy. Germany rejected it.

July 28—Austria-Hungary declared war against Serbia. It wanted to end the Serbian movement, and it assumed Russia would not fight. (This was a mistaken assump-

Archduke Ferdinand is seen arriving at the City Council of Sarajevo in 1914. This was just after being attacked with a bomb, which struck a car following his. After recovering for a while, the archduke and his wife, Sophie, were heading to a hospital to visit the injured from the bombing when a second attacker shot and killed them.

tion.) Russia mobilized against Austria. The Russians had backed down in previous confrontations but felt they could not back down once again. Germany warned Russia that mobilization meant war with Germany since the Germans had a treaty with Austria-Hungary. Germany made Austria agree to discuss Russian changes to ultimatum. Germany demanded Russia demobilize. Russia did not.

August 1—Germany declared war on Russia. France began to mobilize the same day.

August 2—German troops crossed Luxembourg. Germany told Belgium it wanted to cross Belgium to get to France. Belgium refused and called on signers of an 1839 treaty that guaranteed neutrality of Belgium in case of a conflict. This obligated the British to enter the fight.

August 3—Germany declared war on France.

August 4—Great Britain sent an ultimatum to Germany to get out of France. Germany refused. Britain declared war the same day.

None of the countries wanted a major war, yet they stumbled into it. Part of the problem was the interlocking treaties that brought so many countries into what started as a conflict between Austria-Hungary and Serbia.

When the war started, both sides believed that the fighting would be decided quickly. Instead, the fighting spread, involving more countries. Four years of fighting—aided by the airplane, the submarine, tanks, and machine guns—would cause greater destruction than any other war to that date.

What was the Schlieffen Plan?

For decades, German military planners had been devising plans on how to respond to a military crisis in Europe. German field marshal Alfred von Schlieffen (1833–1913) drew up such a plan. He knew that Germany could not fight a two-front war on the East and West. Thus, he devised a plan to attack France quickly and defeat it by driving into the north of France and then sweeping south to capture Paris. Then, the German Army would march east to fight the Russians.

This was what the German military had been planning on and training for four years, so when the conflict broke out in the summer of 1914, it put the plan into operation without even questioning its wisdom. Also, note that the Germans invaded France, where most of the fighting of the war would take place even though the original conflict between Austria-Hungary, Serbia, Russia, and Germany had nothing to do with France.

How well did the Schlieffen Plan work?

In the next weeks, the well-prepared, well-trained, and well-equipped German Army rolled through Luxembourg and Belgium and into France, going around the initial French defensive line further south. However, the Schlieffen Plan had two major flaws. First, despite all their efforts, the German forces could not move fast enough and remain strong enough. Second, the Russians showed up sooner than expected in the East, forcing the Germans to pull troops out of France and send them east.

The Germans pressed on into France while French and British troops fell back, suffering great losses. However, at the Marne River, thirty miles outside of Paris, the French troops held their ground and stopped the German advance. This became known as the First Battle of the Marne in September 1914.

The Schlieffen Plan failed. In World War II, the German blitzkrieg into France in 1940, with better equipment and a far faster-moving army, did what the Schlieffen Plan had failed to do two decades earlier.

What happened after the First Battle of the Marne?

Both sides were stuck and could not move forward, so they started to dig trenches. Then, both the French and Germans tried to outflank each other repeatedly. To flank an enemy force is to try to go around it on the side.

The result of flanking and counterflanking was the digging of more trenches. Eventually, over 200 miles of trenches stretched from Switzerland to the coast of northern France. A stalemate then ensued, with neither side able to break the enemy's lines.

What are five of the most famous battles of the war in Europe?

- The First Battle of Ypres in Belgium, October and November 1914.

- The Second Battle of Ypres in Belgium was fought in April and May 1915. This battle featured the first use of poison gas.

- The Battle of Verdun was fought from February to December 1916. The Germans wanted to draw the French into a bloody battle in which the French would lose many troops. However, a huge number of Germans also died.

- The Battle of the Somme, July to November 1916. This became one of the bloodiest battles in history.

The Belgian city of Ypres was the unfortunate location of several battles during the Great War, leaving it a rubble-strewn ruin after the war.

- The Third Battle of Ypres, July to November 1917, also called the Battle of Passchendaele. The allies attacked over a rain-soaked battlefield of mud. It was a disaster.

What was the effect of these major battles?

Most of the major battles of the war followed the same course: One side would build up massive forces and supplies to break through the enemy line. They would then attack and make a little progress until halted by the enemy's defenses. The fighting would go on for days, weeks, or months, with the trench lines moving very little. In the end, tens or hundreds of thousands would be dead, with neither side gaining a strategic advantage.

Part of the problem was the nature of modern warfare. Before launching a major offensive, one side would launch a massive bombardment on the enemy's defenses. However, such bombardments could never wipe out the enemy. Enough of the enemy would survive in their dugouts below ground to come out with machine guns to slow the attack.

Also, the massive bombardments blew so many holes in the ground that it was very difficult for that attacking army to move troops and supplies forward. Lastly, as the advancing army moved forward, their supply lines were stretched, making it harder to receive ammunition, supplies, and fresh troops. At the same time, the defending army backed up, so their supply lines became shorter, making it easier for them to receive ammunition, supplies, and fresh troops.

What famous book told the story of the war?

All Quiet on the Western Front (1928) by Erich Maria Remarque describes the experience of Paul Bäumer, a German soldier. It is considered by many to be one of the greatest war novels of all time.

What alliances were forged during World War I?

Austria-Hungary had been joined in early August 1914 by its ally Germany, which together formed the Central Powers. In October 1914, Bulgaria and the Ottoman Empire—including modern-day Turkey—joined the Central Powers.

France, Britain, and Russia threw their support behind Serbia and together were known as the Allies. The Allies declared war on the Ottoman Empire in November 1914 after Turkish ships bombarded Russian ports on the Black Sea and Turkish troops invaded Russia. Eventually, twenty more nations joined the Allies, including the United States, which entered the war in 1917.

Was World War I fought only in Europe?

Important battles of the war took place in the Mediterranean and the Middle East in campaigns by the Allies against the Ottoman Turks. One important event was the Gallipoli campaign in which troops from Britain, Australia, and New Zealand tried to destroy Turkish defenses so the Allies could open the shipping route from the Mediterranean Sea to the Black Sea. The Gallipoli campaign was a disaster for the Allies.

What movies show the Gallipoli campaign?

A young Mel Gibson starred in the 1981 movie *Gallipoli*, which shows the experiences of Australian soldiers in the battle. There is also a 2005 documentary called *Gallipoli* by Turkish filmmaker Tolga Örnek.

What did the *Lusitania* have to do with World War I?

World War I was already underway when in May 1915, a German submarine sank a British passenger ship, the SS *Lusitania*, off the coast of Ireland. When it sank in the North Atlantic, 1,200 civilians, including 128 American travelers, died. President Woodrow Wilson (1856–1924) warned Germany that another such incident would force the United States into entering the war. Germany heeded the warning but only for a time.

However, the *Lusitania* carried hundreds of tons of war munitions headed for Britain in violation of the rules of neutrality for ships. In the eyes of the Germans, this made the ship a legitimate military target. In time, the memory of the sinking of *Lusitania* would be one factor in the American decision to enter the war.

Why did the United States get involved in World War I?

When war broke out in Europe in August 1914, Americans opposed the involvement of U.S. troops, and President Woodrow Wilson declared the country's neutrality. But as the fighting continued and the German tactics threatened civilian lives, Americans began siding with the Allies.

After the sinking of the passenger liner SS *Lusitania*, Germany adopted restricted submarine warfare. However, early in 1917, Germany again began attacking unarmed ships, this time American cargo boats, goading the United States into the war. German U-boats (submarines) were being positioned to cut off shipping to and from Britain in an effort to force the British to surrender.

Tensions between the United States and Germany peaked when the British intercepted, decoded, and turned over to President Wilson a telegram Germany had sent to its ambassador in Mexico. The so-called "Zimmermann note," which originated in the office of German foreign minister Arthur Zimmermann (1864–1940), urged the German officials in Mexico to persuade the Mexican government into war with the United States—in order to regain lost territory in Texas, New Mexico, and Arizona. The message was published in the United States in early March. One month later, on April 6, 1917, the U.S. Congress declared war on Germany after President Wilson had asserted that "the world must be made safe for democracy."

What was the effect of American entry into World War I?

Though the United States had been little prepared to enter the war, the American government mobilized quickly to rally the troops—and the citizens—behind the war effort.

In April 1917, the U.S. Regular Army was comprised of just more than 100,000 men; by the end of the war, the American armed forces stood some five million strong. It was the arrival of the U.S. troops that gave the Allies the manpower they needed to win the war.

In November 1918, after years of fighting in the trenches of Europe, which left over ten million dead, Germany agreed to an armistice (an end to the fighting), and the Central Powers finally surrendered. In January 1919, Allied representatives gathered to draw up the peace settlement at the Paris Peace Conference.

How were Europe's lines redrawn as a result of World War I?

The treaties that came out of the Paris Peace Conference (1919–1920) redrew Europe's boundaries, carving new nations out of the defeated powers. The Treaty of Versailles forced Germany to give up territory to Belgium, Czechoslovakia, Denmark, France, and Poland. Germany also forfeited all of its overseas colonies and turned over coalfields to France for the next fifteen years.

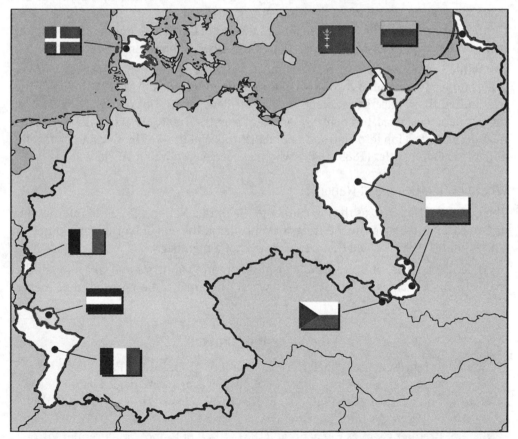

The victorious nations blamed Germany for the onset of the Great War. The Versailles Treaty punished the nation, divvying up parts of Germany to its neighbors (land areas in white). This action was one reason for resentment among Germans and contributed to the rise of the Nazis.

The treaties of St. Germain and Trianon toppled the former empire of Austria-Hungary and created the separate nations of Austria and Hungary, each occupying less than a third of its former area. Their former territory was divided among Italy, Romania, and the countries newly recognized by the treaties: Czechoslovakia, Poland, and the kingdom that later became Yugoslavia.

The Treaty of Sèvres took Mesopotamia (present-day Iraq), Palestine, and Syria away from the Ottoman Empire, which three years later became the Republic of Turkey. Finally, Bulgaria lost territory to Greece and Romania. However, these new borders would serve to heighten tensions between some countries, as the territorial claims of the newly redrawn nations overlapped with each other.

How did the Treaty of Versailles pave the way for World War II?

In the aftermath of World War I, Germany was severely punished. One clause in the Treaty of Versailles even stipulated that Germany take responsibility for causing the war. In addition to its territorial losses, Germany had to pay for an Allied military force that would occupy the west bank of the Rhine River, intended to keep Germany in check for the next fifteen years. The treaty also limited the size of Germany's military. In 1921, Germany received a bill for reparations: it owed the Allies $33 million.

While the postwar German government had been made to sign the Treaty of Versailles under the threat of more fighting from the Allies, the German people nevertheless faulted their leaders for accepting such strident terms. Not only was the German government weakened, but public resentment over the Treaty of Versailles would in the next decades develop into a strong nationalist movement—led by German chancellor and führer Adolf Hitler (1889–1945), who had been a corporal in World War I.

What was the League of Nations?

The League of Nations was the forerunner to the United Nations. It was an international organization established by the Treaty of Versailles at the end of World War I. Since the United States never ratified that treaty, it was not a member.

The league was set up to handle disputes among countries and to avoid another major conflict such as the Great War. However, the organization proved to be ineffec-

Who were the Big Four?

Though representatives of all the Allied nations attended the Paris Peace Conference, which began in January 1919, the decisions were made by four heads of government, called the Big Four: President Woodrow Wilson (1856–1924) of the United States, Prime Minister David Lloyd George (1863–1945) of Great Britain, Premier Georges Clemenceau (1841–1929) of France, and Premier Vittorio Orlando (1860–1952) of Italy.

tive; it was unable to intervene in such acts of aggression as Japan's invasion of Manchuria in 1931, Italy's conquest of Ethiopia from 1935 to 1936 and occupation of Albania in 1939, and Germany's takeover of Austria in 1938.

The League of Nations dissolved itself during World War II. Though unsuccessful, the organization did establish a basic model for a permanent international organization.

What would have happened if the United States had not entered the war?

Although there is no way to answer for certain the "what ifs" of history, this question deserves some reflection. The entry of America into the war guaranteed that the Allies would win. Then, at the Paris Peace Conference, the Allied victors created a very punitive settlement toward the defeated countries. The Treaty of Versailles left many important issues unresolved, and the end of World War I set the stage for World War II. In particular, many national boundaries were drawn without input from the people affected by the new boundaries.

If America had not entered the war, would the exhausted armies and countries of Europe have had to enter into negotiations to end the war on more equal terms that would have led to a better long-term settlement instead of the next world war? Who knows? What do you think?

What was the death toll of World War I?

Between 20.5 to 22 million people died in the war. Half of these were soldiers; the rest were civilians. Death came from weapons but also from famine and disease. Somewhere between twenty and twenty-two million soldiers were wounded.

THE ERA BETWEEN THE WORLD WARS

What was the world like between the world wars?

During the 1920s, with the death toll of the Great War a recent memory, some of the world enjoyed a period of relative peace. (In some parts of Eastern Europe and the Soviet Union, however, there was much turmoil.) In the United States, the decade was known as the Roaring Twenties—ten years of prosperity and even frivolity. The League of Nations had been established to handle disputes among countries and avoid another major conflict.

In 1929, a general downturn began in the world economy, triggered by the U.S. stock market crash of late October. As the United States fell into the severe and sustained economic crisis known as the Great Depression, other industrialized nations—including Germany—also felt the impact. Unemployment jumped to record levels in many countries, and a lack of social welfare programs resulted in the destitution of numerous families. Politicians and economists alike searched for solutions to the crisis, many turning to anti-free trade or isolationist policies to "protect their own."

Meanwhile, postwar efforts to keep peace were proving ineffective as Japan invaded Manchuria (China) in 1931; Italy conquered Ethiopia in 1936; civil war raged in Spain (1936–1939); India became the site of a bitter struggle between British rulers and Indian nationalists; and the Sino–Japanese War (which began in 1937 and would be absorbed by the outbreak of World War II) was fought in Asia.

What were the "fireside chats"?

They were radio broadcasts of President Franklin D. Roosevelt's (1882–1945) messages to the American people. FDR began making the informal addresses on March 12, 1933, during the long and dark days of the Great Depression. In his efforts to reassure the nation, FDR urged listeners to have faith in the banks and to support his New Deal measures. Sometimes beginning his talks with "My friends," the radio broadcasts were enormously successful and attracted more listeners than even the most popular broadcasts during this "golden age" of radio. FDR continued his fireside chats into the 1940s as Americans turned their attention to the war effort.

Why was Eleanor Roosevelt called "the People's First Lady"?

While several first ladies before her had also been active in the nation's life, Eleanor Roosevelt (1884–1962), wife of the thirty-second president of the United States, Franklin D. Roosevelt, stands out as one of the country's most active first ladies and as a woman

President Franklin D. Roosevelt is shown here giving one of his radio "fireside chats" in 1937. The talks were aimed at comforting a nation made uneasy by the Great Depression.

of enormous accomplishment in her own right. During her husband's administration, which began in the dark days of the Great Depression and continued as the world again went to war, Eleanor Roosevelt acted not only as an adviser to the president but as the president's eyes and ears on the nation—traveling in a way that his physical condition prevented him from doing.

From the start, Eleanor Roosevelt remained in constant communication with the American people. She was known for her weekly press conferences, numbering some 350 by the end of the Roosevelt presidency, that were open only to women reporters. In 1934, she began a radio program, which became so popular that she was soon dubbed "the First Lady of Radio." Beginning in 1936, she authored a daily column called "My Day," which was syndicated to newspapers around the country. These forums gave the first lady an unprecedented voice in American life and gave Americans a clear understanding of their first lady and her concerns.

Concerned about the effects of the Great Depression on American children, she was instrumental in creating the National Youth Administration, which helped high school and university students complete their studies before joining the workforce. She was a champion of minority groups, declaring that the right to work "should know no color lines" and resigning from the Daughters of the American Revolution when the group refused to allow black singer Marian Anderson (1897–1993) to perform at Constitution Hall.

Eleanor then arranged for Anderson to sing on the steps of the Lincoln Memorial in Washington, D.C., on Easter Sunday, April 9, 1939, to an integrated crowd of 75,000 people and a radio audience numbering in the millions. (You can hear her performance online.)

Eleanor Roosevelt was known for getting out among the people. She lectured frequently and made other public appearances in which she met and spoke face-to-face with the American people. A famous cartoon depicted a coal miner pausing in his work to exclaim, "For gosh sakes, here comes Mrs. Roosevelt." During World War II, she made a remarkable 23,000-mile trip across the South Pacific, where she untiringly visited American soldiers in field hospitals and on the lines.

Mrs. Roosevelt was an advocate for the people, and it just so happened that she lived in the White House. A beloved first lady who actively supported progressive causes and humanitarian concerns, she has been a model to subsequent first ladies, female politicians, and activists. She chaired the commission that wrote the 1948 Universal Declaration of Human Rights.

THE SPANISH CIVIL WAR

What caused the Spanish Civil War?

From 1936 to 1939, two sides fought for control of Spain: the nationalists and the loyalists. The insurgent nationalists were aristocrats, military leaders, Roman Catholic clergy, and members of a political group called the Falange Party. They were supported by Nazi Germany under Adolf Hitler and fascist Italy under Benito Mussolini in their effort to wrest control. The loyalists were liberals, socialists, and communists who were supported by the Soviet Union under Joseph Stalin.

A number of non-Spanish idealists, who believed saving the republic from the fascist rebels was worth dying for, joined the ranks of the loyalists to form the International Brigade. (In his novel *For Whom the Bell Tolls*, Ernest Hemingway [1899–1961], who had covered the war as a correspondent, wrote about one young American man who took up arms on behalf of the loyalist effort.) The nationalists, under Generalissimo Francisco Franco, won the war when they captured Madrid in March 1939, beginning an era of harsh, right-wing rule. And, as with any war, the fascist victory had come at a dear price: hundreds of thousands dead and massive destruction throughout the country.

Who was Generalissimo Franco?

Generalissimo Francisco Franco (1892–1975) was the fascist leader of Spain from 1939 until 1973. He rose to power in the Spanish Civil War (1936–1939) as he led a rebel nationalist army against the loyalist forces. Capturing Madrid in 1939, Franco assumed the role of head of government. Though he and the nationalists had received considerable help from Nazi Germany and fascist Italy to win the civil war, when fighting broke out in World War II, Spain stayed neutral.

In 1947, with the fighting in Europe over, Franco declared himself monarch of Spain and ruled as an authoritative dictator. Two years before he died, he stepped down as head of state, though he retained the title "generalissimo," meaning "commander in chief." Franco named as his successor Prince Juan Carlos (1938–). When Franco died in 1975, Juan Carlos I became the first Spanish monarch to control Spain since his grandfather was deposed in 1931 to make way for the brief republic that was later overthrown by Franco and the nationalists. King Juan Carlos played an important role in transforming Spain into a modern democracy.

Generalissimo Francisco Franco was dictator of Spain from 1939 until his death in 1975. His forces won the Spanish Civil War with the help of Germany.

THE RISE OF NAZI GERMANY

What was happening in Germany?

In Germany, an extreme sense of nationalism was taking hold. The Treaty of Versailles seriously weakened the nation, allowing the rise of the Nazi Party, led by Adolf Hitler (1889–1945). Nazis were determined to see their beloved homeland rise to power once again, and they found a ready following among the German people.

A dangerous alliance was forged when Germany, Italy, and Japan formed the Axis powers in 1936. Also, by 1933, Germany had become a totalitarian state known as the Third Reich. In 1938, Nazi armies took their first steps toward gaining supremacy when they marched into Austria and claimed it, setting the stage for World War II.

What was the importance of Hitler's beer hall *putsch* trial?

The 1924 trial of Adolf Hitler and nine other men, charged with treason for their attempted coup (in German, *putsch*) of late 1923, marked the beginning of Hitler's seemingly unstoppable rise to power.

As the leader of the Nazi Party (National Socialist German Workers' Party), Hitler had gained enough of a following to believe that he had the support of the people to re-create a powerful German empire and rid it of its "mongrel-like" quality. A speech by Bavarian leader Gustav von Kahr in a Munich beer hall on the night of November 8, 1923, reinforced the belief that many people sympathized with Hitler's message. But in

Were the Nazis socialists?

Although the word "Nazi" is short for "national socialism," the Nazis did not promote socialism. The traditional idea of socialism is to give economic and political power to workers so they can benefit from the wealth created by industrial society. One idea was to give workers control of the "means of production": the factories. Another idea was to give workers power in parliamentary governments so they could create laws and policies to protect and benefit workers and their families with things like better wages, safer working conditions, and insurance for health and old age. Many socialists were active in labor unions in Germany fighting for the rights of workers.

The German economy was a capitalist economy under the Nazis, and as the war progressed, the government exerted more control over it. Under the Nazis, many true socialists—those who asserted workers' rights—were targeted by the Nazis, and many were sent to concentration camps. All the independent labor unions were eliminated, as workers had to join the one labor union controlled by the Nazis, the German Labor Front (Deutsche Arbeitsfront [DAF]).

a march through Munich the following day, the still loyal regular German Army and the Bavarian State Police opened fire on the Nazi demonstrators and their sympathizers, killing sixteen and arresting Hitler and his nine co-conspirators.

Their trial began on February 26, 1924, and over the course of twenty-five days, aided by radio and newspaper coverage, Hitler held forth (in one case taking four hours to respond to a single question), earning him the overwhelming support of the German people. His impassioned appeals turned what ought to have been an open-and-closed case of treason against him into an indictment of the German government. His basic argument was this: "I cannot declare myself guilty. True, I confess to the deed, but I do not confess to the crime of high treason. There can be no question in an action which aims to undo the betrayal of this country in 1918." Hitler was referring to the German surrender in World War I.

Nevertheless, he and nine others were convicted of treason. Hitler was sentenced to five years in prison, where he wrote the first volume of his infamous work *Mein Kampf* (*My Struggle*), which revealed his frightening theories of racial supremacy and his belief in the Third Reich. Released after only nine months, Hitler walked out of prison more popular than he had been before his highly publicized trial.

What was Nazism?

Short for "national socialism," "Nazi" was a derisive abbreviation that held. The Nazi doctrine rested on three sets of beliefs: extreme nationalism, anti-Semitism, and anticommunism. Many Germans felt great anger and resentment over their defeat in World War I, the terms of the Treaty of Versailles, and the diminished power and influence of Germany. For whatever reason, there was little anger against the German military officials who had promoted and directed the war and then lost it. In such a climate, the doctrines of Nazism took hold there, appealing to the masses with promises of a rebuilt Germany.

The "bible" of Nazism was Adolf Hitler's *Mein Kampf* (in English *My Struggle*, published in 1923), which asserted the superiority of a pure Aryan race (Aryans were non-Jewish Caucasians, particularly those of northern European descent), led by an infallible ruler (called "der Führer"); the reestablishment of a German empire (the

Hitler is shown here during a 1938 parade after he annexed the Sudetenland for Germany. During the late 1930s, most Germans did not believe Hitler was leading them to war but was, instead, reunifying their people after being humiliated by the Versailles Treaty.

Third Reich); and the systematic annihilation of people whom Nazis perceived to be Germany's worst enemies, Jews and communists.

Nazis ruled Germany from 1933, when Hitler rose to power as head of the National Socialist German Workers' Party. In their own country, they enforced their policies through a secret police (the Gestapo), storm troops (called the SS), and Hitler's bodyguard (called the SA). Elsewhere in Europe, the Nazis used sheer force in imposing their system.

What was the Munich Pact?

It was a failed effort to appease the territory- and power-hungry German leader Adolf Hitler in the days leading up to World War II (1939–1945). After Germany annexed neighboring Austria in the Anschluss of March 1938, it became known that Hitler had designs on the Sudetenland, a heavily German region of Czechoslovakia. (Despite the German-speaking people in these areas, the land had been given to create Czechoslovakia in the wake of World War I.) With the war a fresh memory, and European nations still recovering from heavy losses, Europe's powers were eager to avoid another conflict.

On September 29 and 30, 1938, British prime minister Neville Chamberlain met with Hitler in Munich; they were joined by Italian dictator Benito Mussolini, a German ally, and French premier Édouard Daladier, a Czech ally. Czechoslovakia did not have any representatives at the conference. The leaders quickly worked out a plan for Germany to occupy the Sudetenland. Chamberlain considered Czechoslovakia's concession a reasonable price to pay for peace on the continent. Chamberlain misread Hitler, and the effort to assuage Hitler was not successful. In March 1939, Germany moved to occupy the rest of Czechoslovakia; on September 1, Germany marched into Poland, and World War II began.

How did World War II begin?

The war began on September 1, 1939, when Germany invaded Poland, which was soon crushed by Adolf Hitler's war machine. While the Nazis moved in from the west, Poland was under attack by the Soviets from the north and east. The events in the Eastern European country had set the stage for a major conflict.

After Poland, the Germans moved into Denmark, Luxembourg, the Netherlands, Belgium, Norway, and France, taking control as they went. By June 1940, only Great Britain stood against Hitler, who was joined by Axis power Italy. Before long, fighting had spread into Greece and northern Africa.

What were the major events of the war?

Year	Events
1939	September: Hitler invaded Poland.
	Britain and France declared war on Germany.
	America remained neutral but sent supplies to Britain.
	The Battle of the Atlantic began as German submarines sank ships taking supplies to England.

Year	Events
1940	Germany began "Blitzkrieg" invasion and quickly conquered Belgium, Holland, and France. Churchill became prime minister of Britain. British forces in France retreated to the city of Dunkirk, where they were evacuated. Germans launched an air campaign to gain air superiority over Britain. This was to prepare the way for a German invasion, or it could force the British to surrender. However, the German Luftwaffe failed to destroy British air defenses, which forced Hitler to cancel his invasion plans.
1941	Hitler began Operation Barbarossa and invaded Russia despite the fact that Germany had signed a nonaggression treaty with Russia in 1939. Germans continued to bomb major cities in Britain. Japan attacked Pearl Harbor. The United States entered the war.
1942	Germany suffered setbacks at Stalingrad and El Alamein in Egypt. Singapore fell to the Japanese in February: 25,000 prisoners taken. At the Battle of Midway, Americans defeated the Japanese Navy. Allies landed forces in North Africa and began to fight German forces. At Auschwitz, Poland, the mass murder of Jews and others began.
1943	The German Army surrendered at Stalingrad. This was Germany's first major defeat. Allies defeated Germans in North Africa and prepared to invade Italy. Italy surrendered. Germans continued to fight in Italy. In Burma, British and Indian forces fought the Japanese.
1944	Allies landed at Anzio in Italy. Soviet offensive gathered pace in Eastern Europe. D-Day: The Allies invaded France. Paris liberated from the Germans. Allies advanced in the South Pacific. The Battle of the Bulge surprised the Allies.
1945	Russians conquered Berlin. Hitler committed suicide. Germany surrendered. Franklin D. Roosevelt died. Harry S. Truman became U.S. president. Atomic bombs were dropped on Hiroshima and Nagasaki. Japan surrendered.

Which countries made up the Axis powers?

The Axis countries were Germany, Japan, and Italy. Nine other countries would join them.

Which countries comprised the Allies in World War II?

The three major Allied powers were Great Britain, the United States, and the Soviet Union. Their leaders, Winston Churchill (1874–1965), Franklin D. Roosevelt (1882–1945), and Joseph Stalin (1879–1953), were referred to as the Big Three. They and their

Soviet Union premier Joseph Stalin, U.S. president Franklin D. Roosevelt, and British prime minister Winston Churchill were the major leaders of the Allies during World War II.

military advisers developed the strategy to defeat the Axis countries. China and some twenty other countries would soon join the Allies.

What was the Lend-Lease Act?

Before the United States entered the war, President Franklin D. Roosevelt proposed the Lend-Lease Act to extend material assistance to the Allied powers fighting the Axis powers. Roosevelt argued that it was imperative for the country to come to the aid of those fighting Germany and Italy—it was similar to helping your neighbor put out a fire in his house by lending the neighbor your garden hose.

Roosevelt was walking a political tightrope. Since many Americans opposed getting involved in another European war, there was opposition to directly giving support to the Allied nations. Thus, Roosevelt sold the concept as "lending" the material needed.

Under the Lend-Lease Act, which was passed by Congress on March 11, 1941, approximately $50 billion of aid in the form of food and supplies, weapons, machinery, and other equipment was provided to the Allied nations—primarily to Britain and the Commonwealth nations first but later to all nations fighting against Hitler's war machine.

The return of the goods was not addressed until after the war had ended. At that time, most people felt the Allies had all contributed everything they had to the war effort and that the sacrifices made by Allied Europe in the days prior to U.S. entry into the fighting were balanced by the contributions made under the Lend-Lease Act.

What was the Atlantic Charter?

On the eve of direct U.S. involvement in World War II, President Franklin D. Roosevelt met with British prime minister Winston Churchill on board a ship off the coast of Canada. The two leaders drew up a program of peace objectives known as the Atlantic Charter, which they signed in August 1941. In addition to other peacetime goals, the charter roughly contained Roosevelt's Four Freedoms. Roosevelt believed that freedom of speech and expression, freedom of worship, freedom from want, and freedom from fear should prevail around the world.

In the Atlantic Charter, the two leaders stated that neither of their countries sought new territories; that they respected the right of the people of each country to choose their own form of government; that no country ("great or small, victor or vanquished") would be deprived access to the raw materials it needed for its own economic prosperity; that countries should cooperate to improve labor standards and social security; that after the "final destruction of the Nazi tyranny, all the men in all the lands may live out their lives in freedom from fear and want"; and that a "wider and permanent system of general security" would be necessary to ensure peace. (This last statement alluded to the future establishment of the United Nations.)

What was Operation Barbarossa?

In 1941, Adolf Hitler ordered the German Army to invade Russia under the code name Operation Barbarossa. The Germans had signed a nonaggression agreement with the Soviet Union called the Molotov-Ribbentrop Pact in 1939. They ignored the pact when they invaded. A very brutal military campaign followed, with parallels to Napoleon's Invasion.

The Russians ultimately repelled the German invasion, pushed the Germans back, and eventually conquered Berlin. The Germans suffered great losses; however, the Rus-

Why did the Germans call their invasion of Russia Operation Barbarossa?

Frederick Barbarossa (c. 1123–1190) was the holy Roman emperor who ruled a vast territory. In Hitler's view, he represented for Germans the First Reich.

The Second Reich was the German Empire, which lasted from 1871 to 1918. It was created by Otto von Bismarck (1815–1898) and ended with World War I.

Hitler called his rule the Third Reich.

sians lost even more lives, representing the greatest loss of life to a nation in war ever in history.

Why did the Japanese attack Pearl Harbor?

There is still disagreement among historians, military scholars, and investigators about why the island nation of Japan made a surprise attack on the U.S. military installation at Pearl Harbor, Hawaii. Very likely, it was an all-or-nothing gamble on the part of Japan to knock out America's navy, so Japan could dominate the Pacific region.

In 1941, Japanese troops had moved into the southern part of Indochina, prompting the United States to cut off its exports to Japan. In the fall of that year, as General Hideki Tojo (1884–1948) became prime minister of Japan, the country's military leaders were laying plans to wage war on the United States. On December 7, 1941, Pearl Harbor, the hub of U.S. naval power in the Pacific, became the target of Japanese attacks, as did the American military bases at Guam, Wake Island, and the Philippines.

What happened at Pearl Harbor?

On the night before the attack, the Japanese moved a fleet of thirty-three ships to within 200 miles of the Hawaiian island of Oahu, where Pearl Harbor is situated. Their goal was

This photo was taken by a Japanese pilot during the attack on Pearl Harbor on December 7, 1941. The attack resulted in the United States entering the war against Japan and, soon after, against Germany and Italy.

to destroy much of the American naval power in the Pacific so they could conquer and control much of the South Pacific. More than 300 planes took off from the Japanese carriers, dropping the first bombs on Pearl Harbor just before 8:00 A.M. on December 7, 1941. There were eight American battleships and more than ninety naval vessels in the harbor at the time. Twenty-one of these were damaged or destroyed, as were 300 planes. However, there were no aircraft carriers—the most important naval asset—at Pearl Harbor.

The biggest single loss of the day was the sinking of the battleship USS *Arizona*, which went down in less than nine minutes. More than half the fatalities at Pearl Harbor that infamous December day were due to the sinking of the *Arizona*. By the end of the raid, more than 2,300 people had died, and about the same number were wounded.

Pearl Harbor forever changed the United States and its role in the world. When President Franklin D. Roosevelt addressed Congress the next day, he called December 7 "a date which will live in infamy." The United States declared war against Japan, and on December 11, Germany and Italy—Japan's Axis allies—declared war on the United States. The events of December 7 had brought America into the war, a conflict from which it would emerge as the leader of the free world.

Why did the U.S. government order the internment of Japanese Americans during World War II?

After the attack on Pearl Harbor, American citizens of Japanese descent were viewed as threats to the nation's security. On February 19, 1942, President Franklin D. Roosevelt signed an executive order directing that they be moved to camps for containment for the duration of the war. More than 100,000 people, most of them from California and other West Coast states, were rounded up and sent to live in secure camps. The action drew immediate criticism.

With thousands of lives interrupted without cause, the chapter is one of the saddest in American history. Later, in 1988, President Ronald Reagan signed the Civil Liberties Act, which made reparations to the victims of the Japanese internment; $20,000 was paid to "internees, evacuees, and persons of Japanese ancestry who lost liberty or property because of discriminatory action by the Federal government during World War II." It also established a $1.25-billion public education fund to teach children and the public about the internment period.

What is the USS *Arizona* Memorial?

Dedicated in 1962, a memorial was built over the sunken USS *Arizona* in Pearl Harbor. The memorial is accessible by boat. Money to build the memorial came from several sources, including $64,000 raised by a benefit concert by the famous singer Elvis Presley. The Revell Model Company gave $40,000 from the sale of plastic models of the ship.

Although most Americans are unaware of it, some 11,500 American citizens of German ancestry were also interred.

When did the first U.S. troops begin fighting in World War II?

Late in 1942, the United States sent its first troops across the Atlantic, making amphibious landings in North Africa, followed by Sicily and the Italian peninsula. The first Allied landings were in Morocco (Casablanca) and Algeria (Oran and Algiers) on November 8 of that year. The combined forces of the initial landing included more than 100,000 troops, launching the American military effort in the Atlantic theater of conflict. One American newspaper headline announced, "Yanks Invade Africa."

Field Marshall Erwin Rommel led the Germans in brilliant campaigns in North Africa. After participating in a plot against Hitler, Rommel was forced to choose between either being disgraced in a trial or committing suicide. He chose suicide.

Who was the "Desert Fox"?

The Desert Fox was the nickname of skilled German military leader Erwin Rommel (1891–1944), who led German forces in the North African campaign of 1940 to 1943. He was known for quick, tactical decisions and excellent strategy. A decorated officer in World War I, Rommel wrote a book entitled *Infantry Attacks* about his various battles in World War I.

He led a Panzer (tank) division, called the Ghost Division, that advanced on French forces at an alarming pace. During the North African campaign, he had many successful battles in the deserts of Egypt and Libya. Rommel actively participated in military campaigns—something that most high-ranking officers do not do.

AMERICAN FORCES IN EUROPE

What happened at Anzio?

Anzio, Italy, was the site of a four-month battle between Allied troops and the Germans during World War II. On January 22, 1944, more than 36,000 Allied troops and thousands of vehicles made an amphibious landing at Anzio, situated on a peninsula jutting into the Tyrrhenian Sea. But German soldiers, led by Field Marshal Albert Kesselring (1885–1960), were able to surround the Allied forces, containing them along the shoreline into May of that year. Fighting was intense, with an estimated 60,000 casualties,

The scene at the beaches of Normandy during D-Day can only be described as incredibly impressive. It was the largest such naval landing operation ever performed up to that point in history.

about half on each side. On May 25, 1944, the Germans withdrew in defeat, enabling the Allies to march toward Rome (thirty-three miles to the north-northwest). The taking of Anzio was a tactical surprise on the part of the United States and Britain, and their eventual victory there was a turning point for the Allies in the war.

What happened at Normandy?

Normandy, a region in northwestern France that lies along the English Channel, is best known for the June 6, 1944, arrival of Allied troops, which proved to be a turning point in World War II. Officially called Operation Overlord (but known historically as D-Day) and headed by General Dwight D. Eisenhower of the United States, the initiative had been in the planning since 1943, and it constituted the largest seaborne invasion in history. After several delays due to poor weather, the Allied troops crossed the English Channel and arrived on the beaches of Normandy on the morning of June 6.

Brutal fighting ensued that day, with heavy losses on both sides. At the end of the day, the Allied troops had taken hold of the beaches—a firm foothold that would allow them to march inland against the Nazis, eventually pushing them back to Germany.

What does the term "D-Day" mean?

The military uses the term "D-Day" to designate when an initiative is set to begin, counting all events out from that date for planning. For example, "D-Day minus two" would be two days before the beginning of the military operation. There were many D-Days during World War II, most of them landings on enemy-held coasts, but it was the June 6, 1944, invasion of Normandy that went down in history as "the D-Day."

While it was a critical Allied victory, eleven more months of bloody conflict would follow. Germany would not surrender until May 7 the following year.

What American general was the first Supreme Allied Commander of Europe?

That honor went to five-star general Dwight D. Eisenhower (1890–1969), who was also chief of staff of the U.S. Army. Eisenhower oversaw Operation Overlord, Operation Torch in North Africa, and Operation Avalanche—the Allied invasion of Italy.

Eisenhower exited World War II as an unquestioned military hero in the eyes of the American public. He later parlayed that into a successful political career, serving as the thirty-fourth president of the United States. (He would serve two terms in office, from 1953 to 1961.)

What was the Battle of the Bulge?

The term refers to the December 16, 1944, German confrontation with American forces in the Ardennes Mountains, a forested plateau range that extends from northern France into Belgium and Luxembourg. Even though Germany appeared beaten at this late point in the war, Hitler rallied his remaining forces and launched a surprise assault on the American soldiers in Belgium and Luxembourg.

It was a desperate move to split the American and British forces. However, the German Army could not sustain the front, and within two weeks, the Americans had halted the German advance near Belgium's Meuse River (south of Brussels). The offensive became known as the Battle of the Bulge because of the protruding shape of the battleground on a map.

Who were Ernie Pyle and Bill Mauldin?

Pyle was a journalist, and Mauldin was a cartoonist. Both tried to show the reality of combat life for ordinary soldiers in World War II. Ernie Pyle (1900–1945), a war correspondent, was best known for his stories about ordinary soldiers in his columns, which were syndicated in hundreds of newspapers across the country. His writings later became books:

179

War correspondent Ernie Pyle (seated, second from right, with crew of the 191st Tank Battalion in Anzio, Italy, 1944) was a Pulitzer Prize-winning journalist who captured the lives and experiences of ordinary soldiers in combat.

- *Ernie Pyle in England* (1941)
- *Here Is Your War* (1943)
- *Brave Men* (1944)
- *Last Chapter* (1949)

Pyle had premonitions about his own death, and he feared that he would not survive the war. In April 1945, on a Japanese island that had not been cleared of enemy soldiers, he was shot.

Bill Mauldin (1921–2003) was an Army soldier but also a cartoonist. In the war, he joined the staff of the *Stars and Stripes*, the soldiers' newspaper, and created the cartoon characters of Willie and Joe, two scruffy soldiers commenting on their experience of war. His cartoons were very popular, and he won a Pulitzer Prize for them.

After the war, he became an important political cartoonist.

What role did cocktails play in the Allied victory over Germany?

President Franklin D. Roosevelt worked very hard leading the American and Allied effort in World War II. However, every afternoon he took time off for cocktails. He and his staff had a break in their work routine to share a drink or two. However, the rule was that no one could talk about the war or politics during the cocktail hour. The idea was to take a break from working in order to work more efficiently when one returned to work. It was also helpful to take a break from the stress of what was going on to better manage the stress. After dinner, Roosevelt would work long into the evening.

Roosevelt's style stands in stark contrast to the world of Adolf Hitler. He never took a break, often working frenetically for long hours in a claustrophobic and paranoid environment. And he regularly consumed barbiturates, methamphetamine, opiates, and cocaine to keep himself going.

Who were Hermann Göring and Albert Göring?

Hermann Göring (1893–1946) was the second-most powerful person in Nazi Germany. Göring had been a pilot in World War I and became an ace, shooting down some twenty Allied aircraft. With the rise of the Nazis, Göring became Hitler's right-hand man and was responsible for many of the Nazi policies and programs. Göring would be convicted of war crimes at the Nuremberg trials after World War II.

On the other hand, his brother, Albert Günther Göring (1895–1966), hated Nazism. Albert did what he could to resist Nazi policies. He helped many Jews and dissidents survive and escape. For example, he sent trucks to concentration camps to get workers. The trucks would then stop in isolated places and allow the prisoners to escape. He even forged his brother's name several times to help people.

Albert was able to get away with these risky activities because of his name. No one dared accuse the brother of Hermann Göring.

THE WAR IN THE PACIFIC

Why is General Douglas MacArthur important?

Two weeks after the Japanese bombing of the U.S. military bases at Pearl Harbor and the Philippines, Japan invaded the Philippine Islands. General Douglas MacArthur (1880–1964), the commander of the U.S. Army forces in the Far East, led the defense of the archipelago. He had begun to organize his troops around Manila Bay when, in March 1942, President Franklin D. Roosevelt ordered MacArthur to leave the islands. When MacArthur reached Australia, he said, "I shall return," in reference to the Philippines. Under new commands, MacArthur directed the Allied forces' offensive against Japan throughout the Southwest Pacific Islands.

After a string of successes, on October 20, 1944, MacArthur made good on his promise, landing on the Philippine island of Leyte accompanied by a great invasion force. By July of the following year, the general had established practical control of the Philippines. When Japan surrendered in August, MacArthur was made the supreme commander of the Allies, and as such, he presided over the Japanese surrender aboard the USS *Missouri* on September 2, 1945.

What was the Bataan Death March?

It was one of the most brutal chapters of World War II. In April 1942, American forces on the Bataan Peninsula, Philippines, surrendered to the Japanese. More than 75,000 American and Filipino troops became prisoners of war (POWs). They were forced to begin a sixty-five-mile march to a POW camp. Conditions were torturous—high temperatures, meager provisions, and gross maltreatment. The troops were denied food and water for days at a time; they were not allowed to rest in the shade; they were indiscriminately beaten; and those who fell behind were killed. On stretches where some troops were transported by train, the boxcars were packed so tightly that many POWs died of suffocation. The forced march lasted more than a week. Twenty thousand men died along the way.

But the end of the march was not the end of the horrors for the surviving POWs. About 56,000 men were held until the end of the war. They endured starvation, torture, and horrific cruelties; some were forced to work as slave laborers in Japanese industrial plants, and some became subjects of medical experiments. In August 1945, Allied forces liberated their POW camp, and the surviving troops were put on U.S. Navy vessels for the trip home. As part of the United States' 1951 peace treaty with Japan, surviving POWs were barred from seeking reparations from Japanese firms that had benefited from their slave labor. This injustice continued to be the subject of proposed Congressional legislation into the early 2000s, with no positive outcome for the veterans.

Why was the Battle of Midway important in World War II?

It was the turning point for Allied forces fighting the Japanese in the Pacific. The battle for Midway Island (actually two small islands situated about 1,300 miles west-north-west of Honolulu, Hawaii) began on June 4, 1942. The Japanese aimed to control Midway as a position from which its air force could launch further attacks on Hawaii. As the Japanese fleet approached the islands, home to a U.S. Navy base (established in 1941), U.S. forces attacked. Fighting continued until June 6. The Japanese were decisively defeated, losing four aircraft carriers; the United States lost one. The victory proved that Allied naval might could overcome Japan's navy.

What happened on Iwo Jima?

In February and March 1945, Allied forces and the Japanese fought for control of Iwo Jima, a small island in the northwest Pacific Ocean, 759 miles south of Tokyo. Japan was using Iwo Jima as a base from which to launch air attacks on U.S. bombers in the Pacific. Capturing the island from the Japanese became a key objective. On February 19, 1945, the Fourth and Fifth U.S. Marine Divisions invaded the island. On the morning of February 23, after a rigorous climb to the top of Mount Suribachi (Iwo Jima's 550-foot inactive volcano), U.S. Marines planted an American flag. Though small, it was visible from around the island. Later that day, five marines and a Navy hospital corpsman raised a larger flag atop Mount Suribachi. American news photographer Joe Rosenthal captured the moment, and it became one of the most famous images of the war.

The fighting on Iwo Jima was brutal and intense. The Japanese had heavily fortified the island and dug eleven miles of tunnels to connect their forces. Some 6,000 Americans and 19,000 Japanese died in the fierce fighting. The story of the battle of Iwo Jima and the raising of the flag is told in the 2006 film *Flags of Our Fathers*. A companion film, *Letters from Iwo Jima,* shows the Japanese experience of the battle.

The iconic photo taken by Associated Press photographer Joe Rosenthal of American soldiers raising the flag after their victory at Iwo Jima was used as the model of the memorial statue erected in Washington, D.C.

What future U.S. Supreme Court justice served in the military and broke enemy codes?

John Paul Stevens (1920–2019) served on the U.S. Supreme Court from 1975 until 2010, serving into his nineties. Stevens was a Navy veteran who enlisted one day before the Pearl Harbor attack. He received a Bronze Star for his work in decoding enemy signals that led to the downing of an enemy Japanese plane in 1943. During his military service at Pearl Harbor, Stevens met Byron White—who would later be his colleague on the U.S. Supreme Court.

What was the *Enola Gay*?

It was the American B-29 bomber that dropped the first atomic bomb ever used in warfare. On August 6, 1945, the *Enola Gay* flew over Hiroshima, Japan, to drop an atomic bomb over the city. The explosion killed an estimated 70,000 people and leveled an area of about five square miles in Hiroshima, an important manufacturing and military center. Thousands more died later from radiation exposure. The total number of deaths would be estimated at between 90,000 and 166,000.

How many were killed by the second bomb dropped on Nagasaki?

The death toll from the explosion, on August 9, 1945, was about 40,000. But, as in Hiroshima, thousands more died later due to radiation exposure from the atomic bomb.

American military strategists believed that the first bomb, on Hiroshima, would force Japan's leaders to surrender. But when they did not, the second bomb was dropped

183

on Nagasaki, an important seaport and commercial city. (However, the Japanese had only been given a couple of days to react to the bombing of Hiroshima.)

The catastrophic attacks on Hiroshima and Nagasaki brought an end to the war.

Were Hiroshima and Nagasaki the only Japanese cities bombed during World War II?

They were the only cities bombed by nuclear weapons, but all the other cities of Japan had been bombed by B-29 bombers with conventional bombs and incendiary devices to start fires, resulting in the deaths of between 241,000 and 900,000 people.

A photo of Hiroshima after the nuclear bomb exploded shows the complete devastation. The same fate came to Nagasaki, but many other Japanese cities were ruined by conventional weaponry as well.

The 2003 documentary *The Fog of War: Eleven Lessons from the Life of Robert S. McNamara* describes the scale of the U.S. bombing campaign of Japan.

WORLD WAR II ENDS

What mistakes did Hitler make?

Although he served in the Army in World War I, Adolf Hitler had no military training beyond that, such as the training in military strategy that officers would receive. During the war, especially as it wore on, he would not listen to his generals, believing that he knew more than they did. For example, Hitler refused the request of General Erwin Rommel (1891–1944) in June 1944 to move his forces to meet the Allied invasion at Normandy. Hitler thought the invasion would come at the French city of Calais, which, of course, proved to be wrong.

Hitler also was intolerant of conflicting views or even true information that went against his own incorrect views. He was very knowledgeable about details, such as production outputs at military factories, and he had a grand vision, yet he lacked the ability to make good and realistic decisions to realize his vision. He was not a military genius. Yet, he micromanaged the generals below him.

Hitler made many mistakes, such as cancelling production of the first assault rifle even though it had proved effective on the Russian front; cancelling production of jet fighters; ordering that the new VI and V2 rockets be directed at civilian targets and not military targets; and putting the Luftwaffe, the German Air Force, under control of Hermann Göring, who made numerous bad strategic and tactical decisions about how to use air power.

Hitler let the British Army escape at Dunkirk in 1940. Then, he chose to invade Russia in 1941 and fight a two-front war that proved disastrous. And he sent German troops into Russia with little preparation to survive the frigid Russian winter. Hitler also declared war on the United States in 1941 after the United States declared war on Japan. Hitler was bound by a treaty with Japan, but he could have reneged—he had done that before with other agreements.

Hitler also never allowed retreat even though retreat is often the smartest strategic decision. In the Battle of Stalingrad in the winter of 1942–1943, he would not allow the 6th Army to retreat to save itself. The Russians destroyed the 6th Army.

Hitler was a terrible person who led the Germans to do many evil things. How much worse would it have been if he had not made so many mistakes?

Who defeated the Germans?

Although the Americans and British played a key role in defeating Germany, the Russians bore the brunt of the fighting. They had five times the number of divisions as the Americans and British combined. A total of 10.6 million Soviet soldiers died in the war, while 407,300 American soldiers died; however, that number includes those who died fighting the Japanese in the South Pacific.

What are V-E Day and V-J Day?

V-E Day stands for Victory in Europe Day, and V-J Day stands for Victory over Japan Day. After the German surrender was signed in Reims, France (the headquarters of General

Who was Tokyo Rose?

During World War II, the Japanese had several women doing propaganda broadcasts to American soldiers to try to undermine their morale. However, none used the name "Tokyo Rose," and most soldiers who heard the broadcasts knew them to be propaganda and did not take them seriously. After the war, the myth developed that there was one woman doing the broadcasts under the name of Tokyo Rose, and the mythical "Tokyo Rose" appeared in American propaganda films and cartoons.

During the war, the Japanese had pressed into service a woman named Iva Toguri (a U.S. citizen caught in wartime Japan) to read over the radio what were intended to be discouraging messages to the Allied troops. Originating in Japan and heard by soldiers and sailors in the Pacific, the broadcasts were either disregarded by their intended audience or were found mildly amusing. When Toguri returned to the United States, the powerful radio and newspaper figure Walter Winchell stirred up a controversy that led to Toguri being convicted of treason and spending six years in prison. In 1977, President Gerald Ford issued an unconditional pardon in the case, which was built on "tainted" facts.

Dwight D. Eisenhower [1890–1969]) in the wee hours of May 7, 1945, U.S. president Harry S. Truman (1884–1972) declared May 8 V-E Day—the end of the World War II fighting in Europe.

But it was not until the Japanese agreed to surrender on August 14, 1945, that World War II ended. September 2, 1945, was declared the official V-J Day since it was then that Japan signed the terms of surrender on the USS *Missouri,* anchored in Tokyo Bay.

Was the Holocaust directed by the German government?

Yes. When fervent nationalist Adolf Hitler (1889–1945) rose to power in Germany in 1933, he quickly established a reign of terror based on his philosophy that the German (Aryan) race was superior to all others. He established a violent policy against Jews and other people deemed as undesirable. Those who did not flee the country were rounded up and sent to concentration camps, where they were kept without cause. This was before Hitler's acts of military aggression in Europe.

But after German troops invaded Poland in 1939 and World War II began, the führer's anti-Semitic campaign was accelerated. Jews in Germany and in Nazi-occupied countries of Europe were severely persecuted. Most of those who were put into concentration camps—including Auschwitz, Treblinka, Buchenwald, and Dachau—were exterminated, many of them in gas chambers. By the end of the war, in 1945, Hitler's "final solution to the Jewish question" had been underway for some twelve years, and six million Jews and millions of others had been systematically murdered by the Nazis during the Holocaust, or *Shoah* (in Hebrew). As his defeat was imminent, the despotic ruler took his own life in 1945. By then, he had destroyed Europe's Jewish community. An international court later tried many of Hitler's leaders at Nuremberg.

THE HOLOCAUST

Where does the word "holocaust" originate?

The word "holocaust" is based on a Greek word used to translate the term "burnt offering" in the Hebrew Bible (the Christian Old Testament), which referred to burning an animal as a sacrifice to God. After World War II, the term was used for the murder of millions of Jews by the Nazis. The term *Shoah*, meaning "destruction," was also used. Today, the term "Holocaust" can be used in two different ways. It can refer to the murder of five to six million Jews under the Nazis. The term can also be used to cover all the other victims of planned and systematic murder by the Nazis.

Who were the victims of the Holocaust?

The victims were not all Jewish. The Nazis killed millions of people in concentration camps who were members of groups they oppressed, as noted in the table below:

Jewish women and children are ushered toward the gas chambers at Auschwitz in this 1944 photograph. The horrors of the concentration camps were an unbelievable crime against humanity perpetrated by the Nazis.

Holocaust Victims

Description of Group	Number of Victims
Jews	5–6 million
Soviet citizens	5.7 million*
Soviet POWs	2.8–3.3 million
Poles	1.8–3 million
Serbs	300,000–600,000
Disabled	270,000
Romani (Gypsies)	130,000–500,000
Freemasons	80,000–200,000
Slovenes	20,000–25,000
Spanish Republicans	7,000
Homosexuals	5,000–15,000
Jehovah's Witnesses	1,250–5,000

*Excluding 1.3 million Soviet Jews, who are categorized under Jews above.

This puts the total at five to six million Jews and eleven million non-Jews.

Who are the Holocaust deniers?

Ever since World War II, there have been those who have denied that the Holocaust happened or that the number of victims has been greatly exaggerated. Often, these claims are linked with anti-Semitic views. This is despite the fact that there is overwhelming evidence supporting what happened in the Holocaust.

Sadly, the coming of the Internet, which should allow the truth to be known, has often had the opposite effect: allowing the spread of misinformation.

The 2016 movie *Denial*, starring Rachel Weisz as Deborah Lipstadt, is based on Lipstadt's book *History on Trial: My Day in Court with a Holocaust Denier*. Lipstadt was sued by David Irving, who filed a libel lawsuit against her and her publisher because she had accused Irving of being a Holocaust denier, which, in fact, he was. She won her court case.

FDR's long tenure as president led to what constitutional amendment?

Franklin D. Roosevelt (1882–1945) was elected to the office of the presidency an unprecedented four times. At that time, there was no official limit on how many terms a president could serve. President George Washington likely could have served at least a third consecutive term but opted not to run. This established a tradition.

But it was a tradition that FDR did not follow, winning four elections. He died shortly into his fourth term. In 1951, Congress passed the Twenty-second Amendment, which begins: "No person shall be elected to the office of the President more than twice...."

THE KOREAN WAR

What is the origin of the two Koreas?

The peninsula of Korea has a very long and complicated history, during which it has been dominated at different times by the Chinese, the Mongols, and the Japanese. Since 1910, it was under Japanese control. After World War II, the United States and the Soviet Union could not agree on how to create one country.

In 1948, a compromise agreement created a North Korea, supported by the Soviet Union, which was to be a one-party state with a centrally planned economy, and a South Korea, supported by the United States, that would be a capitalist democracy. The countries were separated on a line of latitude, the 38th parallel (38 degrees north of the equator).

Who was the first leader of North Korea? How is he related to "Rocket Man"?

The first leader of North Korea was Kim Il-sung (1912–1994). His grandson, Kim Jong-un (1984–), is the current supreme leader of North Korea and has frequently been in the news in recent years. U.S. president Donald Trump (1946–) gave Kim Jong-un the nickname "Rocket Man."

Why did the United States get involved in the Korean War?

During the presidency of Harry S. Truman (1884–1972), America became involved in the Korean War (1950–1953) when the United Nations (UN), only five years old, called upon member countries to give military support to South Korea, which had been invaded by troops from communist-ruled North Korea in June 1950. The United Nations saw the invasion as a violation of international peace and called on the communists to withdraw. Eventually, twenty-one countries sent troops to aid the South Korean armies.

As fighting started, the ill-equipped South Korean troops fell back to a defensive line called the Pusan Perimeter (in South Korea). In a surprising, bold, and risky move, UN forces made an amphibious landing at Incheon in North Korea. North Korean forces now retreated from South Korea, and UN forces drove them north to the Yalu River, the boundary with China.

The tide of the war turned again, and massive numbers of Chinese troops entered the war to defend North Korea. They drove the UN forces back to the 38th parallel, the original boundary before the war. On the ground, a bloody stalemate followed. However, in the air, things were different as the United States undertook a massive bombing campaign. North Korea became one of the most heavily bombed countries ever.

In July 1953, the Korean Armistice Agreement was signed to end the fighting. However, no peace treaty was ever signed. The United States still maintains military forces in South Korea to discourage any further acts of aggression from the north.

The Demilitarized Zone (DMZ) and border between North and South Korea is a place where tensions run high. The two Koreas are technically still at war.

Why was the Kennedy presidency called "Camelot"?

The term was assigned by Jacqueline Kennedy. Shortly after President John F. Kennedy was assassinated (November 22, 1963), the former first lady was talking with a journalist when she described her husband's presidency as an American Camelot, and she asked that his memory be preserved. Camelot refers, of course, to the time of King Arthur and the Knights of the Round Table and has come to refer to a place or time of idyllic happiness. At the time, the musical *Camelot* was popular on Broadway with Richard Burton as King Arthur, Julie Andrews as Guenevere, and Robert Goulet as Sir Lancelot.

John Fitzgerald Kennedy's widow, who with fortitude and grace had guided her family and the country through the sorrow and anguish of the president's funeral, quite naturally held sway over the American public. So when she suggested that the shining moments of her husband's presidency were reminiscent of the legends of Camelot, journalists picked up on it. Despite subsequent revelations that there were difficulties in the Kennedy marriage, public opinion polls indicate that the image of Camelot—albeit somewhat tarnished—has prevailed.

The 2016 film *Jackie*, staring Natalie Portman, depicts the life of Jackie Kennedy in the wake of the assassination of her husband.

How many died in the Korean War?

About three million people died in the Korean War. Exact numbers are not known, but likely over two million of these were civilian deaths. The percentage of civilian deaths was higher than in World War II. Most North Korean cities had been completely destroyed.

U.S. forces suffered 33,686 battle deaths and 2,830 noncombat deaths.

Numerous atrocities and massacres took place during the Korean War. South Korean troops committed the vast majority of them.

What conflicts did President John F. Kennedy have with the Soviet Union and Cuba?

The two conflicts were the Bay of Pigs in 1961 and the Cuban Missile Crisis of 1962. These are described in detail in the chapter "Russia and the Soviet Union."

What happened in the assassination of John F. Kennedy?

President John F. Kennedy, accompanied by his wife, Jacqueline Bouvier Kennedy (1929–1994), was assassinated while traveling in a motorcade through the streets of Dallas, Texas, on November 22, 1963. They were en route to the Dallas Trade Mart, where the president was scheduled to make a lunchtime speech. At 12:30 P.M., shots rang out; the president, who was riding in the back seat of a convertible, was hit in the neck and head. He was rushed to a nearby hospital, where he died at 1:00 P.M.

Abraham Zapruder was in the crowd to watch the motorcade with his 8mm Kodachrome II home movie camera. He filmed the assassination as it took place in front of him. His 27 seconds of film would become one of the most famous film clips ever.

The nation's loss was immediately felt as television and radio stations broadcast the message live that Kennedy had been shot and killed. He was succeeded by Vice President Lyndon B. Johnson (1908–1973), who took the oath of office aboard an airplane just after 2:30 P.M. Lee Harvey Oswald (1939–1963) was arrested for Kennedy's murder but would not live long enough to be tried. A nightclub owner, Jack Ruby (1911–1967), shot and killed Oswald while Oswald was being transferred from police headquarters to a county jail.

Although conspiracy theories regarding Kennedy's assassination have run rampant since the day he died, a ten-month investigation by the Warren Commission concluded that Oswald acted alone.

THE VIETNAM WAR

What caused the Vietnam War?

In the simplest terms, the long conflict in Southeast Asia was fought over the unification of communist North Vietnam and noncommunist South Vietnam. The two separate countries had been established in 1954. Since the late 1880s, Vietnam had been part of the French colony of Indochina. During World War II, Vietnam came under Japanese control. After the war, rather than granting Vietnam its independence, the French reasserted their control despite the fact that France had been under German domination for most of World War II.

Starting in 1946, the Vietnamese forces called the Viet Minh fought to take control of their own country from the French. The United States provided financial support to France, but the French were ultimately defeated in 1954 in the disastrous Battle of Dien Bien Phu. Once France had withdrawn its troops, an international conference was convened in Geneva to decide what should be done with Vietnam. The country was divided into two partitions, along the 17th parallel. This division of land was not intended to be permanent, but the elections that were supposed to reunite the partitions were never held. Vietnamese president Ho Chi Minh (1892–1969) took power in the north, while Emperor Bao Dai (1913–1997), for a while, ruled the south.

But the communist government in the north opposed the noncommunist government of South Vietnam and believed the country should still be united. The North Vietnamese supported antigovernment groups in the south and, over time, stepped up aid to those groups. These communist-trained South Vietnamese were known as the Viet Cong. Between 1957 and 1965, the Viet Cong struggled against the South Vietnamese government. But in the mid-1960s, North Vietnam initiated a large-scale troop infiltration into South Vietnam, and the fighting became a full-fledged war.

China and the Soviet Union provided the North Vietnamese with military equipment but not manpower. The United States provided both equipment and troops to noncommunist South Vietnam in its struggle against the Viet Cong and North Vietnam.

Why did the United States get involved in Vietnam?

The policy of involvement in the Vietnam conflict began in the mid-1950s, when President Harry S. Truman provided U.S. support to the French in their fight to retain control of Vietnam, which was then part of French Indochina. In the Cold War era, government leaders believed that the United States must come to the assistance of any country threatened by communism. Truman's successors in the White House, Presidents Dwight D. Eisenhower, John F. Kennedy, and Lyndon B. Johnson, also followed this school of thought, fearing a "domino effect" among neighboring nations—if one fell to communism, they'd all fall.

Thus, slowly over time, the American entanglement in Vietnam grew, with the United States sending more military personnel and spending more and more money. At the peak, there would be half a million American troops in Vietnam.

What are five of the more important battles of the Vietnam War?

Important Vietnam Battles	Battle Dates	Significance
The Battle of Ia Drang Valley	October 26– November 27, 1965	This was the first major meeting of U.S. and North Vietnamese troops.
Battle of Khe Sanh	January 21– July 11, 1968	This was a long, drawn-out fight to protect an isolated military base. After successfully defending the base, American troops abandoned it.
Tet Offensive	January 30– March 28, 1968	This was a huge offensive by the Viet Cong and North Vietnamese against about one hundred towns and cities in South Vietnam. Although North Vietnam lost many troops, they landed a blow against U.S. morale both among the troops and among Americans at home.
Battle of Hamburger Hill	May 10– May 20, 1969	This was an intense battle to take Hill 937 by American forces. However, the hill had no strategic value, so after being captured, it was abandoned.
The Fall of Saigon	April 30, 1975	Although American troops had been long gone, South Vietnam fell to North Vietnamese forces.

What was the Tet Offensive?

The Tet Offensive was a turning point in the Vietnam War. The assault began during Tet, a festival of the lunar new year, on January 30, 1968. Though a truce had been called for the holiday, North Vietnam and the Viet Cong issued a series of attacks on dozens of South Vietnamese cities, including the capital of Saigon as well as military and air installations. American troops and the South Vietnamese struggled to regain control of the cities, in one case destroying a village (Ben Tre) in order to "save it" from the enemy.

Saigon is shown burning during the Tet Offensive in 1968. Images like this one—and more graphic photos of dead civilians—in the media helped turn public opinion in the United States against the war.

Fighting continued into February. Though the communist north ultimately failed in its objective to hold any of the cities, the offensive was critical in the outcome of the war. As images of the fighting and destruction filled print and television media, Americans saw that the war was far from over despite pre-Tet reports of progress in Vietnam. The Tet Offensive strengthened the public opinion that the war could not be won. It altered the course of the American war effort, with President Johnson scaling back U.S. commitment to defend South Vietnam.

Who was commander of U.S. forces during the time of the Tet Offensive?

The leading American military commander at the time of the Tet Offensive was General William Westmoreland (1914–2005), who was chief commander of American operations in the Vietnam War from 1964 until 1968.

Westmoreland led the United States to many victories in battle, but the United States did not have enough troops to hold down enemy zones permanently. Also, a strategy of attrition simply did not work in the long run.

What was the My Lai Massacre?

It was a horrific chapter in American military history during which U.S. troops fighting in South Vietnam took the small village of My Lai on March 16, 1968. The incident did not come to light until more than a year later, after which time it became clear that the unit of 105 soldiers who entered My Lai that morning had faced no opposition from the villagers. Even so, at the end of the day as many as 500 civilians, including women and children, lay dead. A number of women were sexually assaulted before being killed.

Though charges were brought against some of the men, only the commander of the company, Lieutenant William Calley (1943–), was convicted. His sentence of life imprisonment for the murder of at least twenty-two people was later reduced to twenty years, and he was released on full parole in November 1974.

What journalist broke the story of the My Lai Massacre and cover-up?

Seymour Hersh (1937–) was an investigative journalist who broke the story as an independent freelance reporter. Previously with the Associated Press, Hersh sold the story to Dispatch News Services. He learned of the impending court-martial of Calley and wrote about the horrible incident.

Hersh later wrote a book titled *My Lai 4: A Report on the Massacre and Its Aftermath* about the incident. For his efforts, he won a Pulitzer Prize in 1970 for international reporting.

Why did so many Americans protest U.S. involvement in the Vietnam War?

The Vietnam War (1954–1975) divided the American public. The antiwar movement maintained that the conflict in Southeast Asia did not pose a risk to U.S. security (contrary to the "domino effect" that Washington, D.C., foresaw), and in the absence of a threat to national security, protesters wondered, "What are we fighting for?"

Meanwhile, President Lyndon B. Johnson had slowly stepped up the number of troops sent to Vietnam. Many never came home, and those who did came home changed. Mass protests were held, including the hallmark of the era, the sit-in. Protesters accused the U.S. government of not only involving Americans in a conflict in which the country had no part but of supporting a corrupt, unpopular—and undemocratic—government in South Vietnam.

How did Richard Nixon change the course of the Vietnam War?

As the 1968 election approached, Democratic president Lyndon B. Johnson had negotiated a cease-fire with South Vietnam and North Vietnam that could have ended the conflict and provided a chance to pull U.S. troops out of Vietnam.

Republican Richard Nixon, who was running for the presidency, secretly contacted the president of South Vietnam, Nguyen Van Thieu (1923–2001), telling him to pull out of the deal, promising a better deal in the future. What Nixon did was illegal and treasonous.

Johnson found out but decided not to go public, perhaps fearing that he would have to admit that he had illegally wire-

A war protester offers an MP a flower as a peaceful gesture in this 1967 photograph taken in Arlington, Virginia, at the Pentagon.

tapped Nixon. Thieu pulled out of the cease-fire, Nixon was elected, and the war continued. In the next years, 20,000 more Americans died in Vietnam, and over 100,000 more were wounded. Another million Vietnamese died.

In 1973, Nixon's secretary of state, Henry Kissinger, negotiated a settlement with North Vietnam, similar to what he helped Nixon sabotage in 1968. He received the Nobel Peace Prize for his efforts.

South Vietnam never got the better deal that Nixon offered. In the end, South Vietnam would be conquered by North Vietnam.

How did the war end?

By 1969, there were more than half a million American troops in South Vietnam. This policy was controversial back in America, where protests against involvement in the Vietnam War continued until the last U.S. troops were brought home in 1973. In January of that year, the two sides had agreed to a cease-fire, but the fighting broke out again after the American ground troops left.

On April 30, 1975, South Vietnam surrendered to North Vietnam, and the war, which had lasted nearly two decades, ended. North Vietnam unified the countries as the Socialist Republic of Vietnam.

For its part, the North Vietnamese called the conflict a "war of national liberation": They viewed the long struggle as an extension of the earlier struggle with France. They also perceived the war to be another attempt by a foreign power (this time the United States) to rule Vietnam.

What are the best documentaries that give an overview of the Vietnam War?

Two excellent documentaries on the war are *Vietnam: A Television History*, a thirteen-part documentary produced by PBS, originally broadcast in 1983, and *The Vietnam*

What popular song commemorated the tragedy at Kent State?

"**O**hio," performed by Crosby, Stills, Nash & Young, was written by Neil Young (1945–). It was a dedication to students who were shot dead by national guardsmen at Kent State University, where anti-Vietnam protests were occurring. Nine other students were also wounded.

Tin soldiers and Nixon's comin',
We're finally on our own.
This summer I hear the drummin',
Four dead in Ohio.

The song became a powerful rallying cry against America's military action in Vietnam.

War, a ten-part, 19-hour documentary produced by filmmaker Ken Burns, premiered in 2017.

Was the conflict of the Vietnam War limited to Vietnam?

No, the war greatly affected several countries in Southeast Asia: Thailand, Cambodia, and Laos.

What were the "killing fields"?

The Vietnam War spilled over into the neighboring countries of Laos and Cambodia. Cambodia, which had been a stable and prosperous country, was bombed, and this led to famine, which led to an economic and political disaster. In the chaos, communist leader Pol Pot (c. 1928–1998), head of the Khmer Rouge, took over the Cambodian government in 1975. He ordered a collectivization drive, rounding up anyone who was believed to have been in collusion with or otherwise supported the former regime of Lon Nol (1913–1985). The new government instituted mass executions of enemies and forced labor camps (called reeducation camps).

These horrors and the famine combined to kill one in every five Cambodians—estimated as over two million people—during Pol Pot's reign. He was removed from power in the Vietnamese invasion of 1978–1979, and he died in hiding in 1998. The entry of the Vietnamese stopped the killing.

Several Cambodian leaders, such as Nuon Chea and Kang Kek Iew, were later tried and convicted for their roles in the killings. A number of mass graves exist in Cambodia. The best known is at the village of Choeung Ek, where a Buddhist memorial stands.

RICHARD NIXON

What happened at Watergate?

Watergate is a complex of upscale apartment and office buildings in Washington, D.C. In June 1972, five men were caught breaking into the Democratic Party's national headquarters there. Among these men was James McCord Jr. (1924–2017), the security coordinator of the Committee for the Reelection of the President (CRP). McCord was among those working to get President Richard Nixon, a Republican, elected to a second term in office.

All five men who were caught in the break-in were indicted on charges of burglary and wiretapping, as were CRP aide G. Gordon Liddy (1930–) and White House consultant E. Howard Hunt (1918–2007). Five of the men pleaded guilty to the charges. McCord and Liddy were tried and found guilty.

In February 1972—five months before the break-in at Watergate—President Nixon had traveled to China, becoming the first U.S. president to visit that country. In May, he

Richard Nixon, the only U.S. president to ever resign from office, was under threat of impeachment because of the Watergate scandal and his efforts to cover it up.

traveled to Moscow, where he signed the Strategic Arms Limitation Treaty (SALT-1 treaty), the first such treaty between the United States and the U.S.S.R. When the election was held in November, Nixon won in a landslide victory over the Democratic nominee, South Dakota senator George McGovern (1922–2012).

But early in Nixon's second term, which began in 1973, the Watergate affair became a full-blown political scandal when convicted burglar James McCord wrote a letter to District Court judge John Sirica (1904–1992), charging a massive cover-up in the Watergate break-in. A special Senate committee began televised investigations into the affair. Before it was all over, about forty people, including high-level government officials, were charged with crimes, including burglary, wiretapping of citizens, violating campaign finance laws by accepting contributions in exchange for political favors, the use of government agencies to harm political opponents, and sabotage.

Among those prosecuted were John Dean (1938–), former White House counsel, and Attorney General John Mitchell (1913–1988). It was revealed that members of the Nixon Administration had known about the Watergate burglary and had been involved in covering it up. It was also discovered that the president had taped conversations in the Oval Office. When Dean and Mitchell were convicted, public confidence in President Nixon plummeted. In July 1974, the Judiciary Committee of the House of Representatives was preparing articles of impeachment (including one that charged the president with obstruction of justice) against the president. The impeachment proceedings would not make it as far as the Senate: Nixon chose to resign on August 9, 1974. He was the first and, so far, only U.S. president to resign from office.

Who was Deep Throat?

Deep Throat was the pseudonym given to *Washington Post* reporter Bob Woodard's (1943–) informant, who revealed key information about the Watergate scandal and the involvement of some in the Nixon presidency. More than thirty years after President Nixon's resignation, Mark Felt (1913–2008) revealed himself as the "Deep Throat" source. Felt worked for the Federal Bureau of Investigation (FBI) as its associate director. The term comes from the title of a 1972 pornographic film: *Deep Throat*.

Shortly after taking office, Nixon's successor, Gerald R. Ford (1913–2006), pardoned Nixon. This was a controversial move since many Americans wanted Nixon to be prosecuted for his alleged crimes. Watergate remains a dark chapter in the nation's history.

JIMMY CARTER

What happened during the four years of Jimmy Carter's presidency?

Jimmy Carter was president from 1977 to 1981. He was a Democrat who had been governor of Georgia. Many things happened during his term, both good and bad; however, his accomplishments are often forgotten.

Carter negotiated and signed the SALT II treaty with Leonid Brezhnev in 1979 that put limits on the nuclear weapons of the United States and the Soviet Union and helped slow down the arms race. "SALT" stands for Strategic Arms Limitation Talks. The SALT II treaty put limits on both missiles and warheads.

The SALT I agreement had been signed between the United States and the Soviet Union during the presidency of Richard Nixon in 1972. It seemed like a step forward in reducing nuclear weapons because it limited the number of missiles each side could have. The missiles were called intercontinental ballistic missiles (ICBMs). A ballistic missile is a rocket that shoots up beyond the atmosphere and then falls down toward its target.

However, Nixon had failed to listen to his experts because the SALT I treaty failed to put limits on the number of warheads. One missile could hold as many as ten warheads, called multiple independently targetable reentry vehicles (MIRVs). Each warhead could be sent to a different target. SALT I actually encouraged a nuclear weapons race of warheads.

In 1978, President Carter negotiated a deal with Israeli prime minister Menachem Begin (1913–1992) and Egyptian president Anwar Sadat (1918–1981) to reach an agreement to solve part of the conflict between Israel and its neighbor Egypt. The agreement was called the Camp David Accords. It led to the 1979 Egypt–Israel Peace Treaty. Carter hoped that this would lead to resolving other parts of the Mideast conflict, but it did not.

Carter also began the deregulation of the airline and trucking industries. Normally, Republicans claim they are the ones pushing for less regulation, but it was Democrat Carter who pushed these efforts. Carter also deregulated the beer industry, which led to home brewing and microbreweries.

Carter supported the development of alternative energy sources, such as solar power, to reduce American dependence on foreign oil. He had the federal government provide funds for alternative energy research and even had solar panels put on the White House. When Ronald Reagan became president, the funding was cut and the solar panels removed.

Carter also worked harder than any recent president to cut the budget and limit the growth of government. At the time of his presidency, the federal deficit for each year was a mere $50 billion.

One of the accomplishments of the Carter Administration was the Camp David Accords. President Carter (center) is shown here in 1978 with Israeli prime minister Menachem Begin (right) and Egypt's president, Anwar Sadat.

What was the Iran hostage crisis during Carter's presidency?

Because of a long, complicated history between the United States and Iran, there was resentment in Iran against the American government. After the Iranian Revolution in 1979, Iranian hardliners took over the American Embassy in Tehran. They held fifty-two Americans as hostages for 444 days from November 4, 1979, to January 20, 1981. Every evening on the TV news, the hostage crisis would be remembered with a graphic, such as "Day 295."

Carter tried a rescue mission that failed, adding to his inability to get the hostages released, which made him appear to be ineffective and powerless in the situation.

To remember the hostages and wait for their return, many people displayed yellow ribbons.

What is the origin of the custom of displaying yellow ribbons when waiting for someone to return?

The custom does not have a long history. It was created by the 1973 song "Tie a Yellow Ribbon Round the Ole Oak Tree," sung by the group Tony Orlando and Dawn, which became a worldwide hit. In the song, a man coming home from prison wonders whether the woman he loves will welcome him back. He wrote telling her that if she wanted him back, she should "tie a yellow ribbon round the old oak tree."

Yellow ribbons were also used during the Iraq War by families of military personnel waiting for their loved ones to return.

> ### What did Jimmy Carter do after his presidency?
>
> He started the Carter Center, a human rights advancement organization; acted as a peace ambassador; helped build houses as a volunteer for Habitat for Humanity; and wrote thirty-three books, including *We Can Have Peace in the Holy Land: A Plan That Will Work* (2009) and *A Call to Action: Women, Religion, Violence, and Power* (2014).

GRENADA

What happened in Grenada?

On October 24, 1983, about 3,000 U.S. Marines and U.S. Army rangers landed on the Caribbean island. The number included about 300 military personnel from neighboring islands. The arrival followed the October 12–19 coup in which Prime Minister Maurice Bishop (1943–1983) was overthrown and killed by a hardline Marxist military council headed by General Hudson Austin (1938–).

While the United Nations and friends of the United States condemned President Ronald Reagan (1911–2004) for the action, American troops detained General Austin and restored order on the island. Nominal U.S. forces remained on the island through 1985.

President Reagan justified the tactic by citing that the coup had put in danger American students on the island. However, the students were never in real danger. Some were playing on the beach when the invasion happened.

What was the Iran-Contra affair?

It was a series of actions on the part of U.S. government officials, which came to light in November 1986. The discoveries had the immediate effect of hurting President Ronald Reagan (1911–2004), whose policy of antiterrorism had been undermined by his own executive office. Following in-depth hearings and investigations into "who knew what, when," special prosecutor Lawrence Walsh (1912–2014) submitted his report in January 1994, stating that the dealings with Iran and with the contra rebels in Nicaragua had "violated United States policy and law."

The tangled string of events involved Reagan's national security advisers Robert McFarlane (1937–) and Admiral John Poindexter (1936–), Lieutenant Colonel Oliver North (1943–), Poindexter's military aide, the Iranian government, and Nicaraguan rebels.

The U.S. officials dealt with both the Iranian government and the Nicaraguan rebels with the goal of freeing seven Americans held hostage by Iranian-backed rebels in Lebanon. President Reagan had met with the families of the captives. Under pressure to work to free the hostages, McFarlane, Poindexter, and North arranged to sell an estimated $30 million in spare parts and antiaircraft missiles to Iran (then at war with neighboring Iraq). In return, the Iranian government would put pressure on the terrorist groups to release the Americans.

Profits from the arms sale to Iran were then diverted by Lieutenant North to the contras in Central America who were fighting the dictatorial Nicaraguan government. Congress had already passed laws that prohibited U.S. government aid to the Nicaraguan rebels; the diversion of funds violated those laws.

The Iran-Contra affair led to North's dismissal and to Poindexter's resignation. Both men were prosecuted. Though the hostages were freed, Reagan's public image was damaged.

During the Iran-Contra hearings in 1987, National Security Commission officials revealed that they had been willing to take the risk of providing arms to Iran in exchange for the safe release of the hostages because they all remembered the U.S. government's failed attempt in 1980 to rescue hostages held at the American Embassy in Tehran, Iran.

Nevertheless, the deal with Iran had supplied a hostile country with American arms that could then be used against the United States. In 1987, Iran did launch an offensive when it attacked Kuwaiti oil tankers that were registered as American and laid mines in the Persian Gulf. The United States responded by sending in the Navy, which attacked Iranian patrol boats. During this military initiative, in July 1988, the U.S. Navy accidentally shot down a civilian passenger jet, Iran Air Flight 655, killing 290 people on board, including sixty-six children.

PERSIAN GULF WAR

What did President George H. W. Bush mean when he said the United States had to "draw a line in the sand"?

President George H. W. Bush (1924–2018) was reacting to Iraqi leader Saddam Hussein's (1937–2006) act of aggression when in August 1990, his troops invaded neighboring Kuwait. Iraq had a number of grievances with Kuwait. The United Nations (UN) gave Iraq until January 15, 1991, to withdraw from Kuwait. Iraq failed to comply. The "line in the sand" that Hussein crossed was soon defended.

In January 1991, Operation Desert Storm was launched to liberate the Arab nation of Kuwait from Iraq, whose military dictator had not only invaded Kuwait but proclaimed it a new Iraqi province. Bush averred, "This will not stand," and in order to protect U.S. oil supplies in the country, the president mobilized U.S. forces, which were joined by a coalition of thirty-nine nations, to soundly and quickly defeat Iraq.

Why was the Persian Gulf War important?

The six-week war, telecast around the world from start to finish (February–April 1991), was significant because it was the first major international crisis to take place in the

Destroyed military and civilian vehicles line Highway 80 in this 1991 photo. Called the "Highway of Death," the road Iraqi forces took during their retreat from Kuwait was heavily bombed by U.S. forces and their allies.

post-Cold War era. The United Nations proved to be effective in organizing the coalition against aggressor Iraq. Leading members of the coalition included Egypt, France, Great Britain, Saudi Arabia, Syria, and the United States. The conflict also tested the ability of the United States and the Soviet Union (then still in existence as such) to cooperate in world affairs.

What words of President Bush were used in the movie *The Big Lebowski*?

On August 5, 1990, President Bush stated to reporters: "This will not stand. This will not stand, this aggression against Kuwait." In *The Big Lebowski*, upset by damage to his carpet, the Dude states, "This will not stand, you know. This aggression will not stand, man."

What is NAFTA?

NAFTA is the North American Free Trade Agreement, signed in 1992 by U.S. president George H. W. Bush (1924–2018), Canadian prime minister Brian Mulroney (1939–), and Mexican president Carlos Salinas de Gortari (1948–). The agreement removed trade barriers, including customs duties and tariffs, over the course of fifteen years, allowing commodities and manufactured goods to be freely traded among the three nations. NAFTA also included provisions that allowed American and Canadian service companies to expand their markets into Mexico.

203

What did Ross Perot say about NAFTA?

In the 1992 U.S. presidential election, third-party candidate H. Ross Perot (1930–2019) stated:

> It's pretty simple: If you're paying $12, $13, $14 an hour for factory workers and you can move your factory south of the border, pay a dollar an hour for labor … have no health care—that's the most expensive single element in making a car—have no environmental controls, no pollution controls and no retirement, and you don't care about anything but making money, there will be a giant sucking sound going south.

The giant sucking was the loss of American jobs. Some estimates put the loss of American manufacturing jobs at 700,000 to 800,000.

Americans have been deeply divided on NAFTA. During the 2016 election, candidate Donald Trump railed against NAFTA and blamed it for the loss of so many American manufacturing jobs. As president, he negotiated and, in November 2018, signed the USMCA, the "Agreement between the United States of America, the United Mexican States, and Canada." This treaty makes modifications to the terms agreed to under NAFTA. (As of this writing, the treaty has not been ratified.)

What was the 1993 World Trade Center bombing?

On February 26, 1993, a truck loaded with explosives went off in a garage under the North Tower of the World Trade Center in New York City. The bomb explosion in lower Manhattan killed six people and started a fire that sent black smoke through the 110-story twin towers, injuring hundreds and forcing 100,000 people to evacuate the premises. However, the explosion had been designed to cause the North Tower to collapse into the South Tower to destroy the entire World Trade Center.

Days later, on March 4, twenty-five-year-old Mohammed A. Salameh (1967–), an illegal Jordanian immigrant, was arrested in Jersey City, New Jersey. Salameh was later found to be a follower of self-exiled Islamic fundamentalist leader Sheikh Omar Abdel Rahman (1938–2017), who was wanted by Egypt for having incited antigovernment riots in 1989.

In June, investigators seized Arab terrorists they accused of plotting to blow up several New York City sites, including the UN headquarters and the Holland and Lincoln tunnels. U.S. authorities then arrested Rahman and imprisoned him on suspicion of complicity in the World Trade Center bombing. In 1995, a federal jury found Rahman and nine other militant Muslims guilty of conspiring to carry out a campaign of terrorist bombings and assassinations aimed at forcing Washington to abandon its support of Israel and Egypt.

The 1993 bombing foreshadowed the terrorist strikes of September 11, 2001, which destroyed the landmark twin towers of the World Trade Center.

What was "Black Hawk Down"?

Though the U.S. military uses the term to refer to a crash of a Black Hawk helicopter, the phrase is closely associated with events in Mogadishu, Somalia, on October 3, 1993. American journalist Mark Bowden wrote a book, *Black Hawk Down: A Story of Modern War* (1993), describing a disastrous U.S. raid on a Mogadishu warlord. The book became a 2001 movie directed by Ridley Scott.

The African country of Somalia threw off its colonial constraints in 1960 to become an independent nation. But warring factions within the impoverished east African nation made a stable central government elusive. In 1992, the United Nations (UN) sent peacekeepers to Somalia and launched a humanitarian relief operation. Outgoing U.S. president George H. W. Bush (1924–2018) sent 25,000 American troops to help secure food-supply routes. President Bill Clinton (1946–) reduced the number of troops to less than half.

In June 1993, twenty-four Pakistani soldiers, part of the UN operation, were killed. The warlord Mohamed Farrah Aidid was believed to be responsible. On October 3, U.S. elite forces launched an assault on a Mogadishu hotel believed to be an Aidid hideout. They were met with an ambush. Over the following seventeen hours, U.S. troops, including a military mission to rescue downed Black Hawk helicopter crews, engaged in a battle with armed Somalis in the streets of Mogadishu.

Eighteen American servicemen were killed; the bodies of some were dragged through the streets of the city. Another eighty-four American soldiers were wounded. Hundreds of Somalis were killed in the fighting. Video footage of the chaos was shown on international television. The Battle of Mogadishu, as it is officially called, was the most intense combat firefight experienced by U.S. troops since Vietnam.

President Clinton pulled out all American troops from Somalia in 1994, and UN peacekeepers left in 1995. The country has remained impoverished, strife-ridden, and lawless.

Some military and foreign-affairs experts point to the Battle of Mogadishu as a primary reason for American reluctance to engage troops in the world's hot spots in the 1990s, such as the Rwandan genocide in 1994.

What happened in the Rwandan genocide?

The genocide happened during the Rwandan Civil War, which lasted from 1990 to 1994. On April 6, 1994, unknown attackers shot down the airplane carrying Rwandan president Juvénal Habyarimana (1937–1994) of Rwanda's majority Hutu ethnic group. The event touched off, or was used as an excuse for, what one journalist described as a "premeditated orgy of killing," in which ethnic Hutu extremists carried out a campaign of mass murder against minority Tutsis. The campaign had been planned for some time.

Ten years after the horrific events, the *Chicago Tribune*'s Africa correspondent recounted how Rwanda's "Hutu majority, equipped with machetes and called to action by government radio announcements, slaughtered neighbors, friends, co-workers. Priests killed parishioners who sought refuge in churches. Teachers murdered pupils. Hundreds of thousands of women were raped, children burned or drowned, bodies pushed into mass graves." The massacre continued for three months, ending only when Tutsi fighters managed to seize the capital at Kigali and take power.

In 2004, the Rwandan government released its official estimate of the death toll: between five hundred thousand and one million people were murdered. An estimated 250,000 to 500,000 women were raped. It was the worst ethnic cleansing the world has seen since the Holocaust during World War II. But, unlike the Holocaust, which a dictatorial military machine carried out, the masses carried out the Rwandan genocide.

In the aftermath, more than 150,000 people were accused of participating in the massive violence, though the Rwandan courts had only tried a small fraction of those—no more than 10 percent in ten years. An estimated two million Hutus, many of whom probably feared retribution, had fled to neighboring countries after the Tutsis gained power. The genocide had happened at the hands of many.

In the decade since the Rwandan genocide, Rwandans, and the world, have grappled with difficult and perhaps unanswerable questions. How could so many people (Hutus) have participated in the mass cleansing? Experts point to Rwanda's deeply divided history; the rivalry between Hutus and Tutsis dates back hundreds of years—since the Tutsis first arrived in the central African region in the fourteenth century. How could the world body have "allowed" such an event to happen, particularly with the Nazi Holocaust a not too distant memory? Again, there is no easy answer.

The United Nations withdrew its people when the violence began in April 1994, but some UN officials estimated later that perhaps as few as five thousand troops might have

A convoy of military vehicles are shown bringing fresh water to Rwandan refugees in Kimbumba, Zaire, in this 1994 photograph. The fight between Hutu and Tutsi ethnic groups killed hundreds of thousands of people.

been able to prevent the annihilation. The United States did not intervene in the Rwandan genocide; the recent images of dead American soldiers being dragged through the streets of Mogadishu, Somalia (in October 1993) had left the country reticent to involve itself in the world's hot spots.

What happened in the Oklahoma City bombing?

The attack took place at 9:02 A.M. CST on April 19, 1995, when a truck bomb exploded outside the Alfred P. Murrah Federal Building in Oklahoma City, Oklahoma. Of the 168 people who were killed, nineteen were children. Another five hundred people were injured. The blast, which investigators later learned had been caused by a bomb made of more than two tons of ammonium nitrate and fuel oil, sheered off the front half of the nine-story building and left a crater eight feet deep and thirty feet wide.

Nearby buildings were damaged or destroyed, including a YMCA day care center, where many children were seriously injured. The force of the explosion shattered windows blocks away. Survivors of the blast and others in the vicinity began rescue efforts right away.

Police and Federal Bureau of Investigation (FBI) agents arrested members of an American right-wing militant group, who were suspected of wanting to avenge the April 19, 1993, FBI/ATF raid on the Branch Davidian religious compound in Waco, Texas. Former

army buddies Timothy J. McVeigh (1968–2001), then twenty-seven, and Terry L. Nichols (1955–), then forty, were indicted in August 1995. The two were tried separately and convicted in federal court. McVeigh was found guilty of murder and conspiracy in June 1997, and a federal jury sentenced him to death. He was executed by lethal injection in June 2001. Nichols was found guilty of conspiracy and involuntary manslaughter and sentenced to life in prison.

Officials believe the Murrah Federal Building was targeted in the antigovernment attack because it housed fifteen federal agencies. McVeigh and Nichols wanted to attack the U.S. government.

Why was President Clinton impeached?

Some believe the proceedings were nothing more than a "vast right-wing conspiracy," a term coined by First Lady Hillary Rodham Clinton (1947–) early in 1998. Still, others—including enough members of the

The bomb set off by Timothy McVeigh destroyed the Alfred P. Murrah Federal Building in Oklahoma City, killing 168 people and injuring 680 more.

What is impeachment?

In an impeachment, a legislative body brings charges against a government official. If the official is then convicted of the charges, the official will be removed from office. So, for example, President Bill Clinton was impeached in 1998 but not removed from office.

U.S. House of Representatives to bring eleven counts of impeachment against President Clinton in December 1998—felt the nation's chief had perjured himself and obstructed justice. Many also believed he had jeopardized the authority of the U.S. presidency.

Accused of having an affair with White House intern Monica Lewinsky (1973–), President Clinton vehemently denied it. Upon continued investigation, conducted by special prosecutor Kenneth Starr's office, the allegations proved to be true. Since the president had been so adamant in his statements to the contrary, evidence began to accumulate that he had lied about his relationship with Lewinsky and that he had tried to cover up the matter.

Many believed the charges against Clinton did not constitute the high crimes and misdemeanors called for by the U.S. Constitution to remove a president from office. Nevertheless, in January 1999, the U.S. Senate organized itself to hear the charges against the president. When the trial concluded in February, Clinton was acquitted of both perjury and obstruction of justice. He served out his second term and left office with high approval ratings despite being the subject of the longest criminal investigation of a president in history.

The Clinton impeachment was the first time the federal legislature had convened itself as a court in more than 130 years—since the impeachment hearings of President Andrew Johnson in 1868.

THE TWENTY-FIRST CENTURY

EARLY TWENTY-FIRST CENTURY

How was the attitude of many in the early 2000s?

If you had questioned someone in the early 2000s, you might have heard catchphrases such as "global marketplace," "global village," or "globalization." Modern communications and transportation connected people as never before. Businesses enjoyed broader markets for their goods and services, manufacturing facilities and jobs were located far from the offices of the companies that marketed them, and people of many nationalities, races, and religions had more and more contact with one another every day for both business and pleasure.

Some observers worried that this contact would blur rich cultural differences, diluting diversity. Others believed that globalization would bring tolerance and increased understanding. People were now living their lives on a global stage. The things they bought had labels that read "Made in China" or "Made in Mexico." People continents away talked to each other not just over the telephone but via instant messaging, email, internet chat rooms, and social networking sites, and people communicated on a new international forum called the Internet.

The upsides were many. Modern communications and transportation made it possible, for example, for the world to mobilize aid to victims of the Southeast Asian tsunami of December 2004. But there are downsides as well. Critics said globalization was fueling the exploitation of workers in developing nations, contributing to a modern slave trade, rapidly depleting resources, and wiping out environmental diversity.

These were some of the reasons protesters demonstrated outside meetings of the World Trade Organization, why some people opposed the North American Free Trade Agreement (NAFTA) and Central American Free Trade Agreement (CAFTA), and why many people disliked that American popular culture was marketed around the world. 209

The conflict could be distilled to diversity versus homogeneity. And the resulting culture clashes were not restricted to the realm of scholarly thought; they were making headline news. The enemy was no longer the strong-armed, nuclear-fortified, absolutist government of the Cold War era; the enemy, as the U.S. State Department reminded Americans, was any group of individuals with extremist views.

By 2016, a strong reaction to globalization would appear in America and around the world.

What was the chronology of events on September 11, 2001?

The sequence of events related to the terrorist attacks on 9/11 were as follows (all times are Eastern Daylight Time):

- 8:46 A.M.: A passenger plane crashes into the north tower of New York City's World Trade Center. At first, it is assumed to be an accident. But within hours, it is learned that the plane was American Airlines Flight 11, which had been commandeered by hijackers shortly after takeoff from Boston headed to Los Angeles. It carried eighty-one passengers (including five hijackers) and eleven crew members.

- 9:03 A.M.: A second passenger plane slams into the south tower of the World Trade Center and explodes. United Airlines later announces that this was Flight 175, another Boston–Los Angeles plane; it carried fifty-six passengers (including five hijackers) and nine crew members. Both towers of the World Trade Center are in flames.

- 9:21 A.M.: Bridges and tunnels leading into New York City are closed. Within the hour, Mayor Rudolph Giuliani (1944–) orders an evacuation of Manhattan south of Canal Street.

- 9:25 A.M.: All flights in the United States are grounded. It is the first time in history that the Federal Aviation Administration (FAA) halts all flights.

- 9:30 A.M.: President George W. Bush (1946–), scheduled to speak at a grade school in Sarasota, Florida, remarks that the nation has been the target of an "apparent terrorist attack."

- 9:45 A.M.: A third passenger plane crashes into the east wall of the Pentagon in Arlington, Virginia. The plane was American Airlines Flight 77, carrying fifty-eight passengers (including five hijackers) and six crew members. It originated at Washington, D.C.'s Dulles International Airport and was headed to Los Angeles. After being hijacked, the plane made a U-turn over the Ohio–Kentucky border to return to the Washington, D.C., area, where it hit its intended target.

- 9:45 A.M.: The White House is evacuated.

- 10:05 A.M.: The south tower of the World Trade Center collapses.

- 10:10 A.M.: A large section of the Pentagon collapses.

- 10:10 A.M.: A fourth passenger plane crashes in a field in Somerset County, southwestern Pennsylvania (outside of Pittsburgh). It was United Airlines Flight 93, originating in Newark, New Jersey, and bound for San Francisco. After being hijacked, the plane made a U-turn over Ohio and was headed for a target in Washington, D.C. (probably the U.S. Capitol building). After learning via cell phones of the other hijackings, a group of passengers stormed the cockpit in an effort to take the plane, which crashed in the countryside. The plane carried thirty-seven passengers (including four hijackers) and a crew of seven. There were no survivors.

- 10:24 A.M.: The FAA reports that it has diverted all incoming transatlantic flights to Canada.

- 10:28 A.M.: The north tower of the World Trade Center falls. The collapse of each tower blankets lower Manhattan in smoke and ash, turning the brilliantly sunny day to darkness.

- 10:45 A.M.: All federal office buildings in the nation's capital are evacuated.

- 2:00 P.M.: Senior FBI sources reveal to the media that they are working under the assumption that the four airplanes that crashed were part of a terrorist attack. The FBI later learns the identities of all nineteen hijackers (there were five on board each plane, except Flight 93, which had four).

- 4:00 P.M.: Media reports indicate that U.S. officials have credible evidence tying the morning's attacks to Saudi militant Osama bin Laden (1957–2011).

- 5:20 P.M.: Building 7 (a forty-seven-story structure) of the World Trade Center complex collapses. Nearby buildings are in flames.

Why did the fourth plane crash in a field in Pennsylvania?

The fourth plane, United Airlines Flight 93, crashed in a rural area of Pennsylvania instead of its intended target because of the sacrifice and heroism of several passengers, who stormed the cockpit and overwhelmed the hijackers.

The heroism was exemplified by passengers Todd Beamer (1968–2001), Jeremy Glick (1970–2001), Mark Bingham (1970–2001), and Tom Burnett (1963–2001). Beamer's last words were, "Are you guys ready? Okay, let's roll."

What was the 9/11 Commission?

Congress chose a bipartisan commission consisting of five Republicans and five Democrats to look into how the attacks of September 11, 2001, had happened and how

How many died in the September 11 attacks?

About 3,000 people died: 2,606 people died at the World Trade Center; another 125 died at the Pentagon, outside Washington, D.C.; and 265 died on the four planes (including the nineteen terrorists). Some 6,000 people were injured.

such a tragedy could be avoided in the future. During their investigation, the commissioners and their staff reviewed more than 2.5 million pages of documents, interviewed more than 1,200 people in ten countries, held nineteen days of hearings, and took public testimony from 160 witnesses.

The commission produced a 567-page report that chronicled the events of 9/11, looked at the roots and growth of the new terrorism, reviewed the U.S. response to the

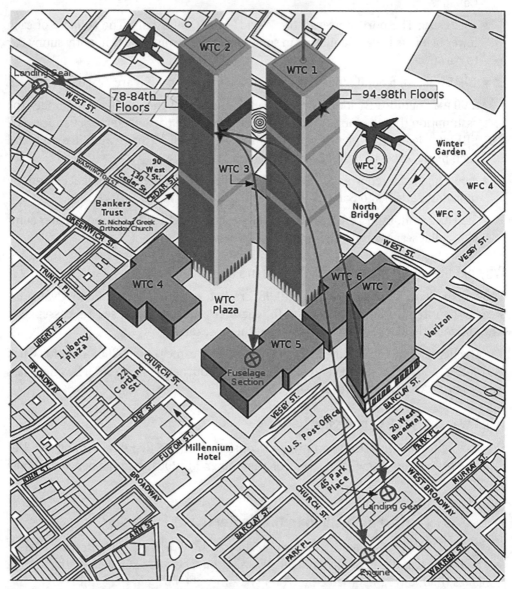

This diagram shows how the planes collided with the two towers of the World Trade Center during the September 11, 2001, attacks. It was the worst attack on American soil since Pearl Harbor in 1941.

attacks and to previous assaults, and recommended changes to prevent further terrorist strikes. (The report is available online.)

Among the key disclosures in the report were that the commission found "no credible evidence that Iraq and al-Qaeda cooperated on the attacks against the United States." In other words, Saddam Hussein had not supported the 9/11 terrorists.

The conclusion: Intelligence errors had overstated Iraq's weapons of mass destruction (WMD) programs. It stated, "The daily intelligence briefings … before the Iraq war were flawed.… This was a major intelligence error." The commission outlined seventy-four recommendations to improve intelligence gathering among the United States' fifteen spy agencies.

Critics of the war argue that the problem was less a failure of the intelligence community and more a case that several key decision makers in the administration had wanted for some time to go to war with Iraq. They wanted to use the claim of WMDs in Iraq as a justification for invasion and, thus, ignored other intelligence that questioned the existence of WMDs in Iraq.

What is the war in Afghanistan?

The war in Afghanistan started in October 2001 under the code name Operation Enduring Freedom. This phase of the war lasted until 2015, when the next phase, Operation Freedom's Sentinel, began. This is the longest war in American history and, as of this writing, continues.

After the withdrawal of Soviet troops from Afghanistan in February 1989, the Taliban took control of the country. (The Soviet Union's invasion and withdrawal from Afghanistan is covered in the chapter "Russia and the Soviet Union.") The Taliban ruled in a tyrannical and often brutal way, insisting on a very conservative version of Islam. For example, in its view, there was no room for treating women as equals. In Afghanistan, the terrorist al-Qaeda group set up training bases. However, during this time, American leaders ignored what was happening in Afghanistan.

Then came the September 11, 2001, terrorist attacks by al-Qaeda members sent by Osama bin Laden, who was living in Afghanistan. The United States demanded the Taliban extradite bin Laden; when the Taliban refused, the Bush Administration sent in military troops.

In Afghanistan, the United States and its allies (forty nations joined the U.S. effort) destroyed the al-Qaeda bases, killing and capturing many al-Qaeda members. However, Osama bin Laden was not captured. At the same time, the Allied Forces went after the Taliban, removed them from power, and took over much of the country. The Afghan Interim Administration was formed under President Hamid Karzai (1957–).

Then, in 2003, as coalition forces were getting close to capturing Osama bin Laden, American strategy shifted its focus to invade Iraq, and military resources were pulled from Afghanistan. Furthermore, the Taliban had not been destroyed. It was rebuilt and fought to take over much of the land of Afghanistan.

Since then, the United States and coalition forces have been caught in a stalemate. The Taliban cannot be defeated and removed. And in many cases, Allied coalition forces have captured land from the Taliban but then been unable to hold it long-term. In September 2014, Ashraf Ghani (1949–) was elected president of Afghanistan.

During the war, 3,500 soldiers of the coalition forces were killed, including 2,420 Americans; 62,000 members of the Afghan National Security Forces and 31,000 Afghani civilians died; and 60,000 to 65,000 Taliban fighters also died.

What is the outlook for Afghanistan?

It looks bleak. The United States has spent many billions of dollars and much effort trying to rebuild Afghanistan and create a healthy country. However, these efforts have had limited success. Part of the problem is that the Afghanistan government that the United States supports is extremely corrupt, and many citizens do not feel loyalty toward that government.

The United States now faces a typical case of "damned if you do, damned if you don't." Most Americans and many military personnel would like the U.S. forces to leave Afghanistan. However, if the United States pulls out, the Taliban will take over and very likely create an oppressive, brutal, and dangerous regime.

Who was Pat Tillman?

Pat Tillman (1976–2004) was a great football player with a great future in the National Football League (NFL). After 9/11, he decided to give up his sports career to join the Army Rangers. Some portrayed him as a patriotic hero. He served several tours of duty in Iraq and Afghanistan. However, on April 22, 2004, in Afghanistan, the men in his unit got separated into two groups when a Humvee broke down, and, in the confusion that followed, Tillman was shot by his fellow soldiers. The military calls this type of incident "friendly fire." However, the Army initially told the family that enemy fire had killed Tillman. In time, the truth came out. Tillman's family was angry and frustrated that the truth of what happened had been covered up to protect the image of the military.

The Tillman Story is a 2010 documentary telling the story of the life, death, and impact of Pat Tillman. It also shows the struggle of his family to get to the truth of what happened.

When did Operation Iraqi Freedom begin?

The U.S.-led, multinational military campaign in Iraq began on March 19, 2003, with air strikes on its capital, Baghdad; ground forces moved into southern Iraq from neighboring Kuwait. After taking the southern city of Basra, U.S. Marines and Army infantry moved northward toward the capital. U.S. troops took control of Baghdad on April 9, after which images of gleeful Iraqis dismantling statues and other symbols of Saddam Hussein's despotic rule flooded the American media.

A Marine Corps tank patrols downtown Baghdad after the fall of the Iraqi capital in 2003.

Coalition forces, American troops, and U.S.-backed Kurdish fighters then pressed into northern Iraq, including Tikrit, Hussein's hometown and a loyalist stronghold. On April 14, Tikrit fell. The war seemed to be near conclusion.

When was Saddam Hussein captured?

The former Iraqi leader, known for his cruelty, was caught in December 2003, eight months after the fall of Baghdad. Hussein (1937–2006) was found about nine miles from his hometown of Tikrit hiding in a hole across the Tigris River from one of his palaces. His six-to-eight-foot bunker was equipped with a basic ventilation system and was camouflaged with bricks and dirt.

A disheveled Hussein had in his possession about $750,000 as well as arms. The former dictator surrendered peacefully. Despite that, Hussein reportedly remained defiant and unrepentant. Later, when asked about the thousands of people killed and dumped into mass graves during his regime, he dismissed his victims as "thieves."

The news of his capture prompted jubilation in Baghdad and across the nation; crowds of Iraqis flooded into the streets to celebrate the end of his brutal rule. But his hometown of Tikrit, considered a loyalist stronghold, remained quiet.

Iraq was given legal custody of the former ruler, who became a criminal defendant instead of a prisoner of war. He was convicted by an Iraqi court of numerous charges of murder and sentenced to death by hanging. He was executed in December 2006.

What was the Abu Ghraib prison scandal?

Abu Ghraib was a prison in Iraq run by the U.S. military that held Iraqi prisoners from the Iraq War (2003–2009). American and British guards at the prison were accused of numerous abuses of prisoners, including physical abuse, sexual abuse, torture, and murder. Many of these abuses were photographed by the guards. The deep troubles first surfaced in spring 2003 when International Red Cross and human rights groups complained that American troops had been mistreating Iraqi prisoners in violation of the Geneva Conventions. In April 2004, photos of abused prisoners appeared in the media and sent shockwaves around the world and sparked an intense debate about how such abuses could have happened. The U.S. Army launched an investigation that later stated that one police company at Abu Ghraib had committed "sadistic, blatant, and wanton criminal abuses." The report also found a rampant lack of supervision of the guards.

While Prime Minister Tony Blair (1953–) apologized for any mistreatment Iraqi prisoners may have suffered at the hands of British troops, President George W. Bush went on Arabic television to denounce the abuses as "abhorrent"; he stopped short of an apology, saying that the mistreatment "does not represent the America that I know."

Both nations moved quickly to bring charges against several soldiers shown in the pictures. Between 2004 and 2006, eleven different American soldiers were court-martialed for their involvement in the scandal. However, a number of critics thought that personnel higher up in the command structure of the military and the Department of Defense should have also been held accountable.

The prison scandals fueled criticism of the controversial Iraq War. They also prompted a deadly backlash as insurgents in Iraq began a series of kidnappings of American and British citizens working in Iraq, many of them ending in ghastly and widely publicized killings. Between spring 2004 and spring 2005, more than 200 foreigners were taken captive in Iraq; more than thirty were killed by their kidnappers.

Why did some observers draw comparisons between the war in Iraq and the Vietnam War?

Critics of the U.S.-led war in Iraq found similarities to American military involvement in Vietnam. Both conflicts seemed to many people to be without ample cause. Critics of the U.S.-led invasion of Iraq charged that there was no compelling reason for Americans to go to war in the Middle Eastern nation; they called the operation hawkish, saying it was an unwarranted expansion of the War on Terror. These arguments were strengthened when no weapons of mass destruction (WMDs) were found in Iraq. (The claim that Iraq had WMDs was the reason given to justify the war.)

Media images of protests against the invasion of Iraq hearkened back to the antiwar demonstrations of the Vietnam era. And, like Vietnam, there seemed to be no clear exit strategy for the U.S. military from Iraq—these were extended operations, or "wars without end."

What was "swiftboating"?

Massachusetts senator John Kerry (1943–) had served during the Vietnam War and was decorated for his actions. He was a commander of a Patrol Craft Fast (PCF), called a "Swift boat," which was used for inland waters. He had been in combat many times and had received a Bronze Star, Silver Star, and three Purple Hearts. He later joined the Vietnam Veterans Against the War.

In 2004, he ran for president against George W. Bush. Kerry hoped his military history would bolster his campaign. However, his opponents created a series of television ads claiming that Kerry had not acted heroically and did not deserve his military decorations. The ads made unsubstantiated claims and included interviews with people who had no contact or very little contact with Kerry during his military service. Supporters of Kerry claimed the ads were a smear tactic to dishonor an American veteran.

Kerry lost the election to Bush. He later served as secretary of state from 2013 to 2017 under President Barack Obama.

When was bin Laden killed?

Osama bin Laden was killed May 1, 2011, by a special U.S. military mission known as Operation Neptune Spear. The operation was directed by the CIA and carried out by a group of highly trained Navy SEALs. The U.S. Special Forces carried out an attack on bin Laden's compound in Abbottabad, Pakistan. President Barack Obama declared to the nation later that evening: "Justice has been done." Obama also declared: "The death of bin Laden marks the most significant achievement to date in our nation's effort to defeat al-Qaeda. But his death does not mark the end of our effort. There's no doubt that al-Qaeda will continue to pursue attacks against us. We must and we will remain vigilant at home and abroad."

What were the three big federal tax cuts in the twenty-first century?

Three times in recent decades, Republicans have made very large tax cuts: in 2001 and 2003 under George W. Bush and then in 2017 under Donald Trump. The promise was that these tax cuts would spur the economy toward greater growth and create more jobs. The claim was also that although the tax cuts would reduce the amount of tax money the federal govern-

The leader of the terrorist group al-Qaeda from 1988 to 2011, Osama bin Laden was the United States' number one enemy until President Barack Obama ordered the CIA and Navy SEALs to take him out at a compound in Pakistan, where he had been hiding.

ment took in, the growth in the economy would ultimately lead to more tax revenue, which would cause deficits to go down. The reality is that the tax cuts led to bigger deficits and added more to the federal debt.

At the same time as the Bush tax cuts, America was engaged in two wars, one in Afghanistan and the other in Iraq. However, to make the U.S. federal budget look better, the cost of the two wars was kept "off budget." The reality was a huge increase in federal debt due to the reduced tax revenues and the expense of two wars.

THE GREAT RECESSION

What was the Global Financial Crisis?

The Global Financial Crisis is the name commonly given to the pronounced economic downturn that began in 2007 and continued for several years. Sometimes referred to as the Great Recession, this economic crisis is considered by economists as the worst since the Great Depression of 1929.

Numerous banks collapsed, and the housing market plummeted. Foreclosures went through the roof, and the government had to bail out many financial institutions. Unemployment skyrocketed, and inflation rose.

Many believe that excesses of Wall Street and the lack of effective oversight contributed to the recession, while others blame the giving of too many high-risk loans in an era of subprime lending.

What happened with the housing market?

There was a boom in the housing market and the financing of home loans. Because of banking deregulation, the old way of getting a home loan from the local bank was replaced by mortgage brokers. Brokers would connect a home buyer with a lending institution for a loan and then the broker would collect a fee for his or her role.

However, there was a big problem. In the old days, a bank making a home loan (a mortgage) would own the loan until it was paid off fifteen, twenty, or thirty years later. Banks were very careful about making mortgages, and they made sure applicants were financially sound and likely to pay off their mortgages. However, with the new system, the brokers never owned the loans; somebody else did. And then, the loans were sold, resold, and combined with other home loans to be sold to other people as investments.

Since the brokers got their commission for making a mortgage deal happen, it did not matter to some brokers whether or not the home buyer could later pay off the loan. It was not the brokers' problem. Many mortgage brokers were honest. But many who were not honest started seeking all kinds of people who were not good loan candidates. Sometimes, brokers faked the buyer's financial info. Some mortgages were sold to people who did not know much English. Often, the mortgages had low monthly payments

> ## What is *The Big Short*?
>
> **A** handful of investors saw the disaster coming and bet against it. To bet against a stock or investment is to "short" it. Although these investors were at times ridiculed, in the end, they were right, and they made lots of money. The 2010 Michael Lewis book *The Big Short: Inside the Doomsday Machine* describes these investors. The book was made into a 2015 movie of the same name, starring Brad Pitt, Christian Bale, Ryan Gosling, and Steve Carell.

for the first years, but then, the payments went up dramatically. Loans were sold to lots of unqualified people who could never pay back the loans. These were called subprime mortgages. But the brokers made lots on commissions.

The mortgages were packaged to investors who could buy them or make bets on how the mortgages would do. It was a disaster waiting to happen. At some point, a lot of people would not be able to make their mortgage payments, which would lead to many, many foreclosures and a collapse of housing prices. That happened between 2007 and 2010. When the subprime mortgage market collapsed, all the various investments built on it went down, too.

THE 44TH AND 45TH PRESIDENTS OF THE UNITED STATES

What did Barack Obama do as president?

Barack Obama was born in 1961 in Honolulu, Hawaii. As a U.S. senator from Illinois, he ran for president in 2008 with Joe Biden as his running mate, and he was reelected in 2012. Obama is the first person of color to become president.

Here are some of the accomplishments of President Barack Obama:

- Signed the Patient Protection and Affordable Care Act (the "Affordable Care Act" [ACA] or "Obamacare")
- Signed the Dodd-Frank Wall Street Reform and Consumer Protection Act
- Signed the Don't Ask, Don't Tell Repeal Act
- Signed the American Recovery and Reinvestment Act and the Tax Relief, Unemployment Insurance Reauthorization, and Job Creation Act; these were designed to lift America out of the Great Recession.
- Urged the lifting of the same-sex marriage ban
- Urged for an assault weapons ban and restrictions on some weapons

President Barack Obama poses with his wife, Michelle, and daughters, Sasha and Malia, in this 2009 photograph.

- Appointed Sonia Sotomayor and Elena Kagan to the U.S. Supreme Court
- Appointed Merrick Garland to the U.S. Supreme Court, but Garland was not given a confirmation hearing because of unprecedented partisan obstruction by the Republican Senate leadership.

What was the birther controversy?

Opponents of Obama made up the false claim that he was not a U.S. citizen, saying he was born in Kenya. These critics claimed that his birth certificate was a forgery.

What is the background of Donald Trump?

The son of real estate developer Fred Trump (1905–1999), Donald J. Trump became nationally known as host of the reality TV show *The Apprentice* (2003–2015). In 2016, he ran for president as the Republican candidate and won a surprise victory over Hillary Clinton. While he had more electoral votes than Clinton (304 to 227), he lost the popular vote with 62,984,828 for Trump versus 65,853,514 for Clinton.

What actions were taken by President Trump?

Here is a list of some of the actions taken by Donald Trump as president:

- Initiated tax cuts in 2017

- Eliminated the individual health insurance mandate of the Affordable Care Act, which required everyone to have health insurance
- Appointed judges Neil Gorsuch and Brett Kavanaugh to the U.S. Supreme Court
- Withdrew from the Trans-Pacific Partnership trade negotiations
- Enacted tariffs on China
- Recognized Jerusalem as the capital of Israel
- Negotiated with North Korea on its nuclear weapons; this effort has stalled
- Put into place great restrictions on legal immigration to the United States
- Attempted to stop illegal immigration and deportations of illegal immigrants
- Removed a number of Obama-era environmental regulations

Why was President Donald Trump impeached?

In December 2019, the House of Representatives impeached him for abuse of power and obstruction of Congress. Trump was accused of withholding military aid to the country of Ukraine until Ukraine investigated Hunter Biden, the son of Democratic presidential candidate Joe Biden, Trump's political opponent. Trump was also accused of obstruction of Congress by withholding documents from the House of Representatives and for not allowing members of his administration to testify before the House.

Impeachment is to bring charges against a president. Donald Trump is the third president to be impeached. Impeachment does not remove a president from office. To remove a president from office requires the Senate to vote to do so.

In February 2020, the Senate took up the case. However, the Republican-controlled Senate refused to allow the calling of witnesses or the presentation of documents as evidence at the trial.

As expected, the Republicans majority voted to acquit President Trump of both charges. The vote was along party lines. The only exception was the vote of Republican senator Mitt Romney of Utah, who voted guilty on the charge of abuse of power.

What is the Mueller Report?

An independent FBI investigation led by former FBI director Robert Mueller (1944–) looked into the allegation of collusion between the Trump campaign and the Russians. A redacted version of Mueller's final report was released to the public. The investigation found over 130 examples of

President Donald Trump has been a highly controversial leader, and many blame him for polarizing the nation between left and right.

What did the Mueller Report say about obstruction of justice?

The Mueller investigation also covered the question of whether Donald Trump had obstructed justice regarding the investigation. The report laid out eleven examples where alleged obstruction of justice had occurred. However, according to a Department of Justice policy, a sitting president cannot be indicted. However, had Donald Trump not been president, it is likely he would have been charged with obstruction of justice. Over a thousand prosecuting attorneys around the country have signed a letter indicating that the evidence uncovered in the Mueller investigation was sufficient to charge someone with obstruction of justice.

At no point did the report exonerate Donald Trump.

contact between the Trump campaign and the Russians. However, "collusion" is not a crime. The question then became, "Was there conspiracy?" The legal requirements to charge conspiracy are quite high, and the Mueller investigation did not find sufficient evidence to support that charge. However, the Mueller Report did not exonerate the Trump campaign of collusion or coordinating with the Russians.

The Mueller Report went into detail showing the myriad ways the Russians interfered with the 2016 election.

Did the Russians interfere in the 2016 election?

According to American intelligence officers of several agencies, evidence shows that Russians did interfere in the 2016 election. This has been validated by the Mueller Report. The Russian goal was to not only disrupt the election and sow discord in the United States but also to promote the campaign of Donald Trump. The following are some of the Russians' activities.

The Russians set up a troll farm called the Internet Research Agency (IRA) in Saint Petersburg, Russia, which created thousands of social media accounts that supported Trump and attacked Hillary Clinton and spread false or made-up information. For example, over 127 million Facebook users got information that originated with the Russians. Other social media platforms, such as Twitter, were also used. The trolls also made efforts to discourage African Americans, a key Democratic constituency, from voting.

The Russians tried to hack into the voting systems of several states. They also hacked into the servers of the Democratic National Committee (DNC), the Democratic Congressional Campaign Committee (DCCC), and the Hillary Clinton campaign. They posted stolen emails from campaign chairman John Podesta to embarrass and discredit Clinton. The stolen emails, posted on WikiLeaks, were strategically timed to do maximum damage to the Clinton campaign. For example, one set was released at the moment that Democrats were drawing attention to the *Access Hollywood* video where Donald Trump boasted of sexually assaulting women.

Did Russian interference win the election for Donald Trump?

There is no way to prove or disprove that the Russians' interference made the difference in Donald Trump's victory. One would have to rerun history with no Russian interference in the election to do so. However, one has to make a judgment about what happened. Looking at the extensive Russian effort and the small numbers of votes that make a difference in the Electoral College system, what do you think?

RUSSIA AND THE SOVIET UNION

Who were the Romanovs?

The Romanov family ruled Russia from 1613 until 1917, when Nicholas II (1868–1918) was overthrown during the Russian Revolution (1905–1917). The dynasty was established by Michael Romanov (1596–1645), grandnephew to Ivan the Terrible. There were eighteen Romanov rulers, including Peter the Great and Catherine the Great.

Why were tsars Peter and Catherine known as "the Great"?

Tsars Peter the Great (1672–1725) and Catherine the Great (1729–1796) are among the best known of the Romanov dynasty, and both had many accomplishments during their reigns. They are also known for having increased their power at the expense of others.

Peter the Great, who ruled from 1682 to 1725, is recognized for introducing western European civilization to Russia and for elevating Russia to the status of a great European power. But he also relied on the serfs (peasants who were little more than indentured servants to the lords) not only to provide the bulk of the funding he needed to fight almost continuous wars but for the manpower as well since most soldiers were serfs.

Peter was responsible for establishing schools (including the Academy of Sciences), reforming the calendar, and simplifying the alphabet. However, he also carried out ruthless reforms. Peter's most vainglorious act was, perhaps, to move the capital from Moscow to the city he had built for himself on the swampy lands ceded by Sweden: Saint Petersburg (called "Petrograd" from 1914 to 1924 and "Leningrad" from 1924 to 1991). Peter succeeded in making the city, his "window on Europe," into a brilliant cultural center.

For her part, Catherine the Great, who ruled from 1762 to 1796, was a patron of the arts and literature (one who corresponded with the likes of French writer Voltaire [1694–1778]), but she, too, increased the privileges of the nobility while making the lives of the serfs even more miserable. Her true colors were shown by how she ascended to power in the first place. In 1744, she married Peter III, who became tsar of Russia in 1762. That same year, Catherine conspired with her husband's enemies to depose him. He was later killed, which led to Catherine rising to power, proclaiming herself tsarina. She began her reign by attempting reforms, but a peasant uprising (1773–1774) and the French Revolution (which began in 1789) prompted her only to strengthen and protect her absolute authority. Like Peter the Great, she, too, extended the frontiers of the empire through a series of conquests. By the end of her reign in 1796, Catherine had reduced even the free peasants to the level of serfdom.

What does the word "tsar" mean?

The word can be spelled as csar, tzar, or czar and is derived from the Latin title for the Roman emperor: "Caesar." Interestingly, the German title "Kaiser" is also based on the Latin title "Caesar."

THE RUSSIAN REVOLUTION

What was Bloody Sunday?

The January 22, 1905, event, which is also known as Red Sunday, marked the beginning of revolutionary activity in Russia that would not end until 1917. A young Russian Orthodox priest, Georgi Gapon (1870–1906), carrying a cross over his shoulder, led what was intended to be a peaceful workers' demonstration in front of the tzar's Winter Palace at St. Petersburg. He had intended to deliver to Tsar Nicholas II a petition on behalf of the workers. But, as a *London Times* correspondent reported that day, when the crowd was refused entry into the common gathering ground of the Palace Square, "the passions of the mob broke loose like a bursting dam."

Father Gapon believed that the Cossack guards and troops on hand for the demonstration would join the protest, but he was wrong. Still loyal to the Romanov tsar Nicholas II (1868–1918), they shot into the crowd of demonstrators, killing about 150 people—children, women, and young people among them.

The event sent shockwaves through the country, where hostilities had been mounting against Nicholas's ineffective government. It also stirred up unrest elsewhere. In the countryside, the peasants revolted against their landlords, seizing land, crops, and livestock. The events foreshadowed the downfall of tsarist Russia.

Who was Rasputin?

Grigori Rasputin (1872–1916) was a Russian mystic and quasi-holy man who rose from peasant farmer to become adviser to Tsar Nicholas II and his wife, Tsarina Alexandra (1872–1918). Rasputin had met Alexandra and demonstrated that he was able to effectively treat the tsar and tsarina's severely hemophiliac son Alexis (1904–1918). Rasputin quickly gained favor with the Russian rulers, but the prime minister and members of the legislative assembly, the Duma, could see Rasputin was a disreputable character, and they feared his influence on the tsar. Rasputin was known for his sexual liaisons with many women.

The charismatic mystic Grigori Rasputin became a close adviser to the Romanov family, and his influence over the royals is what eventually got him assassinated.

By 1913, one year before the outbreak of World War I, the Russian people had become acutely aware of Tsar Nicholas's weaknesses as a ruler—not only was his government subject to the influence of a pretender like Rasputin, but the events of Bloody Sunday had irreversibly marred the tsar's reputation. That year, the Romanov dynasty was marking its 300th anniversary: members of the royal family had ruled Russia since 1613. But public celebrations, intended to be jubilant affairs, were instead ominous as the crowds greeted Nicholas's public appearances with silence.

Russia's entry into World War I proved to be the beginning of the end for Nicholas, with Rasputin front and center in the controversy that swirled around the royal court. During the first year of fighting against Germany, Russia suffered one military catastrophe after another. These losses did further damage to the tsar and his ministers. In the fall of 1915, urged on by his wife, Nicholas left St. Petersburg and headed to the front to lead the Russian troops in battle himself. With Alexandra left in charge of government affairs, Rasputin's influence became more dangerous than ever.

However, in December 1916, a group of aristocrats put an end to it once and for all when, during a palace party, they laced Rasputin's wine with cyanide. Though the poison failed to kill Rasputin, the noblemen shot him and deposited his body in a river later that night. Nevertheless, the damage to Nicholas and Alexandra had already been done.

By that time, virtually all educated Russians opposed the tsar, who had removed many capable officials from government office only to replace them with the weak and incompetent executives Rasputin favored. The stage had been set for revolution.

What movie tells the story of the last years of Nicholas and his family?

The 1971 movie *Nicholas and Alexandra* provides an excellent window into the world of the last Romanov ruler.

What was the Bolshevik Revolution?

It was the November 1917 revolution in which the Bolsheviks, an extremist faction within the Russian Social Democratic Labor Party (later renamed the Russian Communist Party), seized control of the government, ushering in the Soviet age. The event is also known as the October Revolution since by the old Russian calendar (in use until 1918), the government takeover happened on October 25.

The Bolshevik Revolution was the culmination of a series of events in 1917. In March, with Russia still in the midst of World War I, the country faced hardship. Shortages of food and fuel made conditions miserable. The people had lost faith in the war effort and were loathe to support it by sending any more young men into battle. In the Russian capital of Petrograd (which had been known as St. Petersburg until 1914), workers went on strike, and rioting broke out. In the chaos (called the March Revolution),

Russian soldiers fire on protesters during the Bolshevik Revolution in 1917.

Tsar Nicholas II ordered the legislative body, the Duma, to disband; instead, the representatives set up a provisional government.

Having lost all political influence, Nicholas abdicated the throne in March 1918. He and his family were imprisoned and later executed together in July. They were buried in unmarked graves. (In 1979, many of the bodies were found and identified with DNA testing. The remaining bodies were found in 2007.)

Hearing of Nicholas's abdication, longtime political exile Vladimir Lenin (1870–1924) returned from Europe to Petrograd, where he led the Bolsheviks in rallying the Russian people with calls for peace, land reform, and worker empowerment; their slogan was "Land, Peace, and Bread."

The Bolsheviks grew in numbers and became increasingly radical despite efforts by the provisional government headed by revolutionary Alexander Kerensky (1881–1970) to curb the Bolsheviks' influence. The only socialist member of the first provisional government, Kerensky proved ineffective and failed to meet the demands of the people. He also failed to end the country's involvement in World War I, which the Bolsheviks viewed as an imperialistic war.

On November 7, the Bolsheviks led workers and disgruntled soldiers and sailors in a takeover of Petrograd's Winter Palace (the scene of Bloody Sunday in 1905), which had become the headquarters of Kerensky's provisional government. By November 8, the provisional government had fallen.

What was the Red Terror?

The Red Terror was the brutal coercion used by the communists during the tumultuous years of civil unrest that followed the Bolshevik Revolution of November 1917. After the revolution, the Bolsheviks, now called communists, put their leader, Vladimir Lenin, into power.

Delivering on the Bolshevik promise to end the country's involvement in World War I, Lenin immediately called for peace talks with Germany, ending the fighting on the eastern front. Lenin, needing to stop Russian involvement in the war, signed the Brest-Litovsk Treaty in March 1918, which dictated harsh—and many believed humiliating—terms to Russia, which was forced to give up vast territories, including Finland, Poland, Belarus, Ukraine, Moldavia, and the Baltic states of Estonia, Latvia, and Lithuania.

Lenin then disbanded the parliamentary assembly. In its place, Lenin established a dictatorship based on the communist secret police, the Cheka. Furthermore, the radical social reforms he had promised took the form of a government takeover of Russia's industries and the seizure of farm products from the peasants.

Lenin's hard-handed tactics created opposition to the communists—colloquially known as the Reds. The opposition organized their White Army, and civil war ensued. In September 1918, a political opponent nearly assassinated Lenin, prompting his supporters to organize the retaliative initiative that came to be known as the Red Terror.

What is *Doctor Zhivago*?

*D*octor Zhivago was a novel written by Boris Pasternak, first published in 1957, which follows the character of Yuri Zhivago, a poet and physician. The complicated and dramatic story, set against events in Russia from the Russian Revolution into the 1930s, gives a window into this traumatic period of Russian history.

The novel became the 1965 movie *Doctor Zhivago,* directed by David Lean and starring Omar Sharif as Zhivago and Julie Christie, Geraldine Chaplin, and Alec Guinness. The movie won five Oscars, including Best Original Score. The movie's running theme music, known as "Lara's Theme," became the popular song "Somewhere, My Love."

Though thousands of communist opponents were killed as a result, the ruthless repression of the Red Terror lasted into 1924.

THE SOVIET UNION

How was the Soviet Union formed?

The Soviet Union was officially created in 1922, when Russia joined with Ukraine, Belorussia, and the Transcaucasian Federation (Armenia, Azerbaijan, and Georgia) to form the Union of Soviet Socialist Republics (U.S.S.R.). Nine other republics later joined, and territories were redrawn so that by 1940, the union consisted of fifteen Soviet socialist republics: Armenia, Azerbaijan, Belorussia (now Belarus), Estonia, Georgia, Kazakhstan, Kirghiz (now Kyrgyzstan), Latvia, Lithuania, Moldavia (now Moldova), Russia, Tadzhikistan (also spelled Tajikistan), Turkmenistan, Ukraine, and Uzbekistan.

How many leaders did the Soviet Union have?

From its formation in 1922 (just five years after tsarist Russia had fallen in the revolution of 1917), the Union of Soviet Socialist Republics (U.S.S.R.) had only ten leaders. But just five of these had meaningful tenure either due to length of time served or true authority: Vladimir Lenin, Joseph Stalin, Nikita Khrushchev, Leonid Brezhnev, and Mikhail Gorbachev.

After tsarist Russia ended with the revolution of 1917, Bolshevik leader Vladimir Lenin became head of the Soviet Russian government as chairman of the Council of People's Commissars (the communists), dissolving the elected assembly and establishing a dictatorship. This lasted six years.

When Lenin died of a stroke in 1924, an associate of Lenin, Joseph Stalin (1879–1953), promptly eliminated all opposition and in 1929 established himself as a virtual dictator. Stalin ruled the U.S.S.R. during World War II (1939–1945), and though he was aligned with the United States, Britain, and the other Allied nations during that conflict, soon after the war, he began a buildup of power in Eastern Europe, leading to the Cold War (1945–1990). Even though Stalin's domestic policies were extremely repressive and he ruled largely by terror, he remained in power until his death in 1953.

Who was Leon Trotsky?

Leon Trotsky (1879–1940) was a Marxist leader who later joined the Bolshevik Revolution under Lenin's leadership. He was a charismatic leader of the Red Army and later served as the People's Commissariat for Military and Naval Affairs of the Soviet Union under Lenin.

Bolshevik leader Vladimir Ilyich Ulyanov, better known as Lenin, was head of Soviet Russia from 1917 until his death in 1924.

After Lenin's death, Trotsky became opposed to the growing power of Joseph Stalin. Trotsky eventually had to flee the country, as Stalin had him expelled from the Communist Party and exiled from the country. Trotsky first went to Turkey and then later to Mexico, where he lived for more than a decade. He was assassinated there in 1940 by a Soviet agent who used an ice axe, used by mountain climbers, to kill him.

What were the five-year plans?

These were the plans initiated by Premier Joseph Stalin of the Soviet Union to speed industrialization of the U.S.S.R. and organize agriculture under the collective control of the communist government. The first five-year plan began in 1928, and subsequent plans were carried out until 1958, at which time the new Soviet leadership developed a seven-year plan (1959–1965) aimed at matching—and surpassing—American industry.

Later, under Premier Leonid Brezhnev (1906–1982), the five-year plans were reinstated in 1966 and continued until the dissolution of the Soviet Union during 1990 and 1991. Other communist countries also instituted five-year plans, all with the goal of bringing industry, agriculture, and the distribution of goods and services under government control.

What were the gulags?

Gulags were prisons for political dissidents in the Soviet Union; the prisons existed from 1919 into the 1950s. "Gulag" is an abbreviation of the Russian name of the system,

Glavnoye Upravleniye Ispravitelno-trudovykh Lagerey, which translates to "Chief Administration of Corrective Labor Camps." The camps were first used during the collectivization of agriculture in the late 1920s and early 1930s.

Under Soviet leader Joseph Stalin's purges of the 1930s, anyone who posed, or seemed to pose, a threat to his hardline communist regime was rounded up and sent to a gulag. During World War II, prisoners of war were held in the gulags. After the war, Stalin continued to use the camps to punish those who opposed him.

Though exact figures are unknown, it is believed that as many as thirty million people were imprisoned in gulags, where they faced forced labor, grueling conditions, and maltreatment, including starvation. (Official Soviet figures place the number around ten million.) Millions are believed to have died in the gulags. After Stalin died in 1953, the system was dismantled, with some of the prisoners receiving amnesty.

One of the most important writings on the gulag system is the three-volume work *The Gulag Archipelago* (1973) by Aleksandr Solzhenitsyn, who was a gulag prisoner.

THE COLD WAR

Who coined the term "Iron Curtain"? What does the term mean?

The Soviet Union and the territories it controlled in Eastern Europe were closed societies. Travel in and out was greatly restricted, and an intentional effort was made to keep out influences from Western Europe and the United States.

The term "Iron Curtain" was coined by former British prime minister Winston Churchill (1874–1965) to describe the situation. In a March 1946 speech in Fulton, Missouri, he remarked that "an iron curtain has descended across the Continent." The statesman, who had been instrumental in coordinating the Allied victory in World War II, was commenting on Soviet leader Joseph Stalin's tactics in Eastern Europe, which indicated the Soviets were putting up barriers against the West—and building up Soviet domination behind those barriers.

Just as he had issued warnings of the threat posed by Nazi Germany prior to World War II, Churchill astutely observed the rapidly emerging situation in Eastern Europe. In 1946, the Soviets installed communist governments in neighboring Romania and in nearby Bulgaria; in 1947, Hungary and Poland came under communist control as well; and the following year, communists took control of Czechoslovakia. These countries, along with Albania, Yugoslavia, and East Germany, soon formed a coalition of communist allies, and the Eastern bloc was formed. The United States and its democratic allies formed the Western bloc. The stage was set for the Cold War.

Why did the Soviet Union take control of all these countries?

The Soviet Union wanted to keep a buffer between itself and Western Europe. Napoleon had invaded Russia in 1812. The Russians fought the Germans in World War I, and it was

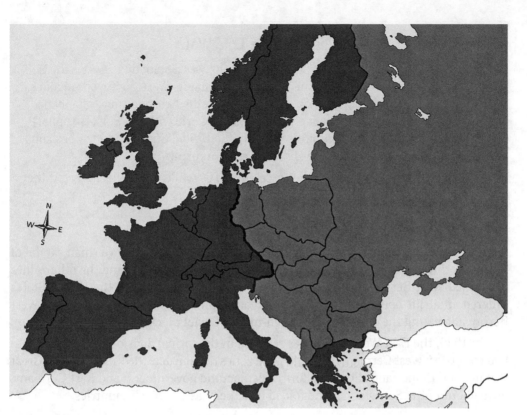

A term coined by Winston Churchill, the "Iron Curtain" was a political and sometimes physical border between NATO and other western countries (dark gray) and the Soviet Union and its communist satellite countries (light gray) in the east.

a disaster for Russia. The treaty that ended Russian involvement in the war resulted in Russia giving up immense territory. And finally, Germany, despite signing a nonaggression treaty with the Soviet Union, invaded the U.S.S.R. in 1941. Although the Soviet Army eventually pushed out Germany and defeated its army, the Soviet Union suffered the greatest loss of human life by any country in war in history.

The Soviet Union lost 10.6 million soldiers who died in the war, ten million civilians who died due to military action or crimes against humanity, and six million civilians who died because of disease and famine caused by the war.

What was the issue with Germany after World War II?

The eroding relationship between the Western powers and the Soviet-led countries of Eastern Europe was in part fueled by disagreements over Germany. At the close of World War II, Germany was controlled by a joint government of the Allies—the Soviet Union, the United States, Britain, and France. But the arrangement quickly proved unworkable. By 1948, Germany was in serious economic straits, and the United States, Britain, and France began to discuss uniting their zones.

233

What was the Cold War?

The Cold War, which lasted from 1945 to 1990, was a standoff between the Soviet Union and its allies and the United States and its Western European allies. It was called "cold" because an open war between the two sides never happened. However, a number of wars happened around the world with the Soviets supporting one side to promote communism, while the United States and its allies supported the other side to stop the spread of communism.

The United States and its allies created NATO, while the Soviets created the Warsaw Pact.

The Soviets ordered a blockade of land and water traffic into the German capital of Berlin. Berlin had been divided: the Soviets controlled East Berlin, and the other Allies controlled West Berlin. To counter the blockade, Great Britain and the United States ordered an airlift operation to provide food and other supplies to the people of West Berlin, alleviating the effects of the eleven-month Soviet blockade.

In 1949, the East-West differences resulted in the formal division of Germany into two countries: West Germany, formed by the zones occupied by the United States, Great Britain, and France and allowed to form a democratic government; and East Germany, formed out of the Soviet zones and folded into the "Eastern bloc" countries.

What is NATO?

NATO stands for the North Atlantic Treaty Organization, a military alliance formed in April 1949, when twelve countries signed the North Atlantic Treaty in Washington, D.C. The original twelve NATO countries were Belgium, Canada, Denmark, France, Iceland, Italy, Luxembourg, the Netherlands, Norway, Portugal, the United Kingdom, and the United States. Each member nation agreed to treat attacks on any other member nation as if it were an attack on itself. In other words, any aggressor would have to face the entire alliance. This was NATO's policy of deterrence, a way of discouraging any attacks by the Soviet Union or other Eastern bloc countries. The organization had the further benefit of discouraging fighting among the member countries.

What is the status of NATO today?

Currently, there are twenty-nine member countries, with NATO headquarters in Brussels, Belgium. However, some have questioned the role and mission of NATO as well as its costs. NATO was originally created because of fear of the Soviet Union during the Cold War. However, the Soviet Union broke apart in 1991.

Although there is much worry about the intentions and actions of Russian president Vladimir Putin (1952–), there is disagreement among its members on the role of NATO in responding to Russia.

The NATO headquarters building is in Brussels, Belgium.

What was the Warsaw Pact?

The Warsaw Pact was the Eastern bloc countries' answer to the North Atlantic Treaty Organization (NATO). Seeing the Western nations form a strong alliance, in May 1955, the Soviet Union and its allies met in Warsaw, Poland, where they signed a treaty agreeing that they, too, would mutually defend one another. The eight member nations were Albania (which withdrew in 1968), Bulgaria, Czechoslovakia, East Germany, Hungary, Poland, Romania, and the Soviet Union. The Warsaw Pact was headquartered in Moscow and, in addition to discouraging attacks from Western bloc/NATO countries, the organization also sought to quell any democratic uprisings in Warsaw Pact nations.

What eventually happened to the Warsaw Pact?

In 1990, the pact and the Soviet Union's control of it weakened as democracy movements in member nations could not be put down. As the former Eastern bloc countries underwent relatively peaceful revolutions, Warsaw Pact members began announcing their intentions to withdraw from the organization. East Germany withdrew when it was reunified with West Germany, and the restored Germany joined NATO (in 1990). The Warsaw Pact was dissolved by the remaining member nations in 1991.

Did the Cold War lead to an arms race?

The United States used two nuclear weapons in 1945. The United States alone had the technology but rejected the idea of creating an international agreement to ban the future use and manufacture of such weapons.

235

In 1949, the Soviets tested their own nuclear bomb. The West was frightened by this development. As a result, an arms race took place between the Soviet Union and the United States that would last some fifty years. Massive amounts of weaponry—both conventional and nuclear—were created at great cost. Enough nuclear weapons were built to destroy life on Earth several times over.

Tragically, much of this weaponry still exists. In the United States, despite the end of the Cold War and the end of the Soviet Union, military budgets have not gone down but have in fact increased dramatically.

What was the Cold War attitude in the West?

In the years following World War II, the nations of Western Europe and the United States became alarmed by Soviet advances into Eastern Europe, and many voiced concerns that communists, led by the Soviet Union, were plotting to take over the world. Political leaders in England, the United States, and elsewhere referred to this new menace in grim terms. In 1947, U.S. president Harry S. Truman (1884–1972) announced a policy of containment of communist incursion into other countries. This policy came to be known as the Truman Doctrine, and it remained an integral part of American foreign policy for the next forty years, ultimately leading to the nation's involvement in the Korean War (1950–1953) and the Vietnam War (1955–1975).

What were the hallmarks of the Cold War era in the United States?

In the United States, the hysteria of the Cold War era reached its height with the so-called McCarthyism of the 1950s; historian Doris Kearns Goodwin described it as "one of the most destructive chapters in American political history." In early 1950, Republican senator Joseph McCarthy (1908–1957) of Wisconsin claimed to possess a list of more than two hundred known communists in the U.S. State Department. The startling accusation launched congressional inquiries conducted by the senator's subcommittee and the House Un-American Activities Committee (HUAC).

Suspicions of communist subversion ran high—even in Hollywood, where a "blacklist" named those who were believed to have been involved in the Communist

Republican U.S. senator Joseph McCarthy of Wisconsin led a witch hunt against people he said were supporters of communism in places such as the U.S. State Department and the acting world of Hollywood. His unsubstantiated accusations ruined many careers.

Party. McCarthy never produced his laundry list of offenders in the State Department, and the sorry chapter was closed when, on live television, the senator's bitter attacks went too far: In televised hearings in 1954, the senator took on the U.S. Army, determined to ferret out what he believed was a conspiracy to cover up a known communist in the ranks.

Faced with McCarthy's slanderous line of questioning, Army counsel Joseph Welch (1890–1960) delivered a reply that finally disarmed McCarthy, saying, "Have you no sense of decency, sir? If there is a God in heaven, your attacks will do neither you nor your cause any good." The retort was met with applause in the courtroom, heralding the end of the communist-in-our-midst hysteria.

Who led the Soviet Union after Stalin?

After Stalin died in 1953, the Soviet Union entered a brief period of struggle among its top leaders. Deputy Premier Georgy Malenkov (1902–1988), a longtime Stalin aide, came to power. In 1955, Malenkov was forced to resign, and he was succeeded by his (and Stalin's) former defense secretary, Nikolai Bulganin (1895–1975). However, Bulganin was a premier in name only, as the true power rested with Communist Party secretary Nikita Khrushchev (1894–1971), who expelled Bulganin and officially took power as premier in 1958.

Khrushchev denounced the oppression of the long Stalin years, which had ended only five years earlier, and worked to improve living standards. On the international front, he pursued a policy of "peaceful coexistence" with the West and even toured the United States in 1959, meeting with President Dwight D. Eisenhower (1890–1969).

What were other effects of the Cold War?

Competition between the Eastern bloc and the West spilled over into athletics, the arts, and the sciences. In 1957, the Soviets beat the West into space with the launch of the first artificial satellite, Sputnik, which they followed in 1961 by completing the first suc-

---

What is the story of Francis Gary Powers and his U-2 spy plane?

In the 1950s and 1960s, U.S. Intelligence agencies had difficulty getting accurate information on what was happening in the Soviet Union, particularly with its nuclear weapons. The United States created the U-2 spy plane to fly over the Soviet Union and take photographs. The plane was designed to fly so high it could not be shot down. However, in May 1962, a U-2 spy plane was shot down over the Soviet Union. Pilot Francis Gary Powers survived the crash and was arrested and convicted of espionage. He was later released in a prisoner exchange.

The story of the shooting down of Powers's U-2 spy plane and the prisoner exchange is told in the 2015 movie *Bridge of Spies*, starring Tom Hanks.

cessful manned space launch. The United States responded by stepping up its space program and vowing to put a man on the moon.

How did the Cold War play out in the Caribbean?

The Soviet Union supported the rule of Fidel Castro (1926–2016) in Cuba. Castro was a communist revolutionary who came to power in Cuba in 1959 as the prime minister. The Soviets gave him both military and financial support, which worried the American government. The United States greatly feared the expansion of communism in the Western Hemisphere. This fear led to the Bay of Pigs disaster.

What was the Bay of Pigs?

The Bay of Pigs is the name of an unsuccessful 1961 invasion of Cuba, backed by the U.S. government. The invasion had been planned under the administration of President Dwight D. Eisenhower (1890–1969). However, his successor, President John F. Kennedy (1917–1963), gave the go-ahead. About 1,500 Cuban expatriates living in the United States had been supplied with arms and trained by the U.S. Central Intelligence Agency (CIA). On April 17, 1961, the group of men who opposed the regime of Cuba's Fidel Castro (1926–2016) landed at the Bahía de Cochinos (Bay of Pigs) in west-central Cuba. Cuban forces captured most of the rebels; the others were killed. The fighters had assumed that when they invaded, the people of Cuba would rise up and overthrow the government of Castro, but that did not happen.

In order to secure the release of the more than 1,100 men who had been captured during the invasion, private donors in the United States accumulated $53 million in food and medicine, which was given to Castro's government in exchange for the rebels' release. The failed invasion came as a terrible embarrassment to the administration of President Kennedy, and many believe the Bay of Pigs incident directly led to the Cuban Missile Crisis.

What was happening in Berlin at the same time?

Germany had been divided into West Germany and East Germany, and Berlin itself was divided. The Soviet Union controlled East Berlin. Yet, many citizens found living conditions very difficult under communist control, and they began fleeing into West Berlin. The East Germans then built a wall with armed guards to isolate West Berlin.

The concrete, electrically fortified wall was first built in 1961 as a barbed wire and cinder block structure. Communist East German leader Walter Ulbricht (1893–1973) convinced Soviet premier Nikita Khrushchev that the wall was needed to prevent people from fleeing communist Eastern Europe. (Before the wall was erected, an estimated 2.5 million people had fled to the free world through West Berlin; after its completion, perhaps 5,000 managed to escape. Hundreds died trying.)

When the wall was complete, it had an average height of twelve feet and ran more than one hundred miles, along which there were posts where armed East German guards stood sentinel, preventing citizens from escaping to the West. The wall completely surrounded West Berlin and divided the German capital into East and West, communism and the free world.

What was Checkpoint Charlie?

There were several crossing points between West Berlin and East Berlin. Checkpoint Charlie (Checkpoint C) became the most famous. It became a symbol for the separation of the communist world from the democratic world.

What was the Cuban Missile Crisis?

The Cuban Missile Crisis, which lasted thirteen days (October 16–28, 1962), developed very quickly, yet nevertheless constituted a major confrontation of the Cold War (1945–1990). After the disastrous Bay of Pigs invasion, the Soviet Union quietly began building missile sites in Cuba as a threat to future possible U.S. invasions. Since the island nation is situated just south of Florida, when U.S. reconnaissance flights detected the Soviet military construction projects there, it was an alarming discovery. On October 22, 1962, President Kennedy demanded that the Soviet Union withdraw its missiles from Cuba. Kennedy also ordered a naval blockade of the island.

Six days later, the Soviets agreed to dismantle the sites, ending the crisis. Part of the agreement was that the United States would remove nuclear missiles in Turkey and Italy

Checkpoint Charlie, as seen from the American side, was the famous crossing point between East and West Berlin.

The 1964 movie *Dr. Strangelove; or, How I Learned to Stop Worrying and Love the Bomb* is a classic satirical dark comedy about the Cold War and fears of nuclear war. Stanley Kubrick cowrote and directed the movie. Actor and comedian Peter Sellers played three different roles in the movie: a British officer, the president of the United States, and ex-Nazi scientist Dr. Strangelove.

that could reach the Soviet Union. The resolution of the crisis showed the importance of good communication between opposing sides and the willingness to negotiate a solution.

How close did the United States and the Soviet Union come to nuclear war in the Cuban Missile Crisis?

Unknown to all but a handful of people at the time was how close the world came to nuclear war. During the Cuban Missile Crisis, the U.S. Navy located a Soviet submarine, *B-59*, and dropped small depth charges, signaling the submarine to surface. The submarine had been out of radio contact with Moscow but had earlier heard news broadcasts from Florida. The officers and crew did not know if a war had broken out.

The submarine commander, Captain Valentin Savitsky, believing that war had started, wanted to launch a nuclear torpedo against the American ships. The political officer on the submarine agreed with the captain. However, the commander of the entire four-submarine detachment, Vasily Arkhipov, was also on board the submarine. Arkhipov refused to approve launching the torpedo without word from Moscow. The submarine surfaced near the American ships and then sailed to Moscow. Had the submarine launched a nuclear torpedo, it could have led to nuclear war with the Soviet Union, which would have destroyed both countries and much of the world.

The story of Vasily Arkhipov is told in the 2012 PBS documentary *The Man Who Saved the World*.

What happened to Nikita Khrushchev?

Khrushchev had to deal with problems in the Soviet Union, such as widespread hunger due to crop failures. His stance on international issues, which included a rift with Communist China, led to his downfall. He was removed from power in October 1964. Khrushchev's ouster (which was

The leader of the Soviet Union from 1953 to 1964, Nikita Khrushchev (left, shown here with U.S. president John F. Kennedy) became unpopular with his party, and he was forced to retire.

240

a forced retirement) had been engineered by his former ally and political adviser Leonid Brezhnev (1906–1982).

With Khrushchev out of the way, technically, Brezhnev was to lead the country along with Premier Alexei Kosygin (1904–1981). But as head of the Communist Party, it was Brezhnev who truly held the power. By the early 1970s, Brezhnev emerged as the Soviet chief—even though Kosygin remained in office until 1980. During his administration, Brezhnev kept tight control over the Eastern bloc (communist countries), built up the Soviet Union's military (continuing the arms race with the United States), and did nothing to try to reverse the downward trend of the Soviet Union's economy.

THE SOVIET INVASION OF AFGHANISTAN

What was the impact of the Soviet invasion of Afghanistan?

In December 1979, the Soviet Union invaded Afghanistan to bolster a pro-communist government. No one could have anticipated the far-reaching effects of this decision. What followed was a ten-year civil war, in which Soviet troops fought Afghan guerrillas, or the Mujahideen. The war in Afghanistan became a jihad, or holy war, and a rallying point for many Muslims, with the conflict drawing young men from across the Muslim world to fight on the side of the guerrillas.

The war was a virtual stalemate for seven years. But a turning point came in 1986 after the United States and Great Britain supplied shoulder-fired, surface-to-air (Stinger) missiles to the Afghan guerrillas. The weaponry gave the scrubby ground forces a fighting chance against Soviet air power. Together with Saudi Arabia, the United States supplied billions of dollars' worth of secret assistance to rebel Afghan groups resisting the Soviet occupation. In April 1988, the Afghans declared victory, and early the next year, the Soviet troops began to withdraw.

The war was over, but it had fueled an extremist Islamic ideology and put into place an infrastructure out of which emerged a powerful and deadly terrorist network. Though most Muslims hold peaceful views, a minority of Muslims view all non-Muslims as unbelievers. It was from this minority, trained and financed in part by the United States, that the global network of terrorists called al-Qaeda emerged. Al-Qaeda terrorists would carry out the 9/11 attacks in 2001.

What is Charlie Wilson's War?

This is the name of the 2003 book *Charlie Wilson's War: The Extraordinary Story of the Largest Covert Operation in History*, written by George Crile III, which became the 2007 film *Charlie Wilson's War*, directed by Mike Nichols and starring Tom Hanks, Philip Seymour Hoffman, and Julia Roberts.

The book and movie tell the story of Charlie Wilson (1933–2010), a Democratic congressman from Texas who served in the U.S. House of Representatives from 1973 to 1997. Wilson sat on key appropriation committees in Congress and was thus able to get funding to buy weapons to support the Mujahideen in their fight against the Soviet Army in Afghanistan. Working with CIA officer Gust Avrakatos (1938–2005), Wilson got enough U.S. government money to create the "largest covert operation in history." A key weapon was the handheld Stinger missile launcher that proved devastating to Soviet helicopters and airplanes.

To this day, questions are asked about the legality, morality, and long-term strategic effects of what Wilson and Avrakatos did. In their efforts to support the Afghans, they also supported many bad actors in Afghanistan and Pakistan who would create serious problems in future years. Wilson himself was a ladies' man and a heavy drinker who died from his alcoholism.

The tragedy of the whole story of Charlie Wilson's War can be seen at the end of the movie and the book when, after the withdrawal of the Soviets, Wilson asks for money to rebuild Afghanistan and try to create a stable society. Despite over twenty billion dollars spent to support the Mujahideen military efforts, Wilson could get no money for such things as schools to rebuild Afghanistan. America ignored Afghanistan, and in the years that followed, Afghanistan would become a breeding ground for terrorists. In 2001, American forces entered Afghanistan to begin the longest war in American history.

What happened when Brezhnev died?

When Brezhnev died in 1982, he was succeeded by Yuri Andropov (1914–1984). However, Andropov died two years later, and Konstantin Chernenko (1911–1985) replaced him as premier. When Chernenko, too, died an untimely death in March 1985, Mikhail S. Gorbachev (1931–) became head of the Communist Party and leader of the Soviet Union.

With Gorbachev, the reign of the old guard of Stalin-trained leaders had come to an end. Gorbachev's policies of openness to the West and economic development led to the disintegration of the Soviet Union, with communist rule ending in 1991 and each Soviet republic setting up its own government.

Gorbachev pulled Soviet troops out of Afghanistan. He also agreed to a treaty with U.S. president Ronald Reagan that banned intermediate-range nuclear weapons (approved in 1987). This was an important step in trying to control nuclear weapons. In 2018, however, President Donald Trump announced that the United States would withdraw from the treaty.

What led to the decline of communism in Eastern Europe?

Anticommunist sentiment among Eastern Europeans was bolstered by the actions and policies of Soviet leader Mikhail Gorbachev. When Gorbachev took office in 1985, the Soviet economy was in decline. In order to reverse the trend, he advocated dramatic reforms to move the economy away from the government-controlled (communist) system and toward a decentralized system, similar to those of Western democracies. Gorbachev's efforts to modernize the Soviet Union were not limited to the economy; he further proposed a reduction in the power of the Communist Party, which had controlled the country since 1917.

Gorbachev's programs for reform were termed *perestroika* (meaning "restructuring"). In the meantime, Gorbachev opened up relations with the West, which included visits with U.S. president Ronald Reagan (1911–2004), who strongly supported the Soviet leader's programs. Gorbachev referred to his policy of openness as *glasnost*. Both Russian terms quickly caught on around the world. While the economic reforms produced a slow and painful change for the Soviet people and Gorbachev had many detractors (including government officials), he also had many supporters—both inside and outside the Soviet Union.

President Mikhail Gorbachev—easily recognizable with his prominent birthmark—tried to modernize the Soviet Union's economy and foreign policies but without much success.

What happened in other communist countries?

People in other Eastern European countries watched with interest the Soviet move toward a more democratic system. Strikes in Poland had begun as early as 1980, where workers formed a free labor union called Solidarity. But the following year, the communist leaders of the Soviet Union pressured the Polish government to put an end to the movement—which it did. After Gorbachev became head of the Soviet Union and initiated sweeping changes, the reform movements in other countries soon realized that the Soviets under Gorbachev would no longer take hard-handed tactics toward anti-communist efforts in other countries.

In 1989, the Polish government ceased to prohibit Solidarity, and the Communist Party there lost influence. The same was true in Hungary, East Germany, and Czechoslovakia. By the end of the decade, most of the Eastern European communist governments were overthrown in favor of democratic-oriented governments. The transition was effected differently in each country: the "overthrow" in Czechoslovakia was so peaceful that it was called the Velvet Revolution, while in Romania, a bloody revolt ensued, and that country's hard-line communist dictator, Nicolae Ceausescu (1918–1989), and his wife were executed.

In 1990, multiparty elections were held in Romania, Czechoslovakia, Hungary, East Germany, and Bulgaria. The noncommunist party that was put in power in East Ger-

243

many agreed to unification with West Germany, again creating one Germany on October 3, 1990. That same year, Gorbachev received the Nobel Peace Prize for his contributions to world peace.

What happened to the Berlin Wall?

The wall was a symbol of communism's oppression and of the Cold War. On June 26, 1963, President John F. Kennedy had delivered his memorable "I am a Berliner" speech in its shadows, saying, "There are some who say communism is the wave of the future…. Let them come to Berlin." He went on to say that the wall was "a vivid demonstration of the failure of the communist system" and that though democracy is not perfect, democratic nations had "never had to put up a wall to keep our people in."

On June 12, 1987, President Ronald Reagan (1911–2004) addressed West Berliners at the wall's Brandenburg Gate; his now famous speech was audible on the East Berlin side of the wall as well. There, Reagan issued a challenge to Soviet leader Mikhail Gorbachev ((1931–), saying, "If you seek peace, if you seek prosperity for the Soviet Union and Eastern Europe, if you seek liberalization … come here to this wall…. Mr. Gorbachev, tear down this wall!"

East Germany's communist government was finally toppled in October 1989. Restrictions between the two Berlins were lifted, and the wall was opened. The resulting celebration brought the wall down, with gleeful Berliners chipping away at the barrier;

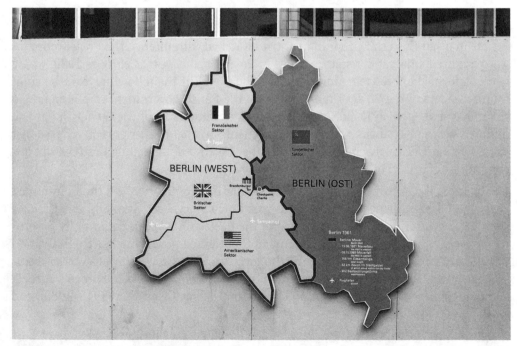

A map at Checkpoint Charlie still shows how the city of Berlin was divided by a wall until 1989.

it was gradually dismantled. A few sections of the wall still stand, many of which have been covered by graffiti artists.

How did the Soviet Union fall apart?

Soviet leader Mikhail Gorbachev's liberal reforms met with the opposition of conservative communist officials who were angered by the hardships produced by the transition to a free-market economy and dissatisfied with the Soviet Union's loss of influence over neighboring countries, where communism had fallen by 1990. In August 1991, communists attempted to overthrow Gorbachev as president of the Soviet Union. Though the effort failed in the face of widespread public opposition, it nevertheless weakened Gorbachev's leadership.

Soon, the fifteen Soviet republics declared independence but indicated their willingness to become part of a loose confederation of former Soviet republics. Though Gorbachev tried to prevent the complete dissolution of the Soviet Union, on December 8, 1991, the republics of Russia, Ukraine, and Belorussia (Belarus) broke away completely from the Soviet Union and formed the Commonwealth of Independent States. All the remaining republics, except Georgia, followed suit. On December 25, 1991, Gorbachev resigned as president, and the Soviet Union ceased to exist.

VLADIMIR PUTIN

Who is Vladimir Putin?

Vladimir Putin (1952–) is the current president of Russia, a position he has held since 2012. He was also the president from 2000 to 2008. In between, he was the prime minister.

After law school, Putin served in the KGB foreign intelligence office for sixteen years and became a lieutenant colonel. (The KGB was the security agency for the Soviet Union from 1954 to 1991. This was the immense spy agency of the Soviets that was known for its use of brutal tactics.) When the Soviet Union broke apart in 1991, Putin went into politics.

With the end of the Soviet economic and political systems, many saw it as an opportunity to create both a democratic society and a free-market economy. However, despite early hopeful signs, this did not happen. A key problem was that all the industries had been previously owned by the Soviet government. When that collapsed, the industries were grabbed up by a handful of people with the right connections and bought for bargain prices. What emerged was an oligarchy of a few powerful people with influence over both the economy and the government. Making things worse is that some of these oligarchs are connected to Russian organized crime. Vladimir Putin is connected to these oligarchs.

Putin has built his economy on exports of oil and national gas. However, this has produced a roller-coaster economy based on the ups and downs of these markets.

As president, Putin has been effective in controlling much of the media in Russia so that it provides a positive image of him with little criticism. Thus, he has remained popular there. (A similar situation existed in the Soviet Union with the state-run news agency TASS.) Russia is not a democracy with free speech. Putin has jailed political opponents. And he is accused of having opponents assassinated.

Under Putin, Russia has tried to influence events and nations around the world. His goals include weakening NATO, tearing apart the European Union, encouraging extremist groups in many countries to weaken those countries, and sowing discord in the United States. Putin is suspected of using influence to bolster support for Brexit, the withdrawal of the United Kingdom from the European Union.

Russia has also tried to interfere with countries created out of the Soviet Union, such as Ukraine. In 2014, Russia took over and annexed the region of Crimea in Ukraine, claiming that it was part of Russia.

Putin has also been accused of interfering in the American 2016 presidential election. (See the chapter "The Twenty-First Century.")

ASIAN HISTORY AND CULTURE

FAMOUS ASIAN RULERS

Why did an ancient Chinese emperor make an army of statues and then bury them in the ground?

The army is called the "Terracotta Army." (Terracotta is made by shaping clay and then baking it, so it remains solid even when wet.) The army was created during the reign of Qin Shi Huang (259–210 B.C.E.), the first emperor of a united China and founder of the Qin dynasty.

Qin Shi Huang created a massive empire by conquering nearby lands. He also instituted political and economic reforms. His workers took existing pieces of defensive walls to create the Great Wall of China. He also had a massive tomb complex built for himself: the site covered thirty-eight square miles! His workers also created the Terracotta Army to protect the emperor in the afterlife.

Workers made life-size statues of over 8,000 soldiers, 130 chariots, and 670 horses. The clothing of the figures matches their military status. The figures originally held real weapons and were brightly painted.

The existence of this huge army buried underground was not known until farmers digging a well discovered it in 1974.

How old is the Great Wall of China?

The immense structure, built as a barricade of protection against invasion, was begun during the third century B.C.E. by Emperor Qin Shi Huang of the Qin dynasty and was expanded over the course of succeeding centuries. The wall stretches 5,500 miles, ranges in height between fifteen and thirty feet (the tallest points are at the fortifications), and

The Great Wall of China remains impressive and is a popular tourist attraction, but although it stretches over five thousand miles, contrary to what some people say, it cannot be seen from outer space.

is between fifteen and thirty feet thick. In the thirteenth century, the Mongols penetrated the wall when they conquered China, expanding their empire across all of Asia.

Who was Genghis Khan?

He was a Mongol conqueror who rose to power to rule over one of the greatest continental empires the world has ever seen. Born Temüjin (c. 1167–1227), he was the first-born son of the leader of a small, nomadic clan. When he was a young boy, a neighboring tribe (the Tatars) killed his father, and, thus, he rose to the status of chief. But instead of allowing a boy to lead them, clan members abandoned Temüjin and his family. He survived the hardscrabbled youth of a destitute nomad.

By the time he was twenty years old, Temüjin had managed to forge alliances with various tribal leaders and claimed the leadership of a small clan. By 1189, he united two Mongol tribes, which he organized to conquer the rival Tatars by the year 1202. At a conference of Mongol leaders in 1206, Temüjin was pronounced the Great Ruler, or Genghis Khan, of the Unified Mongolian State. He began a transformation of the Mongol tribes, dividing them into military units, each one supported by a number of households. He imposed law and order, promoted education, and stimulated economic prosperity. Within five years, Mongol society was changed from a nomadic-tribal system to a military-feudal system. Thus organized, Genghis Khan prepared his troops to expand the Mongol Empire.

Genghis Khan's armies embarked on a series of military campaigns, claiming land and subjugating peoples—sometimes using barbaric methods. By 1213, he controlled northern China to the Great Wall. By 1219, he controlled most of China and began campaigns into the Muslim world. When he died in a field in 1227, Genghis Khan commanded the vast territory from China to the Caspian Sea. He was succeeded by his sons, who continued to expand the Mongol holdings. His grandson was Kublai Khan (1215–1294), under whose leadership the Mongol Empire reached its pinnacle.

Who was Tamerlane?

Tamerlane (1336–1405) was a central Asian conqueror who gained great powers. His Islamic name was Timur; Tamerlane is the English version. He was a barbaric warrior and a brilliant military leader whose fearsome tactics earned him the name Tamerlane the Terrible. By 1370, he was a powerful warlord whose government was centered in the province of Samarkand in present-day Uzbekistan.

In 1383, he launched a series of conquests that lasted more than twenty years and gained him control of a vast region, including Iraq, Armenia, Mesopotamia, Georgia, Russia, and parts of India. He died in 1405 while on an expedition to conquer China. His body was entombed in an elaborate mausoleum. (The tomb, which still exists, is considered a treasure of Islamic art.) After his death, his sons and grandsons fought for control of his dynasty, which remained intact for another hundred years. Tamerlane and his heirs built Samarkand into a great city; in its day, it was a center for culture and scholarship in central Asia.

HISTORY OF CHINA

What are the major dynasties of Chinese history?

Chinese Dynasties

Dynasty Name	Years Reigned
Xia dynasty	2070–1600 B.C.E.
Shang dynasty	1600–1046 B.C.E.
Zhou dynasty	1046–256 B.C.E.
Qin dynasty	221–207 B.C.E.
Han dynasty	202 B.C.E.–220 C.E.
Tang dynasty	618–907 C.E.
Song dynasty	960–1279 C.E.
Yuan dynasty	1279–1368 C.E.
Ming dynasty	1368–1644 C.E.
Qing dynasty	1644–1912 C.E.

What was China called in the twentieth century?

China was called the Republic of China from 1912 to 1949, and it is now called the People's Republic of China. The official name of Taiwan, since 1949, is the Republic of China.

What was the Tang dynasty?

The Tang dynasty (618–907) was a period of great achievements not only in government and business but also in letters and the arts—principally lyrical poetry, formal prose, painting, sculpture, and porcelain pottery. The first published book, the *Diamond Sutra*, was produced during this time (in 868). Considered a golden age of Chinese civilization, Tang was also an age of great expansion. At its height, the empire stretched from Turkmenistan in the west to Korea in the east and from Manchuria to northern India. As a result, trade prospered, with Chinese jade, porcelain, silk, rice, spices, and teas exported to India, the Middle East, and Europe.

One of Tang's innovations was the balance of administrative power. The government was separated into three main branches: the Imperial Secretariat (which organized the emperor's directives into policies), the Imperial Chancellery (which reviewed the policies and monitored bureaucracy), and the Department of State Affairs (which carried out the policies through the administration of six ministries). Add to this triumvirate a

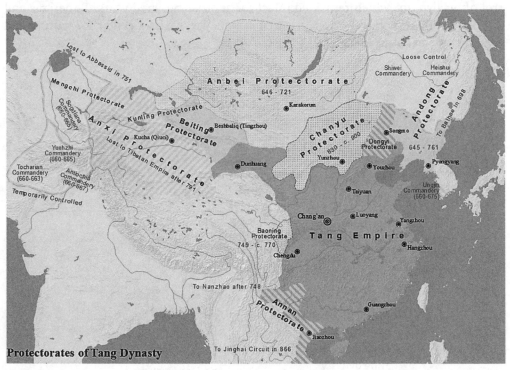

Protectorates of Tang Dynasty

One of the high points of Chinese civilization was the Tang dynasty. Lasting three centuries, it was a time of culture, the arts, and great architecture.

Board of Censors, which ensured that corruption was kept to a minimum. This form of government outlasted the Tang dynasty as subsequent monarchies perpetuated the system into the twentieth century.

Yet another example of the forward thinking of the Tang dynasty was in civil service. Candidates for public service were trained in the Confucian principles before they took an exam that would qualify them for official duty.

What were the highlights of the Ming dynasty?

The focus on Chinese culture that was the hallmark of the Ming dynasty (1368–1644) was both its strength and its weakness. After the foreign Mongols (whose dynasty Kublai Khan established in 1260) were overthrown as rulers of China in 1368, the Ming emperors returned their—and their subjects'—attention to those things that are distinctly Chinese. The focus on Chinese culture produced a flowering in the arts, evidenced by the name *Ming* itself, meaning "bright" or "brilliant." Architects working during this period produced the splendor of Beijing's Forbidden City. Ming porcelain, bronze, and lacquerware are coveted collectors' items today. Additionally, the novel and drama flourished.

Though the Ming rulers promoted this artistic renaissance and reinstated Confucianism and the program of civil service suspended by the Mongols, the rulers' myopia prevented them from seeing the threat of the nomadic Manchu people on the horizon.

In 1644, the Manchus invaded from the north and conquered China, setting up the last dynastic period in Chinese history (the Qing dynasty; 1644–1912). Nevertheless, the Ming was the last great and truly Chinese dynasty.

ANCIENT CHINESE RELIGION

What are the ancient practices of native Chinese religion?

In ancient times, people followed many religious practices, some of which can still be found in modern China. A key practice was ancestor worship. According to this Chinese belief, a deceased ancestor becomes a spirit that can influence events among the living. The living relatives must keep the ancestors happy so the ancestors will benevolently help the living. If the ancestors are offended, however, they can create problems and obstacles. Keeping the ancestors happy includes such things as annual visits to their graves and maintaining a home shrine that lists the names of the ancestors.

Shangdi (or Shang-ti) is an important concept. Shangdi is the deity of the sky, or the spirit of heaven. In centuries past, the main duty of the emperor was to use religious rituals to maintain harmony between heaven and earth.

Yin and Yang is an important concept that holds that everything is made of opposites. Yin represents qualities that are feminine, dark, and cold. Yang represents qualities that are masculine, light, and warm. The goal is to balance Yin and Yang, not that one set of these qualities is bad and the other is good. According to traditional Chinese medicine, illness is caused by too much of either.

In the Yin and Yang symbol, dark and light are balanced. The two dots show that even within light, there is darkness (such as shadows on a sunny day), and even in darkness, there is light (such as the moon and stars).

The Yin and Yang symbol.

Another part of the Chinese religion is divination. One example is the Chinese classic book *I Ching*. Coins are tossed to select one of sixty-four symbols made of six lines. For each symbol, there is a prediction or fortune that goes with it.

Feng shui is another example of divination. Using the principles of feng shui, one tries to find harmony between people and their physical environments. It is often used when choosing the location for a grave or building to find a site with good, positive chi, which is energy. The principles of feng shui allow one to use physical space to enable the flow of good chi. Feng shui is used in designing offices and homes to create prosperous and happy environments.

PHILOSOPHICAL TAOISM

What is philosophical Taoism?

The word "Taoism" can also be spelled "Daoism." Taoism is based on the *Tao Te Ching*, which can also be spelled as *Daode Jing*. Philosophical Taoism is based on the principles of the *Tao Te Ching*. The words *Tao*, *Te*, and *Ching* mean "way," "virtue," and "book"; thus, the title means *The Book of the Way and of Virtue*. According to legend, Lao Tzu is the author of the *Tao Te Ching* (c. 600 B.C.E.)

There are three overlapping meanings of the word "Tao":

1. The Tao is Ultimate Reality, which is beyond explanation: "Those who know don't say; those who say don't know."

2. The Tao is the way of the universe.

3. The Tao is the way to live. One lives life in harmony with the way of the universe, which is in harmony with Ultimate Reality.

Taoists often use the image of a man floating in a stream, who, rather than letting the water take him downstream, fights against the current and is severely battered against the rocks. Taoism is the original version of "go with the flow." Taoists argue that we are unhappy and frustrated because we fight against the way of nature, and, thus, we are fighting with the way of the universe. They suggest we surrender to the universe. We will then find peace and will discover that what we need to do is much easier.

What are some Taoist principles?

Taoists hold certain principles on how to live. These often represent the opposite of the values expressed in modern culture. Thus, these are worth understanding and being thought about by modern people:

- Nonbeing: This is the idea that we are not significant in the big picture. Thus, we should stop promoting ourselves as important. (It is not the idea that one should stop existing.)

- Quietness: According to Taoists, being quiet is more effective than being loud. Sometimes in workplaces, the person who does the most talking gets the least done. Very often, the people getting more done are working quietly.

- Low position: In the Taoist view, being at the bottom is more effective and better than being at the top. Rivers do not flow to the mountaintops; they flow toward valley bottoms.

- Reversion: According to Taoism, anything taken to its extreme will become the opposite. Sharpen a sword too much, and it will become dull.

- Oneness with nature: In Taoism, the goal is to be in harmony with nature; this means not only the natural world but also the very nature of things. Seek to live in harmony with the natural order.

- Spontaneity: Be spontaneous, like nature. It rains in the morning, but the sun comes out. The wind blows this way and then blows the other way.

- *Wu wei*: Sometimes translated as "nonaction," *wu wei* is the principle of doing something so well that it is easy. If you are very skilled at something, it requires little effort.

CONFUCIANISM

Who was Confucius, and what is his teaching?

The teaching developed by Confucius (551–479 B.C.E.) is called Confucianism. "Kung Futzu" (Kung the Master) is closer to the Chinese sound of his name. After his father died, his mother had to sacrifice so her young son could become a scholar. For most of his career, he held minor government positions and worked as a tutor for the sons of gentlemen. He was not well known when he died. However, his followers spread the teachings of their master, and, in time, his ideas would greatly influence Chinese culture and the entire Asian world. His teachings are found in the *Analects of Confucius*. One passage states, "What you do not wish for yourself, do not do to others." Confucian principles would be later explored in writings such as the *Great Learning,* the *Doctrine of the Mean*, and the book *Mencius*.

What are the ideas of Confucianism?

Key to Confucianism is correct understanding of five relationships: Ruler/Subject, Father/Son, Husband/Wife, Elder Brother/Younger Brother, and Elder Friend/Younger Friend. Although these are unequal relationships between a dominant and a subordinate, the key is that there are reciprocal duties going both ways. For example, although a wife must obey her husband, her husband must treat her with benevolence. Both family relationships and Chinese political culture have been shaped by these ideas of Confucius.

Confucius taught the importance of reciprocity: *Shu* is the simple idea of treating others the way you want to be treated. He also taught the five virtues. *Ren* is compassion, the will to seek the good of others. *Yi* is benevolence. *Li* is moral and

Living during the Tang dynasty, philospher Confucius taught that reciprocity is key to all relationships, with dominant and subordinate people each having responsibilities to the other.

religious behavior. *Dhi* is wisdom. *Xin* is faithfulness. A gentleman, or an ideal man, is one who lives out the five relationships and upholds the five virtues.

According to Confucius, the way to create a better society was not with tough laws and punishments. Rather, he thought the key was to teach citizens how to live as good people. For Confucius, that requires that a ruler guide his people by his own personal example of ethical behavior.

RELIGION IN CHINA TODAY

What are the major elements that influenced religion in China today?

The role of religion in China has a very complicated history, and it continues to change. Understanding the place of religion in China today requires that one be aware of nine major elements that shaped it:

- Native Chinese Religion
- Religious Taoism
- Philosophical Taoism
- Confucianism
- Buddhism (from India)
- Christianity (from Europe)
- Islam (from the Middle East)
- Communist Atheism
- Western Materialism
- Government Interference

CONFLICT IN CHINA IN THE NINETEENTH AND TWENTIETH CENTURIES

What was the Chinese–Japanese War?

It was a war fought from 1894 to 1895 over control of Korea, which was a vassal state of China. When an uprising broke out in Korea in 1894, China sent troops in to suppress it. Korea's ports had been open to Japan since 1876, and in order to protect its interests there, Japan, too, sent troops to the island nation when trouble broke out. But once the rebellion had been put down, the Japanese troops refused to withdraw.

In July 1894, fighting broke out between Japan and China, with Japan emerging as the victor, having crushed China's navy. A peace treaty signed on April 17, 1895, provided for an independent Korea (which only lasted until 1910, when Japan took possession) and for China to turn over to Japan the island of Taiwan and the Liaodong Peninsula (the peninsula was later returned to China for a fee after Russia, Germany, and France forced Japan to do so). The war, though relatively brief, seriously weakened China, and in the imperialist years that followed, the European powers scrambled for land concessions there.

What caused the Russo–Japanese War?

From 1904 to 1905, Russia and Japan fought this war over their interests in China (particularly Manchuria) and Korea—areas of strategic importance to each country. Before fighting broke out, Japan moved to settle the conflict, but the overture was rejected by Tsar Nicholas II, and Japan soon severed all diplomatic relations with Russia. Two days later, the Japanese made a surprise attack on Russian ships at Lüshun (Port Arthur), Manchuria.

On February 10, Japan officially declared itself at war with Russia. The battles—both on land and at sea—went badly for the Russian forces, which could not be adequately reinforced or supplied to meet the powerful and disciplined Japanese. Early in 1905, with the war effort already unpopular back home, revolution broke out in Russia, further weakening the country's resolve.

After an eight-month siege at Lüshun, it became clear that Russia could no longer muster a fight. Furthermore, the war was expensive for Japan, which sought the intervention of the United States in settling the conflict. President Theodore Roosevelt (1858–1919) became involved in mediating the dispute; a peace treaty was signed on September 5, 1905, at a shipyard in Portsmouth, New Hampshire, following one month of deliberations.

The terms of the treaty were these: Both nations agreed to evacuate Manchuria; Russia ceded to Japan the southern half of Sakhalin Island, which lies between the two countries (the island was ceded back to Russia after World War II); Korea became a Japanese protectorate; and Russia transferred to Japan the lease of China's Liaodong Peninsula. Japan emerged as a power onto the world scene. Roosevelt received the Nobel Peace Prize in 1906 for his mediation efforts. He was the first U.S. president to win this prize.

What was the May Fourth Movement?

This mass movement emerged in China in 1919, when students in the capital of Beijing protested a decision of the Treaty of Versailles that ended World War I (1914–1918). During the war, Japan had seized German territories in China. Rather than giving this land back to China, the treaty gave it to Japan.

Student demonstrators criticized the Chinese government for allowing this. Following the death of leader Yuan Shih-k'ai (1859–1916), the country's central government crumbled. In northern China, local military leaders (called warlords) rose to power, continually challenging the authority of the capital at Beijing.

Meanwhile, revolutionary leader Sun Yat-sen (1866–1925) had begun promoting his three great principles—nationalism, democracy, and people's livelihood—in southern China, where he gained the support of military leaders in the region. At about the same time, Chinese intellectuals had begun attacking traditional culture and society, urging government reforms and the modernization of industry. The May Fourth Movement fanned the fires of revolution.

In 1919, Sun reorganized the Kuomintang (Nationalist) Party and began recruiting student followers. Two years later, he became president of a self-proclaimed national government of the Southern Chinese Republic, establishing the capital at Guangzhou (Canton). His sights were set on conquering northern China. Intent on toppling the northern warlords to reunify the country, in 1924, Sun began cooperating with both the Soviet Union and the communist groups that students had formed following the 1919 protest. Under Sun's leadership, the Nationalist Party began preparing for war. However, Sun, regarded as the "Father of Modern China," died of cancer in 1925. Under military leader Chiang Kai-shek (1887–1975), the Kuomintang turned on its communist members, whose leaders fled in fear of the Generalissimo Chiang. In 1928, following a two-year military campaign, Chiang led the nationalists to capture Beijing,

What was the Long March?

The Long March began in October 1934 when Mao Zedong (1893–1976) led Chinese communist forces (the Red Army of China), numbering 100,000 men and women, on an epic walk across China. With the Nationalist Army in pursuit, the communist marchers crossed eighteen mountain chains and twenty-four rivers to cover 6,000 miles. Almost all women and children died along the way. In 1935, 20,000 to 30,000 people finally reached Shaanxi (Shensi) Province in the north, where the Red Army established a stronghold.

It was there that Mao, one of the earliest members of the Chinese Communist Party, formulated his own philosophy that came to be known as Maoism. He had adapted Marxism to the Chinese conditions—replacing German politician and socialist Karl Marx's (1818–1883) urban working class with the peasant farmers as the force behind the revolution. The Red Army went on to defeat the nationalists in 1949; Mao was named chairman of the People's Republic of China, a communist state, that same year.

reuniting China under one government for the first time in twelve years. Many millions of Chinese died under the rule of Chiang.

His rule of China lasted until 1949, when communists, who had reorganized in the north and fought back, won control of the mainland, and Mao Zedong (1893–1976) became the first chairman of the People's Republic of China. The expelled Chiang and his followers established a Chinese nationalist government on the island of Taiwan.

What was the Second Sino–Japanese War (*Sino* means "Chinese")?

This dispute between China and Japan (who had previously clashed in the Chinese–Japanese War of 1894–1895) began in 1937 and was absorbed by World War II (1939–1945). The trouble began when Japan, having already taken Manchuria and the Jehol Province from China, attacked China again. Though China was in the midst of internal conflict—with the nationalist forces of Generalissimo Chiang Kai-shek (1887–1975) fighting the communists under Mao Zedong (1893–1976)—China turned its attention to fighting the foreign aggressor. The fighting between the two countries continued into 1941 before war was officially declared by China. In so doing, China was at war not only with the Japanese but with Japan's Axis allies—Germany and Italy—as well. The conflict then became part of World War II.

What was the Nanking Massacre?

One of the most brutal chapters in modern history, the Nanking Massacre, also called the Rape of Nanking, was a mass execution of hundreds of thousands of unarmed Chinese civilians by invading Japanese soldiers in December 1937 and January 1938. No

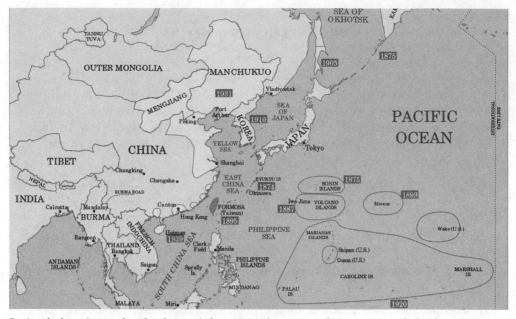

During the late-nineteenth and early twentieth centuries, Japan engaged in a campaign of relentless expansion across Asia and the Pacific.

one knows for certain how many people were murdered in the mass killings, but most estimates place the number at 300,000, with another 80,000 people raped and tortured, including women and children.

On December 13, 1937, the Japanese Royal Army swept into the eastern Chinese city of Nanking (today called Nanjing), which was then the capital of China. In the weeks that followed, the Japanese soldiers went on an orgy of violence. The atrocities were documented on film by the Japanese themselves as well as by helpless foreigners in the city at the time of the seizure. Surviving photos show unimaginable cruelties. It is believed that Japan's military had been trained to carry out the killings and atrocities in order to make an example of Nanking to other Chinese people, thereby facilitating Japan's intended occupation.

What happened at China's Tiananmen Square?

In 1989, Beijing's Tiananmen Square, the largest public square in the world, became the site of a student protest and massacre. Three years before the demonstration, freedom of speech and other democratic beliefs began being espoused on university campuses. Increasing numbers of China's youth were demanding political reform. They found a sympathizer in the general secretary (the highest-ranking officer) of the Communist Party, Hu Yaobang (1915–1989), who adhered to his liberal views, particularly concerning freedom of expression, despite criticism from conservatives in the government.

In January 1987, Hu was removed from his post; he died of a heart attack in April 1989, at which time students organized marches in his honor and demonstrated to call for democratic reforms. On June 4, 1989, Chinese troops fired on the protesters in Tiananmen Square, killing more than 200 and later arresting anyone thought to be involved in China's pro-democracy movement. The actions raised fury around the world.

Since that time, China has tightened many controls to limit free expression. Modern technology has made it much easier to monitor the citizens of China.

Who are the Uyghurs in China?

Islam arrived in China 1,400 years ago, and today, there are two groups in China: Hui Muslims and Uyghur Muslims (pronounced "we-gur"). The Uyghurs, who live in the Xinjiang region in northwest China, have come under suspicion and constant surveillance by the Chinese government, who questions their loyalty to China because of their religious faith in Islam. The Uyghurs are accused of "religious extremism," and actions such as growing a beard or having a prayer rug can get one in trouble.

Perhaps a million Uyghurs have been held in large detention camps called "reeducation camps." The camps are designed to change Uyghur identities and religious and political beliefs. Although the action of the Chinese government is a gross violation of human rights and religious rights, many world leaders and nations have not criticized China.

THE INDEPENDENCE OF INDIA

What led up to the Indian people's fight for independence?

Starting in the 1700s, British companies, such as the East India Company, began taking economic and political control of land in India, which is known today as the countries of India, Pakistan, and Bangladesh. By 1803, the East India Company had its own army of 260,000, which was twice the size of the British Army. After a failed rebellion against the company in 1857, the region came under direct control of the British government. Many Indians felt their land was economically exploited by the British, who dominated Indian society and culture.

One million Indians served as soldiers fighting for the British in World War I. After the war, many Indians began calling for an independent nation of their own.

Why was Mohandas Gandhi called "Mahatma"?

Mohandas Gandhi (1869–1948) was called "Mahatma" (meaning "great-souled") by the common people, who viewed him as India's national and spiritual leader. He is considered the father of his country. He was born in India in 1869. As a young man, Gandhi studied law in Britain. After practicing briefly in India, he traveled to British-controlled South Africa on business. Observing oppressive treatment of Indian immigrants there, he held his first campaign of passive resistance. Gandhi would later become very well known for this method of protest, called *satyagraha* (meaning "firmness in truth").

Back in India in 1915, Gandhi organized a movement of the people against the British government there. After World War I, Indian nationalists fought what would be a long and sometimes bitter struggle for political independence. While Gandhi's protests took the form of nonviolent campaigns of civil disobedience, such as boycotts and hunger strikes, he was more than once arrested by the authorities for causing disorder, as his actions inspired more extreme measures on the part of his followers, whose protests sometimes took the form of rioting.

Mohandas Karamchand Gandhi led the movement for Indian independence from the British Empire.

As a member and, later, the president of India's chief political party, the Indian National Congress, Gandhi led a fight to rid the country of its rigid caste system, which organizes Indian society into distinct classes and groups. In Gandhi's time, not only were there four varna, or social classes, but there was a fifth group of "untouchables," who ranked even below the lowest class of peasants and laborers. Improving the lot of the untouchables was of tantamount importance to Gandhi.

Beginning in 1937, Gandhi became less active in government, giving up his official roles, but he continued to be regarded as a leader of the independence movement. During World War II, he was arrested for demanding British withdrawal from the conflict. Released from prison in 1944, Gandhi was central to the postwar negotiations that in 1947 resulted in an independent India. A believer in the unity of humankind under one god, he remained tolerant to Christian and Muslim beliefs. Amid an outbreak of violence between Hindus and Muslims, Gandhi was on a prayer vigil in New Delhi when a Hindu fanatic fatally shot him in 1948.

How was India divided?

When calling for independence, Gandhi had wanted a united India, with Hindus and Muslims living together in peace. However, when the country of India was created in 1947, the land was divided into two countries: India for the Hindus and Pakistan for the Muslims. Pakistan was divided into two parts: East Pakistan and West Pakistan. Many millions of people had to relocate in the process, and there was much violence.

In 1970, a disastrous cyclone hit East Pakistan. In the wake of the storm, a civil war for independence broke out in 1971. Many people were victims of genocide and famine. A great humanitarian crisis developed. The former Beatle George Harrison held his famous Concert for Bangladesh in 1971 in New York City to raise money for the desperate people of the region, which had become the country of Bangladesh.

Who was Indira Gandhi?

Indira Gandhi served as prime minister of India from 1966 to 1977 and from 1980 to 1984.

After India achieved independence in 1947, the country's first prime minister was Jawaharlal Nehru (1889–1964), who had been a follower of Mohandas Gandhi. During his entire tenure (1947–1964) as leader of India, Nehru was assisted by his only child, Indira (1917–1984), who in 1942 married a man named Feroze Gandhi (no relation to Mohandas Gandhi). Indira Gandhi took an active role in India's national affairs. After her father died, she went on to become prime minister in 1966.

However, hers was a troubled tenure. Found guilty of employing illegal election practices, Gandhi's political opponents ousted her in 1977. Determined to return to power, she was reelected to Parliament in 1980 and again served as prime minister until her death in 1984. She was assassinated by two of her own security guards, Sikhs who were motivated by religious reasons. Her son and successor, Rajiv Gandhi (1944–1991), was also assassinated in 1991.

Who is the current prime minister of India?

Narendra Modi (1950–) is the current prime minister of India (since 2014). During his time in office, he has fought corruption. Modi has taken a conservative approach by investing money in the economy while reducing spending on health care and social welfare programs. He also weakened or removed labor and environmental laws. He has made it harder for workers to unionize.

Modi has remained controversial. He has promoted Hindu nationalism. However, the non-Hindus in India, especially Muslims, feel threatened and marginalized. Some have experienced violence by Hindus. Lastly, a new law passed granting citizenship to people who entered India illegally, fleeing from persecution; however, Muslims were excluded.

PHILOSOPHY

What is philosophy?

Philosophy comes from the Greek words *philo*, meaning "love of," and *sophia*, meaning "wisdom." Thus, philosophy is literally a love of wisdom. In practice, it is the pursuit of understanding the human condition—how, why, and what it means to exist or to be. Philosophers use methods such as observation and questioning to discern the truth. Philosophy is traditionally divided between Eastern thought, originating mostly in India and China, and Western thought, coming mostly from Europe and North America.

Western thought consists of five branches: metaphysics (concerned with the nature of the universe or of reality); logic (the laws of reasoning); epistemology (the nature of knowledge and the process by which knowledge is gained); ethics (the moral values or rules that influence human conduct); and aesthetics (the nature of beauty or the criteria for art).

How old is philosophy?

Philosophy, apart from religion, emerged in the East and the West at about the same time—about 600 B.C.E. It was then that thinkers in Greece began questioning the nature of existence and scholars in China, particularly Confucius and Lao-Tzu, began teaching. Western philosophy is divided into three major periods: ancient philosophy (c. 600 B.C.E.– c. 400 C.E.); medieval philosophy (400s–1600s); and modern philosophy (since the 1600s). Chinese philosophy on how to live has had great influence over China and many surrounding Asian cultures up to the present. (It is covered in the "Asian History and Culture" chapter.)

ANCIENT PHILOSOPHY

Who was the first Greek philosopher?

Many claim that Thales of Miletus was the first major Greek philosopher. Born in 624 B.C.E., Thales was one of the "Seven Sages of Greece" (the others were Cleobulus, Solon, Chilon, Bias, Pittacus, and Periander). Thales discounted mythology and the Greek gods as the source of the universe; instead, he viewed water as the universal source of life and power. He believed that everything was composed of water. Although he was incorrect about water, he raised a question that is still investigated today: What is the one thing that makes up everything?

Like many other great philosophers, Thales was skilled in mathematics, using deductive reasoning to add to the world's understanding of geometry. Some sources credit Thales with successfully predicting a solar eclipse. He also was active in politics.

Who was Solon?

Solon was a Greek politician, philosopher, and poet often credited with creating democratic foundations in the Greek city of Athens. He criticized political and moral decline and sought to improve his world and that of his fellow Athenians. He was a legal reformer and sought to reduce the harshness of criminal punishments instituted by a previous leader named Draco (for whom the word "draconian" is named). Solon also instituted many economic reforms and sought to help those trapped in debt. (Note that reducing the harshness of criminal punishments and helping those in debt are important issues in America today.) Solon is credited with favoring moderation as a way to live one's life.

Who were the Sophists?

The Sophists were a group of Greek philosophers who were skilled in oratory (making speeches) and often charged fees to teach others rhetorical skills and increase their knowledge. According to their critics, they were more motivational speakers than deep thinkers. Leading Sophists included Protagoras, Gorgias, and Prodicus. Plato and Socrates disliked the Sophists, believing that they were not true philosophers. This may explain why the word "sophistry" today carries a negative connotation as the art of using weak arguments to mislead people.

Who are the "big three" ancient Greek philosophers?

Socrates (c. 470–399 B.C.E.), Plato (c. 428–347 B.C.E.), and Aristotle (384–322 B.C.E.) are considered the giants of ancient Greek philosophy.

Who was Socrates?

Although Socrates had many followers in his own time, his ideas and methods were controversial, which led him to be tried before judges and sentenced to death. He was charged with not worshipping the Athenian gods and for corrupting the young. Socrates was allowed to commit suicide by drinking the poison hemlock.

Except for his time in military service, Socrates lived his entire life in Athens, where he was as well known for his disheveled appearance as for his moral integrity, self-control, and quest for wisdom. He walked the streets of Athens, engaging people—including rulers who were supposed to be wiser than he—in conversation. In these conversations, he employed what came to be known as the "Socratic method" or dialectic, a series of seemingly simple questions designed to elicit a rational response.

Through the line of questioning, which usually centered around a moral concept, such as courage, the person being questioned was intended to realize that he did not truly know that which he thought he knew. Socrates's theory was that once

The Greek thinker Socrates was one of the primary founders of Western philosophy.

the person being questioned realized his weak understanding, he could divest himself of false notions and was then free to participate in the quest for knowledge.

These philosophical "disputes," however, gained Socrates many enemies.

Though he left no writings, one of Socrates's students, Plato, wrote down his recollections of the dialogues of Socrates. A staunch believer in self-examination and self-knowledge, Socrates is credited with saying that "the unexamined life is not worth living." Socrates also believed that the psyche (or "inner self") is what should give direction to one's life—not appetite or passions.

What was Plato's relationship to Socrates and Aristotle?

Plato was the disciple of Socrates and later the teacher of Aristotle. These three philosophers combined to lay the foundations of Western thought. Upset about the death of

---

In what popular 1980s movie did Socrates appear?

In *Bill and Ted's Excellent Adventure* (1989), starring Keanu Reeves, Alex Winter, and George Carlin, the title characters travel back in time to find historical figures such as Napoleon Bonaparte and Abraham Lincoln to help rescue their high school history presentation. Bill and Ted also bring Socrates, whom they mistakenly refer to as "Sew-crates." This is still an *excellent* movie that is fun to watch.

Socrates in 399, Plato left Athens and traveled throughout the Mediterranean. He returned to Athens in 387 B.C.E., and, one mile outside of the city, he established the Academy, a school of philosophy supported entirely by philanthropists; students paid no fees. One of the pupils there was a young Aristotle, who remained at the Academy for twenty years before venturing out on his own.

A detail of a fresco by the artist Raphael depicts the philosophers Plato and Aristotle, the next two generations to follow Socrates.

Plato wrote a series of dialogues in which Socrates does most of the talking. The most highly regarded of these is the *Republic*, in which Plato discusses justice and the ideal state. It was his belief that people would not be able to eliminate injustice from society until rulers became philosophers: "Until all philosophers are kings, or the kings and princes of this world have the spirit and power of philosophy, and political greatness and wisdom meet in one, and those commoner natures who pursue either to the exclusion of the other are compelled to stand aside, cities will never have rest from their evils—no, nor the human race." The problem for Plato was that kings and rulers were always promoting their self-interest and the interests of specific groups who benefited, while the rest of the population suffered. Plato thought that philosophers as kings would pursue those things that were good in themselves and would thus benefit the state and the people.

Plato's other works include *Symposium*, which considers ideal love; *Phaedrus*, which attacks the prevailing notions about rhetoric; *Apology*, which is a rendering of the speech Socrates delivered at his own trial in 399 B.C.E.; and *Phaedo*, which discusses the immortality of the soul and which is supposed to be a record of Socrates's last conversation before he drank hemlock and died.

What is Plato's theory of forms?

The theory of forms (also called the theory of ideas) is Greek philosopher Plato's expression of his belief that there are forms that exist outside the material realm and therefore are unchanging—they do not come into existence, change, or pass out of existence. It is these ideas that, according to Plato, are the objects or essence of knowledge. So, for example, there is the idea or form of a tree that exists separate from all the actual trees.

Furthermore, he held that the body, the seat of appetite and passion which communes with the physical world, is inferior to the intellect that communes with the world of ideas. He believed the physical aspect of human beings to be irrational, while the intellect, or reason, was deemed to be rational.

266

Did Aristotle develop his own philosophy?

Yes, despite having studied under Plato for twenty years, Aristotle developed his own philosophy in a different direction. Aristotle rejected Plato's theory of forms. While Aristotle, too, believed in material things and forms (the unchanging truths), unlike his teacher, he believed that it is the concrete things that have substantial being. Aristotle viewed the basic task of philosophy as explaining what things are and how they become what they are. It is for this reason that Aristotle had not only a profound and lasting influence on philosophy but also on science.

What does "epicurean" mean?

While "epicurean" has come to refer to anything relating to the pleasure of eating and drinking, it is an oversimplification of the beliefs of Greek philosopher Epicurus (341–270 B.C.E.), from whose name the word was derived. While Epicurus did believe that pleasure is the only good, and that it alone should be humankind's pursuit, in actuality, Epicurus defined pleasure not as unbridled sensuality but as freedom from pain and as peace of mind, which can only be obtained through simple living.

In about 306 B.C.E., Epicurus established a school in Athens, which came to be known as the Garden School because residents provided for their own food by gardening. There, he and his students strived to lead lives of simplicity, prudence, justice, and honor. In this way, they achieved tranquility—the ultimate goal in life, according to the philosophy of Epicureanism. He further believed that intellectual pleasures are superior to sensual pleasures, which are fleeting. In fact, he held that one of the greatest and most enduring pleasures is friendship. Greek philosopher and writer Lucretius (c. 99–c. 55 B.C.E.) put forth these ideas in his poem "On the Nature of Things." In more recent times, Thomas Jefferson (1743–1826), author and signatory of the Declaration of Independence and third president of the United States, was a self-proclaimed Epicurean.

What was Stoicism?

Stoicism was a philosophy that believed in celebrating virtue, avoiding vice, enduring trials and tribulations, and acquiring wisdom. Founded by Zeno of Cyprus in the late

What famous painting shows Plato and Aristotle?

In 1511, the famous Italian Renaissance painter Raphael (1483–1520) completed *The School of Athens*, which depicts all the famous thinkers, scientists, and philosophers of ancient Greece. In the center stand Plato and Aristotle. Plato, with the orange tunic, points up to the world of forms and ideas. Aristotle, in the blue tunic, reaches out toward the physical world in front of him that can be seen, touched, and described.

third century B.C.E., Stoicism was a remarkably durable philosophy that had many adherents, including the great Roman emperor Marcus Aurelius (121–180 C.E.)

Stoics valued not only wisdom but also bravery, justice, knowledge, and self-restraint. They sought to develop an *askesis*, a faculty that allows one to develop good judgment and an inner peace. They believed that happiness comes from acquiring wisdom and using sound reasoning to understand the workings of the world. Stoics often engaged in meditation and used the Socratic dialogue to test their beliefs and practices.

Stoics accepted that much of what happens to us in life is not in our control. However, one can control one's reactions to life events. One cannot avoid the bad things that happen, but one can control one's thinking and emotions so as not to suffer. Often, our thinking and feeling about what happens is the real source of our suffering.

MEDIEVAL PHILOSOPHY

What was the philosophy of the Middle Ages?

During the medieval period (800–1350), philosophers concerned themselves with applying the works of ancient Greek thinkers, such as Plato and then Aristotle, to Christian thought. This movement was called Scholasticism since its proponents were often associated with universities: the word "scholastic" is derived from the Greek *scholastikos*, meaning "to keep a school." In the simplest terms, the goal of Scholasticism has been described as "the Christianization of Aristotle." Medieval philosophers strived to use reason to better understand their religious faith. Scholasticism was both rational and religious.

Why was Augustine important for medieval philosophy?

Christian medieval philosophers were greatly influenced by earlier writer Augustine (354–430), who lived in North Africa during a time when the last vestiges of the pagan world of the Romans were giving way to Christianity. His theological works, including sermons, books, and pastoral letters, reveal the influence of Plato. Augustine believed that understanding can

Augustine of Hippo (aka St. Augustine) is regarded as one of the greatest philosophers of medieval Europe. Influenced by Plato and the Stoics, St. Augustine's writings on topics like human will and ethics would impact later philosophers, such as Nietzsche, Schopenhauer, and Kierkegaard.

lead one to faith and that faith can lead a person to understanding. His most important writing is called the *Confessions*.

How do you pronounce the name of Augustine?

Roman Catholics call him a saint and tend to put the accent on the first syllable of his name and pronounce the last syllable as "teen," which is how most people pronounce the city named after him: St. Augustine, Florida. Protestants, however, tend to put the accent on the second syllable and pronounce the last syllable as "tin." Many Protestants also drop the saint title.

Who was Anselm of Canterbury?

Anselm is often called the "Father of Scholasticism." He wrote three important works: *Monologion* (the Monologue), *Proslogion* (the Discourse), and *Cur Deus Homo* (Why God Was a Man). He tackled two important questions: Can reason be used to prove the existence of God? Why was the Incarnation necessary? In other words, why did God have to become human in Jesus?

Anselm proposed an argument to prove the existence of God. It would later be called the "ontological argument." God is that which nothing greater can be conceived. According to the *Oxford Dictionary of the Christian Church* (Oxford University Press, 1983): "If we were to suppose that God did not exist we should be involved in a contradiction since we could at once conceive of an entity greater than a non-existing God—an existing God."

According to Anselm, God is the greatest thing we can imagine. Then, he assumes it is better to exist than to not exist. Thus, if one says that God, the greatest thing one can imagine, does not exist, someone could respond that that is not the greatest thing a person could imagine. The greatest thing one could imagine is a god who does exist.

Some people get Anselm's argument; some people do not. His idea is that for God to be the greatest thing, God would have to exist. Some criticize Anselm's argument as being just a play on words.

St. Thomas Aquinas is most renowned for his seminal work the *Summa theologiae*, a comprehensive overview of Catholic theological teachings originally intended for students.

Who was Thomas Aquinas?

Thomas Aquinas (1224–1274) was one of the most influential Christian theologians of the Middle Ages. The most important writing of Thomas Aquinas was his *Summa Theologiae*, a comprehensive overview of all the Christian theological topics of the time. Aquinas is particularly important for integrating the thought of Greek philosopher Aristotle with Christian thought. In the 1500s, during the Protestant Reformation in Europe, many Protestant writers rejected the teachings of Aquinas.

Who were the great Islamic philosophers of the Middle Ages?

At the same time that the Christian scholastic philosophers lived and wrote, several important Islamic philosophers were also making important contributions to philosophy. During the Middle Ages, three thinkers of the Islamic world stood out as important interpreters of Greek thought and, therefore, as a bridge between ancient philosophy and the Scholasticism of the Middle Ages: their Latin names are Avennasar, Averroës, and Avicenna.

Avennasar (c. 878–950), who studied with Christian Aristotelians in Baghdad (Iraq), proved so adept at applying the teachings of Aristotle to Muslim thought that he became known as "the second Aristotle" or "the second teacher." He posited that philosophy and religion are not in conflict with each other; rather, they parallel one another.

Known for his work in interpreting the great Aristotle for the Muslim world, Avicenna (980–1037) is sometimes referred to as "the third teacher." He was also the first to expand the distinction between essence and existence.

Averroës (1126–1198) also was no stranger to Aristotle, writing commentaries on him as well as on Plato. Averroes also wrote on religious law and philosophy as well as religion and logic.

Some people are surprised to learn about these Muslim philosophers. However, in the Middle Ages, the Muslim world was ahead of Europe in translating Greek philosophers and in the study of medicine, navigation, mathematics, and science. Notice that the word "algebra" is an Arabic word and that our numbers 1, 2, 3, etc., are called "Arabic numerals."

Who was Maimonides?

Moses ben Maimon, known as Maimonides (c. 1135–1204), was a Jewish philosopher, scholar, and writer on the Torah (Jewish Law). Born in Cordoba in what today is Spain, he lived in Morocco and Egypt. He wrote a significant work on philosophy called *The Guide for the Perplexed*.

Which philosopher of the Renaissance period contributed much to philosophy and political science?

Niccolò Machiavelli (1469–1527), a native of Florence, Italy, was a master of political philosophy who had an indelible impact on many Western political leaders. In his most famous work, *The Prince*, Machiavelli described how rulers must use any means necessary to attain and keep power. There is much of an "ends justifies the means" rationalization in Machiavelli's political philosophy.

Machiavelli was not trying to describe how things should work or how we want them to work in the political realm. Rather, he was trying to tell how things actually work in the real world. He was trying to be honest about political power. This honesty and candidness is what people love and hate about Machiavelli.

For example, he thought a ruler should only tell the truth when it benefited the ruler, but the ruler should lie when necessary. He also believed that although a ruler should act like he is religious and moral, the ruler should always be ready to act immorally if that was what was needed to further his power.

Machiavelli thought that it was better for a ruler to be feared by his subjects than to be loved by them. If they feared the ruler, the ruler was in control. If the ruler was dependent on the love of the subjects, then he was dependent on them, and they could stop loving the ruler at any time.

Who was Sir Thomas More?

Sir Thomas More (1478–1535) was an English politician, lawyer, and philosopher best known for his relationship with King Henry VIII and for writing *Utopia*. More served as an adviser to the king and served as chancellor. He opposed Henry VIII's separation from the Catholic Church and the king's elevation of himself as the head of the Church of England. For his political heresy, More was executed by beheading. For this reason, many view More as a martyr.

In *Utopia*, More described an ideal state in which the needs of the people were placed above the needs of the privileged few. Many see the work as an attempt by More to criticize aspects of British life in his time.

What is the "doctrine of idols"?

This was a phrase used by English philosopher Sir Francis Bacon (1561–1626) in his written attack on the widespread acceptance of the traditional concepts used in philosophy, theology, and explanations of the natural world. In his 1620 work, *Novum Organum*, Bacon vehemently argues that human progress is held back by adherence to certain concepts, which we do not question. By hanging on to these concepts, or "idols," we may proceed in error in our thinking. In holding to notions accepted as true, we run the danger of dismissing any new notion, a tendency Bacon characterized as arrogance. To combat these obstacles, Bacon advocated a method of persistent inquiry. He believed that humans could understand nature only by carefully observing it with the help of instruments. He went on to describe scientific experimentation as an organized endeavor that should involve many scientists and that requires the support of leaders. Thus, Bacon is credited with no less than formulating modern scientific thought.

271

Why is René Descartes considered the "Father of Modern Philosophy"?

French mathematician and philosopher René Descartes (1596–1650) was living in Holland in 1637 when he published his first major work, *Discourse on Method*. In this treatise, he extends mathematical methods to science and philosophy, asserting that all knowledge is the product of clear reasoning based on self-evident premises. This idea, that there are certitudes, provided the foundation for modern philosophy, which dates from the 1600s to the present.

Considered one of the founders of modern philosophy, French mathematician and scientist René Descartes is often remembered for his famous quote "I think, therefore I am."

Descartes may best be known for the familiar phrase "I think, therefore I am" (*Cogito ergo sum* in Latin). This assertion is based on his theory that only one thing cannot be doubted, and that is doubt itself. The next logical conclusion is that the doubter (thinker) must, therefore, exist. In other words, "If I am doubting, I must be thinking. If I am thinking, I must exist to do the thinking."

The correlation to the concept ("I think, therefore I am") is dualism, the doctrine that reality consists of mind and matter. Since the thinker thinks and is, he or she is both mind (idealism) and body (matter, or material). Descartes concluded that mind and body are independent of each other, and he formulated theories about how they work together.

Descartes's other major works include *Meditations on First Philosophy* (1641), which is his most famous, and *Principles of Philosophy* (1644). His philosophy became known as Cartesianism (from *Cartesius*, the Latin form of his name).

Who was Thomas Hobbes?

Hobbes (1588–1679) was a seminally important English political philosopher who wrote about social contract theory, the sinfulness of the human condition, and the brutality of modern life. He is known for explaining that man in a state of nature will lead to destruction and anarchy. Therefore, man must set up the state to establish order and protect man from himself.

Hobbes explained much of his political philosophy in his work *The Leviathan*, which was influenced by the chaos of the English Civil War (1642–1651). He argues that man's sinful and anarchic nature can be overcome only with a strong, central government. One of the most oft-cited passages from the book is his pessimistic take on human life without such a government: "the life of man, solitary, poor, nasty, brutish, and short."

MODERN PHILOSOPHY

What was the Enlightenment?

The Enlightenment, which is also referred to as the Age of Reason, was a period when European philosophers emphasized the use of reason as the best method for learning the truth. The term "enlightenment" comes from the idea of seeing something clearly in the light. Here, it refers to seeing truth and reaching understanding through reason.

Beginning in the 1600s and lasting through the 1700s, philosophers such as Jean-Jacques Rousseau (1712–1778), Voltaire (1694–1778), and John Locke (1632–1704) explored issues in education, law, and politics. They published their thoughts, issuing attacks on social injustice, religious superstition, and ignorance. Their ideas fanned the fires of the American and French revolutions in the late 1700s.

Hallmarks of the Age of Reason include the idea of the universal truth (two plus two always equals four, for example); the belief that nature is vast and complex but well ordered; the belief that humankind possesses the ability to understand the universe; the philosophy of Deism, which holds that God created the world and then left it alone; and the concept of the rational will, which posits that humans make their own choices and plans and, therefore, do not have a fate thrust upon them. The philosophies put forth during the Age of Reason were critical to the development of Western thought.

René Descartes (1596–1650), who refused to believe anything unless it could be proved, perhaps best expressed the celebration of individual reason during this era. His statement "I think, therefore I am" sums up the feelings of skeptical and rational inquiry that characterized intellectual thought during this era.

Which Enlightenment thinker particularly influenced Thomas Jefferson?

John Locke's writings greatly influenced several of the Founding Fathers, most notably Thomas Jefferson. Locke wrote *Essay Concerning Human Understanding* and *Two Treatises of Government*. His explanation of natural law and the social contract are key progenitors of Jefferson's ideas, reflected in the Declaration of Independence. Locke believed that the government should protect the rights of the people. Jefferson identified this in the Declaration of Independence by declaring that people have certain "inalienable rights," including "Life, Liberty and the pursuit of Happiness."

English physician and philosopher John Locke is considered the founder of Liberalism, the political philosophy concerned with civil liberties that heavily impacted the beliefs of Thomas Jefferson and other Americans.

273

Are the Enlightenment and the scientific revolution the same?

The two terms describe interrelated and sequential European intellectual movements that took place from the 1500s to the 1800s. Together, the movements shaped an era that would lay the foundations of modern western civilization, foundations that required the use of reason, or rational thought, to understand the universe, nature, and human relations. During this period, many of the greatest minds in Europe developed new scientific, mathematical, philosophical, and social theories.

Scientists came to believe that observation and experimentation would allow them to discover the laws of nature. Thus, the scientific method emerged, which required tools. Soon, the microscope, thermometer, sextant, slide rule, and other instruments were invented. Scientists working during this time included Sir Isaac Newton (1642–1727), Joseph Priestley (1733–1804), and René Descartes (1596–1650). The era witnessed key discoveries and saw rapid advances in astronomy, anatomy, mathematics, and physics. The advances had an impact on education. Universities introduced science courses to the curricula, and elementary and secondary schools followed suit. As people became trained in science, new technologies emerged; complicated farm machinery and new equipment for textile manufacturing and transportation were developed, paving the way for the Industrial Revolution.

What is empiricism?

Empiricism is the philosophical concept that experience, which is based on observation and experimentation, is the source of knowledge. According to empiricism, the information that a person gathers with his or her senses is the information that should be used to make decisions without regard to reason or to either religious or political authority. The philosophy gained credibility with the rise of experimental science in the eighteenth and nineteenth centuries, and it continues to be the outlook of many scientists today.

There are three key figures who developed this philosophical approach:

- English philosopher John Locke (1632–1704) asserted that there are no such things as innate ideas: the mind is born blank, and all knowledge is derived from human experience.

- Irish clergyman George Berkeley (1685–1753) believed that nothing exists except through the perception of the individual and that it is the mind of God that makes possible the apparent existence of material objects.

- Scottish philosopher David Hume (1711–1776) took the doctrine of empiricism to the next level: skepticism. We can never know anything for sure. Human knowledge is restricted to the experience of ideas and impressions and therefore cannot be verified as true.

Who was Montesquieu?

Charles-Louis, Baron de Montesquieu (1689–1755) was a French political philosopher credited with advocating a strong belief in the separation of powers between different branches of the government. His philosophy directly influenced many of the Founding Fathers of the fledging United States of America—a country that adopted Montesquieu's philosophy of separation of powers into the U.S. Constitution.

He was well known for his beliefs in legal relativism, that what is good for one may not be good for another. He believed that rulers often must adapt to changing conditions in society and be flexible in their response.

Who was Jean-Jacques Rousseau?

Jean-Jacques Rousseau (1712–1778) was another famous French philosopher, best known for his work *The Social Contract*. Unlike Thomas Hobbes, Rousseau believed in the inherent goodness of man and warned that it was the government that often served as the evil in the world. He lived at a time of authoritarian kings who denied the rights of common people. Rousseau believed that men were born equal and were entitled to freedom and the opportunity for individual self-fulfillment. He wrote: "Man is born free and everywhere he is in chains." He also advocated for a better system of education and warned against authoritarian governments. He is perhaps best known for his writings on equality.

Who is Immanuel Kant? Why is he relevant today?

Immanuel Kant (1724–1804) remains one of the great modern thinkers because he developed a whole new philosophy, one that completely reinterpreted human knowledge. A professor at Germany's Königsberg University, Kant lectured widely and was a prolific writer. His most important work came somewhat late in life—after 1775. It was in that year that he undertook "a project of critical philosophy," in which he aimed to answer the three questions that, in his opinion, have occupied every philosopher in Western history: What can I know? What ought I do? For what may I hope?

Kant's answer to the first question (What can I know?) was based on one important conclusion: What a person can know or make claims about is only his or her experience of things, not the things in themselves. The philosopher arrived at this conclusion by observing the certainty of math and science, and he determined that the fundamental nature of human reality (metaphysics) does not rely on or yield the genuine knowledge of science and math. For example, Newton's law of inertia—a body at rest tends to remain at rest, and a body in motion tends to remain in motion— does not change based on human experience. The law of inertia is universally recognized as correct and, as such, is a "pure" truth, which can be relied on. But human reality, argued Kant, does not rest on any such certainties. That which a person has not experienced with his or her senses cannot be known absolutely. Kant therefore reasoned that free will cannot be proved or disproved—nor can the existence of God.

Even though what humans can know is extremely limited, Kant did not become skeptical. On the contrary, he asserted that "unknowable things" require a leap of faith. He further concluded that since no one can disprove the existence of God, objections to

275

religion carry no weight. In this way, Kant answered the third question posed by philosophers: For what may I hope?

After arriving at the conclusion that each person experiences the world according to his or her own internal laws, Kant began writing on the problem of ethics, answering the second question (What ought I do?). In 1788, he published the *Critique of Practical Reason*, asserting that there is a moral law, which he called the "categorical imperative." Kant argued that a person could test the morality of his or her action by asking if the person was willing for his or her action to become a universal rule applicable to all people: "Act as if the maxim (rule) from which you act were to become through your will a universal law."

For example, is a thief acting morally? A thief might justify his or her stealing, but typically, he or she is not willing to

German philosopher Immanuel Kant was the founder of transcendental idealism, the idea that we do not recognize the outside world as it really is but only as it appears to us through our sensibilities.

make stealing a universal rule such that someone could steal from him or her. Therefore, he or she is not acting morally when he or she steals. Honest people act morally because they are willing to let the rule "speak honestly" and become a universal moral law. Kant concluded that when a person's actions conformed to this "categorical imperative," then he or she was doing his or her duty, which would result in goodwill.

Kant's theories have remained relevant to philosophy for more than two centuries. Modern thinkers have either furthered the school of thought that Kant initiated, or they have rejected it. Either way, the philosopher's influence is still felt. It's interesting to note that among his writings is an essay on political theory (*Perpetual Peace*), which first appeared in 1795. In it, Kant described a federation that would work to prevent international conflict; the League of Nations and the United Nations, created more than a century after Kant, are the embodiments of this idea.

What is the Hegelian dialectic?

It is the system of reasoning put forth by German philosopher Georg Hegel (1770–1831), Kant's most well-known protégé, who theorized that at the center of the universe, there is an absolute spirit that guides all reality. According to Hegel, all historical developments follow three basic laws. First, each event follows a necessary course (in other words, it could not have happened in any other way); each historical event represents not only change but progress. Second, each historical event, or phase, tends to be replaced by its opposite. And third, this opposite is later replaced by a resolution of the two extremes.

This third law of Hegel's dialectic is the "pendulum theory" discussed by scholars and students of history. It says that events swing from one extreme to the other before the pendulum comes to rest in the middle. The extreme phases are called the thesis and the antithesis; the resolution is called the synthesis. Based on this system, Hegel asserted that human beings can comprehend the unfolding of history.

The next important movement is existentialism. Why is it called existentialism?

Existentialism starts by thinking about human existence. This contrasts with thinkers such as Thomas Aquinas, who began by proving the existence of God and then drawing conclusions about how to live based on a belief in God. Existentialists, by starting with human existence, note that the meaning and purpose of life are not obvious. In fact, life often seems meaningless and even cruel.

Existentialists then point out that rational thought cannot prove the existence of God. We cannot know for certain that God exists. At this point, different types of existentialism emerge. Some existentialists move toward atheism, which claims there is no God. Others go to the opposite position that although the existence of God cannot be proven, there can be faith in the existence of God. Faith is essential since proof of God is impossible. Thus, there are several kinds of existentialists.

Some, like Jean-Paul Sartre (1905–1980) and Albert Camus (1913–1960), were atheists. Others, such as Søren Kierkegaard (1813–1855), were believers. Kierkegaard rejected the principles put forth by traditional philosophers such as Georg Hegel, who had considered philosophy as a science, asserting that it is both objective and certain. Kierkegaard overturned this assertion, citing that truth is not objective but rather subjective; that there is no such thing as universal truths; and that human existence is not understandable in scientific terms. He maintained that human beings must make their own choices based on their own knowledge.

Existentialists grappled with the dilemma that human beings must use their free will to make decisions—and assume responsibility for those decisions—without knowing conclusively what is true or false, right or wrong, good or bad. In other words, there is no way of knowing absolutely what the correct choices are, and yet, individuals must make choices all the time and be held accountable for them. Sartre described this as a "terrifying freedom."

However, theologians such as American Paul Tillich (1886–1965) reconsidered the human condition in light of Christianity, arriving at far less pessimistic conclusions than did Sartre. For example, Tillich asserted that "divine answers" exist. Similarly, Jewish philosopher Martin Buber (1878–1965), who was also influenced by Kierkegaard, proposed that a personal and direct dialogue between the individual and God yields truths.

Who was Friedrich Nietzsche? What was his concept of the "will to power"?

German philosopher Friedrich Nietzsche (1844–1900) developed many theories of human behavior, and the will to power was one of these. While other philosophers (including the ancient Greek Epicurus) argued that humans are motivated by a desire to experience pleasure, Nietzsche asserted that it was neither pleasure nor the avoidance of pain that inspires humankind but rather the desire for strength and power. He argued that in order to gain power, humans would even be willing to embrace pain.

However, it's critical to note that he did not view this will to power strictly as a will to dominate others: Nietzsche glorified a superman or "overman" (übermensch), an individual who could assert power over himself (or herself). He viewed artists as one example of an overman—since that person successfully harnesses his or her instincts through creativity and, in so doing, has actually achieved a higher form of power than would the person who only wishes to dominate others.

Friedrich Nietzsche's concept of the superman is a person who asserts power over themselves without regard to social mores, a concept corrupted by the Nazis to justify their actions against Jews and other minorities.

Who was Jeremy Bentham?

Jeremy Bentham (1748–1832) was an English philosopher associated with utilitarianism and the pursuit of pleasure and avoidance of pain. He disagreed with the concept of natural law.

Utilitarianism represents the core belief that the best course of action is the one that produces the most overall happiness. He believed that politicians and public policy in general should serve the interests of the common good and the greatest number of people. He believed in the "greatest amount of happiness for the greatest number."

Bentham was also an important legal reformer who advocated for the separation of church and state, abolition of the death penalty, and equal rights for women.

Who was John Stuart Mill?

John Stuart Mill (1806–1873) was an English philosopher associated with the philosophy of utilitarianism. In fact, in his book *Utilitarianism*, Mill articulated the "greatest happiness principle"—that people should act to produce the greatest total happiness in society, within reason. Mill distinguished between higher and lower forms of happiness. The writings of Bentham and Mill helped to promote the idea that governments should work for what is best for most people and not just promote the interests of the wealthy and powerful.

Mill may be best known for his work *On Liberty* (1841), which is often seen as a progenitor of modern American thought regarding individual liberty and freedom of

What happened to Jeremy Bentham's body?

Bentham wanted to support the development of medical science, which required the use of human cadavers (dead bodies) so doctors could learn through dissection. At that time, there was no system for providing such human bodies. Unfortunately, a black market developed for bodies that were sometimes stolen from graves, or people, such as the homeless, would be murdered so that their bodies could be sold. (The story in Mark Twain's famous book *Tom Sawyer* is built around such a grave robbery.) Bentham encouraged people to donate their bodies, and he set an example by donating his. After his body was used for science, it was stuffed and preserved and put in a glass case. (Do an online image search for "Jeremy Bentham body.")

speech. Mill believed that the government should not censor speech, even false speech, but should allow it to collide with truth and show its errors to society.

Who was Bertrand Russell?

Bertrand Russell (1872–1970) was an English philosopher and Nobel laureate who was arguably the most influential philosopher of the twentieth century. In his early works, he focused more on mathematics, like many of the early Greek philosophers.

He wrote *The Problems of Philosophy*, where he attacked idealism and advanced a theory of empiricism and realism. He advocated a system that he called "logical analysis," where concepts are examined at their roots or atoms to understand their merit and place in the world. He was well known for his politics and his pacifism—including an arrest at a nuclear power plant at the age of eighty-nine. Russell lived to the ripe old age of ninety-eight, making him perhaps the oldest of all famous philosophers.

PHILOSOPHY AND GOVERNMENT

What is natural law?

Natural law is the theory that some laws are fundamental to human nature, and, as such, they can only be known through human reason—without reference to man-made law. Roman orator and philosopher Cicero (106–43 B.C.E.) insisted that natural law is universal, meaning it is binding to governments and people everywhere.

What is the social contract?

The social contract is the concept that human beings have made a deal with their government, and within the context of that agreement, both the government and the people have distinct roles. The theory is based on the idea that humans abandoned a natural free and ungoverned condition in favor of a society that provides them with order, structure, and, very importantly, protection.

Through the ages, many philosophers have considered the role of both the government and its citizens within the context of the social contract. In the theories of English philosophers John Locke (1632–1704) and his predecessor, Thomas Hobbes (1588–1679), the social contract was inextricably tied to natural law (the theory that some laws are fundamental to human nature). Locke argued that people first lived in a state of nature, where they had no restrictions on their freedom. Realizing that conflict arose as each individual defended his or her own rights, the people agreed to live under a common government, which offered them protection. But in doing so, they had not abandoned their natural rights.

On the contrary, argued Locke, the government should protect the rights of the people—particularly the rights of life, liberty, and property. Locke put these ideas into print, publishing his two most influential works in 1690: *Essay Concerning Human Understanding* and *Two Treatises of Government*. These works firmly established him as the leading "philosopher of freedom."

Why are Thomas Paine's philosophies important to democratic thought?

English political philosopher and author Thomas Paine (1737–1809) believed that a democracy is the only form of government that can guarantee natural rights. Paine arrived in the American colonies in 1774. Two years later, he wrote *Common Sense*, a pamphlet that galvanized public support for the American Revolution (1775–1783), which was already underway.

During the struggle for independence, Paine wrote and distributed a series of sixteen papers called *Crisis*, upholding the rebels' cause in their fight. Paine penned his words in the language of common speech, which helped his message reach a mass audience in America and elsewhere. He soon became known as an advocate of individual freedom.

In 1791 and 1792, Paine, now back in England, released *The Rights of Man*, a work in which he defended the cause of the French Revolution (1789–1799) and appealed to the British people to overthrow their monarchy. For this, he was tried and convicted of treason in his homeland. Escaping to Paris, the philosopher

Thomas Paine's *Common Sense* encouraged support for the American Revolution.

280

became a member of the revolutionary National Convention. But during the Reign of Terror (1793–1794) of revolutionary leader Maximilien Robespierre (1758–1794), Paine was imprisoned for being English.

An American minister interceded on Paine's behalf, insisting that Paine was actually an American. Paine was released on this technicality. He remained in Paris until 1802 and then returned to the United States. Though he played an important role in the American Revolution by boosting the morale of the colonists, he nevertheless lived his final years as an outcast and in poverty. Part of his unpopularity in his later years was that he opposed slavery when many supported it, and he was very critical of organized religion.

Who was Michel Foucault?

French postmodernist philosopher Michel Foucault (1926–1984) had little use for Marxism as a political philosophy that explained the history of the world. Foucault devoted much of his career to being a philosophical relativist, showing that truth has changed quite mightily through the ages.

Foucault also wrote about penal systems, the failures of psychology, and sexuality. He attacked many attempts at curing the mentally ill and rehabilitating the prisoner, as he felt that prisons were inhumane institutions. Early in his life, his sexuality caused him distress and led to several suicide attempts. Foucault died of AIDS in 1984.

What is Marxism?

Marxism is an economic and political theory named for its originator, Karl Marx (1818–1883). Marx was a German social philosopher and revolutionary who met another German philosopher, Friedrich Engels (1820–1895), in Paris in 1844, beginning a long collaboration. Four years later, they wrote *The Communist Manifesto*, laying the foundation for socialism and communism. The cornerstone of Marxism, to which Engels greatly contributed, is the belief that history is determined by economics.

Based on this premise, Marx asserted that economic crises will result in increased poverty, which, in turn, will inspire the working class (proletariat) to revolt, ousting the capitalists (bourgeoisie). According to Marx, once the working class has seized control, it will institute a system of economic cooperation and a classless society. In his most influential work, *Das Kapital* (*Capital: A Critique of Political Economy*), an exhaustive analysis of capitalism published in three volumes (1867, 1885, and 1894), Marx predicted the failure of the capitalist system based on his belief that the history of society is "the history of class struggle." He and Engels viewed an international revolution as inevitable.

RELIGION

What are the major world religions?

The major religions of the world include Hinduism, Buddhism, Judaism, Christianity, Islam, and Sikhism. These are described below. A few smaller religions are also covered. The religious tradition of China is described in the "Asian History and Culture" chapter.

HINDUISM

What are the origins of Hinduism?

Along the Indus River (which today is in Pakistan), early Indian society developed many thousands of years ago along with a very diverse religion called Hinduism. The word "Hinduism" was, however, created by later Europeans to describe all the various religious groups and activities in India.

What is the caste system of traditional India?

The traditional Indian caste system consisted of four main groups:

- Brahmins: families of the priests and intellectuals
- Kshatriyas: families of the warriors and political leaders
- Vaisyas: families of the merchants and farmers
- Shudras: families of the servants

Another group also existed that was so low they were not part of the caste system: the "Outcasts." (The English word "outcast" comes from this.) The Outcasts were also called the Chandalas, Dalits, or Untouchables. In the past, many people would not even touch them. The category of Untouchable is no longer legally recognized. However, it still exists in some places, and Dalits often experience injustice, prejudice, and sometimes even violence.

What are the major Hindu writings?

- The Vedas: hymns to Hindu gods
- The Brahmanas: writings about sacrifice
- Two epic poems: the *Mahabharata* and the *Ramayana*
- The Upanishads: writings of Hindu philosophy

In the *Mahabharata,* a battle takes place between two brothers fighting for control of a kingdom. As the battle is about to begin, Lord Krishna gives a long lecture to the warrior Arjuna. This lecture about the meaning of life is often printed as a separate book: the *Bhagavad Gita.*

What is the Hindu belief in reincarnation?

Reincarnation is based on the Hindu belief that humans have souls and that when a person dies, the soul leaves that body and goes into another body, as described in a Hindu saying: "Just as the body sheds worn-out clothes, so the soul sheds worn-out bodies."

In Hindu belief, the soul is caught in a cycle of birth, death, rebirth, and then another death. Hindus call this cycle of continual rebirth and death *Samsara.* The big problem with this cycle is that in between birth and death, we suffer. For Hindus, the goal is to escape from *Samsara* and achieve release, which is called *moksha*, by reaching a state of enlightenment.

What is karma?

Karma guides reincarnation. Often, the term is used when people speak of "bad karma" and "good karma," as if the term meant "bad luck" and "good luck." However, that is not how Hindus understand the concept.

In Hindu belief, karma is the law of responsibility. Everyone is responsible for everything they do, think, or say. Everything bad a person does, thinks, or says will result in bad consequences: the person will suffer. Karma can affect multiple lives. If a person does not suffer in this life, he or she will suffer in future lives.

A person who does good in this life will experience good consequences in future lives. A person who does bad things and "gets away with it" in this life will still suffer in future lives.

A person's thoughts and speech also count, so it is not just actions that matter. An anger-filled person creates bad consequences even if the person keeps his anger inside and never acts on the anger.

What about the Hindu gods?

Hindus believe in thousands of different gods, with the three most important being Vishnu, Shiva, and Brahma. Across India, thousands of temples honor the various gods, and millions of homes have shrines where families pray to them. Certain people honor certain gods. For example, the monkey god Hanuman is a favorite of soldiers.

The three major Hindu gods (left to right), Vishnu, Shiva, and Brahma, are depicted in this tenth-century stone carving.

Although Hinduism looks like polytheism, which is the belief in many gods, it is not actually polytheism in the strict sense because the gods are not seen as separate beings; rather, the gods are manifestations or aspects of an ultimate reality called Brahman.

What is the Hindu understanding of Brahman?

Brahman is Ultimate Reality, but it is beyond understanding. Humans are bound by space, time, and causality, but Brahman is not. Many monotheists believe their god has personhood, awareness, and memory and describe a "personal relationship with God." In Hinduism, Brahman does not have such qualities.

As noted above, in Hinduism, all the various gods are seen as aspects or manifestations of Brahman. However, how does one worship a concept as vague as Brahman? Instead, Hindus worship and pray to the countless manifestations of Brahman: the various Hindu gods.

What are the Hindu concepts of *atman* and *maya*?

In Hindu thought, the gods are Brahman, but so is everything else: humans, animals, plants, and even the physical world. Everyone and everything are one. Hinduism is monism, which means everything is one. You and everyone else are Brahman. The Hindu word for the Brahman that is you is called *atman*.

285

But this raises questions: "If everything is one, then why do humans treat each other so badly?" "If we are part of Ultimate Reality, why do we hurt each other?" Hindus believe that we wrongly think we are all separate. We are caught in an illusion. If we are separate, we might falsely believe we benefit from others' losses. If you take my money, you have gained, and I have lost. In Hindu philosophy, however, you do not gain because you and I are one. Hindus call this illusion *maya*.

Maya is a tricky concept to understand. In Hindu thought, the idea that we are all separate is an illusion. The word "illusion" means the wrong way to see something. For Hindu, the correct way to see reality is that we are all one. But those who are not Hindus believe we are all separate from each other as well as separate from animals and physical things. For monotheists, God is a separate being. Indeed, for them, everything is separate. According to Hindu philosophy, in comparison, this is a completely wrong way to see the world.

What are the four paths or yogas of Hinduism?

In Hinduism, four paths exist to try to achieve *moksha* and release from the cycle of *Samsara*. However, achieving *moksha* is not easy, and it may take several lives.

- Karma yoga
- Bhakti yoga
- Jnana yoga
- Raja yoga

Karma yoga is based on doing one's duty but doing it with detachment. A person's caste and stage in life determine one's duty. The path of devotion to the gods, or to a particular god, is Bhakti yoga. In the third path, Jnana yoga—the intellectual path—devotees use meditation to overcome the illusion of *maya*. Raja yoga is the royal path, which is often chosen by holy men, who devote themselves to meditation and asceticism.

BUDDHISM

What are the origins of Buddhism?

The origin of Buddhism dates back to the man Siddhartha Gautama (c. 563–483 B.C.E.) After his birth, his parents received a prophecy that he would become either a great

---

What is the shortcut to achieve *moksha*?

Hindus believe that one can achieve *moksha* by dying in the sacred city of Benares. This is why sick people often go to Benares to die. Their bodies are cremated on the banks of the Ganges River, and their ashes are then put in the river.

king or a sage (a wise teacher). His parents did not want him to be a sage; they wanted a king, so they raised him in luxury in the palace with all his needs met. He married and had a son. Yet, he was deeply dissatisfied despite his life of luxury.

One day, Siddhartha left the palace to explore the world around him, and he saw four things: a decrepit old man, a sick man in pain, a dead body being taken to be cremated, and an ascetic monk. (An "ascetic" is one who chooses hardships, such as fasting.) Seeing such suffering for the first time, Siddhartha was deeply troubled. In time, he left his home to go seek answers to his questions "Why do we suffer?". and "What can we do to not suffer?" Because he renounced and gave up everything, this period of his life is called the "Great Renunciation."

Although Siddhartha tried Hindu philosophy, he found no answers in it. He

Born to an aristocratic family, Siddhartha Gautama decided to seek wisdom rather than material pleasures in his life. Finding that Hinduism did not satisfy him, he eventually founded his own school of belief, which became Buddhism.

tried denying the body's needs by practicing extreme fasting as an ascetic monk, yet he again found no answers. After several years, he finally gave up and sat down under a Bodhi tree to wait for enlightenment. He sat and waited, and then he got the answers to his questions "Why do we suffer?" and "What can we do to not suffer?" Siddhartha became the Buddha, which means the "Enlightened One." The Four Noble Truths are his answers.

What are the Four Noble Truths of Buddhism?

The core of Buddhist teaching is the Four Noble Truths:

1. Life inevitably involves suffering
2. The cause of suffering is desire
3. To eliminate suffering, eliminate desire
4. To eliminate desire, follow the Eightfold Path

Life inevitably involves suffering. (*Dukkha* is the word for suffering.) Suffering is part of life. We suffer physically, psychologically, and emotionally; to live is to suffer. And it is often very intense. One cause of suffering is *anicca,* impermanence: nothing is permanent. Although we want good things to last, they do not. Family and friends go away or die; our possessions wear out. Even health does not last, as we grow old and die. We suffer because we wish things would last.

The cause of suffering is desire. (*Tanha* is the word for desire.) This idea has several levels of meaning. First, we suffer when we desire things we cannot get, so we become unhappy. Many people can recall being disappointed as a child because they did not get the holiday gift they desperately desired. However, the opposite also happens: we get what we desired but are disappointed by it.

Furthermore, our strong desires cause us to suffer. Addictions can cause great suffering. It can be misery to desperately want something we cannot get.

Since Buddhists believe in reincarnation, there is a further problem with desire: it drives the cycle of birth, death, and rebirth. First, sexual desire drives the cycle by causing humans to be born. Second, when we die, our desires do not disappear. Our desires want to get into a new body so they can seek what they desire.

To eliminate suffering, eliminate desire. The third Noble Truth logically follows from the first two Truths.

To eliminate desire, follow the Eightfold Path. In Buddhism, there are eight principles to help overcome desire.

What are the elements of the Eightfold Path?

- Right View: having the right view of reality
- Right Intention: dedicating oneself to pursuing enlightenment
- Right Speech: avoiding bad speech, such as gossiping or telling lies
- Right Action: avoiding acts of stealing and violence
- Right Livelihood: avoiding any jobs that involve killing of animals or humans
- Right Effort: avoiding negative states of mind
- Right Mindfulness: being aware of what one's mind is doing
- Right Concentration: practicing meditation

What are the two major divisions of Buddhism?

Theravada Buddhism and Mahayana Buddhism are the two major divisions of Buddhism.

What is Theravada Buddhism?

This form of Buddhism is also called "The Way of the Elders" because it is closest to the way the Buddha lived. One must leave ordinary life and become a monk in order to over-

What is the concept of nirvana?

In Buddhism, the goal is to eliminate all desires to achieve a state of bliss called nirvana. An *arhat*, or saint, is one who has achieved this nirvana. Once one reaches nirvana, there will be no reincarnation after one's death.

come desire. Monks give up careers, families, possessions, and money. In a Buddhist monastery, one gives up everything.

As a sign of giving up the outside world, the heads of Buddhist monks are shaved. Since hair is one of the ways we express our identity and individuality, a shaved head is also about giving up one's identity.

Buddhist monks, in trying to overcome all desire, spend their days in meditation. Overcoming desire is difficult. Each day, Buddhist monks walk through nearby neighborhoods, where the people offer food to support them.

According to Theravada Buddhist tradition, the Buddha was an enlightened man but nothing more; he was not a god. The Buddha is an example to follow. In this tradition, it is hard to achieve nirvana.

What is Mahayana Buddhism?

In Mahayana Buddhism, many people can achieve nirvana because they can get help. Thus, this form of Buddhism is called "the Great Boat" or "the Great Raft." Mahayana Buddhists see the Buddha as a divine being; the Buddha who walked on Earth is viewed as an incarnation of a divine Buddha essence. Believers also get help from Bodhisattvas: people in the past who achieved buddhahood. One can pray to such beings.

JUDAISM

What is Judaism?

The religion and culture of Judaism has had a great influence on the world, although there are only about fourteen million Jews today. The word "Jew" is used for both followers of the religion of Judaism and for nonreligious people of Jewish heritage.

Judaism is a monotheistic religion that says there is one god. The Jewish name for God in English is written as YHWH, pronounced "Yahweh." The Hebrew word consists of the four consonants יהוה. (Ancient languages did not have vowels.) Out of respect for God and to follow the commandment "You shall not take the name of the Lord in vain," many observant Jews will not speak the name of God outside of prayer and Torah study. Also, many Jews do not write the word in a casual context and even object to printing the word as it is in this paragraph, so they will instead write the word "God" as "G-d."

At the core of Judaism is a belief that God chose the ancient people of Israel to be His people. The Israelites were not chosen for their greatness; rather, God chose them for their weakness and insignificance.

What is the Jewish Bible?

The Bible of the Jews can be called the Bible, the Jewish scriptures, the Hebrew scriptures, or the Tanakh. The Jewish Bible consists of three sections: the books of law, called the Torah; the books of the prophets, called the Nevi'im; and the books of writings, called the Ketuvim. The first letters of the names for these sections—T, N, and K—become the word "Tanakh."

How does the Jewish Bible compare to the Christian Bible?

The Christian Bible consists of the Old Testament and the New Testament. The Jewish Bible is the same writings as in the Old Testament (the Protestant version).

What happens in the Jewish Bible (the Christian Old Testament)?

The Jewish Bible opens with the Book of Genesis, which tells of the creation of Earth, the first humans (Adam and Eve), and Noah, who builds his ark to survive the flood. The stories of Abraham follow, which are set in about 1800 B.C.E., when God called Abraham to leave his home in

An illuminated page of a Spanish Tanakh, the Hebrew scriptures, from 1476. The Tanakh includes the Torah, the Nevi'im,, and the Ketuvim.

Mesopotamia (modern-day Iraq) and journey to the land of Canaan (roughly the area of (modern-day Israel and the Palestinian territories, Jordan, and the southern parts of Lebanon and Syria). God then made two promises to Abraham: 1) Abraham would have countless descendants, and 2) those descendants would live in the land of Canaan. At the time, Abraham and his wife Sarah were childless and only visitors in the land.

The next important events have to do with the story of Moses, which is set around 1300 B.C.E. Several hundred years had passed since the time of Abraham. Abraham did have many descendants by then, as promised, who would eventually become the twelve tribes of Israel. However, during a famine in Canaan, they went to Egypt and stayed there. By the time of Moses, his descendants had been enslaved by the Egyptians.

God called Moses to lead the Hebrews out of Egypt, an event called the Exodus. Then, as the story is told, Moses climbed Mount Sinai, where he encountered God. God gave Moses the famous Ten Commandments and the other Jewish laws.

According to Jewish tradition, God gave Moses a total of 613 laws. These laws are found in the Torah, the first five books of the Bible: Genesis, Exodus, Leviticus, Numbers, and Deuteronomy. These laws are very important for Jews. The word "Torah" means "instruction," but it is often translated as "law."

The rest of the Jewish Bible tells the story of the creation of the Kingdom of Israel and the first kings: Saul, David, and Solomon (c. 1040–c. 922 B.C.E.). After this time, the kingdom split into two parts: a southern kingdom called Judah and a northern kingdom called Israel (922 B.C.E.). The Assyrians conquered the northern kingdom in 721 B.C.E. and only Judah survived. It is at this point that these people are called Jews, which is derived from the word "Judah." The Jews were repeatedly conquered by the Assyrians (721 B.C.E), the Babylonians (587 B.C.E.), the Greeks (332 B.C.E.), and finally the Romans (63 B.C.E.)

The Tanakh contains the well-known book of prayers called Psalms, a book of wisdom called Proverbs, and books of warning by the prophets about the people's failure to follow God's laws.

What are the core beliefs of Judaism?

Judaism is a monotheist religion based on the belief in the one god of Israel and on following the law given to Moses. Many Jews believe in a heaven, in which faithful Jews will be with God. However, the Jewish Bible does not say much about the afterlife, so Jews have different ideas about what happens when people die. Typically, Jews do not believe in a hell, where souls are punished for eternity.

However, there is great diversity in Jewish religious practice and belief.

What is the Jewish Law?

Judaism is based on the Jewish Bible, the Tanakh, and also on a collection of writings called the Talmud. A typical Talmud is published in several volumes and is over six thousand pages in length. Much of the Talmud is commentary on the law, based on centuries of trying to follow commandments such as "Keep the Sabbath holy." Since the Sabbath is the day of rest, no work is to be done. Many Jews follow complicated rules so as to avoid work on the Sabbath. For example, strict Jews will not use electricity or drive cars on the Sabbath.

What are the major Jewish rituals?

There are many different celebrations and rituals in the Jewish religion: the Sabbath service, seasonal celebrations, and rituals to mark important moments in life.

What is the Sabbath service?

For Jews, the Sabbath, which starts on Friday at sundown and ends at sundown Saturday, is the day of rest. The Sabbath begins with a family meal at home that includes the

What are the major divisions of Judaism?

In Judaism, three major groups exist: Orthodox, Conservative, and Reform. These groups are divided over how strictly they follow the Law of Moses. Reform Jews focus on the moral laws of God, such as "Do not kill." They argue that other rules, such as kosher food rules, are not relevant today because such rules only applied to ancient times. The most strict in following the laws are Orthodox Jews. In between the Reform and Orthodox are the Conservative Jews, who are more strict than Reform Jews but less strict than Orthodox Jews.

lighting of the Sabbath candles and a blessing. For many Jews, synagogue services follow on Friday evening or Saturday morning.

What are the Jewish seasonal rituals?

The Jewish calendar determines the dates to celebrate these holidays, so they are not on the same day each year on the regular calendar. Each fall, the Jewish New Year of Rosh Hashanah is celebrated. In Jewish synagogues, a ram's horn called a *shofar* is blown to announce the New Year.

Rosh Hashanah is the start of a ten-day period called the High Holy Days, which ends with Yom Kippur, the Day of Atonement. To "atone" is to make up for a wrong committed. Jews fast for 25 hours as they reflect on their failure to live up to God's law during the past year.

Jews celebrate Passover in the spring with a meal that remembers the Exodus from Egypt. Called a Seder, the meal includes lamb or fish, unleavened bread called *matzah*, bitter herbs, and a paste of nuts and apples called *haroset*. As the meal progresses, the story of Moses and the Exodus is retold.

Shavuot, which is also called Pentecost, remembers the giving of the Law of Moses. It is held fifty days after Passover.

In the Bible, the Israelites wandered in the desert for forty years after leaving Egypt. They lived in tents. At Sukkot each autumn, Jews remember this history by building a

A Jewish man blows the traditional *shofar* horn during Rosh Hashanah.

shelter in their yard or at their synagogue, in which they eat their meals. Some Jews even sleep in their Sukkot booths.

Hanukkah (also spelled Chanukah or Hanukah), which is held between late November and late December, is an eight-day celebration that remembers the story of the Maccabean revolt against the Greeks in which the Jews retook their Temple in 165 B.C.E. In the Temple stood a lampstand: the Menorah. According to legend, the Jews relit the seven lamps on the Menorah, and although they had only enough oil for one day, a miracle took place, and the lamps stayed lit for eight days.

Jews celebrate Hanukkah over eight days using a candelabrum of eight candles for each day and a ninth candle to light the others. Each day's celebration includes prayers, blessings, gifts, songs, and games.

What are the Ten Commandments?

The Ten Commandments are found in the Tanakh/Old Testament in two places: Exodus 20:1–17 and Deuteronomy 5:6–21. For both Jews and Christians, the Ten Commandments are the foundation of morality.

What are the different versions of the Ten Commandments?

Here is a typical Jewish version:

1. I am the Lord your God, who brought you out of Egypt.
2. You shall have no other gods. You shall have no graven images or likenesses.
3. You shall not take the Lord's name in vain.
4. Keep the Sabbath holy.
5. Honor your father and mother.
6. You shall not kill.
7. You shall not commit adultery.
8. You shall not steal.
9. You shall not bear false witness.
10. You shall not covet your neighbor's wife or possessions.

Here is a typical Protestant Christian version:

1. I am the Lord your God, you shall have no other gods.
2. You shall have no graven images or likenesses.
3. You shall not take the Lord's name in vain.
4. Keep the Sabbath holy.
5. Honor your father and mother.
6. You shall not kill.
7. You shall not commit adultery.
8. You shall not steal.
9. You shall not bear false witness.
10. You shall not covet your neighbor's wife or possessions.

293

CHRISTIANITY

What is the background on Jesus?

In the time that Jesus lived, people would have called him "Jesus of Nazareth" or "Jesus, son of Joseph." Only after his death did early Christians give him the titles of "Messiah" or "Christ."

Our information about Jesus is limited: the four Gospels— Matthew, Mark, Luke, and John—are our main sources. The three Synoptic Gospels—Matthew, Mark, and Luke—give the most details. Surprisingly, there is little additional information on Jesus in the rest of the New Testament, such as in the letters written by Paul.

We do not have precise dates for the life of Jesus. Our best guess is that he lived from 6–4 B.C.E. to 27–33 C.E. in the Roman province of Judaea in a region called Palestine, which today is Israel and the Palestinian territories. Jesus was Jewish.

The region was under Roman control, although the Romans let Jewish kings, such as Herod the Great and Herod Antipas, rule. A Roman governor, Pontius Pilate, would make the decision to execute Jesus. We know almost nothing about the early life of Jesus.

What was the public ministry of Jesus?

Around the age of thirty, Jesus began his public life with his baptism by John the Baptist. The ministry of Jesus involved three main elements. Jesus gathered followers, he taught his followers, and he healed the sick. Jesus chose an inner circle of twelve men called the Apostles or the Disciples. The number twelve was symbolic of the twelve tribes of ancient Israel. However, Jesus had other followers, including several women.

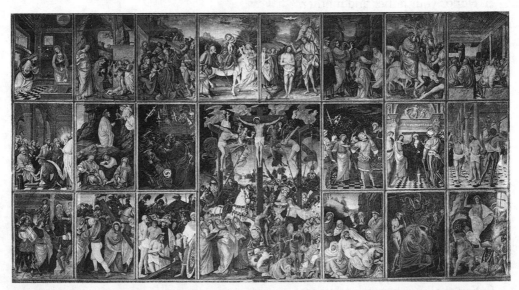

This 1513 fresco by Gaudenzio Ferrari, *Stories of life and passion of Christ*, depicts important events in Jesus' life. The fresco can be seen at the Church of Santa Maria delle Grazie in Italy.

The style of the preaching of Jesus was to give short sayings and tell stories. The three Gospels, Matthew, Mark, and Luke, give us a picture of how Jesus taught. One key theme of his teaching was to invoke God as Father. Jesus used the Aramaic word for father: *abba*.

Jesus frequently spoke of the "Kingdom of God"; however, it is not clear what Jesus meant by this. Over the centuries, Gospel readers have argued over the meaning of the phrase. A careful look at the Gospels shows that Jesus was not talking about heaven after death. Nor did he use the phrase to describe an interior religious experience. Rather, Jesus seemed to be describing a changed relationship with God as Father and changed relationships with other people in the present.

In teaching the Kingdom of God, Jesus turned upside down the values of the world. He rejected power and wealth. Jesus told his followers to love their enemies. He taught, "Blessed are the meek" and "Blessed are the poor." And he gave his own explanation of how to follow the Law of Moses.

The key Gospel texts of the teaching of Jesus are found in the Gospel of Matthew, Chapters 5–7, and the Gospel of Luke, Chapter 6, verses 20–42. (It takes about 10 minutes to read these important passages. Get a Bible or find a Bible online to read them.)

The Gospels speak of Jesus healing people. However, Christians hold different views on how to explain his healings. For some, they are "miracles" or "signs." Several times in the Gospels, the healings are described as driving out demons. At that time, long before science, many thought that illness was caused by demons.

What do we know about the Crucifixion of Jesus?

In the Gospels, Jesus eventually got in trouble with the religious leaders, who turned him over to the Romans to be executed. Very likely, the Romans saw Jesus as a potential leader of an uprising against their authority. A number of Jewish figures called "messiahs" existed at that time who wanted to free Israel from the Romans and create a Jewish kingdom.

Simply put, the Romans used crucifixion because it was the nastiest way to kill someone. It was long, drawn-out, and very painful; some victims lived for days. In the Gospels, after being whipped and stripped, Jesus was nailed to a cross to die.

Many questions about crucifixion remain unanswered. Was a single upright pole used, or was it a T-shaped cross, as most people imagine? Did the condemned person carry the entire cross or just the cross beam, which would then be attached to a standing pole? Was the victim tied or nailed to the cross or both? How did the person typically die: shock, blood loss, asphyxiation, or a combination of these? Very likely, the Romans had no standard procedure on how to crucify someone.

Although Christian art always adds a loincloth when depicting Jesus on the cross, the reality was that victims were stripped naked to further humiliate them. And the Romans would sometimes break the victim's legs to speed up death. Crucifixion was very brutal!

BASIC CHRISTIAN BELIEFS

What are the basic beliefs of mainline Christians?

Seven key beliefs define mainline Christianity: monotheism, Jesus as the messiah, Resurrection, the Trinity, the Bible as a guide, and continuous community. These beliefs held by mainline Christians are stated in the Nicene Creed, which is quoted below.

What is the Christian belief in monotheism?

Christians are monotheists who believe in one god. However, as will be seen below in the concept of the Trinity, their understanding of monotheism is complex.

What is the Christian belief that Jesus was the Messiah?

Jesus is the chosen one of God: the Messiah. Literally, "Messiah" means the "anointed one." In the Old Testament/Hebrew scriptures, anointing was used when a man became king. Perfumed olive oil was poured on his head as a sign of kingship. Christians started using the Greek version of the word as a title for Jesus. It is pronounced as CREE-stos and written as χριστός.

How did the word "Christ" become an important Christian symbol?

The first letter of the Greek word for Christ looks an X and is called *chi*. The second letter, called *rho*, looks like a P. Early Christians combined these to create the symbol called the "chi-rho." In Christian churches that allow art, this symbol is frequently displayed.

From the X for the first letter of "Christ" in Greek comes the custom of abbreviating "Christmas" as "Xmas." Also, the title of "Christ" seems to some to be almost a last name for Jesus. Lastly, the followers of Jesus used the word to label themselves Christians.

What is the Christian belief in Resurrection?

The core Christian belief in the Resurrection of Jesus involves several separate but interrelated pieces.

Mainline Christians believe the Gospels that say Jesus really died and was really alive three days later. They believe Jesus died on the cross and reject explana-

A chi-rho symbol representing the Resurrection rises above two Roman soldiers in this sarcophagus carving from c. 350 C.E.

tions such as the idea that Jesus went into a coma and snapped out of it in the tomb. According to mainline Christians, Jesus died but was seen alive days later.

This is the central belief of Christianity. The logic runs thus: Humans sin and thereby separate themselves from God. However, this sin is so great that humans cannot overcome the distance between God and themselves. The gap can only be bridged by Jesus dying, rising, and paying the price for sin. Jesus brings salvation and redeems humans, who are saved from sin and the penalty for sin. The penalty is to die and not be able to go to heaven. Christians believe that Jesus saved his followers from sin and also the penalty of sin. Hence, Christians call Jesus their "Savior" and "Redeemer."

Christians believe they will be resurrected after they die to live forever in heaven with God.

What is the Christian belief in the incarnation?

The word "incarnation" comes from the Latin word *carnis*, which means "meat," "body," or "flesh." Christians believe in the incarnation, which is the concept that in Jesus, God has taken on a human body. Christians sometimes speak of Jesus as the "Word" or as the "Word made flesh" or even the "Incarnate Word."

Christians who follow the Nicene Creed—mainline Christians—believe that Jesus was both human and divine at the same time. ("Divine" means to be God.) The traditional belief holds that Jesus is one person with two natures: a human nature and a divine nature.

This is not easy to understand. If a person says Jesus was God but not man, that person is disagreeing with the Nicene Creed. If another person says Jesus was just a good man, that person is also disagreeing with the Nicene Creed. Lastly, to say Jesus was an angel is again to disagree with the Nicene Creed.

Mainline Christians believe that Jesus was human and divine. Therefore, to deny that Jesus is also God is a heresy called arianism. On the other hand, to deny that Jesus is also human is another heresy called monophysitism, which means "one nature."

A key argument for incarnation is the belief that Jesus was born of Mary, who was a virgin. According to most Christians, when Jesus was born, his mother, Mary, was still a virgin. By a miracle, God's power entered Mary, and she became pregnant. This belief is based on the first chapters of both Matthew and Luke. The scene is often called the Annunciation because the angel Gabriel announced to Mary that, although a virgin, she would give birth to Jesus.

What is the Christian belief in the Trinity?

Many Christians are confused about the Trinity. It is perhaps the hardest Christian belief to grasp. However, it is a very important belief. The prefix of the word is "tri," which, of course, means "three."

Christians have developed a concept of God as a Trinity: Father, Son, and Holy Spirit, which is symbolized by the dove.

As monotheists, Christians believe in one god. However, according to mainline Christians, this one god. consists of three distinct persons: the Father, the Son, and the Holy Spirit (or Holy Ghost). These are not human persons but divine persons. The traditional belief describes the Trinity as "one god, yet three divine persons."

Interestingly, each of the three persons has a separate awareness. Just as you, as a human, have your own separate awareness and you are a distinct individual, there are three separate "awarenesses" existing within the Trinity. Thus, the Father is distinct from the Son and the Holy Spirit; the Son knows he is the Son and not the Father or the Holy Spirit; and the Holy Spirit knows it is the Holy Spirit and not the Father or the Son.

To better understand the mainline Christian teaching on the Trinity, it is helpful to understand two wrong ideas, or heresies, about "Trinity." First, it is important to recognize that the Trinity is not the same as believing there are three gods (tritheism).

Also, "Trinity" is not "modalism": the idea that one divine being plays three different roles. A mode is a role. For example, people often play different roles in their lives. A woman can be a wife, a mother, an employee or boss, a daughter, and a friend. She is just one person but plays multiple roles, different modes, in her life, each one with different functions and different responsibilities and benefits.

Similarly, according to modalism, there is one divine being who plays three roles: first as the Father, second as Jesus, and then a third as the Holy Spirit. There is only one divine person who plays each role, one at a time.

The easiest argument to use against modalism is to notice the frequent times in the Gospels when Jesus prays to his Father. Jesus and the Father would have to be separate beings, unless somehow, Jesus was praying to himself.

Just to make things clear: mainline Christians consider tritheism and modalism to be heretical ideas.

What do Christians believe about the Bible?

Christians believe that the Bible is the guide for what to believe and how to live. All Christians agree on this point; however, many disagree on all the details of Christianity.

What is the Nicene Creed?

The Nicene Creed was written in 325 C.E. to help clarify and standardize Christian belief. Many Christians hold to the Nicene Creed, and some Christians recite the Creed every Sunday in their services. The seven basic Christian beliefs described above come from the Nicene Creed. However, some people who identify as Christians reject the Nicene Creed or parts of it.

Here is the text in English:

We believe in one God,
the Father, the Almighty,
maker of heaven and earth,
of all that is seen and unseen.

We believe in one Lord, Jesus Christ,
the only Son of God,
eternally begotten of the Father,
God from God, Light from Light,
true God from true God,
begotten, not made, one in Being with the Father.

Through him all things were made.

For us men and for our salvation
he came down from heaven:
by the power of the Holy Spirit
he was born of the Virgin Mary, and became man.

For our sake he was crucified under Pontius Pilate,
he suffered, died, and was buried.

On the third day he rose again
in fulfillment of the Scriptures;

he ascended into heaven
and is seated at the right hand of the Father.

He will come again in glory to judge the living and the dead,
and his kingdom will have no end.
We believe in the Holy Spirit, the Lord, the giver of life,
who proceeds from the Father and the Son.

With the Father and the Son he is worshiped and glorified.

He has spoken through the Prophets.

We believe in one holy catholic and apostolic Church.

We acknowledge one baptism for the forgiveness of sins.

We look for the resurrection of the dead
and the life of the world to come. Amen.

What do Christians believe about continuous community?

Christians hold that the Christian church started with the first followers of Jesus, as described in the New Testament, and that history has shaped it.

What is the Christian Bible?

The Christian Bible has two parts: the Old Testament and the New Testament. The Old Testament starts with the creation stories in Genesis and then describes the history of ancient Israel up to the time before Jesus. The New Testament describes the life of Jesus and then his first followers, who developed and spread the Christian faith.

Among Christians, the Protestant and Catholic versions of the Old Testament are different. While the Protestant Old Testament has 39 books, the Catholic Old Testament has 46 books. The extra books are 1 Maccabees, 2 Maccabees, Judith, Tobit, Baruch, Sirach (also called Ecclesiasticus), and Wisdom.

The New Testament, (also called the Christian Scriptures), has 27 books: the four Gospels, the Acts of the Apostles, twenty-one Letters (or Epistles), and, finally, the Book of Revelation. The Gospels are Matthew, Mark, Luke, and John; however, because the Gospels of Matthew, Mark, and Luke have much in common, they are often called the Synoptic Gospels. ("Synoptic" means "same view.")

What are the major divisions in Christianity?

Thousands of different Christian groups and denominations exist. It can be very frustrating trying to sort them out. To simplify this somewhat, we can group Christian denominations roughly into five different classifications that cover most, though not all, of the various groups.

1. Orthodox Christians (e.g. Greek Orthodox)

2. The Roman Catholic Church

3. Protestant churches coming from Europe (such as Anglican, Lutheran, and Presbyterian)

4. American-born churches that accept the Nicene Creed or the ideas of the Nicene Creed

5. American-born churches that reject the Nicene Creed

ISLAM

What is the meaning of the word "Islam"?

"Islam" is the name of the religion, and a follower of Islam is a "Muslim." The word "Islam" means "submission": submission to the will of Allah. (Allah is Arabic for "God.") Muslims believe in one god and are thus monotheists. Besides "submission," "Islam" also means "peace" and is based on the Arabic word for peace, *salaam*, which is related to the Hebrew word for peace, *shalom*. In Muslim belief, a believer can find peace through submitting to the will of God.

Some people are surprised to learn that the word "Islam" means "peace" because they are aware of Muslim terrorists and extremists in the news committing violent acts. However, what many non-Muslims do not realize is that such Muslim terrorists and extremists are not typical Muslims. Furthermore, most of the victims of such violence are other Muslims. Ordinary Muslims, who do not make the news, want to live peaceful, nonviolent lives.

Who was Muhammad?

Islam begins with Muhammad (570–632), who was born in the city of Mecca in what today is Saudi Arabia. In the center of Mecca stood a shrine, the Ka'ba, where the people worshipped several hundred different gods, including Allah. Both the father and mother of Muhammad had died by the time he was six, so Muhammad was raised by his uncle, Abu Talib, the caretaker of the Ka'ba.

Mecca was a busy place because of its trade in ivory, gold, incense, and silk. Long caravans of camels brought goods to the city. Mecca prospered. Muhammad worked on such caravans, and in his travels, he encountered Christians and Jews. At the age of twenty-five, Muhammad married a wealthy widow, Khadijah, who would give birth to two sons who died in infancy and four girls who survived.

A religious man, Muhammad often went up into the hills around Mecca to meditate. According to Islamic tradition, in the year 610, the angel Gabriel appeared to him in a cave as he was praying. Gabriel gave Muhammad messages that he was to learn and then recite to others. For the rest of his life, Muhammad continued to receive such revelations. He memorized them and taught them to his later followers. Eventually, his followers would write down these messages as the Qur'an, the holy book of Islam.

From these words from Gabriel, Muhammad came to believe in only one god, Allah. He saw that humans needed to submit themselves to Allah. Muhammad also saw himself as the last of the line of prophets that included figures such as Adam, Abraham, Moses, and Jesus.

He began preaching in Mecca that everyone was equal before Allah. He told the people that humans would be judged before God on how they lived and spoke against gambling, drinking alcohol, prostitution, and idolatry. He also criticized the existence of great wealth when there was so much poverty.

Not surprisingly, his preaching was unpopular. Many wanted to continue the practices he condemned. Yet, no one could harm him because he was protected by his family clan. When his uncle and key family members died, however, he no longer had protection.

In 622, Muhammad fled to the nearby city of Yathrib. This event is called the "Hijrah." (622 C.E. became year 1 in the Muslim calendar.) The city was renamed Medinat al-Nabi, "the city of the prophet" (Medina for short). Medina had invited Muhammad to come to resolve the many disputes among the different factions in the city. Muhammad became the political and religious leader of Medina, uniting the various tribes under the Constitution of Medina.

Muslim forces from Medina began raiding caravans en route to Mecca. In retaliation, Mecca sent a force of ten thousand soldiers to attack Medina. Muhammad organized the defense of the city by having a ditch dug around it. This stopped the force from Mecca from taking Medina.

In the 1307 manuscript *Compendium of Chronicles* by the Persian Rashid-al-Din Hamadani, Muhammad is shown receiving his first revelation from the angel Gabriel.

Muhammad then led his own forces in 630 to attack Mecca, but Mecca surrendered without a fight. Muhammad's first action was to go to the Ka'ba and circle around it seven times. Then, he removed all the statues and idols and dedicated the Ka'ba to the one god, Allah. Muslims call this event the "Hajj." (Muslims remember this event by making their own Hajj to Mecca.) In 632, Muhammad died.

What is the Qur'an?

The holy book of Islam is the Qur'an. ("Koran" is the older English spelling.) The Qur'an is divided into chapters, and each chapter is called a "sura." After the first short sura, the rest are organized by size from longest to shortest for a total of 114 *suraat*. (The plural of sura is *suraat*.) In the Qur'an, a number of figures from both the Jewish and Christian scriptures are mentioned, such as Adam, Abraham, Joseph, Moses, Gabriel, Mary, and Jesus.

In Islam, the true Qur'an is in Arabic. Muslims view a translation as not being the Qur'an. Christians, in spreading their faith, have translated the Bible into almost every written language, while Muslims have followed a different path. In spreading their faith, Muslims teach converts Arabic so they can read the Qur'an in its true form.

According to Muslim belief, Muhammad passed on word for word exactly what he heard from the angel Gabriel. He added nothing to the messages. Later, the followers of Muhammad wrote them down as the Qur'an. Muslims call the written Qur'an the "Created Qur'an" and believe it is an exact copy of the "Uncreated Qur'an," which is in heaven.

In Islam, the Qur'an is treated with great respect, and Muslims are offended by any mistreatment of a copy of it.

What are the Five Pillars of Islam?

The Five Pillars, which are the duties of being a faithful Muslim, are key to Islam. They are:

1. Shahada: Shahada is "profession," which is the duty to profess or say one's belief. (Here, "profession" does not refer to one's occupation.) Muslims are required to profess: "There is no god but Allah, and Muhammad is his prophet."

2. Salat: Muslims are required to pray five times daily on a prayer mat facing Mecca. Going to a mosque to pray with others is best; however, if one cannot get to a mosque, then one should pray alone.

3. Zaqat: This is a tax or donation to help the poor.

4. Sawm: During the month of Ramadan, Muslims are required to fast: no food or drink during daylight hours.

5. Hajj: The fifth pillar is to make a pilgrimage to Mecca in Saudi Arabia at least once in one's lifetime, as long as one is in good health and can afford it. In the heart of Mecca is the Ka'ba, a black, cubic building. The high point of the Hajj is to go around the Ka'ba seven times.

What is the concept of jihad, or holy war?

Although jihad is an important concept, it is often misunderstood by non-Muslims. "Jihad" does mean "holy war," and in the long and complex history of Islam, Muslims have fought a number of wars as holy wars. The concept has been used by some Muslim terrorists to justify their actions. However, most Muslims condemn such terrorist actions and do not believe those are holy wars. As noted above, most of the victims of such terrorists are Muslims. Like most people, Muslims just want to live their lives in peace, so the vast majority of Muslims reject this interpretation of Jihad.

As for the morality of warfare, most Muslims believe that only defensive wars are justified. And, thus, their view is very close to the common view of many people around the world.

One final point is important: For many Muslims, the main meaning of the word "jihad" is "holy struggle." According to Muslims, the biggest struggle for most humans is the inner spiritual struggle to submit one's self to the will of Allah. For Muslims, this spiritual struggle is called the "greater jihad," while the struggle against the enemies is called the "lesser jihad."

OTHER IMPORTANT RELIGIONS

What is the Sikh religion?

Because this religion has elements influenced by both Hinduism and Islam, the Sikh religion could be grouped as either an Eastern religion or a Western religion. The teachings of Guru Nanak (1469–1539) form the basis of Sikhism. Nanak lived in the Punjab, a region that today is in both Pakistan and India.

India has a long and complicated history of having both Muslim and Hindu rulers at various times. Muslims and Hindus lived side by side but often in tension. An important influence on Nanak was Kabir (1440–1518), who taught the idea that Muslims and Hindus worshipped the same divine reality. Kabir sought common ground between Islam and Hinduism and saw dogmas and creeds as irrelevant.

Just like the Buddha, Nanak left his home to find answers to his many religious questions. According to Sikhs, Nanak had a vision in which he was taken before God, who told him to preach, "There is no Muslim, and there is no Hindu." God told Nanak to redeem the world by teaching charity, prayer, and clean living. Nanak became a teacher, taking on the title of "Guru."

After Guru Nanak came nine other gurus. Guru Gobind Singh (1666–1708), the tenth, declared he was the last human guru. From then on, the Adi Granth, the Sikh holy book, became the Guru Granth Sahib. In each Sikh temple (called a "Gurdwara"), the Adi Granth becomes the center of worship. It is placed on a raised platform on cushions, and a whisk is waved over it: an ancient sign of honor. When Sikhs enter the Gurdwara, they bow to the Adi Granath. Here is a passage from the Adi Granth:

Why do you go to the forest in search of God?
He lives in all and is yet ever distinct;
He abides with you, too,
As a fragrance dwells in a flower,
And reflection in a mirror;
So does God dwell inside everything;
Seek Him, therefore, in your heart.

Some Sikhs see their religion as monotheism since Sikhs use several tiles for God, including Ek Onkar, which translates as "One Creator." Yet, other Sikhs think that the category of monotheism might be the wrong one for the Sikh tradition because, as the first line of the Adi Granth states: God "cannot be reduced to thought." In the end, perhaps no category fits the Sikh tradition because of the diversity of Sikh religious beliefs.

Sikhs believe that performing good actions is more important than carrying out religious rituals. A Sikh lives a good life by at all times keeping God in heart and mind. Many Sikhs pray two or more times a day. Sikhs also believe in living honestly and working hard. They reject the Hindu caste system because they believe everyone is equal.

Seeing hair as a spiritual crown that is only to be seen by God, Sikh men do not cut their hair. Sikh men wear turbans to cover their hair and have beards.

The Sikh religion was founded in the fifteenth century by the Punjabi Guru Nanak.

What is Jainism?

An offshoot of Hinduism is the Jain religion (also called Jainism). The word "Jain" is pronounced both as "jane" or "jen." Today, over four million Jains live around the world. The founder of Jainism was Mahavira, who lived in the 500s or 400s B.C.E. Mahavira taught the importance of detachment. The goal is to free one's soul from all material attachments. It may take many lifetimes to liberate oneself from the cycle of reincarnation. Some Jains become monks or nuns; many others marry and have families.

What are the three Jain principles?

Jains hold to three principles to free the soul from attachments. 1) Nonviolence: Jains may not kill humans or animals. Many Jains even avoid killing insects. 2) Nonacquisitiveness: Jains avoid owning possessions. 3) Relativity: According to Jainism, truth is relative. What one sees as the truth depends on how one looks at something.

What is Shinto?

Shinto, the traditional religion of Japan, has greatly influenced Japanese culture and moral values. Shinto has no founder and no sacred scriptures. Although very few Japanese identify themselves as Shintoists, most Japanese participate in Shinto rituals. Some 80,000 Shinto shrines can be found in Japan today.

In Shinto, gods are called "Kami," and "Shinto" is "the way of the gods." Amaterasu (the sun goddess) and Izanagi and Izanami (the first man and woman) are three important Kami. Shintoists also believe in a divine presence in all things.

What is Rastafarianism?

In the 1930s, a religious and political movement developed in Jamaica among descendants of African slaves. They called themselves Rastafarians (or Rastas) and consider the emperor of Ethiopia, Haile Selassie I (1892–1975), to be the second coming of Christ. Some saw him as God the Father. Rastafarianism is based on Christianity (especially passages in the Old Testament and the Book of Revelation), African culture, and mysticism.

What is modern paganism?

Modern pagans are a diverse group of people who are interested in Greek and Roman mythology, pre-Christian religions of Europe, folklore, and ethnic religions. Modern pagans might be interested in Norse (Viking) gods, ancient Celtic Druidism, mythology, and nature religions, among other beliefs.

Modern pagan beliefs can be classified as animism, polytheism, or pantheism. Many pagans celebrate seasonal rituals at the spring and fall equinoxes and at the summer and winter solstices.

In their ceremonies, Rastafarians use drumming, chanting, and meditation. To heighten spiritual experiences, marijuana is often smoked. From this movement came Reggae music. Rastafarians grow dreadlocks because they do not cut their hair. Also, Haile Selassie is called the "Lion of Judah," and the dreadlocks thus represent a lion's mane.

What is the Bahá'í religion?

Many people do not know about the Bahá'í faith that was founded in the 1800s by Bahá'u'lláh in Persia (modern-day Iran). Bahá'í teaching emphasizes the unity of religion and of all humankind, believing that God is the source of all religions. Other key Bahá'í teachings promote the equality of men and women, education, and world peace.

Who are the Unitarian Universalists?

Several centuries ago, the Unitarians split from mainline Christians. They did not accept the belief that God is a Trinity. Unitarians insisted that God is one, a unity, so they called themselves "Unitarians." Another group also developed that believed that God would not send anyone to hell forever. They believed that everyone will ultimately go to heaven because in the next life, God's love will transform everyone, even wicked people. Thus, they called themselves "Universalists," believing that salvation is universal.

These two groups joined in 1961 to form the Unitarian Universalist Church. For those seeking a community that avoids the traditional religious doctrines, the Unitarian Universalists are often a good alternative. In Unitarian Universalist congregations, members hold a wide range of beliefs as they search for spiritual growth. Unitarian Universalists do not have any sort of creed telling people what to believe.

THE LAW

ANCIENT LAW

What was the Draconian Code?

The Draconian Code was the body of law, or set of rules, established by the ancient Athenian ruler Draco (seventh century B.C.E.). The code was characterized by very punitive measures implemented for what today would be considered relatively minor offenses. Debtors were penalized severely, sometimes even forced to go into slavery. The death penalty was used for a wide variety of offenses. The harshness of the code explains the etymology of the word "draconian."

What was the debate in ancient China about how to establish an orderly society?

Three main positions emerged in ancient China. Confucius (551–479 B.C.E.) argued that people had to be taught how to live in an orderly society. He stressed the importance of social roles and reciprocal duties between rulers and subjects, husbands and wives, and fathers and sons. Although by modern standards his values seem too traditional and unfair to women, the idea of Confucius was that if people understood their duties, there would be a stable society.

The Mohists, who followed the teaching of Mozi (c. 470–c. 391 B.C.E.), emphasized the importance of impartial care, which meant a person should treat everyone equally regardless of their relationship to the person. Also, actions should be judged as good if they provided general benefit to the people of society.

Lastly, the legalists asserted the importance of tough laws and punishments to create an orderly society.

What was Roman law?

Roman law was the system of law used by the Romans. Justinian the Great (483–565), the emperor of the East Roman Empire, is credited with codifying (writing and organizing) Roman law by ordering the collection of all imperial statutes and all the writings of Roman judges and legal experts.

Justinian appointed the best legal minds in the empire to assemble, write, publish, and update the code; work began early in his reign and continued until the time of his death in 565. The result was the *Corpus Juris Civilis* (*Body of Civil Law*), also called the Justinian Code. It consists of four parts: the Codex (a collection of imperial statutes), the Digest (the writings and interpretations of Roman jurists), the Institutes (a textbook for students), and the Novels (the laws enacted after the publication of the Codex).

Though largely suspended during the Middle Ages, it was kept alive in the canon law of the medieval Catholic Church and was handed down through the centuries. It forms the basis of modern civil law in most of continental Europe and in other non-English-speaking countries.

What is common law?

Common law means case law or judge-made law—the collection of judicial opinions that create a body of jurisprudence. It is the system of justice that prevails in Great Britain and the United States, where the precedents (past decisions) of the courts are used as the basis of the legal system. It is sometimes referred to as customary law since justices consider prevailing practices (customs) in order to arrive at their decisions.

In many countries, the justice system is a combination of the civil law handed down by the Romans under Justinian and the common law formulated in England. Private cases (often and confusingly called civil cases) are largely the realm of civil law (in other words, the written laws prevail), whereas criminal cases (in which crimes have been committed against society) are the realm of common law (i.e., decisions are based on precedent).

What was trial by ordeal?

It was an irrational way of determining someone's guilt or innocence used in the past. After the fall of Rome (476), Roman law gave way to the laws of the various Germanic tribes in Europe. For example, if someone was charged with a crime, he or she was deliberately injured in some way. If the injury (from a heated iron bar or immersion into hot water, for example) healed within a prescribed number of days (usually three), the person was declared innocent. If the wound failed to heal, the verdict was guilty. This method for determining innocence or guilt was also called divination since the court was trying, through the ordeal, to divine whether the accused person was guilty. Divination is the idea that spirits or spiritual forces will indicate who is guilty or not.

Trial by ordeal gave way to a far more practical, and certainly more rational, form of trial, in which judge and jury presided over the presentation of a case and employed written code, precedent, or both to arrive at a verdict. But divination was used as recently as the 1600s, when women in Puritan New England were charged with witchcraft. A suspect was bound up with rope and immersed in water. If she sank, she was innocent; if she floated, she was declared guilty (the "reasoning" being that only someone with supernatural power could float under the circumstances). Those found guilty by this form of trial were put to death.

Trial by ordeal still exists in some places today among some tribal cultures. For example, someone accused of stealing might be burned by a heated piece of metal. If the person flinches, he or she is considered guilty.

How good is trial by evidence?

Although most people consider trials based on evidence to be a superior approach to determining guilt, there have been several high-profile cases in which people argue over whether justice was served, such as the O. J. Simpson trial in 1995 and the initial trial of four Los Angeles police officers for beating Rodney King in 1992.

Also, in recent years, many people convicted in trials have been released when later DNA evidence showed they were innocent. On April 19, 1989, a female jogger was attacked, raped, and severely beaten in Central Park. Eventually, five young men were convicted of the attack and sent to prison. In 2001, a convicted murderer and rapist confessed to the attack. His DNA matched that found on the scene. The charges against the five men in prison were withdrawn.

What was the Code Napoleon?

In 1800, just after Napoleon Bonaparte (1769–1821) had come to power in France, he appointed a commission of legal experts to consolidate all French civil law into one code. The process took four years; the so-called *Code civil des Français* or Code Civil went into effect in 1804, the same year Napoleon named himself emperor of France. The laws thus took on the alternate name of the Code Napoleon or the Napoleonic Code.

The code represented a compromise between Roman law and common (or customary) law. Furthermore, it accommodated some of the radical reforms of the French Revolution (1789–1799). The Code Civil set forth laws regarding individual liberty, property, inheritance, mortgages, and contracts. It had broad influence in Europe as well as in Latin America, where civil law is prevalent. As opposed to the common law of most English-speaking countries, civil law judgments are based on codified principles, rather than on legal precedent. For example, under the Code Civil, an accused person is guilty until proven innocent, as opposed to common law, which holds that a person is innocent until proven guilty.

What is *habeas corpus*?

The writ of *habeas corpus* (which is roughly translated from the Latin as "you should have the body") is considered a cornerstone of due process of law. It means that a person cannot be detained unless he or she is brought in person before the court so that the court can determine whether or not the person is being lawfully held.

What was trial by battle?

Like trial by ordeal, trial by battle was a method of "justice" used predominately during the Middle Ages. When noblemen had disputes, they would engage in a duel with one other. Often, knights on horseback would joust with each other to prove who was innocent and guilty. Such jousts often ended in death. The assumption in trial by battle was that the person who was in the right would have God on his side, and he would emerge the victor in combat. This form of trial was gradually replaced by trial by jury.

Trial by battle ignores the reality that often, the evildoer is stronger and has more power. However, many movies today reinforce the myth that good will always win in the end. The reality is that bad people often win because they have no morals in how they gain and use power. History has shown many examples where God did not intervene to protect those who were good and innocent.

The notion dates back to medieval England. Many historians believe that *habeas corpus* was implied by the Magna Carta (1215). Article 39 states, "No freemen shall be taken or imprisoned … or exiled or in any way destroyed … except by the lawful judgment of his peers or by the law of the land." The writ was reinforced by Britain's *Habeas Corpus* Amendment Act of 1679, which stated that the Crown (king or queen) cannot detain a prisoner against the wishes of Parliament and the courts.

The English introduced the concept in the American colonies. When the U.S. Constitution (1788) was written, it declared (in Article I, Section 9) that *habeas corpus* "shall not be suspended, unless when in cases of rebellion or invasion the public safety may require it." For example, during the Civil War (1861–1865), President Abraham Lincoln suspended *habeas corpus*. During the period after the Civil War known as Reconstruction (1865–1877), it was again suspended in an effort to combat the activities of the Ku Klux Klan, who terrorized African Americans in the South and denied their rights.

The concept of *habeas corpus* is an important human right. It requires that an arrested person be taken before a judge, who determines that a person has been properly arrested and charged with a crime. The right prevents abuses, such as people being arrested and then disappearing in jails with no public acknowledgment that they have been arrested. In societies without *habeas corpus*, arrested people can disappear without anyone on the outside knowing where they are and what happened to them. *Habeas corpus* also prevents people from being held in jail indefinitely with no charges brought against them.

What is divine law?

Many religious people believe in divine law, which is the idea that moral principles ultimately come from God. This is often called the divine command theory. In the divine command theory, God gives the rules of what is right and wrong and enforces them with rewards and punishments. This is why many religious people fear a lack of religion. They feel that if people are not religious, they will not fear the punishments of God and will do bad things.

According to the divine command theory, God enforces morality with rewards and punishments. Religious people often speak of the rewards and punishments both in this life and after death. Many believe that God rewards with heaven those who are good and have faith. In heaven, people will live with God forever in happiness. Many religious people also believe that bad people will be punished in hell forever.

Besides the rewards or punishments after death, many religious people believe that God also rewards and punishes people while they are still living. For example, the Bible has a number of passages saying that God rewards those who are faithful to his laws.

What are the problems with the divine command theory?

There are three difficulties with the divine command theory. First, it does not work with people who do not believe in God. Second, how do believers figure out what God wants? For example, the Bible does not directly address a number of moral issues, such as abortion and the removal of medical life support for a terminal patient. Third, believers disagree on what God's rules are. On every moral issue, such as capital punishments, homosexuality, and war, religious people hold very different views from one another.

INTERNATIONAL LAW

What is international law?

As interpreted by Dutch jurist and humanist Hugo Grotius (1583–1645), natural law prescribes the rules of conduct among nations, resulting in international laws. His 1625 work, titled *Concerning the Law of War and Peace*, is considered the definitive text on international law, asserting the sovereignty and legal equality of all states of the world. But the notion also had its detractors, English philosopher Thomas Hobbes (1588–1679) among them. Hobbes insisted that since international law is not enforced by any legal body above the nations themselves, it is not legitimate.

Since the seventeenth century, however, international law has evolved to be-

English political philosopher Thomas Hobbes argued against the concept of international law because there was no legal body of any kind behind it to enforce such laws.

313

come more than just theory. During the 1800s and early 1900s, the Geneva Conventions (1864, 1906, 1929, and 1949) and the Hague Conventions (1899 and 1907) set forth the rules of war. Today, treaties (between two or among many countries), customary laws, legal writings, and conventions all influence international law, which is also referred to as "the law of nations." Furthermore, it is enforced by the International Court of Justice (a United Nations body) as well as by world opinion, international sanctions, and the intervention of the United Nations.

What is the Universal Declaration of Human Rights?

At the end of World War II, many nations called for an organization to try to prevent future wars and, thus, created the United Nations in 1945. In response to the horrors of the war, many saw the need for a statement of basic human rights. Former first lady Eleanor Roosevelt (1884–1962) chaired the committee of the United Nations charged with writing an international list of human rights. The result was the Universal Declaration of Human Rights, approved in 1948. The declaration contains thirty articles. Here are the first five:

Article 1.

All human beings are born free and equal in dignity and rights. They are endowed with reason and conscience and should act towards one another in a spirit of brotherhood.

Article 2.

Everyone is entitled to all the rights and freedoms set forth in this Declaration, without distinction of any kind, such as race, colour, sex, language, religion, political or other opinion, national or social origin, property, birth or other status. Furthermore, no distinction shall be made on the basis of the political, jurisdictional or international status of the country or territory to which a person belongs, whether it be independent, trust, non-self-governing or under any other limitation of sovereignty.

Article 3.

Everyone has the right to life, liberty and security of person.

Article 4.

No one shall be held in slavery or servitude; slavery and the slave trade shall be prohibited in all their forms.

Article 5.

No one shall be subjected to torture or to cruel, inhuman or degrading treatment or punishment.

The declaration is a statement of ideals since there is no mechanism for enforcement. Also, it is recognized that some of the nations that have signed it have failed to follow its principles. However, it remains an important set of beliefs and values to guide humans.

What are the Geneva Conventions?

The Geneva Conventions are humanitarian treaties that have been signed by most of the approximately 200 nations in the world today. For these treaties, the word "convention" does not mean an assembly of people but rather an international agreement or treaty. The treaties were forged in Geneva, Switzerland, in 1864, 1906, 1929, and 1949. In their entirety, the Geneva Conventions set standards for how signatory nations are to treat the enemy during war.

Convention I (1864) calls for protections for members of the armed forces who become wounded or sick. Convention II (1906) calls for protections of wounded, sick, and shipwrecked members of the naval forces. Convention III (1929) lists the rights of prisoners of war. Finally, Convention IV (1949) deals with the protection of the civilian population in times of war.

The four conventions were followed by three protocols, which were amendments. Protocol I extends protections to victims of wars against racist regimes or wars fought for self-determination. Protocol II extends protections to victims of internal conflicts within a country. (Since it is within a country, it would not be an international conflict.) Finally, Protocol III establishes the Red Crystal as a protective symbol for those performing humanitarian service, such as medical care, in a conflict zone. The Red Crystal is an alternative to the Red Cross or the Red Crescent, which is used in Muslim countries.

The Geneva Conventions, along with the Hague Conventions (1899 and 1907), comprise much of what is called international humanitarian law (IHL). Because so many nations of the world have ratified both the Geneva Conventions and the Hague Conventions, they are considered customary international law, which means they are binding on all nations.

What is The Hague?

The Hague is the capital city of the Netherlands. The name originally referred to the royal residence, hence the use of "The Hague."

What are the Hague Conventions?

They are international treaties (1899 and 1907) covering the laws and customs of war. The first Hague Convention developed out of the Peace Conference of 1899, held in The Hague, the Netherlands, and convened by Russian tsar Nicholas II (1868–1918). Among the original goals was limiting the expansion of armed forces. Though the representatives there, from twenty-six nations (including the United States), failed to agree on a resolution to limit such expansion, they did agree on certain rules of engagement for war on land and at sea.

They also adopted the Convention for the Pacific Settlement of International Disputes. This convention set up the permanent international court of arbitration and justice, still in existence today. The court is in The Hague, where it is housed in the Peace Palace, a gift of American industrialist and philanthropist Andrew Carnegie (1835–1919).

The Peace Palace in The Hague, Netherlands, is the seat of the International Court of Justice.

A later convention, the Second Hague Peace Conference, was held in 1907; representatives of forty-four nations met for a period of four months.

The convention of 1907 modified and added to the first. Delegates resolved to meet again in 1915, but that conference was not held due to the outbreak of World War I. The Hague Conventions were the forerunners of the League of Nations and the United Nations.

U.S. LAW AND JUSTICE

How was the makeup of the U.S. Supreme Court decided?

Article III of the U.S. Constitution (1788) states that the "judicial Power of the United States, shall be vested in one supreme Court." It goes on to describe the high court's jurisdiction, but it does not specify how the court was to be formed or how many justices it would consist of. Congress passed the Judiciary Act of 1789 that created the federal court system. The law provided that the Supreme Court would have a chief justice and five associate justices. The original six were Chief Justice John Jay and associate justices James Wilson, William Cushing, John Blair, John Rutledge, and James Iredell.

Since 1869, the court has consisted of nine members: the chief justice and eight associates who, once named, serve for life. The president appoints the justices, but they must be approved by the Senate (according to Article 2 of the Constitution).

Does the chief justice have additional powers vis-à-vis the other justices?

Yes, the chief justice has additional powers and duties. It has often been said that the chief justice is "first among equals." The chief justice has the assignment power—the power to assign opinions to a justice of his choice—if he or she is in the majority.

The chief justice gives the oath of office to the president, assigns judges to the special Foreign Intelligence Surveillance Court (the FISA court), and presides over the Judicial Conference of the United States. The chief justice also provides reports to Congress on the state of the federal judiciary.

John Jay was the first chief justice of the U.S. Supreme Court.

Who was the first chief justice of the U.S. Supreme Court?

President George Washington appointed John Jay (1745–1829) to the post.

What were the Jim Crow laws?

They were laws or practices that segregated blacks from whites. They prevailed in the American South during the late 1800s and into the first half of the 1900s. Jim Crow was a stereotype of a black man described in a nineteenth-century song-and-dance act. The first written appearance of the term is dated 1838, and by the 1880s, it had fallen into common usage in the United States. Even though in 1868, Congress passed the Fourteenth Amendment, prohibiting states from violating equal protection of all citizens, southern states passed many laws segregating blacks from whites in public places.

In short, the laws were both manifestation and enforcement of discrimination. They permeated all aspects of American society, as whites and blacks used separate bathrooms, different hotels, different railway cars, played in separate sports leagues, and went to separate schools. Blacks were prohibited from many places.

Jim Crow laws were designed to oppress blacks such that they would not have any political power or influence on the society. Perhaps most importantly, Jim Crow laws were designed to keep blacks down so they would be a source of cheap labor. For example, many laws limited educational opportunities for blacks, which meant that many were stuck doing the lowest jobs in society at very low pay.

During the civil rights movement of the 1950s and 1960s, public pressure increased and exposed the unfairness of Jim Crow/segregation laws.

What was the Supreme Court's role in racial segregation?

Though most segregation laws (or "Jim Crow laws") were overturned by decisions of the Supreme Court during the 1950s and 1960s, the court was righting its own wrong. In the late 1800s, during the years following the Civil War and the abolition of slavery, the Supreme Court made rulings that actually supported segregation laws at the state level. The most famous of these was the 1896 case of *Plessy v. Ferguson*, in which the high court upheld the constitutionality of Louisiana's 1890 law requiring "separate-but-equal" facilities for whites and blacks in railroad cars.

The lone dissent in *Plessy v. Ferguson* was authored by Associate Justice John Marshall Harlan (1833–1911), from a slaveholding family in Kentucky, who famously wrote:

In view of the Constitution, in the eye of the law, there is in this country no superior, dominant, ruling class of citizens. There is no caste here. Our Constitution is color-blind, and neither knows nor tolerates classes among citizens. In respect of civil rights, the humblest is the peer of the most powerful.

Because of this dissent and his lone dissent in an earlier case—*Civil Rights Cases* (1883)—Harlan became known as the "Great Dissenter."

Following the *Plessy v. Ferguson* decision, states went on to use the separate-but-equal principle for fifty years, passing Jim Crow laws that set up racial segregation in public schools, transportation, and recreation, sleeping, and eating facilities. This meant there were drinking fountains, benches, restrooms, bus seats, hospital beds, and theater sections designated as "Whites Only" or "Colored." One Arkansas law even provided that witnesses being sworn in to testify in a courtroom be given different Bibles depending on the color of their skin. One big problem with the "separate-but-equal" concept was that conditions were usually very unequal. For example, white schools were typically better funded than black schools.

The U.S. Supreme Court invalidated the "separate-but-equal" doctrine—at least in public education—in its historic decision in *Brown v. Board of Education* (1954). In

What was Operation Falcon?

It was the code name for the mid-April 2005 roundup of more than 10,000 fugitives in one week; the U.S. Marshals Service led the coordinated nationwide effort. Together with officers from 960 federal, state, and local law enforcement agencies, the marshals arrested 10,340 people who were wanted for various crimes, many of them violent. The operation took place during Crime Victims' Rights Week. More than 150 of the fugitives were wanted for murder, 550 for sexual assault charges, and more than 600 for armed robberies. There were also escaped prisoners and criminal suspects among those arrested. Operation Falcon was a landmark in law enforcement because of the sheer number of arrests; previous coordinated efforts had nabbed only hundreds of fugitives.

May 1954, the Supreme Court unanimously ruled that segregated schools violate the equal protection clause, overturning the separate-but-equal doctrine previously upheld by *Plessy v. Ferguson*. The *Brown* decision eventually led to the desegregation of nearly every aspect of American public life—including swimming pools, sporting events, restaurants, hotels, and prisons.

FAMOUS U.S. TRIALS

What were the Salem witch trials?

The Salem witch trials took place in Salem, Massachusetts (just north of Boston) in 1692. The proceedings against 200 people accused of witchcraft became a symbol or allegory for searching out or harassing anyone who holds unpopular views. Indeed, the nineteen hangings that resulted from the witch hunt provide students of history with a cautionary tale about the hazards of mass hysteria.

In the 1600s, people widely believed in witchcraft and that those who wielded its supernatural power could perform acts of ill will against their neighbors. Courts somewhat regularly heard cases involving the malice of witches. Before the notorious trials of 1692, the records of colonial Massachusetts and Connecticut show that seventy witch cases had been tried, and eighteen of the accused were convicted. But nothing had reached the scale of the 1692 witch hunt.

In January of that year, the daughter and niece of Reverend Samuel Parris began exhibiting strange behavior. Upon examination by a doctor, the conclusion was that the young girls (ages nine and eleven) were bewitched. Compelled to name those who had bewitched them, the girls named a Carib Indian slave who worked in the minister's home and two other women—one a derelict and the other an outcast. They were arrested. Hearings were held and others were accused, including upstanding members of the community whose only "crime" seemed to be their opposition to Reverend Parris. By May, jails in Salem and Boston were filled with some seventy accused people.

Through the summer and into September, fifty of the accused confessed to practicing witchcraft, twenty-six were convicted, and nineteen were executed. The colonial governor of Massachusetts, Sir William Phips, became alarmed by the number of convictions and ordered the Salem court to disband, commencing hearings of the remaining cases in a superior court. Of the fifty still accused, the court indicted only twenty-three people

In this 1902 illustration, Mary Walcott is shown accusing a woman of witchcraft during the Salem trials.

and, of these cases, there were only three convictions—all of which were overturned. In 1693, Phips pardoned those whose cases were still pending and declared that witchcraft was no longer an actionable offense.

Who was John Peter Zenger?

German-born John Peter Zenger (1697–1746) was a New York City printer who was accused of seditious libel in 1735. His case changed the definition of libel in American courtrooms and laid the foundation for freedom of the press.

In 1733, New York received a new colonial governor from England, William Cosby (1690–1736), who quickly earned the contempt of the colonists. A prosperous businessman who opposed Cosby and his grievous tactics approached Zenger, offering to back a newspaper that he would both edit and publish. Zenger agreed, and on November 5, 1733, the first issue of the *Weekly Journal* was released. It included scathing criticisms of the royal governor, raising Cosby's ire. After burning several issues of the papers, Cosby had Zenger arrested in November 1734. The editor-publisher continued to operate the journal from inside his jail cell, dictating editorials to his wife through the door.

Zenger's case went to trial in August 1735. Prominent Philadelphia attorney Andrew Hamilton (1676–1741), considered the best lawyer in the colonies, came to Zenger's defense. Hamilton admitted his client was guilty of publishing the papers, but, he argued, that in order for libel to be proved, Zenger's statements had to be both false and malicious. The prosecution contested the definition of libel, asserting that libelous statements are any words that are "scandalous, seditious, and tend to disquiet the people." The court agreed with the prosecution, and Hamilton was therefore unable to bring forth any evidence to support the truth of the material Zenger printed in the *Weekly Journal*.

The defense argument was not heard until Hamilton made his closing statement; his summation stands as one of the most famous in legal history. He accused the court of suppressing evidence, urged the jury to consider the court's actions "as the strongest evidence," and declared that liberty is the people's "only bulwark against lawless power.… Men who injure and oppress the people under their administration provoke them to cry out and complain."

The brilliant attorney closed by urging the gentlemen of the jury to take up the cause of liberty, telling them that by so doing, they will have "baffled the attempt of tyranny." Hamilton's impassioned speech convinced the seven jury members, and they found Zenger not guilty. It was considered one of the earliest cases of jury nullification, a process by which jurors ignore settled law to reach their decision.

Discharged from prison the next day, Zenger returned to his printing business, publishing the transcripts of his own trial. While colonial officials were reluctant to accept the ruling on the definition of libel, the case became famous throughout the American colonies. Once the colonists had thrown off England's royal rule and established a new republic, the nation's founding fathers codified the Zenger trial's ruling in the Bill of Rights, in which the First Amendment to the U.S. Constitution guarantees freedom of the press.

Who was Dred Scott? Why was his court case so important?

The decision in the case of Dred Scott pronounced the Missouri Compromise (1820) unconstitutional and served to deepen the divide between North and South, helping pave the way for the Civil War.

In the mid-1800s, Dred Scott (c. 1795–1858), who had been born into slavery in Virginia, tried to claim his freedom on the basis that he had traveled with his owner in Wisconsin and Illinois, where slavery had been prohibited by the Missouri Compromise of 1820. In the Missouri Compromise, Congress decided to admit Missouri as a slave state and Maine as a free state and declared that the territories north of the 36th parallel (present-day Missouri's southern border) were free, with the exception of the state of Missouri.

After a lifetime of slavery, Dred Scott sued Missouri for his freedom in April 1846. The case, which hinged on Scott's travels in free territories in the North, went through two trials; the second was granted due to a procedural error in the first. In 1850, at the conclusion of the second trial, a Missouri jury ruled Scott a free man based on precedents that indicated residence in a free territory or state resulted in emancipation, regardless of the fact that Missouri itself was a slave state. The lawyer for Scott's owner immediately appealed the decision before the Missouri Supreme Court, where a pro-slavery judge reversed the ruling, rescinding Scott's freedom.

Scott got a new lawyer, who took the case to a federal court. In 1854, a federal circuit court in St. Louis again heard Dred Scott's case, but his freedom was again denied. This decision was appealed to the U.S. Supreme Court, which began hearing the case in 1856.

In March 1857, the Supreme Court, which had a Southern majority, ruled 7–2 that Scott's residence in Wisconsin and Illinois did not make him free, that a black (a "Negro descended from slaves") had no rights as an American citizen and therefore could not bring suit in a federal court, and that Congress never had the authority to ban slavery in the territories. This upended the Missouri Compromise and further stirred up the debate over slavery.

After the ruling, a different family became the owner of Dred Scott, who then gave Scott, his wife, and two daughters their freedom. Dred Scott died a few months later in 1858.

Why was Susan B. Anthony tried?

Susan B. Anthony (1820–1906) was tried for violating federal voting laws. The suffrage movement was in full swing in 1872 when Anthony and fourteen female companions went to the Rochester, New York, voter registration office and demanded to be registered. When the officials refused, Anthony argued with them, showing them the written opinion of Judge Henry R. Selden, who agreed with her (and others) that the Fourteenth Amendment (1868) also protects women's rights, including the right to vote.

She threatened the registrars that she would sue them if they did not allow her to participate in elections. They gave in, and the women signed up to vote. On Election Day, November 5, they did just that. Twenty-three days later, all fifteen women were arrested

Antislavery and women's rights activist Susan B. Anthony was arrested for having the gall to cast a vote in 1872. She believed that the Fourteenth Amendment gave women that right.

for having done so. Bail was set, and eventually, all the women were released.

The following June, Anthony's trial got underway. The U.S. district attorney presented the government's case against her: she had "upon the 5th day of November, 1872 … voted…. At which time she was a woman." She was found guilty and ordered to pay a fine of $100. In another act of civil disobedience, Anthony refused to pay it, saying, "Resistance to tyranny is obedience to God."

In the coming years, the nation's courts continued to narrowly interpret the Fourteenth Amendment to the U.S. Constitution to the exclusion of women. Anthony died twenty-four years before American women were granted suffrage (after the Nineteenth Amendment was ratified in 1920).

Her face would appear on the Susan B. Anthony dollar coin.

Who was the famous Mata Hari?

When Dutch-born Margaretha Zelle MacLeod (1876–1917) was arrested in Paris on February 13, 1917, there was scant hard evidence that this woman, known as Mata Hari, was actually a spy for the Germans during World War I. However, there was plenty of evidence that she had long consorted with the enemy and had been paid by them, but for exactly what, it was never discovered. She was a former exotic dancer, who could count as her lovers a "who's who" of European men.

At the age of eighteen, she married a middle-aged colonial captain in the Dutch Army, who was posted to duty on the island of Java, where his young and beautiful wife, now twenty-one years old, learned not only the Malay language but their native dances as well. Her Javanese friends named her Mata Hari, meaning "the eye of the dawn." Upon returning to Holland, Mata Hari separated from her husband and moved to Paris, where she enjoyed a life of excess and soon became known as an exotic Hindu dancer. She performed throughout Europe, all the while engaging in liaisons with powerful and wealthy men. In 1914, she moved to Germany, where she is believed to have been trained as a spy.

With World War I on, Mata Hari returned to Paris. She renewed her ties with men of influence and, in that capacity, collected information for the Germans. The Allied nations kept a close eye on her; suspecting her of espionage, they set a trap for her. She became a double agent. The French sent her to Spain to work, but there, she reportedly met regularly with German intelligence agents. When the Germans ordered her back to

Paris, Allied officials—having intercepted a German cable for her—awaited her return. They arrested Mata Hari, who was found in possession of a check from the Germans. She was killed by a firing squad on October 15, 1917.

Many questions remain unanswered about whether or not she passed along vital information.

Who were Leopold and Loeb?

Nathan "Babe" Leopold (1904–1971) and Richard "Dickie" Loeb (1905?–1936) were privileged, well-educated, even brilliant, young men who committed what they believed to be the perfect murder. Both were from well-to-do Chicago families. Eighteen-year-old Loeb became the youngest graduate of the University of Michigan. Nineteen-year-old Leopold was a member of Phi Beta Kappa and a law student at the University of Chicago. The two became friends and, as testimony would later reveal, became convinced that they could literally get away with murder—that they could plan it, carry it out, and never get caught.

On May 21, 1924, the pair carried out their dastardly plan. Their victim was fourteen-year-old Bobby Franks, son of a millionaire and cousin to Loeb. Franks's body was found, as were a pair of eyeglasses belonging to Leopold. The spectacles were traced to him, and he and Loeb (who was part of Leopold's alibi) were grilled by the police. They stuck to their story for exactly one day. Then, Loeb, believing Leopold had betrayed him, confessed. They were charged with murder and kidnapping.

Their trial became a media spectacle and was called by some "the trial of the century." Under the advice of noted defense attorney Clarence Darrow (1857–1938), the pair pled guilty, reducing what would have otherwise been death sentences to life in prison plus ninety-nine years.

In 1936, Loeb was killed by a fellow prison inmate. In 1958, Leopold was freed—his sentence had been reduced by Illinois governor Adlai Stevenson II (1900–1965) in exchange for the inmate's contribution to testing for malaria during World War II. He lived out his life in Puerto Rico, where he married, earned a master's degree, performed charitable works, and taught.

What was the background for the Scopes Trial?

In the early 1900s, the fundamentalist movement grew. Fundamentalists insisted on taking everything in the Bible literally, as if it actually happened as described.

Mild-mannered math and science teacher John Scopes was put on trial for teaching evolution to his high school class, which was a violation of Tennessee state law even though the topic was covered in the school-approved textbook.

They feared the scientific teachings of evolution and geology that did not support a literal reading of the first chapters of Genesis. In 1925, the state of Tennessee passed a law prohibiting the teaching of evolution in schools.

What was the Scopes trial?

A key moment in the fight over evolution was the 1925 Scopes Trial in Dayton, Tennessee. It was often called the "Scopes Monkey Trial." A teacher, John Scopes (1900–1970), was tried for breaking the Tennessee law against teaching evolution. He was found guilty, but the decision was later thrown out in an appeals court on a technicality. The one-week trial was the media event of the time.

National figure William Jennings Bryan (1860–1925) came to Dayton to help the prosecuting team. Bryan had run for president three times on the Democratic ticket and had served as secretary of state under Woodrow Wilson (1856–1924) from 1912 to 1915. Famous Chicago attorney Clarence Darrow (1857–1938) joined the defense team. When the judge refused to let Darrow bring in expert witnesses to defend evolution, Darrow pulled a surprise move and called Bryan to take the stand to defend a literal reading of the Bible. Darrow tried to find inconsistencies in Bryan's explanations.

Who was Billy Mitchell? Why was his court-martial so famous?

The 1925 military trial of William "Billy" Mitchell (1879–1936) made headlines because of the defendant's open and controversial criticism of the U.S. military.

A U.S. general in World War I (1914–1918), Mitchell returned from the experience convinced that future military strength depended on air power. In fact, he had commanded the American Expeditionary Force during the war in Europe and had even pro-

Was *Inherit the Wind* an accurate film about the Scopes trial?

The play *Inherit the Wind,* written by Jerome Lawrence and Robert Edwin Lee (not to be confused with the Confederate general Robert Edward Lee), was based on the trial and first performed in 1955. It was made into the classic black-and-white 1960 movie with actors Spencer Tracy, Fredric March, Gene Kelly, Dick York, and Harry Morgan. The movie has some great performances and dramatic scenes. The movie follows the play very closely.

However, the play has numerous inaccuracies. In the actual trial, John Scopes never went to jail. He was not burned in effigy by a hostile town. He did not have a girlfriend, who was brought in as a witness at the trial. William Jennings Bryan did not die in the courtroom. It turns out the play, although built around the actual Scopes trial, was more of a commentary on the controversial McCarthy trials against communism going on in the 1950s.

posed to General John Pershing (1860–1948) that troops be dropped by parachute behind German lines; Pershing dismissed the idea. The war over, in 1921 Mitchell declared that "the first battles of any future war will be air battles." But when the navy and war departments failed to develop an air service, Mitchell was outspoken about it, charging the military with incompetence and criminal negligence and describing the administration as treasonable. Those were fighting words.

Mitchell was charged with insubordination and "conduct of a nature to bring discredit upon the military service," and his trial began in October 1925. Mitchell was found guilty and was suspended without pay from the military for a period of five years. Congress entered the fray, proposing a joint resolution to restore Mitchell's rank, but President Calvin Coolidge (1872–1933) upheld the court's decision. Mitchell resigned from the military.

He returned to civilian life but continued to write and speak about his belief in an air force. He died in 1936, about five years too soon to see his predictions come true. In surprise air raids on December 7, 1941, the Japanese attacked U.S. military installations in the Philippines and Hawaii. Though the U.S. military built an impressive and mighty air fleet during World War II, many observers felt the military could have been better prepared had Mitchell's advice been heeded years earlier.

In 1946 Mitchell was posthumously awarded the Congressional Gold Medal. His story was told in the 1955 movie *The Court-Martial of Billy Mitchell*, starring Gary Cooper.

Who were the Scottsboro Boys?

The Scottsboro Boys were nine African American youths falsely accused of raping two white women aboard a railway car in 1931. They were called the Scottsboro Boys because the event and subsequent trials took place in Scottsboro, Alabama. The young defendants were Clarence Norris, Charlie Weems, Haywood Patterson, Olen Montgomery, Ozie Powell, Willie Roberson, Eugene Williams, Andy Wright, and Roy Wright.

Due to racial prejudice, the youths received a sham trial. Facing the death penalty, the young defendants received legal help from the International Labor Defense (ILD) group and the NAACP (though the NAACP later dropped out). Though convicted, the U.S. Supreme Court reversed the conviction of one of the defendants in *Powell v. Alabama* (1932), ruling that criminal defendants facing the death penalty must have an attorney. Because the defendants did not receive counsel until moments before the trial, the court ruled that their trial violated due process.

Later, in *Norris v. Alabama* (1935), the U.S. Supreme Court reversed a subsequent conviction of another Scottsboro Boy because the jury selection process was filled with racial bias. All-white juries convicted the Scottsboro Boys on several occasions. Eventually, several of the defendants were paroled. Alabama governor George Wallace (1919–1998) pardoned Clarence Norris in 1976.

The plight of the Scottsboro Boys is seen as a national tragedy and a prime example of a miscarriage of justice.

Notorious American gangster Alphonse "Scarface Al" Capone (1899–1947), whose crime syndicate terrorized Chicago in the 1920s, was brought to trial for income tax evasion. After Chicago police had been unable to bring Capone to justice for his criminal activities, which included trafficking bootleg liquor, gambling, prostitution, and murder, the Federal Bureau of Investigation determined that the only way to prosecute the crime boss would be through violation of the tax laws.

In 1931, Capone was found guilty on five counts of tax evasion, sentenced to eleven years in prison, and charged $50,000 in fines and $30,000 in court costs. While his first jail cell, in Illinois's Cook County Jail, allowed him the luxuries of a private shower, phone conversations, telegrams, and even visits by other gangsters, including "Lucky" Luciano and "Dutch" Schultz, Capone was eventually moved to Alcatraz Island in San Francisco Bay, where he received no privileges. Released in 1939, Capone lived out his remaining years with his wife and son in Miami Beach, where his mental health deteriorated due to neurosyphilis.

The 1932 movie *Scarface*, starring Paul Muni, was inspired by the Al Capone story.

Who was tried at Nuremberg?

Following World War II (1939–1945), twenty-four leaders of Nazi Germany were put on trial at Nuremberg's Palace of Justice in 1945 and 1946 by the International Military Tribunal. The site was deliberately selected by the Allies, as the now bombed-out city of Nuremberg was considered a seat of Nazi power.

Though many, including Soviet leader Joseph Stalin (1979–1953), thought that Hitler's henchmen ought only to be tried as a show of justice before they were executed, others, notably U.S. chief prosecutor and U.S. Supreme Court justice Robert Jackson (1892–1954), believed due process of law must be observed. The American view prevailed.

The tribunal indicted twenty-three Nazi leaders on four counts: conspiracy, crimes against peace, war crimes, and crimes against humanity. The case against the Nazis was based on a mountain of written evidence, such as orders, reports, logs, letters, and diaries; the Germans had scrupulously recorded their evil deeds. The presentation of the documents was punctuated with live testimony of a German civilian contractor who, out of curiosity, had followed a Nazi detachment to an embankment where several thousand Jewish men, women, and children were shot and buried in a pit, and of a French woman, a survivor of the horrors of Auschwitz, recollecting a night when "children had been hurled into furnaces alive" since the Nazis had run out of fuel.

The atrocities were rendered unimaginably horrific by the sheer number of Nazi victims. (See "The World Wars" chapter for the statistics on the victims.) The defense was prohibited from employing a "you did it, too" argument, which would have been an attempt to justify their actions by claiming it was all part of war. The Allies were determined to bring the Nazis to justice for their appalling and diabolical acts.

Among those tried at Nuremberg were Hitler's chief deputy, Hermann Göring (1893–1946), whom a *New Yorker* correspondent covering the trials described as "a brain without a conscience"; Foreign Minister Joachim von Ribbentrop (1893–1946); and Armaments Minister Albert Speer (1905–1981). Martin Bormann (1900–1945) was tried and convicted in absentia since it was not known at the time that he was already dead. In the end, ten of those accused were hanged. Seven were given prison terms, ranging from ten years to life. Göring escaped his hanging. Though he was supposed to be closely monitored by his jailers, he managed to secure a vial of cyanide, which he swallowed a few hours before his scheduled execution.

The trials at Nuremberg cemented the principle that wartime leaders are accountable under international law for their crimes and atrocities.

Why was Alger Hiss tried?

U.S. public official Alger Hiss (1904–1996) was tried for perjury during 1949 and 1950. His first trial ended in a hung jury, and the second trial concluded with a guilty verdict and a sentence of five years in prison. Hiss served four years and eight months before he was released and returned to private life. To this day, many believe Hiss was framed by Republican politicians who charged President Harry S. Truman's (1884–1972) administration with employing communists who acted as secret agents for the Soviet Union.

The politically charged case was packed with intrigue, including the testimony of a *Time* magazine senior editor who was later revealed to be a perjurer and who used at least seven different aliases in a fourteen-year period; microfilm evidence stored in a hollowed-out pumpkin in the middle of a farm field; and an old typewriter, which later evidence and testimony revealed was probably a fake.

The case against Hiss was made amid investigations made by the House Un-American Activities Committee (HUAC). It was 1948, and the Cold War between the United States and Soviet Union was on; distrust was running high. When *Time* editor Whittaker Chambers (1901–1961) appeared before the House committee and claimed that Hiss had been a courier who had transported confidential government documents to the Soviets, Hiss, then president of the Carnegie Endowment for International Peace, became the subject of investigation. He was indicted and stood trial.

In spite of Alger Hiss's distinguished career as a public servant (he had served in the State Department for eleven years); a parade of character witnesses who testified of his integrity, loyalty, and veracity; and his own vehement denial of the charges, the prosecution managed to bring enough evidence against him to convince a jury that Hiss lied when he said the charges that he was a secret agent were "a complete fabrication."

Even after his conviction, Hiss's lawyers worked tirelessly to appeal the case; all attempts were denied. In 1957, Hiss published his own account of the case, *In the Court of Public Opinion*, in which he reasserted his innocence. Then, in 1973, during the Watergate hearings, former White House counsel John Dean's (1938–) explosive testimony included the statement that he heard President Richard Nixon say, "The typewriters are always the key.... We built one in the Hiss case." (Nixon had served on the HUAC committee during Hiss's trial.)

In 1988, Hiss published again; the book was titled *Recollections of a Life*. Four years later, at the age of eighty-seven, Hiss appealed to the Russian government to examine their intelligence archives to see what they revealed about him; the response came back that there was "not a single document" substantiating the allegations that Hiss had collaborated with the Soviet Union's intelligence service. That same year, 1992, Hiss's son, Tony, wrote an article for the *New Yorker* magazine; it was titled "My Father's Honor."

Why were the Rosenbergs tried?

Husband and wife Julius (1918–1953) and (1915–1953) Rosenberg were tried for conspiracy to commit wartime espionage. Arrested in 1950, the Rosenbergs were charged with passing nuclear weapons data to the Soviets, enabling the communists to develop and explode their own atomic bomb—an event that had been announced to the American public by President Harry S. Truman in September 1949.

As the realization set in that the United States could now be the victim of an atomic attack, the anxieties of the Cold War heightened. Citizens were encouraged to build bomb shelters, schoolchildren participated in air-raid drills, civil-defense films were screened, and entire towns conducted tests of how residents would respond in the event of an atomic bomb attack.

In the 1940s, top-secret information had been leaked from the Manhattan Project in Los Alamos, New Mexico. The Manhattan Project had developed the atomic bomb, which was dropped on the cities of Hiroshima and Nagasaki, Japan, in 1945. The leaks were traced to New York City machine-shop owner Julius Rosenberg, his wife, and her brother, David Greenglass (1922–2014). The case marked the first time American civilians were charged with espionage, and the trial made international headlines.

Though the Rosenbergs were only two of many involved in the conspiracy, theirs was the heaviest of the punishments handed down in the cases against the spy

Charged with spying for the Soviet Union, Julius and Ethel Rosenberg were sentenced to death for being part of a ring that leaked secrets about nuclear, radar, sonar, and jet-propulsion technology.

ring. For their betrayal and their refusal to talk, the Rosenbergs were sentenced to death. In issuing the sentence, Judge Irving Kaufman (1910–1992) accused the couple of having "altered the course of history." The penalty rocked the world. As Supreme Court justice Felix Frankfurter (1882–1965) put it, they "were tried for conspiracy and sentenced for treason." They were electrocuted one evening in 1953 as New York's Union Square filled with an estimated 10,000 protesters.

What was the lasting effect of the Clarence Earl Gideon trials?

The lasting effect of Clarence Earl Gideon's (1910–1972) famous case was that criminal defendants in state court who are facing felony charges have the right to attorneys. A fifty-one-year-old drifter charged with burglary in Panama City, Florida, Clarence Earl Gideon had two trials, in 1961 and 1963. But it's what happened between the two trials that continues to be important to every American today.

What might have been pretty standard fare in the day-to-day business of the American justice system (Gideon was charged with robbing a cigarette machine and a jukebox), the Gideon case instead made history when the defendant successfully argued that his constitutional rights had been denied when he was refused an attorney. The Sixth Amendment to the U.S. Constitution provides that those charged with a crime should receive the "assistance of counsel." But the question was whether this Sixth Amendment freedom—which technically applied only in federal trials—would be extended to state criminal cases.

Existing law did not support Gideon's claim to an attorney. In *Betts v. Brady* (1942), the U.S. Supreme Court had ruled that the Sixth Amendment right to counsel was not extended to the states via the due process clause of the Fourteenth Amendment. In other words, people like Gideon did not have a constitutional right to an attorney.

However, Gideon kept pressing the issue. Though he had a limited education, after a guilty verdict was handed down in his 1961 trial, Gideon knew enough about his rights to petition the Supreme Court, saying that his right to a fair trial (guaranteed by the Sixth Amendment) had been violated. Since he was not able to hire a lawyer to defend himself, the trial had not been fair. The petition, one of thousands the Supreme Court receives each year, somehow rose to the top.

The high court heard Gideon's case and appointed prominent Washington, D.C., lawyer Abe Fortas (1910–1982) to argue for Gideon at the Supreme Court. (Fortas later became a Supreme Court justice.) The U.S. Supreme Court overruled *Betts v. Brady*, ruling that "any person haled into court, who is too poor to hire a lawyer, cannot be assured a fair trial unless counsel is provided for him." For Gideon, the opinion served to throw out the first trial; for the rest of America, it was assurance that regardless of the crime, a defendant would be guaranteed legal counsel.

With the benefit of that counsel, Gideon's case was retried in 1963. He was acquitted on all charges.

What are Miranda warnings?

Familiar to many Americans from TV police dramas, the Miranda warnings are a reading of the arrested person's rights: "You have a right to remain silent … anything you say can and will be used against you in a court. You have a right to consult with a lawyer … if you cannot afford a lawyer, one will be appointed for you.…"

Reading the defendant his or her rights became a requirement after the 1963 trial of Ernesto Miranda (1941–1976), a young Latino man accused of rape. He was found guilty and sentenced to twenty to thirty years' imprisonment. But Alvin Moore, Miranda's court-appointed lawyer, had revealed through his questioning of a police officer that the defendant had not been notified of his right to the services of an attorney. The same police officer had taken Miranda's written confession following two hours of interrogation.

The case was appealed all the way to the U.S. Supreme Court, which ruled 5–4 in Miranda's favor in June 1966. Chief Justice Earl Warren (1891–1974) reasserted that "prior to any questioning a person must be warned that he has a right to remain silent, that any statement he does make may be used as evidence against him, and that he has the right to … an attorney."

Miranda's first trial was thrown out, and in 1967, he again stood trial in Arizona. But the prosecution secured new evidence—the testimony of his estranged girlfriend that Miranda had confessed to her that he had committed the rape he was charged with. He was convicted and again sentenced to twenty to thirty years in prison. Released on parole, Miranda died in a bar fight in January 1976. Ironically, police officers on the scene found cards in Miranda's pockets in the bar detailing the Miranda rights. Police officers, the courts, and defendants still remember the importance of the case—even if they can't recall Ernesto Miranda's name or crime.

What was the Gang of Four?

The Gang of Four was a group within China's Communist Party that, under the leadership of Mao Zedong's (1893–1976) wife, Jiang Qing (1914–1991), twenty-one years his junior, carried out its own power-hungry agenda and plotted the takeover of the government from Chairman Mao.

A former stage and movie actress, Jiang was also an astute student of politics. In the late 1960s (at which time she had been married to Mao for some thirty years), she became associated with former army commander Lin Biao (1907–1971), and the pair conspired to stage a coup. In 1970, at a Communist Party conference, they announced that Lin had surpassed Mao as the leader of the people; one year later, Lin and Jiang tried to overthrow Mao's government. Failing, Lin fled the country (his plane was later shot down), and Jiang succeeded in covering up her involvement in the affair.

However, she continued her subversive activities, associating with three other members of the politburo (the chief executive and political committee of the Communist Party). In 1974, Mao publicly admonished his wife and her cohorts, Wang Hongwen, Yao Wenyuan, and Zhang Chunqiao, to cease their power-seeking activities. Infighting in the party had already resulted in Mao's loss of influence. Two years later, on September 9, 1976, Mao died. The Gang of Four were arrested and thrown into prison. There they remained for years while the case against them was formulated, resulting in an indictment that consisted of 20,000 words.

Finally, on November 20, 1980, the Gang of Four, expanded to include six other conspirators, were put on trial—charged with counterrevolutionary acts, including sedition and conspiracy to overthrow the government, persecution of party and state leaders, suppression of the people, and plotting to assassinate Mao. During nearly six weeks of testimony, Jiang's machinations were revealed to the 600 representatives who attended the trial, held in an air force auditorium in western Beijing, as well as to the Chinese press (foreign press was prohibited from attending).

Her laundry list of malicious acts as ringleader of the Gang of Four included public humiliation and even torture of Communist Party rivals, execution of her personal enemies, inspiring the fear of the masses, and purging the arts of anything that did not carry a revolutionary theme. Jiang, while not denying many of these acts, insisted that she had all along acted at the behest of her husband, Mao. During the explosive testimony and presentation of evidence, which included tapes and documents substantiating the state's case against Jiang, she made outbursts, was temporarily expelled from the courtroom, was dragged screaming from the courtroom twice, and even taunted her accusers into executing her, saying it would be "more glorious to have my head chopped off."

In the end, Jiang and one other conspirator were found guilty and sentenced to death (later commuted to life in prison), and the eight others were also found guilty and charged sentences ranging from sixteen years to life in prison. Jiang died on May 14, 1991, in what appeared to be a suicide.

What was the "trial of the twentieth century"?

In the twentieth century, several trials received great media attention, be it by newspaper or, later, television. Each trial was claimed by some to be the "trial of the century." Below are some of these famous trials, in addition to those mentioned above.

- The Trial of Harry Thaw: The 1907–1908 trial involved Harry Thaw (1871–1947), whose lawyers went through two trials (the first ended in a deadlocked jury) to convince jurors that Thaw suffered from "dementia Americana," a condition supposedly unique to American men that had caused him to experience an uncontrollable desire to kill a man who had had an affair with his wife; the case took "innocent by reason of insanity" to new heights. The well-to-do, Harvard-educated Thaw was declared not guilty.

- Sacco and Vanzetti: In this 1921 case, Italian-born anarchists Nicola Sacco (1891–1927) and Bartolomeo Vanzetti (1888–1927) were charged with and, amid international uproar, found guilty of murder and robbery. So many people were convinced of the pair's innocence that demonstrations were mounted in cities around the world. They were executed in August 1927, but fifty years later, Governor Michael Dukakis (1933–) of Massachusetts signed a special proclamation clearing their names.

Italian immigrants Bartolomeo Vanzetti (left) and Nicola Sacco (right) were the victims of anti-immigrant sentiments when they were falsely accused of armed robbery and murder. Executed in 1921, they were much later pardoned by Governor Michael Dukakis of Massachusetts.

- 1935 Bruno Hauptmann: In 1935, the German-born Bruno Richard Hauptmann (1899–1936) was convicted of murdering the twenty-month-old son of celebrated aviator Charles A. Lindbergh (1902–1974) and his noted wife, Anne Morrow Lindbergh (1906–2001), after the child was kidnapped from the family's East Amwell, New Jersey, home in March 1932. For two and a half months, the world had prayed for the safe return of Charles Jr., but the toddler's body was found on May 12 two miles from the Lindbergh home. Public outrage demanded justice. Evidence surfaced that implicated Hauptmann, who was tried in January 1935. Found guilty, he died by electrocution. Influential journalist H. L. Mencken noted that the trial, in which the conviction seemed to hinge on circumstantial evidence and which was attended by a "circuslike" atmosphere, was the "biggest story since the Resurrection." Though many remained convinced that officials had acted hastily to bring a case against Hauptmann and maintained that he'd been framed, efforts to clear his name continued to be denied into the 1990s.

- O. J. Simpson: Former football player O. J. Simpson (1947–) was tried and acquitted in the murders of his former wife, Nicole, and her friend Ronald Goldman in this 1995 criminal case. One observer said this trial had it all—"women, minorities, public interest, domestic violence, fallen hero" and, through its live media coverage, had "exposed the legal system to the public." In a subsequent civil trial, Simpson was held liable for the wrongful death of his former wife and Goldman.

ECONOMICS AND BUSINESS

ECONOMICS

What does laissez-faire mean?

From the French, laissez-faire literally means "to let (people) do (as they choose)." As an economic doctrine, laissez-faire opposes government interference in economic and business matters or, at least, desires to keep government's role to an absolute minimum. Laissez-faire favors a free market (a market characterized by open competition). The theory was popularized during the late eighteenth century as a reaction to mercantilism. Noted Scottish economist Adam Smith (1723–1790) was among the advocates of a laissez-faire market.

Who was Adam Smith?

Scottish economist Adam Smith (1723–1790) is popular with conservative economists today because of his work titled *The Wealth of Nations* (written in 1776), which proposes a system of natural liberty in trade and commerce—in other words, a free-market economy. Smith, who was teaching at the University of Glasgow at the time, wrote, "Consumption is the sole end and purpose of all production, and the interest of the producer ought to be attended to, only so far as it may be necessary for promoting that of the consumer."

The Wealth of Nations established the classical school of political economy but has been faulted for showing no awareness of the developing Industrial Revolution. While Smith advocated both free-market competition and limited government intervention, he also viewed unemployment as a necessary evil to keep costs—and therefore prices—in check.

However, Smith also wrote *The Theory of Moral Sentiments,* published in 1759, in which he lays out his views on ethics. He believes that humans need to act with the

333

virtues of prudence, justice, and beneficence (being good to others). He also did not value the amassing of great wealth. *The Theory of Moral Sentiments* is the background for his later book, *The Wealth of Nations*, and it shows that Smith would not be an advocate for unrestrained capitalism.

What is capitalism?

The cornerstones of capitalism are private ownership of property (capital goods); property and capital create income for those who own the property or capital; individuals and firms openly compete with one another, with each seeking its own economic gain (so that competition determines prices, production, and distribution of goods); and participants in the system are profit-driven (in other words, earning a profit is the main goal).

There is no pure capitalist system; national governments become involved in the regulation of business to some degree. But the economy of the United States is highly capitalistic in nature, as are the economies of many other industrialized nations, including Great Britain.

What is mercantilism?

Mercantilism is an economic system that developed as feudalism was dissolving at the end of the Middle Ages. Mercantilism advocates strict government control of the national economy. Its adherents believe a healthy economy can only be achieved through state regulation. The goals were to accumulate gold or silver to be held by the royal government, establish a favorable balance of trade with other countries, develop the nation's agricultural concerns as well as its manufacturing concerns, and establish foreign trading policies.

What is Keynesian economics?

Keynesian economics is the collected theories of British economist and monetary expert John Maynard Keynes (1883–1946), who in 1935 published his landmark work, *The General Theory of Employment, Interest and Money*. A macroeconomist (he studied a nation's economy as a whole), Keynes departed from many of the concepts of a free-market economy. In order to ensure growth and stability, he argued that government needs to be involved in certain aspects of the nation's economic

Considered the founder of modern macroeconomics thought, John Maynard Keynes (pictured here with Russian ballerina Lydia Lopokova) was originally a mathematician, but he became the most influential economist of the twentieth century.

> ## How is the name of Keynes pronounced?
>
> "**K**eynes" is usually pronounced "KAYNZ"; and "Keynesian" is usually pronounced "KAYN-zee-in."

life. He believed in state intervention in fiscal policies, and, during recessionary times, he favored deficit spending, the loosening of monetary policies, and government public works programs (such as those of President Franklin D. Roosevelt's New Deal) to promote employment.

Keynes was a key representative at the Paris Peace Conference of 1919, where the Treaty of Versailles was drawn up, officially ending World War I. He quit the proceedings in Paris, returned to private life in London, and in 1919 published *The Economic Consequences of Peace*, arguing against the excessive war reparations that the treaty required of Germany. Keynes foresaw that the extreme punishment of Germany at the end of World War I would pave the way for future conflict in Europe.

MONEY

When was paper money first used?

Paper money first appeared in China during the Middle Ages. In the eleventh century C.E., Chinese merchants used paper notes as certificates of exchange and, later, for paying taxes to the government. It was not until the eleventh century, also in China, that the notes were backed by deposits of silver and gold (called "hard money").

What were pieces of eight?

Pieces of eight were Spanish silver coins (pesos) that circulated along with other hard currency in the American colonies. Since the settlements in the New World were all possessions of their mother countries (England, Spain, France, Portugal, and the Netherlands), they did not have monetary systems of their own. England forbade its American colonies to issue money. Colonists used whatever foreign currency they could get their hands on. Pieces of eight (from Spain) were the most common, but reals (from Spain and Portugal) and shillings (from England) were also in circulation. The Spanish silver coin was so named because it was worth eight reals and at one time had an eight stamped on it. To make change, the coin was cut up to resemble pieces of a pie. Two pieces, or "two bits," of the silver coin made up a quarter, which is why Americans sometimes refer to a quarter (of a dollar) as two bits.

There were frequent money shortages in the colonies, which usually ran a trade deficit with Europe. The colonies supplied raw goods to Europe, but finished goods, including manufactured items, were mostly imported, resulting in an imbalance of trade. With coinage scarce, many colonists conducted trade as barter, exchanging goods and services for the same.

In 1652, Massachusetts became the first colony to mint its own coins (that year, there was no monarch on the throne of England). Although England strictly prohibited the issuance of coinage by colonists, the Puritans of Massachusetts continued to make their own coins for some thirty years thereafter, stamping the year 1652 on them as a way to circumvent the law.

What were Continentals?

Continentals were the paper money issued by the U.S. government during the American Revolution (1775–1783). Money was needed to buy supplies and ammunition and to pay soldiers. To finance the Revolution, Congress was compelled to issue paper bills, which promised holders future payment in silver. But as Congress issued more and more Continentals, the currency became devalued because there was not enough silver to back up the promised payments. By 1780, there were so many Continentals in circulation that they had become almost worthless. The phrase "not worth a Continental" was used by Americans to describe anything that had no value.

To help solve the financial crisis, some patriotic citizens contributed sums of money; in exchange, they received interest-bearing securities from the government. Eventually, European loans to the United States, notably from France, were instrumental in the American victory in the Revolutionary War.

What were wildcat banks?

Wildcat banks were state-chartered financial institutions that operated in the United States from the early 1800s until the American Civil War. Their free-lending policies and their issue of paper currency could not be backed up by gold or silver (called specie).

The Second National Bank of the United States operated between 1816 and 1836, during which time the federally controlled bank was able to restrain the wildcat institutions, which predominated in the West and South, requiring them to issue only whatever currency they could convert to coin.

However, when the charter of the Second National Bank of the United States expired in 1836, wildcat banks resumed their unsound practices. Paper currency issue and lending went unregulated amid a rush to buy lands on the frontier. The nation's currency wildly fluctuated as the renegade financial institutions loosened and tightened the money supply to suit their own needs. Furthermore, since there were so many banks issuing their own notes, the problem of counterfeiting developed. No one could tell what was true bank currency and what was the product of a good counterfeiter.

With inflation rampant and land speculation at a new high, in 1836, President Andrew Jackson (1767–1845), intent on reining in the wildcat banks, issued the Specie Circular, an order that government agents accept nothing but gold or silver as pay-

What is "rag money"?

Rag money is a derisive term for paper currency. The name comes from the early days of paper money, when paper itself was predominately made with the cotton and linen fibers from rags. Hence, bills were "rag money." Given that valued currency was issued in silver or gold coins by the established governments of Europe, it is not surprising that Americans for many years greeted paper currency—which is nothing more than a promise of future payment in coin—as something to be regarded with skepticism.

ment for new lands. When prospective land buyers (particularly in the West) took their paper bills to the state-chartered banks to be converted to coin, they found the banks' tills empty, and the holders were therefore denied the face value of their notes. Bank after bank closed its doors, causing a financial panic in 1837. But many state banks remained in business, and the issue of regulating paper currency continued to trouble the nation.

What was the National Bank Act?

The National Bank Act of 1863 was designed to create a national banking system, float federal war loans, and establish a national currency. Congress passed the act to help resolve the financial crisis that emerged during the early days of the American Civil War. The fight with the South was expensive, and no effective tax program had been drawn up to finance it. In December 1861, banks suspended specie payments (payments in gold or silver coins for paper currency)—people could not convert banknotes into coins. The government responded by passing the Legal Tender Act (1862), issuing $150 million in national notes called greenbacks. But banknotes (paper bills issued by state banks) accounted for most of the currency in circulation.

To bring financial stability to the nation and fund the war effort, the Senate introduced the National Bank Act of 1863. Secretary of the Treasury Salmon Chase (1808–1873), aided by Senator John Sherman (1823–1900) of Ohio, promoted it to the legislators. The bill was approved in the Senate by a close vote of 23 to 21. The House then passed the legislation. National banks organized under the act were required to purchase government bonds as a condition of start-up. As soon as those bonds were deposited with the federal government, the bank could issue its own notes up to 90 percent of the market value of the bonds on deposit.

The National Bank Act improved but did not solve the nation's financial problems. Some of the 1,500 state banks, which had all been issuing banknotes, were converted to national banks by additional legislation. Other state banks were driven out of business or ceased to issue notes because of the 1865 passage of a 10 percent federal tax on notes they issued, making it unprofitable for them to print their own money.

The legislation created $300 million in national currency in the form of notes issued by the national banks. But since most of this money was distributed in the East, the money supply in other parts of the country remained precarious. The West demanded more money—an issue that would dominate American politics in the years after the American Civil War. Nevertheless, the nation's banking system stayed largely the same—despite the Panic of 1873—until passage of the Federal Reserve Act in 1913.

What is the Federal Reserve?

The Federal Reserve is the central banking system in the United States. It was created in 1913 by Congress. The Federal Reserve Act called for a stable central banking system after the previous system proved ineffective. However, the Federal Reserve is not a government agency; it is a private bank.

The Federal Reserve Act created federal reserve banks in twelve regions: Boston, New York, Philadelphia, Cleveland, Richmond, Atlanta, Chicago, St. Louis, Minneapolis, Kansas City, Dallas, and San Francisco. These institutions operate as "bankers' banks"— member banks (commercial institutions) use their accounts with the Federal Reserve in the same way that consumers use their accounts on deposit at commercial banks.

The Federal Reserve Act also established a Federal Reserve Board of Governors to supervise the system. The board consists of seven members appointed by the president of the United States and approved by the Senate. Members serve fourteen-year terms.

The duties of the Federal Reserve (often called "the Fed") include lending money to commercial banks, directing the reserve banks' purchase and sale of U.S. government securities on the open market, setting reserve requirements (for how much money needs to be in the U.S. Treasury), and regulating the interest rate the Federal Reserve charges commercial banks for loans, called the discount rate. The discount rate affects rates

The Marriner S. Eccles Federal Reserve Board Building in Washington, D.C., houses the offices of the Federal Reserve.

When were ATMs introduced?

The ubiquitous automatic teller machine (ATM) was introduced in 1967 by Britain's Barclays Bank at a branch near London. Two years later, the Chemical Bank opened the first ATM in the United States at Rockville Centre, New York. Self-service banking grew steadily in the 1980s and took off in the 1990s.

---

charged by banks for loans for such things as cars, houses, and student loans. Adjusting the discount rate is the principal way the Fed influences the economy.

In performing these duties, the Federal Reserve can expand (loosen) or contract (tighten) the supply of money in circulation. The Federal Reserve also issues our money. (Look at a dollar bill and see "FEDERAL RESERVE NOTE" at the top.)

TRADE AND COMMERCE

What were indentured servants?

In colonial times in America, two kinds of indentured servants existed: voluntary and involuntary. Voluntary servants were people, often trained in a craft or skill, who could not afford passage to the colonies. In exchange for their passage, they agreed to work for a period of four to seven years for a colonial master. At the end of this period, the servant became a freeman and was usually granted land, tools, or money by the former master.

Involuntary indentured servants were poor people, those in debt, or criminals whose sentence was a period of servitude. Most indentured servants were involuntary. Their period of obligation to a colonial master was longer than that of a voluntary servant, usually seven to fourteen years. But, like their counterparts, the involuntary servants also received land, tools, or money at the end of their contract, and they, too, became freemen.

The arrival of indentured servants in the American colonies addressed a labor shortage of the early 1600s. Many came from England, Ireland, Scotland, and Germany. In European ports, people contracted themselves or became involuntarily contracted to ship captains, who transported them to the colonies, where their contracts were sold to the highest bidder. Roughly half the colonial immigrants were indentured servants.

Colonial laws ensured servants would fulfill the term of their obligation. Any servant who ran away was severely punished. Laws also protected the servants, whose masters were obligated to provide them with housing, food, medical care, and even religious training.

What was the triangular trade?

As described in the chapter "The First Americans," the triangular trade refers to the various navigation routes that emerged during the colonial period. There were numerous triangular paths that ships traveled, ferrying people, goods (both raw and finished), and livestock. The most common triangular route began on Africa's west coast, where ships picked up slaves. The second stop was the Caribbean islands—predominately the British and French West Indies—where the enslaved people were sold to plantation owners, and traders used the profits to purchase sugar, molasses, tobacco, and coffee. These raw materials were then transported north to the third stop, New England, where a rum industry was thriving. (Rum is made by fermenting molasses or sugarcane juice.) There, ships were loaded with the spirits, and traders made the last leg of their journey back across the Atlantic to Africa's west coast, where the process began again.

Other trade routes operated as follows: 1) manufactured goods were transported from Europe to the African coast; enslaved people to the West Indies; and sugar, tobacco, and coffee transported back to Europe, where the triangle began again; 2) lumber, cotton, and meat were transported from the colonies to southern Europe; wine and fruits to England; and manufactured goods to the colonies, where the triangle began again. There were as many possible routes as there were ports and demand for goods.

The tragic result of triangular trade was the transport of an estimated ten million black Africans. Sold into slavery, these human beings were often chained below deck and allowed only brief, if any, periods of exercise during the transatlantic crossing, which came to be called the Middle Passage. Conditions for the enslaved people were brutal and improved only slightly when traders realized that should they perish during the long journey across the ocean, it would adversely affect their profits upon arrival in the West Indies.

After economies in the islands of the Caribbean crashed at the end of the 1600s, many enslaved people were sold to plantation owners on the North American mainland, initiating another tragic trade route. The slave trade was abolished in the 1800s, putting an end to the capture of Africans and their forced migration to the Western Hemisphere.

What Broadway musical described the triangle trade?

The musical *1776*, which premiered on Broadway in 1969, tells about the signing of the Declaration of Independence. The character Edward Rutledge of South Carolina sings about slavery as he mocks Northerners who oppose slavery yet benefit from it:

Molasses to rum to slaves,
Who'll sail the ships back to Boston?
Ladened with gold, see it gleam,
Whose fortunes are made in the triangle trade?
Hail slavery, the New England dream!

How did the American tobacco industry get started?

Tobacco, a member of the nightshade family, is an indigenous American plant. When Christopher Columbus arrived in the West Indies in 1492, he found the native inhabitants smoking rolls of tobacco leaves, called taino. (The word tobacco is derived from the

Spanish *tabaco*, which is probably from taino.) The practice of "drinking smoke" was observed to have a relaxing effect. Columbus took seeds of the plant back with him.

By 1531, tobacco was being cultivated on a commercial scale in the Spanish colonies of the West Indies. In 1565, English naval commander John Hawkins (1532–1595) introduced tobacco to England, where smoking was condemned as a "vile and stinking custom" by King James I (1566–1625) decades later.

Tobacco was not commercially cultivated on the North American mainland until English colonist John Rolfe (1585–1622) carried seeds from the West Indies to Jamestown, Virginia, where he settled in 1610. By 1612, he had successfully cultivated tobacco and discovered a method of curing the plant, making it a viable export item. Jamestown became a boomtown, and England's King James, who collected export duties, changed his mind about the habit of smoking.

The coastal regions of Virginia, Maryland, and North Carolina were soon dominated by tobacco plantations, and the crop became the backbone of the economies in these colonies. Cultivation of tobacco did not require the same extent of land or slave labor as did other locally grown crops, such as rice and indigo, but it depleted the nutrients of soil more rapidly, causing growers to expand their lands westward.

How did the tobacco trade develop?

By 1765, colonial exports of tobacco were nearly double in value the exports of bread and flour. The crop helped define the plantation economy of the South, which prevailed until the outbreak of the American Civil War (1861–1865). During the 1800s, companies such as R. J. Reynolds Tobacco and American Tobacco were founded. Despite the highly pub-

A 1670 painting shows African slaves processing tobacco on a Southern plantation. By that time, tobacco had already become a boom crop that was making Europeans and American colonists rich.

licized dangers of using tobacco (smoking or chewing), tobacco has remained an important crop, and the manufacture of tobacco products is an important industry in the American South. Today, the top four producers of tobacco are China, Brazil, India, and the United States.

Most people are aware of the dangers of tobacco use by smoking, chewing, and as snuff. It is estimated that 100 million people have died from tobacco use. This is more than the number of people who died of war in the twentieth century. Today, there are 1.1 billion tobacco users. Someone dies every six seconds from the effects of tobacco. Cigarette use is the leading cause of preventable death.

What were the Navigation Acts?

Between 1645 and 1761, British Parliament passed a series of twenty-nine laws intended to tightly control trade in the American colonies to the benefit of English interests. The acts stipulated that goods could only enter England, Ireland, or the colonies aboard English (or English colonial) ships. Furthermore, trade between the American colonies was to be conducted entirely aboard English ships. Many goods had to be shipped directly to England.

The intent was to prevent the colonies from trading directly with any other European country, such as France. England required the colonies to sell their materials to English merchants or pay duties on goods sold to other countries. The list of articles included sugar, cotton, tobacco, indigo, rice, molasses, apples, and wool. However, the laws were difficult to enforce, and the colonists easily circumvented them. Smuggling was rampant.

What was the National Road?

The National Road was the first federal road. Today, the path of the great westward route is followed closely by U.S. Highway 40. (Interstate 70 now parallels much of it.) Congress authorized the road in 1806 to answer the cry of settlers who demanded a better route across the Appalachians into the Ohio River valley. Work began in 1811 in Cumberland, Maryland. Progress was slow, and the road did not reach present-day Wheeling, West Virginia, a distance of 130 miles, until six years later. This section was called the Cumberland Road. In 1830, President Andrew Jackson appropriated $130,000 to survey and extend it westward. Jackson called it a "national road" (it was also called the Great National Pike).

At completion in 1852, it extended from Cumberland, Maryland, to Vandalia, Illinois, east of St. Louis. The project cost the government more than $7 million. It spurred development along its route. The overland route was traversed in covered wagons and Conestogas by pioneers and tradesmen. Large quantities of goods, including livestock, grain, and finished products, were transported both east and west. Towns along the route boomed. The National Road is one of many examples that show the importance of government projects and investment in infrastructure to build the economy.

By the end of the century, the road diminished in importance as settlers, new immigrants, and goods were transported along the railroads that had begun to crisscross the nation in 1865. Nevertheless, the National Road heralded the future of federal transportation projects that would knit the nation together. Many of the original stone mile markers still exist. (Do an online image search for "National Road markers.")

The Conestoga wagon has an odd shape. Why wouldn't someone prefer the old version with a flat bottom?

Imagine a flat-bottomed wagon going up or down a hill. The goods inside would start to shift. On a big hill, this could be a problem. The curved bottom of the Conestoga greatly reduced the problem of shifting cargo. Also, the Conestoga was designed to be waterproof if the boards were caulked. It could be floated across streams, or if the wagon was pulled across a stream or river, the goods inside would stay dry. The driver of the Conestoga did not ride but rather walked alongside it.

Who is called the "Father of the Interstate System"?

President Dwight D. Eisenhower (1890–1969) is considered the "Father of the Interstate System" because upon taking office in 1953, he breathed new life into the nation's highway systems. He made it a key priority of his administration to develop better highways. He signed the Federal Aid Highway Act of 1956, popularly known as the National Interstate and Defense Highways Act. This law developed new interstate loops, created new highways, and rebuilt those that had fallen into disrepair. Essentially, the law revitalized the nation's highway system.

Interestingly, Eisenhower got the idea of modern highways from seeing the Autobahn in Germany, which had been built by the Nazis.

Conestoga wagons like this one preserved at the B&O Museum in Baltimore, Maryland, had a curved bottom that was designed to help keep supplies from shifting during travel on rough ground.

343

The state of Missouri was awarded the first contract for the new highway system. Work began on US 40 (now I-70) near St. Charles, Missouri.

What is the impact of the interstate system of highways?

The interstate system would have an immense impact on American society. It made possible the growth and sprawl of suburbs, which often led to the decline of nearby cities. Automobiles became for many their only means of transportation and led to the demise of public transportation in many places. Interstates would make it possible for people to live far from their workplaces and thus would need to commute long distances each day, so interstates even changed how people spent their time.

America would become greatly dependent on oil, which has greatly impacted American political and military strategy around the world. (For example, there would be little interest in countries such as Iraq, Iran, Kuwait, and Saudi Arabia if they were not important oil producers.) Lastly, all those cars driving so many miles on interstates is an important factor contributing to greenhouse gases and global climate change.

What is the Erie Canal?

Completed in 1825, the Erie Canal joined the Atlantic Ocean to the Great Lakes, linking the East with the West, allowing freight and settlers to easily move back and forth between the regions. Begun in 1817, the canal was sponsored by Governor DeWitt Clinton (1769–1828) of New York, who planned and completed the huge building project. Costing over $7 million, the original canal was 363 miles long, 40 feet wide, and 4 feet deep. It had eighty-three locks, which raised vessels 562 feet between the Hudson River and Lake Erie.

A lock is a section of a canal that can be closed to control the water level and is then used to either raise or lower a vessel to another body of water. Beginning at Albany, New York, on the Hudson River (which flows into the Atlantic Ocean at New York City), the canal extends west as far as Buffalo, New York, on Lake Erie (one of the five Great Lakes).

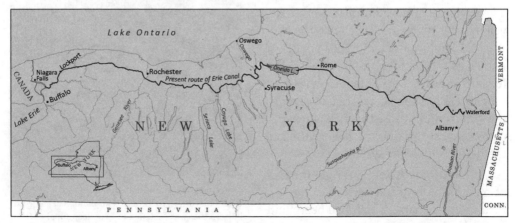

The Erie Canal currently reaches 363 miles (584 kilometers) from Albany to Buffalo, New York.

The waterway could transport passengers aboard boats and move cargo aboard barges, which were pulled by teams of horses and mules walking on the side of the canal. The new transportation route reduced freight rates both eastward and westward, made Buffalo a major port in the region and New York City a major international port, and was a catalyst for population growth in upstate New York and throughout the area that is now Ohio, Michigan, Indiana, Illinois, Wisconsin, and Minnesota. Other states soon built their own canals, opening up the country's interior to development and commerce. Since crops could be shipped from these lush farmlands and as more farms came into existence, the Erie Canal helped supply the newly arrived immigrants in the eastern cities with food; in turn, they shipped manufactured goods west to the farming communities.

The Erie Canal is another great illustration of the role of government in providing infrastructure that helps the economy grow.

Why was the invention of barbed wire important to Western development?

Barbed wire was commercially developed in 1874 by American inventor Joseph Glidden (1813–1906). Consisting of steel wires that are twisted together to make sharp points resembling thorns, the material was quickly implemented in the West to construct fences for cattle. With trees scarce on the Great Plains, farmers had lacked the materials to

What is the famous song about the Erie Canal?

The song is "Low Bridge, Everybody Down," written in 1906 by Thomas S. Allen.

I've got an old mule and her name is Sal,
Fifteen years on the Erie Canal.
She's a good old worker and a good old pal,
Fifteen years on the Erie Canal.

We've hauled some barges in our day,
Filled with lumber, coal and hay.

And ev'ry inch of the way I know
From Albany to Buffalo.

Chorus:

Low bridge, ev'rybody down,
Low bridge, we must be getting near a town
You can always tell your neighbor,
You can always tell your pal,
If he's ever navigated on the Erie Canal.

In some versions, the lyrics are "Fifteen miles on the Erie Canal."

erect wooden fences. Instead, they planted prickly shrubs as a way of defining their lands and confining livestock. However, this was not always effective.

With the advent of barbed wire, farmers could fence in their acreage. Cattle owners became angered by small farmers who put up barbed wire because they had previously let their livestock roam the open plain. Fearing depletion of grazing lands, ranchers also began using barbed wire to fence tracts, whether or not they could claim legal title to them. Disputes arose between ranchers and between ranchers and farmers.

In 1885, President Grover Cleveland (1837–1908) brought an end to illegal fencing, ordering officials to remove barbed wire from public lands and Indian reservations. Legal use of the material to define land claim boundaries brought the demise of the open range and helped speed agricultural development of the prairie.

In the twentieth century, barbed wire was used extensively in wars, such as World War I. It was stretched across battle lines to slow down attacking enemy troops. Barbed wire increased the carnage of World War I.

NATURAL RESOURCES

What was the biggest gold rush?

The greatest American gold rush began on January 24, 1848, when James Marshall (1810–1885) discovered gold at Sutter's Mill in Coloma, California. Within a year, a large-scale gold rush was on. Some 90,000 people arrived in 1949 and were called "forty-niners." (This is the origin of the name of the NFL's San Francisco 49ers.) As the nearest port, the small town of San Francisco grew into a bustling city as fortune seekers arrived from around the world. Due to the influx, by 1850 California had enough people to qualify it for statehood.

This pattern repeated itself elsewhere in the American West, including the Pikes Peak gold rush in 1859, which effectively launched the city of Denver, Colorado. The gold rush led to the discovery of copper, lead, silver, and other useful minerals.

However, the California gold rush was devastating to the Native Americans, who had lived in the area for many generations. Tens of thousands were enslaved, killed, or driven off their land. The Native American population in the area dropped from about 300,000 to 30,000 in about twenty years.

What is the connection between the California gold rush and modern fashion?

In 1853, Bavarian immigrant Levi Strauss (1829–1902) began making and selling sturdy clothing to miners in San Francisco. He and his partner created blue jeans.

THE INDUSTRIAL REVOLUTION:
1700s TO 1800s

When did the Industrial Revolution begin?

The Industrial Revolution began in Great Britain during the 1700s, and by the early 1800s, it had spread to western Europe and the United States. It was brought about by the introduction to manufacturing of waterpower-driven machinery and then steam-power-driven machinery. By the close of the 1800s, most finished goods, which had once been made by hand or by simple machines, were produced in quantity by technologically advanced machinery.

What were the effects of the Industrial Revolution?

The dawn of the Industrial Revolution spelled the end of home- or workshop-based production. Factories were built to house the new machines, causing a population shift from rural to developing urban areas by the mid-1800s as people went where the work was. Factory owners turned to child labor and, in the United States, to the steady influx of immigrants to run the machinery in their plants. As industry grew, it required financial institutions that could provide money for expansion, thus giving birth to a new breed of wealthy business leaders—including the extraordinarily prosperous "robber barons," the industrial and financial tycoons of the late nineteenth century.

Beginning in the eighteenth century, the Industrial Revolution dramatically changed landscapes. This illustration from 1873 shows the "Black Country" in the West Midlands of England.

But as industry evolved, government and policy changes did not keep pace as serious social, political, and economic problems resulted, including poor and often dangerous working conditions, exploitation of workers (including child laborers), overcrowded housing, pollution, corruption, industry monopolies, and a widening gap between the rich and the poor. Change was slow to come, but social activism and government reforms in the late 1800s and during the Progressive Era of the early 1900s, much of which centered around trade unions, alleviated some of these problems. The rapid development of industry caused sweeping social changes. The Western world, which had long been agriculturally based, became an industrial society, where goods and services were the primary focus.

How were finished goods produced before the Industrial Revolution?

Before the factory and machine age were ushered in by the Industrial Revolution, people made many of their own finished goods, bought them from small-scale producers (who manufactured the goods largely by hand), or bought them from merchants who contracted homeworkers to produce goods. The putting-out system was a production method that was used in New England from the mid-1700s to the early 1800s. Merchants supplied raw materials (cotton, for example) to families, especially women and young girls, who would make partially finished goods (thread) or fully finished goods (cloth) for the merchant. These manufactured goods were then sold by the merchant. Homeworkers, who "put out" goods, provided the needed manufacturing labor of the day.

How did the textile industry begin?

The large-scale factory production of textiles began in the late 1700s, becoming established first in Great Britain, where Richard Arkwright (1732–1792) invented a cotton-spinning machine in 1783. In 1790, English-born mechanist and businessman Samuel Slater (1768–1835) introduced spinning mills to the United States. The twenty-one-year-old had worked as a textile laborer for more than six years in an English mill, where he learned the workings of Arkwright's machine, which the British considered the cornerstone of their booming textile industry. Laws prevented anyone with knowledge of the mill from leaving the country.

In 1789, Slater, determined that he could recreate the spinning mill and eager to seek his own fortune, disguised himself to evade the authorities and left the country, sailing from England for American shores. Arriving in Providence, Rhode Island, he formed a partnership with the textile firm Almy and Brown. Slater began building a spinning mill from memory based on the Arkwright machine.

The spinning mill was debuted December 20, 1790, in the village of Pawtucket, Rhode Island, where the wheels of the mill were turned by the waters of the Blackstone River. The machine was a success and soon revolutionized the American textile industry, which previously relied on cottage workers (the putting-out system) to manufacture thread and yarn.

Slater's innovation, which would earn him the title of "Father of the American Textile Industry," spawned the factory system in the United States. By 1815, there were 165 cotton mills in New England, all working to capacity. The early mills were not large-scale, however, and for a time after Slater's introductions, New England mills and merchants continued to rely on homeworkers to weave threads (now produced by the mills) into cloth.

In 1813, the Boston Manufacturing Company opened the first textile factory, where laborers ran spinning and weaving machines to produce woven cloth from start to finish. The advent of machinery had given rise to the factory system. Laborers were shifted from working in their homes to working in factories. An influx of immigrants in the mid-1800s provided the hungry manufacturers with a steady supply of laborers who were willing to work for less money and longer hours.

The key to these early textile mills was waterpower to turn the machine in the factories. At a suitable location, a dam would be built across a river to raise the water level. The falling water from the higher level would be used to turn a water wheel. This turning wheel would be connected to belts and gears to turn the equipment inside the mill to make thread and cloth. In New England today, many of these dams as well as the nearby buildings of the textile mills still exist. Eventually, waterpower would be replaced by steam engines that burned coal.

Within the first three decades of the 1800s, New England became the center of the nation's textile industry. The region's ample rivers and streams provided the necessary waterpower, and the commercial centers of Boston and New York City readily received the finished products. Labor proved to be in supply as well. Since the mill machinery was not complicated, children could operate it—and did. Slater hired children ages seven to fourteen to run the mill, a practice that other New England textile factories also adopted. New England's mills provided the model for the American factory system. Slater had brought the Industrial Revolution to America.

However, although slavery had been outlawed in Northern states, these mills were dependent on it. The cotton that was transformed by these mills into finished clothes was grown in the South on plantations worked by enslaved people.

How did Eli Whitney invent the cotton gin?

American inventor Eli Whitney (1765–1825) is credited with developing the cotton gin, a machine that removes cottonseeds from cotton fibers. A simple cotton gin (called the churka) dates back to ancient India (300 B.C.E.). But Whitney's gin would prove to be far superior. In 1792, while visiting a Georgia plantation, Whitney observed that short-staple (or upland) cotton, which has green seeds that are difficult to separate from the fiber, differs from long-staple (also called Sea Island) cotton, which has black seeds that are easily separated. In 1793, Whitney, who is described as a mechanical genius, completed an invention that removed the seeds from short-staple cotton. He patented it the next year.

The machine worked by turning a crank, which caused a cylinder covered with wire teeth to revolve. The teeth pulled the cotton fiber, carrying it through slots in the cylinder as it revolved. Since the slots were too small for the seeds, they were left behind. A roller with brushes then removed the fibers from the wire teeth. The cotton gin revolutionized the American textile industry.

The increase in cotton production was as much as fifty-fold. One large gin could process fifty times the cotton that a worker—often a slave—could in a day. Soon plantations and farms were supplying huge amounts of cotton to textile mills in the Northeast.

The cotton gin led to a huge increase of cotton production in the South and a simultaneous rise in the number of enslaved people needed to grow cotton. Cotton became the most important crop in the South and the biggest single piece of the economy, becoming known as "King Cotton." Cotton represented 60 percent of all exports coming from the United States.

Most renowned for inventing the cotton gin that changed the textile industry, Eli Whitney was also a prominent gun manufacturer, making weapons for the U.S. Army.

The importance of cotton and the need for enslaved people to grow the cotton, would eventually lead the Southern states into secession, which led to the Civil War.

Why was the invention of the reaper important to the U.S. economy?

Reapers, machines developed in the early 1800s to help farmers harvest grain, such as wheat, dramatically increased overall grain production and consumption in the United States and the rest of the world. The first commercially successful reaper was built in 1831 by Virginia-born inventor Cyrus Hall McCormick (1809–1884). The McCormick reaper was horse-drawn and replaced the use of sickles and scythes in the fields, thus reducing the amount of manual labor required to harvest grain crops. It worked in this way: A straight blade (protected by guards) was linked to a drive wheel. As the drive wheel turned, the blade moved back and forth in a sawing motion, cutting through the stalks of grain, which were held straight by rods. The cut grain stalks then fell onto a platform and were collected with a rake by a worker. The device increased average production from two or three acres a day to ten acres a day.

In 1847, McCormick moved his business to Chicago, where he could transport reapers via the Great Lakes and connected waterways to the east and to the south. Within five years, McCormick's business had become the largest farm-implement factory in the world. Sales of the equipment increased further during the 1850s as Chicago became a center for the nation's expanding rail system.

In 1879, Cyrus McCormick's business became the McCormick Harvesting Machine Company. The reaper was improved over time. In the 1850s, a self-raking feature was added, further reducing the amount of labor required. In the 1870s, a binder was added, which bound the sheaves of grain and dropped them to the ground to be collected. In the 1920s, the reaper (or harvester) was joined with another invention, the thresher, which separated grains from the stalks. The new reaper-thresher machine was called a "combine." Today's combines still use the basic features present in McCormick's revolutionary 1831 invention. His company later became International Harvester (1902) and today is known as Navistar Corporation.

What were bonanza farms?

Bonanza farms were extremely successful, large farms, principally on the Great Plains and in the West, that emerged during the second half of the 1800s. The word "bonanza," which is derived from Spanish and means literally "good weather," was coined in the mid-1800s. It is used to refer to any source of great and sudden wealth—including mines rich in minerals. Large-scale farming had been aided by the development of machinery that greatly increased crop production.

The innovations included reapers invented by Cyrus McCormick and steel plows developed by John Deere (1804–1886). To promote westward settlement, Congress passed the Homestead Act (1862), which allowed for ready and cheap acquisition of vast tracts of land west of the Mississippi. Settlers could buy land for as little as $1.25 per acre, or they could live on a tract and farm it for a period of five years, at the end of which they were granted 160 acres.

The U.S. Army's defeats of Native Americans were followed by treaties that took away much of the Native Americans' land and confined them to reservations. In 1872, the Northern Pacific Railroad arrived at Fargo, North Dakota, allowing farmers to ship their products greater distances. Finally, dry-farming techniques (which allow fields to lie fallow every other year in order to regain their nutrients and moisture to support crops the following year) proved to be a successful method for growing in the Great Plains— previously thought to be too dry for cultivating crops.

All of these factors combined to turn some western farms into "bonanzas"—sources of great wealth for their owners. Encouraged by their success, settlers poured into the West. But not all farmers fared as well, and many were severely hit by the Panic of 1873. A drought in the Great Plains states in the 1880s caused farm prices to drop, further hurting western farmers.

When did the American cattle industry begin?

As a large-scale commercial endeavor, the beef industry had its beginnings in the decades following the American Civil War (1861–1865). Longhorn cattle, a breed of cattle descended from cows and bulls left by early Spanish settlers in the American Southwest, spurred the growth of the industry. Named for their long horns, which span about four

Cattle ranching remains an important industry in the United States, although it is becoming increasingly controversial because of environmental issues and Americans' growing concerns about diet.

feet, by the 1860s, they had multiplied, and great numbers of them roamed freely across the open range of the West. Ranchers in Texas bred the longhorns with other cattle breeds, such as Hereford and Angus, to produce quality meat.

With beef in demand in the Eastern United States, shrewd businessmen capitalized on the business opportunity, buying cattle for $3 to $5 a head and selling them in eastern and northern markets for as much as $25 to $60 a head. Ranchers hired cowboys to round up, sort out, and drive their herds to railheads in places like Abilene and Dodge City, Kansas, which became famous as "cow towns," raucous boomtowns where saloons and brothels proliferated. After the long trail drive, the cattle were loaded onto railcars and shipped live to local butchers, who slaughtered the livestock and prepared the beef. For a twenty-year period, the plentiful longhorn cattle sustained a booming livestock industry in the West. At least six million Texas longhorns were driven across Oklahoma to the cow towns of Kansas.

By 1890, the complexion of the industry changed. Farmers and ranchers in the West used barbed wire to fence in their lands, closing the open range; railroads were extended, bringing an end to the long, hard, and much-glorified cattle drives; the role of the cowboy changed, making him little more than a hired hand; and big business took over the industry. Among the entrepreneurs who capitalized on beef's place in the American diet was New England-born Gustavus Swift (1839–1903), who in 1877 began a large-scale slaughterhouse operation in Chicago, shipping ready-packed meat via refrigerated railcars to markets in the East. The older practice was to ship live animals to the cities in the East. However, the trip was rough, and many animals did not survive.

Key to Swift's success was the creation of refrigerated railcars. The cars had boxes in the roof that held blocks of ice to keep the beef cold. The train would make regular stops on long journeys to replace the ice. The blocks of ice were cut from frozen rivers in the winter and stored in ice houses.

Why was the introduction of canning important?

The advent of canned foods not only created an industry, but it altered the average American diet, helped usher in the consumer age, and saved time. Canning, a process for preserving food (vegetables, fruits, meats, and fish) by heating and sealing it in airtight containers, was developed by French candymaker Nicolas-François Appert (1749–1841) in 1809, though he did not understand why the process worked. Some fifty years later, the pioneering work of French chemist and microbiologist Louis Pasteur (1822–1895) explained that heating is necessary to the canning process since it kills bacteria that would otherwise spoil the food.

Canning was introduced to American consumers in stages. In 1821, the William Underwood Company began a canning operation in Boston. In the 1840s, oyster canning began in Baltimore. In 1853, American inventor Gail Borden (1801–1874) developed a way to condense and preserve milk in a can, founding the Borden Company. And in 1858, American inventor John Landis Mason (1832–1902) developed a glass jar and lid suited to home canning; it became known as the famous Mason jar.

Though early commercial canning methods did not ensure a safe product and many American women avoided the convenience foods, the canning industry grew rapidly, at least in part due to the male market, which included cowboys in the West. Between 1860 and 1870, the U.S. canning industry increased output from five million to thirty million cans. Improvements in the process during the 1870s helped eliminate the chance that cans would burst (a problem early on). And though the canning process changes food flavor, color, and texture, the convenience and long shelf life of canned foods helped them catch on. By the end of the 1800s, a wide variety of canned foods, which had also come down in price, were common to the urban American diet. Companies such as Franco-American advertised in women's magazines, promoting their "delicacies in tins."

What is Bessemer steel?

Developed during the early 1850s, the Bessemer process was the first method for making steel cheaply and in large quantities. It was named for its inventor, British engineer

---

What are some famous movies about cattle drives?

Some great cattle-drive scenes are in the following movies: *Red River* (1948) and *The Cowboys* (1972) with John Wayne; *The Culpepper Cattle Company* (1972); *Lonesome Dove* (1989, a TV miniseries); and *City Slickers* (1991).

Henry Bessemer (1813–1898). The process may also have been developed independently in the United States by William Kelly (1811–1888), who patented the process in 1857. Bessemer experimented with injecting (blowing) air into molten pig iron (crude iron). The oxygen in the air helped rid the iron of its impurities (such as manganese, silicon, and carbon), converting the iron to molten steel, which was then poured into molds. The process was introduced in the U.S. steel-manufacturing industry in 1864. Alloys were also added to the refining process to help purify the metal. Within two decades, the method was used to produce more than 90 percent of the nation's steel and was implemented throughout the industrialized world.

Bessemer converters like this one in England still use the same principles developed by Henry Bessemer and William Kelly in the 1850s to turn crude iron into strong steel.

In the mid-1800s, rich iron ore deposits had been discovered in the Upper Peninsula of Michigan along Lake Superior. The discovery of the minerals and the innovation of the Bessemer process combined to create a thriving steel industry in the United States. At the same time, there was a growing market for the material. Railroads needed to make rails, while the new auto-manufacturing industry used steel to make cars. As a result, between 1880 and 1910, annual U.S. steel production increased twenty times.

One of the early industry leaders was Andrew Carnegie (1835–1919), who in 1873 founded the nation's first large-scale steel plant in Braddock, Pennsylvania. In 1901, Carnegie sold this and other steel mills to the United States Steel Corporation.

What country is the largest producer of steel?

China. Next comes the combined countries of the European Union, then India, Japan, and finally the United States. China produces over ten times the amount of steel produced in the United States.

Who were the "robber barons"?

They were the industrial and financial tycoons of the late nineteenth century, the early builders of American business. Some called them the captains of industry. The "robber barons" included bankers J. Pierpont Morgan (1837–1913, often called J. P. Morgan) and Jay Cooke (1821–1905); oil industrialist John D. Rockefeller (1839–1937); steel mogul Andrew Carnegie (1835–1919); financiers James J. Hill (1838–1916), James Fisk (1835–1872), Edward Harriman (1848–1909), and Jay Gould (1836–1892); and rail magnates Cornelius Vanderbilt (1794–1877) and Collis Huntington (1821–1900). These in-

What U.S. city was known as "Steel City"?

Several American cities have earned the moniker "the Steel City" but perhaps none as prominently as Pittsburgh, Pennsylvania. The city's professional football team in the National Football League is even known as the Pittsburgh Steelers. The city's amateur women's roller derby team is known as the Steel City Derby Demons.

The city began producing steel in 1875 and by 1911 began producing half of the nation's steel supply. Beginning in the early 1980s, the city's steel mills began laying off many workers—more than 150,000. In the early 1980s, 10 percent of the city's workforce worked in the steel industry. Now that number has dwindled, but the image of the city remains the "Steel City."

fluential businessmen were hailed for expanding and modernizing the capitalist system and lauded for their philanthropic contributions to the arts and education.

However, they were also viewed as opportunistic, exploitative, and unethical. For example, Rockefeller was ruthless in destroying all competition in the oil business so he could create a monopoly in oil—the Standard Oil Company. Gould was involved in all kinds of stock and bond manipulations, which cheated many stock investors. He also controlled several railroads for his own financial advantage, which often resulted in total mismanagement of the actual railroads.

Many factors converged to make the robber baron possible. The new nation was rich in natural resources, including iron, coal, and oil; technological advances steadily improved manufacturing machinery and processes; the population growth, fed by an influx of immigrants, provided a steady workforce, often willing to work for a low wage; the government turned over the building and operation of the nation's railways to private interests; and, adhering to the philosophy of laissez-faire (noninterference in the private sector), the government also provided a favorable environment in which to conduct business.

Shrewd businessmen turned these factors to their advantage, amassing great empires. Reinvesting profits into their businesses, fortunes grew. The robber barons, especially the railroad men and the financiers who gained control of rail companies through stock buyouts,, hired lobbyists who worked on their behalf to gain the corporations subsidies, land grants, and even tax relief at both the federal and state levels.

The robber barons converted their business prowess into political might. In Washington, politicians grew tired of the advantage-seeking representatives of for the nation's business leaders. Reform-minded progressives complained that the robber barons lived in opulent luxury while their workers barely eked out a living, their families teetering on despair.

After the robber barons had dominated the American economy for decades, around the turn of the century, the progressives worked to curb their influence. In 1890, the fed-

355

eral government passed the Sherman Anti-Trust Act, making trusts (combinations of firms or corporations formed to limit competition and monopolize a market) illegal; workers continued to organize in labor unions, with which corporations were increasingly compelled to negotiate; the Interstate Commerce Commission (ICC) was established in 1887 to prevent abusive practices; and in 1913, the Sixteenth Amendment was ratified, allowing the federal government to collect a graduated income tax. Though many American businessmen and women would make great fortunes in the twentieth century, by the end of the 1920s, the era of the robber barons had drawn to a close.

Many people see parallels today to the age of the robber barons. In the present, corporations have huge political influence through campaign contributions, lobbyists, and influence on the media. For example, in 2017, the wealthy and corporations received large tax cuts, yet very little of the money they held on to was invested in the economy. In recent decades, the richest people—the 1 percent—have grown even richer, while for most of the rest—the 99 percent—their incomes and wealth have remained stagnant or have declined.

Who was Cornelius Vanderbilt?

Cornelius Vanderbilt (1794–1877) was an extremely wealthy industrialist who made his money in the shipping and railway industries. He owned several steamboats, including the Staten Island Ferry. For his steamboat ownership, he was given the nickname "the Commodore."

But Vanderbilt was more than a rich businessman. He also was a noted philanthropist. Born in New York, he later donated a large sum of money to start a university that was built in Nashville, Tennessee. It was named Vanderbilt University, and its nickname is the Commodores—in honor of its founder.

What is a "Horatio Alger story"?

It is any story about someone who, through sheer determination and hard work, rises from poverty to wealth. During the second half of the 1800s, novels by American clergyman and author Horatio Alger Jr. (1832–1899) were extremely popular. He wrote more than one hundred books, including the *Luck and Pluck* and *Tattered Tom* series. All of the stories center on a boy from inauspicious beginnings who, through hard work, clean living, and a little bit of luck, becomes successful. Though dead for more than a century, Alger's name lives on. Many Americans still describe an honorable person's rise from rags to riches as "a real Horatio Alger story."

However, the irony of many Horatio Alger stories is that often, it is luck rather than the hard work that is the key to success.

Who was "Rosie the Riveter"?

The term referred to the American women during World War II who worked factory jobs as part of the war effort on the home front, where auto plants and other industrial fa-

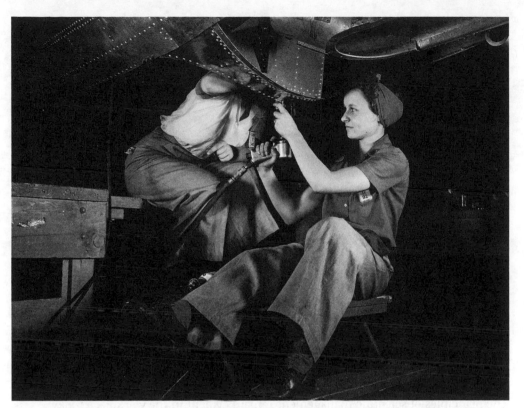

Two women work on an airplane in Long Beach, California, in 1942. "Rosie the Riveter" was the name given to them for the war effort; less known was the term "Wendy the Welder." The riveter name was made famous by popular posters and also by a Norman Rockwell painting.

cilities were converted into defense plants to manufacture airplanes, ships, and weapons. As the war wore on, more and more men went overseas to fight, resulting in a shortage of civilian male workers, so women pitched in. However, at the end of the war, many of these women were displaced as the men returned home to their jobs and civilian life. Nevertheless, the contribution of all the Rosie the Riveters was instrumental to the war effort.

What is the Dow Jones Industrial Average?

The Dow Jones Industrial Average, the DJIA, is a measure of stock prices of thirty important industrial companies. It has been in use since the 1880s. The average is an indicator of the market overall and is used, along with other indexes, by investors, stockbrokers, and analysts to make investment forecasts and decisions. "The Dow," as it is called, was conceived of as a summary measure of the stock market, an index that could be used to analyze past trends, indicate current trends, and even predict future ones. News of fluctuations in the DJIA can affect market prices around the world.

What is the system of scientific management?

A system to gain maximum efficiency from workers and machinery, scientific management, also known as Taylorism, was developed by American industrial engineer Frederick Winslow Taylor (1856–1915). As a foreman in a steel plant, Taylor undertook time and motion studies and conducted experiments to determine the "one best way" to do any given job, developing detailed systems to yield the highest possible productivity levels.

Efficiency was the cornerstone of Taylorism: production processes should not waste time or materials. Taylor published his ideas in the landmark work *The Principles of Management* (1911). Applying his scientific management, manufacturers were able to boost productivity by as much as 200 percent. Since Taylorism broke production processes into individual tasks, each with its own best practice, new workers could be quickly and easily trained, which adherents believed was another benefit of the concept. The principles of scientific management remain evident in the workplace today.

Scientific management also had its detractors. Taylorism was criticized for having a dehumanizing effect on labor. In making every job routine, some charged that the system separated the minds of workers from their hands, eliminated the need for skilled workers, and gave management absolute control over production processes.

Why did the auto industry boom in the postwar era?

In the years following World War II, auto ownership in the United States soared from 27.5 million registered vehicles in 1940 to 61.5 million in 1960. Americans had resumed their love affair with the automobile, inextricably linking the car with the U.S. history of the postwar era. Many factors combined to bring about the automobile's widespread popularity.

During World War II, the car manufacturers curtailed auto production, converting factories to military production and turning out some $29 billion in materials, including trucks, jeeps, tanks, aircraft, engines, artillery, and ammunition. With the conflict ended, automakers stepped up production to fulfill the unmet demand of the war years, and they soon found themselves working to meet new demand, created by an increase in consumer spending and the growth of the suburbs.

The overall prosperity of the late 1940s and 1950s produced a new spirit of consumerism. Government regulations (brought about through the efforts of the labor unions) resulted in increased wages and improved benefits, which meant that Americans, for the most part, had more disposable income. Advertisers took advantage of the new medium of television to reach wide and eager audiences.

The housing industry, largely dormant during World War II, built new neighborhoods around the edges of American cities, making the automobile a necessity rather than a luxury. The Big Three (GM, Ford, and Chrysler) increased capacity to meet the tremendous demand, setting new records for production in 1949 and 1950. By 1960, more than three out of every four American families owned at least one car. The infrastructure raced to keep pace with a nation on wheels; superhighways were built (covering some 10,000 miles of road); motels and fast-food restaurants went up along roadsides; and shopping centers were built outside city centers. While imports would challenge the American automakers in the decades to come, it was the U.S. manufacturers that defined the postwar era.

Why was the introduction of plastic important to industry?

Pioneered in the early 1900s, plastic—which is any synthetic organic material that can be molded under heat and pressure to retain a shape—affected every industry and every consumer. As a malleable material, plastic could be molded for countless uses both for the production of goods and as a material in finished goods. In 1909, Bakelite plastic was introduced, and, over the next three decades, the plastics industry grew, developing acrylic, nylon, polystyrene, and vinyl (polyvinyl chloride or PVC) in the 1930s and polyesters in the 1940s. The applications seemed endless—from household items, such as hosiery, clocks, radios, toys, flooring, food containers, bags, electric plugs, and garden hoses, to commercial uses, such as automobile bodies and parts, airplane windows, boat hulls, packaging, and building materials. The space industry and medicine industry have also found critical uses for plastic products.

Scientists have continued to find new applications for plastics in products such as compact disks (CDs), outdoor furniture, and personal computers (PCs). The material has become essential to modern life.

There is a classic line from the 1968 movie *The Graduate*, starring Dustin Hoffman (1937–) as a recent college graduate, Ben Braddock, who is uncertain of the direction of his life. At a party for the new graduate, a neighbor and Braddock have this conversation:

Mr. McGuire: I want to say one word to you. Just one word.

Benjamin: Yes, sir.

Mr. McGuire: Are you listening?

Benjamin: Yes, I am.

Mr. McGuire: Plastics.

Benjamin: Exactly how do you mean?

Mr. McGuire: There's a great future in plastics. Think about it. Will you think about it?   359

A Netherlands-based environmental group called Ocean Cleanup has taken it upon itself to work toward cleaning plastics out of the world's oceans and rivers using specially designed boats that collect floating debris.

What is the problem with plastics today?

Plastics do not decay and rot away. Some items made of plastic will survive for hundreds of years, while others will break down into tiny pieces of plastic that do not biodegrade. Today, humans use an immense number of plastic items, often for very short times. At a fast-food restaurant, plastic plates, cups, and utensils are used for only a few minutes or less, but the plastic can last for decades or centuries.

What about recycling?

One way to eliminate plastic waste is to recycle plastic to make new plastic items. However, less than 10 percent get recycled. Also, in America, the recycling industry is struggling because much of recycled plastic used to get sent to China. However, China is no longer taking American recycling.

Sadly, many tons of plastic end up being burned, left as litter, or deposited in oceans. Every minute, the equivalent of one garbage truck of plastic winds up in the oceans. An island of plastic has formed in the Pacific Ocean.

MAIL ORDER AND STORES

What was the first mail-order company?

The mail-order business was pioneered by retailer Montgomery Ward & Company, founded in 1872 in Chicago when American merchant Aaron Montgomery Ward (1843–

1913) set up a shop over a livery stable and printed a one-sheet "catalog" of bargains. Midwestern farmers, hurt by low farm prices and rising costs, were a ready market for the value-priced goods, which were shipped by rail to rural customers.

Originally called "The Original Grange Supply House," Montgomery Ward offered thirty dry goods priced at $1 or less and provided special terms of sale for Grange members (the Grange is an association of farmers). Ward bought merchandise directly from wholesalers, and since he did not maintain a store building, overhead was low. By 1876, Ward's catalog had grown to 150 pages; in 1884, it was 240 pages and offered nearly 10,000 products, including household items (such as furniture, cutlery, and writing paper), farm implements (such as harnesses and tools), and fashions (such as ready-made apparel and parasols). Ward offered customers "satisfaction or your money back."

In 1886, American Richard W. Sears (1863–1914) entered the mail-order business, opening operations in Minneapolis. He moved the business to Chicago the following year and sold it in 1889. In 1893, he joined with Alvah C. Roebuck (1864–1948) to found Sears, Roebuck and Company. The Sears catalog, which soon consisted of hundreds of pages and thousands of items, became popularly known as the "Wish Book."

Montgomery Ward and Sears, Roebuck and Company were aided by the U.S. Postal Service's expansion into remote areas. Beginning in 1896, mail could be delivered via rural free delivery (RFD). In 1913, parcel post was added to the postal service's offerings, further benefiting the mail-order houses and their growing lists of customers. Montgomery Ward and Sears, Roebuck offered rural America more than merchandise; the mail-order houses were farm families' link to the greater consumer society that was emerging at the turn of the century. Regardless of geography, rural Americans could purchase "store-bought" goods, manufactured goods that were mass-produced in factories.

The mail-order houses offered customers convenience (since customer purchases no longer had to be deferred until the next trip to a town), variety (since catalogers catered to a nationwide customer base, on-hand inventory included a multitude of products), and low prices (the mail-order houses bought merchandise at reduced rates from the wholesalers). Fashions were no longer restricted to the middle- and upper-class city dwellers who had access to department stores; rural customers became aware of new styles each time the Montgomery Ward and Sears, Roebuck catalogs were delivered, which by the early 1900s was twice a year.

Though both Montgomery Ward and Sears, Roebuck exited the mail-order business to concentrate efforts on their chain-store retail operations later in the century, they set the standard for modern mail-order houses through their early policies addressing merchandise returns, competitive pricing, flexible payment methods, and shipping terms.

When did department stores begin?

Department stores, which offer a wide variety of goods for sale in various departments, emerged in the mid-1800s. Many evolved out of general stores (which offered a variety of goods but were not divided into departments), while others evolved out of dry-goods stores (which sold textiles and related merchandise). The first bona fide department store was established in Paris: Le Bon Marché (French meaning "good bargain") opened its doors in 1838. Between the 1850s and 1880s, numerous department stores opened in American cities—including Jordan Marsh, founded in 1851 in Boston, Massachusetts; R. H. Macy's, founded in 1858 in New York City (the store was known for its creative advertisements); Wanamaker's, founded in 1861 in Philadelphia, Pennsylvania (it successfully implemented fixed pricing so that customers no longer haggled over price); and Marshall Field, founded in 1881 in Chicago (within twenty-five years, it became the world's largest wholesale and retail dry-goods store).

These pioneer department stores, multistoried enterprises located in downtown areas, introduced many innovations to merchandising, including the policy of returnable or exchangeable goods, ready-made apparel, clearly marked prices, and window displays. By the early 1900s, department stores could be found throughout the country.

The timing was right for their emergence. Urban centers grew rapidly at the end of the century, giving department stores a ready clientele; the advent of the telephone, electric lighting, and billing machines helped retailers conduct business efficiently; transportation improvements allowed for the shipment of large quantities of goods; and a variety of finished goods were mass-produced, increasing supply and lowering the cost of production as well as the price to the consumer. By the 1910s, the stores were part of a new mass culture, which was centered in American cities. During the twentieth century, department store sales typically ranged between 6 and 12 percent of total annual retail sales.

When did chain stores first appear?

The innovation of the chain store, technically defined as two or more retail outlets operated by the same company that sell the same kind of merchandise, was made by American businessmen George Gilman (c. 1830–1901) and George Huntington Hartford (1833–1917), who in 1859 set up the Great Atlantic & Pacific Tea Company in New York City. Better known as A&P, the stores proliferated rapidly, and other chain stores, such as F. W. Woolworth (established in 1879) and J. C. Penney (1902), opened their doors for business.

The early twentieth century saw tremendous growth of chain stores. Between 1910 and 1931, the number of A&P stores grew from 200 to more than 15,000. While the department stores, also a by-product of the late 1800s, catered to middle- and upper-class customers, the chain

No. 39 MARKET SQUARE,
NORFOLK, VA.,

One of the 200 stores of that great importing corporation whose signs and busy delivery wagons are to be seen on the streets of every great city in the United States,

The Great Atlantic and Pacific Tea Co.,

not only continues as the acknowledged Headquarters of Tide-water Virginia for the sale of Choice Teas, Select Coffee, Health-giving Baking Powders and Chemically Pure Sugars ; but also dispenses at the lowest possible prices the best

New York State Gilt-edge Butter.

We also wish to call the attention of our patrons to the fact that we are constantly receiving a large amount of imported Majolica China, Glassware, Clocks, etc., which we present to our patrons who purchase our Tea, Coffee and Sugar.

A 1988 A&P advertisement. The Great Atlantic & Pacific Tea Company was the first chain store in the world. It thrived through the first half of the twentieth century but eventually started closing stores and went out of business entirely in 2015.

stores, including Woolworth's "five-and-dimes," served lower-income consumers. (A hundred years ago, many items only cost a nickel or a dime.)

Chain stores' system of centralized and mass buying allowed them to acquire merchandise from manufacturers and wholesalers at reduced costs; this savings was passed along to the consumer, who paid less for the item. Furthermore, they experienced economies of advertising, as a single ad placement promotes all the stores within the chain.

Chain stores would control much of the retail markets for many decades. However, with the rise of Internet sales and deliveries, many long-standing chain stores have gone out of business.

What is the origin of Walmart?

Walmart was created by Sam Walton (1918–1992), who opened his first Walmart store in 1962 in Rogers, Arkansas. In the following decades, his stores showed up all over the United States and then all over the world. Over the years, Walmart has used slogans such as "Always the low prices. Always" and "Save Money. Live Better." Currently, there are over 11,000 Walmart stores in twenty-seven countries. It is the largest private employer in the world and in the United States. It is also the largest grocery retailer in the United States.

In 1983, Walmart opened Sam's Club stores, which are members-only warehouse clubs (stores). Currently, there are about 600 of them in the United States.

Walmart's success is based on efficiency and obsessive cost-cutting. It pioneered how to use handheld store inventory scanners and the information they provided to reduce inventories and make shipping more efficient. Walmart buyers are hard negotiators with their suppliers; they demand low prices for the items they buy to then sell in the stores. Walmart managers work hard to keep down overhead and, especially, labor costs.

Often, Walmart stores have had great impacts on their surrounding communities. For example, when Walmarts have been built near smaller rural towns, often, the existing local businesses could not compete and went out of business.

In the 1980s, Walmart pushed a "Buy America" program that encouraged the purchase of goods made in America; however, they were one of the early retailers to take advantage of the much cheaper cost of goods from China and other countries. They played a key role in shipping so many American manufacturing jobs overseas. For many items, Walmart is the largest importer of foreign-made goods.

BUSINESS CORRUPTION AND BUSINESS FAILURES

Who is Bernie Madoff?

Bernie Madoff (1938–) is an American entrepreneur and financier who committed one of the most egregious examples of financial fraud in history. He bilked many investors out of billions of dollars using an elaborate Ponzi scheme. Eventually, Madoff pled guilty to eleven federal charges in March 2009 and received a 150-year sentence in June 2009.

What was Enron?

Enron was a high-flying energy trading and communications company headquartered in Houston, Texas. It was the seventh-largest corporation in the United States, a favorite on Wall Street, and for six years in a row (1996–2001) was named America's Most Innovative Company by *Fortune* magazine. Then, Enron filed for Chapter 11 bankruptcy in December 2001, rocking the business world and shocking investors and rank-and-file employees. It was, for a short time, the largest bankruptcy in American history.

What is a Ponzi scheme?

In a Ponzi scheme, people invest their money expecting good returns. Early investors do get good returns but not because of the underlying success of the business. In the case of Madoff, there was actually no underlying business. Instead, early investors are paid the money put in by later investors. This works for a while, but eventually, the later investors want their money back, and there is none because it was given to early investors.

The scheme is named for Charles Ponzi (1882–1949), a con artist in the United States and Canada. Although he did not invent this type of scheme, his version of it collapsed in the 1920s with investors losing $20 million, and, thus, his name became linked to any such scheme.

Federal investigators later learned that the company's collapse was caused by fraudulent accounting practices that allowed Enron to overstate earnings and hide debts. The conglomerate had booked billions in profits that did not really exist and created mythical companies to bury heavy losses. Enron's stock price plummeted, there were massive layoffs, employee retirement accounts (heavily invested in Enron stock) were decimated, executives resigned, and criminal indictments followed. Its accounting firm, Chicago-based Arthur Andersen, collapsed under the weight of its involvement in the scandal.

Former chairman Kenneth Lay (1942–2006) and former CEO Jeffrey Skilling (1953–) were charged. In 2006, just months before the trial was to start, Lay died of a heart attack. Skilling was later convicted of multiple felonies and sentenced to twenty-four years in prison.

What was the WorldCom disaster?

WorldCom, a telecommunication giant, was the next colossal business failure. In July 2002, WorldCom, valued at $180 billion and serving fifteen million customers at its 1999 peak, filed for bankruptcy. At the time, it was the largest in U.S. history. (Bigger bankruptcies would come. WorldCom now ranks third and Enron sixth on the list of the largest U.S. bankruptcies in history.)

A *Fortune* magazine writer reflected on the crisis of corporate ethics, saying, "Phony earnings, inflated revenues, conflicted Wall Street analysts, directors asleep at the switch—this isn't just a few bad apples … [it is] a systemic breakdown."

What is the largest bankruptcy in American history?

Lehman Brothers Holdings, Inc., in 2008. Here is the list of the top six bankruptcies:

Company	Bankruptcy Date	Money Lost
Lehman Brothers Holdings, Inc.	9/15/2008	$691,063,000,000
Washington Mutual, Inc.	9/26/2008	$327,913,000,000
WorldCom, Inc.	7/21/2002	$103,914,000,000
General Motors Corporation	6/1/2009	$82,290,000,000
CIT Group, Inc.	11/1/2009	$71,000,000,000
Enron Corp.	12/2/2001	$65,503,000,000

HUMAN RIGHTS ISSUES

CIVIL RIGHTS

What was the Niagara movement?

It was a short-lived but important African American organization that advocated "the total integration of blacks into mainstream society, with all the rights, privileges and benefits of other Americans." Founded in Niagara Falls, Ontario, in 1905, the Niagara movement was led by writer, scholar, and activist W. E. B. Du Bois (1868–1963), who was then a professor of economics and history at Atlanta University.

Observers described the organization as the anti-Bookerite camp, a reference to educator Booker T. Washington (1856–1915), who rose from slavery to found Alabama's Tuskegee Institute (1881) and believed change for black people should be effected through education and self-improvement as opposed to through demand. Washington opposed the social and political agitation favored by some reformers; the Niagara movement, on the other hand, placed the responsibility for the nation's racial problems squarely on the shoulders of its white population.

Though the Niagara organization dissolved in 1909, the National Association for the Advancement of Colored People (NAACP) was heir to its ideology and activism. Du Bois helped found that organization, and from 1910 to 1934, he edited its official journal, *The Crisis*, in which he published his views "on nearly every important social issue that confronted the black community."

Who was W. E. B. Du Bois?

Before W. E. B. Du Bois (1868–1963) rose to prominence as an educator and writer, he chose to leave the security of his home in Massachusetts to attend college at Nashville's Fisk University. There, in 1885, he encountered Tennessee's Jim Crow laws, which

367

strictly divided blacks and whites. He was so intimidated by the "Southern system" that he rarely left the campus, and he ultimately returned to New England to complete his studies at Harvard University. He did, however, go back to the South, becoming a professor of economics and history at Atlanta University (1897–1910, 1932–1944).

As one of the first exponents of full and equal racial equality, in 1909, Du Bois helped found the National Association for the Advancement of Colored People (NAACP), which provided leadership during the civil rights movement. Du Bois wrote extensively. Three of his many books include *The Study of the Negro Problems* (1898), *The Souls of Black Folk* (1903), and *Black Reconstruction in America* (1935).

Educator and author W. E. B. Du Bois cofounded the NAACP.

Were activists the only ones who were vocal about opposing segregation?

No, segregation was opposed at every level of black society as well as by many whites. The voices of the civil rights movement included wage laborers, farmers, educators, athletes, entertainers, soldiers, religious leaders, politicians, and statesmen—all of whom had experienced the oppression of Jim Crow laws and policies in the United States (see "The Law" chapter for more on Jim Crow).

How many race riots have there been in the United States since the Civil War?

Although it is hard to imagine, there have been about 150 incidents of group racial violence in the United States since the Civil War. In many of these, hundreds of people died.

The term "race riot" can be misleading. Some events might be better labeled as "massacres," such as when mobs of whites attacked black neighborhoods, killing and injuring hundreds in such places as East St. Louis, Illinois (1917), and Tulsa, Oklahoma (1921).

In other events, frustrated racial groups vented their anger over injustices, such as in the 1965 Watts riots and the 1992 riot over the acquittal of officers involved in the assault of Rodney King, both in Los Angeles, California.

What is the story of John "Jackie" Robinson?

In 1942, a young Georgia man named John Roosevelt Robinson (1919–1972) was drafted into the military. Robinson applied for Officer's Candidate School at Fort Riley, Kansas, and although he was admitted to the program, he and the other black candidates received no training until pressure from Washington, D.C., forced the local commander to admit blacks to the base's training school.

Later, Robinson became a second lieutenant and continued to challenge the Jim Crow policies on military bases. When the army decided to keep him out of a football game with the nearby University of Missouri because that school refused to play against a team with black members, Robinson quit the base's team in protest. At Fort Hood, Texas, Robinson objected to segregation on an army bus. His protests led to a court-martial.

Acquitted, in November 1944, Robinson was honorably discharged before the end of World War II. The army had no desire to keep this black agitator among the ranks, and, as Robinson later put it, he was "pretty much fed up with the service."

In 1945, Robinson joined the Kansas City Monarchs, a professional baseball team in the Negro leagues. In 1947, "Jackie" Robinson became the first black baseball player in the major leagues when he joined the Brooklyn Dodgers, breaking the color barrier in the national pastime. However, he had to silently endure much racism, such as taunts from the fans.

When were schools in the United States desegregated?

On May 17, 1954, in the case of *Brown v. Board of Education*, the Supreme Court ruled 9–0 that racial segregation in public schools is unconstitutional, as it violates the Equal Protection Clause of the Fourteenth Amendment. The court overturned the "separate-but-equal" doctrine laid down in the 1896 case *Plessy v. Ferguson*. Under this noxious doctrine, schools could be segregated based on race as long as the facilities were roughly equal. This was a fallacy, as schools servicing black students were much poorer and less developed than most schools servicing white pupils.

In a second *Brown* decision in 1956, Chief Justice Earl Warren (1891–1974) ordered the states to proceed "with all deliberate speed" to integrate educational facilities. Un-

Who was Ralph Bunche?

In the postwar years, American diplomat Ralph Bunche (1904–1971) attracted public attention when he rejected an offer from President Harry S. Truman (1884–1972) to become an assistant secretary of state. Bunche, a Howard University professor who had worked for the Office of Strategic Services during the war, explained that he declined the position because he did not want to subject his family to the Jim Crow laws of Washington, D.C. Bunche spoke out frequently against racism, and in 1944 he coauthored the book *An American Dilemma*, which examined the plight of American blacks.

fortunately, there appears to have been more focus on the adjective "deliberate" than the noun "speed." This meant that many schools were not integrated until the early 1970s.

On November 7, 1954, the Supreme Court ordered desegregation of public golf courses, parks, swimming pools, and playgrounds. In the aftermath of these rulings, desegregation proceeded slowly and painfully. In the early 1960s, sit-ins, "freedom rides," and similar expressions of nonviolent resistance by blacks and their sympathizers led to a decrease in segregation practices in public facilities.

Unfortunately, today in many places in America, there is still segregation in many schools. This is not the result of legal policies but rather because of long, complicated histories in many places that have resulted in many neighborhoods that have largely black populations and many neighborhoods that have largely white populations. Often, this situation has been caused by "white flight," where white homeowners fled neighborhoods when African Americans moved in by moving to neighborhoods that were all white, often into the suburbs.

How did the civil rights movement begin?

It began on Thursday, December 1, 1955, as Rosa Parks (1913–2005), a seamstress for a downtown department store in Montgomery, Alabama, made her way home on the bus. Parks sat in the first row that was designated for blacks. But the white rows in the front of the bus soon filled up. Parks was asked to give up her seat so that a white man could sit, but she refused. She was arrested and sent to jail.

Montgomery's black leaders had already been discussing staging a protest against racial segregation on the city buses. They soon organized one, with Baptist minister Martin Luther King Jr. (1929–1968) as their leader. Soon, thousands of black people refused to ride the city buses, which resulted in the Montgomery Bus Boycott. It lasted more than a year and ended only when the U.S. Supreme Court ruled that segregation on buses was unconstitutional. The protesters and civil rights activists had emerged the victors in this—their first and most momentous—effort to end segregation and discrimination in the United States.

Parks, who lost her job as a result of the arrest, later explained that she had acted on her own belief that she was being unfairly treated. But in so doing, Parks had taken a stand and had given rise to a movement.

Who was Emmett Till?

Emmett Till (1941–1955) was a black fourteen-year-old from Chicago who was brutally mutilated and killed in the Deep South in August 1955. The young man was visiting relatives in Mississippi when he allegedly whistled at a white, female store clerk. Till was staying at his uncle's house when two white men came to get him on the morning of August 28; he was not seen alive again. His body was later found in a river, tied to a cotton-gin fan with barbed wire. Till's body was sent back to Chicago, where his mother insisted on an open-casket funeral, so all could see his mutilated body. An all-white jury

Rosa Parks is shown getting fingerprinted after she and dozens of others were arrested in 1956 during the Montgomery bus boycott.

acquitted the store clerk's husband, Roy Bryant, and half brother, J. W. Milman, of the crime. (Bryant and Milman would later admit that they killed Till.) The events stirred anger in the black community and among civil rights proponents in general, contributing to the beginnings of the civil rights movement.

Today, signs mark the sites associated with the killing of Emmett Till. Sadly, some of these signs have had to be repeatedly replaced due to vandalism.

What was the nonviolence movement?

The Reverend Martin Luther King Jr. (1929–1968) was committed to bringing about change by staging peaceful protests. He had studied the works of Mahatma Gandhi and was impressed by Gandhi's nonviolent commitment against injustice. King led a campaign of nonviolence as part of the civil rights movement. King rose to prominence as a leader during the Montgomery Bus Boycott in 1955, when he delivered a speech that embodied his Christian beliefs and set the tone for the nonviolence movement, saying, "We are not here advocating violence.… The only weapon we have … is the weapon of protest." Throughout his life, King staunchly adhered to these beliefs—even after terrorists bombed his family's home. King's "arsenal" of democratic protest included boycotts, marches, the words of his stirring speeches, and sit-ins.

With other African American ministers, King established the Southern Christian Leadership Conference (1957), which assumed a leadership role during the civil rights movement.

The nonviolent protest of black Americans proved a powerful weapon against segregation and discrimination. A massive demonstration in Birmingham, Alabama, in 1963 helped sway public opinion and motivate lawmakers in Washington to act when news coverage of the event showed peaceful protesters being subdued by policemen using dogs and heavy fire hoses. In response to the outcry over the event in Birmingham, President John F. Kennedy (1917–1963) proposed civil rights legislation to Congress; the bill was passed in 1964. That same year, King received the Nobel Peace Prize for his nonviolent activism.

King's policy of peace was challenged two years later when the Student Nonviolent Coordinating Committee (SNCC), tired of the violent response with which peaceful protesters were often met, urged activists to adopt a more decisive and aggressive stance and began promoting the slogan "Black Power." The civil rights movement, having made critical strides, became fragmented, as leaders, including the highly influential Malcolm X (1925–1965), differed over how to effect change.

On April 4, 1968, King was in Memphis, Tennessee, to show his support for a strike of black sanitation workers when he was gunned down outside his hotel room shortly after 5:30 in the evening. As news of King's death swept over the nation, blacks in 168 American cities and towns responded with rioting, setting fire to buildings, and looting white businesses.

Commenting on the terror, radical African American leader Stokely Carmichael (1941–1998) said, "When white America killed Dr. King last night, she declared war on us." The chaos continued for a week; when the rioting ended on April 11, there were

What were the sit-ins?

Sit-ins were a practice of challenging segregation laws by sitting in establishments reserved for whites only. African American students in Greensboro, North Carolina, conducted a sit-in at the lunch counters in Woolworth's stores, which touched off a wave of sit-ins in various cities across the Southeast, including a well-planned wave of sit-ins in Nashville, Tennessee.

The Greensboro sit-in was not the first use of the practice. Some African American activists performed sit-ins in the late 1930s and early 1940s against various segregation laws in places such as libraries, lunch counters, and other places of public accommodation.

forty-six dead (most of them black), 35,000 injured, and 20,000 jailed. Nevertheless, the violent crime that claimed the leader's life and the violence that erupted after news spread of his death have not, decades later, overshadowed King's legacy of peace and his message of the brotherhood of all people.

What were the "freedom rides"?

The "freedom rides" were a series of bus rides designed to test the U.S. Supreme Court's prohibition of segregation in interstate travel. In 1960, in the case of *Boynton v. Virginia*, the Supreme Court ruled in favor of a Howard University student who charged that segregation laws at the Richmond, Virginia, bus station violated federal antisegregation laws. The Congress of Racial Equality (CORE) decided to test the enforcement of the federal law by initiating the freedom rides.

In May 1961, thirteen people, black and white, boarded a bus for the South. Meant as a nonviolent protest against local segregation laws, the riders were nevertheless met with violence. When the bus reached Montgomery, Alabama, on May 20, a white mob attacked and beat the freedom riders. Rioting broke out in the city, and U.S. marshals were sent to restore order. The interracial campaign to desegregate transportation was ultimately successful, but government intervention was required to enforce the laws, as numerous southern whites had demonstrated that they were not going to comply voluntarily.

When did Martin Luther King Jr. give his "I Have a Dream" speech?

The occasion was the March on Washington on August 28, 1963. That summer day, more than a quarter of a million people—lobbying for congressional passage of a civil rights bill—gathered at the Lincoln Memorial to hear speakers, including the charismatic and influential King (1929–1968). His eloquent words defined the movement and still inspire those who continue to work for reforms. Among his words were these: "I have a dream that one day this nation will rise up and live out the true meaning of its creed, 'We hold these truths to be self-evident; that all men are created equal.'" King's call for justice and equality is still relevant today.

Congress passed the Civil Rights Act in 1964 under President Lyndon B. Johnson (1908–1973). The most comprehensive American civil rights legislation since the Reconstruction (the twelve-year period that followed the Civil War), the act outlawed racial discrimination in public places, as-

A close-up of Dr. Martin Luther King Jr. giving his "I Have a Dream" speech in Washington, D.C., in 1963. It was one of the most memorable events of the civil rights movement.

373

sured equal voting standards for all citizens, prohibited employer and union racial discrimination, and called for equality in education.

What other Martin Luther King speech is important?

King delivered his final speech on April 3, 1968, in Memphis, Tennessee, where he was supporting striking trash workers. The last several minutes of King's speech are particularly powerful. The next day, King was shot on the balcony of the Lorraine Motel.

Who was Fred Shuttlesworth?

Fred Shuttlesworth (1922–2011) was an African American leader of the civil rights movement. Based in Birmingham, Alabama, Shuttlesworth was cofounder of the Southern Christian Leadership Conference (SCLC) and pastor of a Baptist church in Birmingham.

He survived several attempts on his life, including a dynamite attack on his home. He was not afraid to speak his mind to fellow civil rights leaders, such as King, or to white authorities. He seemingly had no fear of death, as he vowed to kill segregation—or be killed by it. He later moved to Cincinnati, where he served as pastor of a church there for many years.

Who was Medgar Evers?

Medgar Evers (1925–1963) was a civil rights leader from Jackson, Mississippi, who challenged segregation, voting discrimination, and other unfair practices against African Americans during his short life. In 1963, he was assassinated by Byron De La Beckwith, a member of the White Citizens Council, who was not convicted until 1994. Two previous prosecutions in 1964 had led to hung juries.

What does the letter X in Malcolm X's name stand for?

The influential but controversial African American leader, who was born Malcolm Little, was a staunch defendant of black rights. He took the surname X in 1952 upon his release from prison. He explained that the letter stood for the unknown African name of his ancestors. Malcolm X's family's name, Little, was that given to his slave ancestors by their owner. By adopting X as his surname, it was at once a bitter reminder of his family's enslavement and an affirmation of his (unknown) African roots.

The life of Malcolm X is described in *The Autobiography of Malcolm X*, published in 1965, which was written in collaboration with journalist Alex Haley. Denzel Washington played Malcolm X in the 1992 movie *Malcolm X*.

What horrible event occurred in Philadelphia, Mississippi?

Three civil rights workers—James Chaney, Andrew Goodman, and Michael Schwerner—were murdered in Philadelphia, Mississippi, by members of the Ku Klux Klan, including a deputy sheriff from Neshoba County named Cecil Ray Price. The murders symbolized the injustices occurring against African Americans and other civil rights workers (as Goodman and Schwerner were white). The three victims had been part of "Freedom Summer"—an extensive effort to challenge voting discrimination and other civil rights abuses in Mississippi.

How were southern blacks prevented from voting?

Besides intimidation, there were three different methods used in southern states in the early part of the century to disenfranchise black citizens: 1) the poll tax; 2) literacy tests; and 3) grandfather clauses. The poll tax required a voter to pay a fee in order to exercise the right to vote. Literacy tests were implemented as a prerequisite for voting; this method also kept many poorly educated whites (unable to pass the exam) from casting their ballots as well.

Most southern states also adopted legislation by which voting rights were extended only to those citizens who had been able to vote as of a certain date—a date when few if any black men would have been able to vote. Since these laws made provisions for said voters' descendants as well, they were dubbed "grandfather clauses." Such attempts to deny citizens the right to vote were made unlawful in 1964 (by the Twenty-fourth Amendment, which outlaws the poll tax in all federal elections and primaries), in 1965 (by the Voting Rights Act, which outlawed measures used to suppress minority votes), and in 1966 (when poll taxes at the state and local levels were also declared illegal). Literacy tests and grandfather clauses were also struck down as unconstitutional.

What is the history of the Ku Klux Klan?

The Ku Klux Klan (KKK) is a white supremacist group originally formed in 1865 in Pulaski, Tennessee, when Confederate Army veterans formed what they called a "social club." The first leader (called the "grand wizard") was Nathan Bedford Forrest (1821–1877), a former general in the Confederate Army, who, on April 12, 1864, in the final days of the Civil War, led a massacre of over two hundred black soldiers in service of the Union Army at Fort Pillow, Tennessee.

As the unofficial arm of resistance against Republican efforts to restore the nation and make full citizens of its black (formerly enslaved) population, the Ku Klux Klan waged a campaign of terror against blacks in the South during Reconstruction (1865–1877), the twelve-year period of rebuilding that followed the Civil War. Klan members, cloaked in robes and hoods to disguise their identity, threatened, beat, and killed numerous blacks. While the group deprived its victims of their rights as citizens, their intent was also to intimidate the entire black population and keep them out of politics. White people who supported the federal government's measures to extend rights to all black citizens also became the victims of the fearsome Klan. Membership in the group grew quickly, and the Ku Klux Klan soon had a presence throughout the South. In today's language, the Klan would be called a terrorist organization.

In 1871, the U.S. Congress passed the Force Bill, giving President Ulysses S. Grant (1822–1885) authority to direct federal troops against the Klan. The action was successful, causing the group to disappear—but only for a time. In 1915, the society was newly organized at Stone Mountain, Georgia, as a Protestant fraternal organization (called "The Invisible Empire, Knights of the Ku Klux Klan, Inc."), this time widening its focus of persecution to include Roman Catholics, immigrants, and Jews as well as blacks. Members of all

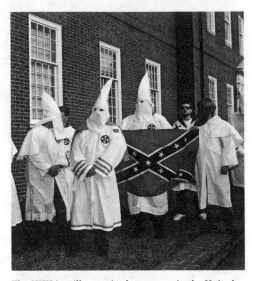

The KKK is still an active hate group in the United States despite the decades that have gone by since the civil rights movement.

of these groups became the target of KKK harassment, which now included torture, whippings, and public lynchings. The Klan also grew using professional publicists and modern marketing techniques.

The group, which proclaimed its mission of "racial purity," grew in number and became national, electing its own members to public office in many states, not just the South. But the organization's acts of violence raised the public ire, and by the 1940s, with America's attention focused on World War II (1939–1945), the Klan died out or went completely underground. The group had another resurgence during the 1950s and into the early 1970s as the nation struggled through the era of civil rights. The Klan still exists today, fostering the extremist views of its membership and staging marches to demonstrate its presence on the American landscape. Such demonstrations are often attended by anti-Klan protestors.

What is the "new Jim Crow"?

The term comes from the 2010 book *The New Jim Crow: Mass Incarceration in the Age of Colorblindness* by Michelle Alexander. Alexander looks at the problem of mass incarceration and the fact that the United States has the world's largest population of people in prison and in its criminal justice system. However, the people in the system are disproportionately African Americans. She sees the system as being a replacement for the old Jim Crow system of racist laws and policies in the South. It is "a stunningly comprehensive and well-disguised system of racialized social control that functions in a manner strikingly similar to Jim Crow."

African Americans make up about 13 percent of the general population yet make up over 40 percent of the prison population even though the crime rate for African Americans is not higher than it is for whites.

One problem has been the enforcement of antidrug policies. More people are in prison for drug crimes than for all other categories. For decades, the penalties for a certain quantity of crack cocaine was 100 times higher than the penalties for the same amount of powdered cocaine. However, African American drug users have tended to use crack, while white drug users use powdered cocaine. In recent criminal justice reforms, the ratio has been reduced, but penalties are still eighteen times higher for the possession of crack cocaine than for powdered cocaine.

WOMEN'S RIGHTS

When did the American suffragist movement begin?

In the 1840s, American women began organizing and, in increasing numbers, demanding the right to vote. The movement was started by women who sought social reforms, including outlawing slavery, instituting a national policy of temperance (abstinence from alcoholic beverages), and securing better work opportunities and pay. These reformers soon realized that in order to make change, they needed the power of the vote.

Among the leaders of the suffragist movement was feminist and reformer Elizabeth Cady Stanton (1815–1902). She joined with antislavery activist Lucretia Mott (1793–1880) to organize the first women's rights convention in 1848 in Seneca Falls, New York, launching the woman suffragist movement. In 1869, Stanton teamed with Susan B. Anthony (1820–1906) to organize the National Woman Suffrage Association.

That same year, a second group, the American Woman Suffrage Association, was formed, led by women's rights and antislavery activist Lucy Stone (1818–1893) and her husband Henry Brown Blackwell (1825–1909). In 1870, the common cause of the two groups was strengthened by the passage of the Fifteenth Amendment, which gave all men, regardless of race, the right to vote. When the two organizations joined forces in 1890, they formed the National American Woman Suffrage Association (NAWSA).

The founders of the American women's movement were followed by a new generation of leaders, which included Stanton's daughter, Harriot Eaton Blatch (1856–1940), as well as Alice Paul (1885–1977), who founded the organization that became the National Woman's Party, and organizer and editor Lucy Burns (1879–1966), who worked closely with Paul.

The suffragists appealed to middle-class and working-class women as well as to students and radicals. They waged campaigns at the state level, distributed literature, organized meetings, made speeches, and marched in parades. They also lobbied federal legislators, picketed, and chained themselves to the White House fence. When jailed, many resorted to hunger strikes and were sometimes met with cruel treatment. The suffragists' fight was a fierce one; the opposition played on the widespread belief that if given the right to vote, women would neglect the traditional duties of wife and mother.

The movement gained strength during World War I (1914–1918). As men went off to fight the war in Europe, the women at home demonstrated themselves to be intelligent and involved citizens in the life of the country. A wartime suffragist poster declared in one long column, "As a war measure, the country is asking of women service as … farmers, mechanics, nurses, doctors, munitions workers, mine workers, yeomen, gas makers, bell boys, messengers, conductors, motormen, army cooks, telegraphers, ambulance drivers, advisors to the council of national defense," and in another short column, it stated, "As a war measure, women are asking of the country … the vote."

By 1918, support for woman suffrage was broad. That year, Congress proposed a constitutional amendment stating that "the right of citizens of the United States to vote shall not be denied or abridged by the United States or by any State on account of sex." It was passed as the proposed Nineteenth Amendment in the House in 1918 and in the Senate in 1919. The amendment was approved by the required number of state legislatures on August 18, 1920, when Tennessee ratified it.

Who was Sojourner Truth?

Sojourner Truth (1797–1883) was a black woman, born as Isabella Baumfree, who was a consistent activist for racial and women's causes during her long life. She had been born

enslaved, but she escaped with her infant daughter. Later, she preached against racial discrimination and slavery for many years.

She also advocated for women's rights. In 1851, in Akron, Ohio, she delivered her powerful "Ain't I a Woman" speech, which attracted much attention. In 1867, she spoke at the American Equal Rights Association convention.

What was the Night of Terror?

It is a little-known episode in the American suffragist movement that took place on November 14, 1917, at the Occoquan Workhouse in Lorton, Virginia.

In January 1917, two months after President Woodrow Wilson (1856–1924) was reelected to a second term in office, activists began picketing daily outside the

An abolitionist and women's rights activist, Sojourner Truth was actually born in New York as a slave whose first language was Dutch! She was also the first black woman to successfully sue a white man for custody of her enslaved son.

White House, demanding the right to vote for women. It was the first time in history that demonstrators had marched at the White House. The suffragists carried banners that read: "Mr. President, how long must women wait for liberty?" and, more radically, "Kaiser Wilson: 20,000,000 American women are not self-governed." In April, a month after Wilson's second term began, the United States entered World War I (1914–1918) to guarantee democracy abroad. Yet, female picketers sought to expose the government's hypocrisy: democracy did not exist at home, where the entire female population remained disenfranchised.

In June, police began arresting demonstrators on minor charges, such as obstructing traffic. But the arrests did nothing to deter the suffragists. Upon their release from prison, they returned to protest at the White House gates. In all, 168 women, including Alice Paul (1885–1977) and Lucy Burns (1879–1966) of the National Woman's Party, were arrested.

On the night of November 14, 1917, guards took thirty-three protesters to the Occoquan Workhouse to be held. Previously, the women had been subject to forced feedings and solitary confinement at Occoquan, but this time, new cruelties awaited them. They were beaten, dragged, choked, and handcuffed. Word leaked out about the atrocities committed at the workhouse. Less than two weeks later, a judge ruled that the women had been brutally treated, yet they had done nothing more than exercise their constitutional right to free speech. The women returned to their fight, now with more weight of public opinion behind them. Nevertheless, it was three long years before the Nineteenth Amendment was adopted, guaranteeing women the right to vote.

In 1982, a historical marker was placed on the prison grounds in tribute to the brave women who endured Occoquan's Night of Terror. In 2019, ground was broken near the Occoquan Workhouse for the Turning Point Suffrage Memorial.

Who was Alice Paul?

Alice Paul (1885–1977) was a groundbreaking feminist before the word "feminist" came into fashion. She has been described as "the architect of some of the most outstanding political achievements on behalf of women in the twentieth century."

Paul was born in 1885 to Quaker parents who instilled in her a belief in gender equality. After completing high school at the top of her class, Paul graduated from Swarthmore College in 1905 and began work toward an advanced degree. In 1906, she traveled to England, where she continued her studies, did social work, and became actively involved in the suffrage movement. She was arrested three times for her involvement in protests.

In 1916, when the American women's suffrage movement was divided and "dead in the water," Paul founded the National Woman's Party (NWP), an organization that spearheaded the campaign for national women's suffrage and that continued working for women's rights and equality into the twenty-first century. Paul's leadership of the suffrage movement was critical in the passage of the Nineteenth Amendment (1920), which guaranteed women the right to vote. She organized thousands of activists to put enormous pressure on the White House and Congress. Paul employed what was then considered a most unladylike strategy of "sustained, dramatic, nonviolent protest." The suffrage campaign was characterized by national speaking tours, marches, and pickets (including the first ever at the White House). When protesters were arrested, they sometimes endured brutal prison conditions and staged hunger strikes.

Called a brilliant political strategist, the forward-thinking Paul authored the first equal rights amendment for women, which she introduced to Congress in 1923. In 1942, she became chairperson of the National Woman's Party. She later added language of gender equality to the charter of the United Nations as well as the 1964 Civil Rights Act. After a life of courageous activism on behalf of women, Paul died in 1977.

Who was Emmeline Pankhurst?

Emmeline Pankhurst (1858–1928), a key figure in the women's suffrage movement, was a militant reformer who waged a decades-long battle to win the vote for women in Great Britain. Pankhurst's sometimes radical campaign greatly influenced her American counterparts. She worked for change primarily through the organizations she founded. In 1889, she organized the Women's Franchise League, and five years later, the group's work secured the right of all women (married and unmarried) to vote in local elections.

She went on to found the Women's Social and Political Union in 1903. The union was known for its extreme tactics. The British suffragist movement culminated in 1928 with the passage of the Representation of the People Act, which gave all women the right to vote in elections. Pankhurst died later that year. (Women in America had gotten the right to vote in national elections in 1920.)

Have all nations of the world granted women the right to vote?

Virtually all nations allow women to vote. The first nations to extend broad voting rights to women were New Zealand in 1893, Australia and South Wales in 1902, and Finland in 1906. Saudi Arabia, a long holdout on the issue, allowed women to vote in 2015. There are several nations where voting is restricted for both men and women.

Vatican City is a unique case. It is both the headquarters of the Catholic Church

Emmeline Pankhurst was a key leader of the women's suffrage movement in the United Kingdom, where the right to vote was granted in 1918, two years before the United States.

What is Title IX?

Considered one of the biggest successes of the modern women's movement, Title IX is part of the Education Amendments of 1972, federal legislation that prohibits any school or college that receives federal funds from discriminating on the basis of sex. The law applies to all aspects of education, including admission, athletics, and curriculum.

and a separate country, although it is only 110 acres in size and has a population of about a thousand people. Only Catholic cardinals can vote to choose a pope, and cardinals must be men.

How old is feminism?

Feminists—people who believe that women should have economic, political, and social equality with men—have existed throughout history; such women are often described in literature and by history as being "women before their time." But as a movement, feminism, which is synonymous with the women's rights movement, did not get underway until the mid-1800s, when women in the United States and Great Britain began organizing and campaigning to win the vote.

Early feminists (and feminists today) were likely influenced by the revolutionary work titled *A Vindication of the Rights of Woman*, published in 1792 by British author and educator Mary Wollstonecraft (1759–1797; her daughter was writer Mary Shelley, of *Frankenstein* fame). Wollstonecraft attacked the convention of the day, charging that it kept middle-class and upper-class women in a state of ignorance, training them to be useless. A staunch promoter of education (she was self-educated), Wollstonecraft is credited with being the first major philosophical feminist.

What is the ERA?

The ERA stands for the Equal Rights Amendment, a constitutional amendment proposed by Congress in 1972. It stated that "equality of rights under the law shall not be denied or abridged by the United States or any state on account of sex." In proposing the amendment, Congress gave the states ten years in which to ratify it.

But by 1982, only thirty-five of the necessary thirty-eight states had approved the amendment, which then died. The failure to ratify the ERA was the result of disagreement over how the language would be interpreted. Supporters believed the amendment would guarantee women equal treatment under the law; opponents feared the amendment might require women to forfeit the financial support of their husbands and require them to serve in the military. The political opposition to the ERA helped create the religious right, which is a potent political force today.

381

Since 1982, five states have rescinded their approvals, and Nevada and Illinois have ratified the ERA after the deadline.

THE BIRTH CONTROL MOVEMENT

How did the birth control movement get started?

Ironically, it was a decline in death rates, which led to an overall increase in the world population, that gave rise to the birth control movement. Scientific advances during the eighteenth and nineteenth centuries resulted in better food supplies, improved control and treatment of diseases, and safer work environments for those living in developed countries. These improvements combined with progress in medicine to save and prolong human lives. During the 1800s, the birth rate, which in earlier times had been offset by the death rate, became a concern to many who worried that population growth would outstrip the planet's ability to provide adequate resources to sustain life.

In 1798, British economist and sociologist Thomas Robert Malthus (1766–1834) published his *Essay on the Principle of Population*, arguing that populations tend to increase faster than do food supplies. He thereby concluded that poverty and suffering are unavoidable. Malthus viewed only war, famine, disease, and "moral restraint" as checks on population growth. In spite of, or because of, Malthus's assertions, during the 1800s, the idea of birth control as a practical method to keep population growth in check gained momentum.

Early in the 1900s, the movement found a leader in American Margaret Higgins Sanger (1879–1966), whose personal experience as a nurse working among the poor had convinced her that limiting family size is necessary for social progress. She became convinced that unwanted pregnancies should be avoided by using birth control methods. The view was—and, to some, remains—controversial. Even though the distribution of birth control information was illegal at the time, Sanger advised people on the subject. In 1914, she founded a magazine called *The Woman Rebel*, and she sent birth control information through the mail. She was arrested and indicted. But she was not deterred.

In 1916 in Brooklyn, New York, Sanger founded the first birth control clinic in the United States. In 1921, she organized the first American Birth Control Conference, held in New York. That same year, she founded the American Birth Control League, which later became the Planned Parenthood Federation of America. As public support for the movement increased, Sanger succeeded in getting laws passed that allowed doctors to disseminate birth control information to their patients.

Margaret Sanger is shown here on the steps of the Brooklyn courthouse in 1917 where she was found guilty of opening a birth control clinic.

In other countries, Sanger's work inspired similar movements, but developed nations continue to have lower birth rates than do developing nations. With the world population now exceeding 7.7 billion, the fear of overpopulation has prompted continued interest in birth control and family planning.

What is the "abstinence only" movement?

Many religious teachers have proposed teaching young men and women about the importance of not having sex until marriage. Such people often oppose the teaching of sex education in schools. They think that teaching young people about contraception legitimizes sex before marriage. Thus, many in this movement oppose the teaching of sex education in schools.

However, numerous studies of "abstinence only" programs show that while young people who undergo such training often delay having sex in the short run, many do not wait until marriage. Yet, since they often were not taught about contraception, they are more likely to become pregnant or to pass along STDs.

ROE V. WADE

Why is the ruling in *Roe v. Wade* controversial?

The 1973 Supreme Court decision in the case of *Roe v. Wade* legalized abortion in the United States and has probably engendered more public controversy than any other recent legal case. The seven Supreme Court justices who issued the majority decision received thousands of letters of hatred, some of them threatening.

The case was brought as a class-action suit by twenty-one-year-old Norma McCorvey (1947–2017). In 1969, under the alias Jane Roe, McCorvey claimed that Texas's abortion law (on the books since 1859) violated her constitutional rights and those of other women.

The other party named in the case was Texas district attorney Henry B. Wade (1914–2001), who argued to uphold Texas state law that punished anyone who gave an abortion.

The lawyer for Roe argued that Texas's ability to compel women to bear children infringed on a woman's right to control her own life. It was therefore a violation of the Constitution (the Fourteenth Amendment), which forbids states to "make or enforce any law which shall abridge the privileges or immunities of citizens."

On January 22, 1973, Justice Harry Blackmun read the majority decision that overturned all state laws restricting women's access to abortions. The decision was based on the court's opinion that existing laws banning abortions had been enacted to protect the health of American women (since abortion had previously been a risky medical procedure) and that with advances in medicine, this protection was no longer necessary or valid.

The court also agreed that the Constitution's implied right to privacy, as found in the "Fourteenth Amendment's concept of personal liberty … or in the Ninth Amendment's reservation of rights to the people, is broad enough to encompass a woman's decision to terminate her pregnancy."

Two justices dissented in the opinion, with Justice Byron White writing that the court had sustained a position that "values the convenience, whim or caprice of the putative mother more than life or the potential life of the fetus."

Protesters at the steps of the Supreme Court building in Washington, D.C., raise their voices against states trying to pass laws that make abortion illegal once a fetus has a heartbeat.

> ## What is the moral issue involved with abortion?
>
> **A**ctually, there are several moral issues involved. When does the fetus become a human being? Does the fetus have rights? What are the rights of a woman in deciding for herself whether to have an abortion or not? What are the special cases that would justify an abortion?

Nearly four decades after the landmark decision, opinion continues to divide along such lines. (In fact, years after the ruling, McCorvey herself reversed her feeling and joined the antiabortion camp as a "right to life" advocate.) In subsequent decisions, the court has upheld various restrictions on obtaining an abortion, but it has never over-ruled the central holding of *Roe v. Wade*.

What are the different views on abortion?

People hold different views on the morality of abortion from strong pro-life advocates, opposing most or even all abortions, to strong pro-choice advocates, believing in the right of women to decide for themselves. Also, many people are indifferent on the issue.

When does a fetus become a human being?

There is no agreement over when a fetus becomes a human being. Everyone agrees that the egg and the sperm are not human beings and that a born baby is. So, when in the nine months between conception and birth does the fetus become a human being? Many pro-life advocates believe it becomes a human life at the moment of conception. Some pro-lifers even oppose scientific research using human embryos, believing them to be human beings. Many religious pro-lifers support their position with the passage from Jeremiah 1:5: "Before I formed you in the womb I knew you, and before you were born I consecrated you; I appointed you a prophet to the nations."

From a legal perspective, the fetus becomes a human being with legal rights at birth. The one exception to this is that in some states, if someone kills a pregnant woman and the fetus also dies, the killer can be charged with two murders.

Other people do not believe that the embryo, and then the fetus in the early stages, is a human being. Many different answers are given as to when it becomes human.

What is the pro-choice position?

Pro-choice advocates focus more on the rights of women in determining whether or not to have an abortion. Given that there is no agreement on when the fetus becomes a human, the decision should be left up to the woman. Also, pro-choice advocates are often very aware of the difficult situations in which women find themselves when they have an unwanted pregnancy.

385

How can we reduce the number of abortions?

The fight between those who oppose abortion and those who support a woman's right to choose is very intense. The issue is constantly fought over in state legislatures and courts. Ironically, both sides agree on the goal of reducing the number of abortions. Many pro-choice advocates are very active in promoting sex education and making contraception more available to reduce the number of unwanted pregnancies.

What is happening in the fight over abortion?

Currently a number of states with Republican legislatures have passed laws to restrict abortions, make it more difficult to get an abortion, or prohibit abortions. The laws have not gone into effect because they go against *Roe v. Wade*, but they will go before the Supreme Court in 2020.

Pro-life advocates have been working to change the makeup of the Supreme Court ever since the *Roe* decision in hopes that new justices would overturn it. Recent conservative justices added to the court, Neil Gorsuch (1967–) and Brett Kavanaugh (1965–), are expected to support restrictions on abortion.

Another strategy to restrict access to abortion is for states to add more regulations to abortion clinics so they cannot function. Often, such regulations are claimed to protect the health of women, but major medical organizations have stated that such regulations are not needed.

POLITICAL AND SOCIAL MOVEMENTS

NATIONALISM

How old is nationalism?

Nationalism, a people's sense that they belong together as a nation because of a shared history and culture and, often, because of a common language and/or religion, emerged at the close of the Middle Ages. By the 1700s, several countries, notably England, France, and Spain, had developed as "nation-states," groups of people with a shared background who occupy a land that is governed independently.

By the 1800s, nationalism had become a powerful force, and the view took hold that any national group has the right to form its own state. However, in many places, nationalist identities did not match political boundaries. For example, in the Austro-Hungarian Empire in Europe, several different nationalities existed within its political boundaries. In the United States, nationalism took the form of manifest destiny, the mission to expand the country's boundaries to include as much of North America as possible.

In the 1800s, nationalist literature began to be written. Also, many composers started writing nationalist music, such as Frédéric Chopin (Polish), Nikolay Rimsky-Korsakov (Russian), Richard Wagner (German), Antonín Dvořák (Czech), and, in the twentieth century, Aaron Copland (American).

Because of the belief called national self-determination, some nations achieved independence. Greece gained freedom from Turkey in 1829, and Belgium became independent from the Netherlands in 1830. Others formed new and larger countries by the unification of numerous smaller states, such as Italy in 1870 and Germany in 1871. The trend continued into the twentieth century with many examples, such as the breakup of the Austro-Hungarian Empire following World War I that resulted in the formation of the independent countries of Austria, Hungary, Czechoslovakia, Poland, and, later, Yugoslavia. Yugoslavia was later broken up into Slovenia, Macedonia, Croatia, Kosovo, Bosnia and Herzegovina, and Montenegro.

While nationalism is a source of pride and patriotism and has had many positive results, some leaders (notably German dictator Adolf Hitler) have carried it to extremes, initiating large-scale movements that resulted in the persecution of other peoples and in the hideous practice of ethnic cleansing.

What is one of the big problems with nationalism?

Political situations become complicated when national identities of a people do not match the political boundaries in which they live. This has been a long-term problem and still exists today in many places. For example, in the country of Spain, the people in the region of Catalonia, which includes the city of Barcelona, speak the language of Catalan. Many see their national identity as Catalan and not Spanish even though they are currently part of Spain. Some want an independent country. In northern Spain is the Basque region that extends into France. Some Basques want an independent country.

THE SOLIDARITY MOVEMENT IN POLAND

What is Solidarity?

It was a worker-led movement for political reform in Poland during the 1980s that contributed greatly to the downfall of communism. The movement was inspired by Pope John Paul II's June 1979 visit to his native Poland, where, in Warsaw, he delivered a speech to millions, calling for a free Poland and a new kind of "solidarity." (As scholar and author Timothy Garton Ash noted, "Without the Pope, no Solidarity. Without Solidarity, no Gorbachev. Without Gorbachev, no fall of Communism.")

Shipyard electrician Lech Wałesa (1943–) became the leader of Solidarity, formed in 1980 when fifty labor unions banded together to protest Poland's communist government. The unions staged strikes and demonstrations. By 1981, Solidarity had gained so many followers that it threatened Poland's government, which responded (with the support of the Soviet

Lech Wałesa (pictured during a 1980 shipyard strike) led a workers' movement in Poland called Solidarity that overthrew the communist government. He served as president of Poland from 1990 to 1995.

Union) by instituting martial law in December of that year. The military cracked down on the activities of the unions, abolishing Solidarity in 1982 and arresting its leaders, including the charismatic Wałesa.

But the powerful people's movement, which had also swept up farmers (who formed the Rural Solidarity), could not be suppressed. Martial law was lifted in mid-1983, but the government continued to exert control over the people's freedom. That year, Wałesa received the Nobel Peace Prize for his efforts to gain workers' rights and prevent violence. Solidarity continued its work for reform.

In 1989, with the collapse of communism on the horizon (people's movements in Eastern Europe had combined with Soviet leader Mikhail Gorbachev's policy of *glasnost* to herald the system's demise), the Polish government reopened negotiations with Solidarity leadership. Free elections were held that year, with the labor party candidates gaining numerous seats in Parliament. In 1990, Wałesa was elected president, at which time he resigned as chairman of Solidarity. Poland's Communist Party was dissolved that year.

In the years following, Poland moved toward becoming a democracy with democratic institutions. However, in 2015, Andrzej Duda (1972–) became president as the candidate of the right-wing Law and Justice Party. Many critics see him as an authoritarian who is moving Poland away from democracy. In particular, he has totally undermined the independence of the judiciary.

APARTHEID IN SOUTH AFRICA

How were the Boer Wars important for the origins of South Africa?

The Boer Wars were conflicts between the British and the Afrikaners (or Boers, who were Dutch descendants living in South Africa) at the end of the nineteenth century in what is today South Africa. The first war, a Boer rebellion, broke out in 1880 when the British and the Afrikaners fought over the Kimberley area (Griqualand West), where a diamond field had been discovered. The fighting lasted a year, at which time the South African Republic (established in 1856) was restored.

But the stability would not last long: In 1886, gold was discovered in the Transvaal, and though the Afrikaner region was too strong for the British to attempt to annex it, they blocked the Afrikaners' access to the sea. In 1899, the Afrikaner republics of the Orange Free State and the Transvaal joined forces in a war against Britain. The fighting raged until 1902, when the Afrikaners (the Boers) surrendered. Part of the British strategy had been to round up Afrikaner women and children and put them in concentration camps. Over 27,000 died in the camps.

For a time after the Boer War (also called the South African War), the Transvaal became a British crown colony. In 1910, the British government combined its holdings in southern Africa into the Union of South Africa. In 1948, the system of apartheid was created, leading to an unequal society with whites at the top and blacks at the bottom.

In 1961, the land became the Republic of South Africa.

What was apartheid? What was the antiapartheid movement?

Apartheid was a system of strict racial segregation in the country of South Africa. (The word "apartheid" means "separateness" in the South African language of Afrikaans.) Under apartheid, which the Afrikaner Nationalist Party formalized in 1948, minority whites were given supremacy over nonwhites. The system further separated nonwhite groups from each other so that mulattoes (those of mixed race), Asians (mostly Indians), and native Africans were segregated. The policy was so rigid that it even separated native Bantu groups from each other.

Blacks were not allowed to vote even though they were and are the majority population. Apartheid was destructive to society and drew protests at home and abroad. But the South African government adhered to the system, claiming it was the only way to keep peace among the country's various ethnic groups.

Who was Stephen Biko?

Stephen Biko (1946–1977) was a black leader in the fight against South African apartheid and white minority rule. In 1969, Biko, who was then a medical student, founded the South African Students' Organization, which took an active role in the black consciousness movement, a powerful force in the fight against apartheid. Preaching a doctrine of black self-reliance and self-respect, Biko organized protests, including antigovernment strikes and marches. Viewing such activities as a challenge to its authority and fearing an escalation of unrest, in August 1977, the white government had Biko arrested.

Within one month, he died in prison. Evidence indicated he had died at the hands of his jailers, a revelation that only cemented antigovernment sentiment. Along with Nelson Mandela (1918–2013), who was imprisoned in South Africa from 1962 to 1990 for his political activities, Biko became a symbol of the antiapartheid movement, galvanizing support for racial justice at home and abroad.

Stephen Biko founded the South African Students' Organization, which actively fought against the injustices of apartheid.

What was the Soweto Uprising?

The Soweto Uprising referred to a protest by South African black school-aged youths

390

that began on June 16, 1976. The youths protested the introduction of Afrikaans, a Dutch language, into their schools. They associated Afrikaans with the government's support of apartheid. More than 20,000 students participated in the protest, which resulted in more than 170 deaths.

June 16 is now a public holiday, called Youth Day, in South Africa.

How did apartheid end?

Protesters against apartheid staged demonstrations and strikes, which sometimes became violent. South Africa grew

South African president F. W. de Klerk shakes hands with Nelson Mandela at the 1992 World Economic forum. Two years later, blacks were eligible to vote, and de Klerk was replaced by Mandela.

increasingly isolated as countries opposing the system refused to trade with the apartheid government. The no-trade policy had been urged by South African civil rights leader and Anglican bishop Desmond Tutu (1931–), who led a nonviolent campaign to end apartheid and in 1984 won the Nobel Peace Prize for his efforts. During the 1980s, the economic boycott put pressure on the white-minority South African government to repeal apartheid laws. It finally did so, and in 1991 the system of segregation was officially abolished.

White South African leader F. W. de Klerk (1936–), who was elected in 1989, had been instrumental in ending the apartheid system. In April 1994, South Africa held the first elections in which blacks were eligible to vote. Not surprisingly, black South Africans won control of Parliament, which in turn elected black leader Nelson Mandela as president, and de Klerk was retained as deputy president. The two men won the Nobel Peace Prize in 1993 for their efforts to end apartheid and give all of South Africa's peoples full participation in government. In 1996, the work of the Truth and Reconciliation Commission, a panel headed by Desmond Tutu and charged with investigating the political crimes committed under apartheid, began work. Its investigations continued into 1999, with many findings proving controversial.

U.S. POPULISM, PROGRESSIVISM, AND THE LABOR MOVEMENT

What was populism in the late 1800s and early 1900s?

Populism was a commoners' movement that was formalized in the United States in 1891 with the founding of the Populist Party, which worked to improve conditions for farmers and laborers. In the presidential election of 1892, the party supported its own political candidate, James B. Weaver (1833–1912). Though Weaver lost, the Populists remained a strong force. In the presidential election four years later, they backed Democratic Party candidate William Jennings Bryan (1860–1925), a self-proclaimed commoner who was sympathetic to the causes of the Farmers' Alliances, and the National Grange movement as well as the nation's workers. (The National Grange movement promoted the economic and political interests of farmers. It still exists; its website is *nationalgrange.org*.)

Bryan lost to William McKinley (1843–1901), and soon after the election, the Populist Party began to fall apart, disappearing altogether by 1908. Nevertheless, the party's initiatives continued to figure into the nation's political life for the next two decades, and many populist ideas were made into laws, including the free coinage of silver and government issue of more paper money ("greenbacks") to loosen the money supply, adoption of a graduated income tax, passage of an amendment allowing for the popular election of U.S. senators (the Constitution provided for their election by the state legislatures), passage of antitrust laws (to combat the monopolistic control of American business), and implementation of the eight-hour workday. Since the early 1900s, political candidates and ideas have continued to be described as populist, meaning they favor the rights of and uphold the beliefs and values of the common people.

What was the Progressive movement?

The Progressive movement was a campaign for reform on every level—social, political, and economic—in the United States. It began during the economic depression created by the financial crisis called the "Panic of 1873" and lasted until 1917, when America entered World War I (1914–1918).

During the first 100 years of the U.S. Constitution (1788), federal lawmakers and justices proved reluctant to get involved in or attempt to regulate private businesses. This policy of noninterference had allowed the gap to widen between rich and poor. The turn of the century was a time in America when early industrialists amassed great fortunes and built fantastic mansions, while many workers and farmers struggled to earn a living.

In urban areas, millions lived in overcrowded tenement buildings in which the living conditions were often squalid. Millions of immigrants were entering the country, and many found it impossible to lift themselves out of poverty. Observing these problems, progressive-minded reformers, comprised largely of middle-class Americans, women, and journalists (often called "muckrakers"), began reform campaigns at the local and state levels, eventually affecting changes at the federal level.

Progressives favored many of the ideas that had previously been espoused by the Populists, including antitrust legislation to bust up the monopolies and a graduated income tax to more adequately collect public funds from the nation's well-to-do businessmen. Additionally, Progressives combated corrupt local governments; dirty and dangerous working conditions in factories, mines, and fields; and inner-city blight. The minimum wage, the Pure Food and Drug Act, and Chicago's Hull House (which served as "an incubator for the American social work movement") are part of the legacy of the Progressive movement.

When did the U.S. labor movement begin?

It began in the early 1800s, when skilled workers, such as carpenters and blacksmiths, banded together in local organizations with the goal of securing better wages. By the time of the Civil War, the first national unions had been founded—again by skilled workers. However, many of these early labor organizations struggled to gain widespread support and soon fell apart. But by the end of the century, several national unions, including the United Mine Workers (1890) and the American Railway Union (1893), emerged.

In the last two decades of the 1800s, violence accompanied labor protests and strikes, while opposition to the unions mounted. Companies shared blacklists of the names of workers suspected of union activities; hired armed guards to forcibly break strikes; and retained lawyers to successfully invoke the Sherman Anti-Trust Act (1890) to crush strikes.

However, the Sherman Anti-Trust Act was being misused. The act was designed to break up large corporations. Now, it was being used against unions, which was not the intent of the lawmakers who had passed the Sherman Act.

In the early decades of the 1900s, unions made advances, but many Americans continued to view organizers and members as radicals. The climate changed for the unions during the Great Depression (1929–1941). With so many Americans out of work, many blamed business leaders for the economy's failure and began to view the unions in a new light—as organizations created to protect the interests of workers.

In 1935, the federal government strengthened the unions' cause in passing the National Labor Relations Act (also called the Wagner Act), protecting the rights to organize and to bargain collectively (when worker representatives, usually labor union representatives, negotiate with employers). The legislation also set up the National Labor Relations Board (NLRB), which is supposed to penalize companies that engage in unfair labor practices.

Unions grew increasingly powerful over the next decade, and by 1945, more than one-third of all nonagricultural workers belonged to a union. Having made important gains during World War II, including hospital insurance coverage, paid vacations and holidays, and pensions, union leaders continued to urge workers to strike to gain more ground—something leaders felt was the worker's right amid the unprecedented prosperity of the postwar era.

But strikes soon impacted the life of the average American, and consumers faulted the unions for shortages of consumer goods, suspension of services, and inflated prices. Congress responded by passing the Labor-Management Relations Act (or the Taft-Hartley Act) in 1947, which limits the impact of unions by prohibiting certain kinds of strikes, setting rules for how unions could organize workers, and establishing guidelines for how strikes that may impact the nation's health or safety are to be handled.

What was the first big union?

The first national union of note was the Knights of Labor, founded by garment workers in Philadelphia, Pennsylvania, in 1869. Recruiting women, blacks, immigrants, and unskilled and semiskilled workers alike, the Knights of Labor's open-membership policy provided the organization with a broad base of support, something previous labor unions, which had limited membership based on craft or skill, lacked. In other words, open membership meant that any worker could join. Previously, unions were organized by industry, such as railway workers and garment workers, or by trade, such as carpenters and laborers.

The official seal of the Knights of Labor bears the motto: "That Is the Most Perfect Government in Which an Injury to One Is the Concern of All."

The Knights of Labor set its objectives on instituting the eight-hour workday, prohibiting child labor (under age fourteen), instituting equal opportunities and wages for women laborers, and abolishing convict labor. The group became involved in numerous strikes from the late 1870s to the mid-1880s.

At the same time, a faction of moderates within the organization was growing, and in 1883, it elected American machinist Terence Powderly (1849–1924) as president. Under Powderly's leadership, the Knights of Labor began to splinter. Moderates pursued a conciliatory policy in labor disputes, supporting the establishment of labor bureaus and public arbitration systems; radicals not only opposed the policy of open membership, they strongly supported strikes as a means of achieving immediate goals—including a one-day general strike to demand implementation of an eight-hour workday.

What happened in Haymarket Square in Chicago?

In May 1886, workers demonstrating in Chicago's Haymarket Square attracted a crowd of some 1,500 people. When police arrived to disperse them, a bomb exploded, and rioting ensued. Eleven people were killed, and more than 1,000 were injured in the melee.

For many Americans, the event linked the labor movement with anarchy. That same year, several factions of the Knights of Labor seceded from the union to join the American Federation of Labor (AFL). The Knights of Labor remained intact for three more decades before the organization officially dissolved in 1917, by which time the group had been overshadowed by the AFL and other unions.

How old is the AFL-CIO?

The roots of the American Federation of Labor-Congress of Industrial Organizations (AFL-CIO), today a federation of national unions, date to 1881, when the Federation of

Organized Trade and Labor Unions was formed, representing some 50,000 members. It reorganized in 1886 as the American Federation of Labor (AFL) and elected Samuel Gompers (1850–1924) president.

Unlike the open-membership policy of the Knights of Labor, the AFL determined to organize by craft. At the outset, its member unions included a total of 140,000 skilled laborers. Gompers had been active in labor for more than two decades. Once chosen as president of the AFL, Gompers remained in that office until his death in 1924. During this nearly forty-year period, he shaped the labor federation and helped it make strides by determining a general policy that allowed member unions autonomy.

Unlike the Knights of Labor, which pursued long-term goals, the AFL focused its efforts on specific, short-term goals, such as higher wages, shorter hours, and the right to bargain collectively (when an employer agrees to negotiate with worker/union representatives).

In the 1890s, the AFL was weakened by labor violence, which evoked public fears. A July 1892 strike at the Carnegie Steel plant in Homestead, Pennsylvania, turned into a riot between angry steelworkers and Pinkerton guards. The militia was called in to monitor the strike, which five months later ended in failure for the AFL-affiliated steelworkers. Nevertheless, under Gompers's leadership, membership of the AFL grew to more than one million by 1901 and to 2.5 million by 1917, when it included 111 national unions and 27,000 local unions.

The AFL-CIO headquarters is located in Washington, D.C. Representing about twelve million employees and retirees, the AFL-CIO is the largest federation of unions in America.

The federation collected dues from its members, creating a fund to aid striking workers. The organization avoided party politics, instead seeking out and supporting advocates regardless of political affiliation. The AFL worked to support the establishment of the U.S. Department of Labor (1913), which administers and enforces statutes promoting the welfare and advancement of the American workforce, and the passage of the Clayton Anti-Trust Act (1914), which strengthened the Sherman Anti-Trust Act of 1890, eventually delivering a blow to monopolies.

The CIO was founded in 1938. In the early 1930s, several AFL unions banded together as the Committee for Industrial Organizations and successfully conducted campaigns to sign up new members in mass-production facilities, such as the automobile, steel, and rubber industries. Since these initiatives (which resulted in millions of new members) were against the AFL policy of signing up only skilled laborers by craft (the CIO had reached out to all industrial workers regardless of skill level or craft), a schism resulted within the AFL. The unions that had participated in the CIO membership drive were expelled from the AFL. The CIO established itself as a federation in 1938, officially changing its name to the Congress of Industrial Organizations.

In 1955, amid a climate of increasing anti-unionism, the AFL and CIO rejoined to form one strong voice. Today, the organization has craft and industrial affiliates at the international, national, state, and local levels, with membership totaling in the millions.

Who were the Wobblies?

The Wobblies were the early radical members of the Industrial Workers of the World (IWW), a union founded in 1905 by the leaders of forty-three labor organizations. The group pursued short-term goals via strikes and acts of sabotage as well as the long-term goal of overthrowing capitalism and rebuilding society based on socialist principles. One IWW organizer proclaimed that the "final aim is revolution." Their extremist views and tactics attracted national attention, making IWW and Wobblies household terms during the early decades of the twentieth century.

Founded and led by miner and socialist William "Big Bill" Haywood (1869–1928) and mine workers agitator Mary "Mother" Jones (1830–1930), the IWW aimed to unite all workers in a camp, mine, or factory for the eventual takeover of the industrial facility. The union organized strikes in lumber and mining camps in the West, in the steel mills of Pennsylvania, and in the textile mills of New England. The leadership advocated the use of violence to achieve its revolutionary goals and opposed mediation (negotiations moderated by a neutral third party), collective bargaining (bargaining between worker representatives and an employer), and arbitration (third-party mediation). The group declined during World War I (1914–1918), when the IWW led strikes that were suppressed by the federal government. The organization's leaders were arrested, and the organization weakened. Haywood was convicted of sedition (inciting resistance to lawful authority) but managed to escape the country. He died in the Soviet Union, where he was given a hero's burial for his socialist views.

The IWW never rose again to the prominent status of its early controversial days. Today, although much smaller in size, the IWW continues to promote its original goal of organizing workers by industry rather than trade. (Its website is *iww.org*.)

Who was Eugene Debs?

Eugene Debs (1855–1926) was a radical labor leader who in 1893 founded the American Railway Union (ARU), an industrial union for all railroad workers. Debs was a charismatic speaker, but he was also a controversial figure. In 1894, workers at the Pullman Palace Car Company, which manufactured railcars in Pullman, Illinois (near Chicago), went on strike to protest a significant reduction in their wages. Pullman was a model "company town," where the railcar manufacturer, founded by American inventor George W. Pullman (1831–1897), owned all the land and buildings and ran the school, bank, and utilities.

In 1893, in order to maintain profits following declining revenues, the Pullman Company cut workers' wages by 25 to 40 percent but did not adjust rent and prices in the town, forcing many employees and their families into deprivation. In May 1894, a labor committee approached Pullman Company management to resolve the situation. The company, which had always refused to negotiate with employees, responded by firing the labor committee members. The firings incited a strike of all 3,300 Pullman workers. In support of the labor effort, Eugene Debs assumed leadership of the strike (some Pullman employees had joined the ARU in 1894) and directed all ARU members not to haul any Pullman cars.

A general rail strike followed, which paralyzed transportation across the country. In response to what was now being called "Debs' rebellion," on July 2, 1894, a federal judge ordered all workers to return to the job. When the ARU refused to comply, U.S. president Grover Cleveland (1837–1908) ordered federal troops to break the strike with the justification that it interfered with mail delivery. The intervention turned violent.

Despite public protest, Debs, who was tried for contempt of court and conspiracy, was imprisoned in 1895 for having violated the court order. Debs later proclaimed himself a socialist and became leader of the American Left, running unsuccessfully for president as the Socialist Party candidate in 1900, 1904, 1908, 1912, and 1920.

He was arrested again in 1918 after giving a speech in Canton, Ohio, in which

Trade unionist, political activist, and socialist Eugene Debs was a founder of the Industrial Workers of the World and ran five times for president of the United States.

he criticized the U.S. war effort and entry into World War I. He was convicted of violating the Espionage Act of 1917 because he compared the draft to slavery and told members of the crowd that they were no better than mere cannon fodder. (The Espionage Act took away the right of free speech for saying anything negative about the war effort.) President Warren G. Harding (1865–1923) commuted his sentence in 1921. Today, the life of Debs can be explored at the Eugene V. Debs Museum in Terre Haute, Indiana.

What happened at the Triangle Shirtwaist Factory in 1911?

The Triangle Shirtwaist Factory occupied the top three floors of a Manhattan office building. (The building still stands as the Brown Building at 23–29 Washington Place in Greenwich Village. A "shirtwaist" was a woman's blouse.) The factory was one of the most successful garment factories in New York City, employing some 1,000 workers, mostly immigrant women. But the conditions were hazardous: The space was cramped, accessible only via stairwells and hallways so narrow that people had to pass single file; only one of the four elevators was regularly in service; the cutting machines in the workroom were gas-powered; scraps of fabric littered the work areas; the water barrels (for use in case of fire) were not kept full; and the no-smoking rule was not strictly enforced. Many exit doors were locked. In short, it was an accident waiting to happen.

On Saturday, March 25, 1911, fire broke out. A total of 146 garment workers—mostly immigrant women aged fourteen to twenty-three—died. However, smoke and fire were not the only causes of death. In the panicked escape, people were trampled, fell in elevator shafts, jumped several stories to the pavement below, and were killed when a fire escape melted and collapsed.

The disaster became a rallying cry for the labor movement. Tens of thousands of people marched in New York City in tribute to those who had died, calling attention to the grave social problems of the day. New York State enacted legislation, and New York City created ordinances calling for fire-safety reforms in factories, including the requirement to install sprinkler systems. The incident illustrated the importance of government regulation to create safe working conditions in factories.

Who was Cesar Chavez?

Mexican American farmworker Cesar Chavez (1927–1993) was a labor union organizer and spokesperson of the poor. Born

Poor working conditions in New York City's garment district led to the tragedy of the 1911 Triangle Shirtwaist Factory fire that killed 146 people. It became a rallying cry for the labor movement.

in Arizona, his family lost their farm when he was just ten years old; they became migrant workers in California, where farm production—particularly of grape crops—depended on temporary laborers. Chavez knew the migrant worker's life intimately, and, as a young man, he began working to improve conditions for his people. In 1962, he organized California grape pickers into the National Farm Workers Association.

Four years later, this union merged with another to form the United Farm Workers Organizing Committee (UFWOC). An impassioned speaker known for squishing bunches of grapes in his hands as he delivered his messages, Chavez went on to lead a nationwide boycott of table grapes since growers had refused to accept the collective bargaining of the UFWOC. By the close of the 1970s, California growers of all crops had accepted the migrant workers' union, known since 1973 as the

Cesar Chavez was a key leader in organizing farmworkers in California. The state honors him annually on Cesar Chavez Day, which is March 31.

United Farm Workers of America (UFW). Like Martin Luther King Jr., Chavez maintained that nonviolent protest was the key to achieving change.

Migrant farmworkers continue to play an important role in the American economy. There are perhaps two to three million farmworkers in America who do work such as handpicking fruits and vegetables. The work is typically physically hard, involving long hours and often unhealthy or dangerous working conditions. Despite some success of workers' unions, many migrant workers still work in harsh conditions for low wages.

Migrant farmworkers are one of the key reasons that many of the fruits and vegetables we buy are not very expensive.

What is "right to work"?

In a union shop, any new worker who is employed has to join the union and pay dues to support the union. The union must protect the worker's rights, and the worker receives the benefits of better wages and working conditions negotiated by the union. In the twenty-seven states that have right-to-work laws, unions cannot negotiate contracts with company managers to require new workers to join the union.

Although "right to work" is often promoted as a freedom issue—that a new worker should be free whether or not to choose to join a union—the real reason for right-to-work laws is to weaken the power of unions to fight for better pay and better conditions for workers. Right-to-work laws reduce union membership and reduce the dues money that supports the unions. However, in right-to-work states, the workers who do not join the union and pay union dues still get the benefits that the unions fought for, such as better pay and union help in settling problems between a worker and employer.

How is the labor movement doing today?

The labor movement in the United States has been struggling for decades. The main reason is that so many unionized jobs have been shipped overseas, where the labor is much cheaper. The NAFTA agreement (1994) sped up the process. Also, many companies have moved their factories to right-to-work states, where unions have less power.

Furthermore, many businesses have worked hard to keep unions out. For example, the largest business employer in the United States is Walmart, with over 1.5 million workers. However, Walmart has worked very hard to keep those workers from unionizing. Also, political forces, especially conservative voices, have worked to sour many people's attitudes toward labor unions.

Lastly, the National Labor Relations Board (NLRB) is an agency of the federal government that is supposed to protect workers' rights to organize. Under Republican administrations, however, it has often promoted the interests of businesses while neglecting the rights of workers.

What are the gains made by unions that benefit most workers?

Unions fought very hard for better working conditions and pay, yet many people, including many nonunion workers, have benefited from them. Here is a list of some of the benefits that unions have provided:

- The eight-hour workday
- The forty-hour work week
- A two-day weekend
- Safe working conditions
- The right to not be fired arbitrarily
- Health insurance
- Retirement benefits
- A banning of child labor
- Good wages so one can enter the middle class

As mentioned above, many good union jobs in America have disappeared as manufacturing has shifted overseas. In most places where these jobs have gone, the workers do not have the benefits listed above. Many of the manufactured goods that Americans consume are made by workers whose rights are not protected. That is why the labor of these workers is so cheap and why the goods we buy are so cheap.

COUNTERCULTURE, CONSUMERISM, AND THE ENVIRONMENT

What was the Beat movement?

The post-World War II era bred unprecedented prosperity and an uneasy peace in the United States. Out of this environment rose the Beat generation, alienated youths who rejected society's new materialism and threw off its "square" attitudes to reinvent "cool." The Beat generation of the 1950s bucked convention, embraced iconoclasm, and attracted attention. Mainstream society viewed them as anarchists and degenerates. But many American youths listened to and read the ideas of its leaders, including writers Allen Ginsberg, William Burroughs, Lawrence Ferlinghetti, and Jack Kerouac, whose novel *On the Road* (1957) was the bible of the Beat movement.

The "Beatniks," as they were dubbed by their critics, believed in peace, civil rights, and radical protest as a vehicle for change. They also embraced drugs, mystical (Eastern) religions, and sexual freedom—all controversial ideas during the postwar era. Beat writers and artists found their homes in communities like San Francisco's North Beach,

Young members of the counterculture of the 1960s and early 1970s were often referred to as "hippies." They were opposed to war, advocated free love, and experimented with sex, drugs, music, and art.

Los Angeles's Venice Beach, and New York City's Greenwich Village. The movement merged—or, some would argue, gave birth to—the counterculture movements of the 1960s, including the hippies. Beat literature is the movement's legacy.

Who were the hippies?

Most hippies of the 1960s and 1970s were young (fifteen to twenty-five years old), white, and from middle-class families. The counterculture (antiestablishment) movement advocated freedom, peace, love, and beauty. Having dropped out (of modern society) and tuned in (to their own feelings), these flower children were as well known for their political and social beliefs as they were for their controversial lifestyle. (Some hippies were called "flower children" since they saw the flower as a symbol of beauty, peace, and natural simplicity.)

Hippies opposed American involvement in the Vietnam War and rejected an industrialized society that seemed to care only about money; they favored personal simplicity, sometimes living in small communes where possessions and work were shared, or living an itinerant lifestyle, in which day-to-day responsibilities were few if any; they wore tattered jeans and bright clothing usually of natural fabrics, grew their hair, braided beads into their locks, walked around barefoot or in sandals, and listened to a new generation of artists, including the Beatles, the Grateful Dead, Jefferson Airplane, Bob Dylan, and Joan Baez.

The hippie movement was in part shaped by the U.S. military draft. Hippie calls for freedom were often in opposition to the draft of young men to fight in the unpopular Vietnam War.

Some hippies were also known for their drug use. Experimenting with marijuana and LSD, some hoped to gain profound insights or even achieve salvation through the drug experience—something hippie guru Timothy Leary (1920–1996) told them was possible. New York City's East Village and San Francisco's Haight-Ashbury neighborhood became havens of this counterculture. The movement began on American soil but was soon embraced elsewhere as well—principally in Canada and Great Britain.

What happened to the hippies?

The conflict in Vietnam ended, flower children grew older, drugs took their toll on some, and by 1980 (and the advent of AIDS), the idea of free love fell into disfavor. Still, a few continued to lead an alternative lifestyle, while at the opposite end of the spectrum, others bought back into the establishment. Still others adapted their flower-child beliefs to the ever-changing world around them and got on with their lives, working at jobs and raising children in the most socially and politically conscious way possible.

What was *Hair: The American Tribal Love-Rock Musical*?

Hair: The American Tribal Love-Rock Musical was the popular rock musical that caught the spirit of the time. With the book and lyrics written by Gerome Ragni and James Rado and music written by Galt MacDermot, *Hair* opened on Broadway in 1968, with songs about race relations, love, sex, drugs, the military draft, air pollution, Vietnam, and astrology.

Act I ended with a very brief scene of the cast onstage in the nude. The scene reflected the freer attitudes toward sexuality of the period. The scene may have also been a ploy to draw bigger audiences, who came to see the nude scene, or because of the controversy about the scene.

Who is Ralph Nader?

Ralph Nader (1934–), an American lawyer, has become the best-known consumer advocate ever. He has even run for president several times. With the help of his research team, called Nader's Raiders, he wrote the landmark book *Unsafe at Any Speed* in 1965; it charged that many automobiles were not as safe as they should be or as consumers had the right to expect them to be. In part, the book was responsible for passage in 1966 of the National Traffic and Motor Vehicle Safety Act, which set motor vehicle safety standards. Nader continued his watchdog work, founding the Public Citizen organization, which researches consumer products, promotes consumer awareness, and works to influence legislators to improve consumer safety. (Public Citizen disassociated itself from Ralph Nader after his 2000 run for president.)

Who were some advocates for consumers before Ralph Nader?

While Nader may be the most recognizable face of consumer advocacy, the movement's roots predate his activism. As the consumer age dawned at the end of the 1800s and early 1900s, when mass-production techniques came into wide use, some observers decried industry standards (or lack thereof) that put the public who used their products at risk. The muckraking journalists of the early twentieth century disclosed harmful or careless practices of early industry, raising awareness and bringing about needed reforms. The prac-

Ralph Nader (shown here in 1975) has been a dominant force in the consumer-protection movement. An attorney, author, lecturer, and former presidential candidate, he is best known for fighting for car-safety regulations.

403

tices attacked included things such as poisons put in foods and so-called medicines. Upton Sinclair (1878–1968) penned the highly influential novel *The Jungle* (1906), revealing scandalous and unsanitary conditions at meat-packing plants.

The public was outraged; upon reading Sinclair's work, President Theodore Roosevelt (1858–1919) ordered an investigation. Finding the novelist's descriptions to be true to life, the government moved quickly to pass both the Pure Food and Drug Act and the Meat Inspection Act in 1906. Industry watchdogs continued their work in the early decades of the century. For instance, in 1929, Consumers' Research, Inc., was founded, and in 1936, Consumers Union (now Consumer Reports) formed; both independent organizations test and rate consumer products. (The monthly magazine *Consumer Reports* can be read online or in the print version.) Such consumer advocacy has served to heighten public awareness, compelling many industries to make changes and improve the safety of products in general.

More consumer-protection laws were enacted in the 1960s and 1970s. Under President Barack Obama (1961–), an effort was made to strengthen consumer protections, especially against such things as predatory loans, for-profit universities that give inadequate educations yet leave students with large debts, and high interest rates on consumer debt.

Under the administration of President Donald Trump (1946–), there has been a systematic effort to remove many regulations that protect consumers. The Trump Administration, seeing government regulation as bad for business, has ignored over a hundred years of history where the U.S. government has regulated industries to encourage good business practices and restrain businesses that make profits by taking advantage of consumers. For example, the Trump Administration wants to remove the number of government inspectors at meat-packing plants. It has also removed regulations against predatory lenders and predatory for-profit universities.

What is the Kyoto Protocol?

It was an environmental agreement signed by 141 nations that agreed to work to slow global warming by limiting emissions, cutting them by 5.2 percent by 2012. Each na-

---

What did *Silent Spring* have to do with the environmental protection movement?

The 1962 book *Silent Spring,* by American ecologist Rachel Carson (1907–1964), cautioned the world on the ill effects of chemicals on the environment. Carson argued that pollution and the use of chemicals, particularly pesticides, would result in less diversity of life. The best-selling book had wide influence, raising awareness of environmental issues and launching green (environmental protection) movements in many industrialized nations.

tion has its own target to meet. The protocol was drawn up on December 11, 1997, in the ancient capital of Kyoto, Japan, and went into effect on February 16, 2005. The United States is not among the signatories due to American officials saying that the agreement is flawed because large developing countries, including India and China, were not immediately required to meet specific targets for reduction. Upon the protocol's enactment, Japan's prime minister called on nonsignatory nations to rethink their participation, saying that there was a need for a "common framework to stop global warming." Environmentalists echoed this call to action.

What is the Paris Agreement?

The next international agreement to take action to slow global warming and climate change was the Paris Agreement, also known as the Paris Accord, adopted in 2015. The agreement calls for nations to take significant steps to reduce greenhouse gas emissions and to take steps to prepare for the effects of climate change. By 2015, 195 countries—the vast majority of countries—had signed it.

In 2017, the Trump Administration gave notice that the United States would leave the Paris Agreement. President Donald Trump has repeatedly denied that climate change is happening and has called it a "hoax." (There is a delay in withdrawing built into the agreement, which means the United States cannot withdraw until perhaps late 2020.)

Demonstrators march in the city of Bayda, Libya, during the summer of 2011, the time of the Arab Spring, when multiple nations saw despotic governments overthrown or drastically changed.

Unfortunately, many of the countries who signed the Paris Agreement have not taken enough action to reduce greenhouse gas emissions to the levels pledged in the agreement.

(Global warming and climate change will be discussed in more detail in the "Disasters" chapter.)

What is the Arab Spring?

The Arab Spring was a movement in the Middle East that began in 2010 seeking to bring about revolutionary change and a more democratic environment in countries such as Egypt, Libya, Tunisia, and Yemen. The protestors sought to rally against government repression and suppression of social media communications.

The first wave of protests began in Tunisia in December 2010 and then spread to Algeria, Jordan, and Egypt. Protests in Libya led to the removal of longtime repressive leader Muammar Gaddafi (1942–2011). A protest in Lebanon in December 2011 led to a significant increase in worker wages. *Time* magazine named "the Protester" its Person of the Year in December 2011 partly as a result of the Arab Spring movement.

However, there was reaction to these calls for reform and democracy of the Arab Spring, and in the wake came what some have called the "Arab Winter," with civil war and/or more oppressive governments in the countries involved. (Only Tunisia has made progress toward democracy.)

THE ANTISLAVERY MOVEMENT TODAY

Is there slavery today?

Yes, slavery continues into the twenty-first century. Estimates range from twenty-one million to forty-six million enslaved humans in the world today, with perhaps ten million of these being children. (At the time of the American Civil War, there were four million enslaved people in America.) It is often called "human trafficking." It is impossible to get exact numbers because there is no precise definition of slavery. Also, since slavery is illegal, much of it is hidden, making it difficult to count how many slaves exist. Making it worse is that enslaved humans are cheap today: they can be bought for as little as $90. Humans are enslaved mostly so the enslavers can make money.

Men, women, and children, especially in developing countries, are forced into labor in sweatshops and fields and into prostitution in brothels. In desperately poor regions of the world, families sell their children into slave labor and forced prostitution.

Sex trafficking is one type of slavery. It is estimated that between 10,000 and 50,000 women and girls are trafficked in the United States each year.

What are the typical types of slavery today?

There are several common types of slavery today:

- Bonded labor (debt bondage)
- Domestic servitude
- Sex trafficking
- Child labor
- Forced marriage
- Government-forced labor
- Prison labor

Bonded labor (debt bondage) is the most common form of slavery of people. These are people forced to work to pay off debts. They cannot leave until the debt is paid, which often never happens. Making it worse is that in many places, economic forces give people so few choices that they end up deeper in debt. This often results in unpaid debts being passed on to future generations.

Domestic servitude happens when one is employed in a home as a maid, nanny, or caregiver of the elderly or infirmed but is unable to leave the situation. These people are often immigrants who were lured into jobs with promises of education, which are never fulfilled. Domestic workers in these situations often become victims of sexual and physical abuse.

LGBTQIA RIGHTS

What is meant by LGBTQIA?

The abbreviation stands for Lesbian, Gay, Bisexual, Transsexual, Queer (or Questioning), Intersex, and Asexual. The I and A were more recent additions in an attempt to include all people.

When did the gay rights movement begin?

On June 28, 1969, New York City police raided a gay bar, the Stonewall Inn in Greenwich Village in Manhattan. At that time, one could be arrested for being gay or being in a place that catered to gays, so few bars openly welcomed gays. Cross-dressing was also illegal. The Stonewall Inn was one of the few places that welcomed gays and lesbians, drag queens, transgender people, male prostitutes, and homeless youth. The bar was run by the Mafia, who had paid off the police to leave it alone. The police did occasionally raid the Stonewall Inn, but usually, the bar knew in advance when they were coming.

However, on that June evening in 1969, when the police showed up, the patrons of the bar, tired of police harassment, resisted. The situation quickly got out of hand, and a riot ensued. More protests and rioting took place the next day as people began to organize to fight for their rights.

This was the beginning of the gay rights movement, and this is why gay pride parades take place in June each year across the country and around the world. The first gay pride marches took place in New York, San Francisco, and Los Angeles on June 28, 1970.

The 1969 event has been called the Stonewall Uprising. The PBS 2010 documentary *Stonewall Uprising* tells the whole story.

Harvey Milk is shown sitting at the desk of Mayor George Moscone of San Francisco. He filled in for the mayor for a day but was usually serving in his Board of Supervisors position.

Who was Harvey Milk?

Harvey Milk (1930–1978) was an activist and politician. He was the first openly gay elected official in California. He had moved to the Castro District of San Francisco in 1972, an area where many gay and bisexual men lived. In 1977, he was elected a city supervisor in San Francisco.

One of his accomplishments was to get a law passed and to change attitudes so that dog owners would clean up after their dog. Harvey played a key role in fighting for gay rights, and as a city supervisor, he fought for legislation to prohibit discrimination based on sexual orientation.

Tragically, Milk and San Francisco mayor George Moscone were shot and killed by a former supervisor, Dan White, a troubled man. Harvey Milk became a martyr for the cause of gay rights.

Milk is a 2008 film biography of Harvey Milk, who is played by Sean Penn.

What is the Transgender Day of Remembrance (TDoR)?

November 20 is a day to remember and memorialize transgender people who have been murdered as a result of transphobia. The murder of transgender people is a problem

---

What is the AIDS Quilt?

The quilt was started in 1985 to draw awareness to the AIDS epidemic and also to remember those who died of AIDS. It is made of 3' x 6' panels. Each is created by friends, partners, or family members of those who died of AIDS. It is also known as the NAMES Project AIDS Memorial Quilt. There are over 48,000 panels. The AIDS quilt web page lists upcoming displays of portions of the quilt.

The quilt played an important educational role in the early part of the AIDS epidemic. It helped lead to a more honest discussion of the scale of the illness.

worldwide. In the United States, there were twenty-four such murders in 2018 and twenty-four in 2019.

OTHER RECENT MOVEMENTS

What is the Me Too or #MeToo movement?

The Me Too movement fights against sexual assault and sexual harassment. The phrase was originally created by activist Tarana Burke (1973–) in 2006. She is a survivor of sexual harassment.

In 2017, as multiple accusations of sexual crimes were made against film producer Harvey Weinstein (1952–), the Me Too term became a hashtag on social media. The goal of using the hashtag was to make people aware of the many, many victims of sexual harassment. The movement has spread worldwide.

What is the Occupy movement?

The Occupy movement was an international movement designed to address social and economic disparities and to make the economic power structure more equitable. The Occupy movement used the slogan "We are the 99 percent," signifying that the power structure and financial empires of world governments serve the interests of the extremely wealthy 1 percent of the world.

Occupy movements or protests occurred throughout the world. For example, 200,000 people protested in Rome, Italy, in October 2011 against economic conditions. Occupy Wall Street, which took place in the Wall Street District in New York City's Zuccotti Park in September 2011, marked the movement in the United States.

Occupy movements sprang up in various cities across the United States. Occupiers camped out on government property, carrying signs and creating symbolic tents to send the message that they will occupy government land until the government responds to the financial wrongs and abuses of the country.

However, in the United States, the occupy encampments were spied on by authorities such as the FBI and then closed by police. Many members of the movement saw this as proof that the ruling elite had the power to suppress free speech and the right to assemble to protest.

What is the Black Lives Matter movement?

The movement began in 2013, when the hashtag #BlackLivesMatter was used after the acquittal of George Zimmerman, who had shot and killed African American teen Trayvon Martin in February 2012. The movement gained national attention after its demonstrations following the 2014 deaths of Michael Brown in Ferguson, Missouri, and Eric Garner in New York City. Both black men were killed by white police officers.

The intent of the movement is to draw attention to frequent deaths of African Americans and, in particular, those who die at the hands of police officers.

What is the Tea Party movement?

The Tea Party, formed in 2009 and named for the Boston Tea Party of 1773, has been vocal in calling for lower taxes and reduced government spending. In particular, the Tea Party opposed the policies of President Barack Obama (president from 2009 to 2017), such as the American Recovery and Reinvestment Act of 2009 (ARRA) and the Affordable Care Act. In particular, Tea Party members opposed the increasing federal debt. Over the next years, they held numerous rallies and protests and got a number of Tea Party supporters into Congress.

Although many supported the election of Donald Trump in 2016, reducing the federal debt seems no longer to be an issue, as the debt has climbed to record levels. In July 2019, Senator Rand Paul of Kentucky declared the Tea Party dead, as the U.S. government debt kept growing.

What is the Southern Poverty Law Center?

The Southern Poverty Law Center is a nonprofit organization that uses the courts to fight white nationalists and extremist groups. It also works to identify and track hate groups and educate citizens about the growing presence of these groups. The center identified 940 groups in 2019. (The list of these groups can be found on its web page, https://*www.splcenter.org/*.)

WESTERN ART, PHOTOGRAPHY, AND ARCHITECTURE

What does the term "Western art" mean?

The term refers to art from Europe and North America. Because there is so much art from around the world, it is impossible to cover it all. The focus here is on Western art since most readers are familiar with many of these artists and their works. Perhaps in the future, you will also explore diverse art from around the world.

FINE ART

Are there any suggestions for exploring this art?

Due to the wonders of the Internet, you can easily see all of the art mentioned below as well as other artworks created by these famous artists and sculptors. As you read, do some online browsing. As you pull up images of this famous art, give each image a moment or two. Look at the image. Look at the detail in the image. What is going on in the image? How do you feel as you look at it?

These pieces of art are famous because people find that they are intriguing and that they stir the emotions. See if you can find what other people over the centuries have found interesting in these artworks. The goal in all of this is for you to find art that is interesting to you. Find what you like!

How long have humans been producing art?

We do not actually know because many forms of art, such as wood carving, decorative clothing, and face painting, have not survived. The oldest surviving art is cave paintings. Cave paintings done by *Homo sapiens* may be 40,000 years old, while cave paintings by Neanderthals are possibly 64,000 years old.

They painted handprints, warrior images, and animals (including bison, horses, and reindeer) on the walls and ceilings of uninhabited caves using red, black, and yellow paints, which were made by mixing powdered earth and rock pigments with water. Among the most famous paintings are those in the caves at Lascaux (in Dordogne, France), Niaux (Ariège, France), Pech-Merle (Lot, France), Gasulla (Castellón, Spain), and Altamira (Cantabria, Spain).

The art of cave painting by *Homo sapiens* is quite sophisticated. If you doubt it, look up images of cave paintings online and try to duplicate them on paper—or on a piece of rock. Now, imagine painting this inside a cave with handheld torches.

RENAISSANCE ART

What is the Renaissance in art?

The Renaissance is a label put on the European world from 1350 to 1600 C.E. During this time, there was a rebirth of interest in the classical world of ancient Greece and Rome. The label "renaissance" was given much later.

In art, there were several direct connections. One was to depict the human body in painting and sculpture. The ancient Romans and Greeks had mastered this in sculpture. During the Middle Ages, with the Catholic Church in control of much of art, the human body was rarely emphasized. The emphasis was on salvation of the soul, not celebration of the beauty of the human body. In the Renaissance, it became common to depict the human body in the nude.

The other connection was a renewed interest in the stories of Greek and Roman mythology. Again, this went against the views of many religious people in Europe—but not all.

In turns out there were two parts of the European Renaissance in art: the Italian Renaissance (centered in Florence and Rome) and the Northern Renaissance (in what today is the Netherlands and Germany).

Who are the most important Italian Renaissance painters?

Four painters stand out from the talented crowd of Renaissance painters: Sandro Botticelli, Leonardo da Vinci, Raphael Sanzio, and Michelangelo Buonarroti.

Who was the painter Sandro Botticelli?

The works of Sandro Botticelli (1445–1510), one of the early painters of the Italian Renaissance, are known for their serene compositions, refined elegance, and spirituality. His most famous painting, *The Birth of Venus* (c. 1482), is known for its elegant figures, use of pictorial space, and decorative detail, which give the painting a tapestry effect.

At the time it was painted, the presentation of a nude Venus was an innovation and controversial since the use of unclothed figures in art had been prohibited during the Middle Ages. Botticelli, however, felt free to render Venus in this way since Florence's powerful Medici family, his patrons, commissioned the work. Under their protection, Botticelli could pursue the world of his imagination without fearing charges of paganism and infidelity.

Botticelli's round painting *Madonna of the Magnificat* (1483) is his most copied work. "Madonna" is the term many Christians use for Mary, the mother of Jesus. In the Gospel of Luke, when Mary meets Elizabeth, who is pregnant with John the Baptist, Mary gives a song of praise: "My soul proclaims the greatness of the Lord; my spirit rejoices in God my savior" (Luke 1:46–55 [New American Bible Revised Edition]). This song is called the "Magnificat."

Why was the Medici family important to Renaissance art?

The Medici family was powerful in Florence, Italy, between the fourteenth and sixteenth centuries. The founder of the family was Giovanni di Bicci de' Medici (1360–1429), who amassed a large fortune through his skill in trade and banking and who virtually ruled Florence between 1421 and 1429. His son, Cosimo de' Medici (1389–1464), inherited his father's wealth and businesses.

Later, Cosimo's grandson, Lorenzo de' Medici (1449–1492), ruled Florence between 1478 and 1492. Though he was tyrannical, he was a great patron of the arts and letters. Lorenzo (also called "the Magnificent") maintained Fiesole, a villa outside Florence, where he surrounded himself with the great talents and thinkers of Florence, including a young artist named Sandro Botticelli (1445–1510). Lorenzo was also a patron of Michelangelo (1475–1564).

The Medici palace, called the Palazzo Medici Riccardi, can be seen today in Florence, Italy.

What can you tell me about Leonardo da Vinci?

Leonardo da Vinci (1452–1519) was a genius interested in science, music, mathematics, engineering, anatomy, and much more. He is the model of a Renaissance man. He created several beautiful and important religious paintings, such as:

- *John the Baptist* (c. 1513–1516)
- *Annunciation* (1475–1480)

- *The Virgin and Child with St. Anne* (c. 1503). According to some Christians, St. Anne was the grandmother of Jesus. Notice the infant Jesus holds a lamb. Many Christians refer to Jesus as the Lamb of God.

- *Virgin of the Rocks* (1483–1486). Mary is the central figure. The infant John the Baptist is on the left side of the painting, and an angel sits behind Jesus on the right. There are two versions of this painting. (You want the one in the Louvre.)

Leonardo's most important painting is *The Last Supper*, which is the most reproduced religious painting in history. The painting shows Jesus and his Twelve Apostles. From left to right as one looks at the painting, the figures are Bartholomew; James the Lesser, son of Alphaeus; Andrew; Judas Iscariot, with dark hair and a beard, holding his moneybag; Peter, with white hair and a beard; John the evangelist; Jesus; Thomas; James the Greater; Philip; Matthew; Jude/Thaddeus; and Simon the Zealot. Judas has knocked over the salt shaker, a sign of bad luck. Da Vinci left a notebook identifying all the figures.

One of Leonardo da Vinci's later self-portraits, c. 1510. A brilliant polymath, he was not only an artist but also an inventor, scientist, engineer, cartographer, musician, and more.

Isn't Mary Magdalene sitting next to Jesus in *The Last Supper*?

Because of the popularity of *The Da Vinci Code*, the 2003 book by Dan Brown, which became a popular movie, many people believe that Mary Magdalene was married to Jesus, had children with him, and was painted into da Vinci's famous *The Last Supper*. But Brown's book is a work of fiction even though it makes many historical references, many inaccurately. According to *The Da Vinci Code*, Leonardo painted Mary Magdalene sitting to Jesus's right.

The figure does appear to be a woman with long hair. If it is not Mary Magdalene, then who is it? It is the Apostle John. Sometime during the Renaissance, the tradition developed of portraying John as a young man, without a beard or long hair, and with somewhat feminine features. This became the standard style for portraying John. Do an online search for paintings of St. John and see what you find. This tradition can also be seen in the stained glass windows in many older churches.

414

What's the big deal with da Vinci's *Mona Lisa*?

Da Vinci's most famous painting, and arguably the most famous painting in history, is the *Mona Lisa*. It is probably a portrait of Lisa Gherardini, an Italian noblewoman. What makes the painting interesting is, first, the look on her face, which is often described as enigmatic. Something appears to be going on in her mind, but the viewer is not sure what. Next comes the background, which is both misty and mystical. It is painted with an immense amount of detail, if you look closely. Lastly, da Vinci uses a technique of adding main layers of paints and tints to achieve subtle variations of color and shape. However, all of these are features that someone who has viewed a lot of art would appreciate but someone new to looking at art might not get. So, if you are not impressed with the *Mona Lisa*, that is okay; go find some art that does impress you.

Why is the painter Raphael important?

Most historians and art critics agree that Raphael Sanzio (1483–1520) most clearly stated the ideals of the High Renaissance. A prolific painter, he was also a great technician whose work is characterized by a seemingly effortless grace. His best-known work is *The School of Athens* (1509–1511), which has been called "a complete statement of the High Renaissance in its artistic form and spiritual meaning."

The painting, which projects a stagelike space onto a flat surface, reconvenes the great minds of the ancient world—Plato, Aristotle, Pythagoras, Heraclitus, Diogenes, Euclid—for an exchange of ideas. Raphael even included himself in this gathering of greatness. The Renaissance was a rebirth of interest in the works of philosophers, mathematicians, artists, writers, and thinkers of the ancient Greek and Roman worlds, many of whom Raphael depicted in this painting.

Raphael's painting *Transfiguration* (1520) is particularly dazzling. The scene is based on a biblical passage from the Gospel of Mark (9:2–8, 14–29). Find the image online along with the Bible passage. Be sure to enlarge the image on your screen to catch all the color.

Also, check out the paintings *Resurrection of Christ* (1499–1502) and *The Madonna of the Meadow* (c. 1506).

MICHELANGELO

What can you tell me about Michelangelo?

Michelangelo Buonarroti (1475–1564) lived in the cities of Florence and Rome, Italy. Some of the most famous works of Michelangelo are his paintings on the ceiling and walls of the Sistine Chapel in Rome, completed between 1508 and 1512. Today, the chapel is part of the Vatican complex in Rome, the headquarters of the Roman Catholic Church.

The Sistine Chapel ceiling looks complicated, but it takes just a moment to figure out all the images. Open this link (*https://www.wga.hu/tours/sistina/index1.html*) to explore the Sistine Chapel ceiling. Simply click on different places for close-up views.

In the center are nine scenes from the first chapters of the Book of Genesis:

- The Separation of Light from Darkness
- Creation of the Sun, Moon, and Planets
- Separation of Earth from the Waters
- Creation of Adam (This painting is one of the most famous images of Christian art.)
- Creation of Eve
- The Fall and Expulsion from the Garden
- Sacrifice of Noah
- The Deluge (the Flood)
- The Drunkenness of Noah

There are four triangle paintings called "spandrels" on each side of the ceiling. Within the triangles are people from the Bible who are ancestors of Jesus.

Between the triangles are seated figures. These seated figures alternate between biblical prophets, such as Isaiah and Jeremiah, and figures such as the Cumaean Sibyl and the Persian Sibyl. There are seven prophets and five sibyls. The sibyls are characters from pagan literature believed to have powers to predict the future.

Another important painting of Michelangelo in the Sistine Chapel is *The Last Judgment*. It is forty-eight feet tall and forty-four feet wide! Jesus is in the center, coming in triumph and judgment. The person to the right of Jesus holding his skin is St. Bartholomew, who had been skinned alive.

The extraordinary achievement of Michelangelo's work in the Sistine Chapel of Vatican City will forever be a testimony to the immortal artist.

What was Michelangelo's technique in painting the Sistine Chapel?

The Sistine Chapel ceiling and walls are fresco paintings. Fresco was a common technique for painting on walls. Oil paints did not come until later, and acrylic paints are very recent.

To create a fresco, the artist starts with a wall with a new layer of plaster. Many people today do not know what plaster is since most houses and buildings are built using drywall on interior walls. Before drywall, the interior walls of buildings and homes were covered with plaster, a paste made of lime, gypsum, or cement. The plaster paste could be smoothed out on the wall or textured, and it would dry to be very hard and durable.

Fresco is a technique for painting on walls while the plaster is still fresh. "Fresco" means "fresh." In fresco painting, pigment, which is colored powder, is mixed with fresh plaster and then painted on. Fresco painting requires careful planning, since the artist needs to complete one area of the painting each day since it is very hard to come back the next day and mix the exact same color to match the color of the previous day.

Did Michelangelo lie on this back while painting the Sistine Chapel ceiling?

He did not. The Sistine Chapel was kept in use during the several years of painting. Michelangelo designed frames along the side walls that held a platform for painting. This platform could be moved along the ceiling as he worked on each part of the painting.

What are the famous sculptures of Michelangelo?

Although he painted the Sistine Chapel, Michelangelo considered himself a sculptor. In fact, Pope Julius II (1443–1513) bullied him into painting the chapel, which is why he signed it "Michelangelo—Sculptor."

Michelangelo created several pieces based on biblical figures, considered some of the greatest sculptures of all time: *Moses*; *David*; and the *Pietà*, which depicts Mary holding the dead body of Jesus. Be sure to look up these images since these statues are so important.

Michelangelo depicts Moses as a powerful figure with muscular arms. The horns on his head are due to a mistranslation of the Bible text of that time, which actually refers to rays of light on the head of Moses.

Michelangelo's *David* might be the most famous sculpture in the world. The statue is eighteen feet tall—three times the height of a six-foot-tall person! This statue is a cu-

What famous movie describes the painting of the Sistine Chapel ceiling?

The 1965 film *The Agony and the Ecstasy* tells the story with actors Charlton Heston (1923–2008) as Michelangelo and Rex Harrison (1908–1990) as Pope Julius II.

rious combination of the biblical story of David presented in the style of an ancient Greek or Roman nude statue. The story of David in the Bible says nothing about him facing Goliath in his birthday suit.

You have mentioned the names of Leonardo, Michelangelo, and Raphael. Aren't these the names of three of the Teenage Mutant Ninja Turtles?

Yes, and Donatello, the fourth Turtle, was named for an important Renaissance sculptor. The creators of the Teenage Mutant Ninja Turtles named them after four famous Renaissance artists.

OTHER IMPORTANT RENAISSANCE ARTISTS

Why is Titian seen as the "Father of Modern Painting"?

During Titian's time (1488/1490–1576, pronounced TISH-en), artists began painting on canvas rather than on wood panels. A master of color, the Venetian painter was both popular and prolific. His work was so in demand that even with the help of numerous assistants, he could not keep up.

His body of works established oil color on canvas as the typical medium of Western painting. Among his best-known paintings are *Sacred and Profane Love* (c. 1515) and *Venus of Urbino* (1538).

Who was Albrecht Dürer?

Albrecht Dürer (1471–1528) was an influential artist. Do an online search for "Dürer woodcuts." In his woodcuts, Dürer would carve an image in a block of wood. This block would be used for printing multiple copies of the image. The block would be covered with ink and then a sheet of paper would be pressed against it. When the paper was removed, it would have the carved image printed on it. Dürer was creating some of the first mass-produced art. His prints of the *Apocalypse* series (1498), based on the Book of Revelation, were very popular in his time. Take a look at his *Four Horsemen of the Apocalypse*. (Do a search online for "Dürer four horsemen.")

Although the image printed from the block was black ink on white paper, color was added to many of these images. A cut-

Capable in many media, German artist Albrecht Dürer is particularly remembered for his finely detailed etchings, such as *Melencolia I* (1514).

out stencil would be made for all parts of the image that would be blue. A painter would paint all the blue parts. Another stencil would be created for all the red parts, which would then be painted. Other stencils were used for other colors. Since the stencils could be reused over and over, multiple color copies could be made. This was one of the first attempts at color printing of multiple copies.

Dürer also did etchings. Instead of carving a wood block, etchings were done by scratching on a copper plate. The finished copper plate would be covered with ink, and paper would be pressed against it to print an image on the paper. Etchings allowed much more detail. Do a search online for "Dürer etchings" to see examples. His most famous etchings are *Knight, Death, and the Devil* (1513) and *Saint Jerome in his Study* (1514).

Around 1508, Dürer did a pen and ink drawing that is called *Praying Hands*. This image has been widely copied and imitated in other paintings and sculptures, such as a thirty-two-foot-tall version in Webb City, Missouri. Dürer also did beautiful watercolors of animals.

Who was Matthias Grünewald?

German painter Matthias Grünewald (c. 1470–1528) is best remembered for his Isenheim Altarpiece. The altarpiece has a number of different panels that originally could be flipped to produce a number of different scenes. Do a search online for "Isenheim crucifixion" to find an online image of the Crucifixion. Mary Magdalene is the kneeling figure. The woman in white is Mary, the mother of Jesus, who is being held by John, one of the disciples of Jesus. Look at some detailed images of the hands and torso of Jesus.

The painting is filled with symbolism. The figure on the right is John the Baptist. He was dead by the time Jesus was crucified, but in the Gospels, he pointed the way to Jesus. Notice that the right hand of John the Baptist points to Jesus. The lamb symbolizes Jesus. Just as lambs were slain as sacrifices for sin, so Jesus was sacrificed for human sin. Notice that the blood of the lamb is flowing into the cup. Many Christians believe that the cup of wine at Mass becomes the blood of Jesus.

Now, search online for "Isenheim Anthony" for images of the two panels *Visit of Saint Anthony to Saint Paul the Hermit* and *Saint Anthony Tormented by Demons*. Be sure to find a large image, so you can see clearly the demons tormenting St. Anthony. Be sure to check out the small demons on the destroyed building in the background. Grünewald created some amazing and bizarre imagery that could easily fit in a science fiction movie today.

BAROQUE ART

What is the Baroque period?

The Baroque period in art and architecture followed the Renaissance. It started around 1600 and lasted for about 150 years. Here are some of the more important painters:

- Diego Velázquez (1599–1660)
- Caravaggio (1571–1610)
- Rembrandt van Rijn (1606–1669)
- Nicolas Poussin (1594–1665)
- Johannes Vermeer (1632–1675)

Many Baroque painters emphasized drama, often showing the key moment when the event depicted took place, and used contrasts of dark and light to heighten the emotional impact of the image.

Part of the impetus for Baroque art was the Catholic Counter-Reformation in Europe. After the Protestants broke away from the Catholic Church, the Church encouraged dramatic art to bring people back to the faith. At the same time, the Church promoted the style of Baroque architecture to create dazzling church buildings to draw in the faithful.

It is hard for some modern people to understand the visual and emotional impact of Baroque art and architecture. Today, many people easily see stunning images. We can travel to see beautiful mountains, the Grand Canyon, or the Eiffel Tower in Paris. We can also see these things in photographs. And we watch movies and TV, which can present amazing images.

Now, imagine a time 400 years ago. There were no movies, TV, or photography. Most people did not travel much, and many spent their entire lives within a few miles of their homes. There was very little to see that was new and interesting. Most of what they saw was ordinary and boring. For such people to walk into a Baroque church with Baroque paintings inside would have been a dazzling experience.

Who was Caravaggio?

The paintings of Caravaggio (1571–1610) are particularly interesting. He wanted to portray the biblical stories with great drama. He designed his scenes and posed the figures in such a way as to increase the dramatic impact. He also used a technique called *chiaroscuro*, which involved contrasting very bright parts of the painting with very dark backgrounds.

Another of Caravaggio's techniques was to paint the Gospel stories with the characters dressed as if they were people living in the time of Caravaggio. This can

Caravaggio was particularly notable in his effective and dramatic use of light in his many paintings with biblical themes, such as *The Conversion on the Way to Damascus*.

be clearly seen in his painting *The Calling of Saint Matthew*. The figures at the table are dressed in fashionable outfits from around the year 1600. They are not wearing clothes from the time of Jesus. Caravaggio wanted the viewers of his time to feel that they were part of the story.

Here are some of Caravaggio's most important religious paintings:

- *The Calling of Saint Matthew* (1599–1600)
- *The Conversion on the Way to Damascus* (1601)
- *The Crucifixion of Saint Peter* (1601)
- *The Supper at Emmaus* (1601)
- *The Incredulity of Saint Thomas* (1601–1602)
- *Ecce Homo* (c. 1605). *Ecce Homo* is Latin for "Behold the Man," the words spoken by Pilate at the trial of Jesus.
- *The Beheading of Saint John the Baptist* (1608)
- *The Raising of Lazarus* (1609)
- *David with the Head of Goliath* (c. 1610)

Caravaggio used his own face for the face of Goliath. Caravaggio also did paintings based on mythology, such as:

- *Bacchus* (c. 1595)
- *Medussa* (1597)
- *Narcissus* (1597–1599)

Who was El Greco?

El Greco (1541–1614) was a famous painter who lived in Spain. He was called "El Greco" because the Spaniards could not pronounce his name, Doménikos Theotokópoulos. He

Were there any important women painters?

Due to cultural constraints of the time, not many women were able to become painters. One exception was Italian Artemisia Gentileschi (1593–1656). She was the daughter of painter Orazio Gentileschi (1563–1639). Both Artemisia and her father often chose to paint dramatic and shocking scenes from the Bible, such as Judith cutting off the head of the Assyrian general Holofernes. (The story of Judith is in the Book of Judith, which is in Catholic Bibles but not Protestant Bibles.) Search for these paintings of Artemisia Gentileschi: *Susanna and the Elders*, *Judith Slaying Holofernes*, and *Judith and Her Maidservant*. She produced multiple versions of each of these. Her paintings are very beautiful, even when depicting scenes of violence. See also her painting *Salome with the Head of Saint John the Baptist* (c. 1610–1615).

was born on the island of Crete in the Mediterranean, and he studied art in Venice. He moved to Toledo, Spain, where he produced his most famous works. His paintings are known for their ghostly quality and his depictions of stretched-out human figures with gray-colored skin. Do an online image search for "El Greco Saint" and see which saints pop up, such as *Saint John the Baptist* and *Saint Francis Meditating on Death*. See also his *The Burial of the Count of Orgaz* (1586).

Why is Rembrandt considered the archetype of the modern artist?

To understand the similarities between Rembrandt van Rijn (1606–1669) and the modern artist, it is important to note that this master portrait-painter, who broke ground in his use of light and shadow, was in his own time criticized for his work. Some thought his work was too personal or too eccentric. Rembrandt's subjects included lower-class people, the events of everyday life and everyday business, and the humanity and humility of Christ (rather than the choirs, trumpets, and celestial triumph that were the subjects of other religious paintings at the time). His portraits reveal his interest in the effects of time on human features—including his own. In summary, the Dutch artist approached his work with "psychological insight and ... profound sympathy for the human affliction." He was also known to use the butt end of his brush to apply paint. Thus, he strayed outside the accepted limits of great art at the time.

Art critics today recognize Rembrandt as not only one of the great portrait painters but also a master of realism. The Dutch painter, who also etched, drew, and made prints, is regarded as an example for the working artist; he showed that the subject is less important than what the artist does with his materials.

Among his most acclaimed works are *The Syndics of the Cloth Guild* (1662) and *The Return of the Prodigal Son* (c. 1665). The first painting shows a board of directors going over the books, and Rembrandt astutely captures the moment when the six businessmen are interrupted, thus showing a remarkably real, everyday scene. *The Return of the Prodigal Son* is one of the most moving religious paintings of all time. Here, Rembrandt has with great compassion rendered the reunion of father and son, capturing that moment of mercy when the contrite son kneels before his forgiving father. Through his series of self-portraits, Rembrandt documented his own history—from the confidence and optimism of his youth to the "worn resignation of his declining years."

Rembrandt's *Return of the Prodigal Son* (c. 1665) is considered one of his finest masterpieces.

ROCOCO AND ROMANTIC PAINTING

What periods of art followed the Baroque period?

The Baroque period was followed by the Rococo period and then the Romantic period. In Rococo art, the painted scenes are not about serious and dramatic subjects but are rather beautiful, delightful, and pleasurable. Three important Rococo painters are:

- Antoine Watteau (1684–1721), who painted *The Feast (or Festival) of Love* (1718–1719) and *The Embarkation for Cythera* (1717);

- Jean-Honoré Fragonard (1732–1806), who painted *The Swing* (1767) and *The See-Saw* (1750–1755); and

- François Boucher (1703–1770), who painted *Venus Consoling Love* (1751) and *Madame de Pompadour* (1756).

Rococo architecture is known for its decorative detail, especially on the interior of buildings. Sculpted moldings and the use of scrolling curves are common, as is the use of gold leaf.

What was the Romantic period? Why was it called "romantic"?

The Romantic period followed, which emphasized passion and feeling. It was a reaction against the Enlightenment and its emphasis on reason and order. Today, the word "romantic" usually refers to strong feelings of love or attraction. In the Romantic period, the word was understood to include all emotions and paintings. Also, Romantics were interested in things and places that were foreign and exotic.

Important Romantic painters include Eugène Delacroix (1798–1863) and Théodore Géricault (1791–1824). Delacroix painted *Massacre at Chios* (1824), *Death of Sardanapalus* (1827), and *Greece on the Ruins of Missolonghi* (1826). Be sure to check out his most famous painting: *Liberty Leading the People* (1830). The French government

Painted when artist Théodore Géricault was only twenty-seven, *The Raft of the Medua* (1818–1819) romantically portrays the naval disaster of the 1816 French ship in which nearly 150 people died.

bought this painting and kept it from public view because it feared that it might encourage the people to push for liberty. The French finally put it on public display in 1848.

Géricault painted *The Charging Chasseur* (1812) and *The Raft of the Medusa* (1819). Other important painters of this era are John Constable (1776–1837), who painted beautiful landscapes, such as *The Hay Wain* (1821); and J. M. W. Turner (1775–1851), whose work included turbulent images of ships at sea, such as *Snow Storm: Steam-Boat off a Harbour's Mouth* (c. 1842) and *The Slave Ship* (1840). The latter career of Turner is portrayed in the 2014 movie *Mr. Turner*.

Was the Romantic period just about painting?

No; at the same time, there was a Romantic period in literature. Some of the great English writers of the time were William Wordsworth (1770–1850), Samuel Taylor Coleridge (1772–1834), Lord Byron (1788–1824), Percy Bysshe Shelley (1792–1822), and John Keats (1795–1821).

Also, there was a Romantic period in music, as described in the chapter "Music, Dance, and Theater."

IMPRESSIONISM

What was the Impressionist period?

The next big period in art was the Impressionist period. Impressionism is rooted in the work of Édouard Manet (1832–1883), who first began experimenting with color and light to bring a more naturalistic quality to painting.

In 1863, Manet exhibited two highly controversial and groundbreaking works: *Dejeuner sur l'herbe* and *Olympia*. Both paintings were based on classic subjects with nude women, but Manet rendered these pastoral scenes according to his own experience, giving them a decidedly earthier and more blatantly erotic quality than the Parisian critics and academicians of the day could accept. He was roundly criticized for his scandalous exhibition and for his style of painting, which some critics thought looked unfinished.

Nevertheless, Manet persevered, and in 1868, with his portrait of French writer Émile Zola (1840–1902), he again challenged the art world and its values. A critic for *Le National* denounced the portrait and cited among his complaints that Zola's trousers were not made of cloth. This, the artists observed, was both truth and revelation: the pants were made of paint. (See Manet's painting *The Fifer*.)

A few years later, in 1870, Manet began experimenting with painting outside in the brilliance of natural sunlight. Manet pioneered many of the ideas and techniques taken up by other Impressionists.

What is the origin of the term "Impressionism"?

The term "Impressionism" was derived by a rather mean-spirited art critic from the title of one of Claude Monet's (1840–1926) early paintings, *Impression, Sunrise* (1872).

How did Claude Monet change how to think about painting?

Prior to Monet, many thought of painting as mostly an attempt to represent something that could be seen, such as a person sitting for a portrait or scene of nature. The goal was to paint the things being seen. Monet changed his understanding of painting by realizing he was not painting objects themselves but rather the light coming from the objects. This changed both his thinking and the look of his paintings. He did a number of paintings of haystacks. However, he painted them in different lights, so the same haystack looked very different in different sunlights.

Monet did some thirty paintings of the Cathedral of Rouen in France, often from the same angle. The object painted (the cathedral) was the same, but the light was different depending on the position of the sun and the weather, and it resulted in many different images. (Do an online image search for "Monet Rouen Cathedral" and notice all the different paintings of the front of the same cathedral.)

Monet's series of *Water Lilies* paintings (1905) are arguably the best known and most highly acclaimed Impressionist works.

Who were other important Impressionist painters?

Pierre-Auguste Renoir (1841–1919), Alfred Sisley (1839–1899), and Frédéric Bazille (1841–1870) are other important painters of this period.

Together, the Impressionist painters paved the way for the art of the twentieth century by treating a painting as a created object on which an artist could explore new and different ways to create images.

How did American Mary Cassatt join the Paris art world of the Impressionists?

Mary Cassatt (1844–1926), the daughter of a wealthy investment banker from Pittsburgh, Pennsylvania, traveled to Paris in 1866 with her mother and some women friends; the young Cassatt was determined to join the city's community of artists. Since women were not allowed to enroll in classes at Paris's Institute of Beaux Arts (the policy was changed in 1897), Cassatt privately studied painting and traveled in Europe, pursuing her artistic interests.

Returning to Paris in 1874, she became acquainted with Edgar Degas (1834–1917), who remarked that the American artist possessed an "infinite talent" and that she was "a person who feels as I do." He made these observations after viewing one of her paintings at the Salon d'Automne in Paris. Cassatt went on to exhibit with the Impressionists in 1879, 1880, 1881, and 1886, gaining her first solo exhibit in 1891.

Georges Seurat's *A Sunday Afternoon on the Island of La Grande Jatte* (1884–1886) is a superb example of pointilism.

An online image search for "Mary Cassatt paintings" will show her many works, most of which are intimate portraits of women, children, or women with children, as she showed the dignity and beauty of the world of ordinary women and children.

Why is Impressionist art so popular?

Impressionist art is popular with many people for two simple reasons. First, impressionist paintings are typically very colorful and beautiful; and second, Impressionists typically depict scenes that are easy to understand. In the next decades, artists would innovate and create many new ways to paint. However, some of the later "modern" paintings would leave many viewers baffled and confused.

What is pointillism?

Georges Seurat (1859–1891) took the painting of light to the next level. He imagined lighted objects to be made up of tiny points of color and not large patches of the same color. The style he developed of painting tiny dots of color to make images was called pointillism. His most famous painting is *A Sunday Afternoon on the Island of La Grande Jatte*. This ten-foot-wide painting can be seen at the Art Institute of Chicago. The painting would be the inspiration for Stephen Sondheim's 1984 musical *Sunday in the Park with George*.

Paul Signac (1863–1935) and Camille Pissarro (1830–1903) followed similar approaches of using points of color. (Do online image searches for each of these names.)

Seurat's thoughts about color and his painting technique are important because the later printing of colored images would be based on printing dots of color. Also, your computer screen and television are based on the same principle of dots of color, called pixels.

VAN GOGH, CÉZANNE, AND MATISSE

Why is the work of Vincent van Gogh so well known?

The work of Vincent van Gogh (1853–1890) is some of the most beloved art ever created and has sold for some of the highest prices in history despite the fact that very little of his art was sold in his lifetime. As with Impressionist art, the subject matter of his paintings is easy to understand, and his paintings are often stunningly beautiful.

When he painted people, van Gogh preferred to paint ordinary people, such as working peasants. His later paintings are known for the use of bright and dramatic color. He was a master of using contrasting colors.

In many of his later paintings, he used streaks of paint, a technique that mimics the way one might draw using repeated lines to fill in areas. In other words, van Gogh was drawing with paint.

What are some of the movies on Vincent van Gogh?

In addition to a number of documentaries, several feature movies depict the life and struggles of van Gogh:

- *Lust of Life* (1956), starring Kirk Douglas as van Gogh and Anthony Quinn as Paul Gaugin, gives an excellent portrait of van Gogh.
- *Vincent and Theo* (1990) explores the relationship between van Gogh and his brother Theo.
- *Loving Vincent* (2017) explores the end of the life of van Gogh and the questions about his death. This experimental film is made of images painted in van Gogh's style.
- *At Eternity's Gate* (2018), starring Willem Dafoe (1955–), shows the struggles of van Gogh in his last years.

Why is Paul Cézanne considered such an important painter?

Many see Paul Cézanne (1839–1906) as a bridge between the work of the Impressionists and the work of the twentieth-century painters, who would take art in many different directions. (Do an online search for "Cézanne paintings," "Cézanne landscapes," and "Cézanne still life.") He did a number of paintings of Mont Sainte-Victoire, a mountain in France. If one looks at several of these paintings, the technique of Cézanne becomes clear in that he composes the piece using small blocks of color. This was revolutionary.

Why were Matisse's paintings considered so shocking when they were debuted?

Even if they seem commonplace to art today, the color and style of the paintings of French expressionist Henri Matisse (1869–1954) were revolutionary in their day.

In 1905, Matisse, along with several other artists, exhibited works at Paris's Salon d'Automne. The wildly colorful paintings on display prompted an art critic to exclaim that they were fauves, or "wild beasts." The name stuck: Matisse and his contemporaries, who were using brilliant colors in an arbitrary fashion, became known as "the fauves." His famous work *Portrait of Madame Matisse*, or *The Green Stripe* (1905), showed his wife with blue hair and a green stripe running down the middle of her face, which was colored pink on one side of her nose and yellow on the other. Matisse was at the forefront of a movement that was building new artistic values. The fauves were not using color in a realistic or scientific manner (as Georges Seurat had done); they were using color in any way they chose.

Throughout his career, Matisse continued to experiment with various art

Portrait of Madame Matisse (1905) is an example of Henri Matisse's experimentation with color that was considered scandalous by conservative art lovers of the time.

forms—painting, paper cutouts, and sculptures. All of his works indicate a progressive elimination of detail and simplification of line and color. So influential was his style on modern art that some seventy years later, one art critic commented that it was as if Matisse belonged to a later generation—and a different world.

MODERN ART

Why is Pablo Picasso so important? What was the style of Picasso?

Picasso did not have one style; he had many. Over his long career, he kept experimenting and changing what he was trying to do with painting. (Find a webpage of Picasso's paintings and explore all of his diverse images. This is better than an image search of "Picasso paintings," which will bring up many images that are not by Picasso but meant to imitate his paintings.)

Many of his paintings make one think that Picasso could not draw at all. Could he actually draw?

Look at Picasso's paintings *Seated Woman* (1937) and his famous *Guernica* (1937). One might conclude that Picasso was a lousy artist, who could not draw or paint. Now, look at Picasso's early paintings, such as *The First Communion* (1896) and *Science and Charity* (1897). Picasso could draw in a realistic style and create beautiful art. But Picasso was not satisfied with such art since this kind of art had been done for centuries, and he wondered why art had to be restricted to realistic images. So, Picasso started experimenting.

He was an artist with a canvas, paint, and an imagination. Why did he have to paint things the way they actually looked? He could do whatever he wanted on the canvas.

Also, he began to explore a simpler way to paint. As he said, "It took me four years to paint like Raphael, but a lifetime to paint like a child." He also stated, "Every child is an artist. The problem is how to remain an artist once he grows up."

Why is Picasso's painting *Les Demoiselles d'Avignon* ("The Young Ladies of Avignon") so important?

In this work, Picasso broke all the assumed rules of paintings. (Find an online image of the painting.) "Paintings are supposed to be beautiful." No, paintings can include ugliness. "Human bodies have to be painted the way they look." No, the painter

Picasso's *Les Demoiselles d'Avignon* (1907) is a brilliant example of his technique of breaking rules and yet creating art.

429

can distort bodies. "Paintings have to make sense." No, he painted masks instead of faces.

What Picasso was embracing was that he was a painter with a canvas who could do whatever he wanted with what he depicted. He could create art that was unsettling and disturbing, but he could also create art that presented things that had never been seen before.

Who are other important artists of this period?

Wassily Kandinsky (1866–1944) and Piet Mondrian (1872–1944) were pioneers of abstract art. Abstract art uses shapes, lines, and colors to create artwork that does not represent something that can be seen in the world.

Georges Braque (1882–1963) and Picasso were key figures in the movement known as Cubism, in which the objects painted would be shown from many angles at the same time.

Who was Jackson Pollock, and why was he important?

Jackson Pollock (1912–1956) broke the rule that painters should produce art with recognizable images, such as people or landscapes. Instead, Pollock, in his later period, laid his canvas on the floor and then threw paint on the canvas. However, the paint was not tossed randomly.

Pull up his paintings on the Internet. Look closely at his paintings, and you can see repeated patterns. Notice that the colors are balanced in his painting; you don't see one side that is mostly red and another side that is mostly blue. The beauty and the draw of Pollock's paintings are that they are just layers of lines and patches of color that are interesting to look at on their own without having any greater meaning.

Jackson Pollock struggled with emotional problems and alcoholism. He died while driving intoxicated; he crashed his car, killing himself and one of the two passengers in his car.

The 2000 film *Pollock*, starring Ed Harris, shows the life, career, and personal problems of the groundbreaking Jackson Pollock.

Why was Andy Warhol so well known, so well liked, and, at times, so controversial?

There is no easy way to summarize the work of Andy Warhol (1928–1987) because in his long and productive career, he produced so many artworks using so many different techniques and styles. Often called a "pop" artist, Warhol took many images from popular culture to use in art: soup cans, Coke bottles, movie stars, and dramatic photos from newspapers. He was fascinated by advertising imagery, celebrity culture, and, in particular, cultural images such as product labels and the faces of famous people. Warhol also innovated by using the process of silk screening for many of his paintings. He also made experimental films.

Do an online image search for "Andy Warhol paintings" and see what you find. Be sure to see his famous image of movie star Marilyn Monroe (1926–1962).

PHOTOGRAPHY

When was photography invented?

The concept of still photography dates back to the tenth century, when Islamic scientists developed the camera obscura (*obscura* is Latin for "dark chamber"), a darkened enclosure with a small aperture (opening) to admit light. The light rays would cast an inverted image of external objects onto a flat surface opposite the aperture. This image could be studied and traced by someone working inside the camera obscura, or the image could be viewed from the outside of the camera through a peephole.

In the sixteenth century, Italian scientist Giambattista della Porta (c. 1535–1615) published his studies on fitting the aperture (opening) of the camera obscura with a lens to strengthen or enlarge the image projected. Made increasingly versatile through additional improvements, the camera obscura became popular among seventeenth- and eighteenth-century European artists.

But the camera obscura could only project (rather than reproduce) images onto a screen or a piece of paper. During the 1800s, scientists experimented with ways of making the images permanent. Among those who made advances in the photographic process were French physicist Joseph-Nicéphore Niépce (1765–1833), who produced the first negative image in 1826, and then French painter Louis Daguerre (1787–1851), who in 1839 succeeded in making a direct positive image on a silver plate, known as the daguerreotype. English scientist William Henry Fox Talbot (1800–1877) developed a paper negative (c. 1841) that could be used to print any number of paper positives, and English astronomer Sir John Herschel (1792–1871) was the first to produce a practical photographic fixing agent and the first to apply the terms "positive" and "negative" to photographic images. All of these milestones made photography a practical way to permanently record real-life images.

When does modern photography begin?

The breakthrough in still photography was the Kodak camera introduced in 1888 by American inventor George Eastman (1854–1932). The Kodak camera used film that was wound on rollers, eliminating the glass photographic plates that had been in use. The box-shaped camera made photography accessible to everyone—including amateurs. By the early 1900s, the Eastman Kodak Company had become the largest photographic film and camera producer in the world. George Eastman has been credited with mass-producing the moment. Before the Kodak camera (a word he made up because he was fond of the letter *k*), photography had largely been the domain of professionals who were commissioned to take portraits of the well-to-do, prominent members of society.

431

Once the Kodak camera became widely available, photographs preserved the faces of ordinary people and the events of everyday life.

When was photography established as an art form?

Alfred Stieglitz (1864–1946) is the acknowledged "Father of Modern Photography." His interest in the medium began when he was just a toddler. At the age of two, he became obsessed with a photo of his cousin, carrying it with him at all times. When he was nine years old, he took exception to a professional photographer's practice of using pigment to color a black-and-white photo, complaining that this spoiled the quality of the print.

Between 1887 and 1911, Stieglitz worked to establish photography as a valid form of artistic expression, a pursuit for which he was sometimes publicly derided. He believed that photography should be separate from painting but on an equal footing as an art form. He also strove to differentiate photography by instilling it with an American essence. The streets of New York City became his subject as he developed a uniquely American art form. Stieglitz also published and edited photography magazines, most notably *Camera Work* (1903–1917).

Why is Ansel Adams so important?

Ansel Adams (1902–1984) made stunning, black-and-white photographs of natural scenes. Do an online image search for "Ansel Adams photographs" to see for yourself. Be sure to open and enlarge the images when you look at them.

When was color photography developed?

A key moment was the introduction of Kodachrome film in 1935 by Eastman Kodak for movies. Colored prints on paper became possible in the 1940s. In the 1960s and 1970s, the cost of taking color photographs went down, while the quality improved. In time, most people with cameras, whether cheap or expensive, were taking color photographs. Polaroid introduced an instant color camera and film in 1963.

When did digital photography develop?

Digital photography had been developing since the 1950s. In the 1990s, digital cameras were available to consumers.

Ansel Adams was famous for his black-and-white photographs of natural scenes of the American West.

What is digital photography?

In a digital camera, when an image is taken, such as a photo of a person, the information is converted into a code made of numbers, letters, and symbols. (Originally, it was just numbers, and numbers are made of digits—hence the word "digital.") The numbers give specific information for each of many dots of an image, such as the location of the dot, the size of the dot, and the exact color. The dots are called pixels. The pixels can be displayed by the camera, shown on a computer or iPhone screen or printed out on paper. A better photograph with a higher resolution has many more dots that are much smaller. (To be more precise, in a photograph, the camera sensor converts light energy into electrical values for each pixel, which are then stored as code.)

Digital photography has all kinds of advantages. Once you own the camera—though some digital cameras are expensive—there is no film cost, so one can take as many images as desired. The only limit is the data storage capacity of the card in the camera. With film cameras, many people had to avoid wasting film. A digital photographer can take lots of digital images, try different angles and poses, and then delete all the unwanted images. And the images are instantly available. With the old film cameras, the film had to be sent away to be developed and printed out.

Also, the digital image is easily manipulated by a computer program, such as Adobe Photoshop. Since the image data is in numbers, the numbers can be easily changed to make the image smaller or larger; to crop (trim) the image; or to change the colors or the lightness or darkness of the image. Focus can be improved, and imperfections can be removed. Making such changes to a digital image is so popular that the word "photoshop" has become a verb, meaning to change a photograph.

ARCHITECTURE

How can one explore the important architectural creations around the world?

Photos of all the important buildings can be found online. Numerous books—usually with great photos—explore architecture. But the best way to explore architecture is to visit these buildings.

However, since there is so much amazing architecture to explore, what follows is a tiny sample of the great buildings of history.

How old is the Great Wall of China?

The immense structure, built as a barricade of protection against invasion, was begun in the third century B.C.E. by Emperor Qin Shi Huang (c. 259–210 B.C.E.) of the Qin dynasty and was expanded over the course of succeeding centuries. The wall stretches 5,500 miles, ranges in height between fifteen and thirty feet (the tallest points are at the fortifications), and is between fifteen and thirty feet thick. In the thirteenth century, the wall was penetrated when Mongols conquered China, expanding their empire across all of Asia.

What is the Parthenon?

The Parthenon is an ancient, white marble temple built in Athens, Greece, between 447 and 432 C.E. It is considered one of the best examples of Greek architecture. The city of Athens was named the Greek warrior goddess Athena, who, according to Greek mythology, was a virgin. Since the Greek word for virgin is *parthenos*, her temple was called the Parthenon. It was built on the Acropolis, a hill overlooking the city of Athens.

Around 500 C.E., the temple became a Christian church; in the mid-1400s, when the region was captured by Turkish Muslims, it was turned into a mosque; and in 1687, when Venetians tried to take the city, the Parthenon was severely damaged; only ruins remain today. Since the 1980s, restoration work has been taking place to stabilize what remains of the Parthenon.

In 1897, a replica of the Parthenon was built in Nashville, Tennessee. It can be seen today and gives the visitor an idea of what the Parthenon in Athens would have looked like to ancient Greeks.

(Do an online image search for both Parthenons. Also, the PBS documentary series *Nova* has an episode called "Secrets of the Parthenon" which describes in detail the restoration of the Parthenon in Greece and all that the workers have discovered about the sophistication of the original builders of the Parthenon.)

How was the Colosseum in Rome ruined?

The Roman structure, begun during the reign of Vespasian (ruled 69–79 C.E.), was disassembled during the Middle Ages when its stones and blocks were removed and used to construct other buildings. The Colosseum, situated in the center of the city of Rome, was a giant, outdoor theater. Between 80 and 404, it was an entertainment center where battles were staged, gladiators competed, and men fought wild animals. It could seat 50,000 spectators, who were separated from the arena by a fifteen-foot wall.

When was London's Westminster Abbey built?

The famed national church of England was begun between 1042 and 1065, when Edward the Confessor (c. 1003–1066) built a

The Colosseum in Rome was the center of the great city's entertainment from 80 to 404 C.E. Gladiator fights, drama, reenactments of battles, animal hunts, and executions were all performed there.

church on the site of the Abbey. King Henry III (1207–1272) began work on the main part of Westminster in 1245. Since the time of William the Conqueror, all of England's rulers, except Edward V and Edward VIII, have been crowned at the church. The Abbey is also a burial place of great English statesmen, literary giants, composers, and scientists. Many notable figures are buried in Westminster Abbey, including Charles Darwin, Charles Dickens, George Frideric Handel, and Isaac Newton.

Why does the Leaning Tower of Pisa lean?

The famous bell tower in Pisa (in northwestern Italy) leans because of the unstable soil on which it was built. Construction began in 1173 on the approximately 180-foot campanile; it began to lean as soon as the first three floors were completed. Nevertheless, building continued, and the seven-story structure was finished between 1360 and 1370. Leaning a bit more each year, by the time it was closed for repairs in 1990, the tower tilted 14.5 feet out of line when measured from the top story. Engineers on the project worked to stabilize the foundation and straighten it slightly. The tower, which was built alongside a church and a baptistery, would probably not be remarkable if it were not for its slant. However, with its characteristic angle, it continues to attract tourists to the small town on the Arno River.

Why is the Cathedral of Notre-Dame famous?

The Paris cathedral was built using the first true flying buttresses. These are masonry bridges that transmit the thrust of a vault or a roof to an outer support. (Do an online

Notre-Dame de Paris, considered one of the all-time great examples of Gothic architecture, is today at risk of being lost forever because fire damage in 2019 was so severe it might not be fixable.

image search: "flying buttresses.") The device allowed the structure to achieve a great height—one of the first Gothic churches to do so. Gothic was a medieval architectural style that predominated in northern Europe.

The buttresses made it possible to put more stained glass windows in the walls. Sadly, Notre-Dame in Paris suffered a devastating fire in 2019. It is currently being restored.

One of the leading examples of Gothic architecture is the Amiens Cathedral (in the northern French city of Amiens), which was begun in 1220. Its soaring nave (the central area of a church) epitomizes the era's drive for height. The Amiens Cathedral is France's largest.

Why is Spain's Alhambra historically important?

The elaborate palace, built east of the city of Granada in southern Spain, was built by Moors, Muslim North Africans who occupied the Iberian Peninsula (Spain and Portugal) for hundreds of years during the Middle Ages. The fortified structure, built between 1238 and 1354, is a monument of Islamic architecture in the Western world.

Its name is derived from an Arabic word meaning "red"; the highly ornamental palace, with decorative columns, walls, and ceilings, was constructed of red brick. Perched on a hilltop, the Alhambra was the last stronghold of the Moors in Spain. In 1492, the forces of Spain's King Ferdinand and Queen Isabella captured the palace.

When was the Brooklyn Bridge completed?

The bridge, which spans New York's East River to connect Manhattan and Brooklyn, was completed in 1883. Upon opening, it was celebrated as a feat of modern engineering and, with its twin gothic towers, as an architectural landmark of considerable grace and beauty. It was designed by German American engineer John Augustus Roebling (1806–1869); upon his death, the project was succeeded by his son, Washington Augustus Roebling (1837–1926).

When the Brooklyn Bridge was finished, it was the longest suspension bridge in the world, measuring 1,595 feet. The bridge hangs from steel cables that are almost sixteen

What tragedy happened to Notre-Dame in 2019?

On April 15, 2019, the Notre-Dame Cathedral caught fire, completely destroying the eight-hundred-year-old wooden roof and the iconic spire. The high altar was also damaged, though the buttresses, south tower, great organ, and rose window survived. At the time of the fire, the cathedral was being restored. Investigators ruled the fire an accident, and it is hoped the ceiling and spire can be rebuilt. However, the historic nature of those structures will be forever lost, as the ancient timbers were irreplaceable.

inches thick. The cables are suspended from stone and masonry towers that are 275 feet tall.

What strange medical problem did the workers face?

To build the two towers, specially designed, watertight chambers called caissons, were lowered to the riverbed. The chambers were filled with pressurized air to keep water from seeping in. Workers entered the caissons through tubes to go down to dig through the silt at the bottom of the river. They went down to 44 feet for the tower on the Brooklyn side and 78 feet for the Manhattan tower. They wanted to get down to bedrock to support the towers.

The project proved to be an enormously dangerous undertaking. Underwater workers suffered from "the bends." While in the caissons, they breathed pressurized air, which meant that pressurized gas was going into their bloodstreams. If a worker left the pressurized space too quickly, gas bubbles would form in his bloodstream. These bubbles cause decompression sickness, which can be fatal.

Decompression sickness can result in great pain in the joints and can cause a victim to bend over; thus, it got the nickname "the bends." It would later be learned that the simplest way to avoid the problem was to limit how much time one spent breathing the pressurized air or go to a chamber to reduce the air pressure very slowly.

Similar problems for workers were discovered when building the Eads Bridge in St. Louis, which was opened in 1874.

When did modern architecture begin?

The term "modern architecture" refers to architecture that turned away from past historical designs in favor of designs that were expressive of their own time. Two "schools" emerged in the late 1800s: art nouveau and the Chicago school. (The following paragraphs include many names of famous architects. If you want, pick one or two and do an online image search for the architect's name and the world "building.")

Art nouveau held sway in Europe for some twenty years and was evident not only in architecture and interiors but also in furniture, jewelry, typography, sculpture, painting, and other fine and applied arts. Its proponents included Belgian architects Victor Horta (1861–1947) and Henry van de Velde (1863–1957) and Spaniard Antonio Gaudí (1852–1926).

But it was the Chicago school that, in the rebuilding days after the Great Chicago Fire (1871), created an entirely new form. American engineer and architect William Le Baron Jenney (1832–1907) led the way. Four of the five younger architects who followed him had at one time worked in Jenney's office: Louis Henry Sullivan (1856–1924), Martin Roche (1853–1927), William Holabird (1854–1923), Daniel Hudson Burnham (1846–1912), and John Wellborn Root (1850–1891). Together, these men established solid principles for the design of modern buildings and skyscrapers where "form followed function." Ornament was used sparingly, and the architects fully utilized iron, steel, and glass.

By the 1920s, modern architecture had taken firm hold, and in the mid-twentieth century, it was furthered by the works of Walter Adolph Gropius (1883–1969), Le Corbusier (Charles-Édouard Jeanneret; 1887–1965), Ludwig Mies van der Rohe (1886–1969), and Frank Lloyd Wright (1867–1959). Modern architecture ended in the 1960s with the deaths of these masters.

What are some examples of modern buildings that can be seen online?

Examples of modern architecture include Chicago's Monadnock Building (1891), Reliance Building (1895), Carson Pirie Scott store (1904), and Robie House (1909); New York City's Rockefeller Center (1940), Lever House (1952), and Seagram Building (1958); Taliesin West (1938–1959) in Scottsdale, Arizona; Johnson Wax Company's Research Tower (1949) in Racine, Wisconsin; and the Lovell House (1929) in Los Angeles, California.

Who invented the skyscraper?

The credit is usually given to American architect William Le Baron Jenney, who designed the ten-story Home Insurance Building, erected on the corner of LaSalle and Monroe streets in Chicago in 1885. The key to these early skyscrapers was to build a steel frame to hold up the building. The walls did not hold up the building! The older method for building used walls of stone to hold up the building. However, to make such a building taller would require much thicker stone walls at the bottom. At some point, the walls would be so thick as to not be practical.

Another key element in creating these new and taller buildings was the invention in 1857 by Elisha Otis (1811–1861) of the safety elevator. He designed an automatic brake so that if the cable holding an elevator broke, the elevator could not fall. (Yes, elevator cars cannot fall if the cable breaks!) Another invention was the creation of central heating systems.

Two other important early buildings are the Rand McNally Building, built in 1889 in Chicago, and the Wainwright Building in St. Louis, designed by Louis Henry Sullivan (1856–1924) and built in 1891.

What New York buildings held the record for tallest building in the twentieth century?

For a short time, the title of world's tallest building was held by Manhattan's cele-

New York City's Chrysler Building (1930) is no longer the world's tallest skyscraper, but it remains a fine example of Art Deco design.

brated Chrysler Building (completed in 1930), considered the height of Art Deco design. The Chrysler Building's 1,046 feet and seventy-seven stories of glory were soon bettered by the Empire State Building (completed in 1931), which boasts a total height of 1,224 feet and 102 stories. That New York City landmark held on to its position for four decades, becoming second tallest with the 1973 completion of the twin towers of the World Trade Center, which consisted of two 110-story towers, one being 1,362 feet tall and the other 1,368 feet. Both were destroyed in the terrorist attacks of September 11, 2001.

What was the next significant innovation in building skyscrapers?

In skyscrapers, the steel structure holds up the buildings. Initially, the walls were built out of brick and stone, but these were veneers since they did not hold up the building. In time, architects began putting in larger windows and eventually creating walls that are entirely glass. This, of course, required the development of glass that was very hard to break and layered glass with a space between the layers to act as insulation. (Next time you are in a large city, look for tall buildings covered entirely with glass.)

Also, glass walls are cheaper than traditional walls of stone or bricks: both the material is cheaper, and the labor required is much less.

What is the world's tallest building today?

The honor belongs to the Burj Khalifa (2010) in Dubai, United Arab Emirates, which soars to an amazing 2,717 feet and 160 stories. Along with the title of world's tallest building, the Burj Khalifa holds a number of other world records: tallest freestanding structure, highest occupied floor, highest outdoor observation deck, highest number of stories, tallest service elevator, and elevator with the longest traveling distance.

The second-tallest building is the Shanghai Tower in China. Completed in 2015, it reaches 2,073 feet. The tallest building in the United States is One World Trade Center. Construction on the site of the destroyed twin towers of the World Trade Center began in 2006 and was completed in 2014. At 1,776 feet, it is the seventh-tallest building in the world.

MUSIC

What is music notation?

Today, if someone creates a new song, it is very easy to record it, so someone in the future can know how to perform the song. Now, imagine a time before recordings existed. How can one pass on a music piece except if someone hears it and remembers how to play it? If no one remembers, the song is lost. The solution to the problem is to create music notation or a musical score in which someone writes down the notes and provides information on how to perform them. We know all the symphonies of Beethoven because he wrote them down with music notation. Music notation is an important invention. It takes a little effort to learn it, but it is not difficult to learn.

When was our system for notating music developed?

Our present system of music notation was developed when Guido of Arezzo (c. 991–1050), an Italian monk, devised a precise system for defining pitch. Guido was a leading music teacher and theorist in his day. As such, he went to Rome to present a collection of religious anthems to Pope John XIX. Guido used a system of four horizontal lines (a staff) on which to chart pitch, and he used the syllables *ut* (later replaced with *do*), *re, mi, fa, sol* (or *so*), *and la* to name the first six tones of the major scale. Before Guido developed his system, singers had to memorize melodies. Guido's famous treatise *Micrologus* was one of the most widely used instruction books of the Middle Ages.

CLASSICAL MUSIC

What are the periods of classical music?

Many people use the term "classical music" to refer to music typically performed by symphony orchestras and to differentiate it from popular music. However, "classical" actually refers to one historical period of this music. Here is a typical list of the periods of musical history:

- Medieval Period: c. 500–1400
- Renaissance Period: c. 1400–1600
- Baroque Period: c. 1600–1760
- Classical Period: c. 1730–1820
- Romantic Period: c. 1780–1910
- Modern Period: c. 1890–1950
- Postmodern or Contemporary Period: 1950–present

What is the importance of the Walt Disney movie *Fantasia*?

A great introduction to classical music is to watch the 1940 Walt Disney movie *Fantasia*. It is an animated film set to several great pieces of music. Its most famous segment is *The Sorcerer's Apprentice,* set to the music of Paul Dukas (1865–1935) and starring Mickey Mouse. The last segment of *Night on Bald Mountain* and *Ave Maria*, written by composers Modest Mussorgsky (1839–1881) and Franz Schubert (1797–1828), is particularly stunning.

Much later, Disney Studios created a sequel, *Fantasia 2000*. The two best segments are *Rhapsody in Blue* with the music of George Gershwin (1898–1937) and *The Firebird* with the music of Igor Stravinsky (1882–1971).

MEDIEVAL MUSIC

What is Gregorian chant?

For some people, Gregorian chant is an acquired taste, which means they have to spend some time with it in order to learn to like it. If you are new to Gregorian chant, you might try listening to short selections at several different times.

Many people find Gregorian chant very soothing. Many people find it provides a nice background for meditation and prayer. It also sounds very religious, especially with a recording made in a church building with lots of resonance. Other people find it to be good background music for work and study.

Gregorian chant is a music style used for prayers and chanting the Psalms that goes back at least to the 700s C.E. and was based on earlier music forms. It gets its name from Pope Gregory I, who died in 604 C.E. Gregory encouraged the development of the liturgy and collected various chants for liturgical use.

Gregorian chant is monophonic, which means that only one melody is sung at a time. Even if there are numerous singers, they all sing the same note. This is different from polyphonic music, where singers sing different melodies that are interwoven. It is also different from singing harmony, where the singers sing different notes of the same chord while singing the same word.

Gregorian chant typically has no instrumental accompaniment. It is sung a cappella, usually by a choir, although sometimes by a soloist. Gregorian chant does have a rhythm, but the rhythm can be very subtle. There is no instrument, such as a drum, to emphasize the beat. It is the exact opposite of rock and hip-hop music, where the beat, emphasized by the drum and bass, predominates. Because Gregorian chant is monophonic with no instruments, it is a very simple style of music, yet it can be very emotionally powerful.

RENAISSANCE MUSIC

Who are the important Renaissance composers?

Some significant Renaissance composers include:

- Josquin des Prez (1440–1521)
- Giovanni Pierluigi da Palestrina (1525–1594)
- Thomas Morley (1557–1602)
- Thomas Weelkes (c. 1575–1623)
- Andrea Gabrieli (c. 1533–1585)

What is polyphony?

Polyphony is music with multiple melodies woven together. Polyphony was used extensively in Renaissance music.

BAROQUE MUSIC

Who was Johann Pachelbel?

Johann Pachelbel (c. 1653–1706) wrote a piece called *Canon in D,* which was popular in his time; however, in the 1970s and 1980s, a new arrangement of the piece became extremely popular.

Who is the most famous Baroque composer?

Without doubt, the most famous and most important Baroque composer was Johann Sebastian Bach (1685–1750), who wrote some 1,100 musical works and has had a lasting and profound influence on music composition. While not famous during his lifetime, J. S. Bach's works and innovations defined music as we now know it. The tempered scale for tuning instruments is among his inventions, and he initiated a keyboard technique considered standard today.

A devout Christian, J. S. Bach believed that all music was to "the glory of God and the re-creation of the human spirit." As a spiritual person and true believer in eternal life, he left behind an impressive body of church music, including 300 cantatas (or musical sermons) as well as passions and oratorios. (The *Merriam-Webster* dictionary defines "oratorio" as "a lengthy choral work usually of a religious nature consisting chiefly of recitatives, arias, and choruses without action or scenery.")

Bach also wrote chamber music, including instrumental concertos, suites, and overtures. Among his best-known and beloved works are "Jesu, Joy of Man's Desiring," "Sheep May Safely Graze," his *Christmas Oratorio*, and *The Saint Matthew Passion*.

I have often heard the famous musical piece the "Hallelujah Chorus." Who wrote it?

Revered as a composer for centuries after his death in 1750, Johann Sebastian Bach is famous for his religious music, including the beloved "Jesu, Joy of Man's Desiring."

A very important piece of Christian music is the *Messiah*, composed in 1741 by George Frideric Handel (1685–1759). Although Handel was born in Germany, he had moved to London, where his career flourished.

Handel's *Messiah* is an oratorio, which means it is a sung piece performed by an orchestra, a chorus, and four singers—a bass, a tenor, an alto, and a soprano. The piece uses every different possible combination of singers and orchestra. The complete piece takes about two hours and twenty minutes to perform.

The best-known part of the *Messiah* is the "Hallelujah Chorus." Most people instantly recognize the piece.

Handel also wrote the Christmas song "Joy to the World."

CLASSICAL MUSIC

Who was Haydn?

Franz Joseph Haydn (1732–1809) is known as the "Father of the Symphony" and the "Father of the String Quartet." He wrote over a hundred symphonies.

Why is Mozart so important?

A child prodigy, Wolfgang Amadeus Mozart (1756–1791) was composing at the age of five. He had been playing the harpsichord since the age of three. His father, Leopold Mozart (1719–1787), was a composer and violinist who recognized his son's unusual music ability and encouraged and taught young Mozart.

Wolfgang Amadeus Mozart's complete output—some 600 works in every form (symphonies, sonatas, operas, operettas, cantatas, arias, duets, and others)—would be enough to fill almost 200 CDs. Among his most cherished works are his operas: *The Marriage of Figaro* (1786), *Don Giovanni* (1787), *Così fan tutte* (1790), and *The Magic Flute* (1791).

Which pieces would be a good introduction to Mozart's music?

Four famous pieces of Mozart stand out:

- *Eine Kleine Nachtmusik* ("A Little Night Music") (1787)

- *Symphony 40* (1788), often called the "Great G minor symphony"

- *Symphony 41* (1788), often called the "Jupiter Symphony"

- *Requiem in D minor* (1791–1792)

A child prodigy, Mozart was a prolific composer throughout his life, which is fortunate since he died when he was only thirty-five years old.

What is a requiem?

A musical requiem is a setting of the Roman Catholic Mass prayers used at a funeral or memorial service. Mozart died before finishing his requiem, so another composer completed it. Mozart's requiem is filled with very powerful music. Two moving parts are *Dies Irae* ("Day of Wrath") and *Lacrimosa*, which means "tears." Mozart's *Dies Irae* is based on an old Latin hymn.

ROMANTIC MUSIC

Was Beethoven really deaf for much of his life?

Yes, Ludwig van Beethoven (1770–1827) suffered a gradual hearing loss in his twenties and lost his hearing altogether in his early thirties. The loss was devastating to the German composer. In a letter to his brother, he wrote, "But how humbled I feel when someone near me hears the distant sound of a flute, and I hear nothing; when someone hears a shepherd singing, and I hear nothing!" At one point, he even contemplated suicide but, instead, continued his work.

He had studied briefly with Mozart (in 1787) and Joseph Haydn (in 1792) and appeared for the first time in his own concert in 1800. While the loss of his hearing later prevented him from playing the piano properly, it did nothing to hold back his creativity.

Between 1800 and 1824, Beethoven wrote nine symphonies, and many believe that he developed the form to perfection. His other works include five piano concertos and thirty-two piano sonatas as well as string quartets, sonatas for piano and violin, opera, and vocal music, including oratorios. It was about the time that he completed his work on his third symphony, the *Eroica* (1804), that he went completely deaf.

A true genius, Beethoven's innovations include expanding the length of both the symphony and the piano concerto, increasing the number of movements in the string quartet (from four to seven), and adding instruments—including the trombone, contrabassoon, and the piccolo—to the orchestra, giving it a broader range.

An 1815 portrait of Beethoven by Joseph Willibrord Mähler.

Through his adventurous piano compositions, Beethoven also heightened the status of the instrument, which was a relatively new invention (1710).

Among his most well-known and often performed works are his third (*Eroica*), fifth, sixth (*Pastoral*), and ninth (*Choral*) symphonies as well as his fourth and fifth piano concertos.

It is remarkable—even unfathomable—that these works, so familiar to so many, were never heard by their composer. A poignant anecdote tells of Beethoven sitting on-stage to give tempo cues to the conductor during the first public performance of his ninth symphony. When the performance had ended, Beethoven—his back to the audience—was unaware of the standing ovation his work had received until a member of the choir turned Beethoven's chair around so he could see the tremendous response.

If you have never listened to Beethoven, you might try listening to his sixth symphony, *Pastoral*. A good way to hear it is in the Walt Disney movie *Fantasia*. In the movie, the symphony is set to images of Greek mythology.

Who are some other important Romantic composers?

- Felix Mendelssohn (1809–1847)
- Frédéric Chopin (1810–1849)
- Franz Liszt (1811–1886)
- Robert Schumann (1810–1856)
- Johannes Brahms (1833–1897)
- Niccolò Paganini (1782–1840)

Why is Richard Wagner important?

Richard Wagner (1813–1883) conceived of the idea of the "total work of art," where music, poetry, and the visual arts were brought together in one stunning performance piece. He had new ideas on how to present opera. In his time, operas were performed with the lights on for the audience. Audience members would eat, drink, and talk during the performances. Wagner changed all this.

He built a special theater with all the seats facing forward. He also built the floor at an angle, so the people in the front rows would be lower and people in the back rows could see over them. He turned out the lights in the theater. He also used the greatest theatrical special effects of the time—fire, smoke, lights, and great sets. Finally, he composed moving and dramatic music for his operas, in which each character had his or her own theme. (Composer John Williams [1932–] in the *Star Wars* movies gave each character an individual theme. Can you hum the beginning of Darth Vader's theme?)

Wagner filled his operas with lush orchestral sounds to tell mythic stories of dwarves, giants, gods, goddesses, superheroes, and humans in a struggle of good versus evil in a world of swords and rings. (All of these components are found in the *Lord of the Rings* movies.)

Wagner's most famous work is "The Ring Cycle," which consists of four operas: *Das Rheingold* ("The Rhinegold"), *Die Walküre* ("The Valkyrie"), *Siegfried*, and *Götterdämmerung* ("The Twilight of the Gods").

However, many people today find his operas difficult to watch. His operas are quite long, and the action develops slowly. Also, the style of singing does not fit modern tastes. But keep in mind that he wrote at a time before recorded music. His audiences were in no hurry, and they knew that they could only hear this music during a live performance. His audiences didn't want a short opera.

MODERN MUSIC

Why did Schoenberg face sharp criticism in his day?

Vienna-born American composer Arnold Schoenberg (1874–1951), now considered one of the great masters of the twentieth century, was derided for having thrown out the rules of composition—for working outside the confines of traditional harmony.

In his youth, he was a fan of Richard Wagner's operas. But just after the turn of the century, Schoenberg set out on his own path. The result was the 1909 composition "Three Piano Pieces," which some music historians argue is the single most important composition of the twentieth century.

The work is atonal, which is to say it is organized without reference to key. Most popular music has a key, and even if you don't know music theory, you often know where the piece is going, and you know when a line of music has reached the end. You recognize when the music has returned to the home key, such as at the end of a verse. However, with Schoenberg, you lose the sense of where the music is going and when it has returned home.

Schoenberg abandoned the techniques of musical expression as they had been understood for hundreds of years. This was no small moment for the music world, and many reacted with vocal and vehement criticism. (Of the outcry, Schoenberg remarked in 1947 that it was as if "I had fallen into an ocean of boiling water.") But he had his followers, too, among them his students. Though he was essentially self-taught as a composer, he became one of the most influential teachers of his time.

Why does the music of Bartók figure prominently in concert programs today?

Béla Bartók (1881–1945) is revered today not only for his ability as a pianist (his teacher compared him to Franz Liszt [1811–1886], who was perhaps the greatest pianist of the nineteenth century) but for his compositions, which are steeped in the tradition of Hungarian folk music. Bartók studied and analyzed Hungarian, Romanian, and Arabian folk tunes, publishing thousands of collections of them in his lifetime.

While ethnic music had influenced the works of other composers, Bartók was the first to make it an integral part of art music composition. His works were unique in that the folk music provided the sheer essence and substance of the music, lending the compositions a primitive quality. Among his masterpieces are his three stage works: the ballets *The Wooden Prince* and *The Miraculous Mandarin* and the one-act opera *Duke Bluebeard's Castle*.

Who was Igor Stravinsky, the composer of *The Rite of Spring*?

The Russian-born American composer Igor Stravinsky (1882–1971) is certainly one of the greatest composers of the twentieth century. Stravinsky wrote concerts, chamber music, piano pieces, and operas as well as ballets, for which he may be most well known.

One of the most important composers of the twentieth century, Igor Stravinsky gained fame early in his life with his ballets.

Between 1903 and 1906, Stravinsky studied under the great Russian composer Nikolay Rimsky-Korsakov (1844–1908). In 1908, Stravinsky wrote his first work of note, the orchestral fantasy *Fireworks*, which caught the attention of Sergey Diaghilev (1872–1929) of the Ballets Russes, who invited the young composer to participate in the ballet company's 1910 season (Ballets Russes had dazzled audiences the year before, bringing new energy to the art form).

In collaboration with Diaghilev, Stravinsky went on to create such masterpieces as *The Firebird* (1910), *Petrushka* (1911), and *The Rite of Spring* (1913). The partnership served to elevate the role of the ballet composer in the art world. *The Rite of Spring* was first performed by the Ballets Russes in 1913, with choreography by the famous dancer Vaslav Nijinsky (1889–1950). But the performance stunned both the music and dance worlds. So extreme was the audience's reaction to this premier work that a riot nearly broke out inside the theater. Stravinsky had composed his music not to express spring's idyllic qualities but rather its turmoil and dissonance—similar to childbirth.

The Rite of Spring as a ballet broke from the rules of what ballet should be. Instead of dancers executing beautiful and elegant movements, the dance movements look harsh, primitive, and unskilled. Instead of the music being harmonic, the music is dissonant, unmelodic, and disturbing. Although the kinds of sound produced by the orchestra in *The Rite of Spring* do not seem shocking today—such sounds are frequently found in movie scores—at the time, the sounds were so disturbing to many listeners that they considered the ballet to be bad music.

Listeners today are still moved by the elevated rhythm of *The Rite of Spring*, which makes an entire orchestra a kind of sustained percussion instrument. Ultimately, most musicians and critics came to regard the watershed work as one of the finest compositions of the twentieth century.

AMERICAN MUSIC: LATE 1800s TO THE PRESENT

Who was Stephen Foster?

Stephen Collins Foster (1826–1864), known as the "Father of American Music," wrote over 200 songs, including classics such as "Oh! Susanna," "Camptown Races," "Old Folks at Home," "Swanee River," "My Old Kentucky Home," "Jeanie with the Light Brown Hair," and "Beautiful Dreamer."

He was the most popular composer of his time. His career was also the beginning of the mass marketing of music, but it was not through CDs or downloads. His music was sold as sheet music, although he never made much money from the sale of his music. At the time, many homes had pianos, so someone could play music as people sang along.

What was the connection of Scott Joplin to ragtime music?

Scott Joplin (1868–1917) was known as the king of ragtime. He wrote forty-four ragtime pieces, including the famous "Maple Leaf Rag" and "The Entertainer." These piano pieces were huge hits at the time, as ragtime was the most popular style of music. Joplin also believed that ragtime music should be taken more seriously and wrote two ragtime operas. (Listen to "Maple Leaf Rag" and "The Entertainer.")

Why is George Gershwin so important?

George Gershwin (1898–1937) was a popular composer who produced many great Broadway and movie hits, such as "Swanee," "Fascinating Rhythm," "I Got Rhythm,"

"The Man I Love," "Embraceable You," and "Let's Call the Whole Thing Off." For many of his songs, his brother, Ira Gershwin (1896–1983), wrote the lyrics.

George Gershwin also wrote the famous *Rhapsody in Blue* (1924), which is an orchestral piece taking jazz to the level of classical music.

Who is Aaron Copland?

Aaron Copland (1900–1990) is the foremost American composer. He wrote an immense body of work in a number of different styles. The best way to understand him is to listen to some of his best-known works, which are the music for three ballets. These pieces are known for having a very "American" sound and include *Billy the Kid* (1938), *Rodeo* (1942), and *Appalachian Spring* (1944).

One of America's greatest composers, George Gershwin is famous for popular songs like "Embraceable You" and the opera *Porgy and Bess*.

The ballet *Appalachian Spring* was written for choreographer Martha Graham (1894–1991). *Appalachian Spring* includes the melody "Simple Gifts," a song written by the American religious group called the Shakers.

Copland also wrote his Symphony No. 3 with "Fanfare for the Common Man" in the fourth movement. Be sure to listen to "Fanfare." (You will love it!)

Who was Leonard Bernstein?

Leonard Bernstein (1918–1990) was a brilliant conductor and composer, best known as the composer of the groundbreaking musical *West Side Story* (1957). He also wrote the music score for the 1954 film *On the Waterfront*, the operetta *Candide,* and the musical *On the Town.*

What are the origins of jazz?

Jazz came out of the complex music scene in New Orleans at the end of the 1800s and early 1900s. One of the early pioneers was the cornetist Buddy Bolden (1877–1931). Ferdinand "Jelly Roll" Morton (real name: Ferdinand LaMothe [c. 1890–1941]), a New Orleans pianist, claimed credit for having invented jazz, but he was a self-promoter who gave himself more credit than he deserved. However, he was the first to write out jazz music scores. His recordings with the group the Red Hot Peppers (1926–1930) are among the earliest examples of disciplined jazz ensemble work.

> ### How can one learn more about jazz?
>
> The filmmaker Ken Burns (1953–) created *Jazz*, a ten-episode documentary exploring the complex history of jazz. *Jazz* includes many samples of the music and many great interviews.

Other key figures in the development of jazz were Bennie Moten (1894–1935), Eubie Blake (1887–1983), Duke Ellington (1899–1974), and Thomas "Fats" Waller (1904–1943).

What about the blues?

Blues music and jazz developed side by side, with blues emerging around the first decade of the 1900s and hitting the height of its early popularity in 1920s Harlem, where the songs were seen as an expression of African American life.

Great blues singers like Ma Rainey (1886–1939) and Bessie Smith (1894–1937) sang of the black reality—determined but weary. During the Harlem Renaissance, the music was a symbol for African American people who were struggling to be accepted for who they were. Poet Langston Hughes (1902–1967) saw the blues as a distinctly black musical genre and as helping to free blacks from American standardization.

As the first person to codify and publish blues songs, American musician and composer W. C. Handy (1873–1958) is considered the "Father of the Blues," with such well-known works as "Memphis Blues," "St. Louis Blues," "Beale Street Blues," and "Careless Love."

When did the big band era begin?

On December 1, 1934, Benny Goodman's "Let's Dance" was broadcast on network radio, which effectively launched the swing era, in which big band music achieved huge popularity. Goodman (1909–1986) was a virtuoso clarinetist and bandleader. His jazz-influenced dance band took the lead in making swing the most popular style of the time.

What are some of the great hits of the big band era?

Here are a few great hits of the big band era. This music was extremely popular among young people. Often, their parents and el-

Band leader and clarinetist Benny Goodman was the "King of Swing" in the 1930s and 1940s.

451

ders disapproved! Some memorable songs include "Sing, Sing, Sing" by the Benny Goodman band, "Begin the Beguine" and "Stardust" by the Artie Shaw band, and "Moonlight Serenade," "In the Mood," and "Chattanooga Choo Choo" by the Glenn Miller Orchestra.

There were hundreds of ballrooms around the country that were very popular to young people. The big bands toured constantly. Keep in mind that in the era before electric instruments, it would take a large band to fill a ballroom with a great sound.

How old is country music?

Old-time music or "hillbilly music," both early names for country music, emerged in the early decades of the 1900s. By 1920, the first country music radio stations had opened, and healthy record sales in rural areas caused music industry executives to take notice. But it was an event in 1925, in the middle of the American Jazz Age, that put country music on the map. On November 28, WSM Radio broadcast *The WSM Barn Dance*, which soon became known as *The Grand Ole Opry*, after the master of ceremonies, George D. Hay, took to introducing the program that way—since it was aired immediately after an opera program.

The show's first performer was Uncle Jimmy Thompson (1848–1931). Early favorites included Uncle Dave Macon (1870–1952), who played the banjo and sang, and Roy Acuff (1903–1992), who was the Opry's first singing star. Millions tuned in, and soon, the Nashville-based show had turned Tennessee's capital city into Music City U.S.A. In the 1960s, and again in the late 1980s and 1990s, country music reached the height of popularity while holding on to its small-town, rural-based audience, who were the show's first fans.

Is bluegrass music a distinctly American genre?

Yes, this style of music developed out of country music during the late 1930s and throughout the 1940s. Bill Monroe (1911–1996), a country and bluegrass singer-songwriter, altered the tempo, key, pitch, and instrumentation of traditional country music to create a new style—named for the band that originated it, Bill Monroe and the Blue Grass Boys (Monroe's home state was Kentucky). Bluegrass was first heard by a wide audience when, in October 1939, Monroe and his band appeared on the popular country music radio program *The Grand Ole Opry*.

Radio was key to the development of bluegrass music. Banjo performers who wanted to attract attention by being different innovated new and more complex ways to play the banjo.

How can one learn more about the history of country music?

In 2019, filmmaker Ken Burns (1953–) released an eight-part documentary, *Country Music,* describing the rise and growth of this popular American music.

DANCE

What are some classic ballets?

Three of the best-known classic ballets were written by Pyotr Ilyich Tchaikovsky (1840–1893): *Swan Lake* (1875–1876), *The Sleeping Beauty* (1890), and *The Nutcracker* (1892). Although many ballet fans consider *Swan Lake* one of the most beautiful ballets of all time, when first performed, critics and audiences hated it. Tchaikovsky was too far ahead of his time.

Which Impressionist painter is known for frequently painting ballet dancers?

Edgar Degas (1834–1917) frequently painted ballet dancers. Sometimes, he showed the dancers in performances, but he also painted dancers in rehearsal, often showing the hard work that goes into creating a good performance. (Do an online image search for "Degas ballet paintings.")

Why is the Ballets Russes famous?

The notoriety of the Ballets Russes began on a May night in 1909 when the dance company, created by Russian impresario Sergey Diaghilev (1872–1929), performed innovative ballet choreographed by Michel Fokine (1880–1942). The Parisian audience, made up of the city's elite, was wowed by the choreography, set design, and musical scores as well as the performances of the lead dancers—the athletic vigor of Vaslav Nijinsky, the delicate beauty of Tamara Karsavina, the expressiveness of Anna Pavlova, and the exotic quality of Ida Rubinstein. Ballet had been freed from the constraints and conventions that had held it captive, and the art form was reawakened.

When it comes to ballet, the Ballets Russes was notable for its innovative techniques invented by choreographer Michel Fokine.

The reforms were on every level: choreography, performance, costuming, and design. The company's chief set designer was Léon Bakst (1866–1924), whose sense of color had influenced not only stage designs but even women's fashions. Soon, Diaghilev and the Ballets Russes were at the center of the art world.

Major twentieth-century painters, including Robert Edmond Jones, Pablo Picasso, André Derain, Henri Matisse, and Joan Miró, created set and costume designs for the dance company. And Diaghilev commissioned music that could match the spectacular dancing, choreography, and decor of his ballets. Some of history's most celebrated composers, including Maurice Ravel, Claude Debussy, Richard Strauss, Sergei Prokofiev, and Igor Stravinsky, provided the scores for the dances performed by the Ballets Russes. The company, under Diaghilev's direction, had created a completely different kind of dance drama, bringing ballet out of the shadows of opera and asserting it as an art form unto itself.

The ballet companies of today are the lasting legacy of the Ballets Russes. Diaghilev illustrated that through a collaborative process, excellent art could be created outside the traditional academy. The Ballets Russes provided twentieth-century dance with the model of the touring ballet company and seasonal repertory.

How did modern dance begin?

American dancer and choreographer Martha Graham (1894–1991) is the acknowledged creator of modern dance. The Martha Graham Dance Group made its debut on April 14, 1929, ushering in a new era in dance performance. The new form of dance dissolved the separation between mind and body and relied on technique that was built from within. Graham is credited with revolutionizing dance as an art form; in her hands, it had become nonlinear and nonrepresentational theater. Choreographing some 180 works in her lifetime, she also taught many students who rose to prominence as masterful dancers, including Merce Cunningham and Paul Taylor.

Who was Dame Margot Fonteyn?

Margot Fonteyn (1919–1991) has been called an "international ambassador of dance." The British-trained ballerina achieved worldwide fame and recognition during more than thirty-four years with the Royal Ballet in London, expanding the company's female repertoire and becoming the model for the modern ballerina.

In 1962, at the age of forty-three, Fonteyn formed a dance partnership with Soviet defector Rudolf Nureyev (1938–1993), challenging traditional assumptions about the ability of mature dancers to continue vigorous performance careers. In her later years, she continued to be active in the world of dance, helping set up dance scholarships, fostering international artistic relations, and encouraging the growth of dance institutions around the world.

Who founded the Dance Theater of Harlem?

The Dance Theater of Harlem, the first world-renowned African American ballet company, was founded by Arthur Mitchell (1934–2018), a principal dancer with the New York City Ballet, along with Karel Shook (1920–1985), a dance teacher and former director of the Netherlands Ballet.

The impetus for the creation of the company came on April 4, 1968, while Mitchell was waiting to board a plane from New York City to Brazil (where he was establishing that country's first national ballet company), and he heard that Martin Luther King Jr. (1929–1968) had been assassinated. Mitchell wondered to himself, "Here I am running around the world doing all these things, why not do them at home?"

Mitchell had spent his youth in Harlem, and he felt he should return there to establish a school to pass on his knowledge to others and to give black dancers the opportunity to perform. The primary purpose of the school was "to promote interest in and teach young black people the art of classical ballet, modern and ethnic dance, thereby creating a much-needed self-awareness and better self-image of the students themselves."

The idea was a success. During the 1970s and 1980s, the company toured nationally and internationally, often performing to sellout crowds and participating in prestigious events, including international art festivals, a state dinner at the White House, and the closing ceremonies of the 1984 Olympic Games.

Today, the Dance Theater of Harlem is acknowledged as one of the world's finest ballet companies. Not only did Mitchell succeed in giving black dancers the opportunity to learn and to perform, he effectively erased color barriers in the world of dance, testimony to the universality of classical ballet.

Who was Alvin Ailey?

Alvin Ailey (1931–1989), dancer and choreographer, created the Alvin Ailey American Dance Theater (AAADT) in 1958 to promote the work of young, modern African American dancers. He wanted to use dance to honor black culture.

How long has the waltz been danced?

Considered the quintessential ballroom dance, the waltz first became popular in

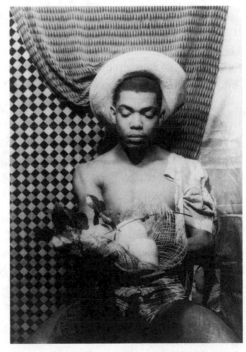

Choreographer, dancer, and activist Alvin Ailey used the dance theater he founded to communicate the African American experience to the world.

Europe in 1813. But it dates as far back as the mid-1700s (the first written use of the word "waltz" was in 1781). In the 1850s, the dance captivated Vienna, and the prolific Johann Strauss (1825–1899), also known as the "Waltz King," produced scores of new waltzes to meet the increasing demand. Many waltzes are written in three-quarter time.

One of the best-known waltzes is "The Blue Danube," first performed in 1867 in Vienna. The new waltz created an immediate sensation.

How did the Charleston get started?

The Charleston, a lively ballroom dance, emerged in 1923 as one of the flashy elements of the period in American history that writer F. Scott Fitzgerald (1896–1940) dubbed the Jazz Age. Other hallmarks of the Jazz Age, also called the Roaring Twenties, were speakeasies (bars where illegal liquor could be purchased during Prohibition), flappers, roadsters, raccoon coats, hedonism, and iconoclasm. The dance was based on the song "The Charleston," composed by pianist James P. Johnson (1894–1955).

THEATER

How old is the dramatic form of tragedy?

Tragedy, a form of drama central to Western literature, dates to ancient times—back to the fifth century B.C.E., when Greeks held a religious festival to honor the god Dionysus (god of fertility, wine, and, later, drama). Famous ancient tragedies include *Oresteia* by Aeschylus (who is credited with inventing tragedy), *Oedipus Rex* by Sophocles, and *Medea* and *Trojan Women* by Euripides.

The philosopher Aristotle observed that tragedy's function is a cathartic one—by participating in the drama, the spectators are purged of their emotions of pity and fear. The well-known Renaissance tragedies of William Shakespeare (1564–1616) hearken back to the works of Roman statesman and playwright Seneca (c. 4 B.C.E.–65 C.E.), who wrote during the first century. Seneca is credited with creating dramatic conventions, including unity of time and place, violence, bombastic language, revenge, and ghostly appearances.

How old is comedy?

Like tragedy, comedy as a form of drama dates to ancient Greece. While tragedy was meant to engage human emotions, thereby cleansing spectators of their fears (according to Aristotle), comedy's intent was simply to entertain and amuse audiences. Athenian poet Aristophanes (c. 446–c. 386 B.C.E.) is considered the greatest ancient writer of comedy. His plays, written for the festival of Dionysus, were a mix of social, political, and literary satire.

Performance vehicles included farce, parody, and fantasy. During the fourth century B.C.E., this old comedy evolved into a new comedy, which was less biting and more romantic and realistic in nature. New comedy, which was marked by strong character development and often subtle humor, includes the works of Greek playwright Menander (c. 342–c. 290 B.C.E.) and those of Roman comic writers Plautus (c. 254–184 B.C.E.) and Terence (c. 195/185–c. 159 B.C.E.), all of whom were influences on Ben Jonson, William Shakespeare, Molière (real name: Jean-Baptiste Poquelin), and other writers of the sixteenth and seventeenth centuries.

What is No drama?

It is the oldest form of traditional Japanese drama, dating to 1383 C.E. It is rooted in the principles of Zen Buddhism, a religion emphasizing meditation, discipline, and the transition of truth from master to disciple. History and legend are the subjects of No plays, which are traditionally performed on a bare, wooden stage by masked, male actors who act out the story using highly controlled movements. The drama is accompanied by a chorus, which chants lines from the play. The art form was pioneered by actor-dramatist Zeami Motokiyo (1363–1443) when he was twenty years old. Zeami had begun acting at age seven and went on to write more than half of the roughly 250 No dramas that are still performed today.

What are the elements of Japanese kabuki theater?

The most popular traditional form of Japanese drama, kabuki, features dance, song, mime, colorful costumes, heavy makeup, and lively, exaggerated movements to tell stories about historical events. The drama had its beginnings in 1575, when Okuni, a woman, founded a kabuki company. In 1603, at Kyoto, women danced at the Kitano shrine, playing men's roles as well as women's. In October 1629, kabuki became an all-male affair by order of the shogun Iemitsu, who decided that it was immoral for women to dance in public.

Just as in Elizabethan England, women's roles were performed by men. The performing art became increasingly popular during the 1600s, eclipsing bunraku (puppet theater), in which a narrator recites a story, which is acted by large, life-like puppets. Today, kabuki remains a viable art form, borrowing from other forms of drama to adapt to changing times.

What is a passion play?

A passion play is a dramatization of the scenes connected with the Passion and Crucifixion of Jesus Christ. The roots of the passion play can be traced to ancient

Dating back to the late sixteenth century, kabuki theater is a form of Japanese drama and dance that emphasizes colorful costumes, makeup, dance, song, and mime.

times. Early Egyptians performed plays dedicated to the god Osiris (god of the Underworld and judge of the dead), and the Greeks also acted out plays to honor their god Dionysus. During the Middle Ages, liturgical dramas were performed. Toward the end of the tenth century, the Western church began to dramatize parts of the Latin Mass, especially for holidays such as Easter. These plays were performed in Latin by the clergy inside the church building. Eventually, the performances became more secular, with laymen acting out the parts on the steps of the church or even in marketplaces.

The liturgical dramas developed into so-called miracle plays or mystery plays. As a symbol of gratitude or as a request for a favor, villagers would stage the life story of the Virgin Mary or of a patron saint. When the plague (also called the Black Death) ravaged Europe, the villagers at Oberammergau, Germany, in the Bavarian Alps, vowed to enact a passion play at regular intervals in the hope that by so doing, they would be spared the Black Death. They first performed this folk drama in 1634 and have continued to stage it every ten years—with a cast of 2,000—attracting numerous tourists to the small town in southern Germany.

In the United States, the Christ of the Ozarks statue in Eureka Springs, Arkansas, reaches 65.5 feet. (The Ozarks is the region of southern Missouri and northern Arkansas.) The grounds of the statue are the site of *The Great Passion Play*, which is an outdoor production of the story of the Crucifixion and Resurrection of Jesus.

What was vaudeville?

Light, comical theatrical entertainment, vaudeville flourished at the end of the nineteenth century and beginning of the twentieth century. Programs combined a variety of music, theater, and comedy to appeal to a wide audience. Scriptwriters attracted immigrant audiences by using ethnic humor, exaggerating dialects, and joking about the difficulties of daily immigrant life in America.

Vaudeville made its way to the American stage by the 1870s, when acts performed in theaters in New York, Chicago, and other cities. Troupes traveled a circuit of nearly 1,000 theaters around the country. As many as two million Americans a day flocked to the shows to see headliners such as comedians Eddie Cantor (1892–1964) and W. C. Fields (1880–1946), singer Eva Tanguay (1878–1947), and French actress Sarah Bernhardt (1844–1923).

During the first two decades of the twentieth century, vaudeville was the most popular form of entertainment in the country. In the 1930s, just as New York opened the doors of its famous Radio City Music Hall, intended to be a theater for vaudeville, the entertainment form began a quick decline. Motion pictures, radio, and, later, television took its place, with numerous vaudeville performers parlaying their success into these new media. Among those entertainers who had their origins in vaudeville were actors Rudolph Valentino, Cary Grant, Mae West, Jack Benny, George Burns, Gracie Allen, Ginger Rogers, Fred Astaire, Will Rogers, and Al Jolson.

Why is the Globe Theatre famous?

The Globe is well known because of William Shakespeare's (1564–1616) involvement in it. In the 1590s, an outbreak of the plague prompted authorities to close London theaters. At the time, Shakespeare was a member of the Lord Chamberlain's Men, an acting company. With other members of the troupe, he helped finance the building of the Globe (on the banks of the Thames River), which opened in 1599 as a summer playhouse.

Plays at the Globe, then outside of London proper, drew good crowds, and the Lord Chamberlain's Men also gave numerous command performances at court for King James. By the turn of the century, Shakespeare was considered London's most popular playwright, and by 1603, the acting group, whose summer home was the Globe Theatre, was known as the King's Men.

A reproduction built near the original location, called Shakespeare's Globe, presents the bard's plays today. (See the "Expressions of Human Culture" chapter for more on Shakespeare's works.)

What are some of the most popular and important musicals?

Hundreds of great musicals have made it to Broadway and, later, most became films. Here are ten great musicals. (There are many more great musicals! People of different ages might come up with different lists for their picks of the Ten Best.)

In 1997, a faithful reconstruction of Shakespeare's Globe Theatre opened to the public in London, England.

Show Boat (1927)

This musical, based on the book by Edna Ferber, played a key role in the development of musical theater, where the music and dialogue work together to create a unified story. Jerome Kern (1885–1945) wrote the music, and Oscar Hammerstein II (1895–1960) wrote the lyrics and the book (the script for the play). The show included the songs "Ol' Man River" and "Can't Help Lovin' Dat Man."

Oklahoma! (1943)

This innovative musical is important for being an early "book musical," in which the songs and dance numbers are fully integrated into the plot and help move the plot along. (In older musicals, the songs and dance numbers often felt stuck into a weak storyline.)

My Fair Lady (1956)

Based on George Bernard Shaw's play *Pygmalion,* Frederick Loewe (1901–1988) wrote the music, and Alan Jay Lerner (1918–1986) wrote the book and lyrics for this classic musical. Rex Harrison (1908–1990) starred as Henry Higgins, and Julie Andrews (1935–) played Eliza Doolittle. This was the first of many big Broadway and film roles for Andrews.

West Side Story (1957)

Set in modern New York, this show, with music written by Leonard Bernstein (1918–1990) and lyrics written by Stephen Sondheim (1930–), retells the story of Romeo and Juliet. Jerome Robbins (1918–1998) did the innovative choreography.

Fiddler on the Roof (1964)

This popular show tells the story of a Jewish family in Russia. Jerry Bock (1928–2010) wrote the music, Sheldon Harnick (1924–) the lyrics, and Joseph Stein (1912–2010) the book. Popular songs include "Tradition," "If I Were a Rich Man," and "Sunrise, Sunset."

The 2019 documentary *Fiddler: A Miracle of Miracles* describes the creation of this famous musical and 1971 film version.

A Chorus Line (1975)

Over the decades, a number of musicals were based on the plot device where a chorus girl gets a lucky break to fill in for the star of the show. The chorus girl then goes on to become famous.

With music by Marvin Hamlisch (1944–2012) and lyrics by Edward Kleban (1939–1987), this musical goes into the realities of being in a chorus line and shows the real-life struggles of the dancers.

Into the Woods (1987)

With music and lyrics by Stephen Sondheim and book by James Lapine (1949–), this musical does a retelling of classic fairy tales.

The Phantom of the Opera (1988)

Andrew Lloyd Webber (1948–) wrote the music to this version of the classic story. He also had a number of other musical hits:

Joseph and the Amazing Technicolor Dreamcoat (1968)

Jesus Christ Superstar (1971)

Evita (1979)

For these three musicals, Tim Rice (1944–) wrote the lyrics.

Lloyd Webber also wrote the popular musical *Cats* (1982).

Big-budget, blockbuster musicals, such as Andrew Lloyd Webber's *The Phantom of the Opera,* have been keeping American musical theater popular for the last several decades.

Lion King (1997)

With music by Elton John (1947–) and lyrics by Tim Rice, this musical, based on the Disney movie, has been the highest-grossing Broadway musical in history.

Mamma Mia (2001)

This musical is built on the hit songs of the famous Swedish pop group ABBA and includes "Super Trouper," "Take a Chance on Me," "Money, Money, Money," "The Winner Takes It All," "SOS," and, of course, "Mamma Mia."

RECENT COMPOSERS

What is the famous music piece called *4'33"*?

This is an experimental piece written by John Cage (1912–1992). It can be performed by any combinations of instruments because the musicians do not play anything; they sit quietly for four minutes and thirty-three seconds. The music of the piece is the sounds the listeners hear in the quiet performance space.

Who is Arvo Pärt?

Arvo Pärt (1935–) is a minimalist composer who has created both classical and religious music. His music often has a haunting quality. His most famous works are *Für Alina* (1976), *Fratres* (1977), and *Spiegel im Spiegel* (1978).

Who is Philip Glass?

Philip Glass (1937–) is also known for writing music in a minimalistic style. His music often sounds very repetitive, with small shifts in the music tones. He has written numerous pieces, including *Glassworks, North Star,* and scores for such experimental movies as *Koyaanisqatsi* (1882), *Powaqqatsi* (1988), and *Naqoyqatsi* (2002).

461

Who is John Adams?

John Adams (1947–) is known for his numerous compositions, including *Shaker Loops* (1978) and *Short Ride in a Fast Machine* (1986). His operas include *Nixon in China* (1987), about President Nixon's visit to China in 1972, and *The Death of Klinghoffer* (1991), about the 1985 hijacking of the passenger ship *Achille Lauro* and the murder of one of its passengers, Leon Klinghoffer.

EXPRESSIONS OF HUMAN CULTURE

WRITTEN LANGUAGE

When did people begin to write?

The oldest writing systems are the ancient Sumerian cuneiform script and Egyptian hieroglyphics that emerged around 3000 B.C.E.

The Sumerians lived in Mesopotamia (present-day Iraq), the valley between the Tigris and Euphrates rivers. Their writing was done on clay tablets that were later fired so they would not again become clay if they became wet. The Sumerians used a pointed stick to make wedge-shaped marks and lines in the clay to represent letters.

Although Egyptian hieroglyphic letters look like actual objects, such as animals, body parts, and ordinary items, the letters are not pictographs, where the foot symbol represents a foot. Rather, the symbols represent sounds. A foot is the *B* sound, a hand is the *D* sound, and an owl is the *M* sound.

When was the first alphabet created?

The earliest form of an alphabet was developed between 1800 and 1000 B.C.E. by a Semitic people of unknown identity. The alphabet consisted of twenty-two characters representing only consonants; the reader had to supply the vowels from his or her knowledge of the language. The first character in the alphabet was "aleph," and the second was "beth." The English word "alphabet" would come from these characters. This early Semitic alphabet would influence the Phoenician alphabet, which would in turn influence the later Greek alphabet and eventually the modern English alphabet.

How was paper invented?

The oldest writing surfaces in existence include Babylonian clay tablets and Indian palm leaves. Around 3000 B.C.E., the Egyptians developed a writing material using papyrus, the plant for which paper is named. Early in the Roman Empire, the long manuscript scrolls that were made of fragile papyrus and used by Egyptians, Greeks, and Romans were replaced by the codex, separate pages bound together at one side and having a cover (like the modern book). Eventually, papyrus was replaced by vellum (made of a fine-grain lambskin, kidskin, or calfskin) and parchment (made of sheepskin or goatskin), both of which provided superior surfaces for writing.

The wood-derived paper we know today was developed in 105 C.E. by the Chinese, who devised a way to make tree bark, hemp, rags, and fishnets into paper. The process used contained the basic elements that are still found in paper mills today. The Moors introduced papermaking to Europe (Spain) in about 1150; by the 1400s, paper was being made throughout Europe. But it was not until the late 1700s that paper was produced in continuous rolls. In 1798, a French paper mill clerk invented a machine that could produce a continuous sheet of paper in any desired size from wood pulp. The machine was improved and patented by English papermakers Henry (1766–1854) and Sealy (1773–1847) Fourdrinier in 1807. The invention spurred the development of newspapers.

What is the oldest-known book?

It was the *Diamond Sutra*, published in the year 868 C.E. Archeologists discovered it in the Caves of the Thousand Buddhas in Kansu (Ganzu), China.

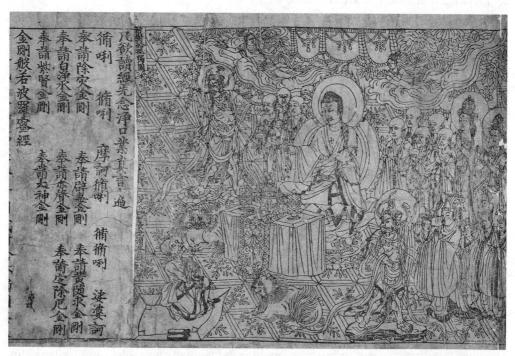

A frontispiece printed in 868 C.E. during the Tang dynasty is an example of some of the earliest sophisticated printing from ancient China.

Who developed printing?

If printing is defined as the process of transferring repeatable designs onto a surface, then the first known printing was done by the Mesopotamians, who as early as 3000 B.C.E. used stamps to impress designs onto wet clay.

Printing on paper developed much later; Chinese inventor Cai Lun (c. 48–121 C.E.) is credited with producing the first examples. During the Tang dynasty (618–906 C.E.), Chinese books were printed with inked woodblocks, and it was the Chinese—not German printer Johannes Gutenberg, as is widely believed—who developed movable type, allowing printers to compose a master page from permanent, raised characters. However, movable-type printing did not catch on in medieval China because the Chinese language has some 80,000 characters; printers found it more convenient to use carved blocks.

What are illuminated manuscripts?

These are books, written by hand, that include colorful paintings and decorations. The word "manuscript" means "written by hand," from the Latin words for hand, *manus,* and *scriber,* "to write." The books were hand copied and typically written on vellum, which is a prepared animal skin. (Do an online search for "illuminated manuscripts.")

When was the first newspaper published?

Newspapers, publications that are issued daily or weekly to notify readers of current events, had their first recorded appearance around 59 B.C.E., when Romans posted a daily handwritten news report in public places (called the *Acta Diurna,* or "Daily Events"). On around 700 C.E., the Chinese developed the world's first printed newspaper, called the *Dibao*; it was printed from carved wooden blocks.

The invention of the movable-type printing press (c. 1450) spurred the development of the newspaper as we know it. In Germany, regularly published newspapers began being circulated in the early 1600s. Newspapers proliferated in the 1800s after the development of a machine that allowed paper to be produced in sheets of any size.

Why is Gutenberg considered the pioneer of modern printing?

Johannes Gutenberg (c. 1400–1468), a German who built his first printing press around 1450, is considered the inventor of

German blacksmith, inventor, and publisher Johannes Gutenberg introduced the printing press to Europe in the fifteenth century.

a lasting system of movable-type printing. He created the first printed Bible, the *Gutenberg Bible*, which is in Latin.

Gutenberg invented a workable system of movable type. Before this, printing a page of text required carving out a wooden board of text for each page, which was impractical. Gutenberg built a wooden frame that held individual metal letters that could be arranged to print a page of text. The letters could be reused by rearranging them for the next page to print.

Eventually, the metal letters were stored on boxes, called cases, with the capital letters in the upper cases and the small letters in the lower cases. From this come the terms "uppercase" and "lowercase" letters.

What were penny newspapers?

The labor-saving machinery developed during the Industrial Revolution was instrumental in lowering the cost of printing newspaper and, hence, the cost of buying a newspaper. The first so-called penny newspaper (or one-cent paper), the daily *New York Sun*, was published by Benjamin Day (1810–1889) in 1833. The American newspaper industry was off and running.

Now reaching a mass audience, publishers worked feverishly to outdo each other to keep their readers. By the late 1800s, news reporting had become increasingly sensationalistic. Population growth, spurred by waves of immigrants, meant there were plenty of readers for the now thousands of newspapers. During the first decade of the 1900s, the number of American newspapers peaked at about 2,600 dailies and 14,000 weeklies.

What is the importance of newspapers?

Today, in the age of the Internet, TV news, radio news, and cable news, it is hard for many to understand the importance of newspapers. However, imagine a time before radio. How would you get current news? Printed newspapers would have the most current news. The telegraph would provide the latest information to be printed in the papers. Big cities often had several competing newspapers. When important breaking news came out after the regular daily edition, a special "EXTRA" edition would be created and newsboys on the streets would sell it, calling out, "Extra! Extra! Read all about it!"

Although customers paid money to buy a newspaper, sales money was never enough to run a newspaper, so newspapers sold lots of advertising to be printed in the newspaper. Also, customers had to pay to put items in the paper, such as "Help Wanted" ads or notices to sell houses or cars. As radio and television came along, newspapers were still very popular because they had so much more depth and detail.

However, the arrival of the Internet had a devastating impact on printed newspapers. Suddenly, newspapers had immense competition as people went online to get their news. And often, people could get the latest news online before it could be printed. But more importantly, most of the advertising money that had supported newspapers went to the Internet, causing many papers to close. Now, job openings could be posted online. Items

> ## What muckraker's book led to the passage of federal laws regarding food safety?
>
> Upton Sinclair (1878–1968) wrote a muckraking novel entitled *The Jungle* that depicted unsanitary conditions in the meatpacking industry in Chicago. The novel touched off a maelstrom of public outcry over unsafe food-handling practices and conditions at meatpacking plants. This led to the passage of the Food and Drug Act and the Meat Inspection Act in 1906.

for sale could be put online for free and reach a much bigger audience. The result was that newspapers have been hurting. Those that survive often struggle to raise enough money to keep going.

What is muckraking journalism?

Muckrakers are journalists who seek out and expose the misconduct of prominent people or of high-profile organizations; they emerged on the American scene in the late 1800s and early 1900s. Crusaders for social change, muckraking journalists wrote articles not about news events but about injustices or abuses, bringing them to the attention of the American public. Published in newspapers and magazines, the articles exposed corruption in business and politics.

While the early muckrakers were sometimes criticized for their tactics, their work succeeded in raising widespread awareness of social, economic, and political ills, thus prompting a number of reforms, including passage of pure food laws and antitrust legislation. American politician Theodore Roosevelt (1858–1919) dubbed the controversial journalists "muckrakers," a reference to a character in *Pilgrim's Progress* (by English preacher John Bunyan [1628–1688]) who rejects a crown for a muckrake, a tool used to rake dung.

What recent movie illustrates the importance of an independent press doing investigative journalism?

The 2015 film *Spotlight* tells the true story of newspaper reporters for the *Boston Globe* who investigated the extent of sexual abuse by Catholic priests in Boston and the cover-up of the abuse by church officials. The film starred Mark Ruffalo (1967–), Michael Keaton (1951–), and Rachel McAdams (1978–). The film's title comes from the *Globe*'s "Spotlight" investigative team. *Spotlight* won Academy Awards for Best Picture and Best Screenplay.

Far less well known is the earlier reporting of the sex-abuse crisis by the *National Catholic Reporter*. The *NCR* is an independent, national newspaper and not an official publication of the Catholic Church. The paper started writing about the sex-abuse crisis ten years before the *Globe* picked up the story.

EDUCATION

When were the first schools established?

The first formal education began shortly after the development of writing (c. 3000 B.C.E.), when both the Sumerians (who had developed cuneiform writing) and the Egyptians (who developed hieroglyphics) established schools to teach students to read and write. The first school that was open to everyone, not just the upper classes, may well have been that established by Chinese philosopher Confucius (Kung Fu Tzu, 551–479 B.C.E.), who taught literature, music, conduct, and ethics to anyone who wanted to learn.

The western model of education is based on the ancient Greek schools, which were founded around the fifth century B.C.E. In the city-state of Sparta, boys were not only trained for the military, they also learned reading and writing and studied music. In Athens, boys learned to read and write, memorized poetry, learned music, and were trained in athletics. In the second half of the fifth century B.C.E., the Sophists (ancient Greek teachers of rhetoric and philosophy) schooled young men in the social and political arts, hoping to mold them into ideal statesmen.

How old is the concept of public schools?

It dates at least as far back as ancient China. The philosopher Confucius was among the first in China to advocate that education should be available to all, stating, "In education, there should be no class distinctions." He never refused a student, "even though he came to me on foot, with nothing more to offer as tuition than a package of dried meat." Confucius asserted that any man—including a "peasant boy"—had the potential to be a man of principle.

However, it was not until the Age of Enlightenment that public schools were widely instituted. In Prussia (present-day Germany), Frederick the Great (1712–1786) was considered an enlightened ruler for starting a public education system. In time, other European countries began instituting systems of public education as they realized that it had been an important factor in Prussia's rise. By the early twentieth century, public elementary schooling was both free and compulsory in most of Europe. Free secondary education was also offered in some nations.

A statue of Jean-Baptiste de la Salle in Paris, France.

In the United States, public schools began during colonial times; in 1647, Massachusetts passed a law requiring the establishment of public schools.

Who was Jean-Baptiste de la Salle?

De la Salle was recognized as a Roman Catholic saint in 1900. However, his influence on education is so important that he should be better known to all people. Jean-Baptiste de la Salle (1651–1719) was a French priest and pioneer in education. He started the first Catholic schools and organized the Institute of the Brothers of the Christian Schools to help support and train teachers. His group is often called the Christian Brothers.

In a time when most people received no education, de la Salle called for universal free education. He saw the importance of educating children of all classes, particularly the poor. Although he experienced great resistance, he organized his own schools where he stopped the teaching of Latin, replacing it with the language of his students. He saw reading as an essential skill and stressed learning practical skills, along with religious instruction. He set up students in classes according to their ability, not age. He also set up Sunday schools for adults, so they, too, could be educated.

When was the first kindergarten?

The world's first kindergarten opened in 1837 in Blankenburg, Germany, under the direction of educator Friedrich Fröbel (1782–1852). Fröbel went on to establish a training course for kindergarten teachers, and he introduced the schools throughout Germany. Such schools and classes, for children ages four to six, are the norm today in much of the world.

The first kindergarten in the United States was started in 1873 by Susan Blow (1843–1916) in the St. Louis, Missouri, neighborhood of Carondelet. She had been influenced by the work of Fröbel.

How did Montessori schools get started?

The schools, found throughout the world, carry the name of their founder, Maria Montessori (1870–1952). She was the first woman in Italy to earn a medical degree and to practice medicine. In 1900, Montessori pioneered teaching methods to develop sensory, motor, and intellectual skills in intellectually disabled kindergarten and primary school students. Under her direction, these "unteachable" pupils not only mastered basic skills, including reading and writing, but they passed the same examinations given to all primary school students in Italy.

Montessori then spent time in the country's primary schools, where she observed the educators' practice of teaching by rote (by using repetition and memory) and their reliance on restraint, silence, and a system of reward and punishment in the classroom. She believed her system, called "scientific pedagogy," which was based on noncoercive methods and self-correcting materials (such as blocks, graduated cylinders, scaled bells, and color spectrums), would yield better results in students. Montessori theorized that children possess a natural desire to learn and, if put in a prepared environment, their "spontaneous activity" would prove educational.

Instead of lecturing to their students, Montessori encouraged educators to simply demonstrate the correct use of materials to students who would then teach themselves and each other. She also believed in community involvement in schools, encouraging parents and other community members to take active roles in the education of the children. When Montessori put these principles into action, she saw highly favorable results.

In 1909, Montessori published *The Montessori Method*, which was made available in English three years later and became an instant best-seller in the United States. Her method, which she believed "would develop and set free a child's personality in a marvelous and surprising way," caught on. For Montessori, who has

Maria Montessori spent her life bucking trends, becoming a physician in an age where women were discouraged from pursuing medical degrees and establishing unique teaching methods in the schools named after her.

been called a "triumph of self-discipline, persistence, and courage," spreading the message about her teaching method became her life's work. She was still traveling, and speaking to enthusiastic crowds the world over, when she died in the Netherlands at the age of eighty-one.

Montessori's beliefs—which were both scientific and spiritual—had a profound effect not only on students in Montessori schools but also on primary education in general. Currently, there are about 20,000 Montessori schools worldwide, 4,500 of which are in the United States.

How has the U.S. separation of church and state affected public schools?

Religion in American public schools continued to be a hot topic throughout the 1900s. But the U.S. Supreme Court rulings in the middle of the twentieth century proved to have the most bearing on religious practices in state-supported schools. On June 17, 1963, in an 8–1 ruling, the Supreme Court decided that prayer and Bible reading in U.S. public schools were unconstitutional, as they violated the Establishment Clause.

The Establishment Clause of the First Amendment provides that "Congress shall make no law establishing religion." It has been interpreted to mean there needs to be separation between church and state.

The Supreme Court first invalidated school-sponsored prayer in public schools in *Engel v. Vitale* (1962) in a 6–1 decision (two justices did not participate). It followed that up the next year with an 8–1 decision in *Abington School District v. Schempp*. These rulings firmly established that public school officials cannot lead students in prayer. Both decisions trace their interpretation of the Establishment Clause to an earlier decision, *Everson v. Board of Education* (1947), in which the court (in a 5–4 vote) defended the use of state funds to transport children to parochial schools but warned that "a wall of separation between church and state" must be maintained.

In later decisions, the Supreme Court invalidated an Alabama moment-of-silence law intended to bring prayer back into school in *Wallace v. Jaffree* (1985), a middle-school graduation prayer in *Lee v. Weisman* (1992), and the practice of announcing prayers over the loudspeakers at Texas high school football games in *Santa Fe Independent School District v. Doe* (2000).

These rulings are still controversial to many Americans—and even some dissenting justices. Chief Justice William Rehnquist, one of the three dissenters in the *Doe* case, wrote that the majority decision "bristles with hostility to all things religious in public life."

When was the first university established in the West?

The first Western university was established in the Middle Ages in 1158 in Bologna, Italy. Other universities were soon created. The universities in Europe at that time were not places or groups of buildings. They were more often groups of scholars and students. The University of Paris, which today includes the renowned Sorbonne, soon became the largest and most famous university in Europe. The Sorbonne was founded in 1250 as a school of theology.

By 1500, universities had been founded throughout the continent. Many of these are still around, such as Cambridge and Oxford in England; those at Montpellier, Paris, and Toulouse in France; Heidelberg in Germany; Bologna, Florence, Naples, Padua, Rome, and Siena in Italy; and Salamanca in Spain. The methods and techniques developed in these early institutions set standards of academic inquiry that remain part of higher education in the world today.

What was the first university in the Western Hemisphere?

It was the University of Santo Domingo, founded in 1538 by the Spaniards in the Dominican Republic (which occupies the eastern half of the Caribbean island of Hispaniola).

What was the first American university?

Harvard University was established in 1636, to be built in New Towne, Massachusetts; however, the town was renamed Cambridge after England's Cambridge University. The university was named for a colonial clergyman, John Harvard (1607–1638), who left the library some 400 volumes and donated about 800 pounds sterling to the college.

The oldest university in the United States is Harvard University, which was established in 1636 by clergyman John Harvard in what is now Cambridge, Massachusetts.

What other educational firsts are notable in the American colonies and early United States?

Harvard University (founded 1636) claims to be the oldest institution of higher education.

The University of Pennsylvania (1740) claims to be America's first university.

The College of William and Mary (1779) claims to be the first college to become a university.

Georgetown University (1789), founded by the Society of Jesus (Jesuits), claims to be the first Catholic higher education institution.

The University of North Carolina at Chapel Hill (1795) claims to be the first state university.

Johns Hopkins University (1876) claims to be America's first research university.

What are the Ivy League colleges?

The Ivy League colleges are:

- Brown University—Providence, Rhode Island
- Columbia University—New York City
- Cornell University—Ithaca, New York
- Dartmouth College—Hanover, New Hampshire
- Harvard University—Cambridge, Massachusetts
- Princeton University—Princeton, New Jersey
- University of Pennsylvania—Philadelphia, Pennsylvania
- Yale University—New Haven, Connecticut

Interestingly, Harvard, Princeton, and Yale were all originally created to train Christian ministers.

What was the lyceum movement?

The lyceum movement was a public-education program that began in the 1820s and is credited with promoting the establishment of public schools, libraries, and museums in the United States. The idea was conceived by Yale-educated teacher and lecturer Josiah

Holbrook (1788–1854), who in 1826 set up the first "American Lyceum" in Millbury, Massachusetts. He named the program for a gymnasium dedicated to Apollo Lyceus—where the ancient Greek philosopher Aristotle (384–322 B.C.E.) taught.

The lyceums, which were programs of regularly occurring lectures, proved to be the right idea at the right time. They got underway just after the completion of the Erie Canal (1825), which connected the harbor at New York to the Great Lakes, opening settlement and shipping to and from the nation's interior, and just as the notion that universal, free education was imperative to the preservation of American democracy took hold. The movement spread quickly.

At first, the lectures were home-grown affairs, featuring local speakers. But as the movement grew, lyceum bureaus were organized, which sent paid lecturers traveling around the country. The lyceum speakers included such noted Americans as writers Ralph Waldo Emerson (1803–1882), Henry David Thoreau (1817–1862), and Nathaniel Hawthorne (1804–1864) as well as activist Susan B. Anthony (1820–1906). After the Civil War (1861–1865), the educational role of the lyceum movement was taken over by the Protestant-led chautauquas. Today, in many old, small towns across America, lyceum halls and theaters still stand.

What was the Chautauqua movement?

The Chautauqua movement was a cultural, religious, and political education movement that began in the 1870s and lasted into the 1920s. An estimated forty-five million Americans participated in the movement, making it a dominant force in American life during its day. Some scholars credit the Chautauqua movement with sowing the seeds of progressive thought in America.

The movement began in 1874 at a Methodist Episcopal campsite on the shores of Lake Chautauqua, New York. ("Chautauqua" was the Native American name for the area.) A young minister, John H. Vincent (1932–1920), wanted to train Sunday school teachers in a summer camp atmosphere. His program grew in popularity and was expanded beyond Bible study and religious training to include lessons in literacy, history, and sociology. Chautauqua-style summer camps, commonly called Sunday school assemblies, began popping up across the nation; all of them featured a general meeting hall or pavilion set in a campground.

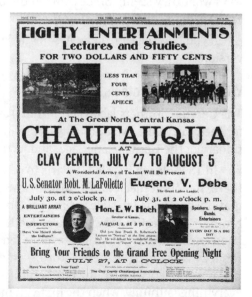

A 1906 advertisement for a Chautauqua gathering in Kansas features a guest lecture from political activist and trade unionist Eugene V. Debs.

473

By 1900, there were 200 pavilions in thirty-one states. Attendees of all ages would attend the summer programs, which featured speakers on a wide variety of subjects, including the arts, travel, and politics. Performances also became part of the movement, with a variety of musicians and entertainers joining the lecturers.

Early in the twentieth century, the Chautauqua movement became less religious. Speakers and performers traveled from town to town, where tents were set up for weeks at a time to house the summer programs. Many Americans saw their first movies in Chautauqua tents. The movement died out in the mid-1920s with the improvement of communication and transportation. Some consider the Chautauqua movement the first form of American mass culture. The Chautauqua Institution in New York State continues to host a summer education program in the spirit of the original.

FOLKTALES

What are Aesop's fables?

The stories date back to the sixth century B.C.E. However, it was not until 1692 that a complete English translation of the stories, which are believed to have been written by a Greek slave, were published in London by Sir Roger L'Estrange (1616–1704). The short, moralistic tales, which were handed down through the oral tradition, include the well-known story of the tortoise and the hare (which teaches the lesson that slow and steady wins the race) and the fable about a wolf in sheep's clothing (people are not always what they seem). Since some of the timeless fables have been traced to earlier literature, many believe it is almost certain that Aesop is a legendary figure.

If you have never read an Aesop's fable, go online and read one or listen to an audio version.

Who were the Brothers Grimm?

The German brothers Jacob (1785–1863) and Wilhelm (1786–1859) Grimm, best known for their fairy tales, were actually librarians and professors who studied law, wrote a dictionary of the German language, and lectured at universities.

In 1805, Jacob traveled to Paris to conduct research on Roman law, and, in a library there, he found medieval German manuscripts of old stories that were slowly disintegrating; he decided the tales were too valuable to lose, and he vowed to collect them. The brothers' interest in fairy tales also led them to search for old traditions, legends, and tales, especially those meant for children. They traveled the German countryside, interviewing villagers to gather stories—most of which were from the oral tradition and had never been written down. The brothers were diligent in their efforts, recording everything faithfully. When the first volume of *Kinder- und Hausmärchen* (which translates as the "Children's Household Tales," but it was known better as *Grimm's Fairy Tales*) was published in 1812, children loved it.

Subsequent volumes were published in German through 1815. The fairy tales collected in the multivolume work included such classics as "The History of Tom Thumb," "Little Red Riding Hood," "Bluebeard," "Puss in Boots," "Snow White and the Seven Dwarfs," "Goldilocks and the Three Bears," "The Princess and the Pea," "The Sleeping Beauty in the Wood," and "Cinderella." Walt Disney would create many movies based on fairy tales, including many stories from the Brothers Grimm.

LITERATURE

What are the *Iliad* and the *Odyssey*?

The two greatest pieces of ancient Greek literature are the *Iliad* and the *Odyssey*. Often, the ancient figure of Homer is identified as the author. However, this cannot be proved, and, making things worse, there are differences in the two writings, causing scholars to think that several authors may have written them. The issue of the role of Homer in these works is called "the Homeric question."

Possibly, Homer, who lived around 800 B.C.E., was a traveling bard or poet who told stories for a living. According to some legends, he was blind. Did he make up the stories that were later written down? Or did he pass along existing oral stories that had been developed by others over a long period of time? Is it possible that the stories were sung to the music of a lyre?

Both stories are set in the Trojan War era. The *Iliad* takes place in the tenth year of the war, and it revolves around a dispute between the Greek king Agamemnon and the Greek warrior Achilles. The *Odyssey* is after the Trojan War and describes the adventures and tribulations of the Greek warrior Odysseus as he tries to get home.

What is the *Aeneid*?

The *Aeneid* was written by Virgil (70–19 B.C.E.), considered to be the greatest Roman poet. The *Aeneid* tells the story of the Trojan hero Aeneas, who escapes from the city of Troy as it is being destroyed by the Greeks in the Trojan War. Aeneas and his followers board ships and sail away to experience many adventures. Aeneas is destined to found a new city, which turns out to be Rome on the Tiber River. In the story, Aeneas and his men wind up visiting some of the same places visited by Odysseus (Ulysses in Latin). Virgil was, in

A mosaic of Virgil from the third century in what is now Sousse, Tunisia (formerly Hadrumetum during the Roman period). Virgil was highly regarded by the Romans for writing the *Aeneid*.

fact, writing a sequel to the *Odyssey*, and, like any good sequel, much of what happens is similar to what happened in the original.

The *Aeneid* was also political propaganda in that it tied the origins of Rome and the line of Roman rulers back to the heroic times of the Trojan War and to the line of Aeneas, who was no mere human. Aeneas was the son of Trojan prince Anchises and the goddess Venus (Aphrodite to the Greeks).

Why is *Beowulf* considered an important work?

Beowulf is the oldest surviving epic poem in English or any other European language. It was written in Old English (the language of the Anglo-Saxons in England) around 1000 C.E., although its author is unknown. *Beowulf* tells the story of a Scandinavian warrior hero who, on behalf of the Danish king, fights and kills the fearsome monster Grendel, then slays the monster's mother, and finally engages a fire-breathing dragon in mortal combat. (This a great story worth reading in a modern English version.)

What is the famous book about the afterlife written by Dante?

In *The Divine Comedy*, Italian writer Dante Alighieri (1265–1321) describes the medieval view of the afterlife. The word "comedy" does not mean it is a humorous story but rather that it has a happy ending. *The Divine Comedy* is a poem made up of 100 parts called "cantos" divided into three sections: *The Inferno* (*Hell*), *Purgatorio* (*Purgatory*), and *Paradiso* (*Paradise*).

In the poem, Dante is led through Hell and Purgatory by Roman writer Virgil. Beatrice, Dante's image of the ideal woman, leads him through Paradise.

Dante's masterpiece is considered the seminal work of Italian literature. At the time that he wrote *The Divine Comedy*, Latin was the undisputed language of science and literature. Italian, on the other hand, was considered vulgar. By skillfully writing this poem in the vernacular (Tuscan Italian) rather than Latin, Dante parted from tradition, marking a critical development for vernacular writing.

What are *The Canterbury Tales*?

The Canterbury Tales were written by Geoffrey Chaucer (1343–1400) between 1387 and 1400. The book is a collection of stories told by pilgrims on their way to the shrine of Thomas Becket in Canterbury, England. *The Canterbury Tales* give a window into the late medieval feudal world. A number of the characters are religious figures, such as the Parson, the Monk, the Friar, the Pardoner, the Summoner, nuns, priests, and the Prioress (a woman in charge of a convent). The characters are all introduced in the Prologue.

Chaucer did not write about ideal models of these various religious roles. Rather, he describes monks and friars who are ignoring the precepts of their religious orders. Chaucer does this because they make more interesting characters. A monk or friar who followed the rules and spent all his time praying would actually be quite boring.

Some of the more popular tales are "The Miller's Tale," "The Reeve's Tale," "The Wife of Bath's Tale," and "The Pardoner's Tale." Although Chaucer wrote *The Canterbury Tales* in English, he used a much older form of English that modern readers find difficult to read. Chaucer also wrote in verse style. So, rather than read the original, most readers today prefer a prose version in modern English. (Verse is short lines, such as in a poem. Prose is in the form of paragraphs.)

Why is William Shakespeare so important?

William Shakespeare (1564–1616) was an English poet, playwright, and actor who is seen by many as the world's greatest writer of plays and the greatest writer of English. No other writer's plays have been produced so often or read so widely in so many countries. Shakespeare's plays are categorized as comedies, histories, and tragedies.

Over four hundred years after his death in 1616, William Shakespeare is still considered the finest playwright and poet England ever produced.

What musical was inspired by Shakespeare's play *Romeo and Juliet*?

Inspired by the story, American composer Leonard Bernstein (1918–1990) wrote the music and Stephen Sondheim (1930–) the lyrics for *West Side Story*, set in New York City. It became a popular hit on Broadway and then a popular movie. In *Romeo and Juliet*, the lovers are separated by two feuding families. In *West Side Story*, the lovers are separated because of two feuding gangs—the Jets and the Sharks. *West Side Story* has many memorable songs, including "Maria," "Tonight," "Somewhere," and "One Hand, One Heart." Directed and choreographed by Jerome Robbins (1918–1998), the show is notable for how dancing is so integrated into the story.

Why is Milton important to English literature?

Except for Shakespeare, the works of John Milton (1608–1674) have been the subject of more commentary than those of any other English writer. Milton is considered one of only a few writers to take their place in "the small circle of great epic writers." For example, in his masterpiece *Paradise Lost* (1667), Milton, like poets Homer and Virgil before him, takes on humankind's entire experience—war, love, religion, hell, heaven, and the cosmos. But rather than having Adam triumph over evil through an act of heroism, he "accepts the burden of worldly existence, and triumphs over his guilt by admitting it and repenting it."

477

Milton's writings also include political discourse, chief of which is the essay "Areopagitica" (1644). Among the ideas that Milton championed were the limitation of the monarchy, dethroning of bishops, freedom of speech, and the institution of divorce. One commentator mused that "the guarantees of freedom in the United States Constitution owe more to Milton's 'Areopagitica' than to John Locke."

What was Goethe's contribution to world literature?

Johann Wolfgang von Goethe (1749–1832) is considered Germany's greatest writer. He also was a scientist, artist, musician, and philosopher. As a writer, Goethe experimented with many genres and literary styles, and his works became a shaping force of the major German literary movements of the late eighteenth and early nineteenth centuries. His masterwork, the poetic drama *Faust* (1808; rewritten 1832), embodies the author's humanistic ideal of a world literature—one that transcends the boundaries of nations and historical periods. Indeed, the story of Faust, a German astrologer, magician, and soothsayer, remains one of universal interest and has been treated often in both literature and music. The legendary figure was believed to have sold his soul to the Devil in exchange for the opportunity to experience all of life's pleasures.

Who was Alexis de Tocqueville?

Aristocrat Alexis de Tocqueville (1805–1859) was only twenty-six years old when he traveled to New York with his colleague and friend Gustave de Beaumont (1802–1866) to study and observe American democracy.

Though Tocqueville set out to study the American penal system on behalf of the French government, he also had the goal of conducting an on-site investigation of the United States as the world's first, and at the time only, completely democratic society. Tocqueville and Beaumont traveled for nine months through New England, eastern Canada, and numerous American cities, including New York City; Philadelphia, Pennsylvania; Baltimore, Maryland; Washington, D.C.; Cincinnati, Ohio; and New Orleans, Louisiana.

The pair returned to France and published their study, *On the Penitentiary System in the United States and Its Application in France*. Tocqueville then spent the next two years writing *Democracy in America* (1835, 1840). The work was soon proclaimed as a classic throughout the Western world and secured Tocqueville's fame as a political observer, philosopher, and, later, sociologist. Tocqueville proclaimed that during his travels, "Nothing struck me more forcibly than the general equality of conditions. All classes meet continually and no haughtiness at all results from the differences in social position. Everyone shakes hands."

Who was the first to write a modern novel?

Most scholars point to Spanish writer Miguel de Cervantes (1547–1616), who wrote *The Ingenious Gentleman Don Quixote of La Mancha* (in two parts, 1605 and 1615). It was the first extended prose narrative in European literature in which characters and events are depicted in what came to be called the modern realistic tradition.

The plot tells of a noble man who has read so many stories of heroic knights that he loses his mind and starts believing that he is the knight Don Quixote of la Mancha. He sets out to right wrongs and bring back medieval chivalry. A farmer, Sancho Panza, becomes the squire of Don Quixote. Many adventures and misadventures follow the pair. At one point, while riding his horse, Don Quixote attacks a windmill, believing it to be giants.

The 1965 musical *Man of La Mancha* was inspired by the life and work of Miguel de Cervantes. The show's most famous song was the popular hit "The Impossible Dream."

How did the novel develop?

Critics and scholars agree that it is French writer Gustave Flaubert (1821–1880) who developed the modern novel into a "conscious art form." Flaubert's *Madame Bovary* is recognized for its objective characterization, irony, narrative technique, and use of imagery and symbolism. American writer (and naturalized British citizen) Henry James (1843–1916) is acknowledged for having enlarged the scope of the novel, introducing dramatic elements to the narrative, developing point-of-view technique,

An illustration by Gustav Doré for Miguel de Cervantes' *The Ingenious Gentleman Don Quixote of La Mancha*, which is considered the first modern novel.

What is the influence of *Don Quixote*?

Considered an epic masterpiece, *Don Quixote* had an undeniable influence on early novelists, including English novelist and playwright Henry Fielding (1707–1754), who wrote the realistic novel *Tom Jones* (1749). *Don Quixote* is also said to have anticipated later fictional masterpieces, including French novelist Gustave Flaubert's (1821–1880) *Madame Bovary* (1857), Russian novelist Fyodor Dostoyevsky's (1821–1881) *The Idiot* (1868–1869), and American writer Mark Twain's (1835–1910) *The Adventures of Tom Sawyer* (1876) and *The Adventures of Huckleberry Finn* (1884).

and advocating realism in literature. James's works include *The American* (1877), *Daisy Miller* (1879), *The Portrait of a Lady* (1881), and *The Ambassadors* (1903).

Irish writer James Joyce (1882–1941), considered the most prominent English-speaking literary figure of the first half of the twentieth century, is often credited with redefining the modern novel. Joyce experimented with the form—and revolutionized it—through his first novel, *A Portrait of the Artist as a Young Man* (1916), and with his masterpiece, *Ulysses* (1922), in which he developed the techniques of interior monologue and stream-of-consciousness narrative.

Writer William Faulkner (1897–1962) was the American counterpart to Joyce's experimentation with the form of the novel. The author of *The Sound and the Fury* (1929), *Light in August* (1932), and *Absalom, Absalom!* (1936), among others, Faulkner, in his acceptance speech for the Nobel Prize in Literature in 1949, stated that the fundamental theme of his fiction is "the human heart in conflict with itself." This he explored by employing a variety of narrative techniques, which, like Joyce's, departed radically from traditional methods.

Why is Jane Austen widely read today?

Austen is considered one of the greatest novelists in English. She wrote just six books during her lifetime, including her best-known works, *Sense and Sensibility* (1811), *Pride and Prejudice* (1813), and *Emma* (1816), but in so doing, she created the novel of manners, which continues to delight readers today. The daughter of a clergyman, Jane Austen (1775–1817) rejected the literary movement of the day, romanticism, opting instead to portray life as she knew it. As such, she was the first realist in the English novel. Austen's works are ripe with shrewd observation, wit, and an appreciation for the charms of everyday life, making her an engaging storyteller for all time.

What about writer Charles Dickens?

The writings of Charles Dickens (1812–1870) were extremely popular in his own time and continue to be popular today. His novels were typically not first published as bound books but, instead, issued in parts, called installments, either weekly or monthly, with illustrations. Dickens's most famous novels are *The Pickwick Papers* (1836/1837), *Oliver Twist* (1838/1839), *David Copperfield* (1849/1850), *A Tale of Two Cities* (1859), and *Great Expectations* (1860/1861).

His story *A Christmas Carol* (1843) has become a classic, with characters Ebenezer Scrooge, Bob Cratchit, and Tiny Tim.

Why is *Moby Dick* considered the greatest American novel?

The 1851 novel *Moby Dick* by Herman Melville (1819–1891), which opens with the familiar line "Call me Ishmael," has been acclaimed as one of the great novels of all time. The story of a whaling captain's obsessive search for the whale that ripped off his leg, *Moby Dick* is both an exciting tale of the high seas and an interesting allegory, interpreted as the human quest to understand the ultimately unknowable ways of God. The work first received notoriety some thirty years after Melville's death.

English author Charles Dickens was prolific and popular in his day and remains so to the present time with such beloved classics as *A Christmas Carol, David Copperfield,* and *A Tale of Two Cities* to his credit.

What has been called our "national novel"?

Harper Lee's (1926–2016) brilliant book *To Kill a Mockingbird* (1960) is considered a national treasure and was called our "national novel" by Oprah Winfrey (1954–). The book tells the story of a young girl named Scout Finch, who learns about the dignity and goodness of her father, Atticus Finch, a lawyer who defends a black man, Tom Robinson, from unjust charges of rape against a white woman. It is perhaps the most widely read book in high schools across the country. Many still consider the book their all-time favorite. The book would become the 1962 film *To Kill a Mockingbird*, starring Gregory Peck.

What is Marcel Proust's claim to literary fame?

Marcel Proust (1871–1922) is generally considered the greatest French novelist of the twentieth century and is credited with introducing to fiction the elements of psychological analysis, innovative treatment of time, and multiple themes. Proust is primarily known for his multivolume work *À la recherche du temps perdu* (1954), which was published in English as *Remembrance of Things Past*. Proust was a creative stylist as well as a shrewd social observer.

In the mid-1890s, Proust joined other prominent artists, including the great French novelist of the nineteenth century, Émile Zola (1840–1902), to form the protest group known as the Revisionists, or Dreyfusards. The artists were staunch supporters of French army officer Alfred Dreyfus (1859–1935) and, therefore, vocal critics of the French military, whom they accused of anti-Semitism for keeping Dreyfus, wrongly accused of treason, imprisoned on Devil's Island.

When did American poetry begin?

As the self-described poet of democracy, Walt Whitman (1819–1892) was the first to compose a truly American verse—one that showed no references to European antecedents (throwing off both the narrative and ode forms of verse) and that clearly articulated the American experience.

His first published poetry was the self-published collection *Leaves of Grass* (1855). In an effort to gain recognition, Whitman promptly sent a copy to the preeminent man of American letters, Ralph Waldo Emerson (1803–1882), and fellow American writers Henry David Thoreau (1817–1862) and Nathaniel Hawthorne (1804–1864). It was a bold move on Whitman's part, but it paid off. While *Leaves of Grass* had been unfavorably received by reviewers, Emerson composed a five-page tribute expressing his enthusiasm for the poetry and remarking that Whitman was "at the beginning of a great career." Thoreau, too, praised the work.

More than a century later, biographer Justin Kaplan acclaimed that in its time, *Leaves of Grass* was "the most brilliant and original poetry yet written in the New World, at once the fulfillment of American literary romanticism and the beginnings of American literary modernism." Whitman's well-known and frequently studied poems include "Song of Myself," "O Captain! My Captain!", "Song of the Open Road," and "I Sing the Body Electric."

Who was Emily Dickinson?

While she was virtually unknown for her poetry during her lifetime, Emily Dickinson (1830–1886) was writing at about the same time as Whitman (the 1850s); she published only a handful of poems before her death. Collections of Dickinson's works were published posthumously, and today, she, too, is regarded as one of the

Emily Dickinson led a reclusive life, and it was only after her death that her poetry came to be appreciated.

great early poets of the United States. Had more of her work been brought out in print, perhaps she would have been recognized as the first truly American poet.

What is Harlem?

Harlem is the famous neighborhood in New York City just north of Central Park. It was originally a Dutch village founded in 1658. In the 1800s, it was settled by Jewish and Italian immigrants. In the 1900s in the Great Migration, millions of African Americans left the South to find better opportunities in the North. Many wound up in Harlem, where they created the setting for the Harlem Renaissance.

The Depression hit Harlem hard, and then, many factory jobs were moved out of New York, leaving great poverty in Harlem and increasing crime rates. Many people fled the neighborhood. Since the 1990s, there has been some revitalization in Harlem.

What was the Harlem Renaissance?

The Harlem Renaissance (1925–1935) marked the first time that intellects and artists gave serious attention to the culture of African Americans. The movement, which had by some accounts begun as early as 1917, was noted in a 1925 *New York Herald Tribune* article that announced, "We are on the edge, if not in the midst, of what might not improperly be called a Negro Renaissance." The first African American Rhodes scholar, Alain Locke (1885–1954), who was a professor of philosophy at Howard University, led and shaped the movement, during which Upper Manhattan became a hotbed of creativity in the post–World War I era.

Not only was there a flurry of activity, but there was a heightened sense of pride as well. The movement left the country with a legacy of literary works, including those by Jean Toomer (his 1923 work *Cane* is generally considered the first work of the Harlem Renaissance), Langston Hughes ("The Negro Speaks of Rivers," 1921; *The Weary Blues*, 1926), Countee Cullen (*Color*, 1925; *Copper Sun*, 1927), Jessie R. Fauset (novelist and editor of *The Crisis*, the journal of the National Association for the Advancement of Colored People, or NAACP), Claude McKay (whose 1928 novel *Home to Harlem* evoked strong criticism from W. E. B. Du Bois and Alain Locke for its portrayal of black life), and Zora Neale Hurston (the author of the highly acclaimed 1937 novel *Their Eyes Were Watching God*, who was the first

Author Langston Hughes, an innovator of jazz poetry, was one of a slew of writers and musicians to arise during the Harlem Renaissance in New York.

> **How big is the *Harry Potter* sensation?**
>
> British author J. K. Rowling's (1965–) *Harry Potter* series, following the adventures of a young wizard, debuted in 1997 and has been so popular with readers that it set new records in the publishing industry. It also made Rowling one of the wealthiest people in the world.

black woman to be honored for her creative writing with a prestigious Guggenheim Fellowship).

The Harlem Renaissance was not only about literature; jazz and blues music also flourished during the prosperous times of the postwar era. During the 1920s and 1930s, Louis Armstrong, "Jelly Roll" Morton, Duke Ellington, Bessie Smith, and Josephine Baker rose to prominence. Their contributions to music performance are still felt by artists and audiences.

How did Dale Carnegie become a best-selling writer?

Dale Carnegie (1888–1955) wrote the 1936 bestseller *How to Win Friends and Influence People*. The books still sells today and has lots of common-sense suggestions on how to be more effective in dealing with people. Carnegie also wrote *How to Stop Worrying and Start Living* (1948).

THE EARLY DAYS OF MOVIES

When was the first movie shown?

On March 22, 1895, the first in-theater showing of a motion picture took place in Paris, when viewers gathered to see a film of workers leaving a factory. The cinematography of inventors Louis (1864–1948) and Auguste (1862–1954) Lumière was a vast improvement over the kinetoscope, introduced in 1894 by Thomas Edison (1847–1931), whose film could only be viewed by one person at a time looking into a box on a stand.

The sixteen-frame-per-second mechanism developed by the Lumière brothers became the standard for films for decades. The following year, 1896, the first motion picture showing in the United States took place in New York. The film was shown using Edison's vitascope, which was an improvement on his kinetoscope.

What are the milestones in the early motion picture industry?

Here are a few of the early film milestones:

- 1903: Edwin S. Porter's *The Great Train Robbery* was the first motion picture to tell a complete story.

- 1910: *Brooklyn Eagle* newspaper cartoonist John Randolph Bray pioneered animated motion picture cartoons.
- 1912: *Queen Elizabeth*, starring Sarah Bernhardt, was the first feature-length motion picture seen in America.
- 1915: D. W. Griffith's *The Birth of a Nation* provided the blueprint for narrative films. (This film was very popular, but it was also extremely racist.)
- 1925: In his movie *Potemkin*, Soviet film director Sergei Eisenstein created a masterpiece by splicing film shot at many locations, an approach subsequently adopted by most film directors.
- 1926: The first motion picture with sound ("talkie") was demonstrated.
- 1927: The first full-length talking picture, *The Jazz Singer*, starring vaudevillian Al Jolson, was released. By 1932, all movies talked.
- 1929: The first Academy Awards (for 1928 films) were held; winners were William Wellman for *Wings*, Emil Jannings for best actor (in *Last Command*), and Janet Gaynor for best actress (in *Sunrise*). Movie columnist Sidney Skolsky dubbed the awards "the Oscars."
- 1929: Eastman Kodak introduced sixteen-millimeter film for motion picture cameras.
- 1935: The first full-length Technicolor movie, *Becky Sharp*, was released.
- 1939: *Gone with the Wind* was released in Technicolor.

What were newsreels?

Newsreels got their start in 1910, when the pioneer film newsreel *Pathé Gazette* was shown in Britain and the United States. French cinematographer Charles Pathé (1863–1957) and his brother Émile (1860–1937) were Paris agents for the Edison phonograph. They visited London to acquire filmmaking equipment and secured financial support in order to set up production units in Britain, the United States, Italy, Germany, Russia, and Japan. These short movies, covering current events, were predominately used during wartime and were shown in theaters before the feature movie. Replaced by television news, the last newsreels were screened in 1967.

What are the Oscars?

The Oscars are awards issued by the Academy of Motion Picture Arts and Sciences for those in the movie and film industry. Many view them as the most coveted of all

Actor Leonardo DiCaprio and director/screenwriter Alejandro Gonzalez Inarritu pose with their Oscars for *The Revenant* in 2016. The Academy Award is one of the highest honors in the film industry.

485

awards. The Oscar is the name for the actual award, though collectively, they are also called the Academy Awards. The five main Oscars are for Best Picture, Best Actor, Best Actress, Best Supporting Actor, and Best Supporting Actress.

The first Academy Awards or Oscars were handed out in May 1929. Do you know who won the recent Academy Awards or what the nominations are for the next Academy Awards? Check them out online.

What was the Motion Picture Production Code?

In the 1920s, many people were concerned that movies often emphasized sexual irresponsibility, crime, and violence. Hollywood producers and directors knew that these elements often made movies more interesting. As the Hollywood producer Jack Warner admitted, "Whenever my directors are stuck for something to do, they make the heroine take off her clothes."

Many people were upset about movie content, as there was no rating system for movies, and children could see any movie shown. Some states and local municipalities started enacting censorship laws. The movie producers did not like such censorship since it varied from place to place, and they feared federal censorship.

In Chicago, FitzGeorge Dineen, S.J. (1866–1944), a pastor in Chicago, led boycotts over film content at local movie theaters. He knew Cardinal George Mundelein (1872–1939), head of the Catholic Church in Chicago. By coincidence, Mundelein had regular lunches with prominent bankers who, because of the 1929 financial collapse, now owned the movie companies. The bankers were also bothered by movie content.

Also concerned about movie content was Martin Quigley (1890–1964), publisher of the *Motion Picture Herald* for movie theater owners and operators. Discussions between Dinneen, Quigley, and Mundelein led to a decision to write a set of guidelines for movies. The code itself was written in Chicago by a Jesuit from St. Louis, Daniel Lord (1888–1955). Due to Mundelein's influence, the Hollywood producers agreed to accept the code in the hope of avoiding federal censorship. The code, called the Motion Picture Production Code, was approved by the producers in 1930. In time, the Hays office, named for Will Hays (1979–1954), chairman of the Motion Picture Producers and Distributors of America, became the enforcer and interpreter of the code. The later impact of the Hays office is a long, complicated, and controversial story.

Daniel Lord's authorship of the code was kept secret. Although a number of Catholic figures were involved in the creation of the code and its later enforcement, there was nothing specifically Catholic or even Christian about the code. Many Protestants, Jews, and other people concerned about movie content supported the code.

Lord was not some sort of moral prude. He got involved because he loved movies and theater. In his lifetime, he wrote over seventy plays, musicals, and pageants. He produced his largest plays with casts of over 1,000 actors. Lord was not opposed to dealing with adult topics; he just thought live theater was the better place.

The code has been controversial from the beginning. Many people have opinions on it, but many people have never read it. As you read it, ask yourself what you agree and disagree with. Also, keep in mind that this code was written almost ninety years ago, when films with sound were brand new and cultural moral values were so different. For example, the majority of people believed that men and women were unequal and should play different roles in society.

What was the Hollywood blacklist?

In 1947, studio executives assembled at the Waldorf-Astoria Hotel in New York City put together a list of alleged communist sympathizers, naming some 300 writers, directors, actors, and others known or suspected to have Communist Party affiliations or of having invoked the Fifth Amendment against self-incrimination when questioned by the House Un-American Activities Committee (HUAC). The "Hollywood Ten" who refused to tell the committee whether or not they had been communists were Alvah Bessie, Herbert Biberman, Lester Cole, Edward Dmytryk, Ring Lardner Jr., John Howard Lawson, Albert Maltz, Samuel Ornitz, Adrian Scott, and Dalton Trumbo. The film industry blacklisted the Hollywood Ten on November 25, and all of them drew short prison sentences for refusing to testify.

The 2015 film *Trumbo*, starring Bryan Cranston, tells the story of Dalton Trumbo, one of the top screenwriters in Hollywood, who was blacklisted. After serving eleven months in prison, Trumbo started ghostwriting scripts to keep his career alive. He eventually wrote screenplays for the blockbuster movies *Spartacus* (1960) and *Exodus* (1960), and the directors of both films publicly recognized him as the screenwriter.

EARLY RADIO AND TELEVISION

What was radio's cultural impact?

It is hard for many people today to understand the impact of radio. However, imagine a time before the Internet, before computers, and before television, when the only mass media was printed material. Although radio technology was developed in the late 1880s, it was in the 1920s and 1930s that radio was woven into the fabric of everyday American life. People across the country—in cities and suburbs and on farms—tuned in for news and entertainment, including broadcasts of baseball games and other sporting events as well as comedy and variety shows, dramas, and live music programs.

President Franklin D. Roosevelt used the new medium to speak directly to the American public during the trying times of the Great Depression, broadcasting his "fireside chats" from the White House. Between the 1920s and the 1950s, gathering around the radio in the evenings was as common to Americans as watching television is today. Also, for the first time, radio created the reality of many people in very different places experiencing the same thing at the same time.

Although people had to buy their own radios, it was decided that radio broadcasts would be free but that they would include advertising. Advertisers would pay to broadcast their commercials, which would pay for the shows. (This was not the only possible option. But this choice is with us today and has become the model for television and for much of the Internet.)

In the 1950s, TV took away much of radio's audience. Radio programmers seized rock music as a way to reach a wide, albeit very young, audience. In the decades since, radio programming has become increasingly music-oriented, though talk and news programming are also popular. Radio has also played an important political role, especially as used by conservative political voices.

What was the immediate impact of television?

By 1947, the four networks that then existed—ABC, CBS, NBC, and DuMont (a short-lived competitor)—could still provide only about ten hours of prime-time programming a week, much of it sporting events. In late 1948, it was estimated that only 10 percent of the population had even seen a television show. However, as the networks stepped up their programming with live-drama programs, children's shows, and variety shows (a format that was familiar and popular to the American radio-listening audience), interest in television grew rapidly. By the spring of 1948, industry experts estimated that 150,000 sets were in public places such as bars and pubs, accounting for about half of the total number of sets in operation. Just a year later, 940,000 homes had televisions. And by 1949, production of sets had jumped to three million.

Which was the first TV network?

The first was the National Broadcasting Company (NBC), founded in 1926 by David Sarnoff (1891–1971), considered one of the pioneers of radio and television broadcasting.

Next came the Columbia Broadcasting System (CBS) in 1928, established by William S. Paley (1901–1990). He built the floundering radio network into a powerful and profitable broadcasting organization.

The American Broadcasting Company (ABC) television network was last, created in 1943 by Edward J. Noble (1882–1958).

Is there a golden age of television?

Yes, people commonly refer to the 1950s as TV's golden age. Critics still hail the programs of the golden age to be the most innovative programming in television history. It was during this decade that an-

Television began to have a big impact on American culture by the 1950s.

thology programs such as *Kraft Television Theatre*, *Playhouse 90*, and *Studio One* made live drama part of the nightly fare on prime-time television with original screenplays such as *Twelve Angry Men* (1954), *Visit to a Small Planet* (1955), and *The Miracle Worker* (1957), written by New York playwrights such as Gore Vidal, Rod Serling, Arthur Miller, and A. E. Hotchner. The live dramas on television attracted the talents of actors George C. Scott, James Dean, Paul Newman, Grace Kelly, Eva Marie Saint, Sidney Poitier, Lee Remick, and Jack Lemmon.

The other cornerstones of 1950 television programming were live variety shows and shows with legendary comedians, such as Jack Benny, Red Skelton, Jackie Gleason, George Burns, Sid Caesar, and "Mr. Television" Milton Berle.

However, live shows were expensive. In time, most were replaced by situation comedies, westerns, and other programs that could be taped in advance and produced in quantity.

What is one of the most famous scenes from television in its golden age?

It is the "Vitameatavegamin" scene from the 1950s television sitcom *I Love Lucy*, which starred Lucille Ball (1911–1989) and Desi Arnaz (1917–1986). The episode was "Lucy Does a TV Commercial," the thirtieth episode of the series, which aired on May 5, 1952.

When was public broadcasting started?

In the United States, the Public Broadcasting Act was signed into law by President Lyndon B. Johnson (1908–1973) in 1967, creating a Corporation for Public Broadcasting to broaden the scope of noncommercial radio and TV beyond its educational role. Within three years, and as a result of federal grants plus funds from foundations, businesses, and private contributions, Public Broadcasting Service (PBS) rivaled the Big Three networks at the time—NBC, CBS, and ABC. Over the years, PBS has presented such famous shows as *Sesame Street*, *Mister Rogers' Neighborhood*, *Masterpiece Theatre*, *Antiques Roadshow*, and *Downton Abbey*.

The website *PBS.org* shows the many programs now being offered. Do you know your local PBS station? As mentioned earlier, the series *American Experience* is a great source for learning American history. Also valuable are the shows *Frontline*, which tackles tough current political and social issues, and *American Masters*, which produces biographies of American performers, musicians, dancers, architects, and much more.

EXPLORATION

FAMOUS ANCIENT EXPLORERS

Who was Hannu?

Hannu (or Hennu) was one of the earliest known explorers in the history of the world. This Egyptian noble, of the twenty-first or twentieth century B.C.E., reputedly made numerous explorations from his native Egypt into surrounding countries, such as Libya and Punt. He encountered the Red Sea on different voyages. He recounted many of these expeditions in stone.

When did Marco Polo travel to the Far East?

Marco Polo (1254–1324) was only in his teens when he left Venice, Italy, in about 1271 with his father, Niccolò, and his uncle Maffeo, traveling an overland route to the East along the Silk Road, eventually reaching China. Marco returned to Venice after twenty-four years of travel and wrote *The Travels of Marco Polo*, describing all that he had seen. His book became a window into the unknown world of India, China, and Japan.

CIRCUMNAVIGATION OF THE GLOBE

Why was Portugal such a force in exploration?

Portugal was the leading seafaring country in the world for a good part of the fifteenth century. For a small country, it has a long coastline and is positioned on the western end of Europe. Another reason for Portugal's predominance was due to Prince Henry the Navigator (1394–1460), the son of King John I of Portugal. Although Henry was neither a sailor nor a navigator, he was the patron and supporter of Portuguese explorers, explicitly urging his father to support various sailing missions to Africa to expand his country's trade. He promoted the development of a ship called the "caravel." Although it was smaller than other ships, it was much faster and highly maneuverable.

However, Henry also played a key role in creating the Atlantic slave trade.

Who was Vasco da Gama?

Vasco da Gama (c. 1460–1524) led an expedition of four ships that left Portugal in 1497 and sailed south from Portugal down the African coast, rounding the Cape of Good Hope at the southern tip of Africa, then sailing north on the other side of Africa to Madagascar, then on to India. The expedition returned to Portugal in 1499. (Do an online image search "map of da Gama route.") Da Gama's voyage opened up the possibilities for trading along the east coast of Africa and with India. His mission around the tip of Africa inspired other explorers and convinced them that it would be possible to circumnavigate the globe (sail around the entire Earth).

Who was Magellan? What did he do?

The expedition of Ferdinand Magellan (c. 1480–1521) was the first to circumnavigate the globe. In 1519, Magellan left Spain with five ships. He sailed around the southern tip of South America, finding a winding waterway that still bears his name, the Strait of Magellan. It had taken a year to get to this point, and along the way, Magellan had had to crush a mutiny by his sailors. Magellan sailed west, reaching the island we know as Guam in March 1521. Ten days later, he discovered the Philippines. On the Philippine island of Cebu, Magellan was killed by the Native peoples. His expedition continued without him, under the direction of Juan Sebastián de Elcano (c. 1476–1526), who in 1522 returned to Seville, Spain, with only one ship, the *Victoria*. Their cargo included valuable spices, which more than paid for the expense of the expedition. Most of the sailors, about 232, died on the expedition. Only eighteen of the original crew survived.

Who was the first Englishman to circumnavigate the globe?

English admiral Francis Drake (c. 1540–1596) set out in 1577 to explore the Strait of Magellan. He did so, investigating the coast of South America (he and his crew plundered coastal Chile and Peru in the process) before continuing into the South Pacific and heading northward. He eventually reached the coast of present-day California.

The *Victoria*—depicted here—was the only ship from Magellan's expedition to make it back safely to Europe.

He continued sailing northward and is believed to have reached Vancouver—still in search of the Northwest Passage that would allow one to sail across the top of North America and reach the Atlantic Ocean. Not finding the Northwest Passage (he was much too far south, explorers would later learn), he sailed westward. He reached the so-called Spice Islands (today known as the Moluccas) in east Indonesia in 1579. Drake also found the Indonesian island of Java before continuing west through the Indian Ocean, rounding the southern tip of South Africa at the Cape of Good Hope and skirting the western coast of Africa northward to Sierra Leone. From there, Drake returned home to Plymouth, England, where he landed in 1580, the first Englishman to travel around the world. He was knighted by the queen one year later.

It is also Drake who, along with his fellow countryman Sir Walter Raleigh (1554–1618), bears the dubious honor of introducing tobacco to his homeland. In 1586, Drake returned from another expedition to North and South America, where he did battle with Spanish fleets for control of lands. He then picked up colonists in Virginia, who carried with them potatoes and the materials and implements for tobacco smoking.

Who was the first woman to circumnavigate the globe?

It was a young Frenchwoman named Jeanne Baret (1740–1807). In 1766, Louis-Antoine de Bougainville (1729–1811), a French naval officer, undertook a successful around-the-world expedition and returned to France in 1769. But the crew made an interesting discovery en route: When the French arrived in Tahiti, the Tahitians immediately noticed something the crew had not—that one of the servants on the expedition was a woman. "Jean" Baret had been hired in France by one of the ship's officers, who did not know Baret was a woman. Her secret discovered by the Tahitians, she confessed, revealing that she was an orphan who had first disguised herself as a boy to get employment as a

What were Captain Cook's discoveries?

British navigator Captain James Cook (1728–1779) was one of the world's greatest explorers, commanding three voyages to the Pacific Ocean and sailing around the world twice. From 1768 to 1771, aboard the ship *Endeavor*, Cook conducted an expedition to the South Pacific, where he landed in Tahiti, and made the first European discovery of the coasts of New Zealand, Australia, and New Guinea, which he also charted. In 1772, Cook set out to find the great southern continent that was believed to exist. He spent three years on this voyage, which edged along the ice fields of Antarctica. On his last voyage, which he undertook in 1776 on a mission to find a passage around North America from the Pacific, Cook charted the Pacific coast of North America as far north as the Bering Strait. He died in 1778 on the Hawaiian Islands. Cook's voyages led to the establishment of Pacific Ocean colonies by several European nations.

valet. When she learned about Bougainville's expedition, she decided to continue the disguise in order to carry out an adventure that would have been impossible for a woman in that day. She was the first woman known to have circled the globe.

Who was the first European to traverse the Bering Strait?

The first European to traverse the Bering Sea was Danish navigator Vitus Bering (1681–1741) in 1728. The explorer, for whom the strait and the sea were named, had been employed by Tsar Peter the Great (1672–1725) of Russia to determine whether Asia and North America are connected. The Bering Strait, which connects the Arctic Ocean and the Bering Sea, is fifty-three miles across at its narrowest point.

EXPLORATION IN THE TWENTIETH CENTURY

What is the Northwest Passage?

The Northwest Passage is the sea passage in the Arctic Ocean between the Atlantic and Pacific oceans that is north of Canada. It had been long sought-after by explorers as a quicker route than sailing around South America. Though it was eventually found through a series of discoveries, it was not completely navigated until 1903 to 1906 by Norwegian explorer Roald Amundsen (1872–1928). What made the passage difficult was all the extensive ice on the water, especially during winter.

Convinced of the existence of such a passage, numerous navigators attempted to find it during the early years of European westward sea exploration. In the process, they made other discoveries:

- The St. Lawrence River, between Canada and the United States, by French explorer Jacques Cartier (1491–1557)

- Frobisher Bay, off the coast of Baffin Island, north of Quebec, by English commander Sir Martin Frobisher (1535–1594)

- Davis Strait, between Baffin Island and Greenland, by English navigator John Davis (c. 1550–1605)

- The Hudson River and Hudson Bay by English navigator Henry Hudson (?–1611)

It took Amundson three years to make the passage aboard the ship *Gjoa*. After a harrowing adventure that saw the *Gjoa* and its crew survive a shipboard fire, a collision with a reef, fierce winter storms, and ice that hemmed them in, Amundsen arrived in Nome, Alaska.

Today, because of global warming and the resulting climate change, there has been a significant decrease of ice in the Northwest Passage with the result that ships, including cruise ships, are now making the journey in the warmer months.

American Robert Peary (left) was the first man to reach the North Pole (in 1909), and Norwegian Roald Amundsen (right) was the first to reach the South Pole (in 1911).

Who was the first person to reach the North Pole?

There has been some dispute over this one. The credit usually goes to American explorer and former naval officer Robert E. Peary (1856–1920), who, after several tries, reached the North Pole by dogsled on April 6, 1909, along with Matthew A. Henson (1866–1955) and three Inuit companions. Unbeknownst to him, five days before this achievement, another American explorer, Dr. Frederick Cook (1865–1940), claimed that he had reached the North Pole a year earlier. Peary and Cook knew each other, as Cook had been the surgeon on Peary's Arctic expedition of 1891 to 1892, which reached Greenland. Cook's claim was investigated by scientists, but the evidence he supplied did not substantiate the claim. Thus, Peary was officially recognized as the first to reach the northern extremity of Earth's axis.

Who was the first person to reach the South Pole?

In December 1911, Norwegian explorer Roald Amundsen (1872–1928) became the first to reach the South Pole. Before earning this distinction, he had achieved another first— sailing the Northwest Passage (1903–1906).

Amundsen's desire to be an Arctic explorer had been with him almost his entire life. As a teen, he is said to have slept with his bedroom windows open year-round in order to become accustomed to the cold. When he was twenty-one, he turned his attention away from the study of medicine to making an Arctic passage. He recognized that many of the previous (and failed) attempts to travel to the Arctic shared a common characteristic—the commanders of these expeditions had not always been ships' captains. He resolved to become an experienced navigator and soon took jobs as a sailor on various ships.

Amundsen then began planning an expedition to be the first person to reach the North Pole; however, when he learned about Peary reaching the North Pole in 1909, Amundsen shifted his sights to reaching the South Pole instead and quietly began to lay plans to do so. In fact, it was not until his expedition left Oslo in September 1910 that he telegraphed his announcement back to Norway that he was, in fact, headed to the South, not the North, Pole. As it turned out, a race was on between the Norwegians and the British. Shortly after Amundsen had set sail, British naval officer Robert Falcon Scott (1868–1912) had left England at the head of an expedition to reach the South Pole.

The Norwegians landed at Ross Ice Shelf, Antarctica, on February 10, 1911. It was not until ten months later, on December 14, 1911, on a sunny afternoon, that they raised their country's flag at the spot their calculations told them was the South Pole. Before heading north again, they celebrated their achievement with double rations. When Scott's expedition arrived at the South Pole on the morning of January 18, 1912, they found the Norwegian flag flying over it. On their way back, the British crew died due to bad weather and insufficient food supplies. Amundsen's Norwegian expedition arrived safely at their base camp.

Who was the first to reach Mount Everest's summit?

New Zealander Sir Edmund Hillary (1919–2008) was the first person to climb to the summit of Mount Everest, the highest mountain in the world. Everest, in the Himalaya

In this 1953 photo, Sir Edmund Hillary (left) is shown with fellow climber Tenzing Norgay not long after completing their ascent of Mt. Everest.

Mountains between Nepal and Tibet, rises nearly five and a half miles (29,028 feet) above sea level.

After numerous climbers made attempts on Everest between 1921 and 1952, Hillary reached the top on May 29, 1953, as part of a British-led expedition; he was followed by fellow climber Tenzing Norgay (1914–1986), a Nepalese sherpa. Hillary took a picture of Norgay at the summit, but Norgay did not know how to work the camera, so there is no picture of Hillary. The "Sir" was added to Hillary's name by Queen Elizabeth II (1926–), who took great pleasure in the fact that the triumph on Everest had been achieved by a British expedition. Having been crowned on June 2, 1953, it was one of her first official acts as queen. The mountain was named for another Briton, Sir George Everest (1790–1866), who served as a British surveyor-general of India from 1830 to 1843. (Tibetans call the mountain Chomolungma, and the Nepalese call it Sagarmatha.)

What is the current problem with climbing Mount Everest?

Climbing Mount Everest has become very popular. About 800 people climb it every year. And things can get crowded on the routes up the mountain. Over 300 people have died trying to climb Everest. In 2014, sixteen people died, and in 2015, twenty-two people died.

Also, when people die on Mount Everest, there is no way to get the bodies down. Most bodies stay there, frozen.

The 2015 film *Everest* describes the 1996 Mount Everest disaster, when eight people died in a blizzard. (Four more people would die that climbing season.)

Why was Charles Lindbergh so important?

On May 21, 1927, at 10:24 P.M., American Charles A. Lindbergh (1902–1974) landed his single-engine monoplane, the *Spirit of St. Louis*, at Le Bourget Air Field in Paris after completing the first solo nonstop flight across the Atlantic Ocean. Lindbergh, declining to take a radio in order to save weight for an additional ninety gallons of gasoline, had taken off in the rain from Roosevelt Field in Long Island, New York, at 7:55 A.M. on May 20.

The plane was so heavy with gasoline (a total of 451 gallons of it) that the *Spirit of St. Louis* barely cleared telephone wires upon takeoff. Lindbergh covered 3,600 miles (about a third of it through snow and sleet) in thirty-three hours, twenty-nine minutes. He won a $25,000 prize, which was offered in 1919, and became a world hero—hailed as the "Lone Eagle." His autobiography, titled *The Spirit of St. Louis* (1953), won the aviator the Pulitzer Prize.

Why was his flight so important?

It is hard to imagine the world of 1927. Today, over 2,000 planes a day cross the Atlantic. It seems like no big deal. But a hundred years ago, in the early decades of flight, crossing the Atlantic seemed impossible. (Crossing the much larger Pacific was even harder to imagine.) There were several attempts to cross the Atlantic, though they had all failed, and several pilots died.

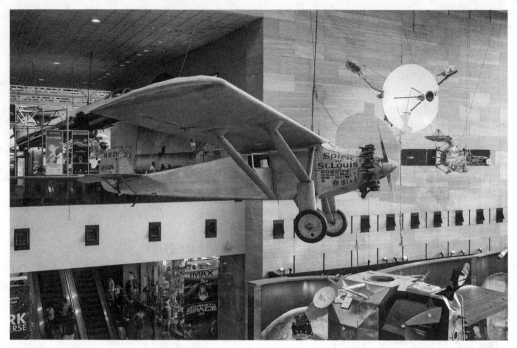

Charles Lindbergh's plane, the *Spirit of St. Louis*, is currently on display at the National Air and Space Museum in Washington, D.C.

Lindbergh was both daring and lucky, which is why he earned the nickname "Lucky Lindy." He did not have a copilot, and his plane had only one engine. There was no backup if either the engine or pilot failed. To reduce weight so he could take more gasoline, he took neither a radio nor a parachute. Yet, he did make it to Paris! He flew across the Atlantic and landed safely.

Who was Amelia Earhart?

American Amelia Earhart (1897–1937), a female pioneer of aviation, was the first woman to fly solo across the Atlantic Ocean. She disappeared in the South Pacific in July 1937 as she and navigator Fred Noonan (1893–1937) attempted an around-the-world flight along the equator.

The Kansas-born Earhart first became interested in aviation, which was very new at the time, during the early 1920s, and she began taking flying lessons. In 1928, she was the only woman on board a transatlantic flight from Newfoundland to Wales. This made her famous as the first woman to cross the Atlantic Ocean by air. She followed that accomplishment in 1932 with a solo transatlantic flight. Earhart took off from Harbour Grace, Newfoundland, Canada, one evening in May 1932; her destination was Paris. However, she encountered a violent electrical storm, the altimeter failed, the wings iced up, and, finally, the exhaust manifold caught on fire. After a fifteen-hour flight, Earhart landed in Ireland. Again, fame and acclaim were hers as the first woman to cross the Atlantic in a solo flight. She then went on to set speed and distance records for aviation and soon conceived of the idea of flying around the world along the equator.

On May 20, 1937, Earhart and Noonan took off from Oakland, California. Reaching Miami, Florida, they stopped for repairs. On June 1, 1937, they departed Miami and headed for Brazil. From there, they flew across the Atlantic to Africa and then across the Red Sea to the Arabian Peninsula. Then, it was on to Karachi, Pakistan; Calcutta, India; and Burma (present-day Myanmar). Earhart reached New Guinea on June 30, and she and Noonan then prepared for the most difficult leg of the journey—to Howland Island, a tiny speck of land only two and a half miles long in the middle of the vast Pacific Ocean.

The next day, July 1, they left New Guinea and began the 2,600-mile flight to Howland Island. On July 2, a U.S. Navy

In this 1936 photo, Amelia Earhart stands next to Purdue University president Dr. Edward Elliott beside her Lockheed Electra.

ship picked up radio messages from Earhart that indicated reports of empty fuel tanks. All efforts to make radio contact with her failed. Though an extensive search effort ensued, no trace of the plane or the two-person crew was ever found, and no one knows for certain what happened.

Although various theories and myths have tried to answer the question of what happened, the most likely possibilities are that the plane crashed into the ocean or that they landed on an island such as Gardner (Nikumararo) Island. Recently, famous ocean explorer Robert Ballard (1942–) has been looking for the wreckage of the plane near this island.

Who discovered the wreckage of the *Titanic*?

Oceanographer and underwater archeologist Robert Ballard (1942–) discovered the wreckage of the *Titanic* in 1985, 13,000 feet below sea level. The U.S. Navy financed Ballard's exploratory hunt for the *Titanic*—provided that the eminent marine archeologist first look for two Navy submarines sunk during the Cold War era.

Ballard found the other sunk ships, including three from World War II:

- The German battleship *Bismarck* (sunk in 1941, found in 1989)

- The American aircraft carrier *Yorktown* (sunk in 1942, found in 1998)

- *PT-109*, the PT boat commanded by John Kennedy, who became president in 1960 (sunk in 1943, found in 2002)

SPACE: THE FINAL FRONTIER

When did the exploration of space begin?

The Space Age began on October 4, 1957, when the Soviet Union launched Sputnik (later referred to as Sputnik 1), the first artificial satellite. The world reacted to the news of Sputnik, which was able to take pictures of Earth, with a mix of shock and respect. Premier Nikita Khrushchev (1894–1971) of the Soviet Union immediately approved funding for follow-up projects. And leaders in the West, not to be outdone by the Soviets in exploring the last frontier, also vowed to support space programs. Four months later, the United States launched its first satellite, Explorer 1, on January 31, 1958. Not only had the launch of Sputnik initiated the Space Age, it had also started the "Space Race." The Soviet and American programs would continue to rival each other, with one accomplishment leapfrogging the other, for about the next three decades.

What was the first animal sent into orbit?

The Soviets immediately followed the success of Sputnik 1 by sending the first animal into space—a dog named Laika. The female Russian Samoyed traveled in a pressurized cabin aboard Sputnik 2, launched November 3, 1957, making her the first living creature to go into orbit. The trip ended badly for Laika, however; she died a few days into the journey.

Before sending humans into orbit, both the Soviets and the Americans needed to prove that animals could survive in outer space. While the Soviets experimented with dogs traveling in space, by the end of 1958, the United States would send a monkey into space (but not into orbit). The following spring (May 28, 1959), two female monkeys, Able and Baker, were launched into space and were recovered alive. They had traveled 300 miles aboard the Jupiter.

Who was the first person in space?

The first person in space was Soviet cosmonaut Yuri A. Gagarin (1934–1968), who orbited Earth in the spaceship *Vostok 1*, which launched on April 12, 1961. The flight lasted one hour and forty-eight minutes. The achievement made Gagarin an international hero.

Who was the first American in space?

U.S. president John F. Kennedy (1917–1963) announced in 1961 that the United States would land a man on the moon before the end of the decade. The first step

Soviet cosmonaut Yuri Gagarin was a national hero for being the first human being to voyage into outer space in 1961. Tragically, his life was cut short in a 1968 plane crash.

toward reaching that goal was made by putting the first American into space. On May 5, 1961, Alan Shepard Jr. (1923–1998) piloted the first U.S. spaceflight, called *Freedom 7*. The suborbital flight reached an altitude of 116.5 miles. Just more than nine months later, the United States put a man into orbit. On February 20, 1962, astronaut John Glenn Jr. (1921–2016) orbited Earth three times in the spaceship *Friendship 7*.

What is the early history of the American space program?

The American space program is run by the National Aeronautics and Space Administration, usually called NASA. The U.S.-manned space program had begun with six flights between May 1961 and May 1963 using the Mercury capsule, which held just one astronaut. The Gemini program followed with ten manned flights between March 1965 and November 1966 with capsules holding two astronauts. The Apollo program with three astronauts in the capsule followed. Eleven manned Apollo missions would follow from October 1968 to December 1972. On six of these missions, astronauts would walk on the moon. (More moon missions had been planned, but these were cut by President Richard Nixon.)

The Space Shuttle program followed.

The Apollo 11 crew: (left to right) Neil Armstrong, Michael Collins, and Edwin "Buzz" Aldrin.

Who was the first man to walk on the moon?

It was American astronaut Neil Armstrong (1930–2012) who, on July 21, 1969, stepped out of the lunar module from Apollo 11 and walked on the moon. Armstrong, who was joined by astronaut Edwin "Buzz" Aldrin Jr. (1930–), uttered the famous words, "That's one small step for a man, one giant leap for mankind." (The live voice transmission had dropped the "a" before "man," but it was added in later.)

What is the International Space Station?

It is a scientific laboratory orbiting about 250 statute miles above Earth. The International Space Station (ISS) is a cooperative project among sixteen nations, led by the United States; the other partners in what is called the most complex science project in history are Russia, Canada, Japan, the eleven nations of the European Space Agency, and Brazil.

The ISS was built through a series of missions, the first of which was the U.S.-designed, Russian-built space module *Zarya (Sunrise)*, launched November 20, 1998. According to NASA's website: "The space station, including its large solar arrays, spans the area of a U.S. football field, including the end zones, and weighs 861,804 pounds, not including visiting vehicles."

Scientists believe that experiments conducted on the ISS will lead to discoveries in medicine and to the development of materials and new science that will benefit people around the world. The space station is also considered a monumental first step in preparing for future human space exploration.

What is the Hubble Space Telescope?

Since the time of Galileo, telescopes have been an essential tool for exploring the universe. In the twentieth and twenty-first centuries, very large telescopes have been built. However, such telescopes must contend with the problem of looking through Earth's atmosphere. This can sometimes distort or put a limit on what can be seen. Also, light pollution from surrounding cities can limit visibility. As a result, most telescopes are placed on mountains in isolated places, such as the Keck telescopes on Hawaii's Mauna Kea.

Who was the first woman in space?

The Soviet Union put the first woman into space. On June 16, 1963, cosmonaut Valentina Tereshkova (1937–) was launched into space aboard the *Vostok 6*. She spent three days circling Earth.

It was twenty years before the United States would match the accomplishment. On June 18, 1983, Sally K. Ride (1951–2012) and four other crew members were launched into space aboard the space shuttle *Challenger*.

However, this does not solve the limitation that Earth telescopes do not see most infrared and ultraviolet light because much of it is absorbed by the atmosphere.

As early as the 1940s, scientists were proposing putting a telescope in space. It took many decades to develop the idea and to get the funding to build the telescope. By 1986, the Hubble Space Telescope had been built and was ready to go into space. It measured 43.5 feet (13.2 meters) in length with a maximum diameter of 14 feet (4.2 meters) and with an internal mirror with a diameter of 7 feet, 10 inches (2.4 meters). However, the explosion of the *Challenger* space shuttle delayed the project. Finally, the Hubble Space Telescope was put into orbit by the *Discovery* space shuttle and started taking pictures.

Unfortunately, it soon became apparent that the photos were not as sharp as expected. It turned out that the mirror that reflected the light from space had been made incorrectly. It took several repair missions to the telescope to fix the problem. The mirror itself could not be replaced, but the equipment that received the light from the mirror could be altered to adjust for the distortions. Soon, the Hubble Space Telescope was providing stunning photos of the universe and helping to greatly increase scientific knowledge. (Do an online search for "Hubble photos" and prepare to be amazed.)

MODERN EXPLORERS OF A DIFFERENT TYPE

What was the Enigma machine?

The Enigma machine was a coding device used by the Germans in World War II. The Germans thought they had an unbreakable code system because the Enigma machine was so sophisticated in creating many different codes.

At the time, messages were sent by radio using Morse code. The enemy could easily hear any message and read the messages. To prevent that, the message was put in a code where each letter was represented by a different letter. However, if one used the same code every day, it would not take long for the other side to decipher the code. The trick was to change the code frequently.

However, that meant that all users would have to have code books with the new codes. What the Enigma machine could do was to create a new code every time it was reset. All that was required was to match the settings on the sender's machine to the settings on the receiver's machine. The Enigma machine allowed the Germans to reset their codes daily. And the machine could produce millions and millions of different codes.

Who broke the codes produced by the Enigma machine?

The person who broke the codes was Alan Turing (1912–1954), a mathematician who worked for British intelligence at a secret site called Bletchley Park in England. He assembled a team of mathematicians and cryptologists to work on breaking the codes pro-

Interior of Bletchley Park building, where Alan Turing and his team created the code-breaking machine (pictured) that helped defeat the Germans in World War II, saving uncounted lives.

duced by the Enigma machine. Turing started building the first computer to help break the codes.

Since the Germans changed the Enigma settings daily to produce new codes, Turing's computer had to be built to break the codes quickly.

However, the Germans sending radio messages also helped. Many German messages ended with "Heil Hitler," which meant that those breaking the code could easily figure out the code for six different letters. Also, there was a problem with radio operators who did not change their six-letter passwords often or used easy-to-figure-out passwords. "HITLER" and "TOMMIX" were popular passwords for the Germans. Tom Mix was an early American cowboy movie star whose films were popular in Europe.

Eventually, Turing and his staff broke the code and could learn of German strategy and military movements. This knowledge helped the Allies win the war.

What movies tell the story of Alan Turing and his struggles in later life?

The 2014 movie *The Imitation Code*, starring Benedict Cumberbatch, and the 1996 television film *Breaking the Code*, starring Derek Jacobi.

Who was Fred Rogers?

Fred Rogers (1928–2003) starred in the beloved children's educational show *Mister Rogers' Neighborhood*, which ran from 1968 to 2001 from WQED in Pittsburgh. He ex-

What are some movies and urban legends about Mr. Rogers?

His story is told in the 2018 documentary *Won't You Be My Neighbor?* In the 2019 *A Beautiful Day in the Neighborhood*, Rogers is played by Tom Hanks.

Several untrue urban legends have been told about Mr. Rogers claiming that he was either an ex-Navy SEAL or an ex-Marine sniper with many confirmed kills. It was also rumored that he had tattoos on his arms, which is why he always wore a sweater. None of these rumors are true.

plored how to use television to connect with and educate young children. The show was beloved by kids because it took seriously the thoughts and feelings of children. Also, Mr. Rogers talked in a slow and easy-to-follow way that children could understand. Adults watching the show might find it dragging and dull, but kids did not.

DISASTERS

How did ancient societies interpret catastrophic events?

Past cultures, long before the science of weather (meteorology) and the science of earthquakes (seismology) had been developed, often used mythology and folktales to explain dramatic weather events or other natural phenomena. For example, the ancient Maya (in what today is Mexico and Central America) believed that earthquakes were the gods' way of thinning out an overcrowded population. One Japanese myth maintained that the entire string of Japanese islands rested on the back of a giant catfish who would grow restless and flop around when the gods were displeased, resulting in an earthquake. According to Hawaiian myth, the volcano goddess Pele causes Mount Kilauea to erupt whenever she has a temper tantrum.

However, it is not just ancient societies that have interpreted catastrophic weather events as religious signs. Pat Robertson (1930–), Jerry Falwell (1933–2007), and other American religious leaders and televangelists stated or implied that certain natural disasters—such as Hurricane Katrina in 2005—were the result of decisions in America that displeased God, such as the policy of allowing abortions.

What are the different kinds of natural disasters?

Typical natural disasters include volcanic eruptions, earthquakes, tsunamis, tropical storms, hurricanes, tornadoes, floods, and blizzards.

VOLCANIC ERUPTIONS

What are the largest known volcanic eruptions?

Scientists measure volcanic eruptions by the amount of material ejected into the atmosphere. Here are the six largest eruptions, from biggest to smallest:

- At the present-day location of Yellowstone Park in Wyoming, c. 600000 B.C.E.
- Toba, Indonesia, c. 74000 B.C.E.
- Tambora, Indonesia, 1815 C.E.
- Santorini, Greece, 1470 B.C.E.
- Laki, Iceland, 1783 C.E. (This eruption produced the largest known lava flow in recorded history.)
- Krakatao, Indonesia, 1883 C.E.

The eruption in Yellowstone is hard to fathom: the volcano left a crater that measured thirty by forty-five miles and released about 10,000 cubic kilometers of material into the atmosphere. The next-largest eruption, at Toba, released only one-tenth that amount, or 1,000 cubic kilometers. The one at Tambora released one-tenth of the Toba amount, one hundred cubic kilometers.

Have there been any recent volcanic eruptions in the United States?

The May 18, 1980, eruption of Mount St. Helens in southwestern Washington State is among the largest known eruptions and is the largest eruption in the modern history of the forty-eight contiguous United States. The eruption created a massive landslide and the emission of 520 million tons of ash across the country. Miles of forest were devastated, and the North Fork of the Toutle River was laden with ash and other volcanic debris up to 600 feet deep. The eruption also claimed fifty-seven lives.

The Mount St. Helens eruption led to more scientific study and monitoring of volcanoes. The United States has nearly 170 volcanoes considered capable of eruption, but until Mount St. Helens, the only modern volcanic eruptions in the United States had been in Hawaii.

Why are there so many volcanoes in Hawaii?

The Hawaiian Islands were created by a line of volcanoes in the Pacific Ocean. Several are still active, including Kilauea, Maunaloa, Hualalai, and Maunakea. Kilauea has erupted continuously since 1983. Visitors can explore Hawaii's Volcanoes National Park to see lava flows. However, Alaska is the state with the most volcanoes.

Mount St. Helens is shown here just a couple days before the 1980 eruption (above) and two years after it erupted (bottom). The explosion took out the top of the mountain and reduced it in height from 9,677 feet (2,950 meters) to 8,363 feet (2,549 meters).

What were the deadliest volcanic eruptions in the modern era?

The 1815 eruption of Mount Tambora in Indonesia was the deadliest yet, killing some 92,000 people. Another Indonesian eruption in 1883 at Karkatoa claimed 36,417 lives.

On the French island of Martinique in the West Indies, Mount Pelée erupted in 1902, and more than 29,000 people perished. A more recent eruption occurred in 1985 at Nevada del Ruiz, Colombia, which claimed 23,000 lives.

Iceland's Skaptar volcano erupted in 1783. Approximately 9,000 people (20 percent of the population) died. The volcano released toxic clouds of hydrofluoric acid and sulfur dioxide, which killed plants and 90 percent of livestock. This led to a famine, which caused so many human deaths.

EARTHQUAKES

What is the strongest earthquake ever measured?

On May 22, 1960, a powerful earthquake hit Valdivia, Chile, measuring 9.5 on the Richter scale. Estimates suggest that between 2,000 and 6,000 people died. More than 3,000 were injured, and two million were left homeless. Damage was $550 million. The quake also spawned tsunamis (seismic waves), which claimed sixty-one lives in Hawaii, 138 in Japan, and thirty-two dead or missing in the Philippines.

Have there been other catastrophic earthquakes in China in recent times?

On July 28, 1976, a quake rocked the Chinese city of Tangshan at four o'clock in the morning. In less than a minute, 89 percent of the homes and 78 percent of the industrial buildings were destroyed, killing 250,000 people, according to the official reports. However, international observers believe the death toll was higher, about 750,000, which means that the quake claimed three-fourths of the area's total population.

A quake had not occurred in that region in six centuries, and the area was considered at low risk for earthquakes. Consequently, the building codes in the region were not stringent enough for the structures to withstand the force of the quake.

What about the earthquake in Haiti in 2010?

On January 12, 2010, a quake rocked the country of Haiti near the city of Leogane. According to the Haitian government, more than 315,000 people perished in its aftermath. The quake impacted the capital city of Port-au-Prince and devastated the economic infrastructure of the country. Mass graves were constructed to deal with the sheer volume of human carnage. It was estimated that the quake destroyed 250,000 residential homes and more than 30,000 commercial buildings. Recovery efforts, aided by billions in foreign aid, attempted to rebuild the country. There were noted successes, but a January 2012 report indicated that still nearly half a million Haitians remain homeless or living in tents.

Tragically, in 2016, Haiti was hit by Hurricane Matthew, which caused more devastation and loss of life.

How disastrous was the San Francisco earthquake of 1906?

The quake struck at 5:12 A.M. on April 18 and registered 8.3 on the Richter scale. Twenty seconds of trembling were followed by forty-five to sixty seconds of shocks. The quake cracked water and gas mains, which resulted in a fire that lasted three days and destroyed two-thirds of the city. The destruction and loss of lives were great. As many as 3,000 were killed; the entire business district was demolished; three out of five homes had either crumbled or burned; 250,000 to 300,000 people were left homeless; and 490 city blocks were destroyed.

The quake was a milestone for American journalism. The offices of the city's newspapers, the *Examiner* (owned by William Randolph Hearst, 1863–1951), the *Call*, and the *Chronicle* had all burned. But the first day after the disaster, the three papers joined forces across the bay in Oakland to print a combined edition, the *California Chronicle-Examiner*. Across the country, Will Irwin (1873–1948) of the *New York Sun*, who had been a reporter and editor at the *San Francisco Chronicle* from 1900 to 1904, wrote a story titled "The City That Was," which he completed from memory alone. Due to the telegraph, the story was picked up by papers around the country and became a classic of journalism. The San Francisco tragedy demonstrated the newfound ability of the American press to create an instant national story out of a local event. The San Francisco earthquake of 1906 remains the worst to ever hit an American city.

Has San Francisco been hit by other serious earthquakes?

The Bay Area was hit again by a large quake in 1989. As millions tuned in to watch the World Series at San Francisco's Candlestick Park (and local interest was high, as the Series featured two Bay Area teams—the San Francisco Giants and the Oakland A's), the TV cameras began to shake. Because of media coverage of the baseball game, the earthquake was broadcast live around the world. As in the 1906 quake, fires resulted from broken gas mains, and the damage was extensive. Named the Loma Prieta earthquake, it registered 7.1 on the Richter scale, claimed sixty-seven lives, and damaged $15 billion worth of property. San Francisco's Marina District was particularly hard-hit because the area was built on a landfill, which included debris from the 1906 quake.

The aftermath of the 1906 San Francisco earthquake leveled 80 percent of the city and killed three thousand people.

What is a tsunami?

Although sometimes called tidal waves, tsunamis are created not by tides but by earthquakes, which produce chains of waves that move across the water at terrific speeds of more than 500 miles per hour. Upon reaching shallow water, the waves grow in height, sometimes up to one hundred feet or more, as was the case in 1883 when tsunamis reaching up to 130 feet hit an Indonesian island, destroying more than 150 villages and claiming some 36,000 lives.

In ancient times, it is believed that a tsunami destroyed the Minoan Greek culture that existed on the island of Crete (in the Mediterranean Sea). In about 1450 B.C.E., Crete was struck by a 200-foot tsunami, which either demolished the island or weakened the population such that they could be taken over by the Mycenaeans, who were Greek mainlanders.

While tsunamis are known to strike along the Pacific Rim, damage has been minimized by sophisticated instruments that help meteorologists monitor and predict disastrous weather, and seismologists track earthquakes that can create tsunamis. This knowledge can be used to alert the public to evacuate from areas of possible danger.

What was the 2004 Indian Ocean earthquake and tsunami?

Warning systems did not exist for the Indian Ocean when a 9.0–9.3 earthquake occurred off the coast of the Indonesian island of Sumatra on December 26, 2004. Witnesses reported that following the earthquake, ocean waters receded from shorelines hours before the giant waves roared in, washing over islands and sweeping through coastal villages in twelve countries, including Indonesia, Myanmar, India, and Sri Lanka. The waves struck as far west as the coast of Africa.

More than 227,000 people died, making the earthquake and tsunami one of the deadliest natural disasters in history. The earthquake that caused the tsunami waves was the third-largest earthquake ever recorded.

Has a tsunami ever hit the United States?

Yes, in fact the tallest tsunami ever recorded hit Alaska in March 1964. It was 220 feet high. The earthquake, called the Great Alaskan Earthquake—which measured 9.2 on the Richter scale—created the tsunami, which hit the southwest part of the state and claimed 107 lives.

Hawaii also sees an occasional tsunami. The most remarkable one hit the islands before Hawaii became a state. In 1946, all the water drained from the three-mile-wide harbor at Hilo, which was immediately followed by a tsunami that rushed onshore, destroying the waterfront. This happened twice, killing 150 people.

TROPICAL STORMS AND HURRICANES

What have been the deadliest tropical storms in the world?

The deadliest tropical storms are not hurricanes but rather the unnamed "super cyclones" that sweep out of the Bay of Bengal (in the Indian Ocean), striking the densely populated Indian subcontinent. These storms have been known to kill 100,000 people or more. The fatalities numbered more than 300,000 when a 1970 cyclone struck East Pakistan (Bangladesh). That storm is still the deadliest cyclone to hit the region.

More recent Indian cyclones have sometimes reached "super cyclone" status. An April 1991 storm packing 160-mile-per-hour winds and twenty-foot waves swept over Bangladesh's low-lying coastal plain. There was no place for residents to seek shelter from the advancing sea. An estimated 140,000 people perished, and ten million were left homeless. Property damage climbed to $1.7 billion.

In October 1999, another devastating cyclone struck the Bay of Bengal region. It was the strongest and deadliest since the 1991 disaster: 10,000 died, and over a million people lost their homes.

What is the outlook for cyclones in the Indian Ocean in the future?

There is much concern about the dangers of cyclones and their damage in the future. Global climate change has altered weather patterns in the Indian Ocean, such as the annual monsoon rains. It is feared that climate change will make storms more unpredictable and more damaging.

The country of Bangladesh is particularly vulnerable because the land elevation is very close to sea level, and many millions of people live in this densely populated country. Bangladesh is especially vulnerable to storms coming off the ocean. Even worse, because of global climate change, the oceans are rising, which means even ordinary storms will affect more land area and endanger more people.

What was the worst hurricane in U.S. history in terms of casualties?

The hurricane that caused the most deaths in U.S. history was the hurricane that struck Galveston, Texas, on September 8, 1900. It claimed the lives of anywhere between 6,000 to 12,000 people. It is also called the Galveston Flood, the Great Galveston Hurricane, and the Galveston Hurricane of 1900.

What happened with Hurricane Katrina?

Hurricane Katrina hit the Gulf Coast in August 2005, becoming one of the most disastrous hurricanes in U.S. history and one of the nation's worst weather disasters. The storm stretched 200 miles in diameter, packed winds of up to 145 miles per hour, produced torrential rain and huge waves, spawned twisters throughout the region, and pushed a twenty-eight-foot storm surge onto the land.

Katrina moved ashore on the Gulf Coast on Monday, August 29. New Orleans, which sits below sea level, had ordered an evacuation, but tens of thousands of people had stayed—some out of necessity (such as law-enforcement and health-care workers), some because they were unable to evacuate, and others because they chose not to leave. Some 23,000 of those who stayed holed up in the aging Superdome sports arena, which was set up as an emergency shelter. The structure barely withstood the lashing winds of Katrina, which blew off portions of the dome.

A NASA satellite image shows the size of Hurricane Katrina as it made landfall over Louisiana in 2005.

513

On Tuesday morning, Katrina ravaged Louisiana, Mississippi, and Alabama before weakening as it moved inland. Officials and news reporters generally agreed that there was unbelievable damage all along the coast, but New Orleans had "dodged a bullet": the Big Easy had not taken the worst of it. Gulfport and Biloxi, Mississippi, appeared the hardest hit. The devastation there was astonishing: 90 percent of the structures along the Gulf Coast were destroyed, and hundreds of thousands of people were displaced.

Later Tuesday, New Orleans's fate changed as levees that protected the city could not hold back a swollen Lake Pontchartrain. The levees broke, and 80 percent of the city filled with water twenty-five feet deep. Officials and volunteers could not get flood victims out fast enough, usually plucking them from rooftops or finding them in attics, where survivors sought refuge as waters rose. The city descended into chaos. Heart-wrenching images of human despair filled the media, touching people around the nation.

Americans responded with donations of money, goods, and time. The American Red Cross launched the largest mobilization effort in its history. The Federal Emergency Management Agency (FEMA, a part of the Department of Homeland Security [DHS]), the Coast Guard (also part of the DHS), and the U.S. military struggled to keep pace with Katrina's aftermath all along the coast.

What other Atlantic hurricanes have set records?

The deadliest Atlantic hurricane of recent times was Hurricane Mitch in 1998 that killed over 11,374 people. The deadliest Atlantic hurricane of all time was the Great Hurricane of 1780, which killed 22,000–27,500 people.

In August 2017, Hurricane Harvey hit Texas and Louisiana. It would tie Katrina as the costliest tropical storm on record. One huge problem was the catastrophic rainfall of the storm that caused massive flooding, especially in the Houston area.

In September 2017, Hurricane Maria, a Category 5 storm, devastated Dominica, the U.S. Virgin Islands, and Puerto Rico. It was the worst natural disaster to hit those islands. These islands have still not fully recovered.

In September 2019, Hurricane Dorian struck the Bahamas. It was the worst tropical storm to ever hit the Bahamas. It was also one of the most powerful hurricanes ever recorded in the Atlantic Ocean, with winds reaching speeds of 185 miles per hour (295 kilometers per hour).

Why are there so many hurricanes that are so intense in recent years?

Scientists studying global climate change have long predicted that climate change would cause storms such as hurricanes to become more frequent, more powerful, and more devastating.

The hurricane also became memorable when U.S. president Donald Trump appeared in a video with a map altered by a Sharpie. He falsely asserted that Hurricane Dorian was headed for Alabama.

What is the origin of the Saffir-Simpson scale?

The scale was created in 1971 by engineer Herbert Saffir (1917–2007) and meteorologist Bob Simpson (1912–2014), director of the U.S. National Hurricane Center. Introduced in 1972, the Saffir-Simpson Scale measures hurricanes, from Category 1, the weakest (with sustained winds of at least seventy-four miles per hour and a storm surge of four to five feet above normal), to Category 5, the strongest (with sustained winds of more than 155 miles per hour and a storm surge higher than eighteen feet).

How long have hurricanes been given names?

Naming hurricanes has a long history. For centuries, Caribbean storms were named according to the saint whose liturgical day it was when the storm hit. This became confusing when hurricanes struck on the same day but in different years, leading to such references as Hurricane San Felipe the Second.

During World War II, the U.S. military began naming storms, giving them women's names. In 1951, the American weather services began naming Atlantic Ocean storms according to a phonetic alphabet (Able, Baker, Charley, etc.). A few years later, forecasters returned to using women's names, and a new list of names was created for each Atlantic hurricane season (June 1 to November 30). Storms in some areas of the Pacific began being named in 1959, and by 1964, all regions of the Pacific were using the naming convention.

Establishing names for storms helps meteorologists track more than one storm at any given time, makes clear the communication of warnings, and facilitates study since the names of major hurricanes are retired to avoid confusion later. In 1979, equality was brought to the naming process, introducing men's names as well as multicultural names to each season's list.

TORNADOES

What were some of the deadliest tornadoes?

The deadliest tornado in world history was the Daulatur-Saturia tornado that struck in 1989 in Bangladesh—a country susceptible to such natural disasters. More than 1,300 people died.

The deadliest tornado in the United States was the Tri-State tornado that struck on March 18, 1925. Called the Tri-State Tornado because it crossed into Missouri, Illinois, and Indiana, it claimed 747 lives.

On May 22, 2011, a massive tornado a mile wide and with winds upward of 200 miles per hour cut a path through Joplin, Missouri, that killed over 150 people and caused $2.8 billion in damage.

What about the Joplin tornado?

The Joplin tornado on May 22, 2011, tore a mile-wide path through the city, killing 158 people. It was the costliest tornado in U.S. history and the seventh-deadliest tornado in the United States.

FLOODS

What was the Johnstown Flood?

The city of Johnstown, in southwest Pennsylvania (east of Pittsburgh), has been the site of numerous floods, but the most disastrous one occurred on May 31, 1889, when the South Fork Dam on the Conemaugh River gave way, releasing a torrent of water. Since the dam was located some fourteen miles into the Allegheny Mountains, the waters rushed into Johnstown at a rate of fifty miles per hour. The water hit with a force strong enough to have tossed a forty-eight-ton locomotive one mile. It killed more than 2,000 people. At the time of the flood, the city's population was about 30,000, meaning between 6 and 16 percent of the population died as a result of the disaster. In 1977, Johnstown was again the site of a disastrous flood, though advance-warning systems helped minimize the loss of life to eighty.

How does the Great Flood of 1993 compare with other floods?

The flood, which occurred in the summer of 1993, was immense: so much of Iowa was under water that a satellite image (monitoring moisture on Earth) made the flooded area look like it was the size of Lake Michigan or Lake Superior. The area that was under water was roughly equivalent to twice the size of Massachusetts. Even so, the Great Flood resulted in a smaller water-covered area than did floods earlier in the century.

Due to heavy rainfall during the spring and summer of 1993, the Mississippi River widened to as much as seven miles at some points, and the Missouri River also overflowed its banks—despite the levee system that had been put in place by the federal government earlier in the century. The flood took fifty lives, displaced 85,000 people from their homes, destroyed 8,000 homes, damaged the contents of another 20,000 homes, stranded 2,000 loaded barges, and resulted in more than 400 counties being declared disaster areas. The property and crop losses totaled $15 billion.

What about the Flood of 2011?

This flood in April and May 2011 was just as bad as floods in 1993 and the flood in 1927 in terms of the amount of water due to unprecedented rainfall.

What is the worst flood in history?

The worst flood to date occurred in China in 1887, when more than 900,000 people died as the Yellow River (Huang He) overflowed. China is particularly susceptible to severe and regular flooding; the Huang He River alone typically floods two out of every three years. And because river valleys are densely populated, the human toll is often great. A 1939 flood in North China claimed more than half a million lives.

BLIZZARDS

What was the harshest blizzard to hit the United States?

Regions of the United States—particularly the Great Plains, Midwest, and New England—typically experience extreme winter weather, but some storms do stand out. In March 1888, the Northeast was hit by a blizzard dubbed the Great White Hurricane. After a warm spell that had caused the buds to open on trees in New York's Central Park, on March 12, the temperature in the city plummeted to 10 degrees Fahrenheit, and winds off the Atlantic built up to forty-eight miles per hour, bringing unpredicted snow that continued intermittently until the early morning of March 14. The three-day accumulation totaled twenty-one inches, and snowdrifts fifteen to twenty feet high halted traffic. The snowfall was even greater elsewhere, averaging forty inches or more in some parts of southeastern New York and southern New England.

Two hundred ships were lost or grounded, and at least one hundred died at sea. A total of at least 400 people died, half of them in New York City.

What about the Great Blizzard of 1993?

The Great Blizzard of 1993 caused loss of life and extensive damage all along the Eastern Seaboard from Maine to Florida. More than 300 people died, almost fifty of them at sea, and economic losses totaled $3 to $6 billion. Wind gusts exceeded seventy-five miles per hour all along the East Coast, while winds exceeding one hundred miles per hour were measured at various points. Tennessee saw the highest snowfall of the storm, with fifty-six inches at Mount LeConte. Snowfall amounts were also heavy in the Northeast, but snow accumulated as far south as the Florida Panhandle. Experts estimated that the amount of water that fell (in the form of snow) was equivalent to forty days' flow of the mighty Mississippi River past New Orleans.

What about the 1975 storm?

Another storm that could easily vie for the title "storm of the century" occurred January 10–11, 1975, in the upper Midwest. The blizzard was accompanied by winds of ninety miles per hour and wind chills as low as minus 80 degrees Fahrenheit. Trains were stranded in snowdrifts, and at least eighty people died. Ranchers and farmers were hard-hit, losing some 55,000 head of livestock.

What was the Dust Bowl?

The Dust Bowl was the most severe drought in U.S. history. In the spring of 1934, with the country in the grips of the Great Depression, farmers across the Great Plains of the United States witnessed two great dust storms. First, in mid-April, after days of hot, dry weather and cloudless skies, forty-fifty-mile-per-hour winds picked up and took with them the dry soil, resulting in thick, heavy clouds. In Texas and Oklahoma, these dirt clouds engulfed the landscape. The next month was extremely hot, and on May 10, a second storm came up as the gales returned, this time creating a light brown fog.

On May 11, an estimated twelve million tons of soil fell on Chicago as the dust storm blew in off the Great Plains, and the same storm darkened the skies over Cleveland. On May 12, the dust clouds had reached the Eastern Seaboard. Between the two storms, 650 million tons of topsoil had blown off the Great Plains.

The resulting Dust Bowl covered 300,000 square miles across New Mexico, eastern Colorado, Texas, western Oklahoma, and Kansas. The damage was great. Crops, principally wheat, were cut off at

The Dust Bowl that struck the U.S. Great Plains states during the 1930s was the result of drought and poor agricultural practices, leading to erosion, loss of crops, and mass migrations and poverty.

ground level or torn from their roots; cattle that ate dust-laden grass eventually died from "mud balls"; dust drifted, creating banks against barns and houses, while families tried to keep it from penetrating the cracks and crevices of their homes by using wet blankets, oiled cloths, and tape, only to still have everything covered in grit. Vehicles and machinery were clogged with dirt. In addition to the farmers who died in the fields, suffocated by the storm, hundreds of people suffered from "dust pneumonia."

What were the effects of the Dust Bowl?

After the dust had settled in the spring of 1934, the reaction among many Great Plains farm families was to flee the devastation. More than 350,000 people packed up their belongings and headed west, their lives forever changed by the disaster. In his 1939 novel *The Grapes of Wrath*, American writer and Nobel laureate John Steinbeck (1902–1968) chronicled the harrowing and sorrowful westward journey of one Oklahoma family that was among the so-called "Okies" who deserted their farmlands in the devastated area of the Great Plains in search of a better life elsewhere.

Nature alone was not to blame for the Dust Bowl. By the end of the nineteenth century, farmers, aided by the advent of large tractors and reapers (harvesting machines), were cultivating the Great Plains, uprooting the native buffalo grass, which holds moisture in the soil and keeps it from blowing away. Even strong winds and extended droughts had not disturbed the land when it was covered by the grassland. When the demand for wheat increased after World War I, farmers responded by planting more than twenty-seven million new acres of the grain. By 1930, there were almost three times as many acres in wheat production as ten years earlier; most of the buffalo grass that had prevented the earth from blowing away had been removed. When the next dry period came and the wind picked up, the Dust Bowl resulted.

The government stepped in to remedy the problem. Soil conservation became the focus of federal agencies, and the U.S. Forest Service undertook a project to plant a "shelter belt" of trees within a one-hundred-mile-wide zone from Canada to the Texas Panhandle. Recovery was aided by the return of the rains. Soon, the buffalo grass grew back, helping to ensure that the Dust Bowl would not recur.

FIRES

How much damage was done by the Great Fire of London?

The fire, which began early in the morning on Sunday, September 2, 1666, and burned for four days and nights, consumed four-fifths of the city (which was then walled), plus sixty-three acres lying just outside the city walls. The blaze began on Pudding Lane near London Bridge and quickly spread through crowded, wooden houses to the Thames wharf warehouses. The destruction included London's Guildhall, the Custom House, the Royal Exchange, and St. Paul's Cathedral. Additionally,

519

forty-four livery company halls, eighty-six churches, and more than 13,000 houses were destroyed.

Though the fire was unquestionably disastrous, London soon rebuilt and became one of Europe's most modern cities. The fire also destroyed thousands of old buildings where lice-infested rats had lived—rats that were partly responsible for spreading the plague through the English city.

What was the impact of the fire at the MGM Grand in Las Vegas?

The November 21, 1980, blaze, which killed eighty-five people and injured more than 600, led to a nationwide revision of local fire codes, giving this tragic event large-scale political significance. The MGM Grand Hotel had, in fact, passed fire inspections, but the building, which was then the world's largest gambling casino, had been eight years in the making. Between the time it was designed and the time it was built, the building no longer complied with the always-improving safety standard for high-rise buildings.

A short circuit started the blaze, which sent thick, black smoke through the air ducts and escape stairwells in the twenty-one floors of guest rooms. Since more people were harmed or killed by smoke inhalation than by the fire itself, the American public became aware of the danger of smoke—sometimes over and above that of fire.

The event was a catalyst for change. Prior to the November blaze, most communities had not required existing buildings to be retrofitted every time fire-safety codes changed and improved. After the fire, many communities chose to require building owners to comply with current protection capabilities.

How bad are the California wildfires?

At this point, the 2018 wildfire season is the deadliest and most destructive on record with 8,527 fires covering 1.9 million acres, which broke the records set during the 2017 California wildfire season. Eighty-five people died in the Camp Fire in November 2018, the worst wildfire in California history.

California has suffered many droughts over time, but the most recent droughts have been the worst on record. Many believe that climate change is the reason.

What was the Australia "Black Summer"?

The 2019–2020 wildfire season in Australia has been worse than what is typical for the continent. Drought—particularly severe because of global warming—led to uncontrollable fires over much of the country, burning some forty-six million square acres (18.6 million hectares), destroying nearly three thousand homes, killing thirty-four people, and causing about $4.5 billion in damages. Perhaps most tragic of all has been the toll on wildlife. Scientists estimate about one billion animals, including many rare and endangered species, have perished in the flames. Koalas, for example, have suffered so much that there is concern the species might never recover.

Kangaroos flee during the Australian wildfire crisis of 2019–2020.

BRIDGES AND TECHNOLOGICAL FAILURES

What happened to the Tacoma-Narrows Bridge?

In 1940, the new 2,800-foot suspension bridge, carrying traffic across Washington's Puget Sound, was hit by high winds, causing it to buckle and undulate. In the simplest of terms, an engineering error allowed one of the suspensions to give way in the wind, and the bridge became ribbonlike, moving in waves. The problem was not the strength of the winds but rather because the frequency of the wind matched the natural frequency of the bridge.

It was ten years before a second span was opened over the body of water. The 1940 accident prompted engineers and bridge designers to be more cautious in the design of suspension bridges.

Which was the first suspension bridge in the United States?

The first wire suspension bridge in the United States was the 358-foot-long, twenty-five-foot-wide Schuylkill River Bridge near Philadelphia, Pennsylvania. Built in 1842 by U.S.

521

civil engineer Charles Ellet Jr. (1810–1862), it was supported by five wire cables on either side. The first chain suspension bridge in the United States was built in 1800.

What is the largest suspension bridge in the world?

It is the Akashi Kaikyo Bridge in Kobe, Japan. It spans 6,500 feet. The famous Golden Gate Bridge in San Francisco, with a span of 4,200 feet, is tied for sixteenth place on the list of largest suspension bridges. The Golden Gate Bridge, built in 1937, had the longest span until the Verrazzano-Narrows Bridge was opened in 1964 in New York, with a span of 4,260 feet.

DISASTERS ON SHIPS

What are the facts about the *Titanic*?

The RMS *Titanic* was the brainchild of Lord William James Pirrie (1847–1924) and J. Bruce Ismay (1862–1937). They wanted to compete with the top-notch Cunard liners by surpassing them both in size and luxury. The ship they planned, the *Titanic*, was built in Belfast, Ireland, along with its sister ship, the *Olympic*. The *Titanic* was 882 feet long, 92 feet wide, and weighed 46,328 gross tons; nine steel decks rose as high as an eleven-story building.

The *Titanic's* size not only allowed more room to accommodate the increasing number of steerage (cheapest-fare) passengers who were immigrating to the United States, but it also featured lavish elegance for first- and second-class travelers. Creature comforts included the first shipboard swimming pool, Turkish bath, gymnasium, and squash court. First-class cabins were nothing short of opulent, including coal-burning fireplaces in the sitting rooms and full-size, four-poster beds in the bedrooms. Additionally, there was a loading crane and a compartment for automobiles. The ship's hospital even featured a modern operating room.

With its steerage full and some of society's most prominent individuals on board, the RMS *Titanic* left the docks at Southampton, England, on April 10, 1912, sailing to New York. On April 14, the ship was traveling in the exceptionally calm and icy waters off the North Atlantic near Newfoundland. At 11:40 P.M., the *Titanic* scraped an iceberg, sustaining damage along the starboard (right) side from the bow to about the middle of the ship. The *Titanic* immediately began taking on water and sank in two hours and forty minutes.

Only 711 of the 2,224 aboard survived; the 1,513 lost included American industrialists and businessmen John Jacob Astor IV, Isidor Straus (of R. H. Macy's), Benjamin Guggenheim, and Harry Elkins Widener. Survivors—mostly women and children who had been traveling as first-class passengers—were picked up by the ship *Carpathia*.

The *Titanic* came to symbolize human arrogance; the shipowners believed the *Titanic* was unsinkable. Consequently, the ocean liner only had enough lifeboats for half

The *Titanic* is shown here leaving the port from Belfast in 1912, leaving for an appointment with tragedy.

the passengers. Since there had been no lifeboat drills on board, many lifeboats were launched only half full.

What low-tech item could have saved the *Titanic*?

The lookouts keeping watch did not have binoculars. The binoculars were in a locker; the person with the key had been reassigned just before the *Titanic* sailed and, by mistake, took the key with him.

What effect did the sinking of the *Titanic* have on sea travel?

The sinking of the *Titanic* brought about new regulations. First, and perhaps most simply, all ships were required to carry enough lifeboats: one spot in a lifeboat for each person on board. New rules required lifeboat drills to be held soon after a ship sails.

Shipping lanes were moved farther south, away from the ice fields, and were monitored by a patrol. Ships approaching ice fields were required to slow their speed or alter their course.

Until 1912, most ships employed only one radio operator. Such was the case on the *California*, which was less than twenty miles from the *Titanic*, when wireless operator Jack Phillips sent out the distress signal. However, the operator on the *California* was not on duty at that hour. Phillips stayed at his station, desperately trying to reach a nearby ship, and eventually went down with the *Titanic*.

In the aftermath of the disaster, the U.S. Congress moved quickly to pass the Radio Act of 1912, which required that radios be manned day and night, that they have an alternate energy source (besides the ship's engine), and that they have a range of at least one hundred miles. Furthermore, operators must be licensed, adhere to certain bandwidths, and observe a strict protocol for receiving distress signals. (This was the beginning of the Federal Communications Commission, or FCC.) These measures were meant to rid the airwaves of those amateur operators who had confused official operators the night of April 15, 1912. One erroneous wireless message transmitted by amateurs that night had the *Titanic* moving safely toward Halifax, Nova Scotia.

When was the wreck of the *Titanic* found?

Oceanographer and underwater archaeologist Robert Ballard (1942–) discovered the wreckage of the *Titanic* in 1985, 13,000 feet below sea level. (See the chapter "Exploration.")

Was the *Titanic* the most disastrous shipwreck of all time?

Though the most famous, it is not the most disastrous. In April 1865, the side-wheel steamboat *Sultana* exploded on the Mississippi River near Memphis, killing 1,547 of the estimated 2,100 people on board, many of whom were Union soldiers who had been released from Confederate prison. The packet steamboat had routinely carried passengers and cargo between St. Louis and New Orleans; however, it was built to hold only 376 passengers.

In 1917, the *Mont Blanc* exploded in the harbor at Halifax, Nova Scotia, claiming 2,000 lives and severely injuring nearly 9,000. The ship, which was a French munitions carrier (World War I was raging at the time), was struck by a Norwegian relief ship, the *Imo*. The *Mont Blanc* was laden with thousands of tons of TNT, acid, and other explosives, which were ignited in the collision. The explosion was so terrific that it laid waste to much of Halifax and generated a tsunami that swept through the city.

Most recently, in 1987, the *Dona Paz* collided with another ship off the Philippines; 1,840 died.

What was the *General Slocum* disaster?

The *General Slocum*, a side-wheel passenger steamboat, caught fire and sank in the East River of New York City on June 15, 1904. On board were members of St. Mark's

What movies are about the *Titanic*?

There have been many films about the sinking of *Titanic*, beginning with 1912's *Saved from the Titanic*. Other memorable movies about the tragedy include *A Night to Remember* (1958), *The Unsinkable Molly Brown* (1964), and, of course, James Cameron's 1997 epic, *Titanic*, starring Leonardo DiCaprio as Jack Dawson and Kate Winslet as Rose DeWitt Bukater. This film won eleven Academy Awards, including Best Picture and Best Director.

Evangelical Lutheran Church on a church picnic. Of the 1,342 people on board, 1,021 died. It was the worst disaster in terms of loss of life in New York until the 9/11 attacks.

The crew on the ship had never practiced fire drills. The water hoses were rotten and fell apart. The life jackets were thirteen years old and in bad shape. Even worse, the manufacturer had put iron weights in the life jackets rather than filling them with the right kind of cork. The passengers, mostly women and children, like most people of that era, could not swim, and their heavy, woolen clothing caused them to sink.

AIRCRAFT DISASTERS

Were there any other airship disasters before the *Hindenburg*?

A British dirigible, R101, burned on October 5, 1930, northwest of Paris while on its maiden voyage to Australia. That disaster claimed forty-eight lives.

The USS *Akron* was destroyed in a thunderstorm off the coast of New Jersey on April 4, 1933, killing seventy-three.

What happened to the *Hindenburg*?

The image of the large airship *Hindenburg* bursting into flames is familiar to many. A German vessel and the largest airship ever built, it exploded while it was trying to land at Lakehurst, New Jersey, on May 6, 1937. The *Hindenburg* had just completed a transatlantic flight and had dropped its mooring lines to the ground crew when the airship afloat caught fire. Within thirty-two seconds, the *Hindenburg* was nothing but smoldering rubble on the ground. Only thirty-five of the ninety-seven people on board survived.

There has been debate over the cause of the fire ever since. Some believe that a spark ignited hydrogen gas leaking from the airship. Others have suggested that a spark ignited the paint, containing both iron oxide and aluminum, which can react together to burn. As for the spark, the airship moving through the atmosphere could pick up an electrical charge, and if it was not discharged properly, sparks could occur.

The *Hindenburg* had actually been designed to be lifted by helium, which does

The explosive end to Germany's *Hindenburg* blimp as it prepared to land in New Jersey in 1937 will always be remembered as one of the most spectacular air disasters in history.

525

not burn. However, the gas was scarce at the time, and the United States refused to sell any to Germany, which had been taken over by Adolf Hitler.

Though travel by airship had been going on for more than twenty-five years and some 50,000 passengers had been transported without a single fatality, the highly publicized crash effectively ended airship travel. Today, airships, or "blimps," are rare except for the Goodyear Blimp seen at sporting events. Some military airships are still used for reconnaissance and patrol.

What is the worst airplane accident in history?

With thousands of accidents since the beginning of aviation history, records differentiate among ground collision, midair collision, and single-aircraft accidents. (Some records differentiate by cause, including pilot error, weather, and fuel starvation.)

The worst ground collision—and the deadliest airplane accident in history—was the Tenerife disaster of March 27, 1977, which killed 583 people. Two Boeing 747 airliners ran into each other on Tenerife in the Canary Islands in the Atlantic Ocean. One was a Pan Am flight, "the Clipper Victor," which originated at Los Angeles International Airport, made a stop at New York's JFK Airport, and was headed for the Canary Islands; it was diverted to Tenerife at the last minute due to a bomb threat at its destination airport on neighboring Las Palmas Island.

The other 747 was a KLM flight, "the Flying Dutchman," originating in Amsterdam; it, too, was diverted away from Las Palmas because of the threat there. On takeoff, the KLM plane slammed into the taxiing Pan Am plane. Heavy fog on the runway contributed to the disaster, but there were communication problems as well. According to tower records, the KLM flight had not yet been cleared for takeoff, yet it took off. Upon collision, the jumbo jets burst into flames; there were only sixty-one survivors (fifty-four passengers and seven crew members), all from the Pan Am flight.

What are some other "worst" airplane accidents?

The worst midair collision happened on November 12, 1996, over Charkhi Dadri, India: 349 people perished when a Saudi Arabian Airlines Boeing 747 collided with a Kazakh Ilyushin 11-76 aircraft. There were no survivors.

The worst single-plane accident happened on August 12, 1985, when a Japan Airlines Boeing 747 crashed into a mountain on a domestic flight, killing 520 people; only four passengers survived.

What are the two tragedies with Malaysia Airlines?

Malaysia Airlines Flight 370 disappeared on March 8, 2014, while flying over the Indian Ocean. All 227 passengers and twelve crew members died. Although some debris has washed up from the plane, the plane itself has never been found. Furthermore, although there are several hypotheses about what happened to the plane, there is no agreed-upon answer as to why it crashed.

Malaysia Airlines Flight 17 was flying from Amsterdam to Kuala Lumpur on July 17, 2014, when it was shot down over eastern Ukraine. All 283 passengers and fifteen crew members died. The plane was shot down by a pro-Russian separatist group in Ukraine using a missile and launcher that had been transported from Russia. Possibly, the rebels who fired the missile thought the airline was a Ukrainian military aircraft.

What happened with the Boeing 737 MAX?

The MAX was the latest redesign of the Boeing 737 airliner. The first 737s entered service in 1968; the 737 MAX entered service in 2017. However, two of the new 737 MAXs crashed:

- October 29, 2018—Lion Air Flight 610, near Jakarta, Indonesia. All 189 people on board died.
- March 10, 2019—Ethiopian Airlines Flight 302 crashed after takeoff from Addis Ababa, Ethiopia. All 157 people on board died.

The crashes were determined to have been caused by a glitch in the automated flight-control software that caused the plane to nosedive in certain conditions. All other 737 MAXs were grounded until the problem was fixed.

SPACE DISASTERS

What happened with Apollo 1?

The American space program is run by the National Aeronautics and Space Administration (NASA). The U.S.-manned space program had begun with six flights between May 1961 and May 1963 using the Mercury capsule, which held just one astronaut. The Gemini program followed with ten manned flights between March 1965 and November 1966 with capsules holding two astronauts. The Apollo program with three astronauts in the capsule followed.

On January 27, 1967, astronauts were training for the first manned Apollo flight in the actual capsule on the launchpad. Tragically, a spark created a fire, which burned quickly in the capsule filled with pure oxygen, asphyxiating the men. Astronauts Virgil "Gus" Grissom, Ed White, and Roger B. Chaffee died in the fire.

The Apollo program was delayed, and many changes were made to the capsules and spacesuits. Eleven manned Apollo missions would follow from October 1968 to December 1972. On six of these missions, astronauts walked on the moon. (More moon missions had been planned, but these were cut by President Richard Nixon.)

What happened on Apollo 13?

On April 13, 1970, a damaged coil caused an explosion in one of the oxygen tanks on the moon-bound U.S. spacecraft, leaving astronauts Jim Lovell, Jack Swigert, and Fred Haise in a disastrous situation. After hearing a loud bang and seeing an oxygen tank empty, the *Apollo 13* astronauts reported to mission control at the Johnson Space Center, "OK, Houston, we've had a problem here." A real-life drama unfolded as the crew moved from the command module into the craft's tiny lunar module, designed to keep two men alive for just two days. They spent four days there with the temperature lowered to 38 degrees Fahrenheit to conserve oxygen and electricity. They returned to the command module and splashed down safely in the South Pacific.

The story of the three astronauts is told in the riveting 1995 movie *Apollo 13*, starring Tom Hanks, Kevin Bacon, and Bill Paxton as the three astronauts.

What happened to the space shuttle Challenger?

On January 28, 1986, NASA launched the twenty-fifth mission of its space shuttle program. The Challenger carried a crew of seven, including Christa McAuliffe (1948–1986), who was to be the first schoolteacher in space. She was slated to broadcast a series of lessons to schoolchildren throughout America. The crew's commander was Francis Scobee. The rest of crew were Michael Smith, Ellison Onizuka, Ronald McNair, Judith Resnik, and Gregory Jarvis.

On that cold and clear January morning, the Challenger's takeoff was delayed by two hours. Freezing temperatures overnight had produced ice on the shuttle and launchpad. At 11:38 A.M., Challenger was launched into space. Just 73 seconds later and at an altitude of 48,000 feet—the craft still in view of the spectators on the ground—Challenger burst into flames. NASA controllers heard crew member Smith utter "uh-oh" just one second prior to the explosion. As the fireball grew bigger and debris scattered, the spectators, including family and friends of the crew, fell silent.

The crew, inside a module that detached from the shuttle during the blowup, evidently survived the explosion but died upon impact after a nine-mile free fall into the Atlantic Ocean. Six weeks after the disaster, the crew module was recovered from the ocean floor; all seven astronauts were buried with full honors.

Investigations into the crash revealed that the O-rings (seals) on the shuttle's solid rocket boosters had failed to work. Due to the low temperatures, the O-rings had stiffened and thereby lost their ability to act as a seal.

Just over a minute after its launch in 1986, the space shuttle Challenger blew up, killing all on board. Later analysis blamed a faulty O-ring that may have been damaged from cold weather conditions before the launch.

Who was the first person to die in space?

Soviet cosmonaut Vladimir Komarov died on April 24, 1967, when the spacecraft *Soyuz I* crashed upon its flight back to Earth. The Soviets and the United States at that time were engaged in what was known as the "Space Race"—which saw the two nations competing to be the first to place a man on the moon, among other ambitious goals in space. Numerous design problems were identified with Soyuz I, but political pressure forced the craft into space before it was ready.

Is it true that the engineers of the Challenger's O-rings warned NASA that the devices might fail?

Yes, but sadly, the advice of the engineers went unheeded. The O-ring manufacturer, Morton Thiokol, gave NASA the go-ahead in the hours before Challenger's takeoff. The night before the planned takeoff, the temperature dropped well below freezing. Thiokol engineers expressed concerns about the O-rings on the shuttle's solid rocket boosters. They feared the rings would stiffen in the cold temperatures and lose their ability to act as a seal.

However, since the space agency was under pressure to launch the shuttle on schedule, NASA managers pushed the manufacturer for a go or no-go decision. The managers of Thiokol, who were aware that the O-rings had never been tested at such low temperatures, signed a waiver stating that the solid rocket boosters were safe for launch.

What happened in the Columbia space shuttle disaster?

The U.S. space shuttle Columbia was lost upon its reentry into Earth's atmosphere on the morning of February 1, 2003. All seven crew members died: Rick Husband, William McCool, Michael Anderson, Kalpana Chawla, David Brown, Laurel Clark, and Ilan Ramon.

The Columbia was in the skies over Texas about fifteen minutes before its scheduled landing at Florida's Kennedy Space Center when, shortly before 9:00 A.M. (EST), ground controllers lost data from temperature controllers on the spacecraft. Over the next several minutes, National Aeronautics and Space Administration (NASA) ground control lost all flight data. At about the same time, witnesses in Texas reported the sound of rolling thunder and debris falling from the sky. Heat-detecting weather radar showed a bright red streak moving across the Texas sky. The shuttle was forty miles above Earth and traveling at eighteen times the speed of sound when it disintegrated, leaving a trail of debris from eastern Texas to western Louisiana.

An investigation later revealed that during takeoff, the left wing of the craft had been damaged by a piece of foam insulation from the external fuel tank. The heat shield of the craft, which was essential to protect the craft during reentry, was damaged. Thus, when Columbia tried to reenter Earth's atmosphere, the craft was torn apart.

INDUSTRIAL ACCIDENTS

What happened at Love Canal?

Love Canal, a community east of Niagara Falls, New York, made international headlines in August 1978. It had already been the subject of local newspaper stories since 1976. More headlines followed into 1980 describing how Love Canal was toxic. Community residents had experienced unusually high incidences of cancer, miscarriages, birth defects, and other illnesses. There were also reports of foul odors, oozing sludge, multicolored pools of substances emerging from the ground, and children and animals returning from outdoor play with rashes and burns on their skin.

Unbeknownst to the residents, beginning in 1947, the Hooker Electrochemical Company had used Love Canal, with its clay walls, to dump 21,800 tons of chemical waste. In 1953, the company sold the canal to the Niagara School Board for the sum of one dollar. The deed acknowledged the buried chemicals, although it did not disclose their type or toxicity. A disclaimer protected the firm from future liability. The canal pit was subsequently sealed with a clay cap designed to prevent rainwater from disturbing the chemicals, and grass was planted.

Soon, Love Canal had become a fifteen-acre field. The following year, a school was built, and in 1955, 400 elementary school children began attending classes and playing on the surrounding fields. Development happened fast with roads, sewers, and utility lines crisscrossing the site, disrupting the soil.

As early as 1958, residents began to notice such problems as nauseating smells and incidences of skin problems. However, in the mid-1970s, the extent of the hazard became evident. Unusually heavy rainfalls caused chemicals to surface. A portion of the school-yard collapsed, strange substances seeped into basements, and trees and gardens died. In October 1976, the *Niagara Gazette* began investigating, and an official investigation began the following April. By this time, the site was a disaster.

Toxins were found in storm sewers and basements, exposed chemical drums leaked substances, and air tests detected dangerously high chemical levels in homes. Further testing identified more than 200 different compounds at the site, including twelve carcinogens (cancer-causing agents) and fourteen compounds that can affect the brain and central nervous system.

The residents of Love Canal organized, forming citizen groups, including the Love Canal Homeowners Association. These groups succeeded in getting media cover-

Love Canal residents confront EPA administrator Lee Thomas about cleaning up their town in this 1985 photo.

age and in pressuring public officials to act. Finally, in August 1978, New York State health commissioner Robert P. Whalen declared Love Canal unsafe. Six days later, President Jimmy Carter (1924–) approved emergency assistance, and New York governor Hugh Carey announced that funds would be used to purchase homes nearest the canal.

While more than 200 families that were perceived to be in danger were moved, in 1980, problems resurfaced when researchers found that blood tests of residents showed abnormally high chromosomal damage. The state recommended that pregnant women and infants be removed from homes—even those that had been certified as safe. In May 1980, conflict ensued between 300 Love Canal homeowners and officials from the Environmental Protection Agency (EPA).

On May 21, President Carter declared a second emergency at Love Canal. This time, the actions were more comprehensive: Almost 800 families were evacuated, and their homes were either destroyed or declared unsafe until further cleanup could be done. Four years later, a new clay cap was installed over the canal. It was also in 1984 that Occidental Petroleum, the parent company of the firm that had dumped chemicals in Love Canal, reached a $20 million settlement with residents.

What impact did Love Canal have?

The effect of the crisis was felt on many levels—by area residents whose lives were forever changed by the hazards, by residents near Love Canal who feared for their own safety, by Americans across the country who lived near other chemical-waste sites, and by Americans for whom Love Canal had become synonymous with the problems posed by hazardous waste.

At the government level, the tragic events at Love Canal helped to speed the passage of the Comprehensive Environmental Response, Compensation, and Liability Act of 1980. Also known as the Superfund, the legislation set up a multibillion-dollar fund to clean up the nation's worst toxic disasters. The Environmental Protection Agency (EPA) assigned cleanup priority to some 1,200 abandoned and potentially contaminated waste sites.

Along with the chemical plant explosion at Bhopal, India, in 1984, Love Canal also contributed to a "community-right-to-know" provision, which was part of the 1985 Superfund Amendments and Reauthorization Act. The new legislation gave all citizens the right to know what chemicals are produced, stored, or buried in their neighborhoods.

What was the worst marine oil spill in history?

The worst marine oil spill in history was the so-called BP oil spill of 2010, which began with the April 20 explosion of the *Deepwater Horizon* rig, which was drilling in a BP project. The explosion killed eleven workers and injured seventeen others. More than 4.9 million barrels of oil flowed into the Atlantic Ocean and the Gulf of Mexico. It is also known as the Deepwater Horizon oil spill. The oil well was not officially sealed until September 2010; however, the well appears to still be leaking.

A key cause was the failure to follow basic safety procedures.

531

What happened at Three Mile Island?

The March 1979 accident—a near-meltdown—at the nuclear power station at Three Mile Island outside Middletown, Pennsylvania (near Harrisburg), was eventually contained. Had it not been, the damage would have been on a level with that of the Chernobyl (Ukraine) disaster, which happened some seven years later. Instead, Three Mile Island served as a wake-up call, reminding the American public and its utility companies of the potential risks involved in nuclear energy.

At 4:00 A.M. on Wednesday, March 28, an overheated reactor in Unit II of the power plant shut down automatically (as it should have); Metropolitan Edison Company operators, guided by indicators that led them to believe water pressure was building (and an explosion was therefore imminent), shut down those pumps that were still operating; the shutdown of all the pumps caused the reactor to heat further; then, tons of water poured out through a valve that was stuck open; this water overflowed into an auxiliary building through another valve that was mistakenly left open. This final procedure, which took place at 4:38 A.M., released radioactivity.

Since there was no cooling system in operation, the reactor in Unit II was damaged. But this was not the end of it. The radiation within the buildings was released into the atmosphere, and at 6:50 A.M., a general emergency was declared. Early that afternoon, the hydrogen created by the uncovered reactor core accumulated in a containment building and exploded. Since hydrogen continued to be emitted, officials feared another—catastrophic—explosion. Worse yet, they feared the reactor would become so

A historic marker informs passersby of the nuclear disaster that was testimony to the failings of the nuclear industry when it came to public safety in the 1970s.

hot that it would melt down. The effect of a meltdown would be that the superheated material would eat its way through the bottom of the plant and bore through the ground until it hit water, turning the water into high-pressure steam, which would erupt, spewing radioactivity into the air.

As technicians worked to manage the crisis, radiation leaked into the atmosphere off and on through Wednesday and Thursday. On Friday, Pennsylvania governor Dick Thornburgh ordered an evacuation of some 144,000 people in the area. The situation inside the plant remained tenuous as a hydrogen bubble developed and increased in size, again raising fear of an explosion. Meantime, public alarm was mounting as the media attempted to monitor the ongoing crisis. Finally, on Sunday, April 1, President Jimmy Carter (1924–) visited the plant. At about the same time, the hydrogen bubble began to decrease in size, ending the crisis.

The other reactor, Unit I, stayed in operation until 2019.

What was the impact of the accident at Three Mile Island?

Prior to the March 1979 events at Three Mile Island, it was thought that the danger of a nuclear meltdown was almost negligible. Though there were safety systems in place, none of them would have prevented a complete catastrophe. Since the accident, the U.S. Nuclear Regulatory Commission (NRC) and utility companies have worked together to resolve the problems that were revealed. Among the efforts and requirements put into place were more stringent licensing procedures for operators; better training of plant operators in the event of an emergency; wider sharing of information on emergency-management systems; efforts to locate new plants outside of densely populated areas; more rigid quality-assurance standards at all plants; strict implementation of the standards, which are subject to review by the NRC; and emergency-evacuation plans that must be approved by the Federal Emergency Management Agency (FEMA). Even with these improvements to safety programs, the accident at Chernobyl in 1986 again produced worldwide concern over the hazards of nuclear power.

What caused the nuclear accident at Chernobyl?

The April 1986 accident—the world's worst nuclear power plant disaster—was caused by explosions at the Soviet power plant, sending radioactive clouds across much of northern Europe. According to the World Nuclear Association, the accident was the result of "a flawed reactor design that was operated with inadequately trained personnel and without proper regard for safety."

The trouble began at 1:24 A.M. on Saturday, April 26, when Unit 4 of the Chernobyl Nuclear Power Plant, about seventy miles outside of the Ukrainian capital of Kiev, was rocked by two enormous explosions. The roof was blown off the plant, and radioactive gases and materials were sent more than half a mile into the atmosphere. Though two workers were killed instantly, there was no official announcement about the hazardous blast. It was the Swedes who detected a dramatic increase in wind-borne radiation, and on April 28—two full days after the accident—news of the event was briefly reported by the Soviet news agency TASS.

Two weeks later, on May 14, First Secretary Mikhail Gorbachev (1931–) went on national television and explained what officials knew about the accident. More details were revealed over the following months. The explosions were caused by an unauthorized test carried out by plant operators, who were trying to determine what would happen in the event of a power outage.

There were six critical errors made by workers during the testing, which combined to spell disaster. Perhaps the most significant of these mistakes was turning off the emergency coolant system. Once the test was underway, further mistakes caused the core to heat to more than 9,000 degrees Fahrenheit, producing molten metal that reacted with what cooling water was left to produce hydrogen gas and steam, resulting in a powerful explosion. A second explosion followed.

As the worst nuclear power plant disaster to date, the Chernobyl accident in 1986 had far-reaching effects. Total fallout from the accident eventually reached a level ten times that of the atomic bomb dropped on Hiroshima, Japan, in 1945, at the end of World War II. Some thirty firefighters and plant workers died just after the accident.

Plants and animals in the immediate area and downwind of the plant were heavily contaminated with radioactive fallout. Even today, food grown in the region has unhealthy levels of radiation.

What was the worst industrial accident?

It was the gas leak at a Union Carbide chemical plant in Bhopal, India, on December 3, 1984. At about 12:30 A.M., methyl isocyanate (MIC), a deadly gas, began escaping from the pesticide plant, and it spread southward, eventually covering approximately fifteen square miles. Within a few hours, thousands of Bhopal residents were affected by the asphyxiating gas. General symptoms included severe chest congestion, vomiting, paralysis, sore throat, chills, coma, fever, swelling of legs, impaired vision, and palpitations. Estimates of the total death toll range from the official government estimate of 2,000 to 10,000, a figure based on what medical professionals described. In total, 500,000 people were directly or indirectly affected by the poisonous gas.

Multinational corporations, including Union Carbide, were vilified in the press; the Soviet news agency accused such companies of marketing "low-quality products and outdated technology to developing countries." Prime Minister Rajiv Gandhi (1944–1991) of India visited the disaster site and announced the immediate creation of a relief fund for victims; he also vowed that he would prevent multinational corporations from setting up "dangerous factories" in India.

What were the long-term effects to people?

In addition to the thousands who died in Bhopal, others suffered from long-term effects, including chronic lesions of the eyes; permanent scarring of the lungs; and in-

534

Experts from the International Atomic Energy Agency inspect the Fukushima Daiichi nuclear plant in this 2013 photo. The region near the disaster will be uninhabitable for about forty years, and radioactive water is still flowing into the Pacific Ocean.

juries to the liver, brain, heart, kidneys, and immune system. In the years after the accident, studies showed that the rate of spontaneous abortions and infant deaths in Bhopal were three to four times the regional rate.

The toxic site of the plant has still not been cleaned up. Soil, groundwater, and well water in residential areas around the plant are contaminated.

What caused the Fukushima Daiichi nuclear disaster?

On March 11, 2011, a horrific earthquake and resulting tsunami devastated the region of Tohoku in Japan. The earthquake registered a whopping 9 on the Richter scale. The earthquake and tsunami impacted the Fukushima I Nuclear Power Plant.

The earthquake did not damage the reactors, which automatically shut down. However, the electricity went out, which stopped the water pumps used to cool the reactors. As designed, the backup diesel generators kicked in. However, the tsunami then hit and flooded the site and shut down the generators. The water pumps stopped, and nuclear reactors overheated. Three nuclear reactors had meltdowns, which were followed by explosions and the release of radioactive contamination. Over 150,000 residents were evacuated from the surrounding communities.

GLOBAL WARMING
AND CLIMATE CHANGE

What is the problem with global warming and climate change? And what is the difference?

The average temperature of Earth's climate system has been rising since the middle of the twentieth century, and this is causing the climate to change. Although the temperature is only going up by a degree or so, it greatly affects the climate. Climate change has caused increases in the frequency, duration, and intensity of droughts, floods, and storms. In some places, these changes are causing economic and humanitarian crises.

For example, currently, the nation of Syria is in a disastrous civil war, which started in 2011. The origin of the war began with climate changes causing a drought, which forced farmers in large numbers to abandon their farms and move to cities, where they could not find work. When they started protesting, the Syrian government of Bashar al-Assad (1965–) began a brutal crackdown. This led to the current civil war.

Isn't there a natural cycle of climate change on Earth?

Yes, there is a natural cycle of ups and downs of global temperatures over very long periods of time, which are typically caused by increases and decreases of the levels of carbon dioxide (CO_2) in the atmosphere. However, what scientists have seen since the rise of industrialization are unprecedented numbers for the amount of CO_2 in the atmosphere. The current levels of CO_2 are far higher than they have ever been in the last several hundred thousand years. Human-created levels of CO_2 in the atmosphere are not natural.

The problem is that we humans are changing the climate by the amount of CO_2 we create and the amount of methane (CH_4) we release into the atmosphere. The increase of these gases in the atmosphere has caused Earth to get warmer.

Humans create CO_2 by burning things such as gasoline in cars and coal in coal-fired power plants to make electricity. Methane, which is the same as the natural gas that people use in stoves and furnaces, often escapes in the process of drilling and transporting natural gas. It is also created by livestock, such as cows. They create methane in their digestive tract, which then gets into the atmosphere. And because we humans eat meat, there are a lot of animals producing methane. These animals also create huge amounts of manure, which produces methane as it rots. That last bad news about methane is that it is thirty times more damaging than CO_2 to the environment. (Coal, oil, and natural gas are called "fossil fuels.")

What is the problem with CO_2 and methane in the atmosphere?

Normally, much of the light and heat that hit Earth bounce back into space. But what CO_2 and methane do is keep more of that heat in Earth's atmosphere. The phenomenon is often compared to the glass in a greenhouse where plants are grown. The glass lets the light and heat from the sun come through, but then, the glass keeps much of the heat from bouncing back into space, so it stays within the greenhouse. This is why global warming is often called "the greenhouse effect."

Who is Greta Thunberg?

Greta Thunberg (2003–) is a young Swedish environmental activist who gained worldwide attention with her remarks at the 2018 United Nations Climate Change Conference. She chastised the listeners with her dramatic words, "How dare you!":

> For more than 30 years, the science has been crystal clear. How dare you continue to look away and come here saying that you're doing enough, when the politics and solutions needed are still nowhere in sight.... How dare you pretend that this can be solved with just "business as usual" and some technical solutions?

She was on the cover of *Time* magazine as the 2019 Person of the Year.

What movies talk about the problem of climate change?

The 2006 documentary *An Inconvenient Truth* features former vice president Al Gore (1948–) as he describes the scope and scale of the problem. This film was followed up in 2017 with *An Inconvenient Sequel: Truth to Power*.

As one young Swedish school kid has pointed out, the adults in charge aren't doing their job. Greta Thunberg has become a prominent voice in world protests about climate change and the inaction of political and business leaders to do anything about it.

Jeff Orlowski directed two films that show the effects of climate change. In *Chasing Ice* (2012), he shows how fast glaciers and ice floes are melting; in *Chasing Coral* (2017), he shows how coral reefs are dying.

What is a helpful web page?

The National Aeronautics and Space Administration (NASA) has a great page on global climate changes: *https://climate.nasa.gov/*.

Under the Trump Administration, other government agencies, such as the Environmental Protection Agency (EPA), have been forced to reduce their online information.

MASS EXTINCTION

What are the five known mass-extinction events?

Long before humans, there have been five mass extinctions of life on our planet Earth. The extinctions had many causes, such as volcanic activity, continental shift, or an asteroid or meteor hitting Earth. All of these caused dramatic climate change, which in turn caused the extinctions to happen.

Mass Extinction Events

Name	When	Results
Ordovician Mass Extinction	440 million years ago	Up to 85 percent of all living species went extinct
Devonian Mass Extinction	375 million years ago	Up to 80 percent of all living species went extinct
Permian Mass Extinction	250 million years ago	Up to 96 percent of all species went extinct
Triassic-Jurassic Mass Extinction	200 million years ago	Over 50 percent of all living species went extinct
K-T Mass Extinction	65 million years ago	Nearly 75 percent of all living species (including all the dinosaurs) went extinct

What is the Sixth Extinction?

This is the current extinction caused by humans through destruction of natural habitat, disease, overuse of resources, pollution, ocean acidification, and global warming causing climate change. The important 2014 book *The Sixth Extinction: An Unnatural History*, written by Elizabeth Kolbert, describes the current threat to animal and human life on the planet caused by humans.

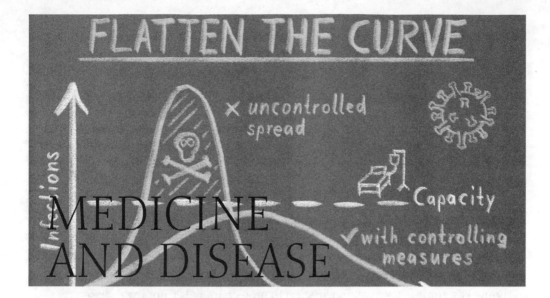

MEDICINE AND DISEASE

EARLY MEDICINE

Who was the first physician in history?

The first physician known by name was Imhotep, an Egyptian who lived around 2600 B.C.E. Also considered a sage, Imhotep lived at a time when the Egyptians were making progress in medicine. The advances included a textbook on the treatment of wounds, broken bones, and even tumors. He also designed the first pyramid for King Djoser. Imhotep was later worshipped as a god by the Egyptians. (Imhotep shows up as a character in the 1999 movie *The Mummy,* starring Brendan Fraser.)

What is the Hippocratic Oath?

The Hippocratic Oath is the pledge taken by many medical students upon graduation or upon entering medical practice. While the text of the oath varies by translation, one important line reads, "I will prescribe regiment for the good of my patients according to my ability and my judgment and never to harm anyone." The vows are attributed to the Greek physician and teacher Hippocrates (c. 460–c. 377 B.C.E.). Unlike his predecessors, who relied

Called the "Father of Medicine," the Greek physician Hippocrates was the first scientist to establish medicine as its own discipline.

539

No, the disease dates back thousands of years, but its potential use as a bioterrorism weapon is relatively recent.

Anthrax is caused by the *Bacillus anthracis* bacterium, spores that can survive in soil for years. It is mainly a disease of grass-eating livestock, but humans who work with herd animals may become infected through exposure. In humans, anthrax occurs as a skin (cutaneous) form, as a lung (pulmonary) form, or as an intestinal infection after the consumption of contaminated meat. In the Bible, the fifth and sixth plagues on Egypt, as described in Exodus, chapters 9 ("Pestilence") and 10 ("Boils"), are consistent with anthrax in livestock and humans. In the late 1800s, scientists made several important discoveries regarding anthrax. The anthrax germ *Bacillus anthracis* was the first germ linked to a particular disease. In 1881, French scientist Louis Pasteur developed an inoculation to protect animals from the disease.

Anthrax emerged as a potential weapon of bioterrorism during the twentieth century. Several countries, including the United States, the United Kingdom, Germany, Japan, Iraq, and the former Soviet Union, experimented with the bacterium.

on superstitious practices in their treatment of patients, Hippocrates believed that diseases were brought on not by supernatural causes but by natural ones. He further believed that disease could be studied and cured; this assertion forms the basis of modern medicine, which is why Hippocrates is called the "Father of Medicine."

It is largely owing to another prominent Greek physician, Galen (129–c. 200 C.E.), who was physician to two Roman emperors, that the oath was handed down through history. He demonstrated that arteries carry blood, not air (as had been thought), and, like Hippocrates, Galen believed in the four humors of the body: blood, yellow bile, black bile, and phlegm. He left medical texts that for centuries were considered the authoritative works on medical practice.

What advances were made in medicine during the Middle Ages?

During the Middle Ages, medicine became institutionalized. The first public hospitals were opened and the first formal medical schools were established, making health care (formerly administered only in the home) more widely available and improving the training of doctors. These developments had been brought on by necessity: Europe saw successive waves of epidemics during the Middle Ages. Outbreaks of leprosy began in the 500s and peaked in the 1200s; the Black Death (bubonic plague) killed about a quarter of the European population; and smallpox and other diseases afflicted hundreds of thousands of people. However, medicine at the time did not have very effective treatments for these diseases. Many hospitals meant to serve the poor were established, as were the first medical schools, some of them associated with universities that were then forming, such as the University of Bologna (Italy) and the University of Paris (France). In 900, the first medical school was started in Salerno, Italy.

European physicians during the period were greatly influenced by the works of Persian physician and philosopher Rhazes (or Rasis; 854–925). Considered the greatest doctor of the Islamic world, Rhazes's works accurately describing measles and smallpox were translated into Latin and became important references in the Christian world. Another prominent Islamic influence, the scientist Avicenna (or Abu Ali Sina; 980–1037), produced a philosophical-scientific encyclopedia, which included the medical knowledge of the time. In the West, the work became known as *Canon of Medicine,* and with its descriptions of many diseases, including tetanus and meningitis, it remained influential in European medical education for the next 600 years.

Were there hospitals before the Middle Ages?

Public hospitals emerged during the Middle Ages as Christianity spread and religious orders set up the facilities to serve the poor. Still, most people received a doctor's care in their own homes. The concept of a public health care facility originated in India as early as the third century B.C.E., when Buddhists established hospital-like installations.

The Middle Ages saw the establishment of facilities more closely resembling modern hospitals, including Paris's Hôtel-Dieu (founded in the 600s); today, it is the oldest hospital still in operation. In 970, a hospital in Baghdad (present-day Iraq) divided physicians into the equivalent of modern-day interns and externs. Its pharmacy disseminated drugs (as well as spices deemed to have medicinal value) from all over the known world.

What advances were made in medicine during the Renaissance?

The chief medical advance of the Renaissance (1350–1600) was an improved understanding of human anatomy. This knowledge was the direct result of dissection, which was prohibited during the Middle Ages. The scientific spirit of the Renaissance saw those laws relaxed, and researchers were free to dissect human corpses for study.

Among those who practiced dissection was Leonardo da Vinci (1452–1519). Da Vinci did dissections because he was curious about the human body but also because he wanted to know what was below the skin so he could paint the human body more accurately. While the Italian artist may be better known for his painting the *Mona Lisa*, he also contributed greatly to the understanding of human anatomy, producing more than 750 anatomical drawings of the human body.

What was the first scientific textbook on human anatomy?

It is a work titled *On the Structure of the Human Body*, written by Belgian physician and professor Andreas Vesalius (1514–1564) and published in 1543, when he was in his late twenties. Like other anatomists during the Renaissance, Vesalius conducted numerous dissections of human cadavers. Publishing his findings and drawings, his textbook soon became the authoritative reference, overturning the works of ancient Greek physician Galen.

When was the first hospital established in North America?

In 1503, the Spanish built a hospital in Santo Domingo in the Dominican Republic (then known as Hispaniola). It is no longer in existence, but the ruins remain.

On the North American mainland, the first hospital was opened in Quebec, Canada, in 1639. The first incorporated hospital in the United States was the Pennsylvania Hospital in Philadelphia, chartered in 1751 with the support of statesman Benjamin Franklin (1706–1790). It is still in operation today.

What is *Gray's Anatomy*?

It is the popular name for *Anatomy of the Human Body, Descriptive and Surgical*, written by English physician Henry Gray (1827–1861). First published in 1858, the

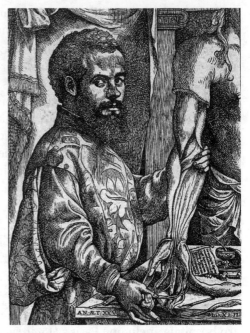

Flemish physician Andreas Vesalius was the author of the first textbook on human anatomy.

tome is still considered the standard work on anatomy, and it is in print today in several editions, including *The Concise Gray's Anatomy*. Gray was a lecturer in anatomy at London's St. George's Hospital and was a fellow of Britain's Royal College of Surgeons. He was thirty-three years old when he compiled the book, which went on to be used by medical students for more than a century. (The title of the popular TV show *Grey's Anatomy*, which premiered in 2005, is an allusion to the famous textbook.)

THE ROOTS OF MODERN MEDICINE

When did modern medicine begin?

The practices of modern medicine have their roots in the 1600s. English physician William Harvey (1578–1657) demonstrated to the scientific community that effective medicine depends on knowledge of the body's structure. He had studied medicine at Padua (Italy) under Italian surgeon Hieronymus Fabricius (1533–1619) and went on to perform numerous experiments to learn how blood circulates through the body. In his studies, Harvey discarded the accepted method of studying parts of a problem and then filling in the gaps with theory; instead, he aimed to understand the entire circulatory system, studying the pulse and heartbeat and performing dissections on cadavers. He accurately concluded that the heart pumps blood through the arteries to all parts of the body and that the blood returns through the veins to the heart. Putting his discovery into writing, Harvey published *An Anatomical Study of the Motion of the Heart and of the Blood in Animals* in 1628.

Another medical development during the 1600s came not at the hands of a physician or surgeon but rather a naturalist, Antonie van Leeuwenhoek (1632–1723). A surveyor to the court of Holland, van Leeuwenhoek began making his own microscopes and used them to study organisms invisible to the naked eye. He had discovered microorganisms. Leeuwenhoek also observed (but did not name) bacteria, and he accurately described red blood corpuscles, striated muscle fibers, and the lens of the eye. This amateur scientist also helped disprove the belief of spontaneous generation.

What is spontaneous generation?

Spontaneous generation, the belief that living things can develop from nonliving things, originated in prehistoric times and held sway throughout the Middle Ages. For example, people noticed that maggots could appear on a piece of meat. They thought that the maggots were able to generate themselves spontaneously. One of the first scientists to test this theory was Italian physician Francesco Redi (1626–1697). He demonstrated that as long as meat was covered, maggots would not "form" on it. (When left uncovered, flies would land on the meat, lay eggs, and, thus, produce maggots.) Despite Redi's findings, the belief in spontaneous generation continued to be held for centuries.

Spontaneous generation was ultimately discredited by the successive experiments of Dutch naturalist Antonie van Leeuwenhoek, French chemist and microbiologist Louis Pasteur (1822–1895), and German physician and pioneering bacteriologist Robert Koch (1843–1910), who together proved that bacteria cause infectious diseases. They helped establish germ theory, which held that certain germs cause diseases, refuting the age-old notion of spontaneous generation. They proved that the microbe, or germ, is a living organism that can cause disease. Koch was even able to isolate certain bacteria as the causes of diseases such as anthrax, tuberculosis, cholera, and rinderpest (a cattle disease). By the end of the 1800s, researchers had discovered the kinds of bacteria and other microbes responsible for the plague, diphtheria, dysentery, gonorrhea, leprosy, malaria, pneumonia, tetanus, and other infectious diseases.

Who invented the vaccine?

English physician Edward Jenner (1749–1823) is credited with inventing the vaccine; however, evidence suggests that vaccination (inoculation of a substance into the body for the purpose of producing active immunity against a disease) was used in China, India, and Persia (present-day Iran) in ancient times.

In modern times, Jenner pioneered the science of immunology by developing a vaccination against smallpox. In 1796, the English physician was practicing medicine in rural Gloucestershire when he observed that dairymaids who had been sick with cowpox did not contract smallpox, suggesting that they had developed an immunity to the often fatal disease, which then occurred in epidemics. Jenner must have been quite certain of his theory, for he chose to test it on an eight-year-old schoolboy, James Phipps, whom Jenner vaccinated with matter from cowpox vesicles from the hands of a milkmaid. Jenner then allowed the boy's system to develop the immunity he had previously observed in the dairymaids. Several weeks later, Jenner inoculated Phipps with smallpox, and the boy did not become even the least bit ill. The experiment was a success. Jenner continued his experiments for two years and then published his findings, officially announcing his discovery of vaccination in 1798.

As Jenner suspected, vaccines provide immunity by causing the body to manufacture substances called antibodies, which fight a disease. Over the course of the twentieth century, vaccination programs have greatly reduced disease, particularly in developed nations where childhood immunization programs are very effective. By 1977, vaccination had virtually wiped out smallpox.

English physician Edward Jenner may not have invented the vaccination process, but he did a lot to make vaccination a common method of fighting diseases such as smallpox.

When was anesthesia first used?

The first use was determined to have been in 1842, when Georgia physician Crawford Williamson Long (1815–1878) became the first doctor to use ether as an anesthetic. He went on to use ether in seven more operations before 1846, when he made a public demonstration of anesthesia. Long published his accounts of the experiences in December 1849.

But Boston dentist William T. G. Morton (1819–1868) disputed Long's claim to have been first in using anesthesia. Morton had begun experimenting with anesthetics at about the same time as Long, and on October 16, 1846, he had arranged the first hospital operation using ether as an anesthetic to remove a tumor from the neck of a patient. Nevertheless, it is Long who gets credit for being the first doctor to use ether during an operation.

When did modern surgery begin?

Modern surgical techniques were developed during the late Renaissance, largely owing to the work of French surgeon Ambroise Paré (1510–1590), called the "Father of Modern Surgery." Prior to Paré's lifework, physicians had regarded surgery as something lowly. They left this "dirty work" to barber-surgeons. As a young man living in the French countryside, Paré became apprenticed to one such barber-surgeon. When he was only nineteen years old, Paré entered Paris's Hôtel-Dieu hospital to study surgery. Becoming a master surgeon by 1536, he later served as an army surgeon and then as physician to four French kings. Paré also built a flourishing surgical practice and authored works on anatomy, surgery, the plague, obstetrics, and the treatment of wounds. Opposing the common practice of cauterizing (burning) wounds with boiling oil to prevent infection, he introduced the method of applying a mild ointment and allowing the wound to heal naturally. Paré was renowned for his patient care, which he based on his personal credo, "I dressed him, God cured him."

FIGHTING GERMS

When were antiseptics first used in surgery?

Antiseptics, which prevent infections, were introduced in the middle of the 1800s and by the end of the century were in widespread use. The introduction in 1846 of anesthetics such as ether and chloroform handled the problem of pain during surgery. Ether and chloroform would be inhaled by the patient, who would then typically lose consciousness. However, even after successful operations, patients were dying or becoming permanently disabled from infections contracted while in the hospital. These infections, which often became epidemics inside the medical facilities, included tetanus, gangrene, and septicemia.

In 1846, Hungarian obstetrician Ignaz Philipp Semmelweis (1818–1865), who was practicing at a Vienna hospital, concluded that infections of childbirth fever (also called puerperal fever or childbed fever) were coming from inside the hospital ward. He noticed that in hospital wards where doctors helped with childbirth, the babies died at three times the rate compared to those babies born in hospital wards for the poorer people, where women midwives delivered the babies. He noticed that the midwives washed their hands before delivery, while the doctors did not. His analysis was met with strong rebuttal. While he began practicing antisepsis (cleanliness to reduce infection) and his statistics showed a decrease in mortality rates, the methods did not gain acceptance in the medical community.

Nearly two decades later, in 1864, English surgeon Joseph Lister (1827–1912) became interested in French chemist and microbiologist Louis Pasteur's work with bacteria. While practicing surgery in Glasgow, Lister replicated Pasteur's experiments and concluded that the germ theory applied to hospital diseases. In order to stave off inflammation and infections in his patients, Lister began working with solutions containing carbolic acid, which kills germs. Observing favorable results, Lister reported his findings in 1867 in the British medical journal *Lancet*.

Many physicians still rejected Lister's claims that antisepsis could reduce the danger of infection. Nevertheless, the medical community began adopting these methods. By the turn of the century, not only had these principles saved lives, they had transformed the way doctors practice medicine. Since doctors could not ensure necessary cleanliness in their patients' homes, hospitals became the preferred place to treat all patients—not just the poor or the very sick.

Who was Louis Pasteur?

Louis Pasteur (1822–1895) may be best known for developing the process that bears his name, pasteurization, but the French chemist and microbiologist made other important contributions to public health, including the discovery of vaccines to prevent diseases in animals and the establishment of a Paris institute for the study of deadly and contagious diseases.

In the 1860s, the hardworking Pasteur was asked to investigate problems that French winemakers were having with the fermentation process. They experienced spoilage of wine and beer during fermentation, which was resulting in serious economic losses for France. Observing wine under a microscope, Pasteur noticed that spoiled wine had a proliferation of bacterial cells that produce lactic acid. The chemist suggested gently heating the wine to destroy the harmful bacteria and then allowing the wine to age naturally. Pasteur published his findings and his recommendations in book form in 1866. The idea of heating edible substances to destroy disease-causing organisms was later applied to other perishable fluids—chief among them milk.

Pasteur later studied animal diseases, developing a vaccination to prevent anthrax in sheep and cattle. The deadly animal disease is spread from animals to humans through contact or the inhalation of spores. In 1876, German physician Robert Koch (1843–1910) had identified the bacteria that causes anthrax, and Pasteur weakened this microbe in his laboratory before injecting it into animals, which then developed an immunity to the disease. He also showed that vaccination could be used to prevent chicken cholera.

In 1881, Pasteur began studying rabies, an agonizing and deadly disease spread by the bite of infected animals. Along with his assistant, Pierre-Paul-Émile Roux (1853–1933), Pasteur spent long hours in the laboratory, and the determination paid off: Pasteur developed a vaccine that prevented the development of rabies in test animals. In 1885, the scientists were called on to administer the vaccine to a small boy who was bitten by a rabid dog. Pasteur hesitated to provide the treatment, but as the boy faced certain and painful death from rabies, Pasteur proceeded. Following several weeks of painful

Louis Pasteur is shown here working in his laboratory. The French scientist after whom the process of pasteurization is named was key in making the medical community understand that microscopic germs caused illness.

injections to the stomach, the boy did not get rabies. Pasteur's treatment was a success. The curative and preventive treatments for rabies we know today are based on Pasteur's vaccination, which has allowed officials to control the spread of the disease.

In 1888, the Institut Pasteur was established in Paris to provide a teaching and research center on contagious diseases; Pasteur was director of the institute until his death in 1895.

When were antibiotics invented?

The great French chemist Louis Pasteur laid the foundation for understanding antibiotics when in the late 1800s, he proved that one species of microorganisms can kill another. German bacteriologist Paul Ehrlich (1854–1915) then developed the concept of selective toxicity, in which a specific substance can be toxic (poisonous) to some organisms but harmless to others. Based on this research, scientists began working to develop substances that would destroy disease-spreading microorganisms. A breakthrough came in 1928 when Scottish bacteriologist Alexander Fleming (1881–1955) discovered penicillin. Fleming observed that no bacteria grew around the mold of the genus *Penicillium notatum,* which had accidentally fallen into a bacterial culture in his laboratory.

But penicillin proved difficult to extract. It was not until 1941 that the substance was purified and tested by British scientist Howard Florey (1898–1968). Another British scientist, Ernst Boris Chain (1906–1979), developed a method of extracting penicillin, and under his supervision, the first large-scale penicillin-production facility was completed, making the antibiotic commercially available in 1945. That same year, Fleming, Florey, and Chain shared the Nobel Prize in Physiology or Medicine for their work in discovering and producing this powerful antibiotic. Penicillin is still used today in the successful treatment of bacterial diseases, including pneumonia, strep throat, and gonorrhea.

The term "antibiotic" was coined by American microbiologist Selman Waksman (1888–1973), who tested about 10,000 types of soil bacteria for antibiotic capability. In 1943, Waksman discovered a fungus that produced a powerful antibiotic substance, which he called streptomycin. The following year, the antibiotic was in production for use in treating tuberculosis, typhoid fever, bubonic plague, and bacterial meningitis. Although streptomycin was later found to be toxic, it saved countless lives and led to the discovery of many other antibiotics, which have proven both safe and effective.

What is the problem with antibiotics today?

The biggest problem with antibiotics is their overuse. Antibiotics kill dangerous bacteria. But sometimes some of the bacteria survive and reproduce bacteria that become resistant to future use of the antibiotic. This is particularly a problem when patients do not take all the antibiotic pills prescribed by their doctor.

Doctors typically prescribe enough pills over enough time to kill all of a particular strain of bacteria in a patient. However, if the patient starts feeling better and does not take all the pills, the surviving bacteria can develop resistance to the antibiotic. In the fu-

No. Antibiotics work on bacterial infections. Influenza—the flu—is an infection caused by a virus. Antibiotics do not work on viruses.

A better approach is to get an annual flu shot.

ture, that antibiotic will not work on that patient. Also, if the bacteria are passed on to another person, such as by coughing, the antibiotics will not work on that person either.

Further complicating the issue is the extensive use and overuse of antibiotics on animals such as cattle and chickens. This often creates drug-resistant bacteria that can travel between animals and sometimes between animals and humans.

One last problem is that a typical prescription for an antibiotic is just one bottle of pills. A pharmaceutical company will not make much money from it compared to a medicine that has to be taken continuously for many years. Thus, there is often little financial incentive for drugmakers to develop new antibiotics.

WOMEN LEADERS IN MEDICINE

Who was Florence Nightingale?

The English nurse, hospital reformer, and philanthropist is considered the founder of modern nursing. The daughter of well-to-do British parents, Florence Nightingale (1820–1910) was born in Florence, Italy. Though she was raised in privilege on her family's estate in England, Nightingale had a natural and irrepressible inclination toward caring for others.

Despite her parents' wishes, Nightingale entered a training program for nurses in Germany. She went on to study in Paris. In 1853, Nightingale became superintendent of a hospital for invalid women in London.

In 1854, Nightingale took thirty-eight nurses with her to the city of Üsküdar near Istanbul, Turkey. There, despite great obstacles, she set up a barracks hospital to treat soldiers who were injured in the Crimean War (1853–1856), then being fought between Russian forces and the allied armies of Britain, France, the Ottoman Empire (present-day Turkey), and Sardinia (part of present-day Italy). Nightingale set about cleaning the filthy hospital facility; established strict schedules for the staff; and introduced sanitation methods that reduced the spread of infectious diseases, such as cholera, typhus, and dysentery. While her methods were considered controversial at first (doctors initially found Nightingale to be demanding and pushy), they got results. Before long, Nightingale was put in charge of all the allied army hospitals in the Crimea.

During the fighting, Nightingale visited the front and caught Crimean fever, which threatened her life. By this time, she had become so well known that Queen Victoria (1819–1901) was aware of and deeply concerned about Nightingale's illness. By the end of the war, Nightingale's care of the sick and wounded was legendary. Known for walking the floor of the hospital at night, tending her patients, she became known as "the Lady with the Lamp."

After the war, Nightingale returned to London, and in 1860, she established a training institution for nurses in London. In 1873, Massachusetts General Hospital in Boston, Bellevue Hospital in New York City, and New Haven Hospital in Con-

Considered the mother of the nursing profession, Florence Nightingale established the first secular school of nursing in the world in 1860.

necticut opened the United States' first nursing schools; all of them were patterned after the London program founded by Nightingale.

Nightingale's fierce determination, which ran contrary to her parents' wishes for her as well as to the social standard of the day, made her a legend—and rightly so. Because of her concern for the sick, the standard of care of all patients improved.

When was the Red Cross founded?

The Red Cross was founded in Switzerland in October 1863 when the delegates from sixteen nations met in Geneva, Switzerland, to create "in all civilized countries permanent societies of volunteers who in time of war would give help to the wounded without regard for nationality." The idea had been described in a pamphlet by Swiss philanthropist Jean-Henri Dunant (1828–1910). In 1859, Dunant was at a battle where French and Italian troops fought Austrian troops. Dunant observed the suffering of the wounded and immediately organized a group of volunteers to help them.

At the 1863 conference, the delegates chose a red cross with a white background as its symbol—the inverse of the flag of Switzerland, where the organization was founded. An 1864 meeting led to the first Geneva Convention, which determined the protection of sick and wounded soldiers, medical personnel, and facilities during wartime.

The Red Cross became a symbol for neutral aid. In Muslim countries, the organization is known as the Red Crescent.

Who was Clara Barton?

This American humanitarian was called "the Angel of the Battlefield" for her work during the Civil War (1861–1865). Clara (Clarissa Harlowe) Barton (1821–1912) was a nurse in army camps and on battlefields, where she cared for the wounded. When the fighting ended, Barton formed a bureau to search for missing men. This demanding work left her exhausted. Recuperating in Switzerland in 1869, Barton learned of the newly formed International Red Cross. She rallied to the aid of that volunteer organization, tending the needs of those wounded in the fighting of the Franco-Prussian War (1870–1871) between France and the German states.

In 1877, Barton began working to form the Red Cross in America. She became the first president of the U.S. branch of the International Red Cross, a post she held from 1882 to 1904. When Johnstown, Pennsylvania, experienced a devastating flood in 1889, Barton took charge of relief work there. She subsequently advocated that a clause be added to the Red Cross constitution stating that the organization would also provide relief during calamities other than war. She was successful. It is because of Barton that the Red Cross has become a familiar and welcome sight in times of disaster.

A nurse during the American Civil War, Clara Barton went on to found the American Red Cross.

NEW DISCOVERIES IN MEDICINE

Who was Karl Landsteiner?

Karl Landsteiner (1868–1943) was an Austrian physician who is known as the "Father of Transfusion Medicine" because he discovered the different major blood types. In 1900, Landsteiner identified four main blood groups—what are known as A, B, AB, and O. He also discovered the polio virus with Constantin Levaditi (1874–1953) and Edwin Popper (1879–1955) in 1909. For his pioneering work, Landsteiner received a Nobel Prize in Medicine in 1930.

Landsteiner's findings enabled others to begin conducting blood transfusions, as he had shown that it was crucial that a person receive blood from a donor with a matching, or compatible, blood type (O negative being the universal donor).

When was insulin discovered?

Insulin, a hormone that regulates sugar levels in the body, was first discovered in 1889 by German physiologist Oskar Minkowski (1858–1931) and German physician Joseph von Mering (1849–1908). They observed that the removal of the pancreas caused diabetes in dogs. Researchers set about isolating the substance, but it was not until 1922 that insulin was used to treat diabetic patients. The first genetically engineered human insulin was produced by American scientists in 1978.

The disease diabetes occurs when the pancreas does not produce enough insulin or the body's cells do not respond properly to the insulin produced. Insulin helps the body regulate the metabolism of fats, proteins, and carbohydrates—especially glucose. Controlling diabetes often involves healthy eating, exercise, and the taking of insulin. In the past, diabetics had to use syringes to inject insulin, often several times a day. Now, many diabetics have insulin pumps that automatically inject insulin.

Who invented the X-ray?

German physicist Wilhelm Conrad Röntgen (1845–1923) discovered X-rays in 1895. However, he did not understand at first what they were—which is how they got their name. In science and math, X refers to an unknown. By the end of the decade, hospitals had put X-rays to use, taking pictures (called radiographs) of bones and internal organs and tissues to help diagnose illnesses and injuries. Using the new technology, doctors could "see" the insides of a patient. In 1901, Röntgen received the first Nobel Prize in Physics for his discovery of a short-wave ray.

Who developed the first MRI machine?

Raymond Damadian (1936–) developed the first magnetic resonance imaging (MRI) machine in 1972—three years after he first proposed the idea of an MRI body scanner. In 1974, he received a patent for his MRI scanner concept. Three years later, he used an MRI scanner on a human being. Today, MRI is an important tool for radiologists and doctors in diagnosing injury and disease.

Who was Albert Hyman?

Albert Hyman (1893–1972) was an American cardiologist who in the 1930s developed what he termed an "artificial pacemaker." Hyman did not invent the pacemaker, as the

How does an MRI work?

Put simply, the MRI moves very powerful magnets to create a very strong magnetic field around a patient. The magnetic field causes most of the hydrogen atoms in a patient to line up. Then, radio wave pulses are sent through the patient, which find the hydrogen atoms that did not line up. These pulses cause the hydrogen atoms to give off energy, which sends a signal that is picked up by the MRI and analyzed by a computer. The information produced can describe what kind of tissue there is at every point in the part of the person being scanned. From this, the computer creates a picture that allows the physician to determine which tissue is healthy and which tissue is unhealthy or damaged.

first person to develop such a tool was an Australian physician named Mark C. Lidwill (1878–1969). However, Hyman popularized the term and used them in his practice.

What did the Curies contribute to medicine?

In 1898, French husband-and-wife team Pierre (1859–1906) and Marie (1867–1934) Curie discovered radium, the first radioactive element, which proved to be an effective weapon against cancer. They conducted further experiments in radioactivity, a word that Marie Curie coined, distinguishing among alpha, beta, and gamma radiation. However, they did not know the dangers of exposure to radiation as they conducted their experiments, and both would experience radium burns and radiation sickness.

Marie and Pierre Curie were French scientists famous for discovering radioactive elements. Unfortunately, unaware of the dangers, they both succumbed to radiation sickness.

Upon Pierre's death in 1906, Marie succeeded him as professor of physics at the Sorbonne. During World War I (1914–1918), Curie organized radiological services for hospitals. In 1918, she became the director of the research department of the Radium Institute of the University of Paris. She died in 1934 due to her exposure to radiation. Even today, her papers are so radioactive that they can only be viewed by someone with protective clothing.

The Curies' daughter, Irène (1897–1956), followed in her parents' footsteps, becoming becoming a physicist and marrying another scientist, Jean-Frédéric Joliot-Curie (1900–1958). He served as director of the Radium Institute for ten years, beginning in 1946. The pair, who were known as the Joliot-Curies, contributed to the discovery and development of nuclear reactors. The Curies and the Joliot-Curies were all Nobel laureates.

What is Jonas Salk known for?

American physician Jonas Edward Salk (1914–1995) was the inventor of the polio vaccine. In 1952, more than 21,000 cases of paralytic polio—the most severe form of polio—were reported in the United States. An acute viral infection, poliomyelitis (also called polio or infantile paralysis) invades the central nervous system. It is found worldwide, mainly in children. It can lead to death or create serious physical handicaps.

In 1953, after years of research that included sorting through all the studies done on immunology since the mid-1800s, Salk announced the formulation of a vaccine, which contained all three types of polio known at the time. Salk tested it on himself first and then on his wife and three children. Experiencing no side effects and finding the vaccine to be effective, it was then tested on 1.8 million schoolchildren in a program sponsored by the March of Dimes (then called the National Foundation for Infantile Paralysis). In April 1955, the vaccine was pronounced safe and effective. Salk received many honors, including a congressional gold medal and a citation from President Dwight D. Eisenhower (1890–1969).

Four years later, American physician Albert B. Sabin (1906–1993) developed an effective polio vaccine that could be taken by mouth instead of by injection. That vaccine contains live viruses (Salk's was an inactive virus vaccine). The two vaccines virtually eradicated polio from developed nations.

Jonas Salk, shown here giving a speech to the Centers for Disease Control in 1988, developed the vaccine for polio.

Who was William Hinton?

William Augustus Hinton (1883–1959) was an African American physician best known for developing the leading test for the detection of syphilis. The so-called Hinton Test was far more accurate—and produced far fewer false positives—than the earlier test for syphilis, the Wasserman Test, which was developed by August von Wassermann (1866–1925).

Who was Charles Drew?

Charles R. Drew (1904–1950) was an African American surgeon who was a leading scientist in the study of blood and plasma. He served as the medical director for the Blood for Britain Project in New York City. This project was created to store large amounts of liquid plasma to send to Great Britain to help treat injured World War II soldiers. He also served as director of a Red Cross program that produced large amounts of dried plasma.

Drew spoke out against the segregation of blood based on race. At that time, blood donations were identified by the race of the donor, and blood was only given to someone of the same race despite the fact that medically, there is no difference. The Red Cross ended its policy of blood segregation in 1950—the very year that Drew died in an automobile accident while driving to a medical conference.

When was the first human organ transplant?

The first human organ transplant occurred on June 17, 1950, at the Catholic Little Company of Mary Hospital in Evergreen Park, Illinois. The doctors who took part in the transplant, Richard H. Lawler and Raymond P. Murphy, tried to keep the highly experimental procedure quiet.

The subject was a forty-four-year-old woman who suffered from polycystic kidney disease. She received a donor organ, a kidney from a cadaver, making the procedure even more controversial for the Catholic hospital. (At the time, the Church was opposed to the idea that tissue could be taken from a dead person and put into a living person and that the tissue would then come to life again.) But the doctors who performed the procedure had the confidence and trust of the sisters running the hospital. The operation was the last resort for the patient, who had seen her mother, sister, and uncle die from the same disease. Word leaked about the operation, and several days after the procedure, when the patient was doing well, the hospital went public with their breakthrough, making headlines around the world.

The transplanted kidney functioned in the patient for about six weeks—enough time for her other kidney to begin working again; she lived another five years before finally succumbing to the disease.

On December 23, 1954, Harvard University physicians, led by surgeon Joseph E. Murray (1919–2012), performed the world's first successful transplant of an organ, a kidney, from a living donor, the patient's identical twin brother. Since the patient and the donor had the same genetic makeup, organ rejection was not an issue. The procedure saved the patient's life, and the well-publicized breakthrough immediately opened up the possibility for similar transplants (between identical twins) as well as for the transplantation of other organs.

Dr. Murray and other Harvard researchers continued working on the problem of rejection, eventually developing new drugs to reduce the possibility that a recipient would reject an organ from a nonrelative.

Today, tens of thousands of organs are transplanted each year in the United States. In October 2004, doctors performed the first organ transplant arranged and brokered over the Internet.

When was the first heart transplant?

The world's first heart transplant took place on December 3, 1967, in Cape Town, South Africa. Surgeon Christiaan Barnard (1922–2001) conducted the operation, after which the patient then lived for eighteen days. Over the next two years, more than a hundred heart transplant operations were performed, but the survival rate was not encouraging.

In the next decades, advances were made in heart transplants, especially the use of various drugs to fight the body's rejection of the new heart. Many thousands have since received heart transplants that added years to their lives. The current problem is that there are far more people needing transplants than there are donors.

Several different models for an artificial heart have been developed. Although there is much hope for these devices, at present they have had only limited success.

When was the first test-tube baby born?

The process of in vitro (artificial) fertilization (IVF), in which doctors retrieve an egg from the mother and mix it with the father's sperm in a petri dish or test tube to achieve fertilization, made possible the birth of Louise Brown on July 25, 1978, in Bristol, England. She became the world's first "test-tube baby." The scientific and medical advance of IVF gave parents who were otherwise unable to conceive another chance at procreation. The procedure has since resulted in countless successful births. Ten years after Louise Brown was born, an infertile couple had a one-in-ten chance of procreating using IVF technology; twenty years later, the chances had increased to one in five.

Why is stem cell research controversial?

Stem cell research raises important bioethical issues. Stem cells have the potential to develop into all body tissues, and they may be able to replace diseased or defective human tissue. The best source for these cell clusters is human embryos, which are destroyed when the stem cells are extracted. Opponents to the research, including many on the religious right who also oppose abortion, argue that the embryo is a potential human life (or is already a human life) and therefore should not be destroyed for the sake of science.

A common source for these embryos comes from the use of in vitro treatments for infertile couples. A doctor will fertilize several eggs from a woman yet place only one fer-

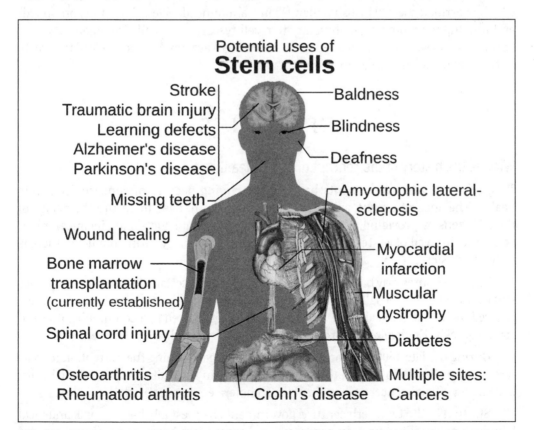

With their ability to replace or fix damaged or missing cells, stem cells have the potential to cure numerous diseases or replace tissues that are no longer viable. Blindness, deafness, and even paralysis might one day be treatable.

tilized egg within the woman. The rest are saved by freezing in case the first effort fails. Often, these other embryos are never needed and remain in freezers. They will never be implanted into a woman.

Proponents of stem cell research say that it could lead to a variety of treatments and cures for diseases. Supporters add that the embryos cannot develop on their own and therefore should be put to use for the sake of better medicine—which could help people who suffer from many different diseases, including diabetes, Alzheimer's, and Parkinson's, thus improving and extending human life.

In August 2001, the George W. Bush Administration moved cautiously forward on the issue by allowing stem cell research as long as it is limited to existing cells, the embryos having already been destroyed. In other words, new stem cells cannot be created strictly for the purpose of laboratory work. Bush said he concluded that federal funding should be used to support research on sixty existing genetically diverse stem cell lines, which have the ability to regenerate themselves indefinitely.

In March 2009, President Barack Obama issued an executive order entitled "Removing Barriers to Responsible Scientific Research Involving Human Stem Cells," which overruled the 2001 Bush policy. Obama announced: "We will lift the ban on federal funding for promising embryonic stem cell research. We will also vigorously support scientists who pursue this research. And we will aim for America to lead the world in the discoveries it one day may yield."

EPIDEMICS

What is the history of the concept of public health?

Through the ages, governments have shown varying degrees of concern for public health. The ancient Greeks, and the Romans after them, tried to ensure the health of their citizens by providing a supply of clean water (via aqueducts and pipelines), managing the disposal of waste, and working to control disease by hiring public physicians to treat the sick.

These measures may have helped prevent the spread of certain diseases, but epidemics still occurred. After the fall of the Roman Empire (c. 476), Europe's civilizations largely ignored matters of public health. Once disease was introduced to a community, it would spread quickly. Epidemics of leprosy, the plague, cholera, and yellow fever ensued.

During the late 1800s, European governments began turning their attention to matters of public health to control the spread of disease. In the United States, public health became an official concern when, in 1866, a cholera epidemic struck the nation.

Starting in the twentieth century, governments have established regional and local laboratories, public education programs, and research programs at universities and other institutions. These combined efforts have made outbreaks of diseases such as diphtheria, dysentery, typhoid fever, and scarlet fever increasingly less common in developed nations. In developing nations, public health officials continue working with international agencies (such as the World Health Organization and other United Nations agencies) to reduce outbreaks and transmission of infectious disease. Despite such efforts, such countries as Italy and the United States have shown themselves to be unprepared for serious pandemics, such as the COVID-19 virus outbreak.

What is the single most important technological development for improving human health?

The single most important factor for improving health and allowing for longer lives for people is good plumbing. Chlorinated water from the tap does not transmit disease. Sewage systems that remove waste water also prevent the transmission of diseases. Diseases such as cholera, typhoid, dysentery, polio, and hepatitis can be gotten from contaminated water, and other diseases can be carried by insects that come in contact with contaminated water.

Sadly, today some 785 million people worldwide do not have access to safe water, and two billion do not have access to a toilet.

What was the Black Death?

The Black Death was the bubonic plague, which comes from the bacterium *Yersinia pestis*. Humans contracted the disease when they were bitten by fleas carrying the bac-

An illustration from 1353 depicts citizens of Tournai, Belgium, burying victims of the Black Death. The massive loss of life from the plague had immense social and economic repercussions.

terium. The plague came in several waves. The worst outbreak peaked in the years 1347–1351, resulting in anywhere from 75 to 200 million people dying in Europe and Asia. This plague had started in Central Asia and then traveled along the Silk Road. It was probably carried by fleas on rats who traveled on ships. The devastation of so many deaths had a tremendous social and political impact.

What is leprosy?

Leprosy is an age-old disease described in many historical texts, such as the Bible. The Christian Gospels contain several stories of Jesus miraculously curing lepers. Leprosy was introduced into Europe in the 400s B.C.E., probably by the Persian Army. By the twelfth century, leprosy had reached epidemic proportions in Western Europe. Explorers and settlers from the European continent later carried the infectious chronic skin disease to the New World, where it was previously unknown.

The cause of leprosy was unknown. While some believed it was contagious, others asserted that it was hereditary or was caused by eating certain foods (even potatoes were at one time blamed for originating the affliction). In many places, leprosy was a very frightening disease. Because of the fear of infection, lepers were often driven from society, sometimes to live in leper colonies. The most famous leper colony was on the Hawaiian island of Molokai. A Catholic priest, Father Damien (later canonized as St. Damien), became famous for his work at the colony.

The first clinical description was not made until 1874, when Norwegian physician Gerhard Henrik Hansen (1841–1912) discovered the leprosy bacterium. Since then, the disease has also been called Hansen's disease. It can now be treated with antibiotics. Today, leprosy afflicts about five million people worldwide. It is endemic (native) to tropical or subtropical regions, including Africa, Central and South America, India, and Southeast Asia.

Untreated, leprosy can lead to disfigurement. The problem is that leprosy can destroy nerve cells, which leads to losing feeling in parts of the body, such as fingers. Without feeling, it is easy to get injured and then, infection results.

What was the first disease conquered by human beings?

Smallpox was the first disease eradicated by medicine. Caused by a virus spread from person to person through the air, smallpox was one of the most feared diseases, and for many centuries, there was no treatment for it. Before the discovery of the New World, smallpox epidemics swept across Africa, Asia, and Europe, leaving victims scarred and/or blind and killing countless millions. When explorers set out to find new trade routes and landed in North and South America, they brought the disease with them, infecting the indigenous peoples.

However, once a person had the disease and survived, he or she would not contract it again. This and other observations led British physician Edward Jenner (1749–1823) to develop a successful vaccine against the disease. The use of Jenner's vaccine quickly

Who was Typhoid Mary?

Typhoid Mary was the name given to Mary Mallon (c. 1869–1938), the first known carrier of typhoid fever in the United States. Though Mallon had recovered from the disease, as a cook in New York City area restaurants, she continued to spread typhoid fever germs to others, infecting more than fifty people between 1900 and 1915. The New York State sanitation department connected her to at least six typhoid fever outbreaks there. Officials finally—and permanently—institutionalized her in 1914 to prevent further spread of the acute infectious disease.

spread. The first vaccine given in the United States was in 1799. During the 1800s, many countries passed laws requiring vaccination. Improvements in the vaccine resulted in the elimination of smallpox from Europe and North America by the 1940s. When the World Health Organization (WHO) was created by the United Nations in 1946, one of its aims was to reduce the instances of smallpox around the world. Immunization programs brought this about. The last natural occurrence of the disease was reported in October 1977 in the African nation of Somalia. When no further cases were documented within the next two years, the disease was considered eradicated.

How did yellow fever get its name?

For most cases, the symptoms of infection of this virus are fever, chills, appetite loss, nausea, body pain, and headaches; however, in severe cases, the liver can be damaged, which causes jaundice, which turns the skin yellow.

The disease was once widespread, afflicting people in tropical climates, such as Central and South America, Africa, and Asia. But with exploration during the 1500s and 1600s and the opening of trade routes during the 1700s, the disease spread to North America by 1699, when there were epidemics in Charleston, South Carolina, and Philadelphia, Pennsylvania; three years later, an epidemic broke out in New York City. Yellow fever first materialized in Europe in 1723. An epidemic in Philadelphia in 1793 was carried there aboard a ship from the West Indies; most of the city's people were afflicted, and more than 4,000 people died in what has been called the worst health disaster ever to befall an American city.

Breakthroughs in controlling yellow fever came in the late 1800s and early 1900s. In 1881, Cuban physician Carlos Finlay (1833–1915) wrote a paper suggesting that yellow fever was transmitted by mosquitoes. This was proved to be true by U.S. Army surgeon Walter Reed (1851–1902), who in 1900 headed a commission sent to Cuba to investigate the cause and mode of transmission of yellow fever. With this knowledge, U.S. Army officer and physician William Gorgas (1854–1920) applied strict measures to destroy mosquitoes in Havana, eventually eliminating yellow fever from the Cuban port city. Serving as chief sanitary officer of the Panama Canal Commission from 1904 to

1913, Gorgas implemented similar measures in the Panama Canal Zone, where the disease had been a menace. His methods proved effective, greatly reducing the instances of yellow fever, which allowed the canal to be completed.

In 1937, the 17-D vaccine was developed by American physician and bacteriologist Max Theiler (1899–1972). The vaccine was found to be effective in combating yellow fever. Conquering yellow fever was one of the great achievements of modern medicine.

Although eradicated in South America, yellow fever has returned. Some mosquito-eradication programs have been abandoned, and climate change has affected the location of mosquito populations. Eradication programs in Africa based on vaccinations have been hit-and-miss, and, thus, the spread of yellow fever in the future is likely.

What was the worst pandemic in history?

The influenza pandemic of 1918–1919 was the worst pandemic in history, killing perhaps 100 million people worldwide. There are many different flu viruses; some are more dangerous than others. This pandemic was particularly deadly for young adults. Normally, the flu is most dangerous for the very young and the very old; however, for this strain of flu, it was different.

The pandemic took place during World War I. In America and Europe, many countries had censorship laws that prohibited saying anything negative about the war or the country or even publishing negative news. Thus, the massive pandemic got little press coverage. However, Spain did not participate in the war, and its newspapers alone gave extensive coverage. As a result, it became known as the Spanish Flu based on the incorrect assumption that it was mostly a Spanish disease.

Perhaps the pandemic started in Kansas, where it took hold at military camps. The subsequent movement of tens of thousands of American troops in the United States and then to Europe helped spread the disease. Over 300,000 Americans died from the pandemic, which is about equal to the number of American deaths in World War II. In some cities in America, there were coffin shortages. However, most Americans are unaware that the pandemic took place.

The PBS show *American Experience* created a 1998 documentary, *Influenza 1918,* describing in detail the pandemic and its impact.

When was AIDS first diagnosed?

The first AIDS (Acquired Immune Deficiency Syndrome) cases were identified in 1981 by physicians in Los Angeles and New York City. Researchers now believe that the infection was first a disease of nonhuman primates, including monkeys, and then jumped to humans in the early 1900s. The human immunodeficiency virus (HIV), which severely damages the body's ability to fight disease, is transmitted through sexual contact, shared drug needles, and infected blood transfusions. Scientists believe that infection began in Africa during the 1960s and 1970s, when significant numbers of people migrated from rural areas to cities. The overcrowding and unemployment that resulted contributed to the spread of sexually transmitted diseases.

AIDS is now considered endemic to many developing nations, where it is spread mostly among heterosexual men and women. In developed nations, education programs have made the public aware of how the disease is transmitted, helping curb the spread of HIV. Drug treatments are still being developed to treat HIV/AIDS; no cure has been discovered.

In 2018, almost thirty-eight million people lived with HIV/AIDS. About 800,000 people a year die worldwide from HIV/AIDS. Sub-Saharan Africa has been the region hardest hit by this disease. About 68 percent of all HIV cases and 66 percent of all related deaths are in this region.

Why is the COVID-19 pandemic so significant?

A type of coronavirus that apparently originated in 2019 in China, where it was transmitted from animals to humans, COVID-19 is a highly infectious, flulike disease that affects the respiratory system. About one percent of the people who contract the virus will die as a result, according to the U.S. Centers for Disease Control and Prevention. There is, as of this writing, no vaccine or cure, so although many people will survive, it has been spreading so quickly that even a one percent death rate could result in millions of fatalities worldwide. In addition, it has the potential of overwhelming hospitals that do not have enough essential equipment, such as ventilators, to treat the ill.

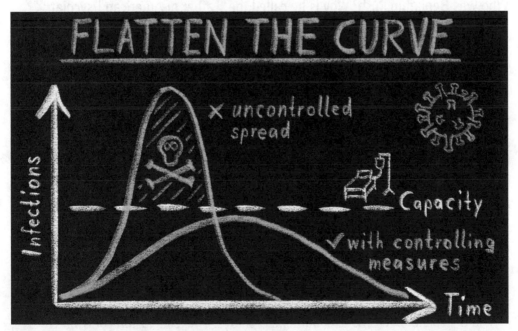

Authorities have been trying to get the message out to "flatten the curve" of the infection rate of COVID-19. The idea is that, although about the same number of people may get the virus, the number won't spike in a way that overwhelms hospitals, which means they will be able to treat people who come for help.

Because of this danger, governments across the globe have been trying to get their citizens to stay home, even if they feel well, whenever possible to reduce the transmission rate. This has had a deep economic impact on many countries. Children, the elderly, and people with compromised immune systems due to other illnesses are particularly vulnerable. There has not been a pandemic this severe since the Spanish Flu in 1918.

PSYCHOLOGY AND MENTAL HEALTH

What is behaviorism?

Behaviorism is a school of psychology that attempts to explain human behavior in terms of responses to environmental stimuli. Influenced by the conditioned reflex demonstrated by Ivan Pavlov, American psychologist John B. Watson (1878–1958) codified and popularized the theory, which discards introspection and consciousness as influences on human behavior. Behaviorism was further studied by American psychologist and Harvard professor B. F. Skinner (1904–1990). Skinner focused his work on patterns of responses to observable stimuli (versus unobservable stimuli, such as introspection and conscience) and external rewards. Applied to human learning, Skinner's theories on behaviorism affected educational methods, which reward good behavior.

Who was Benjamin Rush? Why is he called the "Father of American Psychiatry"?

Benjamin Rush (1746–1813) is called the "Father of American Psychiatry" because he published *Medical Inquiries and Observations upon the Diseases of the Mind* (1812),

Why are Pavlov's dogs well known?

Russian physiologist Ivan Pavlov (1849–1936) carried out famous experiments with dogs, which were intended to demonstrate conditioned reflex. Noticing that the laboratory dogs would sometimes salivate merely at the approach of the lab assistants who fed them, Pavlov, who was already a Nobel laureate for his research on digestion, set out to determine whether he could turn normally "unconditioned" reflexes or responses of the central nervous system into conditioned reflexes. He demonstrated that if a bell is rung every time a dog is fed, eventually, the dog becomes conditioned to salivate at the sound of a bell, even if no food is present. In this way, Pavlov substituted an artificial stimulus (the ringing of the bell) for a natural or environmental stimulus (food) to prompt a physiological reaction (salivation). Based on these experiments, Pavlov concluded that all acquired habits depend on chains of conditioned reflexes. This conclusion contributed to the development of behaviorism.

the first psychiatry textbook in the United States. He advocated for a separate part of the Pennsylvania Hospital to be used for the treatment of those with mental illnesses. His contributions to the field were so influential that the American Psychiatric Association uses his silhouette on its seal.

Rush was a Renaissance man in the truest sense of the word. He signed the Declaration of Independence, served as surgeon general of the Continental Army during part of the Revolutionary War, attended the Continental Congress, and opposed slavery and capital punishment. He was friends with Presidents John Adams and Thomas Jefferson and is given credit for helping the two former political rivals reconcile later in life.

Who was Sigmund Freud? Why was he so important for psychiatry and psychology?

The Austrian neurologist believed that human behavior and all mental states are influenced by repressed and forgotten impressions, many of them from childhood. Sigmund Freud (1856–1939) further believed that by uncovering these impressions, he could affect a cure for his patient. Freud regarded infantile mental processes, including infantile sexuality, of particular importance to the unconscious and, therefore, influential to human behavior.

While he initially used hypnosis (a sleeplike state in which the patient is open to suggestion) as a method of revealing the unconscious, Freud later turned to a new form of treatment called "free association." By this method, a patient talks about whatever is on

his or her mind, jumping from one idea to the next. The memories and feelings that surface through free association are then analyzed by the therapist to find the root of the patient's mental or emotional problem. Freud also interpreted his patients' dreams, which he believed are unconscious representations of repressed desires. Free association and dream analysis are the cornerstones of this method of counseling, which is called psychoanalysis.

In analyzing human behavior, Freud concluded that the mind (or psyche) is divided into three parts: the id, the ego, and the superego. The id is the source of instincts; the ego is the mediator between those instincts and reality—ideally, it uses reason; and the superego is the conscience. The superego functions to reward or punish through a system of moral attitudes and a sense of guilt. The superego often uses the moral values of society. The

The "Father of Psychoanalysis," Sigmund Freud forged new ways to treat people suffering mental and emotional distress using one-on-one dialogue between doctor and patient.

563

theories of psychoanalysis hold that if the parts of the mind oppose each other, a mental or emotional disorder (called a neurosis) occurs.

Freud's theories revolutionized the fields of psychiatry and psychology. They also influenced methods and philosophies of child-rearing and education. While psychoanalysis has been credited with helping millions of mentally ill patients, Freud's theories have also been rejected or challenged by many.

In what popular 1980s movie did Freud's character appear?

As mentioned before, in *Bill and Ted's Excellent Adventure* (1989), starring Keanu Reeves, Alex Winter, and George Carlin, Bill and Ted travel back in time to find historical figures, such as Napoleon Bonaparte and Abraham Lincoln, to help rescue their high school history presentation. Bill and Ted also bring along Sigmund Freud for extra credit, whom Ted greets with, "How's it going, 'Frood' dude?"

What does "Jungian" mean?

"Jungian" refers to the analytical psychology method founded by Swiss psychiatrist Carl Gustav Jung (1875–1961). Jung broke with Freud's theories, establishing his own doctrines of human behavior. Like Freud, Jung believed that the unconscious (that part of the mind of which a person is unaware) affects human behavior. But Jung denied that neuroses have any sexual basis. Instead, Jung believed that many factors influence human behavior, including the personalities of one's parents. He also believed in something he described as the "collective unconscious."

In his revolutionary work *Psychology of the Unconscious*, published in 1912, Jung asserted that there are two dimensions of the unconscious—the personal and the collective. The collective unconscious is made up of those acts and mental patterns that are shared by members of a culture or are perhaps universally shared by all humankind. He theorized that the collective unconscious manifests itself in archetypes—images, patterns, and symbols that appear in dreams and fantasies as well as in mythology, religion, and literature. Jung believed that the collective unconsciousness can serve as a guide to humanity, and, therefore, he taught that therapy should make people aware of it.

A contemporary of Freud, psychiatrist Carl Jung innovated new theories about human behavior that conflicted with those of his esteemed colleague.

Jung's theories of archetypes, or universal symbols, have influenced such diverse fields as anthropology, art, filmmaking, and history.

Jung later developed a system for classifying personalities (into introverted and extroverted types) and distinguishing among mental functions (classifying them as thinking, feeling, sensing, or intuitive). Jung taught that therapists should help their patients balance introversion (relying only on oneself for personal fulfillment) with extroversion (relying on others for personal fulfillment). Jung's system of classifications has been used to develop theories of personality types and their influences on human behavior.

Who was Abraham Maslow?

Abraham Maslow (1908–1970) was an American psychologist best known for developing a list of human needs. Sometimes called "Maslow's hierarchy of needs," the needs range from basic bodily needs, safety, love, and esteem to the highest form—self-actualization. He developed his theory in his 1954 book *Motivation and Personality*.

Maslow believed it was important to study fully functioning human beings—those with excellent mental health—rather than simply focus on those with severe mental issues. He studied individuals' "peak experiences," when individuals are best attuned to their surroundings and in harmony with the world.

Who was Dorothea Dix?

Dorothea Dix (1802–1887) was a philanthropist and among the first American women to become active in social reform. Having been headmistress of her own school for girls in Boston from 1821 to 1836, in 1841 Dix toured Massachusetts state correctional institutions, where she was shocked to see deplorable treatment of the mentally ill. Thereafter, Dix became an impassioned advocate for the mentally ill. Leading a drive to build hospitals for the specialized care of those afflicted with mental illnesses, Dix appealed to the consciences of legislators and philanthropists. She was successful in establishing mental hospitals throughout the United States, Canada, and Europe, many of which still bear her name. Dix's campaign for humane treatment of the mentally ill transformed American attitudes and institutions in the two decades that led up to the Civil War (1861–1865). During the war, she acted as superintendent of the U.S. Army nurses. She also worked to improve prison conditions during her lifetime.

ISSUES IN MEDICINE TODAY

What is the antivaccine movement?

Vaccines are a critical part of fighting many infectious diseases. However, in recent years, a movement has developed claiming that vaccines can cause autism and other health problems. In 1998, Andrew Wakefield wrote an article in the medical journal *The Lancet* that was used to argue a link between the MMR (measles, mumps, and rubella) vaccine

Mothers protesting against being forced to vaccinate their children hold a highly controversial position. Many believe such "anti-vaxxers" are endangering children and contributing to the rise of "superbugs" resistant to treatment.

and the onset of autism. *The Lancet* has since totally discredited and retracted the article. Further scientific investigations show no link between vaccinations and autism. However, many people have stopped having their children vaccinated. As a result, illnesses like measles, which had been eradicated in the United States, are now showing up, and children are dying.

What are the sources of health insurance for Americans?

In 2018, Americans were covered by the following sources of health insurance:

Insurance Source*	# of Americans Covered
Medicare	57.7 million
Employer	178.3 million
Medicaid	57.8 million
Military	8.5 million
Veterans	3.2 million
Self-Purchase	24.1 million
ACA Exchange	10.7 million

*Sometimes, people are covered by more than one insurance program.

How do Americans get medical coverage?

All other industrialized countries of the world have universal health care, where people pay tax money to support a health-care system that provides care for everyone. Canada has such a system and has high approval rates for the system.

In the United States, people get health care through health insurance coverage. Those without insurance often do not get health care. Also, Americans pay more for their health coverage than people do through taxes in countries with universal health care.

Uninsured people totaled twenty-seven million. Medicare is the government program providing insurance for people over sixty-five. Medicaid is for people with very low incomes. CHIP is the Children's Health Insurance Program for low-income children. The "Military" category includes active military personnel and veterans. The "ACA Exchange" is those people who buy their insurance through the Affordable Care Act exchange and typically receive assistance to reduce the monthly premiums.

What did the Affordable Care Act do?

The Affordable Care Act (ACA) was designed to improve health-care coverage in America. Its full title is the Patient Protection and Affordable Care Act, although it is known by many as "Obamacare," named after President Barack Obama (1961–), who signed it into law in 2010. The ACA has been controversial since its passing.

Although it provides great care for some people, America's health-care system does not provide coverage for a significant portion of the population. Canada and countries in Europe have universal health care that ensures everyone gets health coverage. It is paid for by taxes, and no one is left out. In America, lots of people have no health insurance.

During efforts to improve health care in America, a tax-supported universal coverage plan was rejected as being politically impossible. Instead, an approach was developed to provide more health coverage for people through private insurance, employer insurance, and expanded coverage under government programs.

The key issue was that many people did not have health insurance. The Affordable Care Act tried to solve a number of problems. It allowed young people to stay on their parents' health insurance plans until they were twenty-six. This helped many young people who were still in the early parts of their careers and did not yet have employer-provided insurance.

The ACA also expanded Medicaid, which provides health care for the poorest people. The ACA changed the requirements so more people could qualify for Medicaid. However, due to imprecise language in the original legislation, the ACA was taken to the Supreme Court, which decided that states could choose not to participate in this expansion of health care. Thirteen states, mostly in the South, have chosen to not expand Medicaid.

ACA also provided subsidies to reduce the insurance premiums for people with modest incomes. People would select their insurance through the ACA exchange.

The ACA also solved two existing problems with insurance. The first problem was that people with preexisting conditions, those who most needed health insurance, could not get it. Under the ACA, health insurance could not be denied based on previous conditions nor can one be charged higher insurance premium rates.

The second problem was that insurance companies would remove people whose medical care got too expensive. There were limits on many insurance policies. Thus, someone who had bought health insurance for many years but then got a serious illness, such as cancer, could be dropped from his or her insurance plan and then not be able to get coverage from another plan. One of the leading causes of bankruptcy in America was people who couldn't pay their medical bills.

One of the popular provisions in the Affordable Care Act is that insurance companies were forbidden to deny insurance coverage for people with preexisting conditions.

When Congress approved the act, no Republican senators or House representatives voted in favor of it. In the next years, resentment by some Americans would grow and help fuel the rise of the Tea Party. Republicans used anti-ACA sentiment to retake the House of Representatives. However, polls show that most Americans now favor the Affordable Care Act by a significant margin, and furthermore, the opponents of it have not offered a better solution.

In his 2016 presidential campaign, Donald Trump frequently attacked Obamacare and promised to replace it with a much better plan. No such replacement has been enacted into law, and meanwhile, the Trump Administration has taken a number of steps to weaken the Affordable Care Act.

What is the future of the Affordable Care Act?

As of early 2020, the future of the ACA is uncertain. The Affordable Care Act will once again go before the Supreme Court. A lawsuit was brought by its opponents to declare the ACA unconstitutional. At this point, no one knows how the Supreme Court will decide the case.

SCIENCE AND INVENTION

Who was Pythagoras?

Known by students today for the Pythagorean Theorem (the square of the length of the hypotenuse of a right triangle is equal to the sum of the squares of the lengths of the other two sides), Pythagoras (c. 570–c. 495 B.C.E.) was an influential Greek philosopher and mathematician. He left no writings of his own.

Pythagoreans used lines, triangles, and squares made of pebbles to represent numbers. The Latin word for pebble is "calculus," which became the later name for the field of calculus. Pythagoras also worked out how to render astronomy and music in numerical patterns and study them as mathematical subjects. He also suggested that Earth is spherical (not flat) and that Earth, the moon, and the planets revolve around the sun.

Who was Euclid?

The Greek mathematician Euclid (c. fourth century–third century B.C.E.) is considered the "Father of Geometry." He used axioms (accepted mathematical truths) to develop a deductive system of proof, which he wrote in his textbook *Elements*. This book proved to be a great contribution to scientific thinking and includes Euclid's proof of the Pythagorean Theorem.

Euclid's first three postulates, with which he begins his *Elements*, are familiar to anyone who has taken geometry: 1) it is possible to draw a straight line between any two points; 2) it is possible to produce a finite straight line continuously in a straight line; and 3) a circle may be described with any center and radius.

What pupil of Euclid's became one of the greatest mathematicians?

Archimedes (287–212 B.C.E.), who studied at one of Euclid's schools, became a renowned mathematician, physicist, and inventor. He identified the approximate value of π (a key mathematical symbol known as pi that approximates the ratio of the circumference of a circle to its diameter), identified concepts and principles that presaged modern calculus, and published treatises on mathematics that were remarkably advanced.

Archimedes also invented a screw—known as Archimedes' screw—that consists of a screw inside a hollow pipe that is used for irrigation purposes. Legend has it that Archimedes developed this invention after visiting Egypt.

He explained the principles behind a lever. He also explained much about spirals—so much so that the Archimedean spiral is named after him. Archimedes once stated: "Give me a lever long enough and a fulcrum on which to place it, and I shall move the world."

What was the Ptolemaic system?

It was a planetary scheme devised by the ancient Greek astronomer Ptolemy (c. 100–c. 170 C.E.). He proposed a system that placed Earth directly at the center of the universe, with the sun, the moon, and the planets all orbiting around Earth. However, Ptolemy observed that the movement of the planets did not match his scheme, so he added small orbits (called epicycles) to the model to try to make it work. Even though it was erroneous and complicated, the Ptolemaic system was functional enough to make predictions of planetary positions.

The system took hold, influencing thinking for 1,400 years. The Roman Catholic Church adopted the system as part of its doctrine, which the Church hierarchy held to even when Polish astronomer Nicolaus Copernicus (Mikolaj Kopernik; 1473–1543) refuted it in 1543, arguing that the sun, not Earth, is the center of the universe.

While Copernicus (pictured) did upend the scientific and religious communities with his assertion that the sun was the center of the solar system and not Earth, the idea was originally proposed by the Greek astronomer Aristarchus.

What is the Copernican view of the universe?

The Copernican view of the universe argued that Earth was only one of several bodies that orbit the sun. This view was controversial since it rejected the widely accepted Ptolemaic system. Once Copernicus assumed that the sun, rather than Earth, is the center of the solar system and that all the planets orbit the sun, he found that tables of planetary positions could be calculated much more easily—and accurately. Copernicus also argued that Earth itself is small and unimportant compared to the rest of the universe.

However, Copernicus was not the first to put forth such a radical idea: the Greek astronomer Aristarchus of Samos (c. 310–230 B.C.E.) was the first to maintain that Earth rotates on an axis and revolves around the sun.

How did Johannes Kepler improve on the Copernican views?

Copernicus assumed that planetary orbits were circular, which caused problems in predicting planetary orbits. In the early 1600s, German astronomer Johannes Kepler (1571–1630) figured out that planetary orbits were not circles but rather ellipses. Kepler based his work on observations of planetary positions conducted by astronomer Tycho Brahe (1546–1601). In 1609, Kepler published his first two laws of planetary motion: a planet orbits the sun in an ellipse, not a circle, and a planet moves faster when near the sun and slower when farther away.

We also have Kepler to thank for a word that is in everyday use: "satellite." After Galileo discovered the moons of Jupiter, Kepler used a telescope to view them for himself. He dubbed them satellites (*satelles* is Latin for "attendant"), a name that stuck.

What were Galileo's contributions to science and mathematics?

Italian scientist Galileo Galilei (1564–1642) is credited with establishing the modern method of scientific experimentation. He was the first scientist and thinker to try to prove or disprove theory by conducting tests and observing the results. Prior to Galileo, scientific theory was based on hypothesis and conjecture. To conduct accurate tests and make precise observations, Galileo developed a number of inventions, including the hydrostatic balance (a device to measure the density of objects) and the thermometer (one of the first measuring devices used in science).

Although Galileo did not invent the telescope, he improved it. He was the first to use one to study the skies, which led him to make a series of discoveries: the moon shines with reflected light; the surface of the moon is mountainous; the Milky Way is made up of countless stars; and Jupiter has four large satellites. He was even able to correctly estimate the period of rotation of each of these moons, which he named "Medicean stars" (for his benefactor, Cosimo de' Medici). Galileo was also the first to observe the phases of Venus, which are similar to the moon's, and to discover sunspots.

Prior to these astronomical discoveries, Galileo had already made significant contributions to science. When he was only twenty-five years old, he published a treatise on the center of gravity in solids. He studied the motion of pendulums and other objects along arcs and inclines. From these observations, he concluded that falling objects accelerate at a constant rate. This law of uniform acceleration later helped Sir Isaac Newton derive the law of gravity. Galileo also demonstrated that the path of a projectile is a parabola.

Why did Galileo get in trouble with the Catholic Church?

Galileo believed the writings of Copernicus that the sun was the center of the solar system and not Earth. This idea is called heliocentrism. Because his views were controversial, he defended them in his 1632 writing *Dialogue Concerning the Two Chief World Systems*. However, Galileo's *Dialogue* made fun of those who held the older view that Earth was the center of the solar system. Unfortunately, Pope Urban VIII (1568–1644) took offense. This alienated the pope, who had up to that time been a supporter of Galileo.

Galileo was eventually tried for heresy, convicted, and sentenced to house arrest, which meant he could not leave his estate. He never went to prison. Some church officials felt that the heliocentric view went against the Bible and the ideas of the philosophy of Aristotle. The whole episode was a complicated and messy affair involving religion, politics, misunderstandings, and egos—all made worse by Galileo's needlessly antagonizing several of his opponents.

Supporting Copernicus's earlier idea of the heliocentric solar system, Galileo Galilei published the theory, which angered Pope Urban VIII, who accused the astronomer of heresy.

The Galileo affair is often cited as evidence of a fundamental conflict between science and religion, and it is sometimes used to argue that the Catholic Church has opposed science. However, neither point is true. In 1992, Pope John Paul II (1920–2005) admitted that the Church had erred in trying and convicting Galileo.

The trial of Galileo was not part of a witch hunt against science. If there was such an effort, who was the next victim after Galileo? The reality was that most of the scientific thinkers in Europe held religious beliefs, and most were Catholic. A number of Catholic priests were scientists. The Catholic Church would eventually establish a Pontifical Academy of Sciences in 1936.

Is there a conflict between religion and science?

Many people believe there is a fundamental conflict between religion and science. However, this is more of a myth than anything. In fact, the myth was created by two writers in the 1800s, John Draper and Andrew White, who compared the "rationality of science" with the "ignorance of religion."

Admittedly, for some people, there is a conflict. Biblical literalists believe that Earth is only 6,000 years old and there was no evolution. For them, a serious conflict exists between biblical literalism and science. For people who do not read everything in the Bible literally, the problem disappears.

A problem also exists when scientific technology raises moral issues. This is not a fundamental conflict between science and religion but rather a set of religious and moral questions about the use of technology. Some examples of this problem are seen in the debates over using human embryos for stem cell research; cloning of humans; advance genetic testing of fetuses that could sometimes lead to people choosing abortions; or technologies that keep terminally ill patients alive with a very low quality of life. But these are all moral questions, not science questions.

When did Halley's Comet first appear?

Its first noted appearance was in 239 B.C.E., but it was British astronomer Edmond Halley (1656–1742) who noted that the bright comet he observed in 1682 followed roughly the same path as those that had been observed in 1531 and 1607. He suggested that they were all the same comet and that it would reappear in 1758. Though he did not live to see his prediction confirmed, it did reappear, and it was therefore named for Halley.

Before the British astronomer proved, through his observations and previous astronomical data, that comets are natural objects subject to the laws of gravity, people had viewed occurrences of comets as harbingers of doom. Halley's Comet last appeared in 1986, and it will next appear in 2061 and roughly every seventy-six years thereafter.

It's also worth noting that it was Halley who encouraged his friend and fellow scientist Sir Isaac Newton to write his theory of gravity, which he did in *Principia Mathematica,* which is considered a seminal work of modern science. Halley used his own money to publish it.

Did Newton really formulate the laws of motion after observing an apple falling from a tree?

While it may sound more like legend than fact, Newton maintained that it was true. In 1665, Sir Isaac Newton (1642–1727), who had newly graduated from Cambridge University, escaped bubonic-plagued London and was visiting the family farm. There, he saw an apple fall to the ground, and he began considering the force that was responsible for the action. He theorized that the apple had fallen because all matter attracts other matter, that the rate of the apple's fall was directly proportional to the attractive force that Earth exerted upon it, and that the force that pulled the apple was also responsible for keeping the moon in orbit around Earth.

But he then set aside these theories and turned his attention to experimenting with light. In the 1680s, Newton revisited the matter of the apple, taking into consideration Galileo's (1602–1609) studies of motion, from which the Italian scientist had concluded that falling objects accelerate at a constant rate. In 1687, Newton published *Principia Mathematica* (Mathematical Principles of Natural Philosophy), which outlined the laws of gravity and planetary motion. Newton arranged Galileo's findings into three basic laws of motion:

Sir Isaac Newton is the renowned scientist who devised the laws of motion that are the foundation of classical mechanics.

1. A body (any object or matter in the universe) that is at rest tends to remain at rest, and a body in motion tends to remain in motion—moving in the same direction unless acted upon by an outside force (this is the law of inertia).

2. The force to move a body is equal to its mass times acceleration ($F = MA$, where F is force, M is mass, and A is acceleration).

3. For every action, there is an equal and opposite reaction.

These three laws allowed Newton to calculate the gravitational force between Earth and the moon.

Did Newton invent calculus?

Yes, but so did German mathematician Gottfried Leibniz (1646–1716), independently of Newton. Both men had developed calculus in the context of trying to explain the laws of physics. Newton's development of calculus predated that of Leibniz, but he failed to publish it. Leibniz published his results in 1684; Newton followed suit in 1693. Each used different symbols and notations, but Leibniz's were considered superior and were more widely adopted, causing friction between the men. Their conflict became a matter of national pride, with English scientists refusing to accept Leibniz's version. Nevertheless, since Newton's system predated that of Leibniz, he is credited as the originator.

Who was George Washington Carver?

American botanist and agricultural chemist George Washington Carver (c. 1864–1943) won international fame for his research, which included finding more than 300 uses for peanuts and more than 100 uses for sweet potatoes. The son of enslaved parents, Carver was born near Diamond Grove, Missouri, and through his own efforts obtained an education, earning a bachelor's degree in 1894 and his master's degree in agriculture in 1896 from Iowa State University. That year, he joined the faculty of Alabama's Tuskegee Institute (now Tuskegee University), where he served as director of agricultural research until his death.

His first research projects centered on soil conservation and improving farming practices. Carver gave lectures and made demonstrations to southern farmers, particularly black farmers, to help them increase crop production. He then turned his attention to finding new uses for two southern staple crops: peanuts and sweet potatoes.

Agricultural scientist and educator George Washington Carver developed new ways to use crops and to preserve soil better. He taught at the Tuskeegee Institute and was also an environmentalist.

Carver found that peanuts could be used to make a milk substitute, printer's ink, and soap. He also found new uses for soybeans and devised products that could be made from cotton waste. His efforts were all intended to improve the economy in the American South and better the way of life of Southern black farmers.

Carver was lauded for his accomplishments. He was named a fellow of the Royal Society of Arts of London (1916); he was awarded the Spingarn Medal for distinguished service in agricultural chemistry (1923); and he was bestowed with the Theodore Roosevelt Medal for his valuable contributions to science (1939).

Who developed the quantum theory?

German physicist Max Planck (1858–1947) originated and developed the quantum theory, for which he was awarded the Nobel Prize in Physics in 1918. The basic theory is that energy and some other physical properties can exist in tiny, finite amounts (called quanta). Before Planck's work, theories of classical physics held that energy and physical properties varied continuously. Planck experimented with black-body radiation (a black body is any substance that absorbs all of the radiant energy that falls on it, reflecting none of it). He concluded that radiant energy can be divided, and the particles (quanta) would have values proportional to those of the energy source; Planck determined the relationship between the amount of energy that light has and its frequency.

Along with Albert Einstein's (1879–1955) theory of relativity, the quantum theory forms the basis of modern physics. Since it was developed, the quantum theory has been applied

The Swedish chemist Alfred Nobel (1833–1896) invented dynamite in 1866. Even though dynamite improved the safety of explosives, Nobel became concerned with how his invention would be used. A pacifist, he was involved in the explosives industry because it was his family's business. In his will, he set up a fund (bequeathing $9.2 million) to reward people who make strides in the sciences, literature, and promoting international peace. The Nobel Prize has been awarded annually (except for 1940–1942) since 1901. Recipients in any of five categories—physics, chemistry, medicine/physiology, literature, and peace—are presented with a gold medal, a diploma, and a substantial monetary award. A sixth related award is the Prize in Economic Sciences in Memory of Alfred Nobel, first awarded in 1969.

to numerous processes involving the transfer of energy in an atomic or molecular scale, including when it was used by Danish physicist and Nobel laureate Niels Bohr (1885–1962) to explain atomic structure. The theory has been used to explain how electrons move though the chips in a personal computer, the decay of nuclei, and how lasers work.

Why is the equation $E = mc^2$ historically significant?

The famous equation was put forth in 1905 by German-born physicist and Nobel laureate Albert Einstein (1879–1955) and became important to history largely because it, along with the quantum theory developed by Max Planck, laid the foundation for nuclear energy. It is part of Einstein's theory of relativity. In the formula, E is energy, m is mass, and c^2 is a constant factor equal to the speed of light squared. The equation illustrates the relationship between—and the exchangeability of—energy and matter.

In the 1930s, when scientists discovered a way to split atoms (the minute particles of which elements are made), they learned that the subatomic particles that were created have a total mass less than the mass of the original atom. In other words, when the atom was split, part of the mass of the atom had been changed into subatomic particles, but some of it had been converted into energy. Using Einstein's formula $E = mc^2$, the scientists calculated how much energy was produced by splitting an atom.

This atom-splitting method for creating energy is the basis for nuclear energy. The term "nuclear" refers to the atomic process, which uses the nucleus or central portion of an atom to release energy. Today, we live in the nuclear age, where power and weapons are produced using the atomic process for creating energy.

Why did Einstein write to President Franklin D. Roosevelt urging U.S. development of the atom bomb?

Albert Einstein, who was born in Germany and educated in Switzerland, was an ardent pacifist. But being a brilliant observer, he quickly perceived the threat posed by Nazi Germany. Einstein was visiting England in 1933 when the Nazis confiscated his property in Berlin and deprived him of his German citizenship. Einstein decided to move to the United States, where he took a position at the Institute for Advanced Study in Princeton, New Jersey. There, he settled and later became an American citizen (1940).

In August 1939, just before Adolf Hitler's German troops invaded Poland and began World War II, Einstein signed a letter to President Franklin D. Roosevelt (1882–1945), urging him to launch a government program to study nuclear energy. He further advocated that the United States build an atomic bomb, cautioning that such an effort might already be underway in Germany. The letter had been written by Hungarian-born physicist Leó Szilárd (1898–1964), but Szilárd had the far more famous Einstein sign it to get Roosevelt's attention.

Often considered the greatest genius of his generation, Albert Einstein's famous $E=mc^2$ formula led to nuclear energy and the Manhattan Project; his discovery of the photoelectric effect was a vital foundation of what became quantum mechanics.

The president was interested, and he set up the Advisory Committee on Uranium, which eventually led to the development of the atomic bomb, which releases nuclear energy by splitting heavy atomic particles. The program was called the Manhattan Project, and it was centered at Oak Ridge, Tennessee, and Hanford, Washington, where scientists worked to obtain sufficient amounts of plutonium and uranium to make the bombs. The bombs themselves were developed in a laboratory in Los Alamos, New Mexico. The project was funded by the government to the tune of $2 billion.

When were the first atomic bombs used?

The first test of an atomic bomb was done in the desert at Alamogordo, New Mexico, in July 1945. About a month later, on August 6, 1945, the United States dropped an atomic bomb on Hiroshima, Japan. About 70,000 died immediately. By December, more deaths from radiation and injury brought the number of total deaths to between 90,000 and 166,000.

A second bomb was dropped on Nagasaki, Japan, on August 9. Somewhere between 39,000 and 80,000 died from the initial explosion and later from burns, radiation, and injury.

The Japanese agreed to surrender on August 15, 1945.

Were other Japanese cities bombed in World War II by the United States?

As mentioned in the chapter "The World Wars," only two atomic bombs were used late in the war, but dozens of Japanese cities were targeted by B-29 bombers with conventional bombs and incendiary devices to start fires. Many Japanese cities were extensively damaged. Estimates put the death toll at between 241,000 and 900,000 people.

The 2003 documentary *The Fog of War: Eleven Lessons from the Life of Robert S. McNamara* includes a description of the severity of the bombing of Japanese cities using conventional weapons.

Who was Enrico Fermi?

The Italian-born physicist Enrico Fermi (1901–1954) was one of the chief architects of the nuclear age. In 1934, Fermi announced that he had discovered elements beyond uranium, but what he had actually done was split the atom. This process was named nuclear fission.

In 1938, Fermi was awarded the Nobel Prize in Physics and he escaped Italy, where the fascist regime of Benito Mussolini (1883–1945) had taken hold. Fermi became a professor of physics at Columbia University and then joined the Manhattan Project to develop the atomic bomb. In that capacity, he directed the first controlled nuclear chain reaction.

After World War II, he taught at the University of Chicago and continued his research on the basic properties of nuclear particles. In 1953, fermium, an artificially created radioactive element, was named after him.

Why was Oppenheimer investigated for disloyalty to the United States?

American physicist J. Robert Oppenheimer (1904–1967) directed the Los Alamos, New Mexico, laboratory where the first atomic bomb was developed and built. However, he was investigated by the government in 1953 and 1954 because of his opposition to the United States' development of a hydrogen bomb. He was also suspected of having ties with the Communist Party and, therefore, was viewed as a security risk.

After seeing the devastation created by the use of the atomic bomb in World War II, Oppenheimer became a vocal advocate of international control of atomic energy. When the United States began developing the hydrogen bomb (also called a "thermonuclear bomb"), Oppenheimer objected on both moral and technical grounds. He believed the hydrogen bomb was a far more destructive weapon than the atomic bomb, yet it offered no strategic advantage.

In 1953, Oppenheimer was suspended from the U.S. Atomic Energy Commission (AEC) because he was believed to pose a threat to national security. Hearings were held, but the New York-born scientist was cleared of charges of disloyalty. In 1963, the organization gave Oppenheimer its highest honor, the Enrico Fermi Award, for his contributions to theoretical physics.

What is the Big Bang theory?

It is a theory explaining the origin of the universe. According to the Big Bang theory, the universe began as the result of an explosion that occurred about 13.8 billion years ago. Over time, the matter created in the Big Bang broke apart, forming galaxies, stars, and a group of planets that we know as the solar system. The theory was first put forth by Edwin Hubble (1889–1953), who observed that the universe is expanding uniformly and objects that are greater distances away are receding at greater velocities.

In the 1960s, Bell Telephone Laboratories scientists discovered weak radio waves that are believed to be all that remain of the radiation from the original explosion. The discovery further supported Hubble's theory, which puts the age of the universe at about 14 billion years.

Astronomers have observed that the galaxies are still moving away from each other and that they'll probably continue to do so forever—or at least for about the next seventy billion years. If the galaxies did come together again, scientists believe that all of the matter in the universe would explode again (in other words, there would be another Big Bang), and the result would produce another universe.

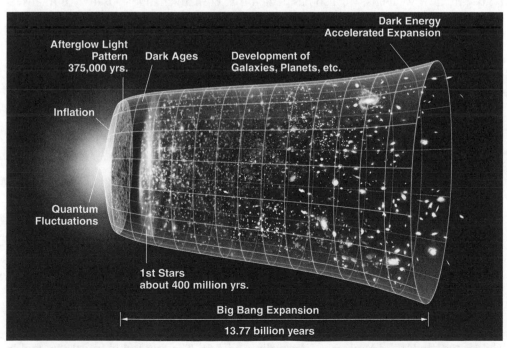

The Big Bang theory states that our universe began around 13.8 billion years ago, when a singularity exploded, rapidly expanding and eventually forming matter, energy, light, galaxies, solar systems, and planets.

What is the Doomsday Clock?

The clock represents the threat of human annihilation. It was created by the directors of the *Bulletin of the Atomic Scientists* in 1947—two years after the United States had used two nuclear weapons against Japan. The scientists wanted to illustrate the threat of total destruction posed by nuclear weapons. On the clock, midnight is the time of destruction. When the clock first appeared, the scientists had set the time at seven minutes before midnight. In the decades since, the clock has been adjusted based on the proliferation of, or agreements to limit, nuclear weapons.

However, in recent years, the threat of ecological disaster brought on by human destruction of the environment—in particular, climate change caused by global warming—has also been considered. Also, of great concern are the threats to democracy around the globe, such as the rise of authoritarian governments, cyberwarfare, and disruptive technologies.

The Doomsday Clock website is *https://thebulletin.org/doomsday-clock*. In 1995, the clock stood at 14 minutes to midnight. It dropped to 6 in 2010, then 5 in 2012. It further dropped to 2 minutes in 2018, and in 2020 it was down to 1 minute and 40 seconds. The drop has been precipitated in part in response to the policies of Donald Trump. Under Trump, the United States has withdrawn from several treaties limiting nuclear weapons, and he has several times threatened to use nuclear weapons. He also has denied that climate change caused by humans exists, halted many U.S. efforts to address climate change, and is withdrawing the United States from the 2016 Paris Agreement on climate change.

A key supporter of the Big Bang theory was British theoretical scientist Stephen Hawking (1942–2018). In 1988, Hawking, who was known for his theories on black holes (gravitational forces in space made by what were once stars), published his ideas in the best-selling book *A Brief History of Time: From the Big Bang to Black Holes*.

NATURAL HISTORY

How did Charles Darwin develop his theory of evolution?

English naturalist Charles Darwin (1809–1882) was attending Cambridge University in England when he was appointed as naturalist aboard the ship the HMS *Beagle*. The around-the-world voyage began in 1831, and Darwin was able to gather data on plants, animals, and geology in the world's southern lands—the South American coasts, the Galapagos, the Andes Mountains, Australia, and Asia. The trip lasted into 1836, and in the years that followed, Darwin published and edited many works on natural history.

Encouraged by Sir Charles Lyell (1797–1875), who is considered the "Father of Modern Geology," Darwin wrote out his theory of evolution. Coincidentally, he received the abstract of an identical theory of natural selection, formulated by English naturalist Alfred Russel Wallace (1823–1913), who had arrived at his conclusions independently of Darwin. Wallace had made his formulation of evolution based on his study of comparative biology in Brazil's Amazon River and the East Indies (Malay Archipelago).

In 1858, Darwin published both his work as well as the abstract written by Wallace. The following year, he backed up his theory in *On the Origin of Species by Means of Natural Selection*, which was found to be scientifically credible. It was widely read by the public, which snatched up so many copies that the first printing of the first edition sold out in only one day. Darwin added to this work in 1871 with *The Descent of Man*.

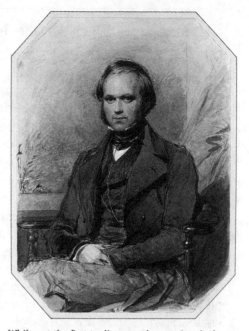

While not the first to discuss a theory of evolution, Charles Darwin explained the concept of natural selection and species change so well in his 1859 book that he would make a profound mark on science.

What Darwin put forth was that all life originated from a simple, primordial protoplasm (the fundamental material of which all living things are composed). Over several billion years, life evolved into ever-more complex animals, as did plants. In his theory of natural selection, Darwin posited that those species that are best adapted to the environment are the species that survive and reproduce.

While organic evolution and natural selection had a profound impact on the world of science (which further studied and supported the concepts), they jarred much of the religious community and created a controversy. Creationists, who believe the origin story put forth in the Bible—the seven-day creation story and the story of Adam and Eve in the Garden of Eden—objected to Darwin's theories.

INVENTION

How old is the compass?

Before the compass, which simply indicates north by means of a magnetic needle that pivots, sailors used the sun, the moon, and the stars to determine direction and navi-

When was the flush toilet invented?

The invention dates to the 1590s and is credited to Sir John Harington (1561–1612), hence its nickname, "the john." A courtier and godson of England's Queen Elizabeth I (1533–1603), Harington installed a flush lavatory in one of the queen's palaces. Though he was a serious scholar and translator, Harington was also a rebel who wrote controversial satire, leading to his banishment. His invention of the so-called "water closet" was not taken seriously in its day. But over the following two centuries, various inventors worked to improve it, ultimately developing the plumbed sanitary toilet, a flush commode that is connected to plumbing and sewers or septic tanks.

Thomas Crapper (1836–1910) is sometimes incorrectly credited with this invention (because his surname would make it a humorous coincidence), but the British businessman only invented the ballcock, which is used to fill the water in a toilet and make sure that it does not overflow. Through his company, Thomas Crapper & Co., he also helped popularize the invention and championed sanitary plumbing practices. Some have claimed that Crapper's prominence with toilets led to the widespread use of the word "crap," though others trace the etymology of the word to the Middle Ages.

gate their ships. The first compass dates to the first century B.C.E., when the Chinese observed that pieces of lodestone, an iron mineral, always pointed north when placed on a surface.

Arab sailors were using compasses as early as 600 C.E., and as Arab influence spread north into Europe, so did the compass. By the fourteenth century, European ships carried maps charted with compass readings. Portugal's Prince Henry (1394–1460), called Henry the Navigator, advanced the use of compasses in navigation by encouraging sailors and mapmakers to coordinate their information to make more accurate maps of the seas.

Italian explorer Christopher Columbus (1451–1506) noticed that as he sailed to the New World, his compass did not align directly with the North Star. (The difference between magnetic north and true north is called declination.)

How old is standard time?

Standard time was introduced in 1884 by an international conference held in Washington, D.C., to consider a worldwide system of time. Earth was divided into twenty-four different "standard" time zones. Within each time zone, all clocks are to be set to the same time.

The building of railroads with trains covering long distances made standard time necessary. Before standard time, each town or city would set its clocks based on solar time, with noon being the highest position of each day. Using solar time made it impossible to coordinate train schedules over long distances, when the time might be different in each town. Standard time solved the problem, and the telegraph made it possible for different cities within a time zone to synchronize their clocks.

Each time zone spans fifteen degrees of longitude beginning at zero longitude (called the "prime meridian"), which passes through the observatory at Greenwich (a borough of London), England. Time kept at the observatory is called Greenwich Mean Time (GMT). Time zones are described by their distance east or west of Greenwich.

The model also dictates that each time zone is one hour apart from the next. However, the borders of the time zones have been adjusted throughout the world to accommodate national, state, and provincial boundaries. The contiguous United States has four time zones: Eastern, Central, Mountain, and Pacific. Waters off the Eastern Seaboard are in the Atlantic Time Zone; Alaska, Hawaii, Samoa, Wake Island, and Guam each have their own time zones.

Who invented the thermometer?

While the Greeks made simple thermometers as early as the first century B.C.E., it wasn't until Galileo Galilei (1564–1642) that a real thermometer was invented. It was an air thermometer in which a colored liquid was driven down by the expansion of air so that as the air got warmer (and expanded), the liquid dropped. This is unlike ordinary thermometers in use today, which rely on the colored liquid of mercury to rise as it gets warmer.

In 1612, Italian physician Santorio Santorio (1561–1636), a friend of Galileo's, adapted the device to measure the body's change in temperature due to illness. (The clinical thermometer wasn't Santorio's only invention. As the first doctor to use precision instruments in the practice of medicine, Santorio also developed the pulse clock.)

It was a full century, though, before thermometers had a fixed scale. This was provided by German physicist Daniel Fahrenheit (1686–1736), who in 1714 invented the mercury thermometer.

Is Thomas Edison the greatest inventor in history?

Some believe that Thomas Alva Edison (1847–1931), the so-called "Wizard of Menlo Park," is the greatest inventor of all time. According to the "Thomas Edison Papers" at Rutgers University, he successfully obtained 1,093 patents during his lifetime and registered another 500 to 600 more that were not granted.

His best-known inventions include an automatic telegraphy machine; a stock-ticker machine; the phonograph (1877); the incandescent light bulb (1878); and the motion picture machine, known as a kinetoscope (1891). Edison also made one major scientific find during his research when he observed that electrons are emitted from a heated cathode (the conductor in an electron tube). The phenomenon is known as the "Edison effect."

When Edison was still in his twenties, he set up a laboratory where fifty consulting engineers worked with him on various inventions. By his own description, the Newark,

Thomas Edison was certainly America's most prolific inventor, making important contributions in such areas as electric power generation, photography, and sound recording, among many other fields. Although he improved upon it, however, he did *not* invent the electric light bulb. The photo is of the reconstruction of his Menlo Park laboratory at Detroit's Greenfield Village (with inset of Edison).

New Jersey, plant was an "invention factory." It operated for six years, during which Edison was granted about 200 new patents for work completed there. The laboratory is regarded by most as the first formally organized nonacademic research center in the United States. By 1876, Edison had outgrown his Newark facilities and arranged for the construction of a new plant in Menlo Park, New Jersey. His most productive work was accomplished at this location over the next decade.

Is it true that Edison had no formal education?

Thomas Edison had little formal education. Edison was born in Milan, Ohio, but his father moved the family to Port Huron, Michigan, in 1854. There, young Edison attended school in a one-room schoolhouse for a few months. The boy grew impatient with his schooling—behavior his teachers interpreted as a sign of mental inferiority.

When Edison overheard his teacher refer to him as "addled," he reported it to his mother, Nancy, who promptly withdrew him from the school. From then on, his mother taught him at home, introducing young Edison to natural philosophy—a mixture of physics, chemistry, and other sciences. He showed an inclination toward science, and by the age of ten, he was conducting original experiments in the family's home.

Edison furthered his education through voracious reading. He sought, and was granted, permission to sell periodicals, snacks, and tobacco to passengers on the train between Port Huron and Detroit, Michigan, some sixty miles away. During the layover in downtown Detroit, Edison spent his time at the public library, where, according to his own recollection, he read not a few books but the entire library. Even though he lacked a formal education, Edison possessed a keen mind and a natural curiosity. Furthermore, he had the benefit of the schooling provided by his mother as well as access to a library, of which he took full advantage.

Then, something happened that changed Edison's life. While still a young man, he lost his hearing. Biographer Matthew Josephson explains that the deafness had two effects on Edison: not only did he become "more solitary and shy," but Edison turned with an even greater intensity toward his studies and began to "put forth tremendous efforts at self-education, for he had absolutely to learn everything for himself."

What are the two systems for electrical current?

They are alternating current and direct current, better known as AC and DC. DC is the current used in batteries. AC is the standard electrical system for buildings. The advantage of AC is that it can send electricity over long distances. The disadvantage of AC electricity is that it is dangerous. Under the right conditions, it can kill a person.

Who has the most patents in history?

As of the writing of this book, Japanese inventor Shunpei Yamazaki (1942–) has 5,536 U.S. patents. Australian inventor Kia Silverbrook (1958–) has more than 4,747 U.S. patents and 9,874 international patents.

Was Tesla a major rival of Edison?

Nikola Tesla (1856–1943) was a brilliant engineer and inventor. He designed the alternating current (AC) electrical system that is widely used today. He was born in what today is Croatia and emigrated to the United States in 1894. Tesla worked under Thomas Edison for a few months but left and went on to design such things as one of the first hydroelectric power plants, which was built at Niagara Falls. He invented the Tesla coil, which is still used in radios today. His fertile imagination foresaw a global system of wireless communication and large electrical towers that would provide free energy for all the world.

Tesla Motors (now Tesla, Inc.), incorporated in 2003, was named after Tesla. Cofounded by Elon Musk (1971–), the Tesla car company designs and builds the latest generation of electric vehicles.

> ## What movie describes the fight
> ## over the choice of electrical systems for America?
>
> The 2017 movie *The Current War* describes the fight between Thomas Edison and George Westinghouse (1846–1914) over whether DC or AC should power the American grid. Benedict Cumberbatch plays Thomas Edison, who pushed for DC, and Michael Shannon plays George Westinghouse, who fought for AC. Spoiler alert: Edison lost!

Most of Yamazaki's inventions have to do with computer-display technology. Many of Silverbrook's patents relate to the digital world—digital paper, digital music, digital commerce, and digital video.

TRANSPORTATION

Who invented the steam engine?

The steam engine had a long evolution. It was first conceived of by Greek scientist Hero of Alexandria in the first century C.E. The mathematician invented many "contrivances" that were operated by water, steam, or compressed air. These included not only a fountain and a fire engine but the steam engine as well. Many centuries later, Englishman Thomas Newcomen (1664–1729) developed an early steam engine to pump water, based on an earlier design.

Scottish inventor James Watt (1736–1819) improved Newcomen's machine and patented his own steam-powered engine in 1776. It was the first practical steam engine and paved the way for the use of the engine in manufacturing and transportation during the Industrial Revolution. Watt's steam engine played a critical role in moving society from an agricultural-based economy to an industrial one. Watt's legacy also includes the terms "horsepower" and "watts" as units of measure.

The steam engine was replaced in the 1800s by more efficient devices, such as the turbine, the electric motor, the internal-combustion engine, and the diesel engine.

Who was Robert Fulton?

American inventor Robert Fulton (1765–1815) was an eminent engineer who many credit as the "Father of the Steamboat", because he developed the first commercially successful steamship. He also designed the USS *Nautilus* while living in France. Approved by Napoleon Bonaparte, the *Nautilus* was the first practical submarine. Fulton also developed torpedoes for the British Navy.

How long have trains been in use?

In the sixteenth century, crude railroads operated in the underground coal and iron ore mines of Europe. These consisted of two wooden rails that extended into the mines. Wheeled wagons were pulled along the rails by men or horses. Early in the eighteenth century, mining companies expanded on this rail system, bringing it aboveground to transport the coal and iron ore. Before long, rails were made entirely of iron.

The high-pressure steam engine developed by Richard Trevithick in 1804 was an important step in the development of the modern railroad.

Meanwhile, the steam engine had been developed. Richard Trevithick (1771–1833), an engineer in the mines of Cornwall, England, built the first high-pressure steam engine. He made quick progress from there, building a road carriage, which on Christmas Eve in 1801 became the first vehicle to convey passengers by steam. Two years later, he had built the first steam railway locomotive.

In 1825, progress in rail transportation was made by another English inventor, George Stephenson (1781–1848), who, after patenting his own locomotive engine in 1815, finished construction on the world's first public railroad. The train ran some twenty miles, carrying passengers from Stockton to Darlington, England. In 1830, Stephenson completed a line between Liverpool and Manchester. Rail travel and shipping by rail caught on quickly.

When did rail service in the United States reach from coast to coast?

In 1869, the last tracks were laid for the United States' first cross-country railroad that reached from coast to coast. Short-run rail lines had been in use since the 1840s, but the nation lacked a method for transporting people, raw materials, and finished goods between distant regions. In the early 1860s, U.S. Congress granted land and extended millions of dollars in loans to two companies to build a railroad from the East Coast to the West Coast. In the West, the route was to run roughly along the 42nd parallel from Omaha, Nebraska, to Sacramento, California. The topography of the landscape along this route would best allow the ambitious project.

The Union Pacific Railroad began work in Omaha, laying tracks westward; the Central Pacific Railroad began in Sacramento, heading eastward, including crossing the Sierra Nevada Mountains. Work began in 1863, and six years later, the two projects met at Promontory in north-central Utah, northwest of Ogden. The Central Pacific Railroad laid 689 miles of track eastward from Sacramento, while the Union Pacific Railroad laid 1,086 miles of track westward from Omaha. Six hundred workers, including numerous Irish, Chinese, and Mexican immigrant workers, attended the May 10, 1869, ceremony celebrating the accomplishment. The last spike driven to hold the railroad track was wired to a telegraph line; when the spike was pounded, a signal was sent around the world to announce the completion of the first transcontinental railroad. By the end of the 1800s, fifteen rail lines crossed the nation.

Did Henry Ford invent the automobile?

No, while Henry Ford (1863–1947) transformed American industry and changed the way we travel, live, and work, he did not invent the automobile. Just before the turn of the century, there were several inventors tinkering with gas-powered vehicles, and by the time Ford had finished his first working car, the Duryea brothers, Charles (1861–1938) and Frank (1869–1967), had demonstrated the first successful gas-powered car in the United States, and Ohio-born inventor Ransom Eli Olds (1864–1950) already had a car, the Oldsmobile, in production. Even prior to the work of these American inventors and entrepreneurs, Europeans had also made strides in developing the automobile.

The automobile is the result of a series of inventions, which began in 1769 when French military engineer Nicolas-Joseph Cugnot (1725–1804) built a steam-powered road vehicle. In the early 1800s, other inventors also experimented with this idea, and the steam-powered vehicle was put into production both in Europe and the United States. In 1899, William McKinley became the first U.S. president to ride in a car—a Stanley Steamer, built by identical twin brothers Francis (1849–1918) and Freelan (1849–1940) Stanley.

A breakthrough in developing gas-powered automobiles came in 1860, when an internal combustion engine was patented by Frenchman Étienne Lenoir (1822–1900). But the car as we know it was born in 1885, when Germans Gottlieb Daimler (1834–1900) and Karl Benz (1844–1929), working independently of each other, developed the forerunners of the gas engines used today. In 1891 and 1892, French company Panhard et Levassor designed a front-engine, rear-wheel-drive automobile. This concept remained relatively unchanged for nearly one hundred years. Until 1900, Europeans led the world in the development and production of automobiles. In 1896, the Duryea Motor Wagon Company turned out the United States's first production motor vehicle. The gas-powered cars were available for purchase that same year.

The development of the car was helped by advances in rubber and in the development of pneumatic tires during the nineteenth century with names like Charles Goodyear (American; 1800–1860), John Boyd Dunlop (Scottish; 1840–1921), and the Michelin brothers (French), André (1853–1931) and Édouard (1859–1940), figuring prominently in automotive history.

The Model T (1910 model shown) was the cornerstone of Henry Ford's auto business in which he determined to make cars that were affordable for average people.

Around 1891, Scottish-born American William Morrison (1855–1927) successfully developed an electric car. Electric cars were soon put into production, and by the turn of the century, they accounted for slightly less than 40 percent of all American car sales.

So why is Henry Ford so important?

Henry Ford refined the idea of assembly-line production to greatly reduce the cost of building a car and the time it took to build one. Prior to Ford, cars were built by a team of workers doing many different tasks to build one car at a time. Under Ford, each worker would be assigned just one small task in making the car, and he would do that same task over and over. He stood on an assembly line, where the car would move along as each worker did his one task.

Ford created the Ford Model T, which was produced from 1908 to 1927 and sold 16.5 million vehicles. The car was inexpensive because of assembly-line production, and the car was very durable and popular.

Who invented the hot-air balloon?

French papermakers Joseph-Michel (1740–1810) and Jacques-Étienne (1745–1799) Montgolfier built the first practical balloon filled with hot air. On June 4, 1783, the Montgolfiers launched a large balloon at a public gathering in Annonay, France. It ascended for ten minutes. Three months later, they safely sent up a duck, a sheep, and a rooster. Later, Étienne went up with the balloon tethered to the ground. Then, scientist Jean-François Pilâtre de Rozier (1754–1785) went up to eighty feet in a tethered balloon. The following month, Jean-François became one of two men to make the first free flight in a hot-air balloon, which ascended to a height of about 300 feet over Paris on November 21, 1783, and drifted over the city for about 25 minutes.

Hot-air ballooning proved to be better than the rival hydrogen-filled ballooning of about the same time and became very popular in Europe. In January 1785, hot-air balloonists successfully crossed the English Channel from Dover, England, to Calais, France.

What does Henry Ford have to do with barbecue?

Wood was an important component in the manufacture of model Ts for the dashboard, floorboards, and wheels. To save money, Henry Ford bought his own timberland in Michigan with the help of Edward Kingsford (1862–1943), a real estate agent. Ford next built a sawmill. But what to do about the waste from the sawmill, such as sawdust and branches? They could be turned into charcoal.

Thomas Edison designed a factory to produce the charcoal, which was originally called Ford Charcoal and only sold through Ford car dealerships. In 1951, Ford sold the charcoal plant, and the product was renamed Kingsford Charcoal.

Hot-air balloons made their debut in the United States in Philadelphia in 1793 before a crowd that included President George Washington.

Who invented the airship?

The airship, a lighter-than-air aircraft that has both propulsion and steering, had a long evolution. The first successful power-driven airship was built by French engineer Henri Giffard (1825–1882), who in September 1852 flew his craft seventeen miles from Paris to Trappes, France, at an average speed of five miles per hour. The airship was cigar-shaped with a gondola that supported a three-horsepower steam engine. Though it included a rudder, the craft proved difficult to steer.

The inventor whose name is most often associated with airships (also called "dirigibles") is Ferdinand von Zeppelin (1838–1917), who designed, built, and flew the first successful rigid airship in 1900. The zeppelin (as the aircraft came to be known) flew at a top speed of about seventeen miles per hour. The German aeronaut steadily improved his craft in the years that followed and in 1906 set up a manufacturing plant where the zeppelins were built. In 1909, Zeppelin helped establish the world's first commercial airline; the transport was wholly via airship. The crafts saw military use during World War I, including the dropping of bombs on cities.

Did the Wright brothers invent the airplane?

The Wright brothers were the first to successfully build and fly an airplane—and both events went virtually unnoticed at the time. The owners of a bicycle shop in Dayton, Ohio, Wilbur (1867–1912) and Orville (1871–1948) Wright were interested in mechan-

The first successful airplane flight at Kitty Hawk, North Carolina, was captured in this 1903 photograph. The plane was called the *Wright Flyer* and was piloted by Orville Wright; his brother, Wilbur, is seen beside the plane.

ics from early ages. After attending high school, the brothers went into business together and, interested in aviation, began tinkering with gliders in their spare time. The brothers consulted national weather reports to determine the most advantageous spot for conducting flying experiments and decided on Kitty Hawk, North Carolina. There, in 1900 and 1901, they tested their first gliders that could carry a person. Back at their bicycle shop in Ohio, they constructed a small wind tunnel (about six feet in length), in which they ran experiments using wing models to determine air pressure. As a result of this research, the Wright brothers were the first to write accurate tables of air pressures on curved surfaces.

Based on their successful glider flights and armed with their new knowledge of air pressure, Orville and Wilbur Wright designed and built an airplane. They returned to Kitty Hawk to try the craft. On December 17, 1903, the Wright brothers made the world's first flight in a power-driven, heavier-than-air machine. Orville piloted the craft 120 feet and stayed in the air twelve seconds.

They made a total of four flights that day, and Wilbur made the longest—fifty-nine seconds of flight time that covered just more than 850 feet. It was not a news event. Despite notice in a few publications, nobody paid much attention to their accomplishment.

The brothers continued their experiments at a field near Dayton, and in 1904 and 1905, they made 105 flights but totaled only forty-five minutes in the air. The Wright brothers persisted despite much public skepticism. In 1908, Orville and Wilbur Wright signed a contract with the Department of War to build the first military airplane. Only then did they receive the media attention they deserved. A year later, they set up the American Wright Company to manufacture airplanes.

The plane piloted by the two brothers in December 1903 near Kitty Hawk is on display at the National Air and Space Museum in Washington, D.C.

When did the first jet airplane take flight?

The aviation event took place in 1939 in Germany, just as World War II was beginning. The development of the jet aircraft was made possible by British inventor Frank Whittle (1907–1996), who built the first successful jet engine in 1937, which the Germans had copied. A jet engine propels an object forward by discharging a jet of heated air and exhaust gases rearward. Whittle's company, Power Jets Limited, built the engine for Britain's first jet plane in 1941, which became the model for early U.S. jets. During World War II, Great Britain, the United States, and Germany all employed jets in limited numbers in their military operations.

After the war ended, aircraft manufacturers began developing jet airliners. The innovator in the field was the de Havilland Aircraft Company (founded in 1920), which produced the Comet, the first commercial jet. In 1958, British Overseas Airways Corporation launched a transatlantic jet passenger service. A U.S. jet airplane passenger service was introduced by American Airlines in 1959; the airline used the Boeing Company's 707 to transport passengers from New York City to Los Angeles.

COMMUNICATION

Who invented the telegraph?

Before the telegraph, the fastest that information could move was the speed of a horse (over short distances) and the speed of a sailing ship (over long distances). For example, the Battle of New Orleans was part of the War of 1812; however, a treaty ending the war had been signed two weeks earlier, but the information did not get to the British forces and American forces in time to stop the battle.

What the telegraph did was allow someone to send two kinds of electrical pulses over a wire by pressing a key either quickly for a "dot" or by holding it slightly longer for a "dash." At the other end of the wire, the person listening did not touch his key, but the incoming electrical pulses caused it to click with the short "dot" sound and the long "dash." The trained listener would recognize the patterns of dots and dashes as letters spelling out words. He or she could then write out the message being sent and then send a response back.

Samuel F. B. Morse (1791–1872) is credited with making the first practical telegraph that could send electric messages across wires over long distances in 1837, although a number of other people had also been working on the problem. He created Morse code, which became a universally recognized code of dots and dashes to each letter, symbol, and number.

By 1861, most major U.S. cities were linked by telegraph wires. The telegraph would play a vital role in the American Civil War. The first successful underwater telegraph cables across the Atlantic were laid in 1866.

Why is the telegraph important?

The introduction of the telegraph marked the beginning of modern communications. The telegraph sent binary signals—a dot or a dash—over long distances to send information. A computer is based on binary code: 1s and 0s. However, now a computer can handle billions of pieces of data in a second.

Who invented the telephone?

Alexander Graham Bell (1847–1922) has been credited with inventing the telephone and receiving a patent for it in 1876. However, an Italian American inventor, Antonio Meucci (1808–1889), had created electromagnetic phones transmitting voices in his home. He even applied for a patent in 1871, but he did not mention electromagnetic voice transmission. Meucci was plagued by financial misfortune, which kept him from developing his devices and promoting them.

In 1876, the first voice transmission via wire was made when Bell had a laboratory accident and called out to his assistant, "Watson, please come here. I want you." Thomas Watson (1854–1934) was on another floor of the building with the receiving apparatus and distinctly heard Bell's message. That same year, the Bell telephone was patented in the United States and exhibited at the Philadelphia Centennial Exposition. The telephone allowed people to speak over long distances by transmitting the voice along a wire.

Today, most people communicate with cell phones that send and receive radio signals. Before cell phones, telephones were connected by wires. Years ago, making a call from New York to California required a continuous connection of wires.

Alexander Graham Bell is shown here in New York City calling Chicago in 1892.

When was the radio invented?

The radio, or "wireless," was born when Italian physicist and inventor Guglielmo Marconi (1874–1937) transmitted telegraph signals through the air from Italy to England in 1896. Marconi then founded Marconi's Wireless Telegraph Company, Ltd., in London and set up radio across the English Channel to France.

In 1900, Marconi established the American Marconi Company. He continued making improvements, such as sending out signals on different wavelengths so that multiple messages could be transmitted at one time. The first transatlantic message, from Cornwall, England, to Newfoundland, Canada, was sent and received in 1901. These early messages were sent using Morse Code. Next, a Marconi wireless station on Cape Cod, Massachusetts, received messages as well as faint music and voices from Europe. That event changed the perception of radio. Before long, Americans became accustomed to receiving "radiograms," messages transmitted via the wireless system.

On Christmas Eve in 1906, the first radio broadcast of voice and music was made from Brant Rock, Massachusetts, and was picked up by ships within a radius of several hundred miles. This resulted from the work of another radio pioneer, American engineer Reginald Fessenden (1866–1932), who patented a high-frequency alternator capable of generating continuous waves rather than intermittent impulses. This was the first successful radio transmitter.

In 1910, American inventor Lee De Forest (1873–1961), the "Father of Radio," broadcast opera singer Enrico Caruso's (1873–1921) tenor voice over the airwaves. In 1916, de Forest transmitted the first radio news broadcast. Westinghouse station KDKA in Pittsburgh, Pennsylvania, was the first corporate-sponsored station and the first broadcast station licensed on a frequency outside amateur bands. Within three years of its first commercial radio broadcast, which announced the election returns in the pres-

What is the origin of the SOS signal?

Radio has often been used to send messages with Morse code. The messages come in clearly, and the messages are very precise. In the early 1900s, a radio distress call using Morse code was created of three dots, followed by three dashes, followed by three more dots. The signal was easy to remember and easily recognized by anyone who received it.

Three dots represent the letter S, and three dashes are the letter O: thus, the signal is SOS. However, the letters have no meaning, such as "Save our ship!"

And, of course, "SOS" is the name of the 1975 hit song by the pop group ABBA.

idential race on November 2, 1920 (Warren G. Harding won), there were more than 500 radio stations in the United States.

Who invented the television?

Television was the outcome of a series of inventions by a cast of international characters. As early as 1872, British engineer Willoughby Smith (1828–1891), inspired by an experiment on selenium rods, imagined a system of "visual telegraphy." Five years later, the tube technology that would make television possible was developed by German physicist Karl Ferdinand Braun (1850–1918). He invented a cathode-ray tube, which improved the Marconi wireless radio technology by increasing the energy of sending stations.

Russian physicist Boris Rosing (1869–1933) proposed using Braun's tube to receive images, which he called "electric vision." Next, Alan Campbell-Swinton (1863–1930) suggested using the cathode-ray tube to both receive and transmit images. Then, the idea of using cathode-ray tubes to scan images for television was proposed, and by 1912, Rosing and a former pupil, Vladimir Zworykin (1888–1982), began working on it in Russia.

In 1923, a competing technology, which was entirely mechanical, reached an early milestone when British inventor John Logie Baird (1888–1946) demonstrated an electrified hatbox with disks, which constituted the world's first working television set. But the race was still on, as Zworykin had moved to the United States in 1919 and was hired by Westinghouse Electronic Corporation. He advanced the tube-based technology when he patented the iconoscope, which would become the television camera. In 1929, Zworykin invented the kinescope (television tube). His inventions together comprised the first all-electronic television.

Regularly scheduled U.S. television began on April 30, 1939, when President Franklin D. Roosevelt opened the New York World's Fair, billed as "The World of Tomorrow," giving a speech that was the first televised presidential talk. The National Broadcasting Company's (NBC) coverage of the fair's opening initiated its weekly television scheduling, a victory for parent company RCA, whose president, David Sarnoff (1891–1971), founded NBC and is considered a broadcasting pioneer.

Sold from 1946 to 1947, the RCA 630-TS was the first mass-produced television set. With its slick looks, ten-inch screen, and a price of about $430 (about the same as a car at the time), it was a popular gadget for post-World War II audiences.

When was color television invented?

In 1940, Hungarian American engineer Peter Carl Goldmark (1906–1977), the head of the Columbia Broadcasting System's (CBS) research and development laboratory, came up with a technology that broke down the television image into three primary colors through a set of spinning filters in front of black and white, causing the video to be viewed in color. His system gave way in the 1950s to an RCA system, whose signals were compatible with conventional black-and-white TV signals.

In 1962, American Broadcasting Company (ABC) began color telecasts for three and a half hours a week. By this time, competitor NBC was broadcasting 68 percent of its primetime programming in color, while CBS had opted to confine itself to black and white after having transmitted in color earlier. By 1967, all three networks were broadcasting entirely in color.

In 1967, color television was first broadcast in England when the British Broadcasting Corporation (BBC) transmitted seven hours of color programming, most of it coverage of lawn tennis from Wimbledon.

When did mobile phones first come into use?

Mobile communication dates back to radiophones used in the 1940s and 1950s. They were two-way radio systems that were powered by car batteries and required operator assistance; they were not very reliable, and the phones were anchored to a place, not a person. The first truly mobile phone call was made on April 3, 1973, by Dr. Martin Cooper of the Motorola Corporation. The device weighed two pounds and had simple dial, talk, and listen features.

The first generation of mobile phones began to be widely used in the 1980s. These large phones were usually installed in a car or briefcase. Transmission was via clusters of base stations, or cellular networks. The next generation of mobile phones appeared in the 1990s; the handset and battery technology improved, allowing for more features in smaller-sized phones and greater mobility; these were reliable phones that people could carry with them.

Who invented the computer?

English mathematician Charles Babbage (1791–1871) is recognized as the first person to conceptualize the computer. He worked to develop a mechanical computing machine called the "analytical engine," which is considered the prototype of the digital computer. He spent much of his life and much of his fortune trying to build such a machine, but he was unable to finish. Nevertheless, Babbage's never-completed "analytical engine" (on which he began work in 1834) was the forerunner of the modern digital computer, a programmable electronic device that stores, retrieves, and processes data. Babbage's device used punch cards to store data and was intended to print answers.

More than one hundred years later, the first fully automatic calculator was invented. Under the direction of mathematician Howard Aiken (1900–1973), the first electronic digital computer, called Mark I, was invented in 1944. (The Mark II followed in 1947.) In 1946, scientists at the University of Pennsylvania completed ENIAC (Electronic Nu-

Who wrote the first computer program?

The first functional computer program was written by Grace Murray Hopper (1906–1992), an admiral in the U.S. Navy and one of the pioneers of computer science. She wrote a program for the Mark I computer (developed in 1944), the first fully automatic calculator. During the 1950s, Hopper directed the work that developed one of the most widely used computer-programming languages, COBOL (Common Business Oriented Language). She is also credited with coining the slang term "bug" to refer to computer program errors. The story goes that her machine had broken down, and when she investigated the problem, she discovered a dead moth in the computer. As she removed it, she reportedly announced that she was "debugging the machine."

However, the very first computer program written, though never used, was also by a woman—English baroness Augusta Ada Byron (1815–1852), the daughter of poet Lord Byron. She wrote it for Charles Babbage's "analytical engine," which was never completed, so the program was not tested.

merical Integrator and Calculator), the first all-purpose electronic digital computer. Operating on 18,000 vacuum tubes, ENIAC was large, required a great deal of power to run, and generated a lot of heat. The first computer to handle both numeric and alphabetical data with equal facility was the UNIVAC (UNIVersal Automatic Computer), developed between 1946 and 1951, also at the University of Pennsylvania.

When was the computer chip developed?

The computer chip, or integrated circuit, was developed in the late 1950s by two researchers who were working independently of each other—Jack Kilby (1923–2005) of Texas Instruments (who developed his chip in 1958) and Robert Noyce (1927–1990) of Fairchild Semiconductor (in 1959). The chip is an electronic device made of a very small piece (usually less than one-quarter inch square) of silicon wafer. Today, there are typically hundreds of thousands of miniature transistors and other circuit components that are interconnected. Since its development in the late 1950s, the number of tiny components a chip can have has steadily risen, improving computer performance. The chips perform a computer's control, logic, and memory functions.

A computer's microprocessor is a single chip that holds all of the computer's logic and arithmetic. It is responsible for interpreting and executing instructions given by a computer program (software). The microprocessor can be thought of as the brain of the computer's operating system.

Many other consumer electronic devices rely on the computer chip as well, including the microwave, calculators, DVD players, MP3s, GPS devices, and, of course, cell phones. The use of computer chips is moving outside the field of electronics; for example, many people have their pets implanted with microchips to help locate them if they are lost.

Who invented the first personal computer?

Development of the personal computer (PC), a microcomputer designed to be used by one person, was first developed for business use in the early 1970s. Digital Equipment Corporation developed the PDP-8 for use in science laboratories.

The credit for development of a computer for home use goes to Steve Wozniak (1950–) and Steve Jobs (1955–2011), college dropouts who founded Apple Computer in 1976. They spent six months working out of a garage, developing the crude prototype for Apple I, which was bought by some 600 hobbyists who knew how to wire, program, and set up the machine. Its successor, Apple II, was intro-

The original Apple I computer made by Steve Wozniak and Steve Jobs in 1976.

duced in 1977 as the first fully assembled, programmable microcomputer, but it still required customers to use their televisions as screens and audio cassettes for data storage. It retailed for just less than $1,300.

That same year, Commodore and Tandy introduced affordable personal computers. In 1984, Apple Computer introduced the Macintosh (Mac), which became the first widely used computer with a graphical user interface (GUI). By this time, International Business Machines (IBM) had introduced its PC (1981), which quickly overtook the Mac.

Why was the Internet invented?

The computer network was invented in the late 1960s so that U.S. Department of Defense researchers could share information with each other and with other researchers. The Advanced Research Projects Agency (ARPA) developed the Internet, and its users, who were mostly scientists and academics, saw the power of the new technology. Wires linking computer terminals in a web of networks allowed people anywhere in the world to communicate with each other over the computer. Even though the government developed the Internet, it is not government-run. The Internet Society, comprised of volunteers, addresses usage and standards issues.

How old is the World Wide Web?

The Web was developed in 1990 by English computer scientist Tim Berners-Lee (1955–), who wrote the Web software at a physics laboratory near Geneva, Switzerland. Berners-Lee wrote a program defining hypertext markup language (HTML), hypertext transfer protocol (HTTP), and universal resource locators (URLs). The Web became part of the Internet in 1991 and has played a major role in the growing popularity of the international computer network, making information more accessible to the user via multimedia interfaces, which allow the presentation of graphics as well as streaming or downloadable audio and video.

Who founded Google?

American computer scientist Lawrence Page (1973–) and Russian American computer scientist Sergey Brin (1973–) cofounded Google in 1998 and made its initial public offering in 2004. Google is predominately known for providing the most popular Internet search engine. Used worldwide, Google has made Page and Brin billionaires. The word "Google" has even become a verb, as in, "Let me google that and get the answer."

Page and Brin met at Stanford University, where both were computer science Ph.D. students. They later dropped out to work on making Google a reality. The group's mission statement was "to organize the world's information and make it universally accessible and useful."

When was email invented?

Short for "electronic mail," email was invented in 1971 by computer engineer Ray Tomlinson (1941–2016), who developed a communications program for computer users at the Advanced Research Projects Agency (ARPA). The result was ARPAnet, a program that allowed text messages to be sent to any other computer on the local network. ARPAnet is now hailed as the Model T of the information superhighway.

Over the next five decades, email would grow to be one of the most powerful tools of the Internet and a key communication tool for billions of people. Many people today find it hard to imagine how workplaces could have functioned before email.

What are interesting books on the effects of technological inventions on our lives?

The 2015 book *How We Got to Now: Six Innovations That Made the Modern World* by Steven Johnson describes the importance of six innovations that have shaped the modern world: glass, cold, clean, sound, time, and light. Companion videos were also created by the BBC.

Another insightful book is *Fifty Inventions That Shaped the Modern Economy* (2017) by Tim Harford.

Further Reading

Alexander, Caroline, and Frank Hurley. *Endurance: Shackleton's Legendary Antarctic Expedition.* New York: Alfred A. Knopf, 1998.

Ambrose, Stephen E. *Citizen Soldiers: The U.S. Soldiers from the Normandy Beaches to the Bulge to the Surrender of Germany, June 7, 1944–May 7, 1945.* New York: Simon & Schuster, 1997.

———. *D-Day: June 6, 1944: The Climactic Battle of World War II.* New York: Simon & Schuster, 1994.

———. *Eisenhower: Soldier, General of the Army, President-Elect, 1890–1952.* New York: Simon & Schuster, 1983.

———. *Nixon: The Education of a Politician, 1913–62.* New York: Simon & Schuster, 1987.

———. *Nixon: Ruin and Recovery, 1973–90.* New York: Simon & Schuster, 1991.

———. *Nixon: The Triumph of a Politician, 1962–72.* New York: Simon & Schuster, 1989.

———. *Undaunted Courage: Meriwether Lewis, Thomas Jefferson, and the Opening of the American West.* New York: Simon & Schuster, 1996.

American Life: A Social History. New York: Macmillan Library Reference USA, 1993.

Anderson, John Lee. *Che Guevara: A Revolutionary Life.* New York: Grove Press, 1997.

Aranson, H. H. *History of Modern Art.* New York: Harry N. Abrams, 1977.

Armitage, Michael, and others. *World War II Day by Day.* Rev. ed. New York: DK Publishing, 2004.

Axelrod, Alan, and Charles Phillips. *What Every American Should Know about American History.* Holbrook, MA: Bob Adams Publishers, 1992.

Bailyn, Bernard. *Voyagers to the West: A Passage in the Peopling of America on the Eve of Revolution.* New York: Alfred A. Knopf, 1986.

Ball, Edward. *Slaves in the Family.* New York: Ballantine Books, 1998.

Barry, John M. *The Great Influenza: The Story of the Deadliest Pandemic in History.* New York: Viking Press, 2004.

Berg, A. Scott. *Lindbergh.* New York: G. P. Putnam & Sons, 1998.

———. *Wilson.* New York: G. P. Putnam's Sons, 2013.

Bernstein, Sara Tuvel, with Louise Loots Thornton and Marlene Bernstein Samuels. *The Seamstress: A Memoir of Survival.* Reprint. New York: Berkley Books, 1999.

Boorstin, Daniel J. *The Americans: The Colonial Experience.* New York: Random House, 1958.

———. *The Americans: The Democratic Experience.* New York: Random House, 1973.

———. *The Americans: The National Experience.* New York: Random House, 1965.

———. *The Creators: A History of Heroes of the Imagination.* New York: Random House, 1992.

———. *The Discoverers: A History of Man's Search to Know His World and Himself.* New York: Random House, 1983.

———. *The Image: What Happened to the American Dream?* New York: Atheneum, 1961.

———, editor. *An American Primer.* Chicago: University of Chicago Press, 1966.

———, and others. *Hidden History.* New York: Harper & Row, 1987.

Boyden, Matthew, and others. *The Rough Guide to Classical Music on CD,* 3rd ed. London: Rough Guides, 2001.

Branch, Taylor. *Parting the Waters: America in the King Years 1954–63.* New York: Simon & Schuster, 1988.

———. *Pillar of Fire: America in the King Years 1963–65.* New York: Simon & Schuster, 1998.

Brokaw, Tom. *The Greatest Generation.* New York: Random House, 1998.

Brown, Les. *Les Brown's Encyclopedia of Television,* 3rd ed. Detroit: Visible Ink Press, 1992.

Brownstone, David, and Irene Franck. *Dictionary of 20th Century History.* New York: Prentice Hall, 1990.

Bruce, Robert C. *The Launching of Modern American Science, 1846–1876.* New York: Alfred A. Knopf, 1987.

———. *Bell: Alexander Graham Bell and the Conquest of Solitude.* Boston: Little, Brown, 1973.

Bryson, Bill. *One Summer: America, 1927.* New York: Doubleday, 2013.

Burrell, Brian. *The Words We Live By: The Creeds, Mottoes, and Pledges That Have Shaped America.* New York: The Free Press, 1997.

Burrows, Edwin G., and Mike Wallace. *Gotham: A History of New York City to 1898.* New York: Oxford University Press, 1999.

Cahill, Thomas. *How the Irish Saved Civilization: The Untold Story of Ireland's Heroic Role from the Fall of Rome to the Rise of Medieval Europe.* New York: Nan A. Talese/Doubleday, 1995.

Cantor, Norman F. *The American Century.* New York: HarperCollins, 1997.

Carey, John, ed. *Eyewitness to History.* Cambridge, MA: Harvard University Press, 1987.

Carnes, Mark C., ed. *U.S. History.* New York: Macmillan Library Reference USA, 1996.

Caro, Robert A. *The Power Broker Robert Moses and the Fall of New York* New York: Knopf Doubleday, 1974.

Carruth, Gorton, ed. *The Encyclopedia of American Facts and Dates,* 10th ed. New York: HarperCollins, 1997.

Carson, Rachel. *Silent Spring.* Boston: Houghton Mifflin, 1962.

Chang, Iris. *The Rape of Nanking: The Forgotten Holocaust of World War II.* New York: Basic Books, 1997.

Chernow, Ron. *Grant.* New York: Penguin Books, 2018.

———. *The House of Morgan: An American Banking Dynasty and the Rise of Modern Finance.* New York: Atlantic Monthly Press, 1990.

———. *Titan: The Life of John D. Rockefeller, Sr.* New York: Random House, 1998.

Churchill, Winston. *The Second World War.* 6 vols. New York: Time, Inc., 1959.

Coles, Harry L. *War of 1812.* Chicago: University of Chicago Press, 1965.

Crile, George. *Charlie Wilson's War: The Extraordinary Story of the Largest Covert Operation in History.* New York. Atlantic Monthly Press, 2003.

Davis, Kenneth C. *Don't Know Much about History: Everything You Need to Know about American History but Never Learned.* New York: Crown, 1990.

de la Croix, Horst, and Richard G. Tansey. *Gardner's Art through the Ages,* 7th ed. New York: Harcourt Brace Jovanovich, 1980.

The Debate on the Constitution. 2 vols. Part One (September 1787–February 1788); Part Two (January–August 1788). Selected and annotated by Bernard Bailyn. New York: Library of America, 1993.

Diamond, Jared. *Guns, Germs, and Steel: The Fates of Human Societies.* New York: W. W. Norton, 1997.

Donald, David Herbert. *Lincoln.* New York: Touchstone/Simon & Schuster, 1995.

Dorson, Richard Mercer. *American Folklore.* Edited by Daniel J. Boorstin. New York: Anchor Books, 1972.

Douglass, Frederick. *Narrative of the Life of Frederick Douglass, an American Slave.* Garden City, NY: Doubleday, 1972.

DuBois, Ellen Carol. *Feminism and Suffrage: The Emergence of an Independent Women's Movement in America, 1848–1869.* Ithaca, N.Y.: Cornell University Press, 1999.

———. *Woman Suffrage and Women's Rights.* New York: New York University Press, 1998.

Einstein, Albert. *Ideas and Opinions.* New York: Crown Publishers, 1954.

Ellis, John Tracy. *American Catholicism,* 2nd ed. Chicago: University of Chicago Press, 1969.

Evans, Harold. *The American Century.* New York: Alfred A. Knopf, 1998.

Ferguson, Niall. *Pity of War: Explaining World War I.* New York: Basic Books, 1999.

Fletcher, Richard. *The Barbarian Conversion: From Paganism to Christianity.* New York: Henry Holt, 1997.

Foote, Shelby. *The Civil War.* 3 vols. New York: Random House, 1958.

———. *Stars in Their Courses: The Gettysburg Campaign, June–July 1863.* New York: Modern Library, 1994 reprint.

Fossier, Robert, ed. *The Cambridge Illustrated History of the Middle Ages.* 3 vols. New York: Cambridge University Press, 1997.

Frank, Anne. *The Diary of a Young Girl.* Translated by B. M. Mooyaart. Garden City, NY: Doubleday, 1967.

Frankopan, Peter. *The Silk Roads: A New History of the World.* London: Bloomsbury, 2015.

Fromkin, David. *The Way of the World: From the Dawn of Civilizations to the Eve of the Twenty-first Century.* New York: Alfred A. Knopf, 1998.

Fussell, Paul. *The Great War and Modern Memory.* New York: Oxford University Press, 1975.

Gandhi, Mohandas Karamchand. *An Autobiography: The Story of My Experiments with Truth.* Translated by Mahadev Desai. Beacon Press, 1993.

Garner, Joe. *We Interrupt This Broadcast: Relive the Events that Stopped Our Lives ... from the Hindenburg to the Death of Princess Diana.* Naperville, IL: Sourcebooks, 1998.

Gibbon, Edward, and others. *The Decline and Fall of the Roman Empire.* 3 vols. New York: Modern Library, 1995.

Gilbert, Martin. *A History of the Twentieth Century.* 3 vols. New York: William Morrow, 1998.

Glazer, Nathan. *American Judaism.* Chicago: University of Chicago Press, 1972.

———. *We Are All Multiculturalists Now.* Cambridge, MA: Harvard University Press, 1997.

Goodwin, Doris Kearns. *The Fitzgeralds and the Kennedys: An American Saga.* New York: Simon & Schuster, 1987.

———. *Lyndon Johnson and the American Dream.* New York: Harper & Row, 1976.

———. *No Ordinary Time: Franklin and Eleanor Roosevelt, the Home Front in World War II.* New York: Simon & Schuster, 1994.

———. *Team of Rivals: The Political Genius of Abraham Lincoln.* New York: Simon & Schuster, 2005.

———. *Wait til Next Year.* New York: Touchstone/Simon & Schuster, 1997.

Goodwin, Jason. *Lords of the Horizons: A History of the Ottoman Empire.* New York: Henry Holt, 1998.

Graeber, David. *Debt—Updated and Expanded: The First 5,000 Years.* New York: Melville House, 2011.

Grun, Bernard. *The Timetables of History: A Horizontal Linkage of People and Events.* New York: Simon & Schuster, 1991.

Gurko, Miriam. *The Ladies of Seneca Falls: The Birth of the Woman's Rights Movement.* New York: Macmillan, 1974.

Gwynne, S. C. *Empire of the Summer Moon: Quanah Parker and the Rise and Fall of the Comanches, the Most Powerful Indian Tribe in American History.* New York: Scribner, 2010.

——— . *Rebel Yell: The Violence, Passion, and Redemption of Stonewall Jackson.* New York: Scribner, 2014.

Halberstam, David. *The Best and the Brightest.* New York: Random House, 1972.

———. *The Children.* New York: Random House, 1998.

———. *The Fifties.* New York: Villard Books, 1993.

———. *Next Century.* New York: Morrow, 1991.

Harbage, Alfred, ed. *William Shakespeare, the Complete Works.* New York: The Viking Press, 1969.

Harris, John F. *The Survivor: Bill Clinton in the White House.* New York: Random House, 2005.

Hibbert, Christopher. *The Virgin Queen: Elizabeth I, Genius of the Golden Age.* Reading, MA: Perseus Books, 1991.

Howard, Michael, and William Roger Louis, eds. *The Oxford History of the Twentieth Century.* New York: Oxford University Press, 1998.

Hunt, William Dudley. *Encyclopedia of American Architecture.* New York: McGraw-Hill, 1980.

Isaacson, Walter. *Leonardo da Vinci.* New York: Simon & Schuster, 2018.

Jennings, Peter, and Todd Brewster. *The Century.* New York: Doubleday, 1998.

Johnson, Paul. *Modern Times: The World from the Twenties to the Eighties.* New York: Harper & Row, 1983.

Johnson, Steven. *How We Got to Now: Six Innovations That Made the Modern World.* New York: Riverhead Books, 2014.

Kean, Thomas, ed. *The 9/11 Commission Report: Final Report of the National Commission on Terrorist Attacks upon the United States.* New York: W. W. Norton, 2004.

Kendi, Ibram. *Stamped from the Beginning: The Definitive History of Racist Ideas in America.* New York: Bold Type Books, 2016.

Kennedy, David M. *Freedom from Fear: The American People in Depression and War, 1929–45.* New York: Oxford University Press, 1999.

Kennedy, John F. *Profiles in Courage.* New York: Harper, 1956.

Kennedy, Paul M. *Rise and Fall of the Great Powers: Economic Change and Military Conflict from 1500 to 2000.* New York: Random House, 1988.

Ketchum, Robert M. *The Battle for Bunker Hill.* Garden City, NY: Doubleday, 1962.

———. *The Borrowed Years, 1938–41: America on the Way to War.* New York: Random House, 1989.

———. *Saratoga: Turning Point of the American Revolution.* New York: Henry Holt, 1997.

———. *The Winter Soldiers: The Battles for Trenton and Princeton.* Garden City, NY: Doubleday, 1973.

Keynes, John Maynard. *The General Theory of Employment, Interest, and Money.* San Diego: Harcourt Brace Jovanovich, 1964.

King, Martin Luther Jr. *Why We Can't Wait.* New York: Harper & Row, 1964.

King, Ross. *The Judgment of Paris: The Revolutionary Decade that Gave the World Impressionism*. London: Walker Books; 2006.

Kluger, Richard. *Simple Justice: The History of Brown v. the Board of Education and Black America's Struggle for Equality*. New York: Alfred A. Knopf, 1975.

Knappman, Edward W., ed. *Great American Trials*. Detroit: Visible Ink Press, 1994.

———. *Great World Trials*. Detroit: Visible Ink Press, 1997.

Lacey, Robert. *Ford: The Men and the Machine*. Boston: Little, Brown, 1986.

———, and Danny Danziger. *Year 1000: What It Was Like at the Turn of the First Millennium, An Englishman's World*. Boston: Little, Brown, 1999.

Lamar, Howard, R. *The New Encyclopedia of the American West*. New Haven, CT: Yale University Press, 1998.

Landes, David S. *The Wealth and Poverty of Nations: Why Some Are So Rich and Some So Poor*. New York: W. W. Norton, 1998.

Larson, Edward J. *Summer for the Gods: The Scopes Trial and America's Continuing Debate over Science and Religion*. New York: Basic Books, 1997

Larson, Eric V. *Casualties and Consensus: The Historical Role of Casualties in Domestic Support for U.S. Military Operations*. Santa Monica, CA: Rand Corporation, 1996.

Lemann, Redemption: *The Last Battle of the Civil War*. New York: Farrar, Straus & Giroux, 2006.

Levi, Primo. *Survival in Auschwitz*. Translated by Stuart Woolf. New York: Summit Books, 1986.

Lewis, David L., ed. *W. E. B. Du Bois: A Reader*. New York: Henry Holt, 1995.

Malone, Dumas. *Jefferson and His Time*. Boston: Little, Brown, 1948.

Manchester, William. *American Caesar: Douglas MacArthur, 1880–1964*. Boston: Little, Brown, 1978.

———. *The Last Lion*. Vol. 1: *Winston Spencer Churchill: Visions of Glory, 1874–1932*.

Boston: Little, Brown, 1983.

———. *The Last Lion*. Vol. 2: *Winston Spencer Churchill: Alone, 1932–40*. Boston: Little, Brown, 1988.

———. *A Rockefeller Family Portrait: From John D. to Nelson*. Boston: Little, Brown, 1959.

———. *World Lit Only by Fire: The Medieval Mind and the Renaissance—Portrait of an Age*. Boston: Little, Brown, 1992.

Mandela, Nelson. *Long Walk to Freedom*. Boston: Little, Brown, 1994.

Matthews, Glenna. *American Women's History: A Student Companion*. New York: Oxford University Press, 2000.

McCullough, David. *Truman*. New York: Simon & Schuster, 1992.

———. *The Wright Brothers*. New York: Simon & Schuster, 2016.

McDougall, Walter A. *The Heavens and the Earth: A Political History of the Space Age*. New York: Basic Books, 1985.

McNamara, Robert S. *In Retrospect: The Tragedy and Lessons of Vietnam*. New York: Times Books, 1995.

McNeill, William H. *The Rise of the West: The History of the Human Community*. Chicago: University of Chicago Press, 1963.

McPherson, James M. *Battle Cry of Freedom: The Civil War Era*. New York: Oxford University Press, 1988.

Meacham, Jon. *Thomas Jefferson: The Art of Power*. New York: Random House, 2013.

Morgan, Edmund Sears. *The Birth of the Republic, 1763–89*. Chicago: University of Chicago Press, 1977.

———. *The Challenge of the American Revolution*. New York: W. W. Norton, 1976.

Mueller III, Robert S. *The Mueller Report: The Findings of the Special Counsel Investigation*. New York: Skyhorse, 2019.

Norwich, John Julius. *A Short History of Byzantium*. New York: Vintage Books, 1999.

Okrent, Daniel. *Last Call: The Rise and Fall of Prohibition*. New York: Scribner, 2011.

Olmert, Michael. *Milton's Teeth and Ovid's Umbrella: Curiouser and Curiouser Adventures in History*. New York: Simon & Schuster, 1996.

O'Neill, Jaime. *We're History! The 20th Century Survivor's Final Exam*. New York: Fireside, 1998.

Peckham, Howard Henry. *The Colonial Wars: 1689–1762*. Chicago: University of Chicago Press, 1964.

Rachlin, Harvey. *Lucy's Bones, Sacred Stones, and Einstein's Brain: The Remarkable Stories Behind the Great Objects and Artifacts of History, from Antiquity to the Modern Era*. New York: Henry Holt, 1996.

Rakove, Jack N. *Original Meanings: Politics and Ideas in the Making of the Constitution*. New York: Alfred A. Knopf, 1996.

Rees, Laurence. *The Holocaust: A New History*. New York: PublicAffairs: 2017.

Remnick, David. *Lenin's Tomb: The Last Days of the Soviet Empire*. New York: Random House, 1993.

Rhodes, Richard. *Dark Sun: The Making of the Hydrogen Bomb*. New York: Simon & Schuster, 1995.

———. *The Making of the Atomic Bomb*. New York: Simon & Schuster, 1986.

Ricks: Thomas E. *Fiasco: The American Military Adventure in Iraq*. New York: Penguin Books, 2007.

Riley-Smith, Jonathan. *The Oxford Illustrated History of the Crusades*. New York: Oxford University Press, 1997.

Rosenberg, Tina. *The Haunted Land: Facing Europe's Ghosts after Communism*. New York: Random House, 1995.

Russ, Martin. *The Last Parallel: A Marine's War Journal*. New York: Rhinehart, 1957.

Schlesinger, Arthur M. Jr. *The Age of Jackson*. Boston: Little, Brown, 1945.

———. *The Age of Roosevelt*. Boston: Houghton-Mifflin, 1957.

———. *The Cycles of American History*. Boston: Houghton-Mifflin, 1986.

———. *A Thousand Days: John F. Kennedy in the White House*. Boston: Houghton-Mifflin, 1965.

———, and Dixon Ryan Fox, eds. *A History of American Life*. Abridged and revised by Mark C. Carnes. New York: Scribner, 1996.

Schlesinger, Arthur M. Sr. *The Birth of the Nation: A Portrait of the American People on the Eve of Independence*. New York: Alfred A. Knopf, 1968.

———. *The Immigrant in American History*. New York: Harper & Row, 1964.

Schom, Alan. *Napoleon Bonaparte*. New York: HarperCollins, 1997.

Shaara, Jeff M. *Gods and Generals*. New York: Ballantine, 1996.

———. *The Last Full Measure*. New York: Ballantine, 1998.

Shaara, Michael. *The Killer Angels*. Demco Media, 1993.

Sheehan, Neil. *A Bright Shining Lie: John Paul Vann and America in Vietnam*. New York: Random House, 1988.

Shipler, David K. *Arab and Jew: Wounded Spirits in a Promised Land*. New York: Times Books, 1986.

Shirer, William L. *Gandhi: A Memoir*. New York: Simon & Schuster, 1979.

———. *The Rise and Fall of the Third Reich*. New York: Simon & Schuster, 1960.

———. *20th Century: A Memoir of a Life and the Times*. New York: Simon & Schuster, 1976.

Smith, Jessie Carney, ed. *Black Heroes of the Twentieth Century*. Detroit: Visible Ink Press, 1998.

Sontag, Sherry, and Christopher Drew, with Annette Lawrence Drew. *Blind Man's Bluff: The Untold Story of American Submarine Espionage*. New York: Public Affairs, 1998.

Strouse, Jean. *Morgan: American Financier*. New York: Random House, 1999.

Suarez, Ray. *Old Neighborhood: What We Lost in the Great Suburban Migration, 1966–99*. New York: The Free Press, 1999.

Swartz, Mimi. *Power Failure, the Inside Story of the Collapse of Enron*. New York: Doubleday, 2003.

Taylor, Alan. *William Cooper's Town: Power and Persuasion on the Frontier of the Early American Republic*. New York: Alfred A. Knopf, 1995.

Thompson, E. P. *The Making of the English Working Class*. New York: Vintage Books, 1963.

Tindall, George Brown, and David E. Shi. *America: A Narrative History*, 4th ed. New York: W. W. Norton, 1996.

Toland, John. *Adolf Hitler*. Garden City, NY: Doubleday, 1976.

———. *Captured by History: One Man's Vision of Our Tumultuous Century*. New York: St. Martin's Press, 1997.

———. *The Last 100 Days*. New York: Random House, 1965.

———. *The Rising Sun: The Decline and Fall of the Japanese Empire, 1936–1945*. New York: Random House, 1970.

Turner, Frederick Jackson. *The Frontier in American History*. Huntington, NY: R. E. Krieger Publishers, 1920.

Von Clausewitz, Carl. *On War*. Edited and translated by Michael Howard and Peter Paret. New York: Alfred A. Knopf, 1993.

Wallis, Michael. *The Real Wild West: The 101 Ranch and the Creation of the American West*. New York: St. Martin's Press, 1999.

Washington, Booker T. *Up from Slavery*. New York: Oxford University Press, 1995.

Weinberg, Gerhard L. *A World at Arms: A Global History of World War II*, 2nd ed. New York: Cambridge University Press, 2005.

Weiner, Tim. *One Man Against the World: The Tragedy of Richard Nixon*. New York: Henry Holt, 2015.

Werner, Stephen, *How to Study Religion: A Guide to the Curious*. Cognella Academic Publishing, 2020

White, Ronald C. *American Ulysses: A Life of Ulysses S. Grant*. New York: Random House; 2016.

Williams, Jonathan, ed. *Money: A History*. New York: St. Martin's Press, 1997.

Wills, Garry. *Lincoln at Gettysburg: The Words That Remade America*. New York: Simon & Schuster, 1992.

Wilson, James. *The Earth Shall Weep: A History of Native America*. New York: Atlantic Monthly Press, 1999.

Wolfe, Tom. *The Right Stuff*. New York: Farrar, Straus & Giroux, 1979.

Wood, Gordon S. *The Radicalism of the American Revolution*. New York: Alfred A. Knopf, 1992.

Woodham-Smith, Cecil. *Florence Nightingale*. New York: McGraw-Hill, 1951.

Worsley, Frank Arthur. *Endurance: An Epic of Polar Adventure*. New York: W. W. Norton, 1999.

Yergin, Daniel. *The Prize: The Epic Quest for Oil, Money & Power*. New York: Touchstone/Simon & Schuster, 1991.

Zhisui Li. *The Private Life of Chairman Mao: The Memoirs of Mao's Personal Physician*. New York: Random House, 1994.

Zinn, Howard. *People's History of the United States, 1492–Present*. New York: Harper-Perennial, 1995.

Index

Note: (ill.) indicates photos and illustrations; *t* indicates table.

A

Roosevelt, Theodore, 149, 149 (ill.), 151, 256, 404, 467
Root, John Wellborn, 437
Rosecrans, William, 134
Rosenberg, Ethel and Julius, 328 (ill.), 328–29
Rosenthal, Joe, 183 (ill.)
Rosh Hashanah, 292, 292 (ill.)
Rosie the Riveter, 356–57, 357 (ill.)
Rosing, Boris, 594
Rough Riders, 149, 149 (ill.)
Rousseau, Jean-Jacques, 70, 273, 275
Roux, Pierre-Paul-Émile, 546
Rowling, J. K., 484
royal houses (England), 62, 68, 78–80
Rubinstein, Ida, 453
Ruby, Jack, 192
Rudolf I, 60
Ruffalo, Mark, 467
Rush, Benjamin, 562–63
Russell, Bertrand, 279
Russia. *See also* Soviet Union
  Bloody Sunday, 226–27
  Bolshevik Revolution, 228 (ill.), 228–29
  Catherine the Great, 225–26
  Communists, 229–30
  Crimean War, 77–78
  interference in 2016 U.S. presidential election, 222–23
  Moscow, burning of, 74–75
  Peter the Great, 225
  Putin, Vladimir, 245–46
  Rasputin, Grigori, 227 (ill.), 227–28
  Red Terror, 229–30
  Romanovs, 225, 228
  Russian Ark, 226
  Russo-Japanese War, 255–56
  tsar, 226
  World War I, 158–59, 161
Russian Ark, 226
Russo-Japanese War, 255–56
Rutledge, John, 316
Rwandan genocide, 205–6, 206 (ill.)

S

Sabbath, 291–92
Sabin, Albert B., 553
Sacagawea, 114
Sacco, Nicola, 331–32, 332 (ill.)
Sadat, Anwar, 199, 200 (ill.)
Saffir, Herbert, 515
Saffir-Simpson scale, 515
Saigon, Fall of, 193*t*
Saint, Eva Marie, 489
Saladin, 49, 49 (ill.), 50
Salameh, Mohammed A., 204
Salat, 303
Salem witch trials, 319 (ill.), 319–20
Salinas de Gortari, Carlos, 203
Salk, Jonas Edward, 552–53, 553 (ill.)
Samara, 284
Samarkand, 249
San Francisco, California, earthquakes, 510, 511 (ill.)

San Juan Hill, 149 (ill.), 149–50
Sanger, Margaret Higgins, 382–83, 383 (ill.)
Santa Anna, Antonio López de, 120, 121, 123
Santayana, George, 3
Santorio, Santorio, 583
Sardinia, 77
Sarnoff, David, 594
Sartre, Jean-Paul, 277
satellites, 571
Saul, 290
Savitsky, Valentin, 240
Sawm, 303
Saxons, 37
scalawags, 142
Schama, Simon, 423
Schlieffen, Alfred von, 159
Schlieffen plan, 159–60
Schoenberg, Arnold, 447–48
Scholasticism, 268
The School of Athens (Raphael), 415
Schubert, Franz, 442
Schultz, "Dutch," 326
Schumann, Robert, 446
Schuylkill River Bridge (Pennsylvania), 521–22
Schwerner, Michael, 375
science. *See also* inventions
  Archimedes, 569–70
  atomic bombs, 576–78
  Big Bang theory, 579 (ill.), 579–80
  calculus, 574
  Carver, George Washington, 574–75, 575 (ill.)
  Copernican view of universe, 570–71
  Darwin, Charles, 580–81, 581 (ill.)
  Doomsday Clock, 580
  $E = mc^2$, 576
  Einstein, Albert, 576–77, 577 (ill.), 578
  Euclid, 569
  Fermi, Enrico, 578
  Galilei, Galileo, 571–72, 572 (ill.)
  Halley's Comet, 573
  humanity's origins, 12–13
  Kepler, Johannes, 571
  laws of motion, 573–74
  Nobel, Alfred, 576
  Oppenheimer, J. Robert, 578
  Ptolemaic system, 570
  Pythagoras, 569
  quantum theory, 575–76
  religion vs., 572–73
scientific experimentation, 571
scientific management, 358
scientific revolution, 274
Scipio Africanus, 29
Scobee, Francis, 528
Scopes, John, 323 (ill.), 324
Scopes Trial, 323–24
Scotland, 65, 124, 339. *See also* United Kingdom and Brexit
Scott, Dred, 321
Scott, George C., 489
Scott, Ridley, 205

Scott, Winfield, 119, 124
Scottsboro Boys, 325
screw, 570
Sears, Richard W., 361
Sears, Roebuck and Company, 361, 362
secession, 135
Second Continental Congress, 107
Second Crusade, 49
Second National Bank of the United States, 336
Second Sino-Japanese War, 257
Seder, 292
segregation, 368
Selden, Henry R., 321
Sellers, Peter, 240
Selznick, David O., 139
Semmelweis, Ignaz Philipp, 545
separation of church and state, 470–71
September 11, 2001, terrorist attacks, 210–13, 212 (ill.)
Serbia in World War I, 158, 161
serfs, 44
Serling, Rod, 489
Serpent Mound (OH), 84
Seurat, Georges, 426 (ill.), 427, 428
1776, 340
Seventh Crusade, 51
Sèvres, Treaty of, 164
sex trafficking, 406
Seymour, Jane, 63
Shaanxi, China, earthquake (1556), 510
Shahada, 303
Shakespeare, William, 477 (ill.)
  comedies, 457
  Elizabethan age, 64
  Globe Theatre, 459
  importance of, 477
  Julius Caesar, 26
  Renaissance era, 57
  Romeo and Juliet, 477
  tragedies, 456
shamrock, 40
Shangdi, 251
Shanghai Tower (China), 439
Shannon, Michael, 586
Shavuot, 292
Shaw, George Bernard, 460
Shelley, Mary, 381
Shelley, Percy Bysshe, 424
Shepard, Alan, Jr., 501
Sherman, John, 337
Sherman, William Tecumseh, 141
Sherman Anti-Trust Act (1890), 393
Shia Islam, 304
Shinto, 306
ship disasters, 522–25
Shiva, 284, 285 (ill.)
Shook, Karel, 455
Show Boat (1927), 460
Shudras, 283
Shuttlesworth, Fred, 374
Siddhartha Gautama, 286–87, 287 (ill.)
Sieyès, Emmanuel-Joseph, 73
Signac, Paul, 427
Sikh religion, 304–5

X–Y

Z